Say this city has ten million souls,
Some are living in mansions, some are living in holes:
Yet there's no place for us, my dear, there's no place for us.

Once we had a country and we thought it fair,
Look in the atlas and you'll find it there:
We cannot go there now, my dear, we cannot go there now.

In the village church yard there grows an old yew,
Every spring it blossoms anew:
Old passports can't do that, my dear, old passports can't do that.

The consul banged the table and said:
'If you've got no passport you're officially dead':
But we are still alive, my dear, but we are still alive.

Went to a committee; they offered me a chair;
Asked me politely to return next year:
But where shall we go to-day, my dear, but where shall we go to-day?

Came to a public meeting; the speaker got up and said:
'If we let them in, they will steal our daily bread';
He was talking of you and me, my dear, he was talking of you and me.

Thought I heard the rumbling in the sky;
It was Hitler over Europe, saying: 'They must die';
We were in his mind, my dear, we were in his mind.

Saw a poodle in a jacket fastened with a pin,
Saw a door opened and a cat let in:
But they weren't German Jews, my dear, but they weren't German Jews.

Went down to the harbour and stood upon the quay,
Saw the fish swimming as if they were free:
Only ten feet away, my dear, only ten feet away.

Walked through a wood, saw the birds in the trees;
They had no politicians and sang at their ease:
They weren't the human race, my dear, they weren't the human race.

Dreamed I saw a building with a thousand floors,
A thousand windows and a thousand doors;
Not one of them was ours, my dear, not one of them was ours.

Stood on a great plane in the falling snow;
Ten thousand soldiers marched to and fro:
Looking for you and me, my dear, looking for you and me.

W. H. Auden, Twelve Songs (1) 1939

THE JEWISH CONTRIBUTION TO THE 20th CENTURY

Also by Alan Symons

Maybe This Time
Dust Never Settles
Behind the Blue Plaques of London

THE JEWISH CONTRIBUTION TO THE 20th CENTURY

ALAN SYMONS

POLO PUBLISHING
LONDON

Published by POLO PUBLISHING
PO Box 108, Hampton, Middx: TW12 3QJ
Fax No: 0181 979 9425

500225547

Copyright © Alan Symons 1997

A catalogue record for this book is
available from the British Library.

ISBN 0-9523751-1-7

Printed and bound in Great Britain by The Bath Press.

First published in 1997 by Polo Publishing, London.

Acknowledgments

In this large undertaking I have enjoyed the support of many organisations, family and friends:

The Israeli Embassy (information department)
Central Office of Information
The Wiener Library
The Staff of Richmond Reference Library, Surrey
The British Council
The British Library
Esperanto Centre
The Sternberg Centre for Judaism
and others

Gilly Adams - for her hospitality & support
Mitchell Symons - for being a mine of exceptional information and advice
Susan Symons - an ever ready ear and suggestions
Jenny Symons - for her constructive criticisms and witticisms
Freddie Knoller - without whose encouragement this book would never have come about
Harvey Spack - for his on-going interest also, Sidney Kempner, Walter Brunn, Eric Lever,
Joy Rack, Liz Sutton - plus many more.....thank you all.

Chris Adams - for his computer genius and patience
Gillian Bromley - for being a wonderful and supportive editor
Tony Maher - for his superb design of page lay-out and cover

Special thanks to The Judaica Philatelic Society, coupled with Freddie Knoller, Clive Rosen, Eric
Sugarman and Gerald Froyd - for their generous loan of postage stamps.

In Memoriam

Of the six million Jews murdered by the Germans as part of their
genocide policy between 1933 and 1945, one and a half million
were children: small children, such as one might see at any
creche, nursery or primary school, anywhere in the world. All
with a right to life and adulthood. This German crime was not
just against the Jewish Nation. The world at large has suffered.
The 1,000 men and women featured here are part of the Jewish
European heritage. So were the murdered children. This
common background prompts the question of what might the full
lives of these children (and their children) have given our century
and beyond. This book, therefore, is dedicated to the Children
of the Holocaust, who never had the chance of making their
contribution.

Introduction

This book contains brief biographies of 1,000 Jews who have made a significant contribution to the 20th century. They come from some 150 different disciplines and many countries and have achieved eminence in many different fields beyond the confines of Judaism or Zionism.

The decision whom to include and whom to omit was unashamedly idiosyncratic but, in practice, only peripherally so. About half of the names were, so to speak, self-selecting. It was the balance that obliged me to exercise my own judgement or, if you disagree with my choices, prejudice. However, I believe that, by and large, each individual included has made a positive contribution in advancing international human welfare or happiness during the 20th century.

What the 1,000 people in this book all have in common is that, regardless of where they were born, they are of Jewish European origin with either one or two Jewish parents. It is true that the Jewish religion does not (save in its most liberal form) recognise as Jewish someone who only has a Jewish father and yet those who fall into that category have been persecuted and slaughtered just as vigorously as the most halachically pure Jew. This may be a reductive criterion, but it remains nonetheless a compelling argument for inclusion.

Inevitably, the shadow of the Holocaust hangs over any book which looks at Jewish achievements this century. With a present world population of 14 million Jews, the figure of 6 million has become so much a part of all our lives that it needs no further qualification save this: as Jews, and in a different place at a different time, those featured here might well have been lost in the Holocaust.

For each person listed here, 1,500 Jewish children were murdered by the Germans. Who knows what they might have achieved?

Alan Symons
London, England.

Sarah Aaronson was born at Zichron Ya'akov, Palestine, at a time when the land was part of the Ottoman empire and ruthlessly controlled from Turkey. Her brother Aaron was important to the Turks, having successfully waged war on the locusts that were causing famine in the region, but was anxious to rid Palestine of its colonial rulers. During the First World War, in which the Turks were allied to Germany, Aaron secretly went to Cairo and offered to form a Jewish espionage group to obtain information on Turkish strength and work to further an Allied victory over Turkey in Palestine. The group became known as Nili.

Sarah, by this time a wife and living in Constantinople, became disillusioned with marriage, left her husband and returned home. She became an expert horsewoman and joined the local Jewish militia formed to protect Jews against Arab and Turkish extremists. Anxious to be taking more positive action, Sarah joined her brother in Cairo. By now Nili had a network of agents all over Palestine and was providing the British with much-needed information.

Nili was asked for up-to-date information concerning the strength of Turkish forces, and Sarah and others volunteered to return to Palestine. They made it to Zichron Ya'akov but, unknown to them, the Turks had shot down a carrier pigeon flying to them with an important message from Aaron. The Turks, enraged by the spy ring in their midst, surrounded the village and arrested Sarah.

Despite four days of constant flogging she remained silent. The Turks decided to take her to Nazareth where more intensive torture could be carried out. Begging to be allowed to wash off the blood, Sarah went to the bathroom, took a pistol from its hiding place and, rather than undergo worse torture and possibly betray British plans, she shot herself. It was 17th October 1917. Shortly afterwards, General Allenby captured Palestine for the British. Without the courage and dedication of Sarah, and the other members of Nili, British casualties in the Palestine campaign would have been very much greater.

Born in Germany, Karl Abraham completed his studies in 1901. In 1905 he joined the Burgholzi clinic in Zurich and worked with Jung. In 1907 he met Sigmund Freud (qv) and joined the famous 'inner circle', going on to become the first German psychoanalyst and founder of the German Psychoanalytic Society. He psychoanalysed many of those who were later to continue his work, including among others Theodore Reik and Melanie Klein (qv). Kind, even-tempered, considerate and optimistic, he was nevertheless often sharply critical. He claimed that a milestone in a child's development is the ability to experience ambivalence, the sense that each parent may have good and bad qualities; in effect, an early recognition of the complexity of relationship. He interpreted myths and fairy tales and noted that communities provided sanctions for what the individual was not allowed to do alone: kill, torture etc. He was highly avant-garde in his writings and observations and trod on many a toe. Time, however, has repeatedly proved him right.

ABRAHAMS, Harold (1899-1978) British Olympic champion

Harold Abrahams was born on December 15th 1899 in Bedford, England. He was one of three brothers, all of whom had a passion for athletics and all of whom were successful at national level. From 1920 to 1923 he studied at Cambridge University, where he had a brilliant athletic career. He failed to win a medal at the 1920 Olympic Games in Antwerp, Belgium, but subsequently devoted himself to the pursuit of selection and success in the 1924 Paris Games. In the course of this preparation he produced an English long jump record. The result was that not only was he selected for the Olympics, he won a gold in the 100 metres and a silver as a member of the British 400 metres relay team. He later stated that neither he or anyone else thought he stood a chance of a gold.

In 1925, injury forced him to retire and he studied to become a lawyer. However, he never gave up his association with athletics. At various times, he was President of the Amateur Athletics Association and chairman, secretary or treasurer of the British Amateur Athletics Board. He sat on one committee for 50 years.

Abrahams became the centre of controversy when in 1936 he refused to take part in a boycott of the Olympic Games to be held in Berlin. Taking the view that he could be more useful to German Jewry by using his contacts in the sporting world, he broadcast for the BBC from the Berlin Olympic Stadium when Hitler opened the Games. He once told an audience that his own experience of anti-Semitism, while at Cambridge, gave him an additional urge to win. He died in London on January 14th 1978.

ABRAHAMS, Ivor (1935-) British sculptor

Ivor Abrahams was born in Wigan, England, and studied at St. Martin's School of Art in London. He became a teacher and was later visiting lecturer at the Royal College of Art. He worked in unusual materials and held his first one-man show in 1962. However, it was not until his New York show at the Museum of Modern Art, in 1970, that his deserved reputation became established. He has subsequently exhibited regularly in the United States, Australia, Britain and Europe. He has acquired international recognition for his three-dimensional prints that incorporate collage techniques. His work can be seen at the Victoria and Albert Museum in London, the Bibliothèque Nationale in Paris, Boymans Museum in Rotterdam and at other museums throughout the world.

His image from a garden suite (1970) is a landscaping design in the style of sculpture. Within his work on the theme of man and nature coming together, Abrahams has found a unique approach which combines these elements and gives continued visual pleasure.

Max Abramovitz was born in Chicago. He qualified as an architect after studying at the University of Illinois, Columbia University and the Ecole des Beaux Arts in Paris. He worked with several firms before being appointed Deputy Director of the United Nations Planning Office (1947-52). He became part of the firm of Harrison and Abramovitz, which designed the United Nations Secretariat building in New York. This famous design incorporated the ideas of an international panel including Le Corbusier and Oscar Niemeyer. The spectacular building, the east and west sides of which were faced almost entirely with glass, became a forerunner for later buildings all over the world.

Other projects included the Alcoa Building in Pittsburgh (1953) and the most unusual Socony Mobil Building in New York (1956). In 1960 Abramovitz designed the 48-storey Time and Life building in New York City. He is probably best known for the Philharmonic Hall, New York (1963; now known as Avery Fisher Hall at the Lincoln Center), in a style often described as American neoclassicism. Also in 1963 he designed the auditorium of the University of Illinois, a vast saucer dome that can accommodate nearly 20,000 people.

Born in Greece in 1903 and brought up in Lausanne, Switzerland, **Abravanel's** Jewish parents wanted him to become a doctor. His own preference, however, was for music: not playing, but conducting. He moved to Berlin in 1922 to study music and composition under Kurt Weill (qv) and was Weill's musical interpreter for over 20 years, in 1930 conducting the first rendering of Weill's *Mahagonny*. As his popularity grew, he frequently conducted the Berlin State Opera. However, as his career was progressing, Hitler's was doing likewise; and as Hitler was finding much favour with the German people, it was Abravanel who had to leave. In 1933 he moved to Paris, where he became musical director of the George Balanchine's Ballet (in 1948 this company would cross the Atlantic to become the New York City Ballet).

Abravanel remained in Paris for three years before moving to the US in 1936. There, at the age of 33, he became staff conductor at the New York Metropolitan Opera. His work on *Samson and Delilah* was considered a great achievement. Unfortunately for Abravanel, he was young and the administrators old; the discrepancy led to clashes and after two years he left to spend the next few years conducting world musical premieres on Broadway, especially the works of Kurt Weill. In 1947 he took on the challenge offered by the job of principal conductor to the Utah Symphony Orchestra, a small, even insignificant body. From this unpromising raw material he achieved extraordinary results. By the time he retired from the post in 1979, not only had the residents of Utah learned much about classical music but their orchestra had the distinction of being the most widely attended in America: no mean feat when considering the opposition, and all due to Maurice Abravanel. Thereafter, despite advancing poor health, he taught musicians at the Berkshire Music Centre in Tanglewood, Massachusetts, where he became artist-in-residence. Although he won many awards, his favourite accolade was the renaming of the Salt Lake City Symphony Hall in his honour. He died in Salt Lake City on September 22nd 1993.

ABZUG, Bella (1920-) US radical

Born Bella Savitsky on July 24th 1920 in the Bronx, New York City, **Bella Abzug** graduated from Hunter College in 1942 and qualified in law from Columbia Law School in 1947. At her law practice she chose to act for many of those named by McCarthy as suspected communists. She also represented the American Civil Liberties Union. In 1960 she was a founder of Women's Strike for Peace and in 1970 was elected to Congress as a Democrat, on behalf of a poor area of Manhattan.

On account of her aggressive style and powerful oratory she was nicknamed, 'Battling Bella'. In this role she fought for women's rights, welfare reform, transport facilities and more. She opposed the US intervention in Vietnam before it became popular to do so. Indeed, on her first day in Congress, she called for the withdrawal of all troops from Indochina. In 1979, her outspoken criticism of Jimmy Carter for paying only lip service to women's rights caused him to dismiss her as an advisor.

Abzug gave up her seat in Congress to run for the Senate but lost, whereupon she returned to her law practice. However, she remained politically active, particularly in the area of equal rights where her example became an inspiration to women all over the world. In 1993 she chaired New York's Commission on the Status of Women.

ADAMS, Franklin Pierce 'FPA' (1881-1960) US journalist

Adams, the son of immigrant Jews, was born in Chicago on November 15th 1881 and began his journalistic career with the *Chicago Journal* in 1903. A year later he was in New York writing for an assortment of newspapers. In 1913 on the *Herald Tribune* he started his 'Conning Tower' column, which he would sign off with his initials, FPA. Interrupted only by the First World War, during which he wrote for the *Stars and Stripes*, Adams continued his witty and well-written column until 1937, telling a series of informal anecdotes concerning the contemporary scene. On Saturdays, he would write in the style of the famous English diarist, Samuel Pepys. This was so popular it even brought about a revival in Pepys' original work. In 1935 Adams published these articles as *The Diary of Our Own Samuel Pepys*.

Adams also wrote a great deal of poetry: not free verse, which he loathed, but light and conventional verse. His first published collection was *Tobogganing on Parnassus* (1911) and his last *The Melancholy Life* (1936). His first experience of broadcasting, in 1938 on the radio show *Information Please*, was the prelude to twenty years as a top radio personality. Adams died in New York on March 23rd 1960.

ADELSTEIN-ROZEANU, Angelica (1921-) Romanian world sports champion

Born on October 15th 1921 in Bucharest, **Angelica Adelstein-Rozeanu** is considered to be the greatest female table tennis player in the history of the game. During her career she won a total of 17 world titles, including the world singles champion six consecutive times, from 1950 to 1955. She won the Romanian national women's championship every year, from 1936 to 1957, excluding the war years of 1940-45, when she was unable to compete because she was in hiding. She was the first Romanian women to win a world title at any sport, and it was directly through her efforts that the national team won the Corbillon Cup five times. In 1939, the antisemitic Romanian government refused to grant her a visa to compete in the world championships held in London. Her greatest year was 1953, when she won the world singles and both world doubles titles, and was a member of the winning Corbillon Cup team.

At home she experienced a mixed reception, showered with honours in some quarters and the victim of anti-Semitism in others. In 1960 she emigrated to Israel, where she represented her new country at the 1961 Maccabiah Games and won.

Often neglected and sometimes maligned, **Adler** was the creative pioneer in psychosomatic medicine. Born in a Vienna suburb on February 7th 1870, the second son of a poor Jewish grain merchant, Adler was a sickly child who did just enough to qualify for medical school. After qualifying, he published a booklet on social medicine claiming that poor working conditions and poverty caused mental disease. In 1902 he met Freud, and was invited to attend his weekly group meetings. Adler became part of the 'inner circle' and invented the phrase, 'inferiority complex'. He publicly disagreed with Freud over his theory of sexual factors in neurosis. Adler believed that the personality developed as a result of a person's self-assertion and determination. In any event, the two men parted company.

Adler dealt with the effects of stress within the family, and explained the possible problems of what he termed 'sibling rivalry'. Early in the 20th century Adler became a Protestant but, with the advent of Hitler and realizing his conversion would not save him from persecution, decided to spend his remaining years in the US. He died in Aberdeen of a heart attack on May 28th 1937, whilst on a lecture tour of Scotland.

The son of Victor Adler, founder of the Austrian Social-Democratic Party, **Friedrich** born in Vienna and educated in Switzerland. There, he concentrated on physics and went on to lecture at Zurich University. At the age of 32 he returned to Austria where, although acknowledging he was a Jew, spurned all forms of religion.

He was violently against the involvement of Austria in the First World War and hated the Socialist Party for supporting it. On October 21st 1916, in an effort to awaken public conscience, he shot and killed the Prime Minister, Count Sturgkh, who was dining with his mistress at a Viennese restaurant. Adler made no attempt to escape but waited calmly for the police to arrest him. The death sentence passed on him was later commuted to one of 18 years' imprisonment. Following the end of the war the Austrian monarchy was dissolved, and during the amnesty that followed, Adler was released.

In 1921 he became one of the founders of the left-wing International Working Union of Socialist Parties, and from 1923 to 1939 was secretary of the influential Labour and Socialist International. Following the arrival of Hitler in Vienna, Adler went to the US. He remained there until the end of the Second World War, when he returned to Austria and the labour movement, becoming a supporter and ally of Bruno Kreisky (qv). Adler died in Vienna in September 1960.

ADLER,
Jankel
(1895-1949)
Polish painter

After training at art schools in Poland, **Adler** went to Germany to live and work. The commission to paint frescoes for the newly opened planetarium in Düsseldorf brought him fame, but with the advent of Hitler, Adler and his work were not wanted. He went to Paris in 1933 and established himself there until the outbreak of the Second World War. During this period he learned his frescoes had been destroyed, and that 27 of his works had been exhibited at the 'Degenerate Art' exhibition held by the Nazis in Munich in 1937. Adler left France for England, where he joined the Polish army, and where he remained after his discharge in 1945.

Following the exposure of the death camps, Adler decided to concentrate on painting scenes concerning Jewish life in pre-war Poland. Several of his paintings are at the Museum of Modern Art in New York. Although often compared with Chagall (qv), his style is essentially Cubist and reflects the influence of Picasso. Adler died in 1949, as a result of wounds received whilst fighting in Italy and heartbreak at the loss of so many close relations in the Holocaust. He has now come to be recognized as one of Europe's leading artists and a continuing influence on today's generation of painters.

ADLER,
Larry
(1914-)
US/British
musician

Adler was born in Baltimore on February 10th 1914. During his education at Baltimore College he taught himself to play the harmonica, for which he won a State prize. In his teens he appeared in revues in New York; then in 1934 he arrived in England, where he remained until the outbreak of the Second World War. He developed the technique of the 12-hole chromatic harmonica which allowed him a wide range. In 1939 he made his debut as a soloist with the Sydney Symphony Orchestra. During the Second World War he toured, entertaining US and Allied forces, all over the world, work he continued in later wars, in Korea (1951) and Israel (1967 and 1973).

Adler was in the forefront of opposition to McCarthy's witch hunts against 'un-American activities', which began in 1953. Blacklisted as a communist, Adler emigrated to the UK, where prominent composers including Malcolm Arnold, Darius Milhaud and Vaughan Williams created solo works for him and his harmonica. Although his achievements for the harmonica in the world of classical music are acknowledged, he will probably be best remembered for composing and playing the music for the film *Genevieve* (1953), which resulted in an Oscar nomination. In 1988, Adler published his autobiography, *It Ain't Necessarily So.*

ADLER,
Stella
(1901-92)
US theatre
teacher

Stella Adler was born on February 10th 1901 in New York into a well-known theatre family. Her parents, Jacob and Sara, ran the independent Yiddish Art Company and her brother was the actor Luther Adler. All this would result in Stella becoming one of the most important and influential film and theatre figures of the 20th century and a leading exponent of method acting. Educated at New York University and the American Laboratory Theatre School, she joined the Group Theatre in 1931 and, after a brief spell in Hollywood, returned to teach theatre at workshops in New York. In 1949, she established the Stella Adler Conservatory of Acting, which specialized in the Stanislavski method.

Stella Adler, tall with blonde hair and large green eyes, was responsible for launching the careers of some of the most celebrated actors of the second half of the twentieth century including Marlon Brando, Warren Beatty, Robert de Niro, James Coburn, Richard Dreyfuss (qv), Anthony Quinn and Martin Sheen. An accomplished actress during the 1940s, in plays by Clifford Odets (qv), she taught from a position of authority. She directed on Broadway and wrote about her work. By 1960, her New York school had grown to a staff of 12 teachers and she opened a branch in Los Angeles. Her teaching methods became legendary. She once said: 'the teacher has to inspire, to agitate. You cannot teach acting. You can only stimulate what is already there.'

Adler was often asked to help out when actors had a mental block while filming. In the film *Meet Me in St Louis*, Margaret O'Brien had to weep but was unable to perform convincingly enough. Next day, on the set, with the cameras ready to roll, Adler quietly told O'Brien that her dog had just been run over. The sobs of anguish that followed were just what the director wanted. Stella Adler died in Los Angeles on December 21st 1992. In the foreword to her book, *The Technique of Acting*, Brando wrote: 'Little did she know that through her technique she would impart theatrical culture worldwide.'

ADORNO, Theodor (1903-69) German philosopher

Born on September 11th 1903 in Germany, **Adorno** was the son of a Jewish wine merchant whose family name was Wiesengrund. Adorno took his mother's maiden name after being expelled from Germany by the Nazis. He came to England and taught at Merton College, Cambridge, before moving on to the US and the University of California.

In 1950, following the Second World War, he wrote that it might be better if the world was in complete ruins so that society could start anew. In 1956 he returned to Germany and Frankfurt University, and came to exert considerable influence on modern psychology and sociology. However, it was not long before the times began to move too fast for him. Although left-wing, Adorno was no revolutionary, and was dismayed when his students registered their disaffection with 'Molotov cocktails' instead of reasoned argument. It became increasingly clear that he was not ready for the 1960s and the emergence of the culture of protest. This is well illustrated by his book *Negative Dialectics*, published in 1966. He found the militant women's movement particularly difficult to accept, leading to a confrontation during a lecture he was giving when three women members of a militant action group rushed the platform baring their breasts. They attacked Adorno with flowers and erotically caressed him. It was all too much. He took himself off to Switzerland to recover, but died of a heart attack three months later, on August 6th 1969.

AGAM,
Yaacov
(1928-)
Israeli painter

Yaacov Agam was born Jacob Gipstein on May 11th 1928 in Rishon-Le-Zion, Palestine. The son of a Russian rabbi, he grew up in a small village settlement and did not receive any formal education until after his bar-mitzvah. He was taught to draw as a child and went on to study at Jerusalem University (1947-48). He continued his studies in Zurich (1949-51) and Paris where, in 1953, he held his first exhibition and where he decided to settle. His works, especially his relief paintings, show merging geometric forms and reflect his concern with time and movement. Besides being an experimental artist, he is also known for his three-dimensional sculpture.

A leading figure in the world of kinetic art, he is a pioneer in branches of non-figurative art that concentrate on movement. Agram often uses both light and sound effects to display his sculptures, which can be rearranged by the sculptor to suit different moods. Examples of his work include *Three Times Three Interplay* (1970-71) and *The Thousand Fates* (1972), which is in Israel's presidential garden in Jerusalem. In Paris, in the Quartier de la Défense, is a very large musical fountain which Yaacov Agam designed in 1975. He continues to be an important force in progressive art.

AGNON,
Shmuel
(1888-1970)
Israeli writer

Agnon was born with the family name of Czaczkes, in Buczalz, Poland on July 17th 1888. His father was a fur merchant and the family middle class. The father would tell his son rabbinical stories and his mother, German stories; little wonder, then, that Shmuel had decided to become a writer by the time he was eight years old, even though he had to wait until he was fifteen before he had anything published. When he was nineteen he went off to Palestine. It was at this time that his story *Agunot* was published, and Shmuel took the name Agnon from that title.

At that time, it was the custom to work the land or engage in other forms of physical labour. Unwilling to do manual work, Agnon moved to Jerusalem and a more intellectual way of life. After a brief sojourn in Berlin he returned to Jerusalem in 1924, a year in which the first of the fires that were to become a feature of his life took place. The house he had recently acquired went up in smoke, in circumstances never fully explained. He lost many books and manuscripts. The next blaze occurred during the Jerusalem riots of 1929; again, he lost his home and many books and papers.

Agnon is best known for his epic trilogy of novels depicting Eastern Jewry in the early 20th century: *Bridal Canopy* (1931), *A Guest for the Night* (1939) and *Days Gone By* (1945). His writings reflect the contrasting influences upon his life and this has led to comparisons with Kafka (*qv*). His style is often surreal and introspective. In 1966, he received the Nobel Prize for Literature and is generally regarded as the greatest writer in Modern Hebrew. His works have been translated into many languages and read world-wide. He died in Jerusalem on February 17th 1970.

Aimée was born Françoise Sorya Dreyfus, in Paris, to middle-class parents, on April 27th 1932. During the German occupation of France the family was constantly on the move in the effort to escape the regular round-up of Jews by the French authorities, eager to show their German masters how efficient they could be. Educated at Bauer-Theroud Drama School, she was soon in demand after the war by the French film industry, that had barely functioned during the years of conflict. Aimée is excellent in portraying sultry, enigmatic ladies, as typified by many of her leading film roles. She has made around 60 films: some great, some good and some best forgotten. The best include *The Golden Salamander* (1949), *La Dolce Vita* (1960) and *The Appointment* (1969). Probably her best-known film is *A Man and a Woman* (1966), for which she won much international critical acclaim. A very talented actress and much admired in the film industry, she was once married to the English actor, Albert Finney. In June 1996 she was on the jury of the Sotchi Film Festival and the Festival's guest of honour.

AIMEE, Anouk (1932-) French actor

Amy Alcott was born in Kansas City on February 22nd 1956. She graduated from Pacific Palisades High School only to discover she preferred golf to university. She had been playing golf since she was nine, taking regular lessons and practising for hours on end. She perfected her swing in front of a large mirror and often spent all day on the golf course before returning home to practise her putting in the garden. She began playing on municipal courses, before joining the Los Angeles Riviera Country Club. In 1973, she won the USGA junior girls' tournament and had won some 150 tournaments by the time she turned professional in January 1975. That same year, she won her first important professional tournament, the 'Orange Blossom Classic', for which she collected $55,000. By mid-1980, Amy had won twelve major tournaments, including the US Women's Open in July 1980, a victory gained by a margin of nine shots. *Golf Magazine* named Amy Alcott the 1980 Player of the Year.

ALCOTT, Amy (1956-) US champion golfer

Her golfing skills earned her a million dollars in 1983, and by 1986 she had completed a decade of professional golf, during which she had played consistently well. In 1988, after winning the Dinah Shore Tournament, her accumulated earnings had soared to over two million dollars, making her one of very few lady golfers to achieve this record. She won the Dinah Shore again in 1991, and by 1993 had 29 LPGA tournament victories under her belt. One more will put her in the Golf Hall of Fame. In August 1996, playing at Woburn in the British Women's Open, she finished joint second.

Born in Brussels on October 19th 1927, **Alechinsky** was elected a member of the association 'Jeune Peinture Belge' at the young age of 20. A year later he was elected a member of the 'Cobra Group'. The son of a Jewish father and Gentile mother, he was able to escape German persecution in the Second World War by living with his mother's family and concealing the Jewish half of his parentage. He studied art in Brussels, at the Ecole Nationale d'Architecture et des Arts Decoratifs. In 1951, he severed his connection with the Cobra Group and went to live and work

ALECHINSKY, Pierre (1927-) Belgian painter

in Paris. His paintings, featured in galleries all over the world, are often described as 'violently explosive' and as evidencing a sense of continuing movement and vigorous expressive abstractions. Alechinsky remains a *force majeure* in the ever-changing world of art.

ALEICHEM,
Sholem
(1859-1916)
Russian writer

Although **Aleichem** lived most of his life in the 19th century, his work only became internationally known in the 20th and, more particularly, after the Second World War. The son of a shopkeeper, he was born in Pereyaslev, in the Ukraine, on February 18th 1859. He started his working career as a rabbi, but abandoned this in favour of his love of writing. He wrote for the Yiddish theatre, but pogroms in Kiev while he was living there prompted a decision to emigrate and he left for the US in 1905. There, he continued writing for the stage, but the Yiddish Theatre in New York had more plays than it could handle. He returned to Europe, visiting many cities and reading his works to adoring audiences. However, he suffered from ill-health and was advised to live in Italy, which he did from 1908 to 1914, returning to the US for the last two years of his life. He died in New York on May 13th 1916.

Aleichem's short stories and plays, which vividly portray 19th-century Jewish life in Russia, were first thrust upon the international scene with Maurice Samuel's *The World of Sholem Aleichem* (1943). This publication led to *Fiddler on the Roof*, the story which became a successful musical show that continues to tour, as well as one of the world's most popular films.

ALEXANDER,
Franz
(1891-1964)
Hungarian/
American
psychoanalyst

Born on January 22nd 1891 in Budapest, where his father was Professor of Philosophy, **Franz** received his MD in 1913 and joined the Austrian-Hungarian army as a front-line medical officer in the First World War. He later worked at the Institute for Psychoanalysis in Berlin, before emigrating to America in 1932, where he founded the Chicago Institute of Psychoanalysis. His great work was the identification of mental factors as causes of physical disorders. He explained the interactivity which was the cause of peptic ulcers, hypertension and rheumatic arthritis. He also expounded on mental stress as a killer. He later became President of the American Psychoanalytical Association. Alexander was also interested in the psyche of the criminal and published *The Roots of Crime* in 1935. He died in Palm Springs, California, on March 8th 1964.

ALEXANDER,
Samuel
(1859-1938)
Australian
philosopher

Born in Sydney on January 6th 1859, the son of a saddler, **Samuel** moved with his family to Melbourne, where he went on to graduate from the city's university. He later became the first Jew to be awarded a college fellowship to Oxbridge. As an academic, he soon became known as an eccentric, beloved by his students, who adored his feigned deafness and his habit of using his sleeve to wipe the blackboard. Fame was thrust upon him in 1920 with the publication of his two-volume book, *Space, Time & Deity*. This work describes the levels of reality on the basis that each level is rooted in the one that precedes it. He retired in 1924 to concentrate on aesthetics and published his results in *Beauty* (1934). He was awarded the Order of Merit in 1930. A bust of Alexander by Sir Jacob Epstein (*qv*) adorns Manchester

University. He was a tall man with a full beard and proud of his shabby clothes. It was Alexander who was responsible for introducing Chaim Weizmann to Arthur Balfour. He died in Manchester, England on September 13th 1938.

Woody Allen was born Allen Stewart Konigsberg in Brooklyn, New York, on December 1st 1935. He is arguably the film world's most original writer, director and actor all rolled into one creative genius. His films have given so such pleasure to so many people in so many countries that he is considered by his many admirers as a legend in his own lifetime. On screen, he is the epitome of the self-doubter. He portrays a neurotic with paranoid tendencies so brilliantly that it comes as no surprise to learn that he has been receiving psychoanalysis over a number of years. His work demonstrates his admiration for such luminaries as Bergman, Tolstoy and Dostoevsky, as well as his fascination with being a short, smart, Jewish New Yorker, as in *Play It Again Sam*. He was educated at New York University - where he failed the film course! In 1965, he was appointed to write and star in *What's New Pussycat?* and this set him on the road to success. He won two Oscars for the direction and screenplay of *Annie Hall* (1977), and two further Oscars for best screenplay with *Interiors* (1978) and *Manhattan* (1979). The list of Oscar nominations is impressive and testifies to his talent; however, Allen himself sets little store by awards and has not yet attended a Hollywood award ceremony.

Allen is still remembered for his work as a stand-up comedian, at the Jewish 'holiday camps' in the Catskills, and for the scripts he wrote and co-wrote for some of the funniest people on radio and television. In 1995 he wrote the second half of the play, *Acts of Murder*, that took 'off Broadway' by storm. His 1995 film *Mighty Aphrodite* was hated by American critics and loved by Europeans. In 1997 he made his first ever musical, *Everyone Says I Love You* has won critical and public aclaim. Woody Allen's throw-away lines are often memorable. 'For a while we wondered whether to take a vacation or get a divorce. We decided that a trip to Bermuda is over in two weeks but a divorce is something you always have.' 'To Catholics, death is a promotion.'

Shulamit Aloni was born in Tel Aviv, Palestine, in 1929, to recently arrived immigrants from Poland. At her parents' urging, she studied to be a teacher. However, she then decided on a career in the law and graduated from the Hebrew University Law School. In 1959, she joined the government party, Mapai. Between 1961 and 1965, she produced a series of radio programmes, designed to help people with their legal problems and the increasing deficiencies of government. It was as a result of these programmes that, in 1965, Israel appointed an Ombudsman to deal with citizens' complaints.

Also in 1965, Prime Minister Levi Eshkol invited Aloni to take a place on Labour's parliamentary list for the forthcoming general election. She agreed, and won a seat, only to find being an MP most frustrating. She provoked the orthodox MPs by appearing in the Knesset wearing low-cut dresses and high heels. Making her point: under no circumstances was she going to be a good, quiet MP toeing the party line. She took on the burden of women's rights, long overlooked in a country dominated by an orthodox religion that claims women are subservient to men.

She fell out with Golda Meir (*qv*) who called Aloni 'a demagogue' and placed her so low on the 1969 party list that she lost her seat in parliament. She became nationally and internationally known, when she invented the 'Shulamit Aloni Marriage': a non-religious contractual agreement between a consenting couple (a man and a woman) and witnessed by a lawyer.

In September 1973 she formed her own political party, the Citizen's Rights Movement, which won three seats in the general election and fought against red tape and senseless bureaucracy. She subsequently gained significant changes. Regarded by some as an opportunist, she joined the government of Yitzhak Rabin (*qv*) to become only the second woman in Israel's post-1948 history to hold a Cabinet post. Her job was Minister without Portfolio; it lasted until Rabin invited the National Religious Party to join his government. In June 1992, Aloni created the Maretz party from an alliance of small left of centre parties. Campaigning on the theme of humanity, they won 12 seats in the Knesset. Now head of the third largest party in the parliament, she aligned with Labour and once again entered the Cabinet, this time as Minister of Education. However, for Rabin her inclusion in the government was the beginning of many problems. Aloni repeatedly attacked his other coalition partner, the ultra-orthodox Shas party, and in 1993 the Shas demanded her resignation. Rabin refused. The Shas said they would leave the coalition. Rabin then explained to Aloni that breaking up the coalition could result in the government falling and the peace talks ending. Aloni reluctantly agreed to resign the education portfolio and become instead Minister for Communications, Science and Technology. She did not stand in the 1996 general election.

ALPERT,
Herb
(1935-)
US musician

Herb Alpert was born in Los Angeles on March 31st 1935 into a highly musical Jewish family. His father played the mandolin, his mother the violin, his sister the piano and his brother the drums. Herb was eight when he joined in on the trumpet. Educated at Fairfax High School, he thought of perhaps becoming a jazz musician; but before he could get his ideas into positive focus, he was conscripted into the US Army for two years. In the army he played trumpet and blew the bugle. Out of the army he recorded his first hit, 'The Lonely Bull' (1962), a song that had started life under the title 'Twinkle Star'. Alpert added a Mexican sound and the crowd noise from a Tijuana bull fight. Jerry Moss, Alpert's business partner in their A&M record label, suggested the record be known as 'Herb Alpert and the Tijuana Brass'. So are legends born. The Brass went on to make another hit, 'A Taste of Honey', and several albums that found their way to Number 1.

April 22nd 1968 saw Alpert given his own television show by CBS. Alpert had the idea of singing a song to his wife on the show. But what to sing? Out of around 50 songs he narrowed it down to one. The music was by Burt Bacharach (*qv*), the lyrics by Hal David: it was 'This Guy's in Love With You'. They recorded it on the beach at Malibu, with Herb Alpert singing it to his wife, Sharon. By the week of June 22nd 1968, it was at the top of the charts and a winner all over the world. A&M, a very successful recording company, with artists of the calibre of Cat Stevens, Procul Harum, The Carpenters, The Police and many others, was sold in 1994 for $500 million. In July 1996, Alpert played his first London concert for 22 years - in the same year that Alpert and Moss created Almo Records. *Second Wind* is Alpert's first album for his new label. He is still in partnership with Jerry Moss and still exercising his influence on the pop scene.

Altman was born on May 19th 1939 in Montreal, Canada. He received his BS in physics in 1960 from the Massachusetts Institute of Technology and his PhD in biophysics in 1967 from the University of Colorado. He became a full professor at Yale University in 1980. During his researches into RNA factors, Altman discovered that RNA could have active enzymatic functions. This new knowledge opened fresh areas of scientific endeavour and prompted scientists to rethink their theories of how life first began on Earth. As a result Altman was awarded the 1989 Nobel Prize for Chemistry.

ALTMAN, Sidney (1939-) Canadian molecular biologist

Andrade was born in London, on December 27th 1887, and graduated from University College, London. He then worked in Manchester, with Rutherford, on measuring the wavelength of gamma rays. During the First World War he served as an artillery officer, and after the war became professor of physics at the Artillery College, Woolwich. He later became head of the physics department at his *alma mater*. In 1935 he was elected a Fellow of the Royal Society. In 1950 he was appointed director of the Royal Institution and the Davy-Faraday research laboratory; but two years later he resigned, over differences with the governors. He went to the Imperial College of Science and there established what became known as 'Andrade's Laws', concerning the flow of metals. He became internationally known when, in 1947, he published *The Atom and its Energy*: the first book to explain atomic energy to laypeople. In 1954, he wrote an outstanding biography of Isaac Newton, which is still the main source on Newton's work and times. Two further books which created wide interest were *Physics for the Modern World* (1963) and *Rutherford and the Nature of the Atom* (1964). Andrade died in London on June 6th 1971.

ANDRADE, Edward (1887-1971) British physicist

Anielewicz was born in the slums of Warsaw and died the hero of the ghetto uprising. In between, he got himself an education and came to believe in socialism in a Zionist atmosphere. He joined the Ha-Shomer ha-Za'ir movement and became one of its leaders. When the Germans arrived in Warsaw, his aim was to get to Palestine, via Romania. However, on the way he was arrested by the Soviets and, when released, was ordered back to Warsaw. Here, in the early days of the occupation, he organized the distribution of underground newspapers. Then the Germans started rounding up the Jews and creating the ghetto. Murder of Jews was commonplace and Anielewicz, together with Polish communists, began organizing Jewish-Polish armed resistance units. Then, as the ghetto closed in on them, Jewish-only units came into being.

ANIELEWICZ, Mordecai (1919-43) Polish resistance leader

Early in 1943, German units, attempting to round up the last 60,000 Jews, came up against fierce resistance and withdrew. The deportations were called off and Anielewicz became the hero of the ghetto. The beleaguered Jews started building defences, for the battle they knew was coming. On April 19th 1943, the Germans arrived in force and a fierce battle raged. The Germans were amazed at the strength of the resistance. They suffered such severe casualties that they were forced to withdraw. The simple exercise of rounding up weak and starving Jews, something that had become commonplace for the German army all over occupied Europe, had become a major problem. German soldiers were being killed and, like the cowards they showed themselves to be when not in numerical superiority or faced only with unarmed people, they fled the scene. Anielewicz, as overall commander of the resistance, was an inspiring figure.

On May 8th, overwhelming German forces, under their new commander General Stroop (hanged by the Poles in 1947 for his war crimes in the ghetto), stormed the barricades. During the ensuing fighting, Anielewicz was killed. Inspired in part by his memory, the battle continued for another month. The Polish People's Guard, impressed by the Jewish resistance, helped the last 50 fighters to escape to the forests and continue the fight in a partisan unit called 'Anielewicz'.

The uprising had an enormous effect on Jew and Gentile alike. It caused Polish resistance to stiffen and provided inspiration for resistance all over occupied Europe. To put Anielewicz's achievements into perspective, it was because of his driving force that the ghetto uprising took place to become the biggest battle in occupied Europe up to 1943. Kibbutz Yad Mordekhai, in Israel, is named after him; a life-size sculpture, by Natan Rapaport, stands at its entrance.

ANTHEIL,
George
(1900-58)
US composer

Antheil was born on July 8th 1900 in Trenton, New Jersey, to Polish-Jewish parents. He studied music in Philadelphia, and also under Ernest Bloch in Europe. For a time he paid his way by playing the piano in a Parisian night club, while composing by day. In 1925 he achieved instant fame with his *Jazz Symphony*. His *Ballet Mécanique* was eagerly awaited but proved to be one of the most difficult works ever produced. It was written for a minimum of ten pianos, an assortment of percussion instruments, anvils, aircraft propellers and many more noise machines. It earned him the soubriquet 'Bad Boy of Music' - a phrase which was later to be the title of his autobiography.

Returning to the US, he became a successful composer of film music, and his opera *Transatlantic* (1930) was well received. As an acclaimed concert pianist he promoted contemporary composers, but in his heart he was devoted to Beethoven. During the Second World War he and his friend, the lovely actress Hedy Lamarr, worked on a device for directing small boats and torpedoes. In 1942 the pair were granted a patent and offered their invention to the US War Department. Much to their regret, their offer was refused. Years later, their patent having expired, the invention was adapted for use in satellite communications by Sylvania, who made no reference to the original inventors. Antheil died on February 12th 1958 in New York City; his constant friend Hedy Lamarr was among the mourners at his funeral.

Born in New York on March 14th 1923 to wealthy Jewish parents, **Arbus** was educated privately and married at the age of 18. She spent the next 20 years working on magazines, designing fashion layouts. In 1960, she separated from her husband and, turning away from her wealthy roots, took her camera to the streets, to photograph life as it really was in the 1960s. Her close-ups, stark and uncompromising, in black and white, showed the other side of the coin to the wealth of Manhattan: poverty, often only yards away from wealth. She showed the deprived, the mentally ill and the older, unattractive, prostitutes. She portrayed people unaware they were being photographed and therefore without the posed mask. She brought her pictures to the world and received public acclamation. She was given an exhibition at the Museum of Modern Art in New York, which received critical praise.

However, this was not enough for Diane Arbus she was becoming increasingly depressed and suffered long bouts of withdrawal. In 1969 she divorced. Her last work was of mental patients dressed up for a formal party. It was all too much. Her depressions returned and, in New York on July 26th 1971, she committed suicide. Her work helped awaken the world to the continuing plight of the weak and disadvantaged. In 1972, she was honoured at the Venice Bienniale, the first American photographer to be so acknowledged.

Ardon was born in Tuchow, Poland, when the family name was Bronstein. His early work was considered good enough to earn him acceptance at the Bauhaus in Berlin for further studies. Later, his work was considered to be of such a high calibre that he was invited to join the 'November Group' and exhibit. This was just before the advent of Hitler. In 1933 he decided to emigrate to Palestine. Despite his job as a director of the Bezalel School, which would produce such artists as Alexander Arikha and Naphtali Bezem, Ardon never stopped painting, and in 1954 he became the first Israeli artist to exhibit at the prestigious Venice Bienniale, where he received the UNESCO prize. His paintings of landscapes and portraits reveal a highly distinctive brush technique, and his very individual style of forms, which mixes the abstract and the symbolist, has brought him an international reputation. His works can be seen at the Tate Gallery in London, the Museum of Modern Art in New York and at museums all over the world.

Though a French writer, **Arega** was born in Poland, his family driven, like many other middle-class Jewish families, by a pogrom to seek sanctuary in Western Europe. Arriving in France only a few years prior to the Second World War, when that war started Arega joined the French army, despite not being a French national. During some fierce fighting he was wounded and captured. Before the war was won, he was to escape from three prisoner of war camps to avoid being handed over to the Gestapo. He received an award for gallantry and was offered French citizenship. He settled in Paris and started writing novels of a secular nature that were well received; a natural storyteller, he became very popular. *Comme Si C'etait Fini*, written in 1946, tells how a foreign Jew volunteers for the French army, only to find that his comrades don't accept him as one of them; then he is captured by the Germans, who won't accept he is a Frenchman. He is in no-man's-land and remains there.

ARENDT,
Hannah
(1906-75)
German
political
philosopher

Born into an upper-class assimilated family on October 14th 1906 in Hanover, **Hannah** was given every advantage. After a university education she chose to leave Germany and the growing menace of Nazism to live in Paris. She became actively involved in getting groups of young people into Palestine and eventually became Director of Youth Aliya. After the fall of France to German forces, she was incarcerated in Gurs concentration camp. Following the personal intervention of President Roosevelt, Hannah and around 100 other intellectuals were allowed to leave for the US.

The Origins of Totalitarianism, a major work that ranges over anti-Semitism, imperialism and totalitarianism, and also traces the decline of Europe that contributed to the emergence of these trends, was published in 1951. It was followed in 1958 by *The Human Condition*, describing man's political abilities in relation to world affairs. Arendt covered Eichman's trial in Israel and then published what proved to be a most controversial work, *A Report on the Banality of Evil*. This was too much for many people to stomach. In it, Arendt argued that Jewish leaders were responsible for the lack of resistance to the Holocaust and claimed that as everyone has the capacity for evil, Eichman was not alone and Israel had no right to try or execute him. This work brought her into the public arena, with mixed results. US Jewry were deeply appalled and very angry. They refused to accept her intellectual theory that the Holocaust was the work of an uncontrollable machine. On the positive side, she became the first woman to hold a full professorship at Princeton University. Her last work, *The Life of the Mind,* was published posthumously in 1979.

Hannah Arendt had an love affair with Martin Heidegger which lasted fifty years, beginning when she was 18 and a student at Marburg University. Heidegger taught philosophy; besides being a devout Catholic he was an active member of the Nazi party from 1933 to 1945. Following the war, and in the face of the truth, Arendt not only forgave him but also protested his innocence and resumed their relationship. She died in New York on December 4th 1975.

ARKIN,
Alan
(1934-)
US actor

Arkin, born in New York on March 26th, 1934, was educated at Los Angeles City College and Bennington Drama College. His feature debut as the Soviet submariner who finds himself in US waters in *The Russians are Coming, The Russians are Coming* (1966) was a winner. He is considered to be a highly versatile actor of proven ability. He has twice been nominated for an Oscar for Best Actor, for *The Russians are Coming...* and for *The Heart is a Lonely Hunter* (1968). He has starred in some excellent films, among which *Wait Until Dark*, with Audrey Hepburn, stands out. *Freebie and the Bean* (1974), a forerunner of the genre of violent comedy films involving police partners, was a great success. Arkin is an innovative actor who relishes starring roles in oddball films that are often extremely good, but have limited audience appeal, such as *Chu Chu and the Philly Flash* (1981). His inimitable style has won him many fans and he is regarded in the film world as an 'actor's actor', especially after his performance in *Glengarry Glenn Ross* (1992), in which he stole attention from the lead actor, Al Pacino. In 1968 he played the part of Clouseau in *Inspector Clouseau*, the exploits of a bumbling

French policeman - the role that made Peter Sellers (*qv*) internationally famous. The winner? Arkin, by a short bumble.

Alan Arkin is also the author of children's stories. *Tony's Hard Work Day* (1972) is about a boy who builds a house and *The Lemming Condition* (1976) is about a young lemming seeking the truth.

Born Hyman Arluck on February 15th 1905 in Buffalo, New York, the son of a cantor and pianist, **Harold** showed exceptional talent for music from an early age. On leaving school, he formed his own band, and by the age of 24 he had turned composer. In 1929, he wrote 'Get Happy' with lyricist Ted Koehler and the two later wrote 'I've Got the World on a String'. Arlen later wrote the score for many of the Broadway shows of the 1930s, 1940s and 1950s. However, it is for the music he wrote for Hollywood films that Harold Arlen is best known: 'It's Only a Paper Moon'; 'Let's Fall in Love'; 'That Old Black Magic'; plus many more. In 1939, he won an Oscar for his 'Over the Rainbow', which Judy Garland sang in *The Wizard of Oz*. Other Arlen songs include, 'Stormy Weather' and 'Accentuate the Positive'. He was nominated nine times for Best Song Oscars, most recently in 1954 for the film, *A Star is Born*, again for Judy Garland. His music has gone around the world and received many honours from film and theatre societies. Arlen died in New York on April 23rd 1986.

Arlosoroff was one of the very few Jews born in Russia with the proverbial silver spoon in their mouths. Despite their wealth, however, the family decided to leave Russia after the pogroms of 1906 that followed the abortive revolution against the Tsar in 1905. They moved to Berlin, where Chaim was educated privately. In 1923, he received his doctorate and decided to involve himself with Zionist politics. He took up the socialist cause and in 1924 settled in Palestine. He built up a rapport with the British running the Mandate, and in particular with Herbert Samuel (*qv*), the serving High Commissioner. He became one of the founders of Mapai or Labour Party and became head of the Political Committee of the Zionist Movement while still only in his early thirties. He was murdered while strolling with his wife on a Tel Aviv beach. No one has ever been convicted of the crime and speculation as to the perpetrators has ranged from Revisionist thugs to Arab terrorists. Every town in Israel appears to have an 'Arlosoroff Street', possibly because he was cut down in his prime, when he appeared to have so much to offer. In a letter to Weizmann written in 1932, and speaking of the British Mandate, he uttered the prophetic warning: 'In the final resort a Jewish homeland would only come about by way of resistance and revolt.' Had he lived, Arlosoroff would doubtless have been an Israeli leader.

**ARNSTEIN,
Karl
(1887-1974)
German/
American
aviation
designer**

Arnstein, born in Germany, was the designer and engineer who, on behalf of the Zeppelin Company, built the airship that flew the Atlantic in 1924. There was of course enormous publicity and Arnstein was a German hero. He went on to build bigger and better machines; but when Hitler arrived, the fact that Arnstein was a giant in the aviation world meant less than the fact he was a Jew. Arnstein packed his bags, arrived in the US and, in 1934, was appointed vice-president of the Goodyear-Zeppelin Corporation. During the Second World War, Arnstein designed and built airships for the US Navy, including the *Los Angeles* and the *Akron*. He retired believing that one day airship travel would predominate over the jet.

**ARON,
Raymond
(1905-83)
French
philosopher**

Aron was born on March 14th 1905 into a Paris-based, middle-class, intellectual Jewish family. He completed his education at the Ecole Normale Supérieure, where he won first prize in philosophy. He then moved to Cologne, to become assistant to Lev Spitzer. While there, he wrote his thesis on *The Limitations of Historical Knowledge*, a philosophical theme to which he constantly returned. He wrote on various subjects, including industrial relations, modern industrial society and the repercussions of the clash of competing political systems. When war broke out in 1939, he was Professor of Social Philosophy at the University of Toulouse. Following a spell in the Resistance, he managed to get to London where, on behalf of de Gaulle, he edited *La France Libre*. The war over, Aron became a columnist for *Le Figaro* and commented on the Cold War thus: 'Peace is impossible; war is improbable.' He later became Professor of Sociology at the Sorbonne, and was one of the few professors who supported the students during the riots of 1968. He urged an end to the war in Algeria and the granting of independence. He was a 'middle of the road' man who, on the one hand, attacked Sartre for refusing to appreciate the real motives of Stalin, and on the other, attacked de Gaulle for his intransigence over Israel. He was outspoken over the world of nuclear balances, claiming the world had shifted from a balance of power to a balance of terror. He described himself as a Jewish agnostic and had little to say on matters Jewish until de Gaulle, following the Six-Day War, made his remarks regarding Jews and Israel; then he wrote *De Gaulle, Israel and the Jews* (1968). The book caused an international stir and brought him national and international attention. His published work is extensive, including *Peace and War* (1966), which caused something of a flurry. His best-known work is probably the two-volume *Main Currents in Sociological Thought* (1968). He died in Paris, on October 17th 1983, and the students he had supported during the riots of nearly thirty years earlier did not forget him: many attended his funeral.

**ARONSON,
Boris
(1900-80)
Russian/
American stage
designer**

Aronson was born in Kiev on October 15th 1900 and trained at the Kiev State Art School. He then worked in Moscow theatres, before going to Berlin and Paris to continue his studies. As a hobby or perhaps as an exercise, he wrote an important book concerning the work of Marc Chagall (1923), at that time emerging as a major artist. In 1924, Aronson arrived in New York and began designing sets for the Unser Theatre's production of *Bronx Express*. In 1930, he and Broadway found one another, and his rapid rise to fame and some fortune followed. By the 1950s he was the top stage designer in the US. His list of production designs is most prestigious and includes such shows as *Three Men on a Horse* (1935); *Cabin in the Sky* (1940); *View From the Bridge* (1955); *Diary of Anne Frank* (1957); and many more. The designs he made for the international hit, *Fiddler on the Roof*, guaranteed him lasting fame. He died in New York on November 16th 1980.

Aronson was born in Latvia, at a time of great anti-Jewish feeling. At school he showed great skill at woodcarving and, after training at the Vilna School of Art, went to Paris for further study. He remained in France until the start of the Second World War, when he escaped to the US; here he was to remain until his death three years later. While in France, Aronson created the definitive bust of Tolstoy. There have been many busts of the great writer but Aronson's is deemed the best. He spent many months with Tolstoy in order to get an insight into his subject's philosophy. After the First World War, Aronson refused a commission from the French government to create busts of the French generals, commenting that he preferred to honour the peacemakers and choosing as his subject Louis Pasteur, the occasion the centenary of the scientist's birth. At the 1937 World's Fair, held in Paris, two major works by Aronson were shown; a sculpture of Beethoven and a large bas-relief, *France and her Colonies*. A particular feature of his work, which became very well known, was the marble heads of young girls. These are regularly shown at museums all over the world.

ARONSON, Naum (1872-1943) French sculptor

Arrow was born on August 23rd 1921 in New York. He graduated from Columbia University and went on to become economics professor at Stanford University (1949-1968), before moving to Harvard (1968-79). His work in the field of economics, in which he specialized, covered the international scene, his central work being his book *Collective Choice Based on Uncertainty and Risk*. In 1962 he was appointed to the Council of Economic Advice in the Kennedy administration. In 1972 he was awarded the Nobel Prize for Economics. 'Arrow's Theorem' holds that, under certain conditions of rationality and equality, it is impossible to guarantee that a ranking of societal preferences will correspond to rankings of individual preferences, when more than two individuals and alternative choices are involved.

ARROW, Kenneth (1921-) US economist

Asch was born on November 1st 1880 in Kutno, Poland. His family was an intellectual one, despite the fact that his father was a horse dealer. In order to read the classics he taught himself German. After traditional schooling he became a professional letter-writer to the illiterate. He spent the First World War in the US, where he wrote *Motke the Thief* (1917) and began to attract notice. Back in Europe, he settled in France, where he wrote his historical novel, *Kiddush Ha-Shem* (1919), following it up with *The Witch of Castile* (1921). His work skilfully interweaves threads of faith and morality, the mundane and the sacred. His stories often concern the hard struggle for survival of East European Jewry, and, among them, some Gentiles. His style changed when he returned to the US in 1938. There, he developed

ASCH, Sholem (1880-1957) Polish/American writer

a secular stance. International fame came when he wrote his trilogy about the founders of Christianity, *The Nazarene, The Apostle and Mary* (1943-49). He interpreted Christianity as the logical extension of Judaism. Orthodox Jewry, who once loved him, now hated him. Asch, however, was not concerned. He had the compensation of being lauded by those whose opinion meant something to him. He died in London on July 10th 1957.

ASCOLI
Ettore
(1873-1943)
Italian soldier

Ascoli was born in Ascona, Italy, to a middle-class Jewish family. Following a formal education he became a professional soldier, eventually receiving a commission in the artillery. In the period immediately prior to the First World War he was a senior instructor at the Modena Military Academy. During that war, Italy fought on the Allied side, and throughout its duration Ascoli held fighting commands. In 1916 he was decorated by several Allied governments for the battle he won when, as commander of an Allied artillery force, he repelled an Austrian attack which, had it succeeded, would have had most serious repercussions. The war over, he was appointed head of military schools with the rank of major-general. In 1937, with Mussolini in power, he was promoted lieutenant-general and given command of an army corps, only to be dismissed his post when anti-Jewish laws were enacted. In 1943, at the age of 70, Ascoli joined the anti-Fascist partisans and was killed fighting the Germans.

ASHENHEIM,
Sir Neville,
(1900-87)
Jamaican lawyer

Ashenheim was born in Kingston, Jamaica, and educated in Britain. Returning to Kingston, he practised as a lawyer until he was appointed to head the Jamaican Industrial Development Corporation (1952-57). He then went into politics and became a member of the Legislative Council (1959). His greatest task was as Jamaica's first ambassador to the US (1962-66). His work in obtaining favourable loans for Jamaica's fledgling industry and building up the tourist industry cannot be overestimated. He was knighted in 1963 and, in 1967, appointed to the Senate as Leader of the House and to the Cabinet as Finance Minister. Despite a busy life, he was always available to discuss matters pertaining to the *Daily Gleaner*, the country's leading newspaper, founded by his grandfather and still owned by a family trust.

ASHKENAZY,
Vladimir
(1937-)
Russian pianist
and conductor

Born on July 6th 1937 in Gorky, into a musical family, **Ashkenazy** graduated with honours from Moscow Conservatory and came to prominence in 1956 when he won the Queen Elizabeth Competition in Brussels. He later won the Tchaikovsky Piano Competition of 1962. Ashkenazy made his London debut in 1963 and decided to stay there; in 1973 he settled in Iceland, where his pianist wife was born. His style is elegant and restrained and his playing and interpretation of such composers as Rachmaninoff and Prokofiev have been favourably acknowledged. Following a brilliant recital career, in the early 1980s he decided to take up the conductor's baton. In 1987, he was appointed Musical Director of the Royal Philharmonic Orchestra. Ashkenazy is considered one of the greats of the musical world, and influential in having brought to public attention the works of less well-known composers.

Asimov was born in Petrovichi, USSR, on January 2nd 1920 and taken by his parents to the US when he was just three years old. At Columbia University he obtained a PhD in chemistry but though he went on to a distinguished career as a biochemist, fame and wealth came to Asimov in large measure from his science fiction writing. He made his initial mark with his famous short story, 'Nightfall', in 1941. His best-known works are the *Robot* novels and the *Foundation* series. He was very prolific, writing many short stories and articles for newspapers and magazines. He brought the world of science to millions of people who would otherwise have sidestepped the subject completely. He reached the status of a seer and added the term 'robotics' to the languages of the world. He died in New York City on April 6th 1992. A man of some humour, he dedicated one of his books to his secretary thus: To Natalie Greenberg, Miss Efficiency.

Tobias Asser was born in the Netherlands, into an old and respected Jewish family, on April 28th 1838. At the turn of the twentieth century, he became the prime mover in the creation of the Permanent Court of Arbitration at The Hague. It was Asser who, in 1900, arbitrated between Russia and America over fishing rights in the Baring Straits. Noted for the Hague Treaties of 1902-1905, concerning family law, as well as other social legislation, Asser was the Netherlands' delegate to the Hague Peace Conference of 1907. In 1911, Tobias Asser was the joint recipient of the Nobel Peace Prize. He died, at The Hague, on July 29th 1913.

Atlan was born in Algiers to Jewish-Berber parents. In 1930 he went to Paris to study philosophy and remained there, studying and working, until the fall of France in 1940. He took up painting as a method of rehabilitation after spending long periods in psychiatric hospitals hiding from the German Gestapo and French police. In 1947, he turned to abstraction and developed a characteristic style of rhythmical forms, in deep and rich colours, painted in a mixture of oils and pastels. Critics claim his work is influenced by both Negro sculpture and pre-Columbia America. He appears to have been fascinated by the primitive, the erotic and the magical. He remains the most mystical of French abstract painters and reached his fullest expression during the last five years of his life. Had he lived longer, he would have doubtless been among the best of the century. In 1953, in the course of an article about starting a painting, he stated: 'At the outset there is a rhythm which tends to develop itself; it is the perception of this rhythm which is fundamental and it is on this development that the vital quality of the work depends.'

Atlas was born in New York and served in the US Air Force during the Second World War. In 1948 he joined the Air Force Research Unit and became chief of the weather radar branch. In 1965 he was appointed Professor of Geophysical Sciences at the University of Chicago. He invented a method for the measurement of atmospheric turbulence and the echoes of lightening channels, which come in on the tops of thunderstorms. His safety device for detecting severe storms was a key advance for air crews; it has subsequently been adopted by the world's leading airlines. It is recognized that the safety of modern air travel is largely due to Atlas's work in the field of radar research, and in developing the Doppler radar systems in the field of agrometeorology, becoming known throughout the world.

ATLAS,
Jechezkiel
(1913-42)
Polish resistance
leader

Atlas was born in Rawa-Mazowiecka, Poland. He qualified as a medical doctor and worked for a time in general practice. Shortly after the arrival of the Germans in September 1939, his parents were murdered. He went to Wiekla-Wola to work and, while there, began gathering together young Jews who had escaped German-controlled ghettoes. He formed a partisan unit, obtained weapons, recruited former Jewish soldiers of the Polish army and took to the Lipiczani forest. The group was 120 strong and linked to a Soviet partisan unit. After the first battle, Atlas was appointed overall commander. During 1942, he led them on raids that attacked and wiped out German garrisons at Dereczy, Kozlowszczyzna and Ruda-Jaworska. The unit didn't take prisoners. They blew up bridges, railway lines and trains. Atlas was killed in action when the Germans launched large-scale reprisals against the partisans. He was an inspiration to all partisan units, who continued their war against the Germans until liberated.

ATTELL,
Abe
(1884-1970)
US world
champion boxer

Abe Attell was born in San Francisco on February 22nd 1884 to Jewish parents lured to California by the gold rush of the 1870s. Abe turned to boxing as a living, as did his younger brother, Monte. Attell's record is considered remarkable. Known affectionately worldwide as, 'the Little Hebrew', he reigned as undisputed World Featherweight Champion from the time he was 18, beating Johnny Regan over 20 rounds in 1903, until he retired undefeated in 1912. In 1905 he lost the title to Tony Sullivan; however, Sullivan soon lost it to Jimmy Walsh, and in 1906 Attell defeated Walsh and went on to defend his title 21 times during the succeeding six years. He was considered the complete fighter: a scientific boxer and a very hard puncher. Over a long career he had 171 professional fights and lost only nineteen of them. Elected to the Boxing Hall of Fame in 1955, he died on February 15th 1970.

AUB,
Max
(1903-)
French/Spanish
writer

Aub was born in Paris to a German Jewish father and a French mother. The outbreak of the First World War meant deportation for Aub senior, so the family moved on to Spain. Although he had Spanish nationality when the Fascist, Franco, took over Spain, Max Aub returned to France. Now it was Hitler's turn to plague him. Following the defeat of France Aub was imprisoned by the Vichy police, before being shipped over to French North Africa. From there he escaped, winding up in Mexico. He had been a well-known figure in Spain, gaining recognition from his well-received play *Narcisco* (1928) and his first novel *Geographia* (1929). Other books followed, dealing mostly with political and social realities within contemporary life. After the Second World War, his books often dwelt on the Spanish Civil War. Probably his most famous work is his play *San Juan*. Written in 1943, the play focuses on a group of Jewish refugees on an old cargo ship, somewhere in the Mediterranean, being refused permission to land anywhere.

Auer was born on June 7th 1845 in Veszprem, Hungary. By the beginning of the 20th century, Auer had settled in Russia and was Professor of Violin at the St Petersburg Conservatory. This was a rare appointment for a Jew, and one possible explanation is that it was not known he was Jewish, being considered just a Hungarian. This supposition is supported by the fact he was knighted, by Nicholas II, and appointed the Tsar's court violinist. Auer left Russia at the time of the 1917 revolution and settled in New York. Tchaikovsky dedicated his violin concerto to Auer; however, the latter claimed the work was unplayable and the dedication went elsewhere. Later Auer changed his mind and was responsible for the concerto becoming very popular in the US. In America, Auer became a teacher of the violin and his pupils included some who were to figure among the greatest violinists of the 20th century: Mischa Elman (*qv*), Jasha Heifetz (*qv*), Efrem Zimbalist and Nathan Milstein (*qv*). Auer wrote several books, including *Violin Playing As I Teach It* (1921) and *Violin Master Works and Their Interpretation* (1923). The title of his autobiography was *My Long Life in Music*. He died in Loschwitz, Germany, on July 15th 1930.

AUER, Leopold (1845-1930) Hungarian/ American violinist

Auerbach, born in Brooklyn, New York, on September 20th 1917, went to George Washington University on a sports scholarship, playing varsity football while he received his education. For a while he played professional basketball, but soon realized that his true role was as a coach. In 1950 he took on Boston Celtic. No one else wanted the job: the team was bottom of the league and likely to stay there. Auerbach thought otherwise. Despite being a Jew in the midst of Irish Catholics, he had his way and Boston Celtic gradually climbed the ladder until, in 1957, they won the title. Proving that this was no fluke, Auerbach did it again in 1959 and every year thereafter until 1966, when he retired. His achievements have never been equalled in any major sport. A quick-tempered, fiery personality, never one to suffer fools gladly, he was named to the National Basketball Hall of Fame in 1968 and appointed life president of Boston Celtic.

AUERBACH, Arnold 'Red' (1917-) US basketball coach

Richard Avedon was born in New York on May 15th 1923. At the age of ten he was experimenting with photographic portraiture. Living in the same New York apartment block at that time was the great composer Rachmaninoff. He and the boy photographer became firm friends and Rachmaninoff was his first sitter. Avedon studied photography while in the US merchant marine and later at the New School for Social Research. After the Second World War he became a professional and a regular contributor to *Harper's Bazaar* (1946-65) before switching to *Vogue* (1966-70). His black and white photographs, usually dealing with fashion, are considered most sophisticated. Often he emphasized elements of his sitters' personalities, with startling effect. His publications included many of his more famous photographs, as in *Observations* (1959), *Nothing Personal* (1974) and *Avedon: Photographs, 1947-1977* (1978). Avedon first began to be involved with motion films and television in 1957 when he was the consultant on *Funny Face*, based on Avedon's life. An acknowledged leader in his fashion and portrait work, and considered one of the finest photographers in the world, he later directed a number of television programmes that dealt with photography.

AVEDON, Richard (1923-) US photographer

AVIGUR,
Shaul
(1899-)
Israeli organizer

Avigur was born in Dvinsk, Russia and taken to Palestine when he was twelve. After a formal education and jobs he disliked, Avigur joined the Haganah during the British Mandate, and made it a career. He became their lead organizer. He arranged for the purchase of illegal arms abroad and organized small workshops to make home products. He organized the Haganah intelligence-gathering unit and created havens for illegal immigrants before, during and after the Second World War. Europe at peace meant hard work for Avigur. He was head of an enormous organization, set up to help the survivors of the horror camps to adjust to a new life. There was one purpose and that was to get them into Palestine. This Avigur achieved, despite the obstructions set by the British army and navy. With the establishment of Israel in May 1948, Avigur had the urgent task of purchasing arms from anywhere he could. This time his job was legal. In 1962 he published his semi-autobiographical *Reminiscences with the Haganah*.

AXELROD,
Julius
(1912-)
US
pharmacologist

Julius Axelrod, born in New York on May 30th 1912, was beset by poverty and Jewish quotas in his attempts to get into university. He was refused admission to medical school and so took an MA in chemical pharmacology instead. In 1955 he was head of the pharmacology section of the National Institute of Mental Health. In 1970 he shared the Nobel Prize for Physiology for his discovery of the substance that inhibits neural impulses. The work he did laid the foundation for essential research in neurophysiology, notably in the search for remedies for hypertension and schizophrenia.

AXEN,
Hermann
(1916-92)
German
politician

Hermann Axen was born in Leipzig, Germany, on March 6th 1916 to Jewish parents. His father was an official of the German Communist Party. By the time Hermann was being educated at a secondary school in Leipzig, Hitler was in power and Hermann a member of the Young Communist League. For most of the twelve years of Nazi rule, Axen was in prison or in a concentration camp. In 1935, there was a round-up of Communists and he was sent to prison for three years. In October 1938 he took off for France and lived in Paris until the German occupation. For two years he was interned by the Vichy French. Then the Germans took over Vichy and Axen was sent first to Auschwitz and then to Buchenwald, from where he was liberated by the Red Army. As he was both a Communist and a Jew, it was remarkable that he survived the war.

In April 1945, after a period of recuperation, Axen became a professional party worker in the German Democratic Republic or GDR. He came to the notice of Erich Honecker, then a senior party official and later the head of state. Honecker took Axen under his wing and Axen gradually climbed the political ladder. A number of appointments followed, and in 1970 he was appointed chairman of the Committee for Foreign Affairs in the People's Chamber, a post he held until 1989. In this position he began appearing on the international scene and at the head of various GDR delegations. In 1977 he was in France; he had talks with Margaret Thatcher in London in 1981 and later with François Mitterrand in Paris; in 1988 he was in Washington DC for talks with Secretary of State Schultz.

Although a powerful figure in the GDR, Axen was also a realist. As a Jew he had to be all things to all people, while keeping one eye on Moscow and one on the party machine. In 1970 he became a full member of the Politburo. When Honecker took over in October 1976, he breathed more easily. In his foreign affairs position he held constant talks with officials from West Germany. Gradually the tensions between the two countries eased, and from 1984 onwards he headed the East German side in the special talks that eventually led to the Berlin Wall coming down. When that event occurred, Axen was in Moscow, having an eye operation; when he returned a few months later, he was arrested and charged with corruption and abuse of office. The charges were designed to take the pressure off a German government being assailed by East Germans wanting an equal standing of living with their new-found West German neighbours. Axen knew about the charges awaiting him, but insisted on leaving Moscow to face them. He knew the accusations were false; in the event, they were withdrawn and Axen allowed the peaceful retirement he so richly deserved. He died in Berlin on February 15th 1992.

Commemorative Stamps

Jankel Adler
Issued by Israel

Shmuel Agnon
Issued by Israel

Pierre Alechinsky
Issued by France

Herbert Baum
Issued by East Germany

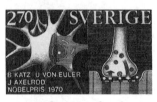

Julius Axelrod
Issued by Sweden

Harold Arlen
Issued by US

David Ben-Gurion
Issued by Israel

Jack Benny
Issued by Grenada

Mikhael Botvinnik
Issued by Republic of Central Africa

B

Babel, born in Odessa on July 13th 1894, is probably the best short story writer in Russian literature. He received a traditional religious education and a secular one to balance it. Following Kiev University, Babel moved to Petrograd where his earliest stories appeared in *Letopis*, a magazine edited by Maxim Gorki. In 1917, Babel welcomed the Bolshevik revolution and fought for the Reds in the civil war that followed. He was appointed a political commissar and rode with the 1st Cavalry Army - probably the only Jew ever to ride and fight with the traditional enemy, the Cossacks.

From 1923 Babel wrote stories, film scripts and plays. International fame came with the publication of two collections of short stories *Konarmiya'* (*The Red Cavalry*) (1926) and *Odessa Tales* (1927). His stories are masterpieces of disciplined prose and vividly convey colour and sound to the reader. Following the success of these two books, Babel fell from Soviet favour. With the death of Gorki in 1936 he was without a voice to speak for him and his work. He was arrested in 1939 and simply vanished in a world that was too violently occupied to look for him. In 1964 his daughter published her biography, *The Lonely Years 1925-1939*, and world interest in Babel's work revived. As our century draws to a close, Babel's stories are still considered most captivating.

Betty Joan Perske came on stage in New York City on September 16th 1924. **Bacall** was a student at the American Academy of Dramatic Art and made her professional stage debut in *Johnny Two-by-Four* in 1942. While working as a fashion model she appeared on the cover of *Harper's Bazaar*. Howard Hawks, the film director, saw the cover and signed her up for the role of 'Slinky' in his film *To Have and Have Not*: thus a legend was born. Her performance was so magical that not only did the public fall in love with her, but so did her leading man, Humphrey Bogart. She and 'Bogie' married in 1945 and starred together in three further films, all winners: *The Big Sleep* (1946); *Dark Passage* (1947); and *Key Largo* (1948). Following Bogart's death in 1957 Bacall turned to her first love, the theatre. She starred in several productions including *The Cactus Flower* (1965) and the long-running *Applause*, for which she received a Tony award. She was a tower of purpose during the infamous McCarthy era and one of the leading marchers in the protest campaign.

Bacall continues to make films and appear in plays; during the summer of 1995 she enjoyed acting in a play by Dürrenmatt at Chichester in England. She is a mother and grandmother; and as her eldest grandson is nearly 30, she could easily become a great-grandmother. This is a woman who has become an icon to women all over the globe, showing how to survive in a world that worships youth. In 1979 she wrote her bestselling autobiography, *By Myself*, and later *Now*, an enjoyable tour of memories. It is not the least part of Bacall's enduring appeal that, considering she is an important figure in the glittering world of entertainment, she doesn't take herself too seriously. This attitude stood her in great stead during the 1997 Academy Award presentations when, despite being the favourite for an Oscar as Best Supporting Actress, it went elsewhere. Bacall remained dignified, serene and smiling.

BACHARACH, Alfred (1891-1966) British chemist

Bacharach was born in London on August 11th 1891 and graduated from Cambridge University before joining the Wellcome Research Laboratories. Later, having moved to Glaxo, he pioneered work on vitamins and their development. He is credited with wiping out the disease of rickets in British children between the two world wars. As well as writing much in his professional field, Bacharach was also passionate about music and in 1957 published *The Music Masters*, which went on to become a textbook on the subject.

BACHARACH, Burt (1929-) US composer

Born in Kansas City on May 12th 1929, **Burt Bacharach** was educated at McGill University in Montreal, Canada. He then went on to Tanglewood Mannes School for Music. During the Korean War he was among those who entertained the forces, as a classical pianist. He drifted along until selected to be Marlene Dietrich's conductor/arranger on her world tour. Global recognition followed when he wrote film music such as the title song for the film *Alfie*, which brought him an Oscar nomination, and 'What the World Needs Now'. For the hit film *Butch Cassidy and the Sundance Kid* (1969) he wrote 'Raindrops Keep Falling on My Head', which brought him another Oscar. All this, plus the music for *Casino Royale*, *What's New Pussycat* and *Arthur*, and much more besides, gives Burt Bacharach an importance that cannot be overestimated.

BACHER, Aron 'Ali' (1942-) South African cricketer

Born into a Lithuanian Jewish family, after qualifying as a doctor of medicine **Bacher** turned his back on what would have been a lucrative white practice and devoted his early years to non-whites. He achieved widespread distinction at cricket which reached godlike proportions when South Africa defeated Australia in 1966. In 1970 he was captain of the side that played England in the test match series. During the sport isolation that came with apartheid, Bacher did his best to keep the cricket flag flying, often in the face of fierce opposition. His dream of multi-racial sport is now a reality and in 1996, after a long interval, England was once again the side Bacher's team faced in South Africa. England lost. Now chief executive of the United Board of South Africa, Bacher is reckoned to be the most dynamic and innovative administrator in world cricket. Bacher's nephew Adam is now flying the flag. A member of the South African test team he was top scorer in their win over Australia in March 1997.

Baer was born on February 9th 1909 in Omaha, Nebraska, the eldest son of a Jewish father. With schooling over and jobs hard to find in the depression of the 1930s, Baer turned to boxing as a career. In 1933, unusually for a contender in a heavyweight non-title fight, he became the centre of world attention. This was occasioned by the fact that Baer was fighting Max Schmeling, a former world champion and a German Nazi, who was personally backed by Hitler. Baer appeared in the ring complete with a Star of David on his shorts and Schmeling, who had been given his orders by Hitler only an hour before, sneered openly. However, things went badly wrong for Hitler's protégé: Baer knocked him out. The following year Baer took on Primo Carnera, an Italian backed by Mussolini and reigning world champion, for the world heavyweight title: again, this time in the eleventh round, Baer knocked his opponent out. Baer lost the title a year later to Jim Braddock and retired in 1941 following his defeat by the legendary Joe Louis. He spent the rest of his life as an actor, appearing on stage, films and television. He died on November 23rd 1959.

BAER,
Max
(1909-59)
US world
champion boxer

Baeyer, born on October 31st 1835 in Berlin of a Jewish mother and a Gentile father, was awarded the Nobel Prize for Chemistry in 1905. His work in organic chemistry as it affected organic dyes and hydro-aromatic compounds, for which the prize was awarded, served the public in so far as it provided for colours to be dyed fast so that they did not run when first washed. He died in Berlin on August 20th 1917.

BAEYER,
Adolph von
(1835-1917)
German
organic chemist

Eduard, the son of poor Jewish tradespeople, was born Eduard Georgiyevich Dzyubin on November 3rd 1895 in Odessa, Russia. At technical school he learned land surveying and in 1917 took part in the Russian Revolution, fighting as a Red Army guerrilla in the Civil War while writing poetry in support of Lenin. The war left him in poor health and he decided to become a full-time poet. His early poetry emulated the Acemist school and was realistic, visual and fresh. However, he soon adopted his own style, unveiled in 1926 when he published an epic poem that had as its hero a Ukrainian peasant named Opanas. *The Lady of Opanas* was considered a masterpiece and a highly skilful piece of work. It was set at the time of the Revolution and is today regarded as the greatest poem of that time. Bagritski's romantic style was out of favour in Soviet Russia where, it was thought, poems should reflect socialist realism. However, he was too popular to suppress, and his poetry continued to exhibit metrical variety and span the spectrum from Classical to Modern. The distinction of his work is his positive and optimistic attitude towards life in general, and his own poor health in particular. He was only 39 when he died in Moscow on February 16th 1934.

BAGRITSKI,
Eduard
(1895-1934)
Russian poet

BAKER,
Josephine
(1906-1975)
American/
French
Entertainer

Josephine Baker was born in St Louis, Missouri, on June 3rd 1906. Her mother was a black St Louis washerwoman, her father a Jewish travelling salesman. She received a minimal education and experienced deep poverty. At sixteen her cheerful, flamboyant personality won her a place in a Philadelphia dance troupe. Little by little, she climbed from the chorus to star spots. In 1925, she was given a job in Paris to dance at the Theatre des Champs-Elysées in *La Revue Negre*, where she introduced to Parisian audiences her 'danse sauvage' style. She became an overnight sensation and decided to remain in France. In 1937 she became a French citizen. By now she was one of the most popular and beloved music-hall entertainers in France and top of the bill at the famous Folies-Bergère. Her performance in *Zouzou* (1934), in which she starred opposite Jean Gabon, brought her film stardom as well; but the Second World War and the German occupation brought her career to a halt. Although few knew about her Jewish father, Josephine had made no secret of the fact, and she would without doubt be classed as an 'Untermensch' (subhuman) on two counts. She joined the French Resistance until she was able to escape from France and join the Free French forces. She then spent the remainder of the war entertaining French troops in Africa and the Middle East. She was awarded the Croix de Guerre and the Legion of Honour, included the rosette of the Resistance. In the 1950s she visited the US only to find she was a victim of segregation, something that did not exist in France. Back home in Les Milandes, south-west France, she established a home for orphaned babies from all over the world. It was, Baker declared, 'an experiment in brotherhood', and she dubbed it her 'rainbow tribe'. Though she retired from the stage in 1956 to devote her time and energies to her 'family', in the 1960s she participated in civil rights demonstrations in America, including the 1963 march on Washington, at the side of Martin Luther King. Josephine Baker died in Paris on April 12th 1975.

BAKST,
Leon
(1866-1924)
Russian painter

Born Lev Samoylovich Rosenberg into a poor Jewish family living in St Petersburg, on February 8th 1866, **Bakst** was destined to become one of the world's most renowned painters. His career began in the world of theatrical design and developed from there. His extravagant designs for Diaghilev at the Ballets Russes included work on *Scheherazade* (1910), and his *L'Après-Midi d'un Faune*, with its exotic colours in fashion and sets, took Paris by storm. More importantly, Bakst's work influenced the Art Deco and Art Nouveau movements. Returning to Moscow, he opened a school for painters; but spent his final years back in Paris designing sets for plays, ballets and operas. He died there on December 24th 1924.

BALCON,
Sir Michael
(1896-1977)
British
film-maker

Michael Balcon was born in Birmingham on May 19th 1896 and educated locally. From an early age he was fascinated by film and it came as no surprise to his family when he declared that film-making would be his career. Over the following 40 years, Balcon was the man who came to shape the British film industry and make it the respected and successful force it now is. The films mentioned here are only a sample. He gave Alfred Hitchcock his first directing job, on *The Pleasure Garden* (1925). He made Alec Guinness a star; and he founded Gainsborough

Pictures and, most famous of all, Ealing Studios. In a long career he produced some 60 films, a list far too long to give in full. Suffice it to mention here *Jew Suss* (1934), *A Yank at Oxford* (1942); *Hue and Cry* (1947); *It Always Rains on Sunday* (1948); *Kind Hearts and Coronets* (1949); *Passport to Pimlico* (1949); *Whiskey Galore* (1949); *The Blue Lamp* (1950); *The Man In the White Suit* (1951); *The Lavender Hill Mob* (1952); *The Cruel Sea* (1953); *The Ladykillers* (1955); *Tom Jones'* (1963). Not all travelled successfully to the US; but, more importantly, they gave the British public a laugh and a lift during the years of austerity and recovery from the Second World War. Sir Michael Balcon died at his home at Upper Parrock, Sussex, on October 17th 1977.

Ballin was the son of a Danish Jew who went to Hamburg to set up a shipping line. Albert was born in Hamburg. By the beginning of the 20th century, with a background in the shipping industry, his political field was economics. He was economic adviser to Kaiser William II and during the First World War organized food supplies for the blockaded Reich. Ballin, by all accounts, was something of a character. A member of the Royal Court, he always insisted on eating kosher food, regardless of whether it was a snack with the Kaiser or a banquet with the General Staff, who loathed him - partly for being Jewish and partly because he was constantly advising the Kaiser to sue for peace. Ballin was the chief German negotiator at the peace talks of 1918, after which he became increasingly depressed by the humiliation being inflicted on Germany. The news that the Kaiser had abdicated and run off to the Netherlands was the final straw for him, and he committed suicide.

BALLIN, Albert (1857-1918) German politician

Thomas Balogh was born in Budapest on November 2nd 1905 and graduated from Budapest University before going on to Berlin University. After spells in the US, including a period at Harvard University, he went to Britain where he was appointed lecturer at University College London (1936-39). During the Second World War he held a lectureship at Oxford, where he was a member of Balliol College, and in 1945 he received a fellowship. After the end of the war he became economic adviser to the United Nations. In this capacity he visited many countries recovering from the ravages of war, as well as underdeveloped countries such as Jamaica and India. Following the Labour victory in Britain in 1964 the Prime Minister, Harold Wilson, appointed Balogh his chief adviser on economic affairs. Wilson did not always take the advice offered but the two men remained friends. It was Balogh who founded the Department for Economic Affairs, which proved its worth many times over as new industries emerged into the computer age. In 1974 he came out of retirement to be a Minister in the Department of Energy under Tony Benn. In 1968 he was created a life peer. He died in Hampstead, London, on January 20th 1985.

BALOGH, Lord Thomas (1905-85) Hungarian/ British economist

Martin Balsam was born in the Bronx, New York, on November 4th 1919. He was educated at the Dramatic Workshop at the New School for Social Research in New York and the Actor's Workshop. Following considerable stage and television work he turned to the large screen. His first film was a small part in *On the*

BALSAM, Martin (1919-96) US actor

Waterfront (1954), where, among some of the greatest film actors of his time, Balsam watched and learned. His first feature part was as the jury foreman in *Twelve Angry Men* (1957). Among his later films were *Psycho* (1960), in which he played the private detective who is murdered, and *The Carpetbaggers* (1964), in which he was the studio chief. He received an Oscar for Best Supporting Actor in the film *A Thousand Clowns* (1965). Although he often played the Jewish businessman, generally with a nagging wife, he also showed a unique ability to play understated characters, as brilliantly demonstrated in *The Taking of Pelham 123* (1974). Although Balsam wasn't a star in the recognized sense he dominated the screen, often drawing attention away from the famous. He died on February 15th 1996 in a Rome hotel.

BALTIMORE, David (1938-) US virologist

David Baltimore was born on March 7th 1938 in New York and graduated from Swarthmore College in Pennsylvania. He trained in virology at the Rockefeller Institute, from where he obtained his PhD in 1964. He worked with Renato Dulbecco at the Salk Institute (1965-68) before returning to the Massachusetts Institute of Technology, as a lecturer. He researched animal cancers and discovered that some viruses are composed mainly of ribonucleic acid (RNA) and can transfer their genetic information to deoxyribonucleic acid (DNA). This DNA in turn alters the hereditary pattern of the cell infected by the virus into a cancer cell. He went on to prove that genetic information always passes from DNA to RNA. For this work he shared the 1975 Nobel Prize for Medicine of Physiology. In 1990 he became President of Rockefeller University in New York, only to resign 18 months later following a petty dispute. However, he remains a member of the main faculty board.

BARANY, Robert (1876-1936) Austrian otologist

Born in Vienna on April 22nd 1876 of Hungarian parents, **Barany** studied medicine at Vienna University, before going on to do research at various German hospitals between 1900 and 1905. He then returned to Vienna and his alma mater, where, as an assistant professor, he continued with his research. He became an acknowledged expert in the working of the human ear and the diseases attached thereto. He was the first to describe the condition known as 'hardening of the ear'; more importantly, he created a method for dealing with it. Further research culminated in his being awarded, in 1914, the Nobel Prize for Medicine. During the First World War, while serving as a surgeon in the Austrian army, he was captured by the Russians; impressed by their prisoner's credentials as a Nobel Prize winner, they released him. Despite his fame and good works he was refused a full professorship in Austria because he was a Jew. In the circumstances, he accepted the offer of a full professorship at the University of Uppsala in Sweden. The rise of Nazism caused him much disquiet and he left his valuable books and papers to the National Library in Jerusalem. He died on April 8th 1936.

Baratz, born in Kamenets in Ukraine, was to become responsible for one of the world's great social experiments - the kibbutz. Arriving in Palestine in 1906, he did the socially correct thing of the time and worked as a labourer. In 1910 he and others founded Deganyah, the world's first kibbutz. Although he went on to hold important national posts, he remained involved with the kibbutz concept all his life, much to the benefit of young people from all over the world, for whom the kibbutz movement was, and often still is, their first taste of adventure.

BARATZ, Joseph 1890-1968) Israeli pioneer

Born in Buenos Aires on November 15th 1942, to parents who escaped Nazi persecution in Europe, **Daniel** was first tutored by his father. He was then taught by Nadia Boulanger, who urged his parents to allow her pupil to give his first public recital, even though he was only seven. Barenboim has gone on to become a world-renowned musical figure and a noted exponent of Beethoven and Mozart, conducting alongside a brilliant career as a soloist. His conducting strength is his interpretation of Wagner; some consider him rather heavy-handed when conducting Mozart. In 1975 he became Director of the Orchestre de Paris, and in 1987 his achievements in this role were rewarded with the Legion of Honour. He is reckoned by Wagner experts to have been the best conductor of a Bayreuth Festival Ring Cycle since the Second World War. He was married to Jacqueline du Pré, a superb cello soloist and beloved of audiences everywhere; her death was a great sorrow to Barenboim, and only the appreciation of his audiences has sustained him. He is musical director of the Chicago Symphony Orchestra, a pinnacle of his profession. In August 1996 he conducted the taxing Wagnerian programme for the Bayreuth Festival. As a counter to the demands of such commitments, he is recently reported to have developed an interest in the tango which emanates from his original homeland, Argentina: a different sort of cycle, perhaps, which has led to an album called *Mi Buenos Aires Querido*. Ethnic music is not an entirely new field for Barenboim, who in 1995 made a record of West African music called *African Portraits*.

BARENBOIM, Daniel (1942-) Argentine pianist and conductor

Barna was born in Budapest and played his first game of table tennis at his bar-mitzvah party. As a teenager he is remembered as a 'scrawny little kid', but he grew into probably the greatest table tennis player ever known. Because of Barna's dedication, the game reached a popularity that it has retained to this day. He was famous for his backhand flip and angled forehand whip. Because of his prowess the Hungarian national team controlled the game for ten years. Barna won five world single titles, eight doubles titles and two mixed doubles. He won the Swaythling Cup, the highest trophy in the sport, seven times. In 1935 he had a car accident, broke his playing arm and never won another title. In 1936 he came to Britain, where he stayed, taking British nationality and touring the music halls giving demonstrations of his art. During the Second World War Barna was in ENSA, entertaining the forces. His younger brother, also a Hungarian table tennis champion, was murdered by the Fascists during the war. A neighbour of Victor hid his trophies during the Nazi regime and returned them after the war; Victor, lamenting his brother's death, cried how he wished it had been the other way around.

BARNA, Victor 'Vicki' (1911-72) Hungarian world table tennis champion

BARNATO,
Woolf
(1895-1948)
British
automobile
racing champion

Woolf was the son of Barney Barnato, the gold and diamond magnate who was alleged to have committed suicide by jumping overboard from the ship that was carrying him home to England from South Africa. As Barney was coming home to a hero's welcome with an awful lot of money it is hard not to believe that he was murdered. It is a fact that he had fallen foul of Cecil Rhodes, and Rhodes was a very vengeful man. He was also the financial backer of the forerunner of the IRA. At the time, it was believed Barney Barnato was murdered on the orders of Rhodes; but this was never proven. Woolf was two years old when his father died and he grew up in the new age of motoring. He adored cars and was a director of Bentley Motors. He also loved car racing and, in a brief career, he won the Le Mans 24 hour Grand Prix three consecutive times from 1928 to 1930. Barnato was the first man to achieve such a record, which was not equalled until 1960-62 and has never been beaten. In 1931, Woolf had a special Bentley made for him in order to tour America, while on honeymoon with his second wife. It was a 45 h.p. 8 litre tourer, capable of a speed of 100 m.p.h. He sold it in 1933. In 1996, the car was discovered in good order, and Woolf's daughter Diane, who during the Second World War was a pilot who delivered fighter aircraft all over the UK, arranged a party to celebrate the car's 65th birthday. Woolf Barnato died in London on July 27th 1948.

BARNETT,
Lionel
(1871-1960)
British
orientalist

Barnett was born in Liverpool on October 21st 1871, into a Sephardic family. He graduated from Oxford in oriental studies, and from 1908 to 1936 was Keeper of Oriental Works at the British Museum. The work allowed him ample time for his travels and so enabled him to produce what have become textbooks on the subject. *Antiquities of India* (1913) and *Hindu Gods and Heroes* (1922) are of particular interest. From 1936 to 1946 he lectured on Indian history at the London University School of Oriental and African Studies. A great influence on his students, he was a most successful lecturer. Beside being an authority on Indian literature, he was a much courted after dinner speaker. He died in London on January 28th 1960.

BARNETT,
Sir Louis
(1865-1946)
New Zealand
medical reformer

Barnett was born in Wellington, New Zealand, on March 24th 1865. He qualified as a doctor and later became a Master of Surgery. In 1905 he was appointed Professor of Surgery at Otago University and here, except for war service in the First World War, in which he was a colonel in the Royal Australian and New Zealand Medical Corps, he remained until 1924. Knighted after the war, Barnett left Otago to become a researcher in matters connected with X-rays and radium for the treatment of cancer. As a result of Barnett's work the incidence of hydatids in New Zealand, and later in Australia, was considerably reduced. He died in London October 28th 1946.

Salo Baron was born in Tarnow, Austria, on May 26th 1895. In 1917 he received his PhD from the University of Vienna and became a lecturer at the Judisches Paedagogium (1919-25). In 1926 he emigrated to the US. In 1930 he became professor of Jewish history at Columbia University, where he stayed until 1963. During this long period he started his *A Social and Religious History of the Jews*. Originally meant to cover three volumes, it had grown to 18 by the time of his death. Other writings included *History and Jewish Historians* (1964) and *Essays on Ancient and Medievil Jewish History* (1972). In 1961 he was the first of the prosecution witnesses at the trial of Adolf Eichman. His evidence centred on the effects of the Holocaust in respect of the background of European Jewry. When he retired from teaching, Columbia University created a new chair in Jewish history in Baron's honour.

Baron's understanding of Jewish history was all-embracing. It was due to his incisive treatment that it became a realistic object of study. He died in New York on November 25th 1989.

BARON, Salo (1895-1989) Austrian/ American historian

Born Lionel Begleiter, in the East End of London, **Bart** embarked on a musical career as soon as he left school. Nineteen fifty-nine was the year it all started going very well. He wrote 'Living Doll' for Cliff Richard and followed this up with *Lock Up Your Daughters*. This was the musical that broke London's reliance on American productions. It was an instant success, as was his next work, *Fings Aint Wot They Used T'be* (1959). Then came *Oliver!* (1960) and the world belonged to Lionel Bart. As a stage show it has been seen all over the world and as a film it won that year's Oscar for Best Picture. *Blitz!* (1962) and *Maggie May* (1964) followed. Then it all went horribly wrong. *Twang!*, a musical about Robin Hood, was a flop; the result was bankruptcy, and a small flat in the poorer part of West London. Here was a man who had given happiness to countless millions, virtually shunned by those who directly profited from his genius. However, in 1995 *Oliver!* was revived in London, to the same rapturous applause it had received 35 years previously.

BART, Lionel (1930-) British composer and lyricist

Born in Camden, South Carolina, on August 19th 1870 and educated in New York, his initial experience of work was as an office boy - but not for long. **Baruch** made a fortune on the stock exchange by the time he was 30 and never looked back. During the First World War he was appointed director of the War Industries Board. Thereafter, he continued to advise successive governments on economic matters. Because Baruch was a practical person, rather than a theorist, his advice was generally pragmatic and sound. It was largely through the efforts of Baruch that Roosevelt was persuaded to co-operate with Winston Churchill and provide the aid that Britain so urgently needed, following the collapse of France, during the Second World War. Baruch had a tough job convincing Roosevelt because Joseph Kennedy, the US ambassador to Britain, was a Hitler fan and thought the UK a lost cause. From this time, Baruch forged a friendship with Churchill which lasted until both men died in 1965. Following the Second World War, Baruch was appointed US representative to the United Nations Atomic Energy Commission. In 1939 he

BARUCH, Bernard (1870-1965) US statesman

advocated a 'United States of Africa' as a solution to the world's refugee problem. He died on June 20th 1965.

BARUK,
Henri
(1897-1988)
French
psychiatrist

After a conventional education, which resulted in a medical degree, **Baruk** decided to concentrate on psychiatry. In 1931 he was appointed Chief Physician at the Charenton Mental Institute. Following the Second World War he became a professor at the Sorbonne. His intensive researches into methods of psychiatric treatments have led to the conclusion that methods of treatment which suppress or diminish the patient's personality, whether by drugs or by other treatment, are to be avoided. His research work has been of the greatest importance and continues to benefit patients all over the world.

BASCH,
Victor
(1863-1944)
French
philosopher

Basch was born in Budapest and educated at the Sorbonne in Paris. At various times he was Professor of Philosophy at Nancy, Remmes and Paris universities and the first Professor of Aesthetics at the Sorbonne (1918). He first came to the public's attention when he championed the cause of Alfred Dreyfus. In 1926 he founded The League of the Rights of Man, a forerunner of today's Amnesty International. He was a socialist and a supporter of the left-wing coalition known as the Popular Front. He was beloved by his students and respected by all. As a reward for his good works on behalf of the common man, he and his wife were executed by the French Vichy government during the Second World War; for they were Jews and Basch, despite his 81 years, was a member of the central committee of the French underground.

BASKIN,
Leonard
(1922-)
US sculptor

Leonard Baskin was born in New Brunswick, New Jersey, on August 15th 1922. Following his studies in the US and Europe he held his first solo show in New York in 1939. In 1947 he won a Tiffany scholarship for sculpture, which was followed by a Guggenheim fellowship to study print-making in 1953. Baskin has designed, in a variety of materials, monumental figures that have become part of the global art canon. Although they are often bleak in style they are most impressive and dominant. These include *Blake* (1955), a homage to the poet William Blake, and *Barlach Dead* (1959) in remembrance of the German expressionist artist whose work was declared degenerate by Hitler. Baskin has completed several works of biblical figures, including *Prodigal Son* (1976) and *Ruth and Naomi* (1978). His woodcuts have a highly distinctive style, *Man of Peace* and *Everyman* being best known. He publishes his own books, complete with excellent illustrations of his woodcuts, under the imprint of Gehenna Press. One of these, published in 1985, under the title *The Raptors and Other Birds*, suggests that birds are messengers.

BASSANI,
Giorgi
(1916-)
Italian writer

Bassani was born on April 4th 1916 in Bologna, the son of a physician. Until 1943 he lived in Ferrara, where much of the action of his novels is set. A major theme of his work since the Second World War, is the suffering of Italian Jews under Fascism. *Five Stories of Ferrara* (1956), which tells of the growth of Fascism and anti-Semitism, is an example of this theme; it brought the author commercial success and the Strega Prize, awarded annually for the best Italian literary work. Bassani is a realist with a poetic style commended for its elegance and favourably compared to Proust (*qv*). One of the most outstanding Italian novelists of our century, with an international audience, probably his best-known book is *The Garden of the Finzi-Continis* (1965), a best-seller that became a prize-winning film directed by Vittorio de Sica. His later work includes *L'airone* (1968), another prize-winning novel, and *The Smell of the Hay* (1972).

Bauer was born in Vienna, the son of a wealthy textile dealer. Like many of his generation who, looking around them, did not like what they saw, he joined the socialist movement. He gained a law degree but did not enjoy the work and decided to launch the political magazine *Der Kampf*. Bauer later became leader of a Marxist socialist party until it was disbanded at the outbreak of the First World War. He then found himself in the Austrian army and was subsequently taken prisoner by the Russians, until freed by the revolution of 1917. In November 1918 he was appointed to be the first Foreign Minister of the new Austrian Republic; but in 1920 his party lost power, and he spent the next fourteen years helping the disadvantaged of Vienna. In 1934 he took part in the workers' uprising against Dollfus, who had suspended parliamentary government. He was forced to flee Austria and went to Paris. In 1938 he warned the world that Jews in Germany and Austria were in mortal danger from Nazi aggression; soon thereafter, on July 4th that year, he died in Paris.

Born in Berlin, **Baum** joined the Communist youth movement while at university. After graduating, he became a full-time party worker at a time when Communists and Nazis were fighting each other in pitched battles on the streets of most large German cities. In 1936, rather than leave what was now Nazi Germany, Baum organized a Jewish resistance cell in Berlin. After the outbreak of war they carried on the fight, distributing leaflets and making contact with foreign workers from Belgium and France. During this time Baum, equipped with false papers, was a normal worker at Siemens. Siemens used a lot of slave labour and Baum was able to organize and encourage the forced labourers to commit acts of sabotage. The directors of Siemens, who took terrible reprisals, were indicted after the war as war criminals. In 1942 Baum and his comrades set fire to the Nazi propaganda exhibit 'Das Sowjet Paradies' at Berlin's exhibition hall. They were soon arrested, tried, sentenced to death and executed. There was one survivor, Charlotte Holzer: after the war, she persuaded the authorities in East Germany to re-inter Herbert Baum and his comrades in the Jewish cemetery at Weissensees in East Berlin.

Baum and his comrades were the real German resistance to Hitler. Those who came after, like von Stauffenberg, backed by general staff officers, were not concerned with humanity; rather, they wanted to take over from Hitler and continue the war on professional lines. The true resistance, like Baum, were working not only for Jewish salvation, but for Germany also.

BAUM,
Vicki
(1888-1960)
Austrian/
American writer

Vicki Baum was born on January 24th 1888 in Vienna and educated at a music school, giving her first recital when she was just eleven. At eighteen she married a writer, only to separate from him the following year. She moved to Berlin and made her living by giving music lessons. She had always enjoyed writing and so took a job as an editor with Ullsteins publishing house. In 1929 she published *Helen Willfuer*, the first of the 25 novels she was to write. Her best-known work, which brought her international fame, was *Grand Hotel* (1930). Published as a novel in many languages, it was also staged as a play all over Europe and in the US, and was turned into a hit film starring Greta Garbo, winning an Oscar for Best Picture. In 1931, Baum visited New York and decided to stay, becoming a naturalized American citizen in 1938. Being Jewish she was deemed decadent, so the Germans and Austrians banned her books and films. Her style was intense and emotional and her characters were said to 'jump off the pages'. More of her books were published after the end of the war and she continued working until her death in Hollywood on August 31st 1960.

BAYLIS,
Lilian
(1874-1937)
British
theatrical
manager

Lilian Baylis was born in London on May 9th 1874, the daughter of Jewish parents who were both musicians. In 1890 the family emigrated to South Africa, where Lilian became a music teacher. In 1898 she returned to London to spend the rest of her working life in theatre management. After serving an apprenticeship under her aunt, Emma Cons, Lilian took over the running of the Old Vic in 1900. With that theatre well established, she turned her attention to the neglected Sadlers Wells Theatre, which she re-opened in 1931 with a gala performance of Shakespeare's *Twelfth Night*. Sadlers Wells later became the home of the Royal Ballet. That both theatres have managed to survive two world wars and countless recessions is a reflection of the strong foundations she laid. In 1929 she was created a Companion of Honour. She died in London on November 25th 1937.

BAZELON,
David
(1910-1993)
US jurist

David Bazelon was born on September 3rd 1910 in Superior, Wisconsin, the youngest of the nine children of Israel and Lena Bazelon. Educated at the University of Illinois and Northwester University, from which he obtained a law degree in 1931, he went on to establish a legal practice which lasted until 1935 when he was appointed an assistant district attorney. Following the Second World War, President Truman named Bazelon assistant Attorney-General. In 1949 he sat on the US Court of Appeal and in 1962 was appointed Chief Judge. It was while he was at the Court of Appeal that Bazelon wrote some of the most famous opinions of the time. In 1954 he ruled on a definition of insanity as it related to criminal cases. During the McCarthy witch-hunts of the 1950s, Bazelon ruled that an individual had the right to refuse to answer questions if they were not pertinent to the inquiry. In 1973 he hit the world's headlines when he ordered Richard Nixon to give up the Watergate tapes, declaring that claims of executive privilege were invalid. This decision led to Nixon's downfall. Later Bazelon declared that tapes used as evidence during the Watergate trials could be freely sold, stating that 'any embarrassment to Mr Nixon is largely that which results whenever misconduct or questionable conduct is exposed'.

Bazelon contributed much to US society and beyond, not least by his ruling in 1966 that mental patients in institutions were entitled to medical treatment. In 1971 he ordered a ban on DDT and in the same year made an order that newspapers could not own radio and television stations in the same area. He retired due to illness in 1985 and died on February 19th 1993 in Washington DC.

BEARSTED,
1st Viscount
(1853-1927)
British
entrepreneur

Bearsted born Marcus Samuel in London's East End on November 5th 1853, was the son of a trader in shells. Educated at Jewish schools in London and Brussels, at the beginning of the twentieth century he founded the Shell Transport and Trading Company, adopting the symbol of a shell, now a familiar sight at filling stations all over the world, because of his father's work. Soon after founding the company, however, Samuel was appointed Lord Mayor of London, and devoted so much attention to his civil duties that he neglected the affairs of Shell. As a result, in 1904, he had little alternative but to amalgamate with the Royal Dutch Petroleum Company. At this point Samuel turned to his commercial interests with renewed energy and became indispensable to the new organisation, of which he was chairman. In 1921 he was created a viscount and took the name Bearsted from the village in which he had lived since 1895. On his retirement, his son became chairman of Shell, now a much bigger company. Marcus died in London on January 17th 1927, just a few hours after the death of his wife Fanny, the only daughter of Benjamin Benjamin of London.

BEASTIE
BOYS
US rock group

The **Beastie Boys** were three Jewish boys from good families who in 1981 decided to form a rock band. The three were: Adam Yauch, born on August 15th 1967 in Brooklyn, New York, and known as MCA (master of ceremonies); Michael Diamond, born on November 20th 1965 in New York and known as Mike D; and Adam Horovitz, born on October 31st 1966 in New York, son of the playwright Israel Horovitz. In August 1983, British Airways gave the group £40,000 compensation for using a snatch of their 'Cookie Puss' as backing for a commercial, without permission. They started including rap in their stage act and, in September 1986, began a tour of the UK. The group made no secret of their intentions, announcing it as the 'Raisin' Hell' tour. Their outrageous act, on and off stage, caused controversy and led to a poor relationship with the British press. In March 1987 their album, *Licensed to Ill*, became the first rap album to top the US chart, where it remained for seven weeks. Their single, 'You Gotta Fight For Your Right To Party', reached the top ten in both Britain and the US. On a British tour in May 1987, Horovitz was arrested in Liverpool and charged with causing actual bodily harm to a fan during their Royal Court Theatre concert in London. He was eventually acquitted but the tabloid press had a field day reporting how the boys went around ripping VW badges off Volkswagens, and much more, resorting to invention when they ran out of facts.

The group continue to entertain and have won a number of awards, including the 1990 Critics Award. In June 1996 Adam Yauch organized a concert to protest against China's continued occupation of Tibet, at which 50,000 Californians turned up at San Francisco's Golden Gate Park.

BECKER,
Gary
(1930-)
US economist

Born on December 2nd 1930 in Pottsville, Pennsylvania, **Becker** was educated at Princeton University and the University of Chicago, from where he obtained his PhD in 1955. He stayed on at Chicago to teach economics until 1957, when he moved to Columbia University; later he returned to the University of Chicago where he was appointed professor of economics and sociology, a position he held until 1983. The core of his theoretical writings is the presumption that rational economic choice, which governs the majority of human behaviour, is based on self-interest. His 1957 book *Economics of Discrimination* examined race preferences in the labour place. In *Human Capital* (1964) he claimed that a person's investment in education is on a par with a company investing in machinery. In 1981 he published *A Treatise on Family*, comparing a household with a factory; his conclusions regarding the role of women were taken on board by the feminist movement of the 1980s. He has also written in the same analytical mould on drug addiction and criminal behaviour. In 1992 Gary Becker was awarded the Nobel Prize for Economic Science.

BEGIN,
Menachem
(1913-92)
Israeli prime
minister

Begin was born in Brest-Litovsk, Poland, on August 16th 1913. His father instilled into his son a pride in all that was Jewish, and an enthusiasm for Zionism, that stayed with him all his life. He grew up in an atmosphere of anti-Semitism that doubtless shaped his future actions. Begin studied law at Warsaw University and, while there, became head of the Betar Zionist Movement. This was in 1931. When the Germans invaded Poland, Begin took off for Lithuania, but was stopped by the Russians who imprisoned him until 1941, at which time he was released to join the Free Polish Army. He was sent to Palestine. On his release from the army, he left the Betar movement and became head of Irgun Zvai Leumi, an organization pledged to remove the British Mandate from Palestine and create a Jewish state by any means possible. Following the Second World War and the decimation of his family in the Holocaust, Begin became active in the war against British forces stationed in Palestine. When the State of Israel was established, Begin founded the right-wing Herut Party and became its leader. In 1973 Herut merged with other parties to form the Likud Front, a right-wing nationalist party. In 1977 he was Prime Minister in a coalition government that sought an accommodation with Egypt. These efforts resulted in the Camp David Accords of 1978, which brought peace between the two countries and has led to further peace initiatives, though the Likud government of 1996-7 appeared to lack the will of Begin in furthering the peace process. Anwar Sadat, the Egyptian leader, and Menachem Begin shared the Nobel Peace Prize for 1978. In 1982 Begin chose to invade Lebanon, but the campaign did not turn out the way he had planned. He claimed that it would take just 72 hours; in the event it took three years, and its failure forced Begin to resign. He died in Israel on March 9th 1992, a broken and depressed man who appeared to take little comfort in the fact that it was his efforts that had got the peace process under way.

Born in Worcester, Massachusetts, on June 9th,1893, **Berhman** was once tagged the 'American Noel Coward'. This was following the successful production of his play, *Second Man*, in 1927, which took him eleven years to get produced. During that time he attempted to keep body and soul together by writing short stories for the *New York Times* and articles for any magazine that wanted them. He went on to write many plays, all in a light and charming style. However, in 1934 he wrote on fascism in *Rain From Heaven*. Criticized in some quarters for not being vehement enough on this subject, he wrote *No Time For Comedy* (1939). In 1952 he turned to writing biographies. His book *Dureen*, based on the life of the British art dealer, was a great success, as was his autobiography, *Worcester Account* (1954). He became to be recognized as one of the stalwarts in new American literature, and in 1964 was one of three writers chosen for the opening session of the Lincoln Repertory Theatre in New York. It was here that he premiered his *Best For Whom Charlie?* Over a 40-year career he wrote over twenty comedies, nearly all of which were hits. Behrman died in New York City on September 9th 1973.

BEHRMAN, Samuel (1893-1973) US writer

Belasco was born in Victoria, British Columbia, Canada on July 25th 1859. He was the son of a Jewish store-keeper and descended from a Sephardic family originally named Velasco. In this century, Belasco wrote *Madam Butterfly* (1900), subsequently turned into the world's most famous opera by Puccini, premiered in Milan in 1904. For good measure he also wrote the play *The Girl of the Golden West* (1905) which Puccini set to music, the result being premiered in New York in 1910. He wrote prolifically and reached the height of his popularity between 1900 and 1920, becoming known as the Stanislavski of the New York stage. He established a new standard of production, seeking a degree of realism for his stage settings that drove directors mad but which the public adored. He died in New York on May 14th,1931.

BELASCO, David (1859-1931) Canadian playwright

Saul was born in Lachine, Quebec Province, Canada on June 10th 1915. He was the son of Russian Jewish parents and was brought up in a Yiddish-speaking household. Soon after Saul's birth the family moved to Montreal, where Saul was educated; in 1924 the family moved once again, this time to Chicago, where Saul completed his education at Northwestern University. His first published novel was *Dangling Man* (1944). It received mixed reviews but a Guggenheim Fellowship resulted and in 1948 Bellow visited Paris and Rome. His list of novels is impressive and well known. In 1962 he was appointed a professor at Chicago University. *The Adventures of Augie March* (1953) won the 1954 National Book Award. *Henderson the Rain King* (1959), about an eccentric millionaire in Africa, became most popular. *Hertzog* (1964) resulted in the 1965 National Book Award. *Humboldt's Gift* (1975) won him the Pulitzer Prize. In 1976 came the ultimate recognition, the Nobel Prize for Literature.

Bellow often writes about Chicago, which he claims is the product of corruption, cynicism and confusion. This is brilliantly depicted in *Dean's December* (1982). His range of style often stretches from the sublime to the absurd but he is always original,

BELLOW, Saul (1915-) Canadian writer

as two of his 1980s books, *More Die of Heartbreak* (1987) and *The Bellarosa Connection* (1989) demonstrate. In 1989 he was married, for the fifth time, to Janice Friedman, who had been a student of Bellow at the University of Chicago. When they married he was 74, the bride was 31.

BELOFF,
Max
(1913-)
British historian

Max Beloff was born in London on July 2nd 1913 and graduated from Oxford University with a degree in modern history. In 1939 he was teaching history at Manchester University when the Second World War broke out. He joined the British Army's Royal Corps of Signals and did not resume teaching until 1946, this time at Oxford. In 1957 he was elected a Fellow of All Souls College. A prolific writer on international relations, he became an authority on relations between Western and Eastern Europe. In 1974, The Open University, the great educational experiment of post-war Britain, was launched. This university, designed for non-qualified, part-time adult students, operates by means of correspondence courses which are integrated with radio programmes, televised lectures, summer schools and a tutorial system. Beloff was appointed Chancellor soon after the University began and he has seen it reach a roll of 50,000 students. In acknowledgement of his services and for the intelligence he was able to bring to the British House of Lords, Beloff was created a life peer in 1982.

BENACERRAF,
Baruj
(1920-)
Venezuelan
physician

Born in Caracas on October 29th 1920, **Benacerraf** received his early education there and only left the country to study medicine in the US. He graduated from Columbia University and qualified as a doctor from the Medical School of Virginia in 1945. In 1950 he moved to the Centre National de Recherche Scientifique in Paris, where he was in charge of research until 1956. Back in the US in 1957, he continued working in broadly the same fields at New York University. Eventually, his researches led him to discover the immune-response genes that regulate immunology, in organ transplants, and prevent infection, leading to the rejection of transplanted organs. For this vital work he was awarded the 1980 Nobel Prize for Physiology.

BENATSKY,
Ralph
(1884-1957)
Czech composer

Benatsky, born in Moravske-Budejovice, studied at Prague Conservatory. He wrote thousands of songs, nearly 100 operettas and the score to something like 250 films. Not a lazy man. However, just one of his operettas has given more pleasure than all the rest of his output. *White Horse Inn* has been performed throughout the world and was the number one show for many generations. Its music is still played. Its success brought fame and fortune to Benatsky and entertainment to millions of people, and it has been the salvation of numerous amateur operetta companies, all over the world.

BENDA,
Julien
(1867-1956)
French writer

Born in Paris on December 26th 1867, **Benda** became the paragon of intellectual thought concerning romantic French philosophy. He particularly disliked Henri Bergson's irrationalism and attacked him on every possible occasion. In 1900 he published his first book, *Dialogues à Byzance*, a broad analysis, in the wake of the Dreyfus Affair, of corruption in French society. He followed it up with *L'Ordination*, a boring anthology of strict moral practices. As someone who constantly defended reason against the idea of intuition, his work showed little imagination; he spent much time rejecting the work of such gifted writers as Romain Rolland, Paul Claudel and his one-time friend, Charles Peguy. His most famous book is *Treasures of Intellectuals* (1928), in which Benda denounces as moral traitors those who betray justice and truth for racial and political purposes. It was both a throwback to the Dreyfus Affair and an expression of conscience over his own departure from Jewish life. Two autobiographical works appeared in 1937 and 1938: *The Youth of an Intellectual* and *A Regulator in His Century*. During the Second World War, despite his isolation from Jewish life, Benda was pursued by the Germans and sought refuge in a remote part of southern France. Following the war, he published his last work, *La France Byzantine; On Le Triomphe de la Literature Pure* (1945). Although often a difficult character to relate to, Julien Benda has an assured place as a man of letters. He died at Fontenay-aux-Roses on June 7th 1956.

Like so many older Israeli politicians, **Ben-Gurion** was born in Poland: in Plonsk, on October 16th 1886, when the family name was Green. His father advised on legal matters to those who could not afford a qualified lawyer. David was brought up in a house that doubled as the local Zionist office. He received a progressive, mostly private education, and immersed himself in politics from an early age. He travelled throughout Poland on behalf of the Po'alei Zion Party, speaking to anyone who would listen to his message. In 1906 he settled in Palestine, where he worked in the orange groves. During the First World War, he served as a soldier in the Jewish Legion against the Turks, who at that time ruled Palestine. From 1921 to 1933 he was general secretary of the General Federation of Jewish Labour and in 1930 was elected leader of the Mapai or Labour party. It was Ben-Gurion who made the historical announcement, in May 1948, that proclaimed the birth of the State of Israel. It was also Ben-Gurion who led his country, against the odds, in the war of survival that followed. He retired from the premiership in 1953, only to take up the mantle again in 1955. In 1963 he finally retired to his kibbutz to enjoy his remaining years as an elder statesman, whose advice was constantly sought. He became the symbol of the new state and an example to politicians all over the world. He died in Tel Aviv on December 1st 1973.

BEN-GURION
David
(1886-1973)
Israeli statesman

Born in Los Angeles, at 18 **Benioff** joined the Mount Wilson Observatory, where he stayed until 1924. He then joined the seismological research department of the California Institute of Technology. It was Benioff who invented the instruments that were essential when measuring movement in the earth's crust on land and sea. He later became a professor of seismology at the California Institute and a consultant to building companies, designing buildings in known earthquake areas all over the world. He was also an adviser to the US Air Force and Navy geophysical departments. Highly regarded as one of the world's leading seismologists and an important lecturer, he continued working right up to the time he died in May 1968.

BENIOFF,
Hugo
(1899-1968)
US seismologist

BENJAMIN,
Ernest
(1900-69)
British soldier

Benjamin was born in Toronto, Canada, and educated in England at the Royal Military Academy at Woolwich and the Staff College, Sandhurst. He was a professional officer and served all over the British Empire. At the commencement of the Second World War in 1939 Benjamin, commander of the Marine Division of the Royal Engineers, was appointed head of the Combined Training Centre for the Middle East and Italy. In 1944 he was promoted to brigadier and put in command of the newly created Jewish Brigade. The Brigade had as its own distinctive emblem a gold Star of David on a background of blue and white stripes. The force, all of whose members were Jewish, was mainly recruited from Palestine, and included men who had previously served in three companies of the East Kent Regiment (The Buffs) as well as troops from the British Army who wished to transfer. The Jewish Brigade, part of the British Eighth Army, consisting of three battalions, first saw action in northern Italy in March 1945. Led by Benjamin, the Brigade spearheaded the attack on a crack German parachute division and succeeded in establishing a bridgehead across the Senio River. Brigade members received decorations, suffered casualties and, on occasion, agreed to take prisoners. Benjamin's biggest problem came when the Brigade was moved to north-east Italy, where it met up with Holocaust survivors. Benjamin, although first and foremost a senior British officer working under strict guidelines, was also a Jew and a humanist. As a result, he simply turned a blind eye to the work the Brigade did to care for and help pitiful refugees who had lost everything. He also disregarded the activities of Brigade members, once the Second World War was over, that led to many of the survivors being smuggled into Palestine. Brigadier Benjamin later served in Hong Kong, and after his retirement from the army in 1950 was honorary treasurer of the Jewish Lads' Brigade.

In the late 1990s it came to light that members of the Jewish Brigade had, soon after the war, formed small vigilante groups that executed out of hand Germans believed to be guilty of war crimes. It is difficult to be certain whether Benjamin was aware of these activities. He was, however, extremely proud of the men he led into battle and well aware of the awe in which the survivors held the tough-looking soldiers with the Star of David flashes.

BENJAMIN,
Walter
(1892-1940)
German
philosopher

Born in Berlin on July 15th 1892, to an upper-class Jewish family, **Walter** was educated at Hanbinda, a countryside boarding school. It was here that he came under the influence of Gustav Wynekau, a radical reformer who was teaching at the school - an influence so strong that, although Benjamin went on to university, it never left him and later led him to found the 'Free Students', with Wynekau as preceptor. In August 1914 Benjamin and his fellow members were among the first to enlist in the Austrian army. A year later, and disillusioned with the ideas he had received from Wynekau, Benjamin resigned from the association and was later demobilized from the army on medical grounds. He moved to Berne, Switzerland, and there studied philosophy. His work as an essayist on the origins of German drama, resulting in his book *Origin of German Tragic Drama* (1928), is still regarded as of the greatest importance in this field. He is now considered as the most important German language-critic operating between the First World War and the Second

World War. He was an early associate of Bertolt Brecht and together they formulated many of the ideas on which Brecht would later write. When the Nazis took over, Benjamin couldn't believe what might happen to him because he was a Jew. He believed his education and background put him into a different category. He was, however, persuaded to leave and made his home in Paris, where he wrote for the Socialist cause. When France fell, he and a group of Jewish refugees made for Spain. There, at Port-Bou on the Spanish border, on September 26th 1940, an official refused them sanctuary, stating they would be returned to France the next day and handed over to the Gestapo. In a fit of wild depression, Benjamin took a mammoth overdose of morphine and promptly died in front of the Spaniard. He, now in a state of deep shock, promptly allowed the rest of the group into Spain.

This very funny man was born Benjamin Kublesky in Waukegan, Illinois, on February 14th 1894. His father ran a saloon and dry goods store and **Jack** helped him before and after school. In his teens he had violin lessons and toyed with the idea of becoming a classical violinist. Instead, at seventeen, he became a vaudeville artist. In 1929 he embarked on a film career that included *Charley's Aunt* (1929) *To Be or Not To Be* (the 1942 version by Ernst Lubitsch, *qv*) and *It's in the Bag* (1945). Benny made his radio debut on the Ed Sullivan show in 1932 and went on to have his own radio show, which ran for many years and was seldom out of the top ten ratings. Benny was unique. He wasn't a stand-up comedian or slapstick artist: the humour was in the character he created. His stare of a martyr-like man, slowly drumming his fingers; his facial expressions; his crippling playing of the violin, particularly 'Love in Bloom'; his reputation for meanness, brilliantly depicted in the radio sketch, when the hold-up man says, 'Your money or your life' and Benny just stands there thinking over the choice; his classic run-ins with Fred Allen; the constant celebration of his 39th birthday - all helped to create the legend. He was simply one of the funniest men ever. His television show, *The Jack Benny Show*, ran from 1960 to 1970 and brought him millions of adoring fans. These shows are now being transmitted again and new generations are becoming hooked, as their grandparents were. Jack Benny loved show business and couldn't stay away. He died in Beverly Hills, California, on December 27th 1974, soon after the broadcast of *Jack Benny's Second Farewell*.

BENNY,
Jack
(1894-1974)
US entertainer

Born in New York on October 15th 1921 and educated there, **Benzer** went on to Purdue University, Indiana, and received his PhD in 1947. In 1965 he moved to the California Institute of Technology. It was Benzer who first demonstrated that genes can be split and recombined. He went on to relate genes as chemical entities with observed and peculiar behaviour in biological systems. It was because of Benzer's original DNA work that we are able to appreciate the difference between individuals based on their hereditary determinants. In 1975 he became the Boswell professor of neuro science at the California Institute.

BENZER,
Seymour
(1921-)
US geneticist

Berenson was born on June 26th 1865 in Vilna, Lithuania. Because of persistent pogroms his father took the family off to the US when Bernhard was 10, changing the family name of Valvrojenski to Berenson. Bernard studied at Harvard and, after graduating, toured the art capitals of Europe. During the First World War, Berenson worked for US intelligence in Paris. He published books on Italian painters, and soon gained a reputation as an expert on Italian Renaissance art. On a visit to London, he claimed that only a small proportion of the 33 paintings attributed to Titian were genuine; the remainder were fakes. The British art establishment howled and never forgave him. Berenson now began a career of advising American collectors and museums on what, and what not, to buy. He wanted to see as much good European art sent to the US as possible, and he sometimes sailed fairly close to the wind when government permissions were required. He came to live in a villa near Settignano, Italy, and accumulated a library of some 40,000 books. Here he entertained, on a lavish scale, artistic luminaries from all over the world. During the Second World War he remained in Italy and kept a diary that he published in 1952 under the title *Rumour and Reflection, 1941-1944*. He was a member of the American Academy of Arts and Sciences and on his 90th birthday received a medal of honour from the Italian government for his contribution to Italian art. Berenson once stated that 'connoisseurship is a guess'. An important writer on his subject, his work includes *The Drawings of the Florentine Painters* (1938), *Aesthetics and History in the Visual Arts* (1948) and - probably his most important work - *Italian Painters of the Renaissance* (1952). He died at Settignano on October 6th 1959, leaving his villa and library to Harvard University.

Jack Berg, born Judah Bergmann on June 28th 1909 in London's East End, became one of Britain's most successful world champion boxers. He grew up in an environment of great poverty, partially alleviated by the establishment of boxing clubs and boxing halls, such as the popular 'Premierland'. A Jewish boxing fraternity emerged in the 1920s and 1930s and it was Jewish boxers who were in the forefront of the sport - unlike the late 1990s, when only Gary Jacobs of Glasgow wears the Star of David on his boxing shorts. In 'Kid' Berg's day it was very different. Boxing was a way out of an East End slum. Berg's style was little more than roughhouse and it was generally only his courage and stamina that saw him gradually wear down a more skilful opponent. He found it difficult to get fights in the welterweight division in Britain, and so, together with his manager, Solly Gold, and his trainer, Ray Arcel, he left London for New York. After several preliminaries he took the world title in 1930 and defended it a record nine times. Back in London, he reigned as British lightweight champion from 1934 to 1936. In all, he had 197 fights, of which he won 157. He fought his last bout in 1945. He then took off for Hollywood and became a stunt man. In his late seventies, he could be seen walking briskly around London's Soho wearing a Stetson hat and combat boots. He was President of the London Ex-boxers' Association. Berg was fortunate in receiving no long-term injuries from boxing. He also kept his money and was an continuing example to the sport of boxing. He died in London on April 22nd 1991.

After graduating with honours from Princeton University, **Berg** joined the Brooklyn Dodgers and played baseball for a living. He continued thus for 16 years, during which time he became known for his intellectual approach to the game. During off-season periods, he studied at the Sorbonne in Paris to become fluent in ten languages. He also earned a law degree from Columbia University. During the Second World War he was an OSS spy in German-occupied Europe, where his linguistic ability allowed him to masquerade as a neutral businessman. His specific mission was to penetrate German nuclear establishments and assess the location of German scientists. Following this employment by the US government, Berg established a law practice and was still at work when he died on May 17th 1972.

BERG,
Moe
(1902-72)
US baseball
player and spy

Berg was born in New York on June 30th, 1926 and educated at Pennsylvania State University, from where he graduated; he then obtained his PhD from Western Reserve University. Further studies took him to Copenhagen before he returned home and took up the appointment as assistant professor of microbiology at Washington University, St Louis (1954-59) He went on to become a professor of biochemistry at Stanford University (1959) and later chairman of the department (1969-74). Berg is responsible for devising a method for introducing 'foreign genes' into bacteria, thereby causing bacteria to produce proteins from the new gene. This type of genetic engineering is of great importance, paving the way for biochemical synthesis of insulin and interferon and enabling antiviral activity to be released by cells in response to virus infection. It all added up to Berg being co-awarded the Nobel Prize for Chemistry in 1980, and the knowledge that a lot of people were alive because of his work.

BERG,
Paul
(1926-)
US biologist

Bergman was born in Vienna, Austria, and took to table tennis before he learned to read and write. His father, who taught Hebrew, was upset that his son preferred sport to learning. In early 1939 Bergman won the world singles title for Austria but left before the Nazis could arrest him. He came to England and, a few months later in the same year, won the world doubles title with Viktor Barna (*qv*), another Jewish refugee, for England. At the commencement of the Second World War Bergman immediately volunteered for the RAF. In 1948 and 1950 he won the world singles title for England, the first Englishman to do so since Fred Perry in 1929. Bergman retired from world competition and joined Barna in giving exhibition matches for the paying public wherever and whenever possible.

BERGMAN,
Richard
(1919-70)
Austrian world
table tennis
champion

Born in Vienna, died in London, usually means one thing in our century: a person who was Jewish and had to leave, if they could, once the Nazis arrived. **Elisabeth Bergner** was such a person. Born Elisabeth Ettel on August 22nd 1900 in Vienna, she was educated at Vienna Conservatory. She decided upon an acting career and success came quickly. By the age of 24 she was an international stage and screen star. Her first film was *Nju* (1924), directed by her husband, Paul Czinner. She played the title role in Reinhardt's brilliant Berlin production of, Shaw's *Saint Joan* and went on to make many films which revealed her talents to the world. The famous French version of *Catherine the Great* (1934), was banned in Germany

BERGNER,
Elisabeth
(1900-86)
Austrian actor

because its star was a Jewess. The following year Bergner won an Oscar nomination for Best Actress, for *Escape Me Never*. In 1936 J. M. Barrie, who wrote *Peter Pan,* wrote a play especially for Bergner, *The Boy David*: it was Barrie's last play. Other films followed including *As You Like It* (1936) and her only American film, *Paris Calling* (1942). After the war she often returned to her homeland and played the theatres on tour. There she became the first actress to win the Schiller Prize (1963). She continued to make films and won awards at the 1963 and 1965 Berlin Film Festivals. Her last film performance was in 1979, in *Der Pfingstausflug*. She died in London on May 12th 1986.

BERGSON, Henri (1859-1941) French philosopher

Bergson was born in Paris on October 18th 1859. His Polish father, son of a Hasidic Jew, was a professional musician and once the pupil of Chopin. His mother was English. Henri was educated in Paris and later became a teacher. He was a brilliant lecturer: light and amusing, he got his message across without sending his audience asleep. He was also a highly original thinker who became a cult figure. He claimed that creative impulse is at the heart of evolution, and that intuition, not analysis, reveals the real world of process and change. His writings influenced Proust, Sorel and Samuel Butler and in 1927 he received the Nobel Prize for Literature. Bergson's doctrine of creative evolution also influenced George Bernard Shaw, who was so impressed by what he read that he travelled to Paris to discover more. Bergson flirted with Catholicism but did not take the final step of conversion. Referring to increasing anti-Semitism, he stated, 'I want to be among those who will be persecuted.' The Vichy French wanted to turn him into some sort of honorary Aryan: his response to this was to return all the medals and honours he had received from numerous French governments. Despite a debilitating illness, he insisted on leaving his sickbed and queuing to register as a Jew. This exertion aggravated his illness and he died shortly afterwards, on January 4th 1941. If someone ever wishes to cite a supreme example of integrity he need look no further than Bergson.

BERKOFF, Steven (1937-) British playwright and actor

A multi-talented man who is equally at home as a stage and film actor, writer and director, **Berkoff** was born in London. Having completed his regular schooling, he went off to Paris and the Ecole Jacques Lecoq, returning to found the London Theatre Group. He is one of best British playwrights of our century, avant-garde, ahead of public understanding but hugely enjoyable. *Greek* (1979), *Decadence* (1981), *West* (1983) and *Kvetch*, for which he won the comedy award of the year, are among his best-known works. In order to subsidize his theatre work, Berkoff plays the principal villain in feature films, the most well known of which include *A Clockwork Orange* (1971), *Beverly Hills Cop* (1983) and the James Bond film, *Octopussy* (1984). His acting is powerful and his writing provocative. Berkoff is at his entertaining best when he combines the two. In 1996 he staged his new play, *Free Association*. His love of words is evident and his gestures are extravagant. As a youngster he was found with a stolen bicycle. It was a first offence, but he was sent to a detention centre for three months by 'an evil, vindictive old sod called Basil Henriques' (*qv*).

Born Milton Berlinger in New York City on July 12th 1908, **Berle** was only five years old when he won a contest that led to parts in silent films. He was in the 1920 Broadway musical *Florodora*, following which he changed his name. His career took off in the late 1940s when television became a fact of everyday life. Between 1948 and 1967 he was the star of six television series that earned him the title of Mr Television and a place in the Television Academy Hall of Fame (1984). In 1986, following a quadruple heart bypass operation, he returned to television, starring in his first situation comedy *Moscow & Vine*. He has appeared in a number of films including *It's a Mad Mad Mad Mad World* (1963), *The Loved One* (1968) and *The Muppet Movie* (1979). He has received three Emmy Awards for his television work. In 1974 he published *Milton Berle: An Autobiography*; he also wrote a book of memoirs in 1988 entitled *B.S., I Love You.* Woody Allen, in the book *Woody Allen on Woody Allen* (1993) by Stig Bjorkman, says of Berle, 'He's very gifted and it's not a mystery why he's been a star for 55 to 60 years in show business. He was a star when he was younger and he *made* television in the US.' In 1991 Berle married Lorna Adams, 33 years his junior.

BERLE, Milton (1908-) US entertainer

It is hard to imagine anyone in the world not knowing at least one **Irving Berlin** song. A legend who lived for over a hundred years, his output was enormous and hugely important. He was born Israel Baline in Siberia, Russia, on May 11th 1888. When he was six, pogroms forced the family out of the country and they finally surfaced in New York. Two years later his father died and Irving, as he was now known, helped out by selling newspapers. He later became a singing waiter and taught himself to play the piano, albeit in the one key of F sharp. He would try out his compositions on the customers. Although his tunes were acceptable, and enjoyed by the diners, they didn't exactly set the pop music world on fire. That happened in 1911 with 'Alexander's Rag Time Band', for which Berlin wrote both words and music. It swept the world and Berlin never looked back. He is credited with having written over 1,000 songs. His hits are far too many to list here; it will suffice to say that he was the forerunner of popular 20th century music. He wrote 'Blue Skies' for the first film talkie, *The Jazz Singer* (1928), as well as probably the most popular song of this century, 'White Christmas', for the 1942 Bing Crosby film *Holiday Inn*. The song won Berlin the Oscar for Best Song. He wrote the music for some of Broadway's greatest musicals, including *Annie Get Your Gun* (1946) and *Call Me Madam* (1950). In 1939, in a fit of patriotic fervour, he wrote the unofficial national anthem of America; *God Bless America*. For this, and other patriotic songs, Berlin was presented with a gold Congressional Medal by President Eisenhower in 1954. Berlin retired in 1962 when only 74, to become a recluse in Manhattan. He died in New York on September 22nd 1989.

BERLIN, Irving (1888-1989) US songwriter

BERLIN,
Sir Isaiah
(1909-)
British
philosopher

Berlin was born in Riga, Latvia, on June 6th 1909 and taken to England as a young lad. He graduated from Oxford University and in 1938 was elected a Fellow of All Souls College. In 1966 he became Master of Wolfson College. A professor of social and political theory, he gravitated to diplomacy and served at the British embassies of Moscow and Washington. He wrote prolifically, his works including *Karl Marx* (1939), *Historical Inevitability* (1954) and *Vico and Herder* (1976). In addition to his philosophical books he has written numerous essays. He stresses the historical dimension of philosophical analysis in contrast to the formality of logical positivism. In 1971 he was awarded the Order of Merit. In 1996 he was involved, with others, in advising the acceptance by Oxford University of a large fund from the Flick Foundation. Unfortunately, the recommendation did not appear to include the fact that the money on offer emanated from the Nazi industrialist who, during the Second World War, used many thousands of Jews and others as slave labourers in order to accumulate the wealth his grandson now enjoys. Later that year, during the course of an interview, Berlin said, 'If I was very ill and I knew I was dying, I would like euthanasia.' In October 1996, Berlin was one of four prominent British Jews who wrote to Israeli prime minister Netanyahu exhorting him 'to revive and implement the peace progress started by Perez and Rabin'.

BERLINER,
Emile
(1851-1929)
US aviation
pioneer

Berliner, the grandson of a rabbi, was born in Hanover on May 20th 1851 and emigrated to the US when he was nineteen. At the start of the 20th century he was working on aviation experiments. In particular he was busy experimenting with the principle of a light engine that would rotate. He wanted to mount the rotating engine on a flying machine, that would become known as a helicopter. Between 1919 and 1926 he built three 'chopper' machines and, although by now in his seventies, he successfully flight-tested them himself. In 1925 he invented an acoustic tile for use in sound studios and concert halls. He died in Washington DC on August 3rd 1929.

BERMAN,
Jacob
(1901-84)
Polish politician

Jacob was the elder of two sons born to Isser Berman, an early advocate of Zionism. Both Jacob and his brother Adolf were socialists and later communists, Adolf in Israel and Jacob in Poland. Jacob graduated as a lawyer and during the Second World War helped to organize the Union of Polish Patriots in the USSR; he later served in the Polish army. Following the war he returned to Poland to become deeply involved with politics. In the period 1952-56 he was a deputy prime minister and a leading member of the Politburo. In 1956, when Gomulka came to power, Berman was accused of 'Stalinism' and removed from office. From then until 1968 he worked as an editor in a publishing house until forced out by one of the periodical bursts of Polish anti-Semitism.

BERMAN,
Pandro
(1905-96)
US film-maker

Berman, born in Pittsburgh, Pennsylvania, on March 28th 1905, was responsible for some 85 films for RKO, including the Ginger Rogers-Fred Astaire musicals. If he had done nothing else in his career, the pleasure he brought with these films alone would have earned him the thankfulness of millions. However, he has achieved some other notable heights. He is responsible for launching Elizabeth Taylor when, in 1940, he produced *National Velvet*. Berman has produced many films that are regarded as distinguished by his peers. In 1934 he saw the Broadway show *Gay Divorcee* and bought the film rights. This film launched the careers of Ginger Rogers and Fred Astaire. He is also responsible for such films as *Blackboard Jungle* (1955), well in advance of national conscience; *Of Human Bondage* (1934), which launched Bette Davis; and *The Picture of Dorian Gray* (1945), which brought an Oscar to Harry Stradling, who photographed it. Berman produced *The Three Musketeers* in 1948 for MGM, by far the best of the six versions so far produced. His *Seventh Cross* (1944) brought an Oscar nomination for Hume Cronyn and is considered the best in its genre. *Ivanhoe* in 1952 was nominated for Best Picture. *Jailhouse Rock* (1957) helped consolidate Elvis Presley's career, while *The Brothers Karamazov* (1958) brought an Oscar nomination for Best Actor for Lee J. Cobb. Elizabeth Taylor picked up the Oscar for Best Actress in Berman's *Butterfield Eight* (1960). In 1962 he produced *The Sweet Bird of Youth*, which gave Ed Begley an Oscar for Best Supporting Actor. Berman followed this in 1963 with *Prize* with Paul Newman (*qv*) and *A Patch of Blue* (1965) with Shelley Winters (*qv*), for which she won an Oscar. In 1977 Berman was awarded the highest honour possible, the Irving G. Thalberg Memorial Award, and in 1985 he was featured in George Steven's documentary *A Filmmaker's Journey*. During a graceful retirement he had the satisfaction of knowing he had been responsible for some of the best films of the century. Married twice and with three children, Pandro Berman died on July 13th, 1996.

Bernard was born in Besançon, France, on September 7th 1866 and began his career as a sports writer. He switched to theatre and wrote good-humoured satire. His observations, mostly witty, originated from the man-in-the-street. He was for ever telling jokes, so much so it was once thought that he was the fountainhead for all French humour. Although he wrote several well-received novels, he is best remembered for such plays as *L'anglais tel qu'on le parle* (1900); *Le Prince Charmant* (1923); *Jules, Juliette et Julien* (1929); *Le Sauvage* (1931); and *Que le Monde est Petit* (1935). The Nazis arrested him during the Second World War but released him following the intervention of influential friends. This experience and the revelations of what happened in the death camps to family and friends less fortunate than himself devastated him, and he died broken of a broken heart in Paris on December 7th 1947.

BERNARD, Tristan (1866-1947) French writer

Bernays has the dubious distinction of being the founder of modern PR. He was born in Vienna, Austria, on November 22nd 1891, a nephew of Sigmund Freud (*qv*), but arrived in the US when he was one year old. He graduated from Cornell Agricultural College in 1912. For a while he worked as a medical journalist before becoming a business publicity agent - a sort of forerunner of what is now termed public relations. It was Bernays who put PR on the map. He used all sorts of techniques, or perhaps ruses, to overcome opposition to a controversial play called *Damaged Goods* written by Eugene Brieux, the French dramatist. Gradually, Bernays

BERNAYS, Edward (1891-1978) US public relations pioneer

acquired a prestigious clientele: Caruso, Otis Skinner, Diaghilev's Russian Ballet and many more, including rising political stars. From 1920 Bernays was recognized as the leading public relations counsellor for major corporations in the US. His book, *Crystallizing Public Opinions* (1929), was the first ever written on the subject. In 1930 he taught the subject as a college course; again, he was the first to do so. For good or bad, PR has become a growth industry with a knock-on effect over millions of lives all around the world. What his grandfather, the rabbi of Hamburg, would have made of all the razzamatazz that accompanies much current PR activity is anyone's guess. What is known is that Bernay's influence on social and political culture has been all-embracing and largely overlooked.

**BERNHARDT,
Sarah
(1844-1923)
French actor**

Born in Paris on October 22nd 1844, **Bernhardt** is arguably the most famous actress who ever trod the stage. She spent two of the most important decades of her life in the 20th century. However, it is a sobering thought that, had Bernhardt lived slightly later, when the French Jews were being shipped off to Eastern Europe, she might well have ended her days in a German gas oven. She founded Theatre Sarah Bernhardt in 1900. In 1915 she had one leg amputated. At that time France was locked into the large-scale battles of the First World War; many thousands of soldiers lost limbs in the carnage and Bernhardt became their inspiration. She was awarded the Legion of Honour in 1914. 'The Divine Sarah' continued her acting even to entertaining troops in the battle zones. She was said to have a voice of liquid gold and to speak verse as the nightingale sings. Her acting was always overpowering, prompting the current phrase: 'Who does she think she is - Sarah Bernhardt?' Sarah died on March 26th 1923 in Paris, while filming.

**BERNHEIM,
Louis
(1861-1931)
Belgian soldier**

Bernheim was born in Saint-Josse-ten-Noode, Belgium, and educated and trained to become a professional soldier. By the begining of the 20th century Bernheim was on the Belgian General Staff. In 1914, at the beginning of the First World War, he took command of the 7th Infantry Grenadiers at Antwerp. Later, commanding a Belgian division, he successfully defended Antwerp against superior German forces, thus keeping the port open for Allied shipping. Although badly wounded, in September 1915 he returned in time to command, with the rank of general, three Belgian divisions that in 1918 fought in the final Flanders battles. At his death he was given a state funeral and a statue was later erected in his honour in a Brussels square. It is interesting to note that two of the fighting generals involved in the war in France were Jewish. The other, of course, was General Sir John Monash (*qv*), Commander in Chief of the Australian and New Zealand armies.

**BERNSTEIN,
Carl
(1944-)
US journalist**

Bernstein was born in Washington,DC on Febuary 14th 1944. Following a conventional education and after graduating from university, Bernstein broke into journalism by getting a job as a copy-boy on the *Washington Star.* In 1966 he switched to the *Washington Post* as a fully fledged journalist complete with by-line. Not unaware of the considerable risk, he and colleague Bob Woodward unearthed the Watergate/Nixon affair by a series of articles. The resulting investigation led to

Nixon resigning in disgrace and several of his staff going to prison. Their work resulted in their winning every journalistic award possible, including the Pulitzer Prize for 1973. They wrote *All The President's Men* in 1974, which went on to become a hit film winning Oscars for Best Writer (William Goldman) and Best Supporting Actor (Jason Robards). It is widely acknowledged that the cause of democracy owes a huge debt to Bernstein and Woodward. *The Final Days* (1976) is a daily account of Nixon's last months in office.

Bernstein was born in Berlin on January 6th 1850, the son of a Jewish family, formerly from Danzig, where his father was a railroad engineer. His uncle, Aaron Bernstein, was editor of the *Berlin Volks-Zeitung,* a working-class newspaper. By 1901, Bernstein was the acknowledged theoretician of the revisionist school in the labour movement. It was his belief that socialism is the natural result of liberal thought and not the result of a revolt against the capitalist middle class. In 1902 he was a member of the Reichstag, to which he was repeatedly re-elected until 1928. He was against his Social Democratic party supporting the war of 1914-18 and equally opposed to those who wanted a revolution like that in Russia in 1917. He strongly believed that a parliamentary republic was the way forward to progress. He was a member of the German Cabinet in 1919 and served as the Secretary of State for Economy and Finance. Social Democracy had at last arrived in Germany, something Bernstein had worked for more than 20 years to achieve. However, while he was able to discourage his fellow Germans from taking the path of revolution, he was unable to stop them supporting fascism, and the German variety, Nazism. Bernstein died in Berlin on December 18th 1932, aged 82. Six weeks later Hitler was elected German Chancellor. The Germany of Eduard Bernstein was over for ever.

Edward Bernstein was born in Bayonne, New Jersey, on December 19th 1904. He was the son of an insurance agent and grew up in New York City. Educated at the University of Chicago, where he gained a degree in economics in 1927, he received his doctorate from Harvard in 1931. He taught economics at the University of North Carolina before joining the US Treasury Department in 1940. Bernstein met John Maynard Keynes at the Bretton Woods conference of 1944, at which Keynes was head of the British delegation and Bernstein was the US technical adviser and executive secretary. At first the two men did not hit it off; then Keynes became impressed with how Bernstein successfully won the US delegation round to his point of view. Keynes fell into line and the post-war international economy benefited accordingly. In particular, the International Bank for Reconstruction and Development (the World Bank) was a direct result of Bernstein's influence. Two years after Bretton Woods he was appointed the bank's first director of research; he stayed with the institution until 1958, when he left to found his own consultancy practice, numbering among his clients several leading banks and multinational companies. Bernstein's clarity of vision and expression enabled him to take on the might of American and British economists and persuade them to his point of view. Decades later he was proved correct. Bernstein died in Washington DC on June 9th 1996.

BERNSTEIN, Eduard (1850-1932) German politician

BERNSTEIN, Edward (1904-96) US economist

BERNSTEIN,
Elmer
(1922-)
US composer

Born in New York on April 4th 1922 and educated at Juilliard and New York University, **Bernstein** studied with Roger Sessions and Stefan Wolpe, two of the greats in 20th century music. Since the mid-1950s he has been the leading writer of film scores. His list of musical credits is formidable: he has written the music to well over a hundred feature films of all sorts, ten of which have won Oscar nominations or awards. They include *Man With the Golden Arm* (1955), *The Magnificent Seven* (1960), *Summer and Smoke* (1961), *Walk on the Wild Side* (1962), *Hawaii* (1966), *Thoroughly Modern Millie* (1967) and *True Grit* (1969). He is noted for his use of solo instruments and the natural use of jazz idioms.

BERNSTEIN,
Leonard
(1918-90)
US composer
and conductor

It is difficult to imagine our century without the music of *West Side Story*, and that was only one contribution from this giant of the music world. **Bernstein's** versatility was a broad platform on which he excelled in brilliant fashion. He was born in Lawrence, Massachusetts, on August 25th 1918 and educated at Harvard and the Curtis Institute of Music. He came to fame overnight in dramatic fashion in 1943, when the legendary Bruno Walter was taken ill and the 25-year-old Bernstein was given two hours' notice to take his place and conduct the New York Philharmonic. He wrote prolifically, including three symphonies, of which *Kaddish* (1963) is the best known. His musical comedy *On the Town* (1944) became a hit film starring Gene Kelly and Frank Sinatra. *West Side Story* has been staged all over the world and the film version won seven Oscars. However, Bernstein was first and foremost a classical musician, who enjoyed delving into show business. He was a brilliant lecturer, as his 1950s programme of Young People's Concerts testifies. These were later televised, thus introducing millions of people to the beauty of the classics. He was appointed music director and conductor of the New York Philharmonic in 1958, an association which continued until his death. in New York on October 14th 1990. A great musician, his music and performances will be remembered with affection and gratitude.

BERNSTEIN,
Lord Sidney
(1899-1993)
British media
magnate

Sidney was born in Essex on January 30th 1899 into a Jewish family with Swedish and Russian backgrounds, and grew up in two traditional Jewish strongholds: Ilford and Crickelwood. His father was in the quarry business and as a sideline had an investment in London's emerging cinema world. Little could Bernstein senior imagine how prophetic his investment would become. Sidney left school at fifteen, and by the time he was 22 he was running his father's cinemas. The cinema in general was on the verge of revolution, with the advent of talkies. Bernstein gradually built up a chain of cinemas in Britain and named the company 'Granada' to recall happy walking tours of Spain. A merger with Gaumont-British followed that allowed Bernstein to launch his 'super cinemas' in 1930. These were 1,000-seaters with a great organ that rose when the house lights came on and descended when the lights went down. In addition, these cinemas often provided live cabaret between the two parts of a double feature bill. For Bernstein what the public wanted was more important than profit, although the two often went hand in hand.

In the late 1930s Bernstein was an outspoken critic of Hitler and, nearer home, Hitler's British supporter, Oswald Mosley. During the Second World War, Bernstein was film advisor to the Ministry of Information. In 1945, during the last throes of the war, Bernstein engaged Alfred Hitchcock to supervise film footage taken by Allied cameramen during the liberation of the concentration camps. Following the war, Bernstein had to decide between building up a television empire or going wholeheartedly into film production. He had made a few films, notably *Rope*, directed by Hitchcock in 1948, but he knew that television would become the major entertainment medium of the century. So Granada Television was born, and grew to become the finest commercial channel in the UK, often rivalling the BBC in excellence of production: a sure sign that Sidney's hand was on the tiller. In 1969 he was created a life peer and in 1972 he retired. He was known as shy, generous and above all a gentleman. Government, for reasons best known to themselves, kept Bernstein's concentration camp film footage locked away for some 40 years. That amount of time did not diminish the shock and pain when the film was at last shown. Sidney Bernstein died in London on February 5th 1993.

Leopold was born in Vilna, Lithuania, into a family of orthodox Jews. At the age of fourteen he ran away to Paris to study drawing. He then turned to sculpture and studied under no less a figure than Rodin. Bernstein-Sinaieff produced statues, portraits and groups as well as busts of the important people of his day. He was awarded the Order of the Legion of Honour and his sculpture *Ezra in Mourning* was acquired by the French government. He then spent ten years working on a large work, *Youth and Age*, which was rapturously received - and smashed by the Germans when they conquered Paris during the Second World War. As an additional reward for his great work the Nazis sent him to an extermination camp. As he was 77 at the time he was murdered, he was unlikely to have been much of a threat to the Germans. He was simply an old Jew whose talents meant nothing to them.

BERNSTEIN-SINAIEFF, Leopold (1867-1944) French sculptor

Born in St Petersburg, Russia, on January 24th 1891, **Besicovitch** went on to work under Markoff at the city's university. Following the 1917 revolution, he first moved to Perm in the Urals; then, in 1925, he emigrated to Britain and Cambridge University. Besicovitch became responsible for something that was very important to those in the upper strata of intellectual brilliance: the solution to the famous mathematical conundrum known as 'Kekeya's problem', the determination of the least area swept out by a straight line which is reversed in direction by a continuous motion in the plane. This problem was solved by Besicovitch who satisfactorily proved that there is no 'least area'. The importance of his work was reflected in his election as a Fellow of the Royal Society and the award of its Sylvestor medal. He was also well known for producing apparently simple problems that were fiendishly difficult to solve. He wrote many books, of which *Almost Periodic Functions* (1955) is the best known. He died in Cambridge on November 2nd 1970.

BESICOVITCH, Abraham (1891-1970) Russian/British mathematician

BETHE,
Hans
(1906-)
German/
American
physicist

Bethe was born on July 2nd 1906 in Strassburg, Germany, before it lost an 's', gained an 'o' and became French. He studied physics at the University of Frankfurt and did research work in theoretical physics at the University of Munich, where he obtained a doctorate in 1928 with a thesis on the theory of electron diffraction. His work on crystal splitting, in 1929, illustrated how the symmetrical electric field, by which an atom in a crystal is surrounded, affects its energy condition. In 1931 he worked with Enrico Fermi in Rome, returning to Germany in 1932 to lecture at the University of Tübingen. In 1933, as the son of a Jewish mother, he was forced out of his job and advised to leave the country. He spent a year in England before emigrating to America in 1935 to serve as an assistant professor of physics at Cornell University, becoming a full professor two years later. Ithaca, New York, became his home until 1975. He had become a US citizen in 1941 in time to work on the Manhattan project at Los Alamos, New Mexico. After the atomic bomb was dropped he was one of the scientists who keenly felt their responsibility in ensuring that an atomic war never happened. Bethe was one of the contributors to the *Bulletin of the Atomic Scientists*. In addition, he lectured and wrote on the danger of the nuclear threat, thereby increasing public awareness. Beside being awarded the Max Planck medal in 1955 he was a foreign member of the Royal Society of London and a member of the US National Academy of Sciences. In 1967 he was awarded the Nobel Prize for Physics for discoveries on the energy production of stars. In 1980 he wrote his autobiography, *Hans Berthe, Prophet of Energy*.

BETTELHEIM,
Bruno
(1903-90)
Austrian/
American
psychologist

Born on August 28th 1903 in Vienna, Austria, **Bettelheim** studied at Vienna University and had just qualified in medicine when the Nazis arrived and he was arrested. Imprisoned in Dachau and later transferred to Buchenwald, he was freed in 1939 following the intervention of Eleanor Roosevelt, wife of the US President. Safely in America, Bettelheim worked with the Progressive Education Association of Chicago University. He later became director of the Orthogenic School in Chicago, where he stayed for 30 years. He soon became known for his radical techniques in the treatment of emotionally disturbed children. It is thought he was able to relate to the pain suffered by such children to that which he had suffered and witnessed in the concentration camps. Today many of his ideas are incorporated in treatment methods in all parts of the world. His writings concerning the Holocaust have aroused much controversy. He claims that many Jews were partially responsible for their own fate at the hands of the Germans, because of what he terms 'ghetto thinking': a type of docility and compliance adopted in order that they might survive in an alien culture. He stated: 'the Jews who marched "like lemmings" to the death camps were permitting themselves to be punished, not for what they did but for who they were and therefore they were already dead by their own decision . . .' In 1976, in an article entitled 'Surviving', he wrote that those who had survived the death camps were able to do so because they believed in some cultural or religious ideal that helped them transcend themselves. Many thought that these pronouncements were too pat to describe situations too horrific to contemplate, and perhaps were the excuses put forward by someone rescued from a situation the majority couldn't escape. Bettelheim, for reasons that are unknown, took his life, while in a nursing home in Silver Springs, on March 13th 1990. It was the 52nd anniversary of the German occupation of Austria.

Ellen Bischoffsheim was born on September 1st 1857 in London, the eldest daughter of Jewish parents; her father was a well-known merchant banker. In 1881 she married the Earl of Desart. He died in 1898. However, Ellen decided to remain in Kilkenny and she began taking an active part in local events. She became involved in politics and in the continuing campaign for Irish freedom. She supported the Easter Rebellion of 1916 and ignored antisemitic and anti-Irish comments from English landowners who lived in her area. When the Irish Free State became a fact in 1921, as Lady Desart, Ellen was nominated by President Cosgrave to become a Senator in the Irish parliament. She was the first woman to win such an honour in Ireland and it reflected her well-known work to protect and advance that country's cultural and economic heritage. She died in Dublin on June 29th 1933.

BISCHOFFSHEIM, Ellen, Lady Desart (1857-1933) Irish politician

Black was born in Baku, Russia, on October 16th 1910 and moved to Britain as a young child. He trained as an architect and concentrated on exhibition design. He designed the famous Kardomah cafes of the inter-war and post-war years, sadly no longer with us. He was co-founder of the Industrial Design Partnership (1935). He designed radio and television cabinets for EKCO, so beloved of today's Art Deco collectors. He was among the pioneers in exploring the possibilities of plastics. In the Second World War he worked as an exhibition designer for the Ministry of Information. Here he met Milner Gray, with whom he set up the highly successful Design Research Unit. Black was the designer for the 'Britain Can Make It' exhibition held at the Victoria and Albert Museum in 1946. In 1951 he was co-designer of the Festival of Britain, an enormously successful exhibition that dominated the South Bank of the Thames. His design work for the early years of British Rail is considered outstanding. He also designed the interiors of London buses. In 1959 he became professor of industrial design at the Royal College of Art, where he stayed until 1975. As a reward for his design work he was knighted in 1972. He died in London on August 11th 1977.

BLACK, Sir Misha (1910-77) British designer

George Blake was born in Rotterdam in 1922 to middle-class Jewish parents. The family name was Behar. During the Second World War Blake worked for British intelligence, including MI6. It is generally presumed that in the 1950s, following time spent in Korea, he was sent to Berlin and there recruited to become an agent for the Russian KGB. After a successful career as a double agent, playing off one master against the other, Blake was caught and charged by the British. Found guilty, he was sentenced to 42 years in prison. Blake subsequently escaped from the maximum security Wormwood Scrubs prison in what was described at the time as 'one of the most famous escapes of all time'. The fact that it was accomplished by an overweight, unfit man in his forties was conveniently overlooked. It is now thought probable that his escape was 'aided' in order to effect a swap with a British or

BLAKE, George (1922-) British spy

American spy being held by the Soviets. In any event, Blake was smuggled out of Britain and into Russia. The publication in 1991 of *No Other Choice*, in which he told of his years working with MI6 as a middle-ranking spy, caused a furore in government circles, and during 1996 the British government went to the High Court in an effort to recover some £90,000 Blake is reputed to have made from publication. This issue has still not been publicly resolved. Doubtless a secret deal has been or will be the method used to settle the affair. It is, after all, the way these things are done.

BLANC,
Mel
(1908-89)
US voiceover

Mel Blanc was born on May 30th 1908 in San Francisco, California. From an early age he was interested in music, and he became proficient on the violin and the sousaphone. In 1933 he was working on a daily radio programme. One of the features audiences enjoyed was the radio play. The difference here was that Blanc provided all the voices: he *was* the cast. Over the ensuing years Mel Blanc became the voices of some of the greatest characters created by the cartoon industry. He was Woody Woodpecker, Daffy Duck, Tweety Pie, Sylvester the Cat and Bugs Bunny, complete with 'What's up, Doc?'. He also provided the voice for the French skunk, Pépé le Pew. Warner Brothers, who had a cartoon subsidiary, used Mel Blanc for some 90 per cent of their characters. One way and another, he provided voices for around 3,000 cartoons. In the 1960s he co-produced *The Bugs Bunny Show.* For the *Flintstones* he was Dino the Dinosaur. For the feature film *Who Framed Roger Rabbit?* (1988) he re-created many of the voices he had used during his 50 years in show business. His autobiography, *That's Not All, Folks: My Life in the Golden Age of Cartoons and Radio*, was published in 1988. He died on July 10th 1989 in Los Angeles.

BLANKSTEIN,
Cecil
(1908-)
Canadian
architect

Born in Manitoba, Canada, the son of a pioneer architect, **Cecil** followed in his father's footsteps. In a full career he is credited with many major projects that have enhanced the Canadian lifestyle, among them a 1,000-bed hospital at Ste Anne de Belloac, Quebec, the National Art Gallery, and the world-famous housing project known as 'Habitat'. Blankstein first exhibited this project, in model form, at the Montreal International Expo of 1967. This type of architecture has influenced architects and designers all over the world in the construction of their future housing projects. In 1976, a Canadian stamp was issued honouring Blankstein for his work.

BLOCH,
Ernest
(1880-1959)
Swiss/American
composer

Born in Geneva, Switzerland, on July 24th 1880, **Bloch** studied the violin at Geneva Conservatory before going on to conservatories in Brussels, where he studied with the noted violinist Eugene Ysaye, Frankfurt and Munich. Between 1911 and 1915 he taught at the Geneva Conservatory, and first made a name for himself with *Trois Poems Juifs* (1913). In 1916 he toured the US with the dancer Maud Allen; the touring company ran into financial difficulties and Bloch settled in the US. Between 1920 and 1925 he was director of the Cleveland Institiue of Music. In 1925 he went westwards and directed the San Francisco Conservatory until 1930. He was in Paris when his opera *Macbeth* received its premiere. In 1916 the first of his Jewish music, *The Israel Symphony*, was performed, followed in 1923 by the suite *Baal Shem*. He became a US citizen in 1924 but went back to Europe in 1930, not returning until 1938. He wrote *Sacred Service* (1930-33) for baritone, chorus and orchestra. His symphonies include the epic rhapsody *America* (1926), which won him first prize in a national competition. During the period 1941-52 he taught at the University of California at Berkeley. Bloch was an advocate of both music and art. While living in the Swiss village of Poveredo-Capriasca he wrote *Avodath Hakodesh*, and said of it: 'though intensely Jewish in its roots, this message seems to be above all a gift of Israel to whole of mankind.' Bloch died in Portland, Oregon, on July 15th 1959.

Bloch was born on October 23rd 1905 in Zurich, Switzerland, the son of a wholesale grain merchant. In 1924 he started to study engineering but soon decided on a career in physics. In his new department he met Erwin Schrodinger, who at that time was in the throes of formulating quantum mechanics. Bloch worked in Leipzig University for some years, but with the arrival of Hitler he left for the US. A year later he was professor of theoretical physics at Stanford University, a post he held from 1934 to 1971. Although Bloch never contributed to the formulation of quantum mechanics, all his work was in its direct application, and today's students of physics learn about 'Bloch states' and 'Bloch functions'. At Stanford, Bloch conceived a method for detecting neutrons. During the Second World War he worked on the early stages of the development of the atomic bomb, but then switched to work on methods of countering radar detection of aircraft. In 1952 Bloch received the Nobel Prize for his work on nuclear magnetic resonance. He was the first director-general of the European Commission for Nuclear Research, based in Geneva. Over the last four decades nuclear magnetic resonance techniques have become increasingly important in diagnostic medicine. Bloch died in Zurich on September 10th 1983.

BLOCH, Felix (1905-83) Swiss/American physicist

Born in Paris, **Bloch** in his youth was stirred by the anti-Semitism shown in the Dreyfus Affair. Educated at the Sorbonne, he became a teacher of history and literature. In 1912 he wrote *Levy*, a story dealing with the effects of the Dreyfus case on an ordinary Jewish family. His most powerful work was probably *Et Compagnie* (1918), written in the realistic style made famous by Emile Zola. He served during the First World War in the French army and was wounded three times. He joined the Communist Party in 1921 and in 1931 co-founded the Communist daily, *Ce Soir*. During the Second World War Bloch was an active member of the Resistance and in 1941 eluded the Gestapo by escaping to Moscow. There he worked in radio, broadcasting to the French people. He returned to France in 1945. He was the brother-in-law of Emile Herzog, better known as André Maurois.

BLOCH, Jean-Richard (1884-1947) French writer

BLOCH,
Konrad
(1912-)
US biochemist

Bloch was born in Neisse, Germany, on January 21st 1912 and educated at the Technische Hochschule in Munich, graduating in 1934. Although most Aryan looking, with fair hair, blue eyes, regular features and an athletic bearing, Bloch the Jew was not wanted by the new regime. He took off, first to Switzerland and then to the US and Columbia University. Here he obtained his doctorate in 1938. He stayed on as a member of staff and began his long affair with the biological origins of cholesterol. Between 1946 and 1954 he taught at the University of Chicago. In 1954 he became professor of biochemistry at Harvard, but still found time to pursue his research. His work on cholesterol, and its relation to fatty acids, led to his discovering the complex sequence of the molecule in the human body, a discovery that had an important bearing on finding a cure for arterio-sclerosis or hardening of the arteries. This most important advance in knowledge earned the man the Germans didn't want a half share in the 1964 Nobel Prize for Medicine.

BLOCH,
Marc
(1886-1944)
French
historian

Bloch was born Leopold Benjamin on July 6th 1886 in Lyon, the son of a professor of ancient history, and was educated at the Ecole Normal Superieure in Paris and at the universities of Leipzig and Berlin. Before going into the French army for the First World War he was a teacher. After the war he became a professor of medieval history at Strasbourg and co-founded *Annales d'Histoire Economique et Sociale*, a periodical which transformed historians' view of their work. In 1936 he was appointed professor of economic history at the Sorbonne. In 1939, on the outbreak of the Second World War, Bloch rejoined the army so becoming the oldest captain in the French forces. Following France's defeat Bloch taught for a while but soon gave it up for the Resistance movement. His skill at deciphering secret codes was most important and he became one of those most wanted by the Germans. In 1944 he became their prisoner. They tortured him before standing him in front of a firing squad. His last words were 'Vive La France'.

His writings were of high technical merit and he warned his students to ask questions constantly and not take what was told them for granted. His last book, *L'Etrange Defaite*, was published posthumously in 1946. Here Bloch discussed his relationship with Judaism and, inter alia, stated: 'by birth I am a Jew but not by religion for I have never felt the need for any sort of religion. I never stress my heredity save when I am the presence of an anti-Semite. I was born in France. I have drunk the waters of her culture. I have made her past my own. I breathe freely only in her climate.'

BLOCH,
Pierre
(1905-)
French
Politician

Pierre Bloch was born in Paris. After graduating from university he joined the left-wing journal *Populaire*. In 1936, he was elected Socialist deputy for the Aisne Department and in 1938 was chairman of one of the many commissions of inquiry set up to investigate the Algerian problem. At the outbreak of the Second World War, Bloch joined the army and was taken prisoner. He escaped to join the Resistance, becoming one of the leaders of the banned French Socialist party. In 1941 his fellow Frenchmen in Vichy condemned him to death for organizing parachute drops of arms into occupied France. Once more Pierre Bloch escaped his captors and in 1942 arrived in London, where he became head of French counter-espionage. After the war he rejoined the French Socialists. He was a prolific writer and published several books, many of which were critical of de Gaulle at a time when such a stance was not fashionable.

Born in London on February 15th 1931, **Claire** received her training at two of London's best dramatic institutions, the Guildhall School of Music and Drama and the Central School of Speech and Drama. She is a classic actress who first made her reputation on the stage in Shakespearean roles. Her exceptional talent and elegant, cool looks have kept her busy on stage, screen and television. At seventeen she was Ophelia; at nineteen she was playing alongside Richard Burton (her first lover) and John Gielgud in *The Lady's Not For Burning*. Her starring role in Charlie Chaplin's *Limelight* (1952) received international acclaim. She has since distinguished herself in such films as Laurence Olivier's *Richard III*, *Look Back In Anger* (1959), *A Severed Head* (1970), *Sammy and Rosie Get Laid* (1987) and Woody Allen's *Crimes and Misdemeanours* (1989). She married actor Rod Steiger in 1959, a traumatic union that lasted ten years. Her next marriage, to producer Hillard Elkins, was disastrous. Her third, to writer Philip Roth, was the worst of the three and ended in divorce. Laurence Olivier, who was also her lover, cruelly rejected her from those theatrical parts that, by virtue of talent alone, were rightfully hers. Olivier was not above the odd antisemitic jibe, and this, along with the fact that, as his autobiography shows, he did not much like women, especially his own former lovers, was probably his petty reason. In 1996 Claire Bloom published her biography, *Leaving a Doll's House*. The title reflects her triumph in Ibsen's play which became a film in 1973.

Bloomfield, born in Chicago on April 1st 1887 to immigrant Jewish parents, was educated locally before graduating from Chicago University. He later received his doctorate from Harvard. He went on to teach linguistics at several major universities including Chicago (1927) and Yale (1940). He began by studying the details of Indo-European, mainly Germanic, speech sounds and word formations, and went on to study many of the rarer Asian dialects, becoming an expert on Malay and Polynesian languages. Because of Bloomfield's efforts, linguistics became an independent scientific discipline. His major literary work on the subject, *Language* (1933), is now considered outdated; however, it has continued to provide a basic approach to language as a subject of scientific inquiry. Bloomfield's contribution to our understanding of the language of many of the Native North American tribes is of the greatest importance. He died in New Haven, Connecticut, on April 18th 1949.

Mike Bloomfield was born in Chicago on July 28th 1944. His musical education came from sitting at the feet of the great Chicago-based blues guitarists. He haunted the clubs and learned from the likes of Muddy Waters and Albert King. By the middle to late 1960s he was considered the best white blues guitarist in America. He provided the backing for Bob Dylan's (*qv*) hits of the 1960s. He was part of the Paul Butterfield Blues Band until 1967, when he formed the short-lived Electric Flag group. In 1968 his album, *Super Session*, with Stephen Sills and Al Kooper (*qv*), became a best-selling record. The Bloomfield style is described as clean, crisp, sparse and emotional. His technique was unique, and it was said he could sustain a note better and longer than any other player, pop or classical. He shunned publicity. He would follow a hit by a long period of seclusion. His life was very varied and the ultimate in independence. He would back the greatest recording stars in music history and score the music for pornographic films. He taught music at Stanford University in San Francisco and he was a drug addict. He hated touring, because he needed the security of home. He once said: 'Playing in front of strangers leads to idolatry and idolatry is dangerous because the audience has a preconception of you, even though you cannot get a conception of them.' In 1975, much against his will, he became part of the group KGB. It didn't last. In 1977, now playing acoustic music, he released five albums including *If You Love These Blues, Play 'Em As You Please*. On February 15th 1981 he was found dead in his car. An accidental drug overdose was given as the cause. It was a sad end to a star performer who always fought the limelight to preserve his integrity.

Born in Paris on April 9th 1872, to a Jewish Alsatian family, **Blum** was educated at the Ecole Normale Superieure before going on to the Sorbonne, from where he graduated with the highest honours. Blum registered two firsts in his life, being both the first Jew to be Prime Minister of France and the country's first socialist Prime Minister. As a lawyer he was horrified by the Dreyfus Affair. It propelled him into politics and he became a deputy in the French parliament in 1919. In May 1936 he was elected Prime Minister, and within weeks of taking office he made good his electoral promises: paid holidays, a 40 hour working week and nationalization of the Bank of France. The French public, and the world beyond, saw that Blum was a man of his word. He organized the various left-wing factions together, and in 1938 headed a Popular Front government; however, it lasted only a few months. Blum refused to serve in the Daladier government that was in office at the start of the Second World War. Following the fall of France, he was arrested by the Vichy French and prosecuted for leading France to war. Blum conducted such a brilliant defence that Vichy's German masters ordered the case to be halted and Blum was taken to Germany and interned. In 1945 he was freed by US troops. Back in France, he was given an enthusiastic welcome. He now became his country's 'elder statesman'. In 1946 he again headed a socialist government, but it only lasted a month. In 1948 he was deputy prime minister, a post he held until a month before his death. Leon Blum is undoubtedly one of the great figures, not just of the French socialist movement, but also of the international scene during this period. In 1907 he wrote an essay on marriage in which he advocated that young girls should enjoy as much freedom as young men, and he recommended 'trial marriages'. Leon Blum died, in Jouy-en-Josas, on March 30th 1950.

René Blum was the younger brother of Leon Blum (*qv*) the French premier. He was initially a teacher; having become editor of the periodical *Gil Blas*, he then gave up journalism for art and ballet - especially the ballet. In 1929, when Diaghilev died, Blum was asked to succeed him as director of the Ballet de l'Opéra de Monte Carlo. Blum filled the post brilliantly, and under his aegis the company prospered, to become one of the major ballet companies in the world. Then came 1940 and the Germans. Following the occupation, Blum refused to go to the so-called safe zone of Vichy. Early in 1942 he was interned, together with a thousand other French-Jewish intellectuals, and was eventually entrained for Auschwitz where, in September 1944, he died. Just before his arrest he wrote his memoirs and delivered them to his publishers. They have never been found.

BLUM, René (1878-1944) French ballet producer

Blumberg was born on July 28th 1925 in New York, and graduated from Union College, Schenectady, New York, in 1945. With looks that resembled a boxer, rather than a research professor, he went on to get an MD from Columbia University in 1951 and a PhD from Oxford University in 1957. Thus academically equipped, he joined the Clinical Research Institute for Cancer Research. During the 1960s and 1970s Blumberg was professor of medicine and genetics, at the University of Pennsylvania. Blumberg's work led to him create a test for hepatitis viruses in donated blood and, in turn, an experimental vaccine against the disease. In 1963 he discovered in the blood serum of an Australian aborigine an antigen that he eventually determined to be part of a virus for possible hepatitis B transmission. Blumberg shared the award of the 1976 Nobel Prize in Physiology of Medicine for his work on the origins and spread of infectious diseases. In 1982 a safe vaccine, based upon the use of the Australian antigen, became available in the US.

BLUMBERG, Baruch (1925-) US physician

Born in New Jersey on Febuary 12 1938, **Judy Blume** has become probably the most controversial American writer of teenage fiction, as well as the most popular. It was her third book, *Are You There God? It's Me, Margaret* (1970) that launched her international career. It brought acclaim for the candid approach she took to the onset of puberty. She has a natural, unsubtle style and her explicitness in dealing with problems peculiar to those in the 10-14 age group has brought her into conflict with the narrow minded. Her readers, however, rejoice in Blume's readiness to tackle subjects previously considered taboo. Her other books include *Then Again, Maybe I Won't* (1971); *It's Not the End of the World* (1972); and *Forever* (1975).

BLUME, Judy (1938-) US writer

BLUME,
Peter
(1906-92)
Russian/
American
painter

Peter Blume was born in Smorgon, Russia, on October 27th 1906, and taken to the US when he was five years old. Under the Federal Arts Project of the 1930s he produced many murals and won high praise. This project, which started in 1935 and ended ten years later, was designed to aid artists hit by the Depression. The murals, on public buildings all over the States, were designed to give people a lift from the drabness and decay in their lives, as well as providing a possible continuing interest in art. Blume's meticulously detailed dreamlike canvases earned him a place among the best-known American painters of the first half of the century. His style constantly underwent changes as he reflected the changes around him, from the careful composition of the early days, through horrifying and fantastic paintings in his middle years to the rapid, almost lazy style of his late years. Following the award of a Guggenheim scholarship he headed for Italy and there produced his best-known work, *The Eternal City* (1937), having recently come to prominence after being awarded the first prize in the 1934 Carnegie International Exhibition, for his painting, *South of Scranton*.

The Rock (1948) was a giant painting on which the artist worked, on and off, for seven years, saying that it was meant to symbolize man's continuing rebuilding of his devastated world. In the 1970s, he produced a group of bronzes based on known classical themes. Although his later work was not of the type of his earlier years and did not arouse much controversy, he was nevertheless regarded throughout his career as a master.

BOAS,
Franz
(1858-1942)
German/
American
anthropologist

By the beginning of the twentieth century **Boas** was living in the US. Born in Minden, Germany, on July 9th 1858 he is considered to be the man who established anthropology in America. His main purpose was to bring together ethnology, physical anthropology, archaeology and language in order to save details of culture from becoming extinct. He wrote much. His best-known books of this century are *The Mind of Primitive Man* (1911); *Primitive Art* (1927); *Anthropology in Modern Life* (1928); and *Race, Language and Culture* (1940). These books were later forbidden in his country of birth and burnt. Hitler ordered that the PhD conferred upon him by Kiel University be cancelled. Boas lent the full force of his scientific knowledge to the fight against German racism. In 1933, following Hitler's appointment as German Chancellor, Boas wrote a pamphlet, *Aryans and Non-Aryans*, which was distributed widely in Germany by the underground movement. While speaking at a luncheon being given in honour of a colleague in New York on December 22nd 1942, Boas collapsed and died. Boas claimed that neither race or geography has the primary role in forming human beings. It is due to his influence and writings that this proposition is now overwhelmingly accepted.

BODENHEIM,
Maxwell
(1893-1954)
US poet

Born **Maxwell Bodenheimer** on May 26th 1893 in Hermanville, Missouri, he spent his early twenties in Chicago, during the period that became known as the Chicago Renaissance. Mostly self-educated, he met up with Ben Hecht (*qv*), and together they edited the *Chicago Literary Times*, which began and ended inside a year. They also wrote some plays together before falling out, following a public row.

They then resorted to mentioning each other in their respective writings, Bodenheim appearing in Hecht's *Count Bruga* (1926) and Hecht in Bodenheim's *Ninth Avenue* (1926). Bodenheim's poetry originally appeared in *Poetry* magazine in 1914, then in a collection entitled *Minna and Myself* (1918). He contributed considerably to the Modernist movement, as reflected in *Selected Poems, 1914-44* (1946). In the late 1920s he was living in New York's Greenwich Village and mixing in a Bohemian circle. He produced some of the best proletarian writings of the 1930s and his novels, *Rollerskates* and *New York Madness*, were considered brilliant at the time. He was a complicated person with a complex personality that gradually reduced him, in the late 1940s, to begging in the bars and cafes of the Village, while reading his poems to whoever would listen. He and his third wife were reduced to living in the poorest lodgings imaginable. It was a sleazy and dangerous life which came to an end when the couple were murdered by a former mental patient. The funeral costs were paid by Ben Hecht who later, in 1958, wrote fondly of Bodenheim in his play *Winkelberg*. Bodenheim's unfinished autobiography, *My Life and Loves in Greenwich Village*, was published in 1954.

BOHR, Aage (1922-) Danish physicist

Like father, like son, to an amazing degree: both were born in Copenhagen, both were famous physicists and both were awarded the Nobel Prize. **Aage**, the son, was born on June 19th 1922 and educated at the Universities of Copenhagen and London. In 1946 he went to work for his father at the Institute of Theoretical Physics in Copenhagen. From 1963 to 1970 Aage was director of the Institute, now renamed the Niels Bohr Institute. Together with Ben Mottelsom (*qv*), he researched the work of Leo Rainwater's collective model of the atomic nucleus. All three shared the 1975 Nobel Prize for Physics. Aage Bohr later became director of the Nordic Institute for Theoretical Atomic Physics.

BOHR, Niels (1885-1962) Danish physicist

Neils, born in Copenhagen on October 7th 1885, was the son of a Gentile father and Jewish mother. At school he competed academically against his younger brother Harald, and lost. Harald went on to become a well-known mathematician. However, at the University of Copenhagen Niels was found to be most perceptive and his first research project resulted in a gold medal from the Royal Danish Academy of Sciences. In 1911 he gained his doctorate and went to England to join Ernest Rutherford, the man who discovered the workings of the atomic nucleus. Niels Bohr took Rutherford's work a stage further and applied the quantum theory. Rutherford, for his part, found it difficult to appreciate the logic of Bohr's assertions. He was eventually persuaded and the concept of the 'Rutherford-Bohr atom' of nuclear physics was established. Bohr continued with his work on atomic structure, which earned him the 1922 Nobel Prize for Physics. His thinking was often at odds with other scientists. Einstein, his friend for over 30 years, claimed Bohr was constantly departing from the norm and it was a matter of deep sorrow to both men that they could not come to terms with each other. Only very recently, long after the death of both of them, has Bohr's view been confirmed. By the mid 1930s the main focus of scientific interest was nuclear physics, and here Bohr played a major part with his appreciation of nuclear fission. In September 1943 Bohr was tipped off that the Germans were about to arrest him and his family. That night they escaped the Nazis by travelling to Malmo, Sweden, in an old fishing boat. In Sweden, Bohr successfully persuaded the King to offer an unconditional sanctuary to all the Jews of Denmark. Desperately wanted by the Allies to work on the Manhattan Project, the making of the atomic bomb, Bohr was flown to England the following month laying in the bomb rack of an unarmed RAF Mosquito fighter/bomber. Bohr, who was satisfied that the uranium atom split by Hahn and Strassman in 1938 was the rare isotope U-235, was of major importance to the overall success of the project. However, after Hiroshima, he saw the atom bomb as a threat to the whole of mankind and spent the rest of his life working for peace. This did not prevent Bohr from seeing a positive use for atomic energy, for peaceful purposes, and he encouraged its development for use as an energy source. In 1957 he was awarded the first 'Atoms for Peace' prize by the Ford Foundation. He died in Copenhagen on November 18th 1962.

**BOLAN,
Marc
(1947-77)
British singer/
songwriter**

Born Mark Feld on September 30th 1947 in Hackney, London and educated at the same primary school as Keith Reid of Procul Harum, he was a male model at fifteen. Deciding to pursue a career in the world of pop music, he flopped as Toby Tyler. Calling himself Mark Bowland, he earned a spot on television's *Ready, Steady Go* but nothing came of it. He met up with Simon Napier-Bell who, in June 1966, became his record producer. Three unsuccessful singles later, Bolan decided to form a duo with Steve Peregrine Took on percussion, and in July 1968 as Tyrannosaurus Rex the pair launched their single, *My People Were Fair and had Sky in Their Law, But Now They're Content To Wear Stars on Their Brow*. It reached the top twenty in the UK, but by October 1969 they had still not had a major success and Took left, to be replaced by Mickey Finn. Their concert tours were successful; then, in October 1970, Marc Bolan decided to abbreviate the name to T-Rex and record *Ride a White Swan*. The single roared up to No. 2. By the end of the year the duo had become a quartet. Until 1977 T-Rex was an important part of the pop music scene, with many of their releases reaching the top twenty. Then, on September 16th 1977, while Bolan was being driven home in the early hours of the morning, the car crashed on a bend on Barnes Common and he was killed. He was two weeks short of his 30th birthday and still striving for a number one. Every year, on the anniversary of his death, an unknown person ties a yellow ribbon around the oak tree into which the car crashed.

**BOMBERG,
David
(1890-1957)
British painter**

Bomberg was born in Birmingham on December 5th 1890, but was brought up in Whitechapel in London's East End. For a time he was apprenticed to a lithographer. He worked there by day and attended evening classes at the Slade School of Art. In 1914 he became a founder member of the London Group, an exhibiting group that still exists, having known wide swings of popularity. Bomberg, needing a change of scenery, took off for Paris where he met the avant-garde artists Modigliani and Picasso. Both had a strong influence on him, leading to such large compositions as *Vision of Ezekiel* (1912, Tate Gallery, London) and *The Mad Bath* and *The Hold* (1913-14). He travelled much prior to the Second World War and produced considerable work, some of which he managed to sell. After the war, Bomberg held art classes at the Borough Polytechnic in South London, which aroused an unprecedented degree of enthusiasm. His influence on the artists who would find fame in the second half of the century cannot be denied. In 1957 he returned to Spain and produced his best-known work, *Hear O Israel*. He died shortly thereafter, on August 19th 1957. In 1967 the Tate Gallery in London held a comprehensive exhibition of his work.

Bondi was born in Vienna on November 1st 1919, leaving in 1936 for reasons that are all too familiar. He came to Britain and received his MA from Trinity College, Cambridge. Then, following the outbreak of the Second World War, he was shipped off to Canada as an enemy alien. Fortunately for Britain's war effort, someone somewhere saw sense and he was returned in 1941 in order to undertake secret research on radar for the Admiralty. During this period he met up with Fred Hoyle, the astronomer, so beginning his ongoing interest in cosmology. In 1948 Bondi and Hoyle advanced their cosmological theory of a steady-state universe. In 1954 Bondi was appointed professor of applied mathematics at Kings College, London, where he stayed until 1985. In 1967 he was granted leave of absence to become director-general of the European Space Research Organization and in 1970 was appointed the Ministry of Defence's Chief Scientist. In 1959 he had been elected a Fellow of the Royal Society. He wrote much on a variety of inter-related topics connected with cosmology and continued to take a great interest in the role of mathematics in Britain's secondary school education programme. He has published several books, including *Cosmology* (1952); *The Universe at Large* (1960); *Relativity and Commonsense* (1964); and *Assumption and Myth in Physical Theory* (1967). Awarded a knighthood in 1973, he became chairman of the Natural Enviroment Research Council.

BONDI, Sir Hermann (1919-) Austrian/British mathematician

Daniel was born in Atlanta, Georgia, on October 1st 1914. Educated at Harvard, he won a Rhodes scholarship to Oxford University where he studied law. He was admitted to the English Bar in 1937 but never practised. Back home in the US, he became senior historian at the Smithsonian Institution, then director of the National Museum of History, before becoming professor of American History at Chicago University (1944-69). He has travelled much and wrote *The Lost World of Thomas Jefferson* (1948); *The Genius of American Politics* (1953); and the first two volumes of his historical analysis of American history, *The Americans*. He later wrote the final volume. In 1958 he published *The Colonial Experience* and in 1973 *The Democratic Experience*, for which he won the 1974 Pulitzer Prize. He was head of the Library of Congress in Washington DC from 1975 to 1987.

BOORSTIN, Daniel (1914-) US writer

BORGE,
Victor
(1909-)
Danish/
American
entertainer

Victor Borge was born in Copenhagen, Denmark, and educated at the Royal Danish Academy of Music in Copenhagen. He made his debut as a classical pianist when he was seventeen. In 1933 he started working in revues and, at the outbreak of the Second World War, and just one step ahead of Hitler, left Denmark for the US. Since then he has worked in radio, in the theatre and on television. He has appeared with leading symphony orchestras worldwide and has an enormous following for his zany theatrical shows. Now in his eighties, he is still performing and creating laughter.

BORN,
Max
(1882-1970)
German/British
physicist

Born on December 11th 1882 in Breslau, Germany, his father a professor of anatomy at Breslau University, **Max** received his PhD from Göttingen in 1907 and became a teacher in Berlin. He was a lecturer of physics at Frankfurt before being appointed a professor of theoretical physics at Göttingen in 1921. This was the centre where the theory of quantum mechanics was being formulated. It was propounded in 1927, by which time Born was already a respected physicist who had written over a hundred research papers on the subject as well as six books. His contribution to the appreciation of quantum physics cannot be overestimated, and he is generally acknowledged as the originator in this field of physics. The theory was centrally concerned with the essence of probability, which Born introduced as an inherent feature of physics. It represented a departure from current thinking; Albert Einstein (*qv*) was never able to agree with this formula and a correspondence ensued between the two men. Niels Bohr (*qv*), however, gave Born's theory guarded acceptance. In 1933 Born was described by Hitler as a practioner of 'Jewish physics' and dismissed from his post at Göttingen. As a Jew he and his family were in considerable danger and were forced to flee. The family went to Britain, where he continued to teach, at Edinburgh and Cambridge universities. His home at Cambridge became the gathering place for scientific minds and here he indulged his passion for art and literature. It was also the place where his daughter later gave birth to his granddaughter, who grew up to become the singer, Olivia Newton-John (*qv*). In 1953 Born returned to Germany and retired in Heidelberg. In 1954 he was awarded the Nobel Prize for Physics, in recognition of the work he had done on quantum mechanics in 1926. It appeared he couldn't keep away from Göttingen and he died there on January 5th 1970.

BOTVINNIK,
Mikhail
(1911-95)
Russian world
chess champion

Botvinnik was born in St Petersburg on April 17th 1911 and trained to be an electrical engineer. At the age of fourteen he defeated the then world chess champion in an exhibition; ten years later he did it again in reality. During the Second World War his work as an electrical engineer was acknowledged by numerous decorations and awards. Following the war, his main field of interest was the chess board. In 1948 he became world champion and went on to defend his title successfully three times, the last in 1963. If one man could be described as promoting chess in the Soviet Union and making that country the world leader in the game, it is Botvinnik. He has devoted much time and energy training to young people and developing chess software for computer use. He is regarded by his fellow Grandmasters as the best Russian chess player of this century. His style is eclectic. He trains for championships in noisy, smoky rooms in order not to be put off by distractions. He died on May 5th 1995.

Brandeis was born in Louisville, Kentucky, on November 13th 1856, the son of a Czech immigrant. He graduated from Harvard Law School and went into private practice in nearby Boston. He was a lawyer for public causes and was often referred to as 'the People's Attorney'. In 1912 Woodrow Wilson, the newly elected US President, sought the aid of Brandeis in promoting political and social reform. In 1916 Wilson nominated him for the Supreme Court. Conservative and vested interests in the Senate, together with an antisemitic faction, opposed the nomination of Brandeis, but they were defeated. Brandeis' zest for reform was balanced by his judicial opinions, which were considered and authoritative. Brandeis, together with his friend and colleague, Oliver Wendell Holmes, was nearly always in the minority on the Court as he fought to maintain minimum wages, price controls and trade unions free from gangster control. He earned the gratitude of millions of working-class Americans. Slowly, the Supreme Court adopted his views and by the time he retired in 1939 he was often in the majority. He died in Washington DC on October 5th 1941. In 1948 Brandeis University was inaugurated in Waltham, Massachusetts.

BRANDEIS,
Louis
(1856-1941)
US lawyer

Brandes was born in Copenhagen to a family named Cohen, on February 4th 1842. By 1900 he was an established writer and, following his discovery of Nietzsche, took to hero worship. This led directly to his writing about famous individuals, with books on *Voltaire* (1916), *Julius Caesar* (1918) and *Michelangelo* (1921). Georg Brandes is often considered Denmark's greatest writer, and his influence on Danish culture is still in evidence. He lived in an ambivalent world: on the one hand he rejected all things Jewish, while on the other he abjured persecution of Jews. It is probably true to say that the Danish fondness for Brandes was one reason why the Danes, following the German occupation in the Second World War, did so much for their Jews. Brandes died in Copenhagen on February 19th 1927.

BRANDES,
Georg
(1842-1927)
Danish writer

Marcel Breuer was born on May 21st 1902 in Pecs, Hungary. From 1920 to 1928 he studied at the Bauhaus School of Design and later taught there. He was influenced by Walter Gropus and his enthusiasm for unit construction, which prompted him to design the chromium-plated tubular steel chair that became famous as the Wassily Chair, and continues to be copied and reproduced some 70 years on. In 1928 he opened a private practice in Berlin. Between 1934 and 1936 he designed the Dolderthal Apartments in Zurich. Following his expulsion from Germany for the capital offence of being Jewish, he went to London. There he entered into partnership with F. R. Yorke and in 1935 designed, for the Isokon Furniture Company, his laminated plywood chair, a form of chaise-longue which has repeatedly been copied. In 1937 he went to Harvard University, to teach architecture, and practised with Gropus in Cambridge, Massachusetts (1938-41). Their mixture of Bauhaus internationalism and New England timber influences resulted in a timber frame type of domestic

BREUER,
Marcel
(1902-81)
Hungarian/
American
architect

architecture which revolutionized the American scene. Among his fine public buildings, Breuer's design for the Whitney Museum of Modern Art in New York, built in 1966, stands out. His buildings adorn many other countries, and include the UNESCO building in Paris (1953-58), the De Bijenkorf department store in Rotterdam (1955-57) and the Headquarters of the Department of Housing and Urban Development, in Washington DC (1963-68). Breuer retired in 1976 and died in New York City on July 1st 1981.

BRICE,
Fanny
(1891-1951)
US entertainer

Born Fanny Borach on the Lower East Side of New York on October 29th 1891, she was spotted in 1910 by the great Ziegfeld (*qv*), who heard her singing in a burlesque show and put her into his Follies. During the 1920s and 1930s she appeared in many of his shows. As a singer, probably her best-known songs are 'Second Hand Rose' and 'My Man'. She was an extrovert with a lifestyle to match. Her first husband was Nicky Arstein, the gangster; her second, Billy Rose, the night-club king. In 1960 *Funny Girl*, was a musical hit, telling the story of Fanny Brice. The film version launched another singer: Barbra Streisand (*qv*). Fanny Brice died in Los Angeles on May 29th 1951.

BRISCOE,
Robert
(1894-1969)
Irish politician

Briscoe was born in Dublin, Eire. His father, an immigrant from Lithuania, thought he had reached the US, because the ship's captain said so. Robert was educated in both Ireland and England and then sent to Germany, his mother's homeland, to study electrical engineering. During the summer of 1914, Robert was travelling to Austria to join his parents on holiday. On a warm August day the First World War was declared, and Robert and his parents were arrested as enemy aliens.. After a short time in prison, the Briscoes were released and allowed to make their way home to Ireland, but Robert had to promise he would never join the British army and fight the Austrians. This was no problem for Robert, for he was a fervent Irish nationalist. In any event, Robert went off on a business trip to New York and stayed until 1916, when, seeing the newspapers full of the 'Easter Rising', he left the US at once to return home and join the Irish Republican Army. He was given the nickname 'Captain Swift', because of the deft way he handled his briefs. On one occasion, needing to transport important secret dispatches, he hid them in his baby's diapers. He organized and smuggled shiploads of arms into Ireland, often right under British noses. Briscoe was honoured by the occupying British with a 'wanted' poster that stated 'he was unlike most Irish rebels and had a gentlemanly appearance'. The 1921 signing of the 'Articles of Agreement' led to civil war. Briscoe was opposed to Michael Collins and the agreement, because under it the British retained six counties that would become Northern Ireland. Briscoe returned to New York to raise money for the cause, but when, in 1923, a political compromise was reached, he returned to Dublin to take charge of the family business. Briscoe, a member of Fianna Fail, won a seat in the Irish parliament, the Dail, in 1927. He remained an MP for 38 years. In 1958 he was elected Lord Mayor of Dublin, the first Jew ever to have held the post. During his year of office he was guest of honour at the St Patrick's Day Parade in New York. At the gala dinner that followed, he made a speech in which he confirmed he was an Irish Jew, explaining he was one of the 'lepre-cohens'.

Leon Brittan, born in London on September 25th 1939, was educated at Trinity College, Cambridge and at Harvard University in the US. He qualified as a barrister and continued the political activities he had begun at Cambridge. He entered the House of Commons in 1974 as Tory member for Cleveland and Whitby. In 1979, under Margaret Thatcher, he received his first ministerial post. He was Home Secretary in 1983, leaving that post to become Trade and Industry Secretary in 1985. He resigned a year later over the Westland Helicopters affair and returned to the backbenches. He later became the UK's Commissioner to the EEC. In 1989 he was appointed a Vice-President of the European Community. Often in conflict with some of his former Tory colleagues, his is a powerful voice that a continuing European partnership is vital to Britain's future and the future of Europe.

BRITTAN, Sir Leon (1939-) British politician

Broch, born in Vienna to well-off parents on November 1st 1886, studied science and engineering and went on to make a career for himself in textiles; but his heart was elsewhere. In his early forties he finished with business, and started writing. He established his reputation with *The Sleepwalkers* (1932), a trilogy about decaying values. Broch has James Joyce, the Irish writer of *Ulysses* fame, to thank for his freedom from a Nazi prison and a visa for the US. In Princeton, where he settled, he completed his best work, *The Death of Virgil* (1945). Broch's style is an acquired taste. He is highly individual and often morbid. He deals with man's inevitable end and gives little room to humour. In 1950 his *The Innocents* created quite a stir, as did his 1953 book, *The Seducers*, published posthumously. An internationally recognized writer, his work is said to be 'multidimensional'. He died in New Haven, Connecticut, on May 30th 1951.

BROCH, Hermann (1886-1951) Austrian writer

Max Brod was born in Prague on May 27th 1884 and studied at the German University there. While Brod has enjoyed a certain amount of success on his own account during a long literary career, it is as Kafka's 'Boswell' that he is world-renowned. Brod was the first to recognize Kafka's genius, and brought him to the world's notice. Kafka, aware of his approaching death, appointed Brod his literary executor with explicit instructions to destroy his unpublished manuscripts. Brod disobeyed. Instead, he devoted much time and effort to editing, translating and publishing his friend's work. For over 40 years Brod called the world's attention to the work of Kafka and it was Brod who had all Kafka's work published. It is therefore due to Brod that Kafka enjoys his justified fame. Nor did Brod restrict himself to aiding Kafka: he did much the same for Janacek's music, translating his librettos in order to further his popularity. And it was Max Brod who revealed the genius of Jaroslav Hasek, author of *The Good Soldier Schweyk*. In 1921 Brod published his two-volume work *Heidentum, Christentum and Judentum*, which attracted the attention of serious readers who had previously enjoyed his writing of specialized serious historical novels. A man who got his relaxation by helping others,

BROD, Max (1884-1968) Czech writer

he escaped the Germans by emigrating to Palestine in 1939, to become drama adviser to the Habima Theatre. He died in Tel Aviv on December 20th 1968.

BRODSKY,
Isaac
(1884-1930)
Russian painter

Brodsky was born in St Petersburg and lived most of his life there. He studied at Odessa's School of Fine Arts and later at the Academy. He rejected all influences and concentrated on his own methods to develop his talents. Following the 1917 revolution, Brodsky gradually emerged as Soviet Russia's most successful portrait painter. His portrait of Lenin for the Smolny Institute brought him fame, following the demand for mass reproduction. Depictions of other popular Soviet leaders followed. Interestingly, his work has stood the test of time to a greater degree than that of any other modern Russian painter. This may be because of his early interest in Flemish and Dutch art which, the critics claim, can be detected in his work. Most of his major paintings survived the Second World War and are in the Tretyakorrkaya Gallery in Moscow.

BRODSKY,
Joseph
(1940-96)
Russian/
American poet

Brodsky was born in Leningrad on May 24th 1940. He was the only son of Jewish parents and it was they who instilled in him a love of books and writing. At 15 he left school and worked first in an armaments factory, then in a morgue. Whenever he had some spare time, he wrote poetry. Following the publication of four poems in an anthology, Brodsky became recognized as a new voice in Russian poetry. However, his poetry was not popular with everyone and it certainly wasn't politically correct. He was 24 when he was sentenced to five years imprisonment for 'parasitism'. The state claimed he wasn't working and wasn't a registered member of the Writer's Union. He was an individualist who, during his trial, had the following Kafkaesque dialogue.

Prosecutor: What is your occupation?
Brodsky: I am a poet.
Prosecutor: Who included you in the list of poets?
Brodsky: Who included me in the list of human beings?

He served eighteen months in prison and spent the time reading the works of many poets, including W. H. Auden, an episode that changed his life. Of particular significance to him was Auden's elegy to W.B. Yeats, written in 1939:

Follow, poet, follow right
To the bottom of the night,
With your unconstraining voice...
In the prison of his days,
Teach the free man how to praise.

Brodsky began developing his mind, and his imagination, developing his lifelong optimism concerning good art and good actions. He once said 'evil, especially political evil, is always a bad stylist'. He learnt to speak and write English and started a correspondence with Auden. In June 1972 Brodsky was expelled from the Soviet Union with a one-way ticket to Tel Aviv, via Vienna, where he met and stayed with Auden. *Selected Poems* was published in 1973. He later moved to the US and held visiting professorships at Michigan and Columbia universities. He received an honorary doctorate from Yale and in 1981 received a grant from the MacArthur Foundation. His parents tried to leave Russia, but to no avail, and Joseph was not allowed to return for his mother's funeral. He recalls this event in his moving essay, 'In a Room and a Half', that tells the story of growing up in a tiny apartment in war-torn Russia. In 1986 he published, *Less Than One: Selected Essays*. This book, and his accumulated poetry, resulted in the 1987 award of the Nobel Prize for Literature. Joseph Brodsky died on January 28th 1996. He was only 55 but a heavy drinker and a chain smoker who continued the habit despite having open-heart surgery in 1979 and two subsequent heart attacks. His somewhat bizarre lifestyle often reflected his work. Probably one of the greatest poets of the century, his two last works were published posthumously in October 1996: *On Grief and Reason: Essays by Joseph Brodsky* and *So Forth*, his final collection of poems. Brodsky once declared: 'literature started with poetry'.

BRONOWSKI, Jacob (1908-1974) Polish/British mathematician

Born in Poland on January 18th 1908, **Bronowski** and his family arrived in Britain when he was twelve. He won a scholarship to Cambridge University from where he received his PhD in 1933. He became a lecturer in maths at the University of Hull in 1934, a post he held until 1942. During the Second World War, he was sent to Washington DC to work with the Joint Target Group, an Anglo-American think tank. In 1948-49 he was UNESCO's Head of Projects and in 1950 he headed the British Coal Board research department; 1964 saw him as deputy director of the Salk Institute for Biological Studies in the US. Bronowski had a sideline. He was an expert on William Blake, the English poet, and wrote *William Blake: A Man, a Mask* (1944). He was also a writer of radio plays and won the international 'Italia' prize in 1951 for *Face of Violence*.

All this, one might imagine, would be enough for any man. Perhaps; but not for Jacob Bronowski. In one swoop he reached millions of people and enthralled them, winning critical acclaim and for himself the knowledge he was responsible for awakening an interest in a subject long thought too boring to be in the least bit entertaining. What he was about to launch belonged to an educational channel, and a small number of viewers. Instead the BBC, to their eternal credit, put on, at a peak viewing time, a major 13 part series entitled *The Ascent of Man* (1973), and gave the lecturing part to an expert on the subject, despite the fact that he spoke English with a foreign accent, did not have a film star's looks and had the barely pronounceable name of Bronowski. What he did have was a passion for his subject and the ability and charisma to get it all across. The series was a winner and Jacob Bronowski became a household and international name. He died in East Hampton, New York, on August 22nd 1974, while on a visit to the US.

BRONSTEIN,
David
(1924-)
Russian chess
Grandmaster

Bronstein was born in Kiev. After service in the armed forces during the Second World War, he emerged on to the world chess scene in 1946 with victory in his first major tournament. There followed numerous other wins, particularly when he won the play-off in the Candidates Tournament, defeating Isaac Boleslavski, in Budapest in 1950. This gave him the right to enter the final stages of the world chess championship. In the final he drew against the reigning champion, Botvinnick (*qv*) who, under the rules, as reigning champion retained the title. Bronstein's success was his originality. His big problem was that he put so much mental effort into his middle game that he was too tired for the endgame. However, he was always a force to be reckoned with and was a continuing example to younger would-be champions.

BROOKNER,
Anita
(1928-)
British writer

Anita Brookner was born in London on July 16th 1928, the daughter of Jewish immigrants from Poland. She grew up with parents who found it difficult to adjust to an English way of life and she deeply felt the difference between her home life in South London and the world outside. She was educated at James Allen's Girls' School in Dulwich and Kings College, London, where she read history but preferred art. She received a BA and went to Paris to study art history and write a thesis on the work of Jean-Baptiste Greuze. She then spent five years (1959-64) lecturing on the history of art at Reading University. Her expertise on 18th and 19th century art led to an invitation to become the Slade Professor of Fine Arts at Cambridge, a unique role for a woman. A decade later, she was the professor of art history at the Courtald Institute in London. She started writing novels in 1981; her first was *A Start in Life*, telling the story of Ruth Weiss and her interest in Balzac. Since then Anita Brookner has written many books, often focusing on lonely women during their 'mid-life crisis'. She gently unravels their fears and hopes. The heroine of *Providence* (1982), Kitty, is a woman of mixed English, French and Russian descent. A Brookner heroine is generally analytical, intelligent and intellectual. *Hotel du Lac* (1984) takes place in a Swiss resort where a Virginia Woolf type works away on a romantic novel and lives out her days dreaming of her lover in London. Brookner's characters are brilliantly drawn and her own romance comes shining through. She writes a book a year. They are not thick books; just long enough to tell the story in a fashion that is sometimes reminiscent of Charlotte Bronte. The difference perhaps lies in Brookner's subtle ability to attach importance to very ordinary situations.

BROOKS,
Mel
(1926-)
US film-maker

Films: he writes them, produces them, directs them and often stars in them. **Mel Brooks**, whose work film buffs either love or hate, is someone who never allows himself to be ignored. He was born Melvin Kaminsky in Brooklyn, New York, on June 28th 1926, and the only way he could go was up. He started off as a stand-up comedian, and was a very good one. What is so refreshing about Brooks is that he is as zany today as he was when he wrote *The Producers* (1967), his first film and probably his best. It brought him an Oscar for Best Original Story and Screenplay. The many films made through his production company, Brooks Films, include *The Elephant Man* (1980) and *84, Charing Cross Road* (1986), both of which featured Anne Bancroft, Brook's wife, in starring roles. He wrote, directed, produced and starred in *Blazing Saddles* (1974), which enhanced his reputation and brought Oscar nominations for Best Story. *Young Frankenstein* (1974) was a success; Brooks didn't appear in it but it was nominated for Best Story. In 1983 Mr and Mrs Brooks starred in *To Be or Not To Be*, judged a fair successor to the original version by the great Lubitsch (*qv*). Not everything Brooks does is great, and he has had his share of the 'not so goods'; but no matter, the balance sheet is well in credit and film fans are the richer. In recent years Brooks has lectured on the subject of films. The venues are always full and the question and answer sessions eagerly anticipated.

BROWN,
Georgia
(1933-92)
British singer

Born Lillie Klot on October 21st 1933 in the East End of London, her parents were Russian Jews who encouraged their daughter in her ambition to be a singer and dancer. She was educated at the Central Foundation Grammar School for Girls in London and later took singing lessons. Her first big public appearance was at the famous Stork Club in Mayfair. She was seventeen and her style was a cross between Ella Fitzgerald and Billie Holiday. Television, variety shows and tours of US army bases throughout Britain and Europe followed. The nightclubs of Europe became her real teacher and it was while appearing in such a venue that Sam Wanamaker (*qv*) found her and gave her the part of Lucy in Brecht's *Threepenny Opera* at London's Royal Court Theatre. It transferred well to the Theatre de Lys in New York. Then followed a slack time which saw her unwanted in Los Angeles and broke in New York. She returned to London. In 1960 she was once again playing at the Royal Court Theatre in *The Little White Boys*. There she met up with Lionel Bart (*qv*). They struck up a rapport: they came from the same background, they were Jewish, they enjoyed music and it was the sort of music in which Georgia excelled. The result was that she was cast in the role of Nancy in Bart's *Oliver!* The show was a triumph and Georgia Brown became an international star when the show eventually hit Broadway. There she was nominated for a Tony award. She hoped to be considered for the film version, but the role went elsewhere. The excitement died down and she continued as before: some television work, some nightclub shows and some straight acting on television and in theatre. Back at the Royal Court, she played in Brecht's *Man is Man* (1971). In 1974 Georgia, her husband and son took off for the US. Here she appeared in the hit *Side by Side* by Sondheim (1977). In the 1980s she wrote her own successful one-woman show, *Georgia Brown and Friends*, she became popular on both sides of the Atlantic again as Madame Lazora in *Cheers*. She came to London to take part in a tribute show for Sammy Davis Junior, but was suddenly taken ill and hospitalized for an exploratory operation. She never recovered and died in London on July 5th 1992.

BROWN,
Herbert
(1912-)
US chemist

Herbert Brown, was born Herbert Brovarnik on May 22nd 1912 in London, but by the age of two was playing with his toys in a Chicago apartment. Despite financial hardships Herbert made it to Chicago University from where, in 1938, he received his PhD. He then taught at Wayne State University in Detroit until 1947, going on to become professor of organic chemistry at Purdue University in Indiana. Brown, who has been the recipient of many awards and a member of the most important associations, reached the pinnacle of his career in 1979 when he was awarded the Nobel Prize for Chemistry for his work on the application of borohydrides and diborane to organic synthesis. This work had a revolutionary impact on the world of chemistry and considerable beneficial effects for humanity. His publications include *Hydroboration* (1962) and *Organic Syntheses via Boranes* (1975).

BROWN,
Michael
(1941-)
US geneticist

Michael Brown was born in New York on April 13th 1941. He graduated from the University of Pennsylvania in 1962 and obtained his MD from the university's medical school in 1966. While working as an intern at the Boston General Hospital he met Joseph Goldstein (*qv*). Between 1968 and 1971 the two conducted research at the National Institute for Health and later at Southampton Medical School at Dallas, Texas. There they investigated the genetic factors that are the reason for high levels of cholesterol in the bloodstream. They were able to determine a genetic defect in patients and a deficiency in cell receptors for low-density lipoproteins (LDL), the primary cholesterol carrying particles. Their work resulted in their being awarded the 1985 Nobel Prize for Medicine or Physiology for the explanation of a key link in the metabolism of cholesterol in the human body. Brown and Goldstein later collaborated in developing drugs in order to lower high levels of cholesterol. From 1977 onwards Brown was director of the centre for Genetic Diseases in Dallas, Texas.

BRUCE,
Lenny
(1925-66)
US entertainer

Lenny Bruce was born Leonard Schneider on October 13th 1925 in Long Island, New York. His parents divorced when he was five, and for many years he was shuttled between his father, a shoe salesman, and his mother, a bit-part actress. The day after Pearl Harbor, Lenny Bruce lied about his age and joined the US Navy: he was sixteen. After seeing action at the Salerno and Anzio landings he was transferred to the navy entertainment section. Bruce now started to build his act. He gradually went from conventional to radical, culminating in what became known as 'sick humour'. In 1959 his act brought him a 'Grammy' award. He performed all over the US until he started getting arrested on narcotics charges as well as on obscenity charges. Bruce became very depressed at the way things had gone so wrong for him: partly because he wouldn't compromise with society's demands and partly because he was so upset by the puritanical attitude of conservative America. By 1965 he had lost all the money he had made and was declared bankrupt. His home was repossessed by the bank and no one seemed to care. In a fit of acute depression he took an overdose of heroin and on August 5th 1966 he died. Lenny Bruce, a great performer, was ahead of his time. Thirty years on, what he said and did appears so ordinary and so inoffensive. 'Every day people are leaving the church and going back to God.' 'My mother-in-law broke up my marriage. My wife came home from work one day and found me in bed with her.'

Jerome Bruner was born in New York on October 1st 1915. His father was a watchmaker who died when Jerome was twelve years old. Jerome was educated at Duke University in Durham, North Carolina, and obtained his BA in 1937; a PhD from Harvard University followed in 1941. During the Second World War he was with the US Army in France working as an expert on psychological warfare. In 1945 he returned to Harvard, becoming professor of psychology, and from 1960 to 1972 was director of the Centre of Cognitive Studies. In 1972 he was at Oxford University as professor of experimental psychology. His work as an educator has had a great influence on education generally, and on the American system in particular. Some of his conclusions have had and continue to have far-reaching effects. His publications reflect his philosophy. His book *The Process of Education* (1960), published in several languages, was a most important study of the reforms that were required. He argues that any subject can be taught to any child and at any stage provided it is presented in a proper manner. Bruner explains that all children have a natural curiosity and a wish to became competent at whatever they undertake; however, if the task set is too difficult the child will become bored. Therefore a good teacher is one who will set schoolwork at a level to challenge the child's present developmental level. His later books include

The Relevance of Education (1971), *Communication as Language* (1982), *Child's Talk* (1983) and *Actual Minds, Possible Worlds* (1986).

Buber was born on February 8th 1878 in Vienna. He studied philosophy at the universities of Vienna, Berlin and Zurich. In 1901 he became the editor of *Die Welt*. In 1916, during the First World War, he founded *Der Jude* (The Jew), which became a most important journal for German-speaking Jewry, reflecting his philosophical attitudes to long-established practices, both civil and theological. A complicated man, he appeared to have difficulty on the one hand in accepting God, and on the other in alienating himself from the Jewish life of the period in favour of Hasidim. His great philosophical work was, *Ich and Du*, translated as 'I and Thou' in 1937. Buber creates two basic forms of relationship in the world, I-it and I-thou. I-thou results in the individual engaging in a dialogue with another subject. His work had considerable impact on Jewish and Christian 20th century theology. In 1938 he emigrated to Palestine to become professor of social philosophy at the Hebrew University. He advocated the creation of a binational state, in which Jews and Arabs would live side by side. Buber became the first president of the Israeli Academy of Sciences and Art. He died on June 13th 1965 having completed, with Franz Rosenzweig, a new German translation of the Bible.

BRUNER,
Jerome
(1915-)
US child
psychologist

BUBER,
Martin
(1878-1965)
Austrian
philosopher

**BUCHALTER,
Louis, 'Lepke'
(1897-1944)
US criminal**

Louis Buchalter, better known as 'Lepke', was born in New York on February 12th 1897, one of 11 children of poor Jewish immigrants. His mother would call him 'Lepkeleh', an affectionate Yiddish term for Louis. The shortened version, Lepke, was to remain with him all his life. Small in build, softly spoken, quietly dressed, Buchalter was one of the most vicious of the mobsters operating in the US during the 1920s and 1930s. His career took the classical path from membership of the local gang upwards, rising in stages to the top, usually by killing off the opposition. Lepke chose to make his crooked name and fortune in labour racketeering, rather than the usual bootlegging that characterized the Prohibition era. He collected an army of gangsters and together they brought terror and violence to the workplace. He took over the garment industry, mostly run by fellow Jews, and the docks, where nothing was unloaded without Lepke getting his share. No one worked without his getting a percentage from the wages of workers already on low pay. He took over bona fide trade unions and made them his own. Anyone who didn't like it ended up dead. Lepke was a sadist who enjoyed hurting people and watching them die slowly. He was involved with other Jewish gangsters of the time as they fought the Irish, German and Italian mobs to keep their share. The result was the formation of the National Crime Syndicate that included Murder Incorporated. Lepke was the boss of Murder Inc.; It was his domain to keep order among the mobs and hit whomever the syndicate decreed should be killed. Lepke was responsible for the death of dozens of people. The money poured in and Lepke disported himself in the style of the multimillionaire he had become. All was fine until 1941. Then he was indicted for the murder of a truck driver and convicted. Lepke was executed by the electric chair in Sing Sing prison on March 4th 1944. Because of Buchalter's reign of terror and his labour racketeering, the trade union movement underwent a programme of reconstruction to eliminate gangster manipulation.

**BUCHTHAL,
Hugo
(1909-96)
German/British
art historian**

Hugo Buchthal was born in Berlin on August 11th 1909 to well-off Jewish parents. Educated at the Sorbonne, where he read philosophy and art history, he took his doctorate at Heidelberg University. Buchthal was forced to leave Germany by the advent of the Nazis, but not before he had completed his thesis on the Paris Psalter. This work, on medieval religious art, later became a textbook. He made his home in London. In 1957 he published *Miniature Painting in the Latin Kingdom of Jerusalem*, an authoritative work that analysed palaeographical and religious miniature works of art. He also wrote on Byzantine art, and his *Studies of the Warburg Institute* (1938) is still a work of reference. Buchthal was the librarian at the Warburg for many years as well as a lecturer. He later became professor of fine arts at the New York Institute of Fine Arts (1965-75), where he moulded the ideas of future generations of art historians. He returned to London and watched with more than passing interest as his students went on to fill top academic posts in America and elsewhere overseas. A sought-after lecturer, he fulfilled engagements all over the world. He died in London on November 10th 1996. His wife, Amalia, died a week later. They had been married for 56 years.

Born in Mount Vernon, New York, on October 20th 1925, **Art Buchwald** was in the US Marines by the age of seventeen. The end of the Second World War found him in Paris, where he stayed to be a reporter for *Variety*. In 1949, still in Paris, he switched to the *New York Herald Tribune*. In 1957 he wrote a column on the briefings by White House press secretary, James Hagerty, and Buchwald's reputation spread. After fifteen years overseas, he returned to the US, moved to Washington DC and has been satirizing American politics, in his widely syndicated column, ever since. His books include *Son of the Great Society* (1966); *I Never Danced at the White House* (1973); *While Reagan Slept* (1983); *You Can Fool all of the People All of the Time* (1985); and *I Think I Don't Remember* (1987). In 1988 he successfully sued Paramount Pictures for stealing his idea for the film, *Coming to America*. In 1982 he won the Pulitzer Prize for Commentary, and is known as one of the funniest and perceptive journalists on American affairs.

BUCHWALD, Art (1925-) US journalist

Born in Leipzig, Germany, **Bucky** was head of the radiology department at Berlin University from 1918 to 1923. Then America beckoned and off he went, only to find he was homesick. After seven years he returned, as boss of the Rudolph Virchow Hospital's cancer and radiological department. Three years later Hitler arrived and Bucky was off to the US again. This time he wasn't homesick! He was professor of radiology at Bellevue Hospital, when he came up with the invention that would ensure his fame in medical circles everywhere: the Bucky Diaphragm for roentgenography. It was a wonderful invention that cleared the grid lines, preventing secondary rays from reaching the X-ray film and thereby achieving better definition. He went on to invent a camera for medical colour photography, and was the originator of grenz ray therapy using infra roentgen rays, called Bucky Rays.

BUCKY, Gustav (1880-1963) German/ American radiologist

Tamara, known as Tania, was born in Buenos Aires, Argentina. The daughter of a German communist and a Polish Jewess, her parents had left Germany in 1934 because of the Nuremberg race laws. In 1952 the family moved back to Europe and East Germany. In 1959, Tania became Che Guevara's official interpreter, when the revolutionary leader made an official visit to East Germany. In 1961, following Fidel Castro's historic victory in Cuba, Tania decided to go to work in Havana at the Ministry of Education. She was fired both by wanting to see Guevara again and by Castro's vow to teach every Cuban how to read and write. In 1962 she was involved in the civil war in Nicaragua, on the side of the guerrillas fighting the fascist government. Two years later she was in Bolivia, hoping to overthrow the corrupt Bolivian right-wing government to prepare the way for Che Guevara, as he and Castro had done in Cuba. In 1966 Guevara arrived; four months later he was killed in an ambush. Tania stayed, joined another fighting group until, in 1967, she was killed in action. Unfortunately, there are no set recipes for revolution and the Bolivian adventure failed. In 1971 the Cuban government honoured her memory by dedicating International Journalists Day to her. This honour was accompanied by a set of three Cuban postage stamps, showing her picture.

BUNKE, Tamara, 'Tania' (1937-67) Argentinean radical

BUNSHAFT,
Gordon
(1909-90)
US architect

Bunshaft, born on May 9th 1909 in Buffalo in New York State, decided from the time an aunt bought him a set of bricks that he wanted to be an architect. He was educated at the Massachusetts Institute of Technology and later travelled throughout Europe and North Africa on fellowship. In 1952 his major work, the Lever Building in New York, was unveiled. This design, later much copied, established Bunshaft as a major designer of large commercial buildings. He was the first to use glass cladding on exterior walls. As a partner in the firm of Skidmore, Owings and Merrill from 1937 to 1979, he built many galleries and libraries, providing additions to established institutions such as the Library for Manuscripts and Rare Books at Yale University. This type of design, that linked old and new, required a high degree of blending, and has always been considered the hardest type of design work to achieve. Bunshaft is credited with being the most capable at this strand of work. His designs for extensions to the University of Texas in Austin (1971) are exceptional and continue to excite. Bunshaft designed all over the world; his work includes the Banque Lambert in Brussels (1965) and the outstanding design of the Haj Terminal and Complex at Jidda International Airport (1981). Bunshaft died in New York on August 6th 1990.

BURNS,
Arthur
(1904-87)
US economist

Arthur was born in Stanislau, Austria, on April 27th 1904, but the family arrived in the US while he was a young boy. He graduated from Columbia University in 1934 with a PhD in economics, and went on to become presidential adviser in US economics to four Presidents: Eisenhower, Nixon, Carter and Ford. Burns is credited with having played a central role in shaping America's economic policy. From 1957 to 1967, he was president of the National Bureau of Economic Research. As chairman of the Board of Governors of the US Federal Reserve System in 1969, his economic theory was simple and pragmatic: if inflation was on the increase, tighten the economy; if inflation was too low, loosen the purse strings. The problem was that in 1974, when inflation was in double figures, his advice was to raise interest rates, which caused a recession. Burns wrote much on his subject and was universally accepted as an authority. It must have given him particular pleasure when, in 1981, he was appointed US ambassador to Germany, for it had been anti-Semitism that had driven his parents to leave that part of the world in the first place. Now he was back. He remained at his post until 1985, when he retired to the US. He died there two years later.

BURNS,
George
(1896-1996)
US entertainer

He was born Nathan Birnbaum in New York on January 20th 1896, but he also had two further names, Eddie DeLight and Ted Jackson, before hitting on **George Burns**. Following a limited education and after several failed attempts to get into vaudeville, he had the good fortune to meet Gracie Allen. Nice Roman Catholic girl meets nice Jewish boy. Their marriage was, by and large, a happy one. They had an even better stage partnership, when Burns realized he was cut out to be the straight man. They played the vaudeville circuit all over the States, and even went to England, to play the London Palladium in the early 1930s. They also made some instantly forgettable films. However, they were a hit on radio until Gracie was forced by cancer to retire in 1958. George carried on as a solo act, telling anecdotes and waving his big cigar. Then, in 1975, he reluctantly and nervously agreed to star in a Hollywood film, alongside Walter Matthau, called *The Sunshine Boys*. This had been a very successful Broadway production, but there was some doubt as to whether it would transfer well to the silver screen. It did, and Burns picked up the Oscar for Best Supporting Actor. His acceptance speech brought the house down when he explained that this award was generally for newcomers and he was 80 years old. In 1977 he made *Oh God*, with his old friend Carl Reiner directing. Even in his late nineties, he was still giving advice about women, still smoking his big cigars and still cracking jokes. A natural wit who made people laugh, he spent his last twenty years telling jokes about Gracie and tales about the old days of vaudeville. He died on March 9th 1996, 100 years young. His quips concerning old age are legendary; 'I was brought up to respect my elders and now I don't have to respect anybody' covers them all.

BURROUGHS, *Abe* *(1910-85)* *US director/ writer*

Born Abram Solman Borowitz on December 18th 1910 in New York City, by the time he was in his early twenties he had changed his name and was an acknowledged gag writer for radio as well as a successful night-club performer. In 1950 he had his first Broadway hit, *Guys and Dolls*. With Frank Loesser (*qv*) he wrote *How to Succeed in Business Without Really Trying* (1962) for which they received the Pulitzer Prize, a Tony Award and the New York Critics Award. Burroughs wrote the book and directed while Cole Porter wrote the music for *Can Can* (1953) and *What Makes Sammy Run* (1964). He directed *Cactus Flower* in 1965 and *Forty Carats* in 1968. Burroughs was sometimes called 'Doc Burroughs', so often was he consulted on rewriting and restaging other people's work. His autobiography was published in 1980 under the title *Honest Abe, Is There Really No Business Like Show Business?* He died on May 17th 1985 in New York.

BURTON, *Sir Montague* *(1885-1952)* *British industrialist*

Burton was born on August 15th 1885 in Russia and arrived in Leeds as a young man. He changed his name and, after working as a tailor for some while, came to the realization that what separated the classes, besides one lot having more money than the other, was the way they dressed. He had the idea of giving the working-class man the opportunity of having his clothes made to measure, at the same sort of price he was paying for inferior ready-made clothes. It took time, but eventually Burton had shops all over the country where a man could go to select the cloth and style he wanted before being measured up. One fitting, or perhaps two, and the man in the street was the equal of the chap who went to Savile Row. His shops were of a distinctive design and there was a large factory in Leeds to back them. At the height of his success, Burton employed over 20,000 people. Burton employees were happy workers. They had good working conditions and fair welfare schemes. Burton made a large fortune and continued his good industrial practices by establishing chairs at universities in this discipline. He was also interested in international relations, and established chairs at Oxford, London and Nottingham universities. Burton was a good man, who made a fortune without hurting anyone and then gave it away. He was knighted in recognition of his good works. Burton died in Leeds on September 23rd 1952.

Commemorative Stamps

Henri Bergson
Issued by the Popular
Republique of Congo

Robert Barany
Issued by Austria

Georg Brandes
Issued by Denmark

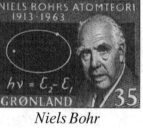

Niels Bohr
Issued by Greenland

Martin Buber
Issued by West Germany

Leon Blum
Issued by France

Max Born
Issued by West Germany

Otto Bauer
Issued by Austria

Ernest Bloch
Issued by Israel

C

James Caan was born in Queens, New York, on March 26th 1939. He was educated at Michigan State University and Hofstra University, New York. He studied acting at the Neighbourhood Playhouse in New York and began his film career in 1963, in an uncredited part in *Irma La Douce*. Ten years later he became a national and international star. National recognition came in 1971 with a made-for-television feature, *Brian's Song*, in which Caan played a cancer-stricken footballer. International fame followed when he played the hot-tempered elder son in *The Godfather*. His screen presence was such as often to eclipse his more famous co-stars. Indeed, he was nominated for an Academy Award as Best Supporting Actor. He has made several films of note including *The Godfather, Part II* (1974), *Gambler* (1974), *Funny Lady* (1975) and *Rollerball* (1975). In 1977 he had a starring role in *A Bridge Too Far*. In 1980 he starred in and directed *Hide in Plain Sight*. This was Caan's first attempt at directing and the result was said to be 'smoothly handled'. In 1990 he starred in *Misery*, in which his co-star, Kathy Bates, won the Oscar for Best Actress. Caan was superb as the helpless author kidnapped by a crazed fan. The role re-established Caan as a powerful screen actor.

CAAN, James (1939-) US actor

Sid Caesar was born in New York on September 8th 1922. Educated at Yonkers High School, he graduated in 1939 and worked in the theatre district as a doorman. He studied music with the idea of becoming a professional saxophone player. In 1940 he played with a variety of dance-hall bands and learnt his craft. He also worked in the Catskill Mountains, the holiday area favoured by New York's Jews. There he wrote sketches and on occasion worked as a comedian. In 1942 he joined the US Coastguards for the duration of the Second World War. The war over, Caesar stayed on in Los Angeles and took small roles in several low-budget films. In 1948 he returned to New York to spend a year on Broadway in the show *Make Mine Manhattan* (1948). He then became part of the new and exciting world of television. He rapidly became the number one television personality with *Your Show of Shows* (1950-54), *Caesar's Hour* (1954-57) and *The Sid Caesar Show* (1963-64). His sketch writers have become legends in their own right: Woody Allen (*qv*), Mel Brooks (*qv*) and Neil Simon (*qv*). In the 1970s his problems led him to depend on alcohol and pills; in his autobiography *Where Have I Been?* (1982) he describes these times and how, by his own endeavours, he recovered to resume working in films and television. In 1996 Neil Simon's play, *Laughter on the 23rd Floor,* with Gene Wilder (*qv*), was based on writers working for *The Sid Caesar Show* in the 1960s.

CAESAR, Sid (1922-) US entertainer

One day someone is going to write a doctoral thesis on the subject of Jewish songwriters in the 20th century. Such a work would have to include **Sammy Cahn**, born in New York on June 18th 1913. He lived in the same area as the Gershwins and Irving Berlin (*qv*). He was the only boy among five children born to poverty-stricken parents, and naturally his mother hoped her son would become a doctor or a lawyer; instead, Sammy decided to leave school early and become a musician. His instrument was the violin and he worked in the burlesque houses that proliferated in the Bowery area of New York. As the strippers stripped, Sammy would parody the popular songs of the day. He was just fifteen. He went on to have many jobs ranging from liftman to tinsmith, all aimed at supporting himself and his family. Realizing he had no future as a violinist - he couldn't stand his own playing - he teamed up with pianist Saul Chaplin to write songs. They had their first hit in 1936 with 'Shoe Shine Boy', performed by Louis Armstrong. The same year they wrote, 'Bei Mir Bist du Schoen' and sold it to the Andrew Sisters, who in turn sold a million copies of the sheet music and a million records. It launched all their careers. In 1940, Cahn moved to Los Angeles and teamed up with Julie Styne (*qv*). Following America's entry into the Second World War in December 1941, Cahn tried to enlist but was turned down because of stomach ulcers. He spent the next three years with the USO, performing for the troops all over the world. In the 1940s he wrote 'Let it Snow, Let it Snow, Let it Snow'; 'I'll Walk Alone'; 'Only Five Minutes More'; and 'Things We Did Last Summer'. Cahn and Steyne gave Doris Day her first hit with, 'It's Magic'. Sammy Cahn, with various partners, wrote some of Frank Sinatra's best songs, including among others 'All the Way'; 'Three Coins in the Fountain'; 'High Hopes'; 'Call Me Irresponsible'; 'My Kind Of Town'; and 'Come Fly With Me'. With Jimmy van Heusen, Cahn wrote the music for the hit film, *Throughly Modern Millie* (1967). 'Love and Marriage' launched the career of Britain's Alma Cogan. Although the money was pouring in Cahn, wasn't satisfied; he wanted to be a performer. In 1974 he wrote a one-man show, called it *Words and Music* and successfully toured with it all over the world for nearly 20 years. He died a happy man on January 15th 1993 in Los Angeles, having written some of the all-time great songs, picked up four Academy Awards, been nominated for another 26 songs and written a best-selling autobiography, *I Should Care*, published in 1974. He was once asked: 'Would you, for example, have liked to have been a successful architect?' Cahn thought and then replied: 'Nothing wrong with that, but who walks down the street humming a building?'

CALMAT,
Alain
(1940-)
French world
figure skating
champion

Born Alain Calmanovich in Paris on August 31st 1940, he is one of only two Frenchmen to have won the World Figure Skating Championships during their 100 year history. Giletti was the first, in 1960; Alain Calmat the second, in 1965. When it happened it was no great surprise because Calmat had been runner-up in 1963 and 1964. He was also European figure skating champion in 1962, 1963 and 1966, and won a silver medal for France in the Winter Olympics of 1964. In 1965 he won the gold medal at the Winter Olympiad in Innsbruck and was later awarded the Legion of Honour. In 1968, at the Winter Olympics in Grenoble, Calmat had the singular honour of carrying the Olympic torch and lighting the Olympic flame. He later qualified as a surgeon, but by 1984 had moved into politics and was Head of the Sports and Youth Ministry in the administration of Laurent Fabius (*qv*).

Calvin was born in Minnesota, to Russian-Jewish immigrants, on April 8th 1911. After receiving his doctorate from the University of Minnesota, Calvin decided to teach. He joined the faculty of the University of California and stayed, in one position or another, until 1971. During the Second World War he worked on the Manhattan Project in the field of atomic fission and after the war spent considerable time away from teaching researching the role of chlorophyll in photosynthesis. During his studies he developed a system of using the radioactive isotope carbon-14 as a tracer element and as a result could stop the growth of plants at various stages. Calvin was awarded the Nobel Prize for Chemistry in 1961 for his work on photosynthesis. He later researched aspects of life based on radiation chemistry and in 1963 joined the US Academy of Science. He was also a foreign member of the Royal Society. An experienced and popular lecturer, constantly expressing new ideas, he was also a prolific writer who published some 500 papers and books. He died in Berkeley, California, on January 8th 1997.

Canetti was born in Rustschuk, Bulgaria, on July 25th 1905. The first language he spoke was Ladino. He spent his formative years moving between Switzerland, Germany, Austria and England. In 1927 he was part of the mob responsible for the protest burning of the Justizpalast in Vienna. In 1938 he decided to plant roots. Considering what was happening to Jews in Europe, he wisely decided upon England. The books for which he is perhaps best known are *Auto-da-Fe* (1935), a warning about the growth of totalitarianism, and the study on mass behaviour, *Crowds and Power* (1960). In recent times his autobiographies, *The Tongue Set Free* (1977) and *Torch in My Ear* (1980) have explained the origins and reasons for his work. Perhaps his most imaginative works are his plays; *The Wedding* (1932), *Comedy of Vanity* (1950) and *The Numbered* (1964). In 1981 Canetti was awarded the Nobel Prize for Literature.

Dyan Cannon was born Samille Diane Friesen in Tacoma, Washington, on January 4th 1937, the daughter of a Baptist father and Jewish mother. She was educated at the University of Washington, were she studied anthropology. She decided to make acting her career and later, described as a zany, sexy, dizzy blonde, she came across as a flighty comedienne with a sure touch in some of the trendiest films of the 1970s and 1980s, including *Bob and Carol and Ted and Alice* (1969), for which she received an Oscar nomination, *Doctors' Wives* (1970) and *Such Good Friends* (1971). In 1965 she married Cary Grant; they had a child and then divorced in 1968. In 1976 she directed, wrote, produced and edited the award-winning short film *Growing Pains: Number One* on the theme of children's natural curiosity about their bodies and how adult values stifled them. This film was nominated for an Academy Award. Dyan Cannon was nominated for another Oscar following her excellent performance in *Heaven Can Wait* (1978). In 1990 she wrote and directed her first feature film, in which she also acted: *The End Of Innocence*, a semi-autobiographical story. Since the late 1970s Cannon has shown much skill in the selection of the roles she plays. She is also the first woman to be nominated for an Academy Award as both director and actress (1977 and 1979).

CANTOR, Eddie (1892-1964) US entertainer

Born Isidor Iskowitch on the Lower East Side of New York City on January 30th 1892, in 1907, he blacked his face, called himself 'The Chocolate Coloured Coon' and won a music contest. He never looked back. He took his act all over the US and topped the bill in the Ziegfeld Follies of 1917, 1918 and 1919. Famous for his 'banjo eyes', his face became known all over the world following his entry into films, with starring roles in, for example, *Whoopee* (1930). The feature song, 'Making Whoopee', became his trademark and a hit. He also scored with *Roman Scandals* (1933) and *Ali Baba Goes to Town* (1937). *Thank Your Lucky Stars* (1943) was produced to raise the spirits of soldiers and civilians alike during the heart of the Second World War. Cantor's rendering of 'They're Either Too Young or Too Old' was memorable. After the war, 1948 saw 'If You Knew Susie' and another hit song for Eddie Cantor. Television brought more fame, Cantor's singing and comedy routines delighting audiences everywhere. In 1964 President Johnson awarded Cantor a presidential medal for his services to the US and humanity. Cantor died a few weeks later, on October 12th 1964, in Beverly Hills; he was mourned by the nation.

CAPA, Robert (1913-54) Hungarian/ American photo-journalist

Robert Capa was born Andrei Friedmann on October 22nd 1913 in Budapest, Hungary. As a young man, he took off for Paris to work as a freelance photographer. In 1935, at the start of the Spanish Civil War, Capa was unexpectedly asked by the editor of the London photo magazine *Picture Post* to cover the conflict. The photos he sent back were brilliant and shocking. Besides showing soldiers in combat he also depicted, probably for the first time, the effect of war on civilians. He appeared to get into the very centre of the battle. His photo of a Loyalist soldier taken at the moment of his death is still considered one of the greatest war photos ever. After Spain, he covered the 1938 attacks on China by the Japanese, and in 1939, having emigrated to the US, the North African campaign. In June 1944 he was with the troops on the first day of the Normandy landings, swimming ashore; his were the first photos showing US soldiers in close-ups that didn't require words to describe the horror of battle. Following the Second World War, he and two friends, Henri Cartier-Bresson and David Seymour, founded Magnum Photos, an international photo agency. In 1948, during Israel's war of independence, Capa was with David Marcus in the battle for the road link with Jerusalem. On May 25th 1954 Capa was covering the French war in Indo-China for *Life* magazine when he stepped on a landmine and was blown up. He thus became the first American casualty of what was to become the Vietnam War. His death would have made a photograph Capa would have been proud of.

Al Capp was born Alfred Gerald Caplin in New Haven, Connecticut, on September 28th 1909. He studied landscape architecture at the Designers Art School in Boston and the Pennsylvania Academy of Fine Arts in Philadelphia. He worked as assistant to Budd Fisher, the originator of 'Mutt and Jeff' (1930). Later Al Capp gave birth to L'il Abner, a shy country lad, and the legend of the hillbilly people and Daisy Mae's perpetual chase of her bashful hero began. The stories of L'il Abner and the gang appeared in daily newspapers all over the US. A satire of the American political scene, it has provided the basis for two feature films and numerous animated cartoons. It even became a staged musical. The feature was so popular that at one time it was the main reason the newspaper was bought, to start the day off with a laugh. The saga came to an end when Daisy Mae finally caught Abner in 1977, the year Capp retired. He died in New Haven on November 5th 1979.

Anthony Caro, born in London on March 8th 1924, studied engineering at Cambridge before switching to sculpture. Following service in the Royal Navy during the Second World War he studied at the Royal Academy School from 1947 to 1952, before becoming an assistant to Henry Moore. Caro's early work was based on modelling in preference to carving. Then, in 1960, following a meeting with David Smith (probably the most original American sculptor of the century), Caro switched to metal sculpture using such diverse materials as aluminium tubing, propeller blades, steel plates, etc. An example of this phase of his work is *Midday* (1960), a painted steel structure that is at the Museum of Modern Art in New York. Many of his works express a significant mood, generally conveyed by the title, e.g. *Early One Morning* (Tate Gallery, London), *Slow Movement* and *Away* (MOMA, New York). Later work shows how Caro has dispensed with the plinth or pedestal: the work is straight 'off the ground', which he claims involves the spectator more closely. His work continues to have a deep influence on young artists as well as having kept faith with Smith's pioneering work.

Cassin was born in Bayonne on October 5th 1887, the son of a well-known Jewish family that had links with pre-Inquisition Spain. He was educated at Aix and Paris universities and studied law. During the First World War he served in the French army, was badly wounded, and was decorated with the Croix de Guerre as well as the Medaille Militaire. In 1920 he became professor of law at Lille University, where he stayed until 1929. He then went to the University of Paris, taking time off to be part of the French delegation to the League of Nations. At the beginning of the Second World War, Cassin was involved at the highest possible level in discussions with foreign governments before the collapse of France. During the war years he was in London, serving in the French government-in-exile. He represented France at the founding of the United Nations, later becoming, together with Eleanor Roosevelt, the first president of the UN Commission on Human Rights. He went on to hold many public posts. In 1968 René Cassin was awarded the Nobel Peace Prize. The large cash prize that accompanied this honour he donated to the work of the Human Rights Institute at Strasbourg. He died in Paris on October 5th 1976. In October 1987 his remains were transferred to the Pantheon in Paris: a signal honour.

CASSIRER,
Ernst
(1874-1945)
German
philosopher

Cassirer was born in Breslau, Poland, on July 28th 1874, the son of a successful merchant. He was educated at various German universities before obtaining his doctorate from the ancient University of Marburg. Beginning his academic career as a professor at Berlin University, he was elected Rector in 1930 only to be thrown out by Hitler in 1933 for having been born a Jew. His philosophical theories were partially based on Immanuel Kant. In his book *Substance and Function* (1910), he advances the theory that 'the concept of substance should be replaced by that of function'. He also developed the thesis that language, mythology and science are all different symbolic expressions for understanding the world. Cassirer, deciding the Nazis were there to stay, took off for Oxford University. Here he taught for two years before leaving for Sweden to teach at Gothenburg University, where he spent six years. When he celebrated his 65th birthday he was a Swedish citizen and as such had to retire. Not yet ready for slippers and sleep, he voyaged to America during the hazardous days of 1941 to spend two years at Yale University and the rest of his life at Columbia. He wrote much, including *Language and Myth* (1946), *The Philosophy of the Enlightenment* (1951) and his three-volume *The Philosophy of Symbolic Forms* (1953-57). He died in harness, his mind constantly seeking out the mysteries of life and trying to provide the answers, in New York City on April 13th 1945.

CASTILLO Y
ALBORNOZ,
Jose
(1854-1940)
Ecuadorean
pioneer

Castillo y Albornoz was born in Ambato, Ecuador, into a distinguished Jewish family. After fighting against the dictator Vintimilla, as a colonel in the Liberal army, he was wounded and forced to retire. He founded *El Telegrafo*, Ecuador's first liberal newspaper, and through that journal fought for the causes he believed in. He often had to leave the country to take sanctuary in a neighbouring state; but he always returned. In 1920 he bought an aeroplane, called it 'El Telegrafo' and established the first airmail service on South America's west coast. In 1922 he was once again forced into exile. This time he chose San Remo on Italy's Mediterranean coast as his refuge, staying there until 1928. Back in Ecuador, following Hitler's election, Castillo y Albornoz did much to help rescue Jews from Germany, and later Austria, and take them into Ecuador. On the 30th anniversary of the first airmail flight, Ecuador postal authorities issued stamps to commemorate the event.

CELAN,
Paul
(1920-1970)
Romanian/
French poet

Born Paul Antschel in Cernauti, Romania, on November 23rd 1920, **Celan** survived the Holocaust but lost his parents. His experiences in a Romanian labour camp, and the Holocaust generally, coloured his post-war work. He spent the years 1945-47 working in Bucharest for a publisher; then he moved to Vienna, where he published his first book of poetry, *The Sand From the Urns* (1948). In 1948 he moved to France and settled in Paris. Having been virtually unknown before the war, he now forged his reputation by a mixture of reality and refinement. He describes the horrors he has experienced and makes them come alive. He has come to be regarded as the most authentic poet writing in German. Some of his poetry is influenced by surrealism and the Jewish mystical tradition; other poems are mainly concerned with the nature of words. A lecturer at the Ecole Normale, he once told his students that 'language was the only thing that remained intact'. He translated

Shakespeare and other poetic works into German and published his second book of poetry, *Poppy and Memory*, in 1952. However, it was apparently not enough for him, and he committed suicide in Paris, on May 1st 1970, at the age of 49. *Speech-Grille and Selected Poems* was published posthumously, the following year, to mark the first anniversary of his untimely death.

Marc Chagall was born Mark Segal in Vitebsk, Russia, on July 7th 1887. He studied at St. Petersburg's School for the Imperial Society for the Encouragement of the Arts: a long, high-sounding name which meant that Chagall, as a Jew, had a long walk each day, for he was not allowed to live inside the city. Extremely poor, he had to trudge to and from the Academy each day. Later, thanks to a rich patron, Chagall went to Paris. There, he was accepted by his contemporaries and flourished. His colours were so exuberant they were said to sing. In May 1914 Der Sturm Gallery in Berlin held a one-man exhibition of his work. In July he was back home in Vitebsk; two weeks later the First World War started, and Chagall was drafted into the Tsar's army to fight Germany. On leave, he got married and was lucky enough to find himself a desk job. This meant he could continue his painting. Following the 1917 Russian Revolution Chagall was appointed Commissar of Fine Arts and director of the Vitebsk Art Academy; and, best of all, the state bought twelve of his paintings. Two years later, Chagall was replaced and the whole family moved to Moscow. Here he designed theatrical sets and costumes and painted his largest work yet: a mural for the Jewish theatre. In 1922 he left for Berlin, did not much like what he saw and went on to Paris. He produced many circus paintings and was most upset when some, such as *Bouquet with Flying Lovers* (1934-37, Tate Gallery, London) became part of the 'degenerate art' exhibition held in Berlin in 1937.

Following the German occupation of France Chagall was in considerable danger, and was lucky to arrive in New York in 1941. Americans loved his work and loved his humour. Someone asked him why he had a milkmaid's head floating above her body. Chagall replied, 'In the first instance I had to fill in an empty space. In the second I had to create one.' The Second World War had a profound influence upon his work. The death of his wife in 1944 was one blow, and the revelation of the death camps nearly finished him off. In 1947 he returned to France, first to Paris, then to St Jean, Cap-Ferrat, finally settling in Vence.

He has been honoured and exhibited all over the world. His work is instantly recognizable and he stands alongside Picasso as probably one of the most important painters of the 20th century. His major works are awesome, especially his works in stained glass, such as *The Twelve Tribes of Israel* at the Hadassah Hospital, Jerusalem, *The Peace Window* for the UN in New York, and windows for the Vatican. He painted the ceiling of the Paris Opera House and created two large murals for the Lincoln Center, New York. As a 90th birthday present he was given an exhibition at the Louvre, Paris, the first time this has ever been done for a living artist. In 1981, at the age of 92, he returned to Moscow after an absence of 60 years. The occasion was an exhibition of his work at the Treyiakov Gallery. Although many of his paintings were Jewish in character, the appeal was universal.

CHAGALL, Marc (1887-1985) Russian/French painter

During the Six-Day War of 1967 in Israel, four of his stained glass windows, at the Hadassah Hospital, were smashed. Chagall, when told by the Israelis what had happened, replied, 'You take care of the war, I'll take care of the windows.' He was as good as his word and two years later he had replaced them. Chagall died in Saint-Paul, France, on March 28th 1985.

CHAIKIN,
Sol
(1918-91)
US labour
leader

Sol Chaikin was born in New York City on January 9th 1918, the son of Russian Jews who escaped the tyranny of Tsarist times and arrived in the US in 1910. Sol's father worked in one of the garment sweatshops that proliferated in the ghetto of the Lower East Side. Sol grew up in an atmosphere in which the worker had little alternative but to accept bad conditions or starve. Being above average ability, Sol secured a place at Townsend Harris School, from where he graduated at sixteen and went on to take a degree at the City College. In 1940 he obtained a law degree from St Lawrence Law School. Instead of becoming a successful corporation lawyer he chose to work full-time for his parents' trade union, the ILGWU. It was Sol's way of saying ' thank you' to his parents. They had given him every advantage in life; now he was putting his talents to work on their behalf. He spent the next three years working and negotiating for better conditions; then, in 1943, he joined the US Air Force, serving two years of combat duty in the Pacific, China and India. In 1946 he was demobbed and returned to his union career. In 1965 he was elected international vice-president of the ILGWU. Over a period of some 30 years he acquired a wealth of experience and was beloved by the rank and file. In 1977 he was elected the union's president and remained in that post for three terms. However, by the 1980s the union no longer had a mass membership. The American fashion industry now found it cheaper to import ready-made clothes from countries where wages were much lower than in the US; and cheap immigrant labour, from Hispanic backgrounds, had replaced the Jews and Italians of the earlier times, who had now moved on to more salubrious places. Chaikin now used his best endeavours to stem the tide of imported goods and negotiate better deals that would encourage manufacturers to turn to home production. There was a contradiction in these efforts, but Chaikin knew his back was to the wall, with union membership dropping by some 50 per cent in a decade. He remained an executive council member until 1986. Chaikin could have been a financial giant had he chosen the corporate path; he chose, instead, to look out for the poorer members of society. He died in New York on April 1st 1991.

CHAIN,
Sir Ernst
(1906-79)
German/British
biochemist

Chain was born in Berlin on June 19th 1906, son of a chemical engineer. He grew up in an atmosphere which insisted that the only worthwhile occupation in life was the pursuit of intellectual activity. Moreover, any career that wasn't university-based was unthinkable. Chain originally wanted to be a musician but was persuaded into a career of science. He received his PhD from the Pathological Institute of Berlin in 1927. In 1929 he became most interested in Fleming's discovery which later, after Chain's work, would be known as penicillin. This interest, plus Hitler's attitude to the Jews, gave Chain the impetus to go to England. He taught at Cambridge

University for two years, after which he joined Howard Florey in Oxford. Chain is acknowledged as the key figure in the isolation and purification of penicillin. Because Britain was concentrating on the war it was left to three American companies to mass-produce, by arrangement, what would become known as a 'miracle drug': the first antibiotic. Chain's discovery and Florey's commercialism made it possible for hundreds of thousands of Allied personnel to be treated for wounds that would otherwise probably have killed them. After the war, the drug gradually became available for civilian use, all over the world. In 1948 Chain, Fleming and Florey shared the Nobel Prize for Physiology or Medicine. Ernst Chain was knighted in 1969 and served as professor of biochemistry at Imperial College London from 1963 to 1971. He died in Ireland on August 12th 1979.

Born Tula Ellice Finklea on March 8th 1921 in Amarillo, Texas, she was known as Lily Norwood until an agent came up with the name **Cyd Charisse**. Unlike most Hollywood sex symbols, Charisse had the talent to match her looks. She started her career as a dancer and broke into films to play opposite such stars as Fred Astaire and Gene Kelly. Besides television, she has made some 40 feature films, the first in 1943, the last in 1990. Her best-known film has to be *Singin' in the Rain* (1952). *Band Wagon* came a year later. It was nominated for three Oscars and reckoned to be the best musical of the decade. *Silk Stockings* (1957), opposite Astaire, and *Party Girl* (1958), with Robert Taylor, followed. She starred with Kirk Douglas (*qv*) and Edward G. Robinson (*qv*) in *Two Weeks in Another Town* (1962) and held her own. Many of her films were rubbished by the critics, but given a good dramatic role with a well-written script, she was as good as any other actress - besides which, she was reckoned to have the best legs in Hollywood.

CHARISSE, Cyd (1921-) US actor

Georges Charpak was born in Poland on August 1st 1924. He was seven years old when the family moved to Paris. During the Second World War Charpak fought with the Resistance until captured by Vichy police. Because he was a Jew they handed him over to the Germans who incarcerated him in Dachau concentration camp. In 1945 the camp was liberated by US troops and Charpak gradually recovered his health. The following year he became a French citizen and ten years later received his PhD from the Collège de France in Paris. In 1959 he joined CERN, the European Organization for Nuclear Research based in Geneva. In 1968 he built the first multiwire proportional chamber and was able to record up to one million tracks per second, sending the data directly to a computer for analysis. This discovery revolutionized high-energy physics and has applications in medicine and industry. For his invention of subatomic particle detectors, Charpak received the 1992 Nobel Prize for Physics.

CHARPAK, Georges (1924-) Polish/French physicist

Born Sidney Aaron Chayefsky on January 29th 1923 in the Bronx district of New York he was educated at CCNY. He first began writing in hospital, recovering from wounds received while serving with the US Army during the Second World War. After the usual rejections he began selling some short stories to magazines.

CHAYEFSKY, Paddy (1923-81) US writer

Earning hardly enough money to live on, he wrote a television play which he called *Marty* (1953), and the world smiled upon him. Two years later *Marty* became a feature film and collected three Oscars, for Best Actor (Ernest Borgnine), Best Picture and Best Screenplay (Paddy Chayefsky). In 1957 he wrote *The Batchelor Party* for television, and that too became a feature film with Carolyn Jones picking up an Oscar nomination. *A Catered Affair* (1956) with Bette Davis also first saw life on the small screen. He wrote *The Hospital* in 1971 and *Network* in 1976, both taking a critical look at a slice of American life. Chayefsky won an Oscar for *Hospital*. *Network* nearly cleared the board. It collected four Academy awards: Best Actor (Peter Finch), Best Actress (Faye Dunaway), Best Supporting Actress (Beatrice Straight) and of course Paddy, for Best Original Screenplay. In 1980, Ken Russell took Chayefsky's novel and screenplay, *Altered States*, and so mucked around with it that the author refused to allow his name to be listed in the credits. It appears with 'screenplay by Sidney Aaron'. Paddy died in New York on August 1st 1981.

CHERNYAKH-OVSKI,
Ivan
(1906-45)
Russian soldier

Chernyakhovski was born in Uman, near Kiev, the grandson of a rabbi. Rather than going to university, Ivan preferred the Kiev Military College. He was top of his year and joined a tank regiment. At the outbreak of the Second World War, at the age of 33, he was in command of a tank corps. For his part in the Russian counter-offensive in 1943, when the Dnieper was crossed to liberate Kiev, Chernyakhovski was made a Hero of the Soviet Union and promoted to full general. In June 1944, now in command of the 3rd Belorussian Army, he went on to liberate Minsk, Vilna and Grodno. In August 1944 his was the first Russian army fighting on German soil. The German SS general commanding the army opposite him, was aware his enemy was a Jew and sought to sow disaffection in the Russian army by announcing this fact over mobile loudspeakers. If the ploy had any effect at all it was to increase the determination of the Russians. Shortly after his forces captured Koenigsberg, the capital of East Prussia, Ivan Chernyakhovski was killed in action. The following day the BBC in London cancelled its scheduled programme and in its place broadcast a tribute to General Chernyakhovski. Following the end of the war the town of Insterburg, in East Prussia, was renamed Chernyakhovski; in memory of the highest-ranking Allied officer to die in action during the Second World War.

CHOMSKY,
Noam
(1928-)
US political
philosopher

Chomsky was born on December 7th 1928 in Philadelphia, the son of a Hebrew scholar. He rounded off his education with a four-year fellowship at Harvard. In 1955 he taught modern languages at the Massachusetts Institute of Technology. Six years later he was a full professor. In his book, published in 1957, *Syntactic Structures*, he began his linguistic revolution. He wrote much on this subject but later concentrated on political problems. He was especially critical of American involvement in Vietnam and of the role of the CIA, whose meddling in foreign countries he saw as often resulting in civil war. He crusades against poverty and the increasing menace of giant multinational corporations that owe allegiance only to themselves. He lectures all over the world and is in much demand. A prolific writer, his works include *American*

Power and the New Mandarins (1969); *Language and the Mind* (1972); *Pirates and Emperors* (1986); and *Language and the Problems of Knowledge* (1988). He is often held to be a voice in the wilderness and is considered by many to be the greatest intellectual in the world today.

Citroën was born in Paris on February 5th 1878 and educated locally. His father was a small-time diamond merchant who had come to Paris from Poland, via Amsterdam. By 1908 André had established himself in the fledgling automobile industry, making a lot of money by patenting various manufacturing processes, and that year he took over the ailing Mors Automobile company. Ten years later he had increased annual sales tenfold. During the First World War he was in charge of a large part of French war production and created the giant munitions factory on the Quai de Javel. After the war, Citroën put into operation his plan to manufacture French cars on the assembly line principle, and so mass-produce cheaply enough for the working man to purchase. He earned the nickname 'the French Henry Ford'. It was well deserved, and he sold his car, the Citroën, all over the world. André Citroën was always on the lookout for a deal, and in return for permission to advertise his cars on the Eiffel Tower he agreed to organize the installation of traffic lights in Paris. In 1922 he sponsored the first crossing of the Sahara by automobile and in 1934 introduced the front-wheel drive. Adverse financial problems caused Citroën to hand his company over to Michelin. However, sixty years later the company he started still exists, and still bears his name. André Citroën died in Paris on July 3rd 1935.

CITROEN, André (1878-1935) French industrialist

Hélène was born in Algiers, the daughter of an orthodox Jewish family, and was educated at the Lycée Bugeaud in Algiers before moving to Paris in 1955 to teach. She was a lecturer at the Sorbonne at the time of the 1968 student uprisings. Unlike most of her colleagues, she took an active part in the riots that followed, and was much admired by her students for the stand she took with them. Later, as professor at Vincennes, she established experimental literature courses and based her research on psychoanalysis as it affects women. She continues to have a profound influence in educational circles and on the continuing campaign for women's equality. Her writings include *Dedalus*, which won her the 1969 Prix Medicis.

CIXOUS, Hélène (1937-) French academic writer

Born in New York on September 18th 1901, **Clurman** was to become a major force in American theatre for over 50 years. In 1931 he co-founded the Group Theatre in New York, and there directed plays by many young writers, some of whom would go on to number among the greatest in the world. Clurman gave them their chance. They included Clifford Odets (*qv*), Arthur Miller (*qv*), William Saroyan and Irwin Shaw. He developed the careers of Lee J. Cobb (*qv*) and John Garfield (*qv*) and introduced the Stanislavsky method of acting to the US. He directed many hit plays including *Awake and Sing* (1935), *Member of the Wedding* (1950) and *Tiger at the Gates* (1955). From 1953 he was drama critic for *The Nation*. His several books include *On Directing* (1972) and *The Divine Pastime* (1974). In

CLURMAN, Harold (1901-80) US drama critic and director

1974 he published his autobiography, *All People Are Famous*. He died in New York on September 6th 1980.

COBB,
Lee, J.
(1911-76)
US actor

Lee J. Cobb, born Leo Jacob in New York on December 8th 1911, was the Best Supporting Actor never to have won an Academy Award, though he was nominated twice. Educated as an accountant, he turned to acting and in 1935 joined Lee Strasbourg's Group Theatre. He appeared in Clifford Odet's *Waiting For Lefty* and *Golden Boy*. His notices were so good that he was invited to Hollywood in 1937. He was a powerful actor, sometimes too powerful for the top actors he appeared with. He made around 70 films; while not all were good box office, some were superb. *Song of Bernadette* (1943) saw Jennifer Jones getting an Oscar for Best Actress and rave notices for Cobb. *The Three Faces of Eve* (1957) had Cobb starring with Joanne Woodward, who won the Best Actress award. He was a powerhouse in Preminger's *Exodus* (1960). In *On The Waterfront* (1954) he more than held his own when he played the gangster boss opposite Marlo Brando, Rod Steiger and Karl Malden; indeed, he was nominated for Best Supporting Actor. In the event the film collected four Oscars, but nothing for Cobb. In *Twelve Angry Men* (1957) he played the intransigent bigot opposite Henry Fonda. Cobb was once more nominated for Best Supporting Actor for his role in *The Brothers Karamazov* (1958). His portrayal of Willy Loman in Arthur Miller's *Death of a Salesman* has never been bettered or even equalled, and there have been some impressive attempts. He died on February 11th 1976.

COEN,
Joel
(1955-)
and Etham
(1958-)
US film-makers

Etham and **Joel Coen** were born at St Louis Park, Minnesota. Together, it is reckoned, they form the most imaginative talent currently at work in the field of film-making. Etham was educated at Princeton University, where he studied philosophy, and now acts as the producer and screenwriter part of the duo. Joel, who was educated at Simon's Rock College, Massachusetts, and New York University film school, is the director and also a screenwriter. The brothers are steeped in cinematic history. *Blood Simple* (1984) was their first big film effort. It is a tribute to the *film noir* genre and creates a tight atmosphere of suspense. *Crimewave* (1985) followed, but did not live up to expectation. *Raising Arizona* (1987), a crazy comedy, restored their inspirational reputations. *Miller's Crossing* (1990) was a stylish film that echoed the work of Dashiel Hammett and confirmed the Coen Brothers as a creative force. Their 1996 feature film, *Fargo*, is said to be based on a true story. In any event it is quite unusual and took the Cannes Film Festival by storm. Their vast international public look forward, with more than general interest, to future productions from the Coen Brothers.

COHEN,
Sir Andrew
(1909-68)
British colonial
administrator

Andrew Cohen was born in Berkhamsted, Hertfordshire, on October 7th 1909; one of twins, his father was Walter Cohen, a financier. Educated at Malvern College and Trinity College, Cambridge, he obtained a double first in the Classics tripos (1930-31). He joined the Colonial Service and spent several years among the African tribes. As a result, he came to sympathize with the Africans who were under British rule, rather than with his colleagues, the rulers. During the Second World War, he was in charge of organizing supplies to Malta, as well as deputizing for the Governor when he was away from the island, which was under constant attack by German and Italian air forces. The Labour victory in the general election of 1945 saw Cohen appointed assistant under-secretary of the African section of the Colonial Office. For Cohen it was vital that the African colonies should become independent as soon as was feasibly possible. He persuaded the minister, Creech Jones, to his point of view with the result that the Gold Coast received independence in 1948. Cohen secured the release from prison of Kwame Nkrumah, so enabling him to become prime minister of Ghana. Nigeria followed and a domino effect ensued, with West Africa becoming independent in 1951, Central Africa in 1953. Cohen's plan, designed to educate the national movement into gradual responsibility, bore fruit. Andrew Cohen was now appointed Governor of Uganda. Through his efforts that country was ready for independence by 1957. Cohen now hoped for a Labour seat in Parliament, but instead he was appointed to the Trusteeship Council of the United Nations. In 1959 he published *British Policy in Changing Africa*. With this book he set the wheels turning to generate co-operative aid to modernize Africa. He developed ideas for American aid for British schemes to develop East Africa, especially university education. In 1964 the Ministry of Overseas Development was born. Cohen, as its permanent secretary, established the programme with dynamic enthusiasm. A big man with a boyish charm, his vision and energy dismantled the old colonial ways and paved the way for Africa to govern itself. For his important work he was appointed a knight in 1952. He died suddenly in London on June 17th 1968.

Cohen was born in Amsterdam. In 1902 he was professor of inorganic chemistry at Utrecht University. Cohen was the man who found the explanation for the previously mysterious 'tin disease'. He went on to research the various aspects of iodides. He founded the Dutch Society for the History of Medicine and was the first president of the Dutch Chemical Society. He wrote many books and was an accepted authority on his subject. In 1941, his property was seized by the German army of occupation, and he was forbidden to teach. Two years later, at the age of 73, he was arrested and sent to a concentration camp. Released following pressure from the Dutch Chemical Society, he was advised by his friends to leave the Netherlands. Unhappily, with the Germans surrounding the country, Cohen had nowhere to go. The Germans re-arrested him, entrained him for Auschwitz, and gassed him to death.

COHEN, Ernst (1869-1945) Dutch chemist

Harriet Cohen, born in London on December 2nd 1901, had become a top soloist by the age of 20. She was a virtuoso, whose interpretation of the great piano works was judged remarkable for the clarity she brought to the keyboard. British composers Bax, Elgar, Vaughan Williams and Walton all wrote for her. During the Second World War, she entertained the forces both at home and overseas. In 1948 she suffered a serious accident, which left her right hand virtually powerless. Two

COHEN, Harriet (1901-67) British pianist

years later she was back on the concert hall circuit, playing a piano concerto for the left hand especially composed for her by Sir Arnold Bax. She continued giving piano recitals until 1960, at which time she began holding master classes for students of the piano. She died in London on November 13th 1967.

COHEN, Henry (1900-77) British physician

Cohen, born in Birkenhead on February 21st 1900, became one of the pioneers of the British National Health Service, founded in 1948. Cohen had graduated from the University of Liverpool Medical School and, by the age of 34, was a professor of medicine. In the early days of the health service he became its chairman, and the foundations he laid then enabled the NHS to become the envy of the world. He was knighted for his services and created a life peer in 1956, taking the title Lord Cohen of Birkenhead. A small man with a soft voice, he commanded attention whenever he spoke in the upper chamber. In 1974 he was made a Companion of Honour. He died in Bath, Avon, on August 7th 1977.

COHEN, Israel (1912-95) US retailing pioneer

Israel Cohen was born in the US on January 14th, 1912. In 1936, during the Great Depression, Cohen and his father inaugurated the first ever supermarket, a store where everything could be bought under one roof. The venue was Washington, the weather foul, and the idea novel; there was little or no money for advertising the event. Despite these handicaps, the result was positive. The public wanted what the Cohens had to offer. It was hard work and Israel would often drive from wholesaler to store several times a day, keeping the shelves stocked up. It wasn't long before their company, Giant Foods, began opening branches all over the country and soon their concept was being copied. Supermarkets became ever bigger, as more and more lines were included for sale. Eventually the Cohens controlled some 160 stores nationwide. Their concept has taken over the shopping habits of people in every corner of the world. Israel Cohen died in Washington DC on November 22nd 1995.

COHEN, Leonard (1934-) Canadian composer/ singer

Born in 1934 in Montreal, **Leonard Cohen** came to public notice following a great debut with *Songs of Leonard Cohen* in 1968. 'Suzanne' was a particularly great hit. Although he acknowledges he has been inspired by Bob Dylan (*qv*), his style is unique. Such collections as *Songs From a Room* (1969) and *Songs of Love and Hate* gaver rise to his nickname as 'bard of the bedsits'. He gradually acquired the confidence required for live performances and the result was a series of concerts that formed the basis for his album *Live Songs* (1972). His basic acoustic guitar playing and gravelly voice distinguish him and allows the quality of his song writing to come through. In 1974 his *New Skin for the Old Ceremony* was considered a work of genius. However, *Death of a Ladies Man* (1977) is considered his best of the decade. Other recordings include, *Recent Songs* (1979), *Various Positions* (1985) and Jennifer Warne's, *Famous Blue Raincoat* (1986). *Chelsea Hotel*, Cohen now admits, was written for Janis Joplin. More recent releases include *I'm Your Man* in 1988 and *The Future* in 1992. A poet of some distinction, his book *Beautiful Losers* is considered excellent.

Morris Cohen was born in the East End of London, often the sanctuary of East European Jews, when they first arrived in Britain. Cohen attended the Jews' Free School, but at 10 years of age was sent to a Borstal establishment for thieving and being out of control. By the time he was released Cohen was a teenager, for whom Borstal had done nothing save make him tough and shrewd. His long-suffering parents thought it would be best all round if he went off to Canada. Morris genuinely tried going straight. He ranched in Saskatchewan but found it boring. He became an expert shot and took to wearing a revolver, especially when he went gambling in one of the many saloons. On one occasion he shot two cowboys who called him a dirty Jew. Then, like so many Jews who have failed in their original work, he thought he would try his hand at property. He looked around and settled in Edmonton, Alberta. Here he discovered the Chinese were being ripped off by the whites. Cohen befriended the Chinese, learnt their language and handled their property deals. He made a fortune, the Chinese made a fortune and Cohen was their hero. In 1910 Sun Yet Sen, the Chinese revolutionary leader, came to Canada to enlist support for his Kuomintang party. The two men met and got on well with each other, and Cohen accompanied Sun on his Canadian lecture tour as his bodyguard. In 1914, on the outbreak of the First World War, Cohen enlisted in the Irish Guards. He was put in command of the Chinese Labour Battalions who built the trenches in France and suffered high casualties.

The war over, Cohen joined Sun in Peking and was given command of the Presidential Bodyguard. He now became known as 'Two Gun Cohen' on account of the brace of pistols he always wore. The weapons were essential, as on several occasions he used them to save Sun Yet Sen from assassination. Sun then entrusted Cohen with the intricate job of buying arms and recruiting officers for his army, as well as setting up an international banking system. When in 1925 Sun died, Chiang Kai-Shek succeeded him and Morris Cohen was promoted to general. He was given the task of equipping, training and organizing a modern army. It was due to Cohen's dedication that the Japanese invasion of the 1930s was not the easy task Too, the Japanese War Minister, said it would be. The Japanese hated General Cohen and when they captured him in Hong Kong in 1941 they treated him quite brutally. He was sentenced to be shot, only to be reprieved at the last minute. Following the Second World War and the civil war in China, Chiang was ruling in Taiwan and Mao Tse-tung on the mainland. Cohen tried to bring the two together but eventually admitted failure and returned to England. He died peacefully in bed in his Manchester home after a full, dangerous and eventful life. He always claimed that he loved the Chinese people because they alone had never persecuted the Jews. During 1995, a memorial to the members of the Chinese Labour Battalions who died during the First World War was dedicated; some eighty years on.

COHEN, Morris (1887-1970) Chinese Army General

Cohen was born in Brooklyn, New York, on November 17th 1922. He was educated at Brooklyn College, where in 1943 he received a BA, then at the University of Michigan, from where he obtained a PhD in 1948. He joined up with Levi-Montalcini (*qv*) at Washington University, St Louis in 1952 as a researcher. He

COHEN, Stanley (1922-) US biochemist

worked on the nerve growth factor and went on to discover a cell within this factor, which he termed epidermal growth factor (EGF). Later it was shown that EGF influences a range of developmental events in the body. He also discovered the mechanisms by which EGF is taken into and acts upon individual cells. In 1967 he was appointed professor of biochemistry at Vanderbilt University, Nashville, Tennessee. In 1986 he shared the Nobel Prize for Physiology or Medicine with Rita Levi-Montalcini.

COHN,
Edwin
(1892-1953)
US biochemist

Cohn, was born in New York on December 17th 1892. He received his PhD from the University of Chicago in 1917, and chose a career in research. In 1935 he was appointed professor of biological chemistry at Harvard University, becoming head of the department three years later. His area of research was the chemistry of liver, plasma and tissue proteins. He developed a method, which later became known as 'Cohn Fraction', by which liver extract could be produced that was active against pernicious anaemia. Edwin Cohn wrote extensively concerning the chemical process of amino acids, proteins and phospholipids as well as the separation of gamma-globulin. His discovery of a new method for the production of blood plasma was most important, coming as it did just prior to the Second World War. During the war he introduced serum albumin, gamma globulin and fibrin and oversaw satisfactory production on behalf of the US Navy. Following the war the result of Cohn's work was of benefit world-wide. His major books were *Proteins, Amino Acids and Peptides as Ions and Dipoler Ions* (1943) and *Research in the Medical Sciences* (1946). For his work Cohn received many awards from numerous foreign governments and in 1948 was awarded the Medal of Merit from the US government. He died in Boston on October 1st 1953.

COHN,
Harry
(1891-1958)
US film pioneer

Cohn, born in New York on July 23rd 1891, came to the world of films after a series of unlinked jobs. These ranged from vaudeville performer to a fur salesman, taking in on the way song plugger, streetcar conductor and secretary. In 1918 he joined his brother Jack in Hollywood and they, together with Joe Brandt, formed their own motion picture company. It was called CBS but in 1924 it changed its name to Columbia Pictures. Later, following a boardroom row with his brother and Brandt's resignation, Harry was left in complete charge. A ruthless man, he had a certain flair which resulted in Columbia becoming Hollywood's most profitable studio. Cohn had the ability to recognize talent and exploit it to his advantage. During the 1930s, thanks mostly to Frank Capra's efforts, numerous Oscars came Columbia's way, and films such as *It Happened One Night* (1934), *Mr Deeds Goes to Town* (1936) and *Mr Smith Goes to Washington* (1939) were box-office hits. Cohn's personality was rude and rough, attracting the sobriquet 'white fang' from writer Ben Hecht. No aspect of film production was safe from Cohn's incursions. He told Bogart, 'he had no talent for films and do something else'. The fact that he admired Mussolini explains a lot. But he produced hits for Columbia and hits meant profits. *The Jolson Story*, *From Here To Eternity*, *The Bridge On The River Kwai* and *On The Waterfront* are examples of the films he authorized. When he died in Phoenix,

Arizona, in 1958, a friend of Ben Hecht expressed his surprise at the size of the funeral crowd. Hecht replied: 'They want to be sure he's dead.'

'Danny the Red' was how the world knew him during the 1960s student riots in Paris. He was born in France of German-Jewish refugee parents. The French Communist Party found him an embarrassment and their newspaper, *L'Humanité*, called him a 'German anarchist'. The French students, however, adored him, and claimed 'We are all German Jews'. Influenced by socialist and anarchist policies, he was anti-Stalin. The aims of the group he led, called 'Group 22', unified the left wing, in French politics. The riots started with the refusal of the education authorities to widen the educational sphere and drop outdated traditional practices, but then embraced wider issues . Cohn-Bendit, with his flaming red hair and explosive personality, was an exciting figure who spoke three languages fluently and gave television interviews. Following the students' failure to achieve their aims, Daniel lived for a while in London. He later went to live in Frankfurt where he has played a leading role in the Green Party and runs a current affairs magazine entitled *Pflaster-strand*.

For a brief time in French history, Cohn-Bendit brought together the workers and the students in a common cause and against the policies of the middle-right government of de Gaulle. They nearly brought down the French government and the world held its breath.

Joan was born in London on May 23rd 1933, the daughter of a Jewish businessman. Following a general education she was admitted to the Royal Academy of Dramatic Art in London. She showed some acting talent, but relied on sultry appeal to see her through her early films. Although she has appeared in numerous films she achieved world fame for her creation of Alexis Carrington in the television soap, *Dynasty*, a role she played with extreme authority. Joan Collins, a glamourous lady who attracts great media attention wherever she goes, gives enormous encouragement to older women on the basis of 'well, if she can so can I'. Unfortunately, very few can. She has married four times, the best-known of her husbands being Anthony Newley, whom she wed in 1963. At that time she described Newley as 'a half-Jewish cockney git' and herself as 'a half Jewish princess from Bayswater via Sunset Boulevard'. In the early 1980s Joan was broke. She took a pragmatic view and quit Hollywood for home. She worked in British repertory theatre and survived. She was thinking of a career change when the part of Alexis Carrington was offered by Aaron Spelling and Joan Collins became a household name. In 1996 she published the latest edition of her autobiography, *Second Act*. In the 1997 New Years Honours list Joan Collins was awarded the OBE.

COMDEN,
Betty
(1919-)
and
GREEN,
Adolph
(1915-)
US writers

Betty Comden, née Cohen, was born on May 3rd 1919 in Brooklyn, New York. **Adolph Green** was born in the Bronx, New York, on December 2nd 1915. They came together in 1938, having met while haunting the offices of theatrical agents.. A bohemian night club in Greenwich Village, The Village Vanguard, was the venue for a hastily formed group that included Comden, Green, Judy Tuvim, Alvin Hammer and John Frank. Their revue was a great success and engagements followed. Judy Tuvim became Judy Holliday (*qv*). In 1944 Comden and Green wrote *On The Town* with music by Leonard Bernstein (*qv*) and choreography by Jerome Robbins (*qv*). It later became a very popular film, reckoned to be one of the best musicals to come out of Hollywood. For many of their future musicals they wrote the story and the lyrics and Jule Styne (*qv*) wrote the music. This highly successful collaboration produced *Two on the Aisle* (1951), *Peter Pan* (1954), *Bells Are Ringing* (1956 and a hit film in 1960), *Say, Darling* (1958), *Fade Out, Fade In* (1964) and *Lorelei* (1974). In 1953 Comden and Green wrote another musical with Bernstein, *Wonderful Town* . It won them their first Tony awards. They wrote several film scripts, including *Singin' in the Rain* in 1952, voted by The American Film Institute the best film musical of all time. They also wrote many popular songs including 'Just in Time' and 'The Party's Over'. In 1980 Comden and Green entered the Songwriters' Hall of Fame.

COPELAND,
Lillian
(1905-64)
US world
athletic
champion

Lillian Copeland was born on November 25th 1905 in New York City and grew up to become one of the world's greatest female athletes. In the 1928 Olympic Games, the first that allowed women to compete in track and field events, she won a silver medal in the discus and threw 37.08 metres. In the 1932 Olympics, she won a gold medal and threw 40.58 metres, achieving a new world record. She was at Southern California University where she won every track and field event she entered. She won the National US Championships nine consecutive times, beginning in 1925. In 1926 she won three national and world titles for shotput, javelin and discus and held the world record. She was part of the 1935 US team that entered the Maccabiah Games and won four gold medals. Selected for the 1936 Berlin Olympic Games in Berlin, Lillian Copeland refused to compete. Later in life she became a teacher. She died in New York in July 1964.

COPLAND,
Aaron
(1900-90)
US composer

Copland was born in Brooklyn, New York, on November 14th 1990 to Russian Jewish immigrants, and was educated at local public schools. His elder sister taught him to play the piano and encouraged his musical ambitions. After an attempt to learn harmony via a correspondence course, he took the more established route. Copland's father sought out Rubin Goldmark, who had taught George Gershwin (*qv*), to teach Aaron. Copland found Goldmark too inflexible and scrimped to save enough money to go to Paris. In Paris he studied under Nadia Boulanger, who would later be the soloist when Copland's Organ Symphony was included by Serge Koussevitsky in the Boston Symphony Orchestra's programme. In 1924 he returned to the US to receive a Guggenheim Fellowship. He won much acclaim for his American-inspired compositions, especially those that featured in his ballets: *Billy* the Kid (1938), *Lincoln Portrait* (1942) and *Appalachian Spring* (1944). His involvement with music was total and included active association with many musical societies. He was president of the American Composers' Alliance (1937-45) and involved with the founding of the Berkshire Music Centre at Tanglewood in 1940. He taught music at Harvard and was the first composer to deliver the Norton Lectures. He was often invited as the guest conductor of great orchestras, especially to conduct his own works. Besides writing numerous film scores, he wrote books on music designed for mass appeal. *What to Listen For in Music* (1957) was a best-seller. Koussevitsky once declared of Copland: 'He is the leader to whom young composers bring their compositions.' Copland made no secret of his left-wing views, especially at the time of the McCarthy hearings. This did not appear to do him any harm, as the later award by the American government of the Medal of Freedom showed. Copland had a special relationship with Leonard Bernstein; it is said they were lovers. Both men died in 1990, Copland in North Tarrytown, New York, on December 2nd.

Courant, born in Lublinitz, Germany, on January 8th 1888, studied at Breslau, Zurich and Göttingen, from where, in 1910, he received his doctorate. His work was disrupted during the First World War while he served in the German army. In 1920 he became professor of mathematics at Göttingen, but he was sacked by the Nazis following the burning of his books in 1933. He went to England and taught at Cambridge University before deciding to settle in the US. There he became head of the mathematics department of New York University, a post he held until his retirement in 1958. Between 1953 and 1962 he wrote *Methods of Mathematical Physics*, a work that advanced the subject of quantum mechanics. He developed methods of applying the theories of quantum mechanics to the problems of physics and he is credited with having paved the way for the practical use of electronic computers. During the Second World War, Courant was part of a team of scientific scholars working on military projects. In his honour, New York University established the Richard Courant Lecture. Speaking of Courant at the time of the lecture's inauguration, Niels Bohr, the Swedish Nobel Prize winner, said: 'every physicist is in his debt for the vast insight he has given us into mathematics methods for comprehending nature and the physical world'. In 1941, together with H. Robbins, Courant co-wrote *What is Mathematics?*, an attempt to explain a complex subject to lay people. Courant died in La Rochelle, New York, on January 27th 1972.

COURANT, Richard (1888-1972) German/ American mathematician

Born in Union Hill, New Jersey, on June 24th 1912 to middle-class Jewish parents, **Cousins** studied at Columbia University's Teachers College and then became managing editor of *Current History* before joining the *Saturday Review* in 1940. He was their editor from 1940 to 1971 and again from 1973 to 1977 He expanded the journal's area of intellectual interest and encouraged readers' interest in such events as world government and a ban on nuclear tests. He boosted its circulation from 20,000 to 660,000. Cousins spent much time on lecture tours and was on the board of *Encyclopaedia Britannica*. He wrote several books including *Modern Man is Obsolete* (1945) and his autobiography, *Present Tense* (1968). A victim of

COUSINS, Norman (1912-90) US editor

cancer and heart disease, he bravely chronicled the events in, *Anatomy of an Illness* (1980), *The Healing Heart* (1983) and *The Pathology of Power* (1987). He died in Los Angeles on November 30th 1990.

COWEN,
Sir Zelman
(1919-)
Australian
lawyer and
administrator

Cowen, born in St Kilda, Victoria, on October 7th 1919, joined the Royal Australian Navy and served throughout the Second World War before going to Oxford University to study law. In 1947 he was a Fellow of Oriel College; he returned there as Provost in 1982, remaining until 1990. In between, he was Dean of the Law Faculty at Melbourne University from 1951, becoming emeritus professor in 1967. In 1977 he was appointed Governor-General of the Commonwealth of Australia. It was a difficult time in relations between the UK and Australia following the constitutional row involving Sir John Kerr, the previous Governor, and Gough Whitlam, the then Prime Minister. Cowen began the healing process and succeeded in re-establishing the warm relationship that had previously existed by the time he left office in 1982. Cowen was knighted for his efforts. In 1991 he was appointed Chairman of the Press Council. Cowen wrote an authoritative biography in 1967 on the life of Sir Isaac Isaacs, Governor-General of Australia from 1931 to 1936.

CRANKO,
John
(1927-73)
South African
choreographer

Cranko was born in Rustenburg, South Africa, on August 15th 1927 to a well-known Jewish family. His father, Herbert, hoped John would follow him and become a lawyer. John's heart, however, was set in the world of dance and while at Cape Town University he joined the Ballet Club. His first production there was *A Soldier's Tale* (1942). At nineteen he was at Sadlers Wells Theatre Ballet in London; he stayed for fifteen years. From 1950 he was resident choreographer and responsible for such radical productions as *Pineapple Poll* (1951) and *Prince of the Pagodas*, with music by Benjamin Britten (1957). He also wrote the critically acclaimed *Cranks* (1955). In 1961 he went to Germany as artistic director of the Stuttgart Ballet. Cranko is responsible for turning an average provincial company into a sought-after international force. He was a master at giving drama and an extra physical dimension to classical works. His production of *Romeo and Juliet* (1959) placed him among the greatest choreographers of the century. During the 1960s he toured the Soviet Union with the Stuttgart Ballet. In Moscow his production of *The Taming of the Shrew* took the home of ballet by storm. The applause lasted for 20 minutes. In 1973, while returning from New York with the Bavarian State Opera Ballet, following a successful tour of the US, Cranko collapsed and died as his flight was landing in Dublin. It was June 26th 1973.

CREMIEUX,
Benjamin
(1888-1944)
French writer

Cremieux was born in Narbonne, France. The family originated in the Midi, and was one of the oldest Jewish families in France. During the First World War, while serving in the French army, Cremieux was wounded three times. Following the war, he became a recognized authority on Italian literature and an expert on the works of Pirandello, which he translated into French. Cremieux's best known works are *Le Vingtième Siecle* (1924) and *Inventaires: Inquietude et Reconstruction* (1931). For some years he was secretary of the French PEN club. He only wrote one novel, *Le Premier de la Classe* (1921). It tells the story of young Blum, son of a Jewish tailor, who maintains his ancestral allegiances. Following the collapse of France in 1940 Cremieux joined the Resistance, becoming a leader of the Maquis. In 1944 he was betrayed, captured by the Germans and summarily executed by a firing squad.

Crohn was born and educated in New York City. His major contribution to 20th century medicine was the description he gave in 1932 of the disease regional ileitis and granulomatous colitis. It has since become known as Crohn's Disease of the Colon. He wrote extensively for the lay person, notably *Affections of the Stomach* (1927) and *Understand Your Ulcer* (1943).

Crystal was born on March 14th 1947 at Long Beach, New York, and educated at Marshall University. He then went on to the Theatre College, part of New York University. An open, fresh-faced personality, he is multi-talented. He has followed the well-tried formula: the comedy circuit as a stand-up comedian, captivation of the 'borscht belt' with his Jewish and secular humour. Television gave him his first big break. He played a homosexual in the sit-com, *Soap* (1977-81). To the world at large he is best known as a film actor, although his movie career nearly went horribly wrong. His film debut was in *Rabbit Test* (1978), playing the part of the world's first pregnant man. It was a complete flop, berated by the critics who described it at best as 'dreary, tasteless, stupid'. Crystal returned to being a stand-up comedian. It was nearly ten years before he returned to Hollywood to make a film: this was *Throw Momma From The Train* (1987), in which he starred opposite Danny De Vito. Crystal could now call himself a film actor. He and the film were well received. A year later, Crystal became a star with the box-office success of *When Harry Met Sally*, and Crystal was in demand. *City Slickers* (1991) won a Best Supporting Actor Oscar for Jack Palance and plaudits for Billy Crystal. In 1995, *Forget Paris* was one of the 'feelgood' films of the decade; and 1996 saw the release of *Mr Saturday Night*, a brilliant autobiographical film which he wrote, produced, directed and starred in. The title is drawn from his experience in the television show *Saturday Night Live* as a stand-up comedian. In 1997 he appeared as the first grave-digger in Kenneth Branagh's film of *Hamlet* and earned critical appreciation of his acting.

Cukor was born in New York on July 7th 1899 and started his career in the theatre world of Broadway. After becoming a leading stage director he turned his attentions to Hollywood. He made his film debut with *Grumpy* (1930), but although this was originally a Broadway hit it did not transfer well to the screen. Notwithstanding, Cukor was on his way. He appears to have had a natural affinity with women players. He knew how to direct them in order to get the maximum reaction possible and the actresses responded well. Katherine Hepburn is a good example. Cukor first directed her in 1933 in *Little Women* and received an Oscar nomination for the result. Over a 50 year period Cukor directed some 50 films and there is ample evidence that his female characters are shown as strong and intelligent.

The 1930s was a particularly good period. Besides *Little Women* there was *David Copperfield* (1935) and *Camille* (1937). At the end of the decade he was named as director of *Gone With The Wind* - and in 1940 he was fired. It was said Clark Gable feared that Cukor's ability with actresses would show him up. So instead, in 1940, Cukor directed Hepburn in *The Philadelphia Story* and, in 1949, Hepburn and Spencer Tracy in *Adam's Rib*. The 1950s kicked off with Judy Holiday in, *Born Yesterday*, followed by Judy Garland in *A Star Is Born* (1954). In the 1960s he made *My Fair Lady* (1964), which earned Cukor his first Oscar. During the 1970s, *Travels With My Aunt* (1972), adapted from Grahame Greene's novel, was not well received. Cukor, by now into his 70s, had slowed down, but his record speaks for itself. In 1981, aged 82, he directed his last film: *Rich and Famous*. It would be part of the Hollywood legend if this film had been a winner. It wasn't, but Cukor undoubtedly was.

**CURTIS,
Tony
(1925-)
US actor**

Born Bernard Schwartz on New York's Lower East Side on June 3rd 1925, after a teenage spell of running wild he served in the US Navy during the Second World War. The war over, he joined the Drama Workshop of the New York School for Social Research. He learnt his trade in a small theatre off 'off' Broadway and gradually worked his way into the centre, reaching off Broadway before getting the call to Hollywood. He pottered along at Universal for many years before his appearance in *Sweet Smell of Success* (1957), in which he played opposite Burt Lancaster as a crawling press agent, gave him the lift his career needed to take off. *The Defiant Ones* (1958) directed by Stanley Kramer (*qv*), won him an Academy nomination for Best Actor. The memory of his impersonation of Cary Grant in *Some Like It Hot* (1959) lives on today. He has starred in over a hundred films from the worst to the best. In his later years he has won a reputation as a useful painter. In 1995, Curtis was awarded the French Chevalier Order of Arts and Letters, in recognition of his work as an actor and painter. His first wife of several was the brilliant actress Janet Leigh; their daughter is the star actress, Jamie Lee Curtis, now married to an English peer and known as Lady Haden-Guest. Curtis has five other children. In 1993, at the age of 67, Curtis married Lisa Deutsch, a US lawyer, his fourth wife and 37 years his junior.

D

Sheila van Damm, born in London on January 17th 1922, was in every way a larger than life character. The youngest daughter of Vivian van Damm, the boss of London's famed Windmill Theatre, she had a minimal education that ended when the Second World War broke out. She joined the Women's Auxiliary Air Force (WAAF) as a driver, then transferred to the Voluntary Reserve and trained as a pilot, after which she spent the remainder of the war ferrying new aircraft from the factory to the airfield. After the war her father, as a PR exercise, encouraged Sheila to enter for a car rally as part of the Rootes team. She came third. Having been reluctant at the outset, she was now hooked. She went on to win some of the most prestigious events open to women in the world of motor rallying, including the Coupe des Alpes and Alpine Rally (1953-4), the Great American Road Rally (1953), the Women's European Touring Championship (1954) and the Coupe des Dames in the Monte Carlo Rally of 1956. In the same year she won the toughest event of all, the Mille Miglia. Sheila van Damm retired as the most successful woman rally driver of her time and a great example to those she inspired. She took over the management of the Windmill Theatre, following the sudden death of her father. Her biography, published in 1957, was entitled *No Excuses*. Sheila, a friendly, jovial personality, was considered an early example to women of what they might achieve if they tried. She died at her home in Sussex on August 23rd 1987.

DAMM, Sheila van (1922-87) British rally driver

Walter Damrosch was born in Breslaw, Germany, on January 30th 1862. By the turn of the century he was living in the US and reorganizing the New York Symphony Society. He was its conductor until 1927, when it combined with the Philharmonic. He was an enthusiast of the Romantic composers and he presented the first American performance of many works by Brahms and Tchaikovsky. Between 1928 and 1942 he pioneered concerts on radio and gave musical lectures and appreciation talks over the airwaves. He gained particular renown as the conductor of the New York Metropolitan Opera. As a composer, Damrosch wrote several operas including the famed *The Scarlet Letter*. At Fontainebleau in France, following the First World War, he founded the American Conservatory. He died in New York on December 22nd 1950.

DAMROSCH, Walter (1862-1950) German/ American conductor

Yuli, the famous son of a famous father, M. Daniel (1897-1944), who fought in the Russian Revolution and wrote Yiddish plays in the days when the Yiddish Theatre flourished, was born in Kharkov and joined the Red Army on his eighteenth birthday. Badly wounded during the Second World War, in 1946 he was admitted to Kharkov University and graduated as a teacher in 1951. Years before he became a household name in the USSR he had an international reputation under the pseudonym of Nikolai Arzhak. His manuscripts were smuggled out and during the early 1960s were published in the West. *This is Moscow Speaking and Other Stories* appeared in English in 1962. In 1966 he and others featured in a Moscow trial that received worldwide attention. It resulted in Daniel being imprisoned for five years. He had been convicted of slandering Soviet society, by his accusation that anti-Semitism was rife in the USSR. On his release in 1970 he was refused permission to live in Moscow, being allowed no nearer than 90 miles from the capital. However, the ban was waived when he needed to go to Moscow for medical treatment, and he died there in hospital on December 30th 1988.

Dassault was born Marcel Bloch in Paris on January 22nd 1892. His father was a Jewish doctor. Of his two brothers, to whom he was very close, one would become a French army general and Governor of Paris while the other, a famous surgeon, would die in the Holocaust. As a small child Marcel was fascinated by flying and after seeing one of the Wright Brothers in flight was inspired to follow a career in aeronautics. He graduated from the Ecole Nationale Supérieure de L'Aeronautique in 1913. During the First World War he concentrated on designing propellers, one of which, 'The Guynemer', is commemorated in a monument in the Place des Invalides. He was largely responsible for the successful French fighter plane, SEA4, that appeared during the latter part of the war. Following the First World War, orders for aircraft failed to materialize and Dassault turned to building houses. In 1930 the French government realized that its aircraft industry was lagging behind the rest of Europe. The Air Ministry ordered a new three-engined type of aeroplane for the postal service, and Dassault was back in the aircraft business. Air France started operating in 1938 with a two-engined aeroplane Dassault built in metal. During the Second World War, following the fall of France, Dassault, as a Jew, was sent to Buchenwald concentration camp. A large secret bribe, sent by a group in Switzerland to Himmler in Germany, ensured that Dassault remained in Buchenwald and was not sent to a death camp. However, a few days prior to liberation he caught diphtheria. It took six months of intensive treatment to render him fit enough to return to work. Up to this time he had been known as Marcel Bloch; now he took the name Dassault. It had been his brother Darius' code-name while in the Resistance. The success of his new company was phenomenal. The Dassault 315 was considered excellent and 300 were built. The Mystère IV was the first European plane to break the sound barrier. The delta-winged fighter plane known as the Mirage was popular with air forces all over the world. Dassault also built passenger aircraft. All in all, the Dassault company helped France become a top exporting country and its founder became a very wealthy man. From 1951 to

1955, and again from 1957 to 1958, he was a deputy in the National Assembly. In 1986 he was elected yet again, but he died shortly thereafter in Paris, on April 18th 1986. When Dassault was liberated from Buchenwald, he was so ill he was included in the mercy flight to an army hospital. It was the only time he ever flew.

Born in Middletown, Connecticut, on December 18th 1911, **Dassin** started his career as an actor in the Yiddish Theatre. After experiencing the secular theatre and radio, he went to Hollywood to learn his future trade of film director. Following *Brute Force* (1947) and *The Naked City* (1948) he was beginning to get a name for himself when he fell foul of the McCarthy witch-hunt and was blacklisted. It was a blessing in disguise. He moved to Europe where, in France in 1955, he directed and co-wrote *Rififi*. The film was critically acclaimed and a box-office success. Dassin followed this with *Never on a Sunday* (1959), featuring his Greek wife Melina Mercouri. Dassin produced it, directed it, wrote it and starred in it. The film won an Oscar for its title song and again Dassin had a hit on his hands. He then returned to the US to continue his career, but he was never able to match the success he experienced in Europe.

*DASSIN,
Jules
(1911-)
US film-maker*

David was born in Bombay, the son of a Bene Israel family. The author of some 100 plays, that cover all Indian languages, he aimed to bring to the masses a feel for the theatre. He was also the producer for the Parsi Imperial Theatre Company for 15 years. He was later able to reflect, with some satisfaction, how his efforts had raised the level of the Urdu-Hindu stage to international standards. In 1931 he wrote the screenplay for India's first feature length talking film, *Alam Ara*. The film was a success and laid the foundation for the world's largest film industry.

*David,
Joseph
(1876-1948)
Indian Writer*

Davidson was born on January 4th 1883 in New York's Lower East Side. Despite the poverty he experienced and the family's need for money, Jo refused to take a dead-end job and devoted himself to the pursuit of his ambitions. He studied at the Arts Students League in New York and the School of Fine Arts in New Haven. Jo decided that sculpture was the path for him and, following a short time at Yale, he began an apprenticeship with Herman MacNeil. He exhibited at the 1906 exhibition, held at the Art Students League, where he sold a statuette of *David*. He managed to acquire sufficient funds to get to Paris and the Ecole des Beaux Arts. Returning to the US, he rented a studio and started work. Among others, he sculpted US Presidents Woodrow Wilson, during the First World War, Roosevelt, during the Second World War, and Eisenhower, while he was in office. Many famous people sat for him including US General Pershing, French Marshall Foch, Albert Einstein, the Hindu poet Rabindranath Tagore, and Golda Meir. Davidson also sculpted some of the greatest writers of his time, including James Joyce, Arthur Conan Doyle and Arnold Bennett. Gertrude Stein would read her manuscripts to Davidson to keep herself awake while he worked on her. In 1940, having worked on it for fourteen years, he completed the bronze statue of the legendary Will Rogers, which now stands in the Statuary Hall of the Capitol Building in Washington DC. Following the

*DAVIDSON,
Jo
(1883-1952)
US sculptor*

Second World War, Davidson worked on creating memorials to the town of Lidice in Czechoslovakia, which was razed to the ground and its citizens murdered in reprisal for the execution of SS General Heydrich. Other works commemorated the Holocaust. Davidson's style was natural; he claimed it was the result of the rapport he created between himself and his subject. Mahatma Gandhi, upon seeing the bust of himself for the first time, declared, 'You make heroes out of mud.' Davidson's autobiography, *Between Sittings*, was published in 1951. He died on March 30th 1952.

DAYAN,
Moshe
(1915-81)
Israeli soldier
and politician

Dayan was born on May 20th 1915 in the Jezreel Valley, Palestine. His home was on the first kibbutz or co-operative farm and he was educated at a teachers' seminary. An early member of the Haganah, the illegal Jewish army, he was jailed along with others in 1939 by the British authorities for the illegal possession of arms. During the Second World War, as the German army approached Cairo, the British army planned to evict from Syria and Lebanon the pro-German Vichy French forces. In June 1941 Dayan and his comrades were released from Acre prison to form part of the raiding force. Acting as a scout, Dayan was shot by a sniper, lost an eye and gained a black patch. Following the creation of the State of Israel in 1948 and the war that followed, Dayan was in command of the forces that captured Lod and stopped the Egyptian attack on the southern front. In November 1953 he was appointed Chief of Staff and set about reorganizing the Israeli Defence Forces. He created special strike forces and strengthened paratroop units.

He was in command during the Suez War of 1956 and was responsible for the capture of Gaza and Sinai. Two years later he was out of the army and studying at the Hebrew University. In 1966 he wrote his Sinai memoirs, *Diary of the Sinai Campaign.* He entered politics in the Labour cause, was elected to serve in parliament in 1959 and never left. In 1967, Israel had a government of national unity. To this government Dayan was appointed Minister of Defence, despite opposition from Golda Meir and other Labour party veterans. Dayan provided the leadership his predecessor, Levi Eshkol, had lacked and was seen as the hero of the Six-Day War. He was a member of the government of Golda Meir (1969-74) and was blamed for the unpreparedness of Israeli forces at the time of the Yom Kippur War in 1973. Although he was exonerated by a commission of inquiry, somehow his image appeared stained. In 1977 he left the Labour party, on whose behalf he had been elected, and joined the Likud Prime Minister, Menachem Begin (*qv*), as Foreign Minister. Dayan played an essential part in the negotiations that led to the Israel-Egypt peace accords of 1978. He resigned from the Cabinet in 1979, having come to the conclusion that the Likud regime would never implement measures to create a Palestinian state. Dayan once said: 'Never ask permission. Do it, and then argue from a position of strength.' Dayan said in an interview with US envoy Cyrus Vance, quoted in *The Observer* on August 14th 1977: 'Whenever you accept our views, we shall be in full agreement with you.' He published his autobiography, *The Story of My Life*, in 1976. Dayan, a larger than life character, died in Tel Aviv on October 16th, 1981.

Day-Lewis's mother is actress Jill Balcon, daughter of Sir Michael Balcon (*qv*) of Ealing Studios fame. Daniel, born in London on April 20th 1958, received his training at the Bristol Arts Centre and the Bristol Old Vic. He came to notice in *My Beautiful Launderette* (1985) and progressed rapidly to become a box office favourite, starring in *A Room With a View* (1986) and *My Left Foot* (1989), for which he won the Oscar for Best Actor. In 1992 he made *The Last of the Mohicans*. In this film, as in all his roles, Day-Lewis puts himself right into the mould of his character. The result is a highly believable performance. In November 1996, while filming Arthur Miller's *The Crucible,* Day-Lewis met, fell in love with and married Miller's daughter.

He was born Abram Moiseyevich Ioffe in Upyna, Russia on June 16th 1881. His family was described as petit bourgeois; they were also Jewish and Abram was often the recipient of anti-Jewish feeling. He joined Lenin's Bolshevik movement in 1903 while at the University of Bern, from where he graduated in 1908. Following the revolution, he was appointed to the Sverdlov University in 1921, where his theories concerning Marxist philosophy and materialism found much favour. He published books on the subject: *Lenin and the Crisis of Modern Physics* and *Philosophy and Marxism*, both published in 1930. However, during the Stalin regime he fell out of favour. He was accused of separating philosophy from practice and ejected from his educational posts. While waiting for Stalin to die he maintained himself and his family by working, in a low-key position, for the Academy of Sciences (1931-53). With Stalin dead he was able to publish further books: *Sociopolitical Doctrines of Modern Times* (1958) and *Philosophy and Politics* (1961). He died in Moscow on March 8th 1963.

Michel Debré was born in Paris on January 15th 1912, the grandson of a chief rabbi. His father was Professor Robert Debré, a leading children's specialist and President of the Medical Association in 1958. Michel was educated at the Faculté de Droit of the Sorbonne and later came first in the entrance exams for the French Civil Service. In 1938 he was working for Paul Reynaud, the Finance Minister, when he first came into contact with Charles de Gaulle. He joined the army in 1939 and was taken prisoner by the Germans. In 1941 he escaped to Morocco and joined the Free French Army. Soon after France was liberated, Debré was given the job of setting up the National School of Administration. The school was created with the aim of training a new breed of people who would eventually become the post-war governing elite of the civil service and replace those tainted by Vichy. In 1948, as a senator, he backed de Gaulle. In 1958 he was appointed Minister of Justice. While in this post he drafted the new constitution that became the basis for the Fifth Republic, a brilliant piece of work that took into account those who would come after de Gaulle. A year later, in January 1959, he was Prime Minister. He stayed at this post until 1962. Thereafter, at differing times, he held the ministerial posts of finance, foreign affairs and defence. In 1978 he was elected to the European Parliament. In 1981 Debré stood for the presidency; he polled 1 per cent of the vote. He remained in parliament until 1988 and between 1966 and 1989 was mayor of Ambroise. He died in Montlouis-sur-Loire on August 2nd 1996. He left a wife and four sons, two of whom have followed him into politics.

DE GRUNWALD Anatole (1910-67) Russian/British film-maker

De Grunwald was born in St.Petersburg, Russia, and came to the UK in the 1930s. His adaption of the play *French Without Tears* (1939) into a successful film was the start of his British film career. In 1942 he wrote *The First of the Few*, which told the story of R. J. Mitchell, designer of the Spitfire fighter plane. *The Way to the Stars* (1945), which he produced and co-wrote, is said to be the finest film made concerning the Second World War. *The Winslow Boy* (1946) was most successful, as was *Queen of Spades* (1948). *The VIPs* (1963), with Richard Burton and Elizabeth Taylor, was an international box office success that brought an Oscar for Best Supporting Actress to Dame Margaret Rutherford. De Grunwald followed this with *The Yellow Rolls Royce* (1965), another winner. The majority of De Grunwald's productions were written by Terence Rattigan. The understanding between the two men was outstanding and resulted in an excellent boost for British films.

DELAUNAY-TERK, Sonia (1885-1979) French painter

Sonia was born to Jewish parents in Russia. By the time she was 21 she was living and working in Paris. She married Wilhelm Uhde, the original dealer in Picasso's work, but the marriage was short-lived. In 1910 she married Robert Delaunay whose work was a mixture of cubism, abstraction and expressionism. Sonia was responsible for the advancement of orphism, a type of abstract painting in which colour is the principal method of expression. Paul Klee and Fernand Leger were keen exponents of this method. In the 1920s, Sonia designed fabrics which were hand-painted, and for which there was a great demand from the international couturiers. In the 1930s she returned to painting and was a member of the well-known Abstraction Creation Association, with a membership of some 400 artists. In 1978 an exhibition was held at the Musée d'Art Moderne de la Ville de Paris, that revived the work of the association. In 1964, the Louvre exhibited 58 of Sonia Delaunay-Terk's works, making her the first woman to be exhibited, during her lifetime, at the Louvre. She died in Paris in 1979.

DELVALLE, Max (1911-) Panamanian politician

Max Delvalle, born in Panama to Jewish parents, was involved in politics from his early teens. He was eventually elected to the National Assembly and in 1964 was vice-president of the Republic. In 1968 Delvalle was, for a brief time, President of Panama. Following a court ruling, Delvalle was replaced by the former President, causing a governmental crisis. In the general election that followed both men were ousted. Delvalle is credited with protecting and organizing the sugar workers who, together with immigrants and mestizo workers, are among the most disadvantaged groups in the country.

Deutsch was born in Vienna, Austria. His family had little interest in things Jewish and it was not until Felix was assailed by anti-Semitism, while at university, that being a Jew had any sort of influence upon his lifestyle. In his early twenties and now a doctor, Deutsch set up a clinic to deal with the problems attached to physical illness and, in particular, the emotions that ill-health engendered. As a result, Felix Deutsch became a pioneer, and later an expert, on psychosomatic medicine. As a result of the welcome the Austrians gave Hitler, in 1935 Deutsch moved to the safety of the US. At Harvard University he became a research fellow in Psychiatry. In the course of his considerable number of varied publications, Deutsch uses such phrases as 'associative anamnersic', 'sector psychotherapy' and 'posturology'. These expressions have since become part of the psychiatrist's vocabulary.

DEUTSCH, Felix (1884-1964) Austrian/ American psychiatrist

Deutscher was born in Cracow, Poland. As the son of an orthodox Jew he grew up in an atmosphere of Judaic learning. By the time Isaac was ten he was a child prodigy on the works of Talmud. His father sent him to the Hasidic rabbi of Gur in order he complete his studies. However, by the time Isaac reached his bar-mitzvah, he was asking questions to which he was not getting answers. A year later he was actively rebellious. On Yom Kippur he went to the cemetery and, standing by the grave of a rabbi, he ate a ham sandwich on buttered bread. After this there was no going back. He took to writing poetry and had some published. Thus encouraged, he went to Warsaw. He now rejected Judaism and embraced Marxism. In 1927 he was editor of the Communist publishing unit, but in 1932 he was expelled from the party for exaggerating the danger of Nazism and thus spreading panic. In 1939 he became London correspondent for a Polish-Jewish newspaper but the job vanished a few months later when the Germans invaded Poland. Forced to remain in England, he learnt English with the same dedication he had shown as a child. He joined the Polish army stationed in Scotland and served in it until 1942. He was then discharged for 'subversive activities' because he had protested about rampant anti-Semitism in the Free Polish Army. He went to work on the London *Observer* under the pseudonym, 'Peregrine'.

DEUTSCHER, Isaac (1907-67) Polish historian

Over a ten-year period (1954-63) he wrote a trilogy on Leon Trotsky. For this purpose he obtained special permission from Trotsky's widow to use Harvard University's Trotsky archives. These now remain closed until the year 2000. The Trotsky trilogy, *The Prophet Armed*, *The Prophet Unarmed* and *The Prophet Outcast*, is all-embracing and is considered the best work written on the man. Deutscher had an ambition to write the definitive biography on Lenin, but died on a visit to Rome before he could embark on the project. A year after his death his autobiography was published. It is called *The Non Jewish Jew*.

Neil Diamond was born in Brooklyn, New York, on January 24th 1941 and educated at Erasmus High School. At a summer school when Neil was sixteen, Pete Seeger performed and several children showed him the songs they had written. Diamond then and there had the notion he could write songs. He returned home, bought a guitar, took a course of lessons and started writing. His childhood was

DIAMOND, Neil (1941-) US singer/ songwriter

spent moving around, attending assorted schools and not making many friends. Writing music was his means of expressing himself. He received a fencing scholarship from New York University where his major was in biology and his minor in chemistry. He thought of becoming either a doctor or a music writer; fortunately for the world at large, music won. A series of jobs with music publishers followed and when nothing happened he rented a storage room above a night club in Manhattan, bought a cheap piano and took a year off to write songs. He wrote two hits for The Monkees, 'I'm a Believer' (1966) and 'A Little Bit Me, A Little Bit You' (1967). He later decided to sing as well as write; there followed a small success with 'Solitary Man' and then, with 'Cherry Cherry' a hit. His career now started to take off, and he achieved a string of hit singles that included, 'Girl, You'll Be a Woman Soon' and 'Sweet Caroline'. With 'Cracklin' Rose' Diamond had his first Number One hit, followed in July 1972 by 'Song Sung Blue'. 'He Ain't Heavy, He's My Brother' and further hits such as 'I Am, I Said' and the *Jonathon Livingstone Seagull* album kept him at the top. In a duet with Barbara Streisand (*qv*) he more than held his own in their Number One hit, 'You Don't Bring Me Flowers' (1978). At the Grammy Awards event that followed the presentation, the audience went wild when the duo entered the stage from opposite ends, singing their winning song. They hadn't expected it because Streisand dislikes singing in public, but Neil Diamond held them together. In 1980 he had the star role in the remake of *The Jazz Singer*. His 1982 album *Heartlight* was most successful, as was his world concert tour that resulted in 'sold out' notices at most venues. Later albums have included *Primitive* (1984) *Headed For the Future* (1986) and *Hot August Night* (1987). *Lovescope* followed in 1991 and *The Greatest Hits, 1966-1992* took the number one spot in the UK. A successful world tour in 1996 testifies to his enduring popularity.

DIETZ, Howard (1896-1983) US lyric writer

Howard Dietz was born in New York on September 9th 1896. He graduated from Columbia University in 1917 and joined an advertising agency. One of his first assignments was to devise a logo for MGM. His university mascot was a lion and this became his idea for the MGM roaring lion, whom he called Leo. Thereafter it has always been Leo who appears to introduce an MGM film. Dietz also suggested their motto: 'Art for Art's Sake' sounded better in Latin, as 'Ars Gratia Artis'. Dietz joined the MGM company as advertising and publicity director in 1919 and stayed for 40 years. In his spare time he wrote lyrics and was acknowledged as having written the words to over 500 songs. He collaborated with Arthur Schwartz from 1929 and they wrote several Broadway musical shows, including *Three's a Crowd* (1930), *The Band Wagon* (1931), *Revenge With Music* (1934) and *The Gay Life* (1961). However, his most acclaimed work was his translation of John Strauss's operetta *Die Fledermaus*. Dietz died in New York on July 20th 1983.

DOCTOROW, Edgar (1931-) US writer

Doctorow was born in New York City on January 6th 1931 and educated at Bronx High School of Science and Columbia University. Between 1960 and 1964 he was the editor of *The New American Library* and also held a number of teaching posts. His first novel, *Welcome to Hard Times*, was published in 1961 and in 1966 he wrote *Big as Life*. *The Book of Daniel* (1971) is based on the story of the executed Rosenbergs (*qv*). It was, however, *Ragtime* (1975), which blends fact and fiction in American life prior to the First World War, that shot Doctorow on to the international scene, especially after it was filmed in 1981. He wrote *Loon Lake* in 1980 and *Billy Bathgate* in 1989, and *Waterworks* was published in 1994.

Dorati was born to Jewish parents on April 9th 1906 in Budapest, Hungary. By the age of fourteen he was at the Royal Academy of Music, studying piano. Four years later he graduated, and at eighteen was appointed the conductor of the Budapest Royal Opera House. In 1932 he was became musical director to the Ballet Russe in Monte Carlo. He and they toured internationally until 1940, when the Second World War put a hold on ballet performances in Europe. Dorati now made his home in the US. Between 1941 and 1945 he was the music director of the American Ballet Theatre. In 1947 he acquired US citizenship. He was to conduct first the Dallas Symphony Orchestra, then the Minneapolis Symphony Orchestra in a relationship that ran from 1949 to 1960. Together they made many distinguished recordings that received critical acclaim. This success led Dorati being offered the post of chief conductor to the BBC Symphony Orchestra, where he remained until 1966. For some time he lived and worked in Sweden, and between 1966 and 1970 he conducted the Stockholm Philharmonic. He then returned to the US and the National Symphony Orchestra in Washington DC. Dorati was a specialist in the works of Bartok and Stravinsky and did much to promote performance of their work. In 1973 Dorati completed the Herculean task of recording all 107 Haydn symphonies. Some had never before been performed. In 1979 he published his autobiography, *Notes of Seven Decades*. He retired the following year to Gerzenssee, Switzerland, where he died on November 13th 1988.

DORATI, Antal (1906-88) Hungarian/ American conductor

Kirk Douglas was born Issur Danielovitch in Amsterdam, New York, on December 9th 1916. His father was a tough, hard-drinking ragman. Douglas has described Amsterdam as a WASP town and himself as a nobody, meaning the son of an illiterate Russian Jewish immigrant who had a son, six daughters and a wife to feed. Following a basic education Douglas, now using the name Izzy Demsky, enrolled at St Lawrence University in Canton. At college he became educated and a wrestling champion. A love of theatre, and an urgent need to act, now drove him. Good enough to be accepted by the American Academy of Dramatic Arts, he worked as a waiter to help pay for his tuition. Following the attack on Pearl Harbor on December 7th 1941, Douglas volunteered for the air force as a pilot but was considered too old at 25. The medical also revealed that his eyesight was not good enough to be a pilot. He returned to the theatre, exercised his eyes, and joined the navy. After midshipman school he served as an naval officer until the end of the war.

In a small theatre off Broadway Hal Wallis, a Hollywood film producer, saw Douglas in the play *Wind is Ninety*. Much impressed, Wallis chose Douglas to star opposite Barbara Stanwyck in *The Strange Love of Martha Ives* (1946). The film was well received and Kirk Douglas was on his way. Following *Champion* (1949),

DOUGLAS, Kirk (1916-) US actor

Douglas became a star and termed 'bankable'. He and Burt Lancaster are considered to have been the top Hollywood stars of the post-war era. *Young Man With a Horn* (1950), *Detective Story* (1951), *Ace in the Hole* (1951), *The Bad and the Beautiful* (1953), *Lust for Life* (1956) and *Paths of Glory* (1957) were all films that made the name Kirk Douglas known throughout the world. In 1960 he decided to become a player/producer. With *Spartacus* he announced that Dalto Trumbo would script the film. Trumbo was still on the McCarthy blacklist but Douglas didn't care; so far as Douglas was concerned the witch-hunt was over. He has made some 70 films. A top star and an excellent actor, he has been nominated three times for an Academy Award as Best Actor; but the Oscar still eludes him. In 1963 he returned to the stage in *One Flew Over the Cuckoo's Nest*. It was later turned into a major film by his son Michael and it was a great disappointment to Kirk that he wasn't given the role of McMurphy. It went to Jack Nicholson, 21 years his junior, and Nicholson won the Oscar for Best Actor. Kirk Douglas has also been a successful writer of novels, and his autobiography, *The Ragman's Son*, has become a best-seller.

DOUGLAS, Melvin (1901-81) US actor

Matinee idol **Melvin Douglas** was born Edouard Hesselberg in Macon, Georgia, on April 5th 1901. Tall, suave and sophisticated, he was the ideal leading man. In 1931 he made his film debut with *Tonight or Never*. It was the first in a string of great performances. His film career encompassed five decades and over 100 films. His first Oscar came in 1963: the award for Best Supporting Actor in *Hud*. In 1970 he received an Academy Award nomination for Best Actor for his role in *I Never Sang For My Father*. In 1979 he once again won the Best Supporting Actor Oscar for *Being There*. Douglas enjoyed a great career and was well regarded by his contemporaries. However, because his father was a Jew Hitler banned his films from being shown. Douglas's answer was to enlist in the US army. He was 40 years old at the time. In June 1981 he was filming in Los Angeles when he died suddenly.

DOUGLAS, Michael (1944-) US actor

Michael, son of Kirk, was born in New Brunswick, New Jersey, on September 25th 1944. Having graduated from the University of California, he enrolled at a series of acting schools, followed by a spell in theatre. In the 1960s he worked as an assistant director on several of his father's films. It was however, the television series *Streets of San Francisco* (1972-77) that taught him to become a first-class actor and excellent producer. His production debut was *One Flew Over The Cuckoo's Nest*: It took five Oscars including Best Picture. Nowadays the public know him for his acting, although in *The China Syndrome* (1979), *Romancing the Stone* (1984) and *Jewel of the Nile* (1985) he produced as well. Other successful films include *Fatal Attraction* (1987), *War of the Roses* (1989), *Basic Instinct* (1992) and *The American President* (1995). In 1987 he won the Oscar for Best Actor in *Wall Street*. His role interpretations have deservedly brought him much international fame and continue to do so. The ragman's grandson, like the son, has achieved a great deal.

Dovator was born in Moscow. Following university he became a teacher at a Jewish school. In the mid-1920s he joined the Red Army and in 1929 was commissioned into the Cossack cavalry. In the late 1930s, he was seconded to the Army Command School. In early 1941, during the Second World War, when the German army was advancing on Moscow, Dovator, now a major-general, was in command of a sector on the flank of the Moscow defence system. On December 19th 1941, Dovator led his Cossack cavalry in an attack on the Germans across the River Rusa. As he reached the further bank, Dovator was shot and died instantly. His troops successfully completed the mission. Dovator was posthumously awarded the title of Hero of the Soviet Union, the highest award for bravery possible. Following a hero's funeral he was buried in Moscow.

DOVATOR,
Lev
(1909-41)
Soviet general

Dressler was born in Vienna, and educated there. He qualified as a doctor of medicine and decided to specialize in cardiology. He was an early advocate of the use of electrocardiology in the early diagnosis of heart problems. As a Jew, he was forced to flee Austria when Hitler made it part of Greater Germany. He arrived in the US in 1938 and, until his retirement in 1967, was the head of the cardiology clinic at Maimonides Medical Centre. In 1942 he published *Clinical Cardiology*. This became the authoritative work and an aid in diagnosing cardiac illness. Dressler's international claim to fame, however, is that he diagnosed the problems associated with post-myocardial infarction syndrome. This later became known as, 'Dressler's Syndrome'.

DRESSLER,
William
(1890-1969)
Austrian/
American
physician

L'Affair **Dreyfus** continues to reverberate long after the personalities involved in the episode have died. Dreyfus was born in Mulhouse, Alsace, on October 19th 1859. This area came under German control following the Franco-Prussian war of 1870-71. Dreyfus senior, as an act of French patriotism, moved the family to Paris and Alfred was educated at the Ecole Polytechnique. He later joined the army as an engineer with the rank of lieutenant. He overcame anti-Jewish sentiment to gain promotion to captain and subsequently elevation to the general staff. What happened next has been well stated in books, articles, plays and films. Suffice it to say that Dreyfus was the victim of a plot that would blame him for the activities of others. As Dreyfus was a Jew, he was also an outsider and the tale against him would therefore be readily believed. The plot succeeded and Dreyfus was found guilty of treason. The public clamour against him, promoted by the antisemitic press, made any other verdict most unlikely. He was incarcerated on Devil's Island in South America for many years. At the end of the 19th century French society was split over the validity of the original verdict - until Emile Zola, the famous novelist, published what is probably the most famous letter to a newspaper ever written. His letter, entitled 'J'Accuse', printed in the newspaper *L'Aurore*, created an uproar. Zola was himself accused of impeaching the military authorities and sentenced to imprisonment. Instead he fled to South Norwood, a suburb of London. The authorities reviewed the case against Dreyfus and reduced his original sentence of life imprisonment to ten years. This didn't satisfy the liberal President of France, Emile

DREYFUS,
Alfred
(1859-1935)
French soldier

Loubert, who, outraged, a week later granted Dreyfus a pardon. It was, however, another seven years before Captain Dreyfus was finally acquitted by the court of appeal. In 1906 Dreyfus was reinstated in the army with the rank of major. A year later he resigned. However, on the outbreak of the First World War in August 1914 he rejoined the army on active duty. In 1916 he was promoted to lieutenant-colonel and awarded the Legion of Honour.

The Dreyfus Affair had the most dramatic effect on French society and led directly to the separation of Church and State. The effects of the affair were not confined to France. Theodore Herzl, one of many moved by what had happened to Dreyfus because he was a Jew, advanced the cause of a need for a Jewish homeland. It was the beginning of political Zionism. It had cost the Dreyfus family a million francs to clear Alfred's name. He died in Paris on July 12th 1935. In 1995, 101 years later, the French Army authorities finally admitted they had been wrong.

**DREYFUSS,
Richard
(1947-)
US actor**

Dreyfuss was born in Brooklyn, New York, on October 29th 1947, and educated at San Fernando State College, California. His father, a lawyer, hoped his son would follow in his footsteps. However, Richard had been attracted by the theatre from the age of nine, while acting in the plays produced at the West Side Jewish Centre in Los Angeles. He was just sixteen when he started working professionally in the theatre. For ten years he performed both on and off Broadway before starting a film career. *American Graffiti* (1973) was a hit both critically and financially. It cost $750,000 to make and took $55 million at the world's box offices. The following year he starred in *The Apprenticeship of Duddy Kravitz*, and Dreyfus was on his way. Following *Jaws* (1975), *Close Encounters of the Third Kind* (1977) and *The Goodbye Girl* (1977), for which Dreyfus won the Oscar for Best Actor, he became established as a major star. He starred in several films during the 1980s and 1990s including *Down and Out in Beverly Hills* (1986), *The Tin Men* (1987), *Always* (1989) and *What About Bob?* (1991). Later in the 1990s, he achieved his ambition to direct a Shakespeare play, when he was given a free hand at Birmingham Theatre in the UK. In 1996 he starred in *Mr Holland's Opus*, a 'feelgood' type of film: not one for the critics but the box-office was happy. An old-fashioned liberal, he has during his career known many ups and downs, both in his work and in his private life. In an interview he once said, 'Regrets? Oh yes, I regret things. There are certain experiences in life it is simply better not to have.'

**DRUCKER,
Peter
(1909-)
Austrian/
American
educator**

Drucker was born in Vienna on November 19th 1909 and received a law degree from the University of Frankfurt. He worked as a journalist until in 1933 he experienced sufficient anti-Semitism to convince him that emigrating was a good idea. He chose the US and became an adviser to British banks doing business in the States as well as financial correspondent to several European newspapers. He became a naturalized citizen and professor of management at New York University from 1950 to 1972. He wrote much, and his books echo the progress of a 20th century phenomenon. In 1939 he wrote *The End of Economic Man* and in 1950 *The New Society*. These books reflect the type of industrial society existing between two world wars. *The Concept of the Corporation* (1946) and *The Practice of Management* (1954) propound ideas relevant to modern business management. *America's Next Twenty Years* (1957) and *Technology, Management and Society* (1970) focus on the results of technical development. His later books, *Managing in Turbulent Times* (1980) and *The Changing World of the Executive* (1982) deal with problems of corporate management. Drucker is now acknowledged as a world authority in the field of management education.

Dubinsky was born in Brest-Litovsk, Russia, on February 22nd 1892, the youngest of nine children. The family moved to Lodz in Poland, where David's father established a bakery in a small basement. David received elementary schooling until he was eleven, then went to work to learn the bakery trade. At the age of fourteen he was considered a master baker. David became involved with politics via the Bakers' Union, which was part of the General Jewish Workers Union. Following a successful strike for better wages the leaders of the union, including Dubinsky, who was now the union secretary, were arrested and imprisoned. It was the first of many arrests and eventually Dubinsky was ordered to be banished to Siberia. However, now aged nineteen, he escaped and eventually arrived in the US. There the trade union movement beckoned and before very long he was in the leadership of the International Ladies' Garment Workers' Union. In 1932 he became president of the now nearly bankrupt organization; by the time he resigned, in 1966 after 40 years service, it was flourishing and an example to the American trade union movement as a whole. He pioneered pensions, paid holidays and welfare. David Dubinsky was considered a driving force and a pragmatic arbitrator. He died in New York on September 17th 1982.

DUBINSKY, David (1892-1982) Russian/ American trade union leader

Emile Durkheim was born in Epinal, France, on April 10th 1858. It was thought he would become a rabbi, but the early death of his father forced him out into the world of teaching. By the beginning of the 20th century he was professor of social philosophy at the University of Bordeaux. He was also the founder of *L'Année Sociologique*, a review magazine of sociological matters from all over the world as well as reports on anthropology experiments. He philosophized that suicide appeared less frequent where the individual was closely integrated with his culture and therefore concluded that suicide could be explained through social forces. The Dreyfus Affair affected him deeply and he took an active part in pressing for the exoneration of the Jewish army officer. As a result, Durkheim was not elected to the prestigious Institut de France, despite having written *The Rules of Sociological Method*, a work that had brought him international fame and influence. However, in 1902 he was appointed professor of social philosophy at the University of Paris. His attempts to teach teachers modern methods would not bear fruit until after his death, and his attempts at educational reform and reducing the influence of religion in society brought him into conflict with the establishment. His work in this field was not published until 1938, when it appeared under the title *Pedagogical Evolution in France*. It is still the best-informed and most impartial work on the French education system. The

DURKHEIM, Emile (1858-1917) French social scientist

outbreak of the First World War came as a shock to Durkheim, whose sociological insights led him to think that war had been overtaken as a solution to international problems. He became depressed that so many fine young men were being killed for no good purpose. The crunch came when his only son was killed in action in 1916 and 'patriots' were calling him 'German' and accusing him of teaching a 'foreign' subject at the Sorbonne. It was all too much and his heart was heavy with despair. He died in Paris on November 15th 1917, but not before he had laid the foundation for the entire field of sociology.

DUVEEN,
Lord Joseph
(1869-1939)
British art
dealer

Duveen was born on October 14th 1869 in Hull, England, the son of a Dutch Jew who was expert on Delft pottery. Growing up in such atmosphere it was no surprise that Joseph would choose the art world for a career. By the turn of the 20th century he was an accepted dealer in fine art. His clients, in the main, were American millionaires who came to rely on Duveen as to what they should buy. Duveen educated them and the best European art left for the US, often at very high prices. He specialized in the English masters of the 18th and 19th centuries, often buying up whole collections and taking his time selling them off piece by piece. He would tell his clients, 'when you pay high for the priceless, you're getting it cheap'. Following his purchase of two French collections for eight million dollars, he sailed for the US and opened a gallery in New York. In 1919 he was knighted for services to art and in 1933 was created a peer. He had built a new wing for the Tate Gallery in London's Millbank; so Duveen took for his title Lord Duveen of Millbank. He later endowed the British Museum with a gallery to house the Elgin Marbles. Duveen died in London on May 25th 1939.

DYLAN,
Bob
(1941-)
US singer/
songwriter

Born Robert Zimmerman in Duluth, Minnesota, on May 24th 1941, **Dylan**, at an early age, came under the influence of Woody Guthrie. In 1955 he formed his own rock band, then moved on to a more blues type music in the mould of Pete Seeger. Dylan was one of the most important people associated with the revival of folk songs that dominated the 1960s. Bob Dylan has composed songs that have become classics: *'Blowing in the Wind'* (1962) and *'The Times They Are a-Changing'* (1964). In the 1970s he produced combination music that blended rock with folk. More recently his work has become a blend of folk and Country and Western, with *'Tambourine Man'* and *'Like a Rolling Stone'*. In the 1970s Dylan found Christianity appealing and it became his faith; in the 1980s, however, he returned to Judaism. Dylan, who has been at centre stage for decades, is still a powerhouse in song writing and performance. In June 1996, at London's Hyde Park, he was the star of an open air concert in aid of the Prince's Trust before an audience of some 200,000 people. In November 1996 he upset fans by permitting his famous protest song, *'The Times They Are a-Changing'*, to be used in an advert by a Canadian bank.

Dymshyts, born in Moscow, was educated at the Moscow Technical Institute and qualified as an engineer. Following the Second World War he gained a central government position, with special responsibilities in respect of Soviet aid to India. On a practical basis he oversaw the satisfactory completion of the Bhilai steel plant. Upon on his return to the Soviet Union Dymshyts was appointed chairman of the State Planning Committee, as well as being given the post of deputy Prime Minister. In 1962 he became head of the National Economics Council, dealing with the day-to-day problems that were constantly occurring in the management of the economy in an enterprise as enormous as the USSR. Dymshyts evolved the plan and headed the committee set up to modernize distribution, the enduring problem of the Soviet economy. A deputy to the Supreme Soviet and a leading figure in the Communist Party, Dymshyts was the most senior Jew in the Soviet regime.

DYMSHYTS,
Veniamin
(1910-)
Soviet politician

Commemorative Stamps

Renee Cassin
Issued by The Republic of
Malagasy

Andre Citroen
Issued by The Republic of
Gabon

Al Capp
Issued by US

Marcel Dassault
Issued by France

Alfred Dreyfus
Issued by Israel

Ernst Chain
Issued by Dominica

Kirk Douglas
Issued by Maldives

Moshe Dayan
Issued by Israel

Lev Dovator
Issued by USSR

E

Born Aubrey Solomon in Cape Town, South Africa, on February 2nd 1915, he was educated at Cambridge University where he became President of the student's Union. Eban was the name of his stepfather, a doctor who practised in London and married Aubrey's widowed mother. During the Second World War Eban was a liaison officer, with the rank of major at Allied HQ. Following the war he changed Aubrey for Abba and went to live in Jerusalem, where he worked as the political information officer of the Jewish Agency, collaborating in the final stages of the British Mandate on Palestine.

In 1947 he moved to New York where he represented the Agency at the UN. Following the creation of the State of Israel, Eban was appointed by Ben-Gurion to be Israel's ambassador to the UN. Here he represented Israel's case so often, receiving much publicity and making so many television appearances, that he was getting the sort of attention usually accorded a film star rather than a politician. He served as Israel's ambassador to the US from 1950 to 1959, after which he returned to Israel, a seat in the Knesset and a post in the Cabinet. He was Foreign Minister from 1966 to 1974, a period that included the Six-Day War (1967) and the Yom Kippur War (1973). Out of government, Eban has been a powerful advocate for a just peace and the establishment of a Palestinian state. His published works include *The Tide of Nationalism* (1959); *My People* (1969); *An Autobiography* (1977); and *Personal Witness* (1992).

EBAN, Abba (1915-) Israeli Statesman

Edelman was born in New York on July 1st 1929. He was educated at the Medical School of Pennsylvania, from where he obtained his MD in 1954. In 1960 he received his PhD from the Rockefeller University in New York. Edelman and his team created a model of the antibody molecule and discovered a four-chain structure containing some 1,300 amino-acids. They were then able to identify the exact locations on the molecule where antigenic binding occurs. As a result Edelman was awarded the 1972 Nobel Prize for Medicine or Physiology for explaining the chemical structure of antibodies. In 1975 he discovered the proteins called the cell-adhesion molecules, which work to attach individual cells to one another to make tissues. In 1987 he published *Neural Darwinism: The Theory of Neuronal Group Selection.*

EDELMAN, Gerald (1929-) US biochemist

EDELSTEIN,
Jillian
(1957-)
South African
photographer

Jillian Edelstein was born on August 21st 1957 in Cape Town. The daughter of middle-class Jewish parents she was educated at the University of Cape Town and later at the London College of Printing. While working as a social worker in a poor district of Cape Town she was captivated by the lives of the people, so different from her own background, and began photographing them and their environment. This led her to deciding to become a working photographer. She worked for the *Rand Daily Mail* and *The Star* during the early 1980s, and by 1985 she was in London. There she obtained a job on *The Times* just as the paper's owner, Rupert Murdoch, temporarily closed it down. For Jillian it was the opportunity to escape newspaper photography in favour of portrait work. Her experimental work has included photographing personalities together with their idea of their soulmates. It was an experiment fraught with problems but it has produced great results. Her work is a continuation of that of Diane Arbus (*qv*) and has resulted in exhibitions, some solo, some shared, at Johannesburg's Museum of Africa and the National Portrait Gallery in London. In 1990 she was voted Photographer of the Year and in 1993-4 the London *Sunday Telegraph* featured her *Affinities/Soulmates* series.

EHRENBURG,
Ilya
(1891-1967)
Russian writer

Ehrenburg, born to a non-religious Jewish family in Kiev, Russia, on January 15th 1891, became internationally known as the leading Soviet writer of Russian literature. He took part in the Revolution and joined the Red Army. His literary achievements are well known. What is less well known, perhaps, is that he exiled himself for a long period in France (1921-36). In the latter year he returned to Moscow, but left again for Paris in 1939, following Stalin's pact with Hitler. After the fall of France, however, Ehrenburg returned home. Following the German invasion of Russia, he became the head of the anti-Nazi propaganda unit. His bitter satirical articles were circulated to millions and his popularity grew until his name was a household word. A leading member of the Jewish anti-fascist committee, he left no one in doubt as to his identity. Following the Second World War, Ehrenburg's anti-Zionist views received world-wide notice. His view was that Jews in every country of the world should be accepted as Jews of that country.

His extensive writings have earned him a place among the greatest writers of modern times. *The Extraordinary Adventures of Julio Jurenito* (1921) is a satire on life following the First World War. *The Fall of Paris* (1941) and *The Storm* (1947) were both Second World War novels. *The Thaw* (1954) graphically described the post-Stalin period. His autobiography appeared in six volumes (1960-66) and was entitled *People, Years, Life*. Ehrenburg lived through difficult times; that he survived is a tribute to his genius as a writer and his friendship with Stalin. He died in Moscow on August 31st 1967.

EHRLICH,
Eugen
(1862-1922)
Austrian scholar

Eugen Ehrlich was born in Czernowitz, Austria, on September 14th 1862. By the beginning of the 20th century he was an associate professor of Roman law at the University of Czernowitz. In 1913 he published his major work, *The Sociology of the Law*, which influenced the rule of law thereafter. In this he expounded his fundamental principles, based in part on the conception of free law or sense of justice, in part on legal history and precedents and on 'living law', as shown by current social custom, and backed up by formal law. Following the end of the First World War anti-Semitism prevented Ehrlich from teaching. Content that he had contributed much to the post-war world, he occupied himself with writing essays on a variety of topics. He died in Vienna on May 2nd 1922.

Ehrlich was born to a Jewish family on March 14th 1854 in Strehlen, Germany, now the Polish town of Strzelin. At the turn of the 20th century, he was director of the Royal Prussian Institute for Experimental Therapy at Frankfurt. He had pioneered research on haematology and chemotherapy and as a result had synthesized Salvarsan as a treatment for syphilis. This discovery was considered to be the most important since the identification of syphilis some 400 years previously. Ehrlich's discovery was the beginning of modern chemotherapy and earned him the award of the Nobel Prize for Physiology in 1908. His discovery became known as 'The Magic Bullet' after the appearance of a Hollywood feature film entitled *Dr Ehrlich's Magic Bullet* (1940), with Edward G. Robinson (*qv*) as Dr Ehrlich. When Ehrlich, a German, died during the First World War even the London *Times* stated in its obituary that 'the whole world was in his debt'.

EHRLICH, Paul (1854-1915) German bacteriologist

Einstein was born in Ulm, Germany, on March 14th 1879, the most famous person ever to be born there. This fame came about after he published his work on the principle of relativity, which revolutionized not only science but the wider world also. In 1921 he was awarded the Nobel Prize for Physics: not for his work on the theory of relativity but for explaining the photoelectric element of the quantum theory. No one in Ulm had previously ever won anything of note, and here was one of her sons carrying off the most spectacular award possible. A few years later the citizens of Ulm showed the respect and affection in which they held their great and world-renowned Albert Einstein. They held a special ceremony in his honour and burned his books. There were 530 Jews living in Ulm at the time. In 1938, when the town worthies burnt the synagogue, there were little more than 100 left. These were later sent to Theresienstadt: four returned.

EINSTEIN, Albert (1879-1955) German physicist

Fortunately Einstein had left Ulm, and the position he held at the Royal Prussian Academy of Sciences, and was living in the US. It was also fortunate for the Americans, because Einstein was the moving spirit that led to the Manhattan Project and the atomic bomb. Einstein and his fellow Jewish scientists were particularly concerned that Germany might well be the first country to create an atomic weapon. They knew that would mean the end of the civilized world. This fear led to the urge to get there first. However, once many of the scientists, Einstein included, discovered that the race had not only been won but that Germany was not an atomic threat, they were opposed to the dropping of the atomic bomb on Japan. They said so in a letter to President Roosevelt that arrived as he died. Truman's view was a pragmatic one, and two atomic bombs later Japan surrendered.

Following the Second World War, Einstein urged the outlawing of atomic weapons. He refused to testify before McCarthy and his Committee on Un-American

Activities and urged his fellow scientists to take the same stance. The authorities found it difficult to pursue the man the world recognized as the greatest scientist of the century, and they quietly and wisely left him to his continuing research. In a *New Statesman* interview given on April 16th 1955, discussing his part in the development of the atom bomb, Einstein said: 'If only I had known, I would have become a watchmaker.' He died in Princeton, NJ, on April 18th 1955.

When Albert was a teenager his father went to see his headmaster. Einstein Senior asked the teacher what profession his son should take up. The headmaster replied: 'It doesn't matter, he will never make a success of anything.'

EISENSTEIN,
Sergi
(1898-1948)
Russian
film maker

Eisenstein was born Sergey Mikhaylovitch in Riga, Russia, on January 23rd 1898. He trained as a civil engineer, then served in the Red Army before, during and after the Russian Revolution (1916-18). He was appointed the revolution's documentary film-maker and made several small propaganda films before he embarked on the feature film that would make him the foremost film-maker of the 20th century. *The Battleship Potemkin* (1925) is considered the greatest film ever made. It was produced to mark the 25th anniversary of the 1905 naval mutiny and was meant as yet another propaganda film. Instead it received a world-wide distribution and the rest is legend. Despite this success, Eisenstein had to put up with considerable interference from party officials and jealous colleagues. He was often accused of concentrating too much on artistic values to the detriment of the 'party message'. *Alexander Nevsky* (1938), the historical epic that included the fantastic battle scene on ice accompanied by Prokofiev's music, was also a world-wide success and enhanced Eisenstein's reputation. *Ivan the Terrible,* made during the desperate times of the Second World War in 1944, was intended to be part one of a trilogy. Part 2, subtitled *The Boyars' Plot*, was made in 1946, but Stalin disliked it, with the result that it was not released until three years after his death. Unfortunately, Eisenstein died before he could finish Part 3. During the Second World War Eisenstein, together with other Jewish artists, demonstrated to show their pride at being Jewish and protested at the German treatment of Jews. He died in Moscow on February 11th 1948.

EISENTAEDT,
Alfred
(1898-1995)
German/
American
photojournalist

Alfred Eisentaedt was born in Prussia, Germany, on December 6th 1898. He was a well-known photographer in Germany, and worked with the Associated Press in the early 1930s. In 1935 he was, as a Jew, invited to leave the country. By this time he had already made and completed his photographic study of Goebbels, revealing his venomous personality, at the League of Nations in Geneva in 1933. Eisentaedt joined *Life* magazine and became one of their early staff photographers, remaining there from 1935 to 1972. An expert at the candid shot and at capturing detail of expression, he became famous in the 1930s with his pictures entitled 'Feet of an Ethiopian Soldier' and 'Nurses Attending a Lecture' and in 1945-6 with his photos from a defeated Japan. Following the war, Eisentaedt photographed hundreds of individuals: famous people, poor farmers, dictators, kings and nobodies. His books reflect his work and include *Witness to our Time* (1966). His most provocative photograph of Sophia Loren, dressed only in a see-through negligée, sat quite comfortably with his portrait of a pensive Albert Einstein. His other books include *The Eye of Eisentaedt* (1969), *People* (1973) and *Eisentaedt's Album* (1976). In 1981 he returned to Germany and produced *Eisentaedt: Germany*. He published his autobiography, *Eisentaedt on Eisentaedt*, in 1985. Besides being one of the world's greatest photographers, he is known as the 'father of photojournalism'. Probably his most famous photograph was the one entitled 'VJ-Day at Times Square, New York City, August 15th, 1945'. It shows a sailor spontaneously kissing a nurse in celebration. 'Eisie', as he was affectionately known, claimed the picture would be his epitaph and so it has proved. He died on August 23rd, 1995. He had no children and his wife predeceased him.

Kurt Eisner was born in Berlin on May 14th 1867. By the beginning of the 20th century he was enjoying the plaudits that greeted the publication of his philosophical treatise, *Friedrich Nietzsche and the Apostle of the Future*. After opposing German aid to Austria in its fight against Serbia, Eisner was caught up in the Great War. As a freelance journalist he was much in demand, when in 1917, he began to oppose the war. He became leader of the Independent Social Democratic Party; he was arrested, charged with incitement and released before trial. In November 1918, following the Armistice, he successfully organized a revolution that overthrew the Bavarian monarchy. He proclaimed a Bavarian Republic. As both Prime Minister and Foreign Minister he made deals with various socialist parties. He later resigned these posts and accepted the appointment as President of Bavaria. His aim was to unite, in the common cause, reform and economic progress. A reactionary student thought otherwise and assassinated him in Munich on February 21st 1919.

EISNER, Kurt (1867-1919) German statesman

Elek was born in Budapest, Hungary. When he was six, his family moved to Paris and Tamas was educated at the Lycée Louis Le Grand, but he never graduated. Insulted by a fascist student, Tamas knocked him out, left college and joined the French Resistance, more specifically, Group Manouchian. Tall, blond and blue-eyed, he looked a typical Aryan rather than a hunted Jew. On October 15th 1942, Tamas casually walked into the German Information Library in Paris and, on the pretext of looking for a book, placed explosives and nonchalantly left. The centre of German propaganda in France was completely destroyed. Several more missions followed, and Tamas was wounded. Upon his recovery he rejoined his unit, now known as the 23 Group. An active thorn in the German side, the Group was their number one target. Following great efforts by the Vichy French police, the whole group was captured and handed over to the German Gestapo. Following a staged trial all 23 of its members were sentenced to death and executed in Paris on February 21st 1944. Group 23 in general and Tamas Elek in particular were a continuing inspiration for the Resistance in their fight against the German forces in their midst. In Hungary, in 1974, Tamas Elek was among those commemorated by a postage stamp in the series 'Hungarian Heroes of the French Resistance'.

ELEK, Tamas (1924-44) Hungarian/ French patriot

ELION,
Gertrude
(1918-)
US biochemist

Gertrude Elion was born in New York on January 23rd 1918, the daughter of immigrant Jewish-Russian parents. Her parents explained to their teenage daughter, that educated men wanted educated wives. She soaked up knowledge and discovered a preference for science. She obtained a scholarship to Hunter College. Watching her grandfather slowly dying from stomach cancer gave her the urge to become a biochemist. She graduated in 1937 only to find that a lack of money, combined with being a woman, made it very difficult to obtain a place to study for a PhD so that she could continue her chosen career. A series of incidents affected her. She was forced to become a secretary in order to live, and then her fiancé died. She spent the next seven years grieving for her lost love and doing all sorts of jobs to accumulate sufficient money to pays the fees demanded by New York University.

The Second World War helped her. The war caused a labour drain and, male chemists being in short supply, research laboratories turned to women. Gertrude Elion got a job with Burroughs Wellcome, a British company, in a research laboratory in Tuckahoe, New York. She and a colleague, George Hitchings, did radical research that resulted in developing drugs that interrupted the life cycle of abnormal cells while leaving healthy cells intact. At night she studied for a doctorate at Brooklyn Polytechnic Institute. However, two years into her course the Dean decided he wanted Elion to leave her job and become a full-time student. She was refused and dismissed from the Institute. A short time later, in 1950, without a doctorate, Elion became responsible for the discovery of two major cancer treatments. One was a purine compound that interfered with the formation of leukemia cells. Although her discovery required further investigation, childhood leukemia could be cured in 80 per cent of all cases as a direct result of Elion's work. The second was a drug called Imuran used to prevent rejection following kidney transplants.

In 1968 Hitchings retired and Elion was appointed head of the Department of Experimental Therapy for Burroughs Wellcome. She spent as much time as possible researching an anti-virus drug. She achieved her ambition with the discovery of a drug called Zovirax which is effective against herpes, shingles and chicken pox. Billion-dollar sales resulted from this discovery. Gertrude Elion retired in 1983, but continued working as a consultant. Her previous research work was instrumental in producing a drug called Azidothymidine, now used to treat patients with the AIDS virus. On October 17th 1988 she heard she had been awarded a third share of the 1988 Nobel Prize for Chemistry for her work demonstrating the differences in nucleic acid metabolism between healthy and diseased cells. In 1991 she was the first woman elected to the National Inventors' Hall of Fame; and she still hasn't obtained her doctorate.

ELKAN,
Benno
(1877-1960)
German/British
sculptor

Elkin was born on December 2nd 1877 in Dortmund, Germany. After studying art for several years he went to Paris and in 1905 declared himself a sculptor - albeit self-taught. Influenced by the French sculptor, Paul Bartholme, Elkin returned to Germany and started work making bronze statues and sculptures from coloured stone. The work results can be found in museums all over the world, particularly in

Europe. With the rise of Hitler in the early 1930s and the resulting increase in anti-Semitism, Elkin moved to England. There he was commissioned to create busts of such people as Winston Churchill, Lord Samuel, Lord Keynes and others. He sculptured large bronze candelabra, to which he added popular biblical characters, for New College, Oxford, and King's College, Cambridge. He later contributed to the beauty of Westminster Abbey with his imposing twin candelabra showing 24 groups of biblical figures. The Menorah, presented by the British House of Commons to the Israeli Knesset in 1956, stands magnificently in Jerusalem. It was Benno Elkin's finest and final work. He died on January 10th 1960.

Elman was born in Kiev, Russia, on January 20th 1891 and was originally taught the violin by his father. When just six years old he was at the Odessa Music Academy. In 1902, now aged eleven, he required royal permission to be allowed, as a Jew, to live in St Petersburg while attending the Conservatory there. He made his concert debut two years later in Berlin, and the following year he was the soloist at a London concert. At both venues the audiences were enthralled by his sweet playing. The critics decided his technique was superb, sweet-sounding with brilliant technical bowing. 'The Elman Tone' was a phrase now used to describe his playing. He played with the leading orchestras of the world and was privileged to premiere works for the violin by several leading composers. In 1911 he arrived in the US, and here he stayed. In 1926 he formed the well-known Elman String Quartet. One of the great violin virtuosos of the century, who toured the world playing with the greatest orchestras, Elman died in New York on April 5th 1967.

ELMAN, Mischa (1891-1967) US violinist

Born Harry Finkleman on May 26th 1914 in Philadelphia, he learned to play various brass and reed instruments while still a child. In 1936 he joined Benny Goodman's (*qv*) band to become part of one of the best three-man trumpet sections of the swing era. When Harry James (*qv*) left the trio, Elman was a featured soloist until he too left Goodman; but not before he had found fame with 'Who'll Buy My Bublitchki?' For a while he worked with Joe Venuti and Tommy Dorsey, then in the late 1940s he formed his own band and had a hit record with, 'And the Angels Sing'. He worked in film studios but ill-health dogged him and he had little success. In 1961 his financial position was revealed in court when his ex-wife was claiming an increase in alimony. He agreed with his wife's lawyer that many people around the world thought him the world's greatest trumpet player, but added, 'I still can't get much work.' He had seven bank accounts: six had credits of between $1.19 and $11.00 while the seventh was overdrawn. He died on June 26th 1968, mourned by millions in Europe and America who recalled his playing in the forties and fifties.

ELMAN, Ziggy (1914-68) US jazz musician

Elsa was born in Vienna, Austria, the daughter of Baron Wilhelm Isak von Guttman, a wealthy Jew ennobled by the Austrian Emperor. Following a failed marriage in her late teens, she secretly married Prince Francis of Liechtenstein in 1921. He was considerably older than she was, but he was rich and royal. In 1929 he became ruler of the principality and Elsa ruled at his side. Elsa's serenity and

ELSA, Princess of Liechtenstein (1875-1947) Jewish Princess

purchasing power came to an abrupt halt when Hitler took over Austria in 1938. Her husband was advised to abdicate, because he had a Jewish wife and that was unacceptable to the German people. Shortly after, Lake Vitlan in Switzerland became the home of the Prince and Princess; two months later the Prince died. The Princess remained in Switzerland, relying on the small pension her husband's family provided. When, in May 1947, she died, the Liechtenstein postal authorities remembered her with a 2 franc stamp entitled 'Death of Princess Elsa'.

EMBDEN,
Gustav
(1874-1933)
German
biochemist

Embden was born in Hamburg, Germany, on November 10th 1874. In 1914 he was professor of physiology at Frankfurt University, Here he researched the chemistry of the human muscular contraction. He came to the conclusion that carbohydrate is degraded within the cell structure. This biochemical pattern, now known as the Embden Syndrome, is typical of most living cells. He was later influential in establishing the significance of phosphoric acid in relation to the metabolism of sugars. Embden was a pioneering researcher into fat metabolism, and his work was later to prove most valuable in future research into the enduring question why some people become fat while others remain slim. He died in Nassau, Germany, on July 25th 1933.

EPHRON,
Nora
(1941-)
US writer

Nora Ephron was born in New York on May 19th 1941, the eldest of four daughters born to Henry and Phoebe Ephron who, with a little money and a lot of hope, took the family off to the West Coast in 1950. By the mid-fifties they had written two of the decade's most popular films, *Carousel* (1956) and *Desk Set* (1957). Nora was educated at Wellesley College, Massachusetts, and has written extensively; her work, often with a feminine bias, has taken her to the top of her profession. Among her screen credits are *Silkwood* (1983), for which she was nominated for an Oscar for Best Screenplay, and *Heartburn* (1986), for which she wrote the screenplay from her novel of the same name. *Cookie* (1989), for which she was both executive producer and screenwriter, did little to further her career. However, in 1989 she more than made up for it writing the screenplay for the hit film *When Harry Met Sally* and getting another Oscar nomination for Best Screenplay.

In the 1990s she turned to directing as well as writing. *Sleepless in Seattle* (1993) one of the first of the 'feelgood' films of the decade, was a world-wide winner and Nora picked up yet another Oscar nomination. Nora Ephron, three times married (once to Carl Bernstein, *qv*), is reputed to be moulded in steel, probably a result of the experience of having parents who were neurotically and financially flawed by the need to keep their, and their children's heads, above the turbulent Hollywood waters. With Nora at their head, the children virtually brought themselves up, and Nora probably still finds she has the need to stay ahead of her siblings. For much of her working life Nora worked in the shadow of her father and was always looking for his approbation. He died in 1992, since when, it is stated, she has become her own complete person. She is certainly one of the forces of Hollywood, having accomplished much and thought to have a lot more to come.

Brian Epstein was born in Liverpool on September 19th 1934. His family had a chain of furniture shops, and after his education Brian went to work managing the record department of their Liverpool store. When he started being asked by customers for a Beatles record, he was surprised to discover the group regularly appeared locally at the Cavern Club. He went to hear them on August 21st 1961 and, despite his lack of interest in pop music, was quite fascinated. With their permission, Brian Epstein went to work on getting The Beatles known. He smartened up their act, taught them to be reliable and disciplined, sacked their drummer for Ringo Starr and organized a contract with Parlophone. Epstein went all the way for the Beatles - indeed, he was considered the fifth Beatle.

Epstein was an excellent and painstaking manager but when The Beatles became the biggest act ever to hit the US he was out of his depth in the world of very big money. In 1965 he allowed the US rights for Beatles merchandising to go for very little. With The Beatles successfully launched, knowing his contract had only two years to run and uncertain whether it would be renewed, Epstein began managing other Liverpudlian acts: Cilla Black, Gerry and the Pacemakers, Billy J. Kramer and others. Gradually Epstein's life was taken over by drugs and his homosexuality, neither of which brought him the happiness he craved. He was not mentally equipped to handle the demands of the crooked elements of the pop world. He had been threatened with violence by accumulated enemies and it culminated on the night of August 26th/27th 1967 when in London he put an end to the pain by taking his own life. His death shocked The Beatles, especially John Lennon, who knew how Epstein felt about him. Lennon publicly stated that without Brian Epstein, 'The Beatles would never have made it'. The *New York Times* called him 'the man who revolutionized pop music in our time'. His autobiography, *A Cellar Full of Noise*, was published in 1964.

EPSTEIN, Brian (1934-67) British pop manager

Epstein was born in the Lower East Side of New York, on November 10th 1889, to Jewish parents recently arrived from Poland. He studied at the Art Students League and survived by selling drawings of ghetto people. He came to the notice of writer Hutchins Hapgood, who asked him to provide the illustrations for his book, *The Spirit of the Ghetto*. From his share of the royalties, Epstein was able to travel to Paris and study at the Ecole des Beaux Arts. In 1905 he emigrated to the UK and became a British citizen. In 1913 he completed his *Torso in Metal from the Rock Drill* (Tate Gallery, London). Much of his subsequent work caused considerable controversy. In particular, his symbolic sculptures *Genesis* (1930), *Ecce Homo* (1934) and *Adam* (1939) were accused of being indecent and blasphemous. He modelled many famous heads, including Einstein, Conrad, Menuhin and Shaw. In the last years of his life Epstein completed what is considered his best work: *Christ in Majesty* at Llandaff Cathedral and *St Michael and the Devil* at Coventry Cathedral. In 1952 an exhibition of Epstein's work at the Tate Gallery in London attracted 10,000 visitors a week. Much of his work was ahead of public opinion and it was not until the late 1940s that he was accepted widely. He was knighted in 1954. Epstein was always passionate about people and in one of his books writes: 'the whole

EPSTEIN, Sir Jacob (1889-1959) US/British sculptor

integrity of art lies in its tradition. Tradition does not mean surrender of originality.' Sir Jacob Epstein died in London on August 21st 1959. In October 1996 it was announced that a new art gallery to be built in Walsall, England, would be ready in April 1997 to house, among other works, 43 pieces of Epstein's sculpture.

ERIKSON,
Erik
(1902-94)
German/
American
psychoanalyst

Erik Erikson was born in Frankfurt, Germany, on June 15th 1902 and studied at the Vienna Psychoanalytic Institute, where he was himself psychoanalysed by Anna Freud (*qv*). At that time he had problems of identity and found growing up in Germany as the son of a Danish Jew, most difficult. Hitler's anti-Jewish propaganda didn't help and in the mid-1930s he emigrated to America. There he taught at Harvard (1934-35), Yale (1936-39) and the University of California at Berkeley (1939-51). During the Second World War he worked with servicemen who were experiencing extreme emotional problems. Here he found his experiences as a child psychoanalyst most valuable. This work led to the publication of his *Eight Psycho Stages of Life From Infancy to Old Age. Child of Society* (1950) has become the textbook of the science. His work also explores the psychological development of historical figures, including a 1942 study on the effects of Hitler's speeches on German children and the lasting emotions produced. His books *Young Man Luther* (1958) and *Gandhi's Truth* (1969) reflect this study. Erikson introduced his theories on identity into the field and invented the phrase 'identity crisis'. He went on to show that people grow mentally by experiencing a series of crises that equate to his original eight examples: trust, anatomy, initiative, competence, identity, generavity, integrity and acceptance. Erikson was the first psychoanalyst to explain how a well-adjusted person functions. His later writings include *The Life Cycle Completed* (1982) and *Vital Involment in Old Age* (1986). He died on May 12th 1994.

ERLANGER,
Joseph
(1874-1965)
US physiologist

Erlanger was born on January 5th 1874 in San Francisco, California. In 1900 he graduated from John Hopkins University and later became professor of physiology at the Washington School of Medicine in St Louis, where he did much of his research work. The results of this work contributed greatly to existing knowledge concerning the cardiovascular nervous system and the investigative methods that might be used. Erlanger invented a graphic method for measuring blood pressure and did pioneer work on what is today called the fibrillator. In 1944 he received the Nobel Prize for Physiology or Medicine for the work he did concerning nerve fibres and impulse transmission. He died in St.Louis, Missouri, on December 5th 1965.

ERNST,
Max
(1891-1976)
German/French
painter

Max Ernst was born on April 2nd 1891 in Bruhl, Germany. Between 1909 and 1911 he studied philosophy at the University of Bonn. In 1913 he visited Paris and there met Jean Arp, who would become his lifelong friend. A self-taught painter, he met many of the avant-garde artists of the time and became a member of the Dada movement. On his return to Germany, he founded a Dada group in Cologne and worked for a time under the name Dadamax. He was responsible for adapting collage techniques to a surrealist use. His *The Elephant Celebes* (1921, Tate Gallery, London) is regarded as a surrealist masterpiece, while his earlier work, *Zivot V*

Dome (1913, Jewish Museum, Prague) gave an idea of what was to come. He went on to produce what became known as 'collage novels', such as *The Woman with 100 Heads* (1929) and *A Week of Goodness* (1933), of which the best is probably *Une Semaine de Boute* (1934). In 1925, now living in Paris, he held his first surrealist exhibition. His vivid works of disturbing images often reflect his fascination with the art of the insane. Richard Dadd's work dazzled him. During the Second World War he was briefly interned as a enemy alien. Upon his release, concerned about his Jewish background, he left for the US. In New York he worked on his *Europe After the Pain* (1940-42, Wadsworth Atheneum, Hartford, Connecticut). He also worked on the magazine *VVV*, which published the work of artists expelled by Hitler, and married the third of his four wives, Peggy Guggenheim (*qv*). In 1949, divorced, he returned to Paris and became a French citizen in 1958. Now his paintings became more lyrical and abstract. Retrospective exhibitions have established Ernst as one of the great masters of the 20th century. He died in Paris on April 1st 1976.

Commemorative Stamps

*Elsa von Gutterman
Princess of Lichtenstein
Issued byLichtenstein*

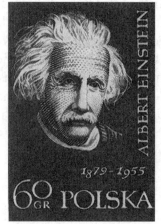

*Albert Einstein
Issued by Poland*

*Sergi Eisenstein
Issued by Republic of Congo*

*Paul Ehrlich
Issued by West Germany*

*Anne Frank
Issued by Holland*

*Bobby Fischer
Issued by The Republic of
Central Africa*

*Sigmund Freud
Issued by Austria*

*Lion Feuchtwanger
Issued by East Germany*

*Casimir Funk
Issued by Poland*

F

Laurent Fabius was born in Paris on August 20th 1946, the son of a wealthy Jewish art dealer. Educated at the Ecole Normale Superieure and later at the Ecole Nationale d'Administration, he joined the Socialist Party and before long was one of François Mitterrand's inner circle of advisers. In 1978 he was elected to the National Assembly to represent the Seine-Maritime constituency. He managed Mitterrand's campaign for President in 1981 and subsequently served in the Cabinet, as Budget Minister and Industry Minister, before being appointed Prime Minister in July 1984. In March 1986 the Socialist Party lost the general election and Jacques Chirac became Prime Minister. Between 1988 and 1991, Fabius served as President of the National Assembly. He then became First Secretary of the Socialist Party (1992-93). All of this was achieved within his first fifty years.

FABIUS, Laurent (1946-) French prime minister

Born in Warsaw, Poland, on May 27th 1887, **Fajans** obtained a doctorate in physics from Leipzig University. Following teaching posts at numerous universities in Switzerland and England, he returned to Germany to be a lecturer in physical chemistry at the Technische Hochschule, Karlsruhe. Later, at Munich University, he researched the effect of radioactive forces and optical properties on natural substances. As a result, he discovered 'brevium' element 91 or uranium x 2. This element analysis was important to the gathering knowledge connected with understanding the atom. In 1936 Fajans was forced to leave Germany by the edict prohibiting Jews to be teachers. That same year he was appointed a professor of chemistry at the University of Michigan, where he stayed until he retired in 1957. Besides being a popular educator he was instrumental in many discoveries, especially the quanticle theory of electronic molecular structures. A prolific writer, he was also an active member of the American Physical Society and chairman in 1947 of the American Chemistry Society. Although Fajans was to receive many awards and prizes for his work in chemistry, in both Europe and America, the one that pleased him the most was the Kasimir Fajans Award for Chemistry instituted by the University of Michigan to mark his retirement. He died in Ann Arbor, Michigan, on May 18th 1975.

FAJANS, Kasimir (1887-1975) Polish/American chemist

Peter Falk was born in New York on September 16th 1927. He was three years old when he developed a tumour in his right eye that led to an operation and a glass eye. This disadvantage has never appeared to affect him unduly and during his schooldays he was an excellent athlete. During the Second World War he served

FALK, Peter (1927-) US actor

for some two years in the Merchant Marine, after which he went to college and obtained a BA in political science (1951). He went on to Syracuse University and gained a Masters degree in public administration. He was 28 when he started his acting career and made his theatrical debut off Broadway, gradually getting noticed. His film career has included some notable roles, generally in the company of John Cassavetes, for example in *Husbands* (1970), *A Woman Under the Influence* (1972) and *Opening Night* (1978). Other well-known films in which he has appeared are *Murder Inc.* (1960 and an Oscar nomination), *A Pocketful of Miracles* (1961 and another Oscar nomination), *Robin and the Seven Hoods* (1964) and *Murder by Death* (1976). In Wender's *Wings of Desire* (1987) he plays himself and gives one of his finest performances. He is however, best known for the long-running television series *Colombo*, in which he plays the role of the scruffy bumbling detective who always solves the case.

FAST, Howard (1914-) US writer

Born Walter Ericson on November 11th 1914 in New York City and educated there, he grew up in the Great Depression, which was to make a lasting impression on him. He worked at many jobs and his early writings were unsuccessful. In 1937, following the success of a short story in a magazine, he published his full-length novel *Place in the City* and became recognized. He followed it with *Conceived Liberty* (1939), *Citizen Tom Paine* (1943), *Freedom Road* (1944) and much more in the 1940s and early 1950s. All his books have a left-wing bias - not surprising in a writer who was an active and open member of the American Communist Party. In 1950 he was imprisoned for alleged contempt of Congress. In 1953 he won the Stalin Peace Prize. In 1960 his book *Spartacus* (1952) was made into a feature film by Kirk Douglas (*qv*). His later novels include *The Immigrants* (1977) and *The Dinner Party* (1987).

FEIFFER, Jules (1929-) US cartoonist

It was not until a comic strip called 'Feiffer' appeared in New York's *Village Voice* in 1956 that **Feiffer** began to receive the recognition his work demanded. He was born in New York on January 26th 1929 and educated at the Art Students League, New York, and the Pratt Institute. His satirical wit and distinctive style have become most popular, and the wonderful illogical monologues that appear to come from the mouths of worried figures are enjoyed throughout America and beyond. In 1961 he won an Academy award for his animated cartoon, *Munro*, which tells the tale of a four-year-old who is drafted into the US Army. A versatile artist, Feiffer has published several volumes of his cartoons including, *Sick, Sick, Sick* (1958) and *Passionella, and Other Stories* (1959). These were followed by *Feiffer's Album* (1963) and *Feiffer's Children* (1986), with much in between. He writes for the theatre and his plays include *The Explainers* (1961), a musical review of his cartoons, *Little Murders* (1967), *The White House Murder Case* (1970) and *Elliot Loves* (1990). Two of his screenplays, *Carnal Knowledge* (1971) and *Popeye* (1980), were most popular. He was an outspoken critic of the Vietnam War as well as of the nuclear arms race. In 1986 he was awarded the Pulitzer Prize for editorial cartooning.

Born in Brooklyn, New York, on December 21st 1919 **Feld** received his BS from City College, New York, when he was only nineteen. He then went to Columbia University, but he did not get the PhD he was working for until 1945. In 1941 Leo Szilard (*qv*) explained a project he was working on involving nuclear chain reaction. Would Feld be interested? Feld was interested, with the result that he became one of the team working on creating the atomic bomb. However, the experience so influenced his life that Feld, haunted by the horror he helped to create, decided to work for nuclear energy for peaceful purposes only. Following the war Feld took up a position at the Massachusetts Institute of Technology. Here he became active in the effort to control nuclear proliferation. Feld and his colleague Albert Wattenberg devoted themselves to getting the McMahon Bill through Congress, a measure which called for the civilian control of nuclear energy. With that success under his belt, Feld began his crusade in atonement for his part in the making of the bomb. In 1955 he met up again with fellow nuclear scientist Joseph Rotblat (*qv*), and together encouraged by the Russell-Einstein manifesto which called for scientists to share their knowledge, they sought a method for involving like-minded scientists from all over the world in stopping the arms race in nuclear weapons. Out of the blue a Canadian millionaire industrialist, Cyrus Eaton, offered to finance their work provided the proposed conference was held in Pugwash, Nova Scotia. So was born the movement which would give meaning to the remainder of Feld's life. He served on the council of Pugwash and was its chairman in the US from 1963 until he was elected to be the secretary-general in 1973. As head of Pugwash, Feld covered the world, at one time travelling to 21 countries in 18 months. He would later say it was the most rewarding part of his life. He was editor of the *Bulletin of Atomic Scientists* and created the satirical 'doomsday clock' which calculated how near the world was to nuclear destruction. He never allowed the opposition to get away unchallenged. He claimed his inclusion on President Nixon's list of enemies was one of his greatest accomplishments. Despite his work for peace, he found time to continue working in the field of physics and to write significant papers on a variety of topics, including his discovery that the previous held theory relating to the law of reflection symmetry did not hold in the decay of strange mesons. Having been concerned in the building of the atomic bomb he spent the rest of his life trying to prevent its use. He died, as he was born, in Brooklyn, on February 19th 1993. His Pugwash partner, Joseph Rotblat, was awarded the 1995 Nobel Peace Prize for his part in the great movement. Feld, had he lived, would probably have shared it with him, but unfortunately the Prize is never awarded posthumously.

FELD,
Bernard
(1919-93)
US physicist

Eliot Feld was born in New York on July 5th 1942. He trained at the traditional School of American Ballet before moving on to the High School for the Performing Arts to study modern dance. After spending some years as one of the most outstanding dancers in the country, he switched to choreography. In 1963 he had his first success with *Harbinger.* In 1968 he formed his own group, the American Ballet Company; it lasted three years. In 1973 Feld started again with a group he called Eliot Feld Ballet. This company has gone on to achieve an international

FELD,
Eliot
(1942-)
US
choreographer

reputation in the field of modern ballet; specializing in Feld's art of choreography and direction. His well-known works include *Intermezzo* (1969), *Jive* (1973), *Mazurka* (1975) and *Papillon* (1979).

FERBER,
Edna
(1887-1968)
US writer

Edna was born on August 15th 1887 in Kalamazoo, Michigan, to a middle-class Jewish family. Her earliest writings showed her love of America, a feeling that was to permeate her work. Following graduation from high school she discovered her father was financially unable to send her on to university. She got herself a job with the local paper until an illness laid her low and she was unable to work. During the long convalescence that followed she turned to writing. As a pilot she wrote a short story that featured a girl called Emma McChesney and sent it to *America* magazine. The magazine commissioned a series from Edna and she was on her way. A short while later she moved to New York and there became part of the literary scene. She travelled extensively throughout the States and Europe; always writing. In 1924 she published *So Big*, which won her the Pulitzer Prize. *Show Boat* (1928) was not only a best-selling novel but was adapted by Jerome Kern and Oscar Hammerstein into a blockbusting musical and popular film. In 1952 *Giant*, the film version of which featured James Dean, was another best-seller. She researched briefly and used what she discovered as a base, drawing on her imagination and library for the flesh. Edna Ferber also wrote for the theatre, collaborating with George Kaufman on *Dinner at Eight* (1932) and *Stage Door* (1936). She wrote two biographies, *A Peculiar Treasure* (1947), in which she describes growing up in a small Jewish community, and *A Kind of Magic* (1963). Edna Ferber died in New York on April 16th 1968.

FERBER,
Herbert
(1906-91)
US sculptor

Herbert Ferber was born on April 30th 1906 in New York. He obtained a degree in dentistry but never practised. While at medical school he was attending evening classes at the Beaux-Arts Institute of Design in New York. Then he followed the usual route taken by young artists with indulgent parents and went off to Europe. There he met up with expressionist art and Romanesque sculpture. He returned to New York and somehow combined the two styles to produce, in wood, massive nude sculptures. His first one-man show was at New York's Midtown Gallery in 1937. Then he turned to using metal, having come under the influence of Julio Gonzales, the great Spanish sculptor. He went on to work in a variety of metals and in a wide variety of shapes. He came to fame following his work for the B'nai Israel Synagogue in Milburn, New Jersey. The sculpture Ferber created, called *And The Bush Was Not Consumed*, depicted the story of Moses and the burning bush. The commissions came flooding in. He went on to produce the first sculptures concerning the environment and his *Interior* - a structure that allows spectators to share in its space - was commissioned by the Whitney Museum, New York. It was followed by his series of 'Calligraphics'. Ferber's work was carried by museums all over America as well as overseas. However, what made his name a household word in the art world was his accusation of theft against the executors of Mark Rothko (*qv*) and his taking them to court. Ferber was the guardian of Rothko's daughter Kate and he took his role seriously. The court eventually decided that there had been a conspiracy between the executors and Marlborough Gallery, New York. Ferber held a number of solo exhibitions and was an undoubted influence on young sculptors, as one of the first artists to present sculpture in a free form. He died in North Egremont, Massachusetts, on August 20th 1991.

Sandor was born in Miskole, Hungary. He became interested in the new science of hypnosis and in 1900 began a practice based on neurology and psychiatry. He and Sigmund Freud were close friends and it is reckoned that over 1,000 letters passed between them. In 1909 he accompanied Freud on his US tour. In 1911 Ferenczi set out to examine the difference between passive and active homosexuality and the bearing this had on paranoia. In 1913 he founded the Hungarian Psychoanalytic Society and in 1919 was appointed professor of psychoanalysis at the University of Budapest. Ferenczi, who gradually drew away from conventional methods in favour of more radical ideas, explained his position in his book *The Development of Psychoanalysis* (1924). The book was a source of controversy among his colleagues all over the world. Ferenczi believed that the wish to return to the womb, and the comfort provided by the amniotic fluids, really demonstrates that the individual wishes to return to the origin of life, the sea. He formulated the theory that the therapist should be loving and caring, in order to counter any rejection and emotional deprivation the patient received from his parents. This was a radical departure from the norm and caused Freud to distance himself from the man who had formerly been his best friend.

FERENCZI,
Sandor
(1873-1933)
Hungarian
psychoanalyst

Born into a middle-class Jewish family living in Munich, Germany, on July 7th 1884, **Feuchtwanger** studied philology and literature at Berlin University and took his doctorate in 1918. In the same year he launched a newspaper, *Der Spiegel.* His chief interest, however, lay with the theatre and, following his meeting with Bertolt Brecht, the two men collaborated on three plays. When Feuchtwanger published *Jew Suss* in 1926 it was an immediate success and led to a 1934 Hollywood film. Further novels followed, including *Ugly Duchess* (1927) and the *Josephus* trilogy (1932-42). At the time Hitler came to power, Feuchtwanger was on a lecture tour of the US. He never again returned to Germany but made his home in the South of France. When this area came under the control of the fascist Vichy regime he was put into a local concentration camp. With external assistance he escaped over the Pyrenees into Spain and from there made his way to the US. Living in California, he continued to write best-selling novels. He accumulated a library of some 30,000 books and left the collection to the University of Southern California, where it is known as the Feuchtwanger Memorial Library. He died in Los Angeles on December 21st 1958.

FEUCHTWANGER,
Lion
(1884-1958)
German writer

FEYNMAN,
Richard
(1918-88)
US physicist

Feynman was born on May 11th 1918 in New York City. Educated at Massachusetts Institute of Technology, he obtained his degree in 1939 and went on to Princeton University, where, in 1942, he obtained his doctorate. While at Princeton Feyman was recruited to work on the Manhattan Project. A year later he was at Los Alamos in New Mexico, where he stayed until the atom bomb had become part of post-war life. As a professor at Cornell University, Feynman worked on a revised theory relating to quantum electrodynamics. He started from a base structure, so disregarding existing theories. The work he did is covered by the diagrams he invented and which later became known as Feynman Graphs. From 1950 until he died, he was professor of physics at the California Institute of Technology. During this period Feynman researched various physical phenomena and published his results. Though a man who didn't much care for rewards, he won the Einstein Award in 1954 and the Niels Bohr Gold Medal in 1973. He shared the Nobel Prize for Physics in 1965 and commented, 'I won the prize for shoving a great problem under the carpet.' Feynman was a character much beloved by his students and much given to practical jokes. During his time at Los Alamos, if he wanted a report out of office hours he would crack open the combination locks - all nine of them - take what he wanted and return the file with a note: 'I borrowed document No. LA 4321 - Thanks - Feynman the safe cracker.' He died in Los Angeles on February 15th 1988.

FIEDLER,
Arthur
(1894-1979)
US conductor

Fiedler was born in Boston, Massachusetts, on December 17th 1894. He received a classical musical education and between 1911 and 1915 studied violin, piano and conducting at the Royal Academy of Music in Berlin. He returned to Boston and joined the violin section of the symphony orchestra. A little later he moved to the viola section and stayed there for a very long time (1917-30). However, he wasn't just a viola player. In 1924 he founded the Arthur Fiedler Sinfonietta and in 1930 he was appointed conductor of the Boston Pops - a symphony orchestra without the principal players. Fiedler went to become the best-selling classical conductor of all time, selling over 50 million records, tapes and CDs. His purpose was to give audiences the world over a good time, to make them happy. Fiedler was a great exponent of making popular songs symphony material. The Beatles songs are a great example. He died in Brookline, Massachusetts, on July 10th 1979.

FIELDS,
Jackie
(1908-84)
US world boxing
champion

Born Jacob Finklestein on February 9th 1908 in Chicago, he was sixteen years old and had only recently left school when, in 1924, he won the gold medal at the Paris Olympic Games for boxing in the featherweight division. A few years later he turned professional and, in 1929, became undisputed world welterweight champion. In 1930 he lost the title to Jack Thompson who subsequently lost it to Lou Brouillard of Canada. In 1932 Jackie won back the title only to lose it the following year to Young Corbett of Italy. In 1962 Jack Kearns, the legendary fight manager, called Fields the 'best all-around battler the United States has ever produced'. Jackie Fields died in 1984.

Harold Montague Finniston was born in Glasgow, Scotland, on August 15th 1912. His Jewish parents were poor and lived in a poor section of Glasgow, and Monty was their fifth son; nevertheless he received an excellent education that culminated in his obtaining a doctorate in metallurgy from the Glasgow Royal College of Science and Technology (now Strathclyde University). On the outbreak of the Second World War Finniston joined the Royal Navy Scientific Service. Here his expertise eventually brought him into the nuclear energy programme. For ten years he was chief metallurgist for the UK Atomic Energy Authority at Harwell. There he was the leader of a young team who were researching new materials for a new era. In 1959 Finniston switched to the private sector. Then, in 1965, a Labour government nationalized the steel industry as British Steel. With Finniston as chief executive, and two years later its chairman, British Steel spent millions on bringing the company into modern times. The previous private owners had neglected the industry for decades, with the result that Britain was well down the scale of steel-producing countries.

Finniston allowed only a minimum of governmental interference while he selected the best equipment available. In 1976 there was a blistering row between Finniston, the boss of British Steel, and Tony Benn, the government minister who was Finniston's boss. The result was that Finniston's contract was not renewed. However, Benn also lost his job and the new minister appointed Finniston to be chairman of a committee of inquiry to investigate the engineering profession. The result was the Finniston Report, which outlined the steps that needed to be taken to stop the industry sliding downhill while the service sector expanded. The formation of the Engineering Council, without teeth, followed and, as Finniston had predicted, there was mass unemployment in the industry. Britain, with an arts-biased culture, always regarded engineering as a low-status enterprise. Finniston did his best to redress the balance. Knighted in 1975, he was associated with many universities and was Chancellor of Stirling University from 1978 to 1988. He died in London on February 2nd 1991.

FINNISTON, Sir Monty (1912-91) British engineer

Fischer was born on March 9th 1943 in Chicago, Illinois, the son of a Jewish father who taught him chess before he could read or write. In 1958 Bobby became the youngest player in the world to achieve the rank of Grandmaster. His impatience and brilliance made him a favourite with the American public and as a result the game of chess received wide popularity. He finished high school at sixteen and gave up further education for the chess board. In 1972, in Reykjavik, Iceland, Fischer became the first US player to hold the title of chess champion of the world, defeating the Russian champion Boris Spassky. For this victory, gained through his surprising play, regardless of attack or defence, he won $150,000. In 1975, after refusing to defend the title against Karpov of the Soviet Union, the World Chess Federation took away his title and declared Karpov the winner by default. For the next 20 years Fischer became a recluse, until 1992, when he beat Spassky in a privately arranged match.

FISCHER, Bobby (1943-) US chess Grandmaster

FISCHER,
Gottfried
(1897-1995)
German
publisher

Gottfried Fischer was born Gottfried Bermann in Silesia on July 30th 1897. After qualifying as a doctor of medicine, he joined the famous publishing firm of S. Fischer in 1925. Many of the great writers of the century were published by Fischer, including Thomas Mann, Tolstoy, Ibsen and Herman Hesse. In 1926 Gottfried married the boss's daughter, Brigitte, and tacked Fischer on to his name. In 1931 he succeeded his father-in-law as chairman. Fischer tried to continue publishing after 1933, with Hitler in power, but it was a difficult path and in 1936 he gave up. Forced to hand over the business to an 'Aryan' partner, so that it might continue its world-wide activities, the Fischers left Germany for Sweden, but were moved on when the Swedish authorities thought they were spying for the Allies. Following a highly adventurous journey that took them the length of Russia to Japan, they eventually arrived in America. Here Fischer started again, publishing work by German writers in exile. The war over, Fischer returned to Germany and tried to recover his business. However, Peter Suhrkamp, the Aryan left in charge, refused to return the company. Fischer had little alternative but to start all over again. The new company became very successful, thanks mainly to Fischer's policy of publishing works of literary merit in paperback that most people could afford. It was due to Fischer that Germans enjoyed a post-war intellectual life and it was Fischer who published books that dealt with the Holocaust. In 1967 he retired to Lucca in Italy. Here he pursued his hobbies of painting, sculpting and playing tennis. He died in Lucca on September 17th 1995.

FISCHER,
Louis
(1896-1970)
US journalist

Fischer was born on February 29th 1896 in Philadelphia. Initially a teacher, he tired of this work and journeyed to Palestine during the First World War. There he joined the Jewish Legion, part of the British Army. He followed this by spending fourteen years in the Soviet Union as a freelance correspondent. No foreign journalist ever came to know so many of the Revolution's leaders. His first book, favourable to the new regime, was *Oil Imperialism* (1926). He was given top-level co-operation and in 1930 published *The Soviets in World Affairs*. In the 1930s many of Fischer's friends were caught up in the Stalin purges. He left the Soviet Union to become the first American to join the International Brigade being set up to fight for the Republican cause in the Spanish Civil War (1936-39). Following the victory of the fascist leader Franco, Fischer travelled the world. In India he became a close friend of Gandhi and Nehru. Because of the madness of Stalin and others, who Fischer believed had betrayed the Revolution, he became disenchanted with the Russian brand of Communism. He was considered an important writer whose insights on his subject set him apart. His published works include *Soviet Journey* (1935); *The War in Spain* (1937); *Stalin and Hitler* (1940); *Gandhi and Stalin* (1947); *The Life of Mahatma Gandhi* (1950); *The Life and Death of Stalin* (1952); *America and the World* (1961); and *The Life of Lenin* (1964). For today's student of 20th century history these books are a must. Fischer, an acknowledged authority on the Soviet Union, gradually became disillusioned by what he saw at first hand. He died on January 15th 1970.

Born **Edwin Fisher** on August 10th 1928 in Philadelphia, at the age of eighteen he was singing of Budely Morrow and Charlie Ventura. His strong melodic voice and handsome appearance made him a target for the bobbysoxers of the 1940s and 1950s, who screamed and shouted and sometimes mercifully fainted. Known as 'Sonny Boy' because he loved to sing Al Jolson (*qv*) songs, he received nationwide publicity when, in 1949, he appeared in the Eddie Cantor (*qv*) radio show. In 1952-53, his career came to a temporary halt whilst he served in the US Army in Korea. Then it took off again and he had a string of Number One hits that included, 'Tell Me Why'; 'I'm Yours'; 'Wish You Were Here'; 'Oh My Pa-Pa'; 'I Need You Now'; and 'Cindy, Oh Cindy'. He had five gold discs before the 1950s were over. In 1956 he starred with his wife, Debbie Reynolds, in the film *Bundle of Joy* . In 1960 he was starring with wife no. 2, Elizabeth Taylor, in a non-singing role in *Butterfield 8*. For Fisher, the 1960s was generally a time of drugs and financial problems. His third wife was Connie Stevens, whom he married and divorced before the decade was out. His best work was in the 1950s, when he was known around the world and gave much pleasure to millions. He has made several comebacks to little purpose; however, his autobiography, *Eddie: My Life and Loves*, was very well received.

FISHER, Eddie (1928-) US singer

He was born Chaim Reeven Weintrop on October 14th 1896 in London's East End, the fifth son and the youngest of ten children born to Jewish parents from Poland. His father had a barber's shop and Chaim, now known as Robert, was educated at Petticoat Lane School. At the age of twelve he made his theatrical debut in an amateur talent contest, performing conjuring tricks as 'Fargo - the Boy Wizard'. In 1910, aged just sixteen, he walked to Southampton and, passing himself off as an electrician, sailed on the SS *Majestic* for New York. There he jumped ship and spent the next five years in a variety of jobs, from messenger boy for Western Union to a street-corner newspaper seller. Then he joined a vaudeville act called 'Campus Days' and toured America. In 1912 he acquired a partner and the new double act went off to perform in Australia, New Zealand and South Africa. With the First World War under way he decided to return to the UK, where he joined the army and the Royal Artillery. Wounded and temporally blinded, he was sent to an army hospital in Deauville, France. He returned home in 1919 and decided his stage name would be Bud Flanagan, as an act of revenge against his former anti-Jewish sergeant-major of the same name.

By 1922 he was broke and driving a London taxi. However, in 1926 he met up with Chesney Allen, whom he had first met in the army. They decided to team up under the name Flanagan and Allen. Thus was born the act which was destined to last for the next 20 years. They had several hiccups before they made a name for themselves, but gradually they climbed higher and higher up the billing. In 1930, they appeared in their first Royal Command Performance, before King George V and Queen Mary at the London Palladium. Later the duo teamed up with Nervo and Knox, Naughton and Gold and Eddie Gray to become 'The Crazy Gang'. By the time the Second World War arrived the Crazy Gang was the number one variety

FLANAGAN, Bud (1896-1968) British entertainer

turn, starring in several musical comedies. Immediately after D-Day, Flanagan and Allen went off and entertained the forces all over Britain and in France. In 1945 Chesney fell ill and for two years Bud Flanagan was a solo act. To everyone's relief the Crazy Gang got back together and, from 1947, with Flanagan their undisputed leader, they were back at the top.

Flanagan also appeared on his own in several long-running musicals including *Knights of Madness* (1950), *Jokers Wild* (1954) and, in 1956, *These Foolish Kings*, which ran for nearly 900 performances. In 1963 Bud Flanagan retired and was awarded the OBE. He and Allen made several comedy films that were very popular in Britain but didn't travel well. Bud Flanagan wrote several hit songs, including *Underneath the Arches*. Bud Flanagan, who gave so much pleasure to so many people, suffered the terrible loss of his son: Buddy was only 29 when he died from leukemia. Flanagan established his own fund to raise money to fight the disease. Bud Flanagan died in Sydenham, London, on October 20th 1968.

FLATOW, Alfred (1869-1942) German Olympic champion

Alfred Flatow was born in Berent, Germany. In 1896 the first modern Olympic Games were held in Athens, and Alfred and his cousin Gustav (1875-1945) represented Germany in the gymnastic events. By the end of the Games, Alfred had won four gold medals, an individual gold in the parallel bars and the other three in team events, and his cousin two, also in team events. In 1903 Alfred Flatow was co-founder of the Judische Turnerschaft, the pioneering Jewish sports organization in Europe. He was the leader of the German gymnastic world, until his expulsion in 1933 for being a Jew. Surplus to requirements, Flatow, now aged 73, was sent to Theresienstadt concentration camp and murdered. His cousin Gustav was 70 when he too was murdered in the same German camp.

FLEG, Edmond (1874-1963) Swiss/French writer

Born in Geneva, Switzerland, **Fleg** only became aware of matters Jewish following the Dreyfus Affair. At the time of the First World War, Fleg was already a successful playwright and still a Swiss national when he volunteered for active service in the French Foreign Legion. Following the war, Fleg accepted French nationality and settled in Paris. His writings include poetry, biographies and accounts of religious experiences. During the Second World War he refused to take refuge in Switzerland, but lived secretly in the Midi region of France. There he wrote what has become known as *Fleg's Creed*, detailing his life as a Jew in a secular world. Fleg's writings had a significant influence on French writers of all faiths and he was responsible for founding the Christian-Jewish Fellowship. Towards the end of his life Fleg was made an officer of the French Legion of Honour and elected a member of the French Academy.

FLEISCHER, Max (1883-1972) US cartoonist

Fleischer was born in Austria on July 17th 1883 and arrived in the US five years later. He and his family lived in Brooklyn, where he attended various schools including a local drawing class. He went to work as a cartoonist on the *Brooklyn Daily Eagle* and later as the art editor of a monthly magazine. Here he developed an interest in animation. He went to Los Angeles where he developed a technique for producing what would become the world's first animated cartoon feature. Max and his brother Dave (1894-1979) founded the Fleischer Studios and did a deal with Paramount Pictures that ensured distribution of their product over the next 20 years. It was during this period that Max Fleischer invented the characters that would become part of the folklore of the 20th century. Popeye and his girlfriend Olive Oyl first saw the light of day in newspaper comic strips. Then Max made cartoon feature films and Popeye and Olive Oyl were elevated to star status to become national and international personalities. Fleischer invented various pieces of machinery that became essential to the animation industry, the most famous being the 'Rotoscope'. Max Fleischer is responsible for animated feature films becoming an important part of the movie world. He died in Woodland Hills, California, on September 15th 1972.

FLEISCHER, Nat (1887-1972) US writer

Fleischer was born on the Lower East Side of New York on November 3rd 1887. After an education at the City College of New York, he combined his hobby of athletics with writing on sport. He showed early promise as a promoter by organizing his school's first university basketball team. Then he discovered boxing and his love affair with that sport pushed all others to one side. Again he twinned his interest and his writing career to produce *The Ring*. This magazine started life in 1922 as a monthly and succeeded in becoming the bible of boxing. *The Ring Record* was an annual which sold around the world. *Boxing Encyclopaedia* carried on from there. In all, Fleischer wrote some 50 books on boxing and is still considered the outstanding authority on the sport. He also, on occasions, acted as a ringside judge. One such occasion was the second fight between Sonny Liston and Muhammad Ali. The referee, the famous Jersey Joe Walcott, missed a time out by the timekeeper on Liston at the beginning of the seventh round. Fleischer ordered Walcott to stop the fight and award Muhammad Ali the victory. Nat Fleischer died on June 25th 1972 at Atlantic Beach, New York.

FLEXNER, Abraham (1866-1959) US educator

Flexner was born on November 13th 1866 in Louisville, Kentucky, to an orthodox Jewish family. By the beginning of the 20th century he was at Harvard University, studying psychology, science and philosophy. He had a continuing interest in education and travelled extensively in Europe, investigating comparative systems. In 1908, Flexner published a book on higher education that caused a stir in educational circles. As a result, he was commissioned by the Carnegie Trust to investigate the qualities of 155 medical colleges. The resulting report, known as the Flexner Report, rated each college, so laying the ground for reforms at medical schools all over the US. He was connected with the education board of the Rockefeller Foundation for some 20 years and was responsible for the supervision and allocation of resources to educational and medical establishments. This included the founding of the Institute for Advanced Study at Princeton University. He became the Institute's first director (1930-39). Here in 1933 he gathered together the country's foremost scientists to meet the recently arrived Albert Einstein (*qv*). Flexner died at Falls Church, Virginia, on September 21st 1959.

FORD,
Harrison
(1942-)
US actor

Harrison Ford was born on July 13th 1942 in Chicago. His father was an Irish cabinet-maker who taught his son skills that would later come in handy, his mother Jewish. Educated at Ripon College, Wisconsin, he later became an actor. When, after several small film parts, it appeared his film career was not going to take off, he kept going by earning his living as a carpenter. In 1977, Ford was cast as the cynical Han Solo, the pilot, in *Star Wars*. The huge success of this film resulted in Harrison Ford becoming internationally known. He has since appeared in some of the biggest box-office hits of the second half of the 20th century, and his craggy features and often humorous style have given much pleasure to many millions all around the world. His cult movie role as the robot-killing cop in *Blade Runner* (1982), then his more humane acting in *Witness* (1988) and *Presumed Innocent* (1990) testify to his range. His nonchalant role as Indiana Jones will long be remembered. Other films of note include *Patriot Games* (1992), *The Fugitive* (1993) and, in 1994, *Clear and Present Danger*. In 1997 *The Devil's Own* was criticized because it was a film concerning the IRA without expressing a moral standpoint. Ford's acting however was not an issue and he continues to be most bankable and an exponent of the charisma long expected of Hollywood stars.

FOREMAN,
Carl
(1914-84)
US film-maker

Foreman was born in Chicago, Illinois, on July 23rd 1914. Educated at the University of Illinois and Northwestern University, he served in the US Army throughout the Second World War. He started writing while recovering from war wounds in hospital and decided to make it his career. That career took off when he wrote the screenplay for *Champion* in 1949 and received an Oscar nomination. *Home of the Brave* (1949) followed; then came *High Noon* in 1952, and he was once again nominated for an Oscar; sadly for Foreman, it went elsewhere. It was now the time of the McCarthy witch-hunts and Foreman refused to testify before the Committee on Un-American Activities. Placed on the blacklist that prevented him from working, he went to live in Britain. There he wrote the screenplay for *The Bridge On The River Kwai* (1957): the film won four Oscars, including that for Best Screenplay for Foreman. He now started his own production company and wrote and produced *Guns of Navarone* (1961); besides being a box-office success it was nominated for Best Film, but suffered from being made in the same year as *West Side Story*! In 1963 he wrote, produced and directed *Victors*, a story of the Second World War which won critical acclaim and is considered to be one of the best in its genre. Foreman went on to produce, among others, *Born Free* (1965), *Mackenna's Gold* (1969) and *The Virgin Soldiers* (1969). His last film of note was *Young Winston* (1972), which he wrote and produced and which resulted in another Oscar nomination for Best Screenplay. During the late 1960s and early 1970s he was President of the Writer's Guild of Great Britain and a board member of the British Film Institute. Despite his long stay in London, in his last years he returned to the US and Beverly Hills, where he died on June 26th 1984.

Milos was born on February 18th 1932 in Caslav, Czechoslovakia, the son of Jewish parents who perished in the Holocaust. He graduated from FAMU, part of the University of Prague, and started work in his local film world. Not content to follow the norm, he made films of a different style on challenging themes, showing powers of observation and an ironic sense of humour. *Loves of a Blond* (1965) and *The Fireman's Ball* (1967) illustrate what he was trying to achieve. When the Russians invaded his country in 1968, Milos Forman left for the US and Hollywood. Although he was known in the film world it wasn't until 1975 that he achieved true international fame. *One Flew Over The Cuckoo's Nest* swept the board with five Oscars including one for Forman as Best Director. He followed up with *Hair* in 1979, *Ragtime* in 1981 and *Amadeus* in 1984, for which he received another Oscar for Best Director. It has been said of Milos Forman that he is one of the few established foreign directors to find consistent success within the American film industry. In 1977 he directed the controversial film, *The People v Larry Flynt*.

FORMAN, Milos (1932-) Czech film-maker

Fortas was born on June 19th 1910 in Memphis, Tennessee, the son of a religious British Jew. Abe, educated at Southwestern College, worked as a shop assistant by day and a violin player in a jazz band by night. In between, he managed to do sufficient work to win an offer of a place at Yale Law School. He graduated top of his class of 1933 and remained at Yale as an assistant professor before accepting a minor post in government. Several minor posts further on, in 1941 Abe was seconded to the Department of the Interior. Within a year he was under-secretary. In 1945 he was closely associated with the founding of the UN. He then resigned from government work and went into private practice in Washington.DC. Here Fortas began to attract attention while defending victims of the McCarthy witch-hunt. In 1963 he won a landmark victory in the case of *Gideon* v. *Wain*. The Supreme Court upheld his assertion that poor defendants in criminal cases had the right to free legal counsel. Abe Fortas, a close friend of President Johnson, received his nomination to the Supreme Court in 1965 and so became part of the liberal majority. Unfortunately for Fortas, he was unable to enjoy his elevation for long. In 1968 Johnson nominated him to succeed Chief Justice Earl Warren, but the nomination was blocked by Republicans and others, said to be antisemites, with the result that his nomination did not receive Senate approval: the first time such an event had occurred. Worse still was the revelation the following year that Fortas was receiving an annual fee from a securities dealer, one Louis Wolfson, a convicted fraudster. This revelation resulted in a storm of protest against Fortas, who was forced to resign from the Supreme Court. It was another first. He returned to private practice and died in Washington DC on April 19th 1982.

FORTAS, Abe (1910-82) US lawyer

**FORTES,
Meyer
(1906-83)
South African/
British
anthropologist**

Fortes was born on April 25th 1906 in Britstown, South Africa. Educated at Cape Town University, he obtained his PhD in psychology from the London School of Economics in 1930. Two years later he started studying anthropology. In 1934 he worked in Ghana and upon his return in 1937 became lecturer in social anthropology at the London School of Economics. Later he was a research lecturer at Oxford University. Following the Second World War he was appointed professor of social anthropology at King's College, Cambridge, where he remained for 20 years. His main interest was in the structure of African tribes, especially the Tallensi. He studied the tribal system and wrote on its political and cultural significance. Most of his research was conducted in the countries of coastal Africa. He wrote extensively and his books continue to influence students of anthropology. They include *The Dynamics of Clanship Among the Tallensi* (1945), *Kinship and Social Order* (1969) and *Time and Social Structure, and other Essays* (1970). Fortes died in Cambridge, England, on January 27th 1983.

**FOSS,
Lukas
(1922-)
German/US
conductor**

Born Lukas Fuchs in Berlin on August 15th 1922, he has become widely known for his experiments in music. He studied in Paris and Berlin before leaving for the US, following threats on his life by fellow students. In the US he studied under Hindemith and Serge Koussevitsky and published his first work at the age of sixteen. In 1945, he became the youngest composer to win a Guggenheim Fellowship. In 1957, while a professor of music at the University of California in Los Angeles, he founded the Improvisation Chamber Ensemble. This he created as a platform on which he could put into practice his experimental ideas in music. In 1963 he was appointed conductor of the Buffalo Philharmonic Orchestra, where he stayed for seven years. At the same time he founded the Centre for Creative and Performing Arts at the State University of New York. In 1981 he was music director of the Milwaukee Symphony Orchestra. He has written much, ranging from neo-classical music to the avant-garde and from symphony to ballet, opera and chamber music. His best-known work is probably *America Cantata*, written in 1977 for tenor, soprano, two speakers, chorus and orchestra.

**FOX,
William
(1879-1952)
US film pioneer**

Fox was born Wilhelm Fried on January 1st 1879 in Tulchva, Hungary, of German-Jewish parents, and arrived in New York shortly before his first birthday. At eleven he left school in order to work and help support the family. Various jobs and high-risk ventures led to his buying in 1904 a nickelodeon - something we now call a cinema or movie house. Although little more than a fleapit, it was the foundation of a chain of cinemas and the establishment of an independent film distribution company. A legal victory against a monopoly consortium gave him the financial muscle to enter the world of film-making. His company, the Fox Film Corporation, later 20th Century Fox, was formed in 1915 and rapidly took off. By 1930 Fox had most of the best directors and stars working in Hollywood under contract. His company was the first to use a sound-on-film system, so that his Movietone newsreels allowed American audiences to 'hear and see', months before *The Jazz Singer* was screened. Fox now controlled cinemas across the States as well as in Europe, and bought a controlling interest in Loews Inc., the company that owned MGM. This, however, marked the beginning of his downfall. Anti-trust issues were raised and Fox had to let go of Loews Inc. Unable to deal with matters on a day-to-day basis because of an automobile accident, Fox was forced to rely upon others. The result was that his quoted shares fell from a high of $119 a share to $1. Fox's success crumbled. In 1936 he was declared bankrupt. Worse was to follow: in 1941 he was convicted of attempting to bribe the bankruptcy hearing judge and sent to prison for six months. On his release he attempted a film-making comeback, but it never happened. However, thanks to the patents he had from his original sound-on-film inventions, Fox had a comfortable retirement. He died in New York on June 3rd 1952.

James was born on August 26th 1882 in Hamburg and studied chemistry at Berlin University. He spent many years researching the reaction of bombardment of electrons on the ionization of atoms. This important work won him the Nobel Prize for Physics in 1925, and would bear fruit during the race for the atom bomb during the Second World War. He was physics professor at the Göttingen Institute when, in 1933, in protest at Nazi policies, he resigned his post and went to Denmark. Two years later he was a professor at John Hopkins University, Baltimore, in the US, before moving on to Chicago University in 1938. Here he carried out important research into photochemistry which was used in the aircraft industry during the Second World War. Franck worked on the development of the atom bomb and was one of the few who appreciated its devastating power. He urged that a demonstration be given in an unpopulated area in order to demonstrate that power. During the latter part of his life he returned to Germany and the Göttingen Institute; he died in Germany on May 21st 1964.

FRANCK,
James
(1882-1964)
German
physicist

Anne Frank is the child who became the symbol of the Holocaust. Her diary of events involving her and her family during the Second World War, while they hid from the Germans, has become a world best-seller. She was born Annelies Marie Frank in Frankfurt on June 12th 1929. Following Hitler's arrival in power in 1933, the family moved to Amsterdam. She and her family went into hiding in 1942, although her father, Otto, had prepared for such an event in 1940, when the Germans invaded the Netherlands. Their sanctuary was a sealed-off back office room. For nearly two years, former employees of Otto Frank kept the refugees supplied with the essentials of life. During all this time Anne kept her diary describing their daily lives. The diary takes the form of notes to an imaginary friend, Kitty. It is a full and candid diary and includes phrases and quotations she enjoyed hearing and using. The family were eventually betrayed and arrested by the Gestapo on August 4th 1944, two months after D-Day, as the Allies were speeding to the liberation of the Netherlands. The Germans burst into 263 Princengracht, found the annexe and took away Anne and her sister to Belsen, where in March 1945 they died of typhus following starvation and neglect. It was one month before British troops liberated the camp. Anne's mother Edith and her father were taken to Auschwitz. Otto Frank was the only

FRANK,
Anne
(1929-45)
Dutch diarist

member of the family to survive. Following the arrest of the family, Otto's secretary, Miep Gies, searched the annexe and took various papers and the diary away for safe keeping. She returned all these to Otto. In 1947 excerpts of the diary were published under the title *The Annex*. The full diary was published in June 1952 as *Anne Frank's Diary*. Some 20 million copies have been sold in dozens of languages. A Broadway version of the diary was staged in 1955 and won the Pulitzer Prize for the best play of the year. It has since been staged, in some form or another, all over the world. In 1959 a film version was produced. Anne Frank's diary has been, and continues to be, an inspiration to people everywhere. Otto Frank, his children dead, became the 'father' to thousands of lonely children all over the world. They wrote to him and Otto Frank replied to each. The family hideaway is now a museum and there is an Anne Frank Foundation that exists to teach about the evils of racism. In a TV interview, following his release from prison, Nelson Mandela told of how reading Anne Frank's diary gave him hope for the future. In 1997 the Foundation published the unexpurgated version of Anne Frank's diary, called *The Diary of a Young Girl: The Definitive Edition*. It contains items relating to Anne's sexual awakenings that her father thought would shock a 1947 readership. On April 11th 1944 Anne Frank, aged fourteen, wrote in her diary: 'I don't believe that the big men, the politicians and the capitalists alone are guilty of the war. Oh, no, the little man is just as keen. There is an urge and rage in the people to destroy, to kill, to murder and until all mankind, without exception, undergoes a great change, wars will be waged.'

FRANKFURTER, Felix (1882-1965) US lawyer

Frankfurter was born on November 15th 1882 in Vienna, Austria. His family moved to New York when he was twelve years old; he was educated at New York College and Harvard University, from where he graduated as a lawyer. He spent the years 1914-39 teaching at Harvard Law School. He was then appointed by President Roosevelt an associate justice of the US Supreme Court, on which he sat from 1939 to 1952. Frankfurter founded the American Civil Liberties Union and was a prominent supporter of civil liberties generally. He provoked much controversy with his dictum that judges should consider whether lawmakers had acted reasonably in creating the law under discussion. Frankfurter's fight on behalf of Sacco and Vanzetti, and his ruling in favour of membership of trade unions, accentuated his deserved reputation as a caring liberal. While teaching at Harvard he was also legal adviser to the National Association for the Advancement of Coloured People as well as consultant to the National Consumer League. The twenty years that Frankfurter spent with Oliver Wendell Holmes on the bench of the Supreme Court are considered a high point of 20th century jurisprudence. In 1963 President Kennedy awarded Frankfurter the US Medal of Freedom. Frankfurter was a prolific author. His major works are *The Business of the Supreme Court* (1927), *The Public and its Government* (1930) and *Of Law and Men* (1956). He died in Washington DC on February 22nd 1965.

Frankl was born in Vienna and educated at the university there, from where he obtained doctorates in philosophy and medicine. His life has been influenced by the years he spent (1942-45) in the German concentration camps of Auschwitz and Dachau. He wrote of these experiences in his book *From Death Camps to Existentialism* (1959). In 1947 he joined his former university as professor of neurology and psychiatry. He developed the concept of logotherapy, the theory that the underlying need of human existence is to find the meaning of life. Probably his best-known book on this subject is *Man's Search For Meaning: An Introduction to Logotherapy* (1962).

Rosalind was born on July 25th 1920 in London, the daughter of Ellis Franklin, a member of a distinguished Jewish family that arrived in Portsmouth from Germany in 1784. She studied chemistry at Cambridge, before working in Paris and London. While at the Laboratoire Central des Services Chimiques de l'Etat in Paris, she used various methods of X-ray diffraction and noted the structural changes that would later be termed carbon fibre technology. It was at this time that Franklin was acknowledged as an expert in the field of crystallography. In 1951 she was part of a small research team at King's College, London, where she worked on advanced X-ray diffraction. This led directly to her work on DNA and she was partly responsible for determining a full structure of DNA and its relation to molecular biology. At the time of her death in London on April 16th 1958, aged 38, a close colleague discovered Rosalind Franklin's laboratory notes. He found she was so advanced in her research she was judged to be just two steps from deciphering the whole DNA structure. Two years after her death, her two co-workers were awarded the Nobel Prize for their part in discovering DNA. Unfortunately the Prize is never awarded posthumously.

Born Arthur Grossman in Charleston, South Carolina, on September 9th 1894, after a basic education **Freed** decided to become a song writer and just about kept body and soul together. With the establishment of talkie films, he joined MGM and went on to produce the best musicals of the forties and fifties. He had the knack of recognizing talent and utilizing it. Gene Kelly, Cyd Charisse (*qv*), Frank Sinatra and Judy Garland were just some of the stars he launched via his great productions. This production list includes *Strike Up The Band* (1940); *Lady Be Good* (1941); *For Me and My Girl* (1942); *Cabin in the Sky* (1949); *Meet Me In St Louis* (1944); *On The Town* (1949); and *Singin' in the Rain* (1952). For *An American in Paris* (1951) he won the Oscar for Best Picture. He did it again with *Gigi* in 1958. Many of the musicals he produced contained some of his song lyrics. The debt the film world owes to Arthur Field is acknowledged by the many television hours given over to his films all around the world.

Freedman was born in London on May 19th 1901, the son of Jewish immigrants from Russia. A sickly child, he was sent to a local authority boarding school where the countryside air was deemed to be better than that in an East End slum. He received a minimal education, spending the years from nine to fourteen in hospital, but during this period he read a lot and taught himself to draw and paint. At fifteen he was thought well enough to have a job and found one as a trainee draughtsman in an architect's office. He discovered an interest, that almost became a passion, for lettering and typography. After work he attended evening classes at the St.Martin's School of Art and after much persuasion he gained a scholarship to the Royal College of Art. He left the College in 1925 and tried to earn a living as a painter; the result was near poverty. However, his work gradually became known and today galleries like the Tate and the Victoria and Albert in London and the Fitzwilliam in Cambridge exhibit Freedman's work. He turned to design as an alternative to painting, and his work included the 1935 silver jubilee postage stamp and book jackets for classics including *War and Peace*, *Anna Karenina*, *Oliver Twist* and *Wuthering Heights*.

Although never in the best of health, during the Second World War Freedman was an official war artist. He was with the British Expeditionary Force in France at the time of Dunkirk, with the Royal Navy on the battleship *Repulse'* when it was on Arctic convoy duty to Russia, and in submarines. Much of his work is in the Imperial War Museum in London, including his famous painting of the beach landing at Arromanches following the D-Day landings of June 6th 1944. After the war he returned to his main love, lithography, and passed on his knowledge and expertise to future generations. He had an eccentric sense of the absurd and revelled in his cockney dialect and independent mind. Although he received awards and decorations (a CBE in 1946), he was most pleased by the award of the Royal Society of Arts' highest honour. A portrait of Freedman by Sir William Rothenstein (*qv*) hangs in the Tate Gallery, London. Freedman died in London on January 4th 1958.

Maurice Freedman was born to middle-class Jewish parents in London on December 11th 1920. He was educated at King's College, London, but the Second World War interrupted his studies. Freedman joined the Royal Artillery, and completed his degree course after the war. As a postgraduate student, he chose to study anthropology at the London School of Economics, where, following extensive fieldwork experience in Singapore, he became a lecturer. In 1965 he was appointed a professor. Freedman's studies of Chinese matters fall into several sections. The first is his Singapore research, including work on Chinese family and marriage, Chinese law, religion and community organization. The second phase of study covers the early 1950s, when he reconstructed traditional Chinese society as it affected family relationships and marriage. The third stage was devoted to what Freedman termed 'residual China', particularly Hong Kong and Taiwan. The fourth and final part was the study and explanation of the intellectual history of sinological anthropology. To this end he diagnosed the events of the early attempts to understand Chinese society. He wrote much upon his subject, including *Chinese Family and Marriage in Singapore* (1957), *Chinese Lineage and Society* (1966) and *Sinology* *and the Social Sciences* (1975). In 1970 he accepted a chair at Oxford University which he held until July 14th 1975, when he died suddenly in London.

Anna was born on December 3rd 1895 in Vienna, the youngest daughter of Sigmund Freud. As a young woman she was a teacher in an elementary school and made a point of observing children's actions and habits. In 1925 she became chairperson of the Vienna Psycho-Analytic Society and wrote a paper on her proposals concerning child psychoanalysis. In 1936 she published *Ego and Mechanisms of Defence* that gave a new role to ego psychology. In 1938 Anna and her immediate family escaped to London, where she worked as a nursery school teacher during the Second World War and published important books concerning children evacuated in a war atmosphere: *Young Children in Wartime* (1942), *Infants Without Families* (1943) and *War and Children* (1943). In 1947 she opened the Hampstead Child Therapy Clinic and was its director from 1952 to 1982. Anna Freud claimed that children at play equated to their idea of reality but not necessarily as a revelation of unconscious conflicts. She worked closely with parents and believed analysis should have an educational influence on children. In 1968 she wrote *Normality and Pathology in Childhood*, which reflected her fieldwork. She died in London on October 9th, 1982.

Lucien, the grandson of Sigmund, was born in Berlin and was part of the family that left for London in 1938. Once safe in London, Freud finished off his education at progressive schools, and following the outbreak of the Second World War served in the Merchant Navy until 1942. Lucien is now regarded as a great artist and a leader of realism in painting. His portraits of chunky naked people are well known. *Naked Man, Back View*, painted as recently as 1992, is at the Metropolitan Museum of Art in New York. An important work is his *Leigh Under the Skylight*, described as a massive claustrophobic masterpiece, showing the bald, overweight, naked Leigh Bowery in full frontal view. Freud's work is often considered too brutal, disconcerting to the viewer. However, his attention to detail, his rewarding technique and use of colour have resulted in even the most reluctant of critics acknowledging Freud as one of the finest realist painters alive today.

In June 1996 his show at the Abbot Hall Art Gallery in Kendal in the Lake District featured his painting called *Pluto and the Bateman Sisters*. The show also included his 1986 *Double Portrait*, which shows a reclining woman and a sleeping dog. One of the nude sisters is Nicola, whom Freud featured in his 1993 painting, *And The Bridegroom*. Also in 1996, his *Portrait on Grey Cover*, on exhibition in a New York art gallery, received offers of $1,000,000. The sale had been delayed, pending funds being made available to enable the painting to remain in Britain. However, the required funds never materialized and the painting was later sold in New York.

FREUD,
Sigmund
(1856-1939)
Austrian
founder of
psychoanalysis

Freud was born on May 6th 1856 in Freiberg, Moravia (now Pribor, Czech Republic). In 1902 he became professor of neurotic diseases and neurology at the University of Vienna. His work on hysteria led him to believe that this disorder was in fact the expression of repressed sexual energy. He claimed that patients thought to have brain disease were in fact suffering from mental disorders brought on by psychological factors. Freud, known as the founder of psychoanalysis, was revered in his lifetime. One of the great figures of the century, he was nevertheless a victim of German persecution and forced to flee for his life. The Germans only gave him an exit visa following President Roosevelt's direct appeal to Hitler. He came to Britain in 1938 and made his home at Hampstead in London. By now he was seriously ill, although he continued to see patients. He died a few months later, on September 23rd 1939. His many published works include *The Interpretation of Dreams* (1900), *The Ego and Id* (1923), *Moses and Monotheism* (1938) and *The Outline of Psycho-Analysis*, published shortly after his death. In 1933, together with Albert Einstein, he wrote *Why War?*

Freud himself suffered from a phobia. He had an inordinate fear of train travel known as siderodromophobia.

FRIED,
Alfred
(1864-1921)
Austrian
publisher

Fried was born on November 11th 1864 in Vienna. At the beginning of the 20th century he was living in Berlin, where he worked as a publisher and for peace. To this end he published much and founded peace societies in Germany and Austria. As secretary of the International Institute for Peace he did much to stave off the clouds gathering for what would be the First World War. In 1911 he was rewarded with the Nobel Prize for Peace. During the war of 1914-18 he was forced to flee to Switzerland, accused by the Austrians of high treason because of his continuing pacifist work. In Switzerland he busied himself caring for prisoners of war. Following the war and the demise of the monarchy, Fried returned to Vienna, where he spent the remainder of his life preaching peace and the need for a European Union. He died in Vienna on May 5th 1921.

FRIEDMAN,
Betty
(1921-)
US feminist
writer

Born Naomi Goldstein in Peoria, Illinois, on February 4th 1921, in 1942 she obtained a BA in psychology from Smith College, Northampton, Massachusetts. She married in 1947 and had three children. Her role as housewife and mother did not satisfy her intellectual abilities, and divorce ultimately resulted in 1969. Meanwhile her book, *The Feminine Mystique*, had appeared in 1963. A best-seller it brought her directly into the feminist movement. In 1966 she co-founded NOW, the National Organization of Women, and was its first president. In 1976 came her second book, *It Changed My Life*, a description of her involvement in NOW. *The Second Stage*, dealing with the status of women's movements, was published in 1981. Her writings and deep involvement with feminist issues have had a great and continuing influence in the US and beyond.

Jerome Friedman was born in Chicago on March 28th 1930. Educated at the University of Chicago, he received his PhD in 1956. A teacher and a researcher, he began his teaching career at the Massachusetts Institute of Technology in 1960, becoming a full professor in 1967 and head of the department of physics in 1983. His research career started while he was at Chicago and continued later at Stanford University. He and two colleagues, Richard Taylor and Henry Kendall, carried on where Murray Gell-Man (*qv*) left off, confirming Gell-Man's hypothesis of 1964 regarding the existence of fundamental particles, known as quarks. For their experimental work in this field, Friedman and his associates shared the Nobel Prize for Physics in 1990.

Friedman was born in Brooklyn, New York, on July 31st 1912 and educated at Rutgers University. In 1946 he received his PhD from Columbia University and joined the faculty of the University of Chicago. Friedman, a leading advocate of monetarism, expounded his right-wing economic theories in *Capitalism and Freedom* in 1962. This work and subsequent books greatly influenced economic trends in the US and, during the 1980s, in Britain when Prime Minister Margaret Thatcher adopted his ideas and made him her guru. His advice was partially responsible for the great recession of the late 1980s, which continued to have repercussions in the 1990s. However, he won the Nobel Prize for Economics in 1976. His autobiography, *Free to Choose* (1979), was co-written with his wife Rose. In 1996 the US finally dropped Friedman's philosophy on economic policy. At a lecture given in 1973 he said, in answer to a question, 'There is no such thing as a free lunch.'

Frisch was born on October 1st 1904 in Vienna. His aunt was Lise Meitner (*qv*), with whom he was to work on elements connected with the development of atomic structures. He worked in Berlin but left when the Nazis took over in 1933 to work in Copenhagen under Niels Bohr (*qv*), while his aunt was working in Stockholm. In 1939, just before the outbreak of the Second World War, Frisch arrived in Britain whose scientific establishment warmly welcomed him. They were especially impressed by the work he did in 1933, when he and two colleagues successfully measured the magnetic moment of the proton. Within months of his arrival in Britain he had named the process of atomic energy 'fission' (later, 'nuclear fission'). For a time during the Second World War he worked in New Mexico on the atom bomb project. After the war, Frisch returned to the UK and was appointed head of the physics department of the UK Atomic Energy Unit at Harwell. From 1947 he taught at Cambridge University and was director of physics at the Cavendish Laboratory. He was elected a Fellow of the Royal Society in 1948. He wrote much on his subject but did not write a definitive autobiography. However, his *The Nature of Matter* (1968) contains elements of his life story. He died in Cambridge, England, on September 22nd, 1979.

FROMM,
Erich
(1900-80)
German/
American
psychoanalyst

Fromm was born on March 23rd 1900 in Frankfurt, Germany; his grandfather was a rabbi. He was educated at the University of Heidelberg, from where he received his PhD in 1922. He trained in psychoanalysis at Munich University and at the Institute in Berlin. He started practising in the Freud tradition but found he was at variance with many of his ideas. Fromm preferred to believe that there are individuals whose personality is dependent upon their culture and biological make-up. By the time Hitler arrived in 1933, Fromm was ready to leave for the US. There his reputation had preceded him with the result that pro-Freudian circles were ready to ridicule his theories. The years 1934-41 saw Erich Fromm on the faculty of Columbia University. Here his views diverged so markedly from orthodox beliefs that he was known as controversial in the extreme. Between 1951 and 1961 he held two posts at the same time: professor of psychoanalysis at the Universidad Nacional Antomona de Mexico in Mexico City and a similar post at Michigan State University. In 1962, he was appointed professor of psychiatry at New York University, where he remained until he retired. He wrote extensively on his subject, winning round the world of psychiatry to his point of view. Perhaps his most notable contribution was *The Sane Society* (1955). Here he argues that modern man has encapsulated himself in the consumer society to the detriment of his natural personality. Fromm's continuing message is for a new society that allows individuals to become fulfilled within a society of social brotherhood. He died in Muralto, Switzerland, on March 18th 1980.

FUNK,
Casimir
(1884-1967)
Polish/American
biochemist

Funk was born on February 23rd 1884 in Warsaw, Poland, and received his PhD from Berne University in 1904. In 1910 he was engaged in research at the Lister Institute in London. His work was painstaking and often disappointing to him. However, in 1912 Funk identified that the anti-beriberi substance found in unpolished rice was an amine, an organic derivative of ammonia. Funk considered his discovery to be of the utmost importance and suggested his discovery be termed a *Vitamin*. After a period as head of the Cancer Research Unit, Funk went to the US; then, from 1928 to 1939, he ran his own biochemistry establishment at Malmaison, France. Forced to leave France following the German occupation, he returned to the US and worked with the US Vitamin Corporation and the Funk Foundation for Medical research. Funk's theory on the importance of vitamins A,B,C and D led the way in the research of nutrients and diet requirements for children and adults alike. As a boy he had a dislocated hip which, despite constant treatment, left him with a marked limp. Funk claimed that this infirmity left him more time for research and the eventual cure of beriberi by means of vitamin B1. He died on November 19th 1967.

G

Born Naum Neemia Pevsner in Bryansk, Russia on August 5th 1890, he was the older brother of Antoine Pevsner (*qv*). Gabo, who used that name from 1915 to distinguish himself from his brother, first studied medicine but was introduced to avant-garde art by his brother in Paris during 1913-14. In 1915 Naum began experimenting with geometrical construction in Oslo, Norway, where he had gone to avoid the First World War. In 1920 both brothers were back in what was now Soviet Russia. There they issued their now famous 'Realistic Manifesto' which outlined the basic principles of 'Constructivism'. In 1923, this form of art was discouraged by the state and the brothers left Russia, Antoine for Paris and Naum for Berlin. Over the next decade, Naum Gabo worked to further the cause of Constructivism. In 1932 he left Germany and joined his brother in Paris. Between 1932 to 1935 Gabo was very active in the abstraction-creation movement; then he went to England, where he remained until 1946, having been co-editor of *Circle* from 1937. In 1946 he went to America and over the next 30 years became renowned as a major force in sculpture. From 1953 to 54, he taught at the Harvard School of Architecture. His works, the titles of which indicate the type of sculpture, include *Spiral Theme* at the Museum of Modern Art, New York; *Translucent Variation on Sphere Theme* (1951) at the Guggenheim Museum in New York; and *Linear Construction in Space, Number 4* (1957/8) at the Whitney Museum of Modern Art in New York. Probably his most impressive work is the sculpture commissioned for the Bijenkorf building in Rotterdam in 1957. Naum Gabo and his brother are credited as the originators of kinetic art. Naum died in Waterbury, Connecticut, on August 23rd 1977.

GABO, Naum (1890-1977) Russian/ American sculptor

Gabor was born on June 5th 1900 in Budapest, Hungary, and educated at Budapest University. He taught at the University of Berlin for two years and from 1926 to 1933 worked as a research engineer at Siemens. Forced to flee Germany, he found sanctuary in London where he worked for the company of Thomson-Houston. In 1947 he had the notion of holography; by using filtered light sources, he developed the notion to a basic technique. Holography was not, however, really feasible until the laser was demonstrated in 1960. In 1958 Gabor was professor of applied electron physics at Imperial College, London, where he carried out research into high-speed oscilloscopes, physical optics and television; he invented a colour television tube of greatly reduced depth, so making colour television sets for the home a practical proposition. During his career, Gabor was granted some 100 patents

GABOR, Dennis (1900-79) Hungarian/ British physicist

and was awarded the Nobel Prize for Physics in 1971 for his invention of holography or three-dimensional photography. He died in London on February 8th 1979.

Serge Gainsbourg was born Lucien Ginsberg in Paris on April 2nd 1928. His Jewish parents were Russian emigrés. His father Joseph was a night club pianist and taught his son to play the piano. That stood Serge in good stead, when he was forced to leave the Lycée Concorcet for bad behaviour: the harbinger of things to come. He enrolled at the Ecole Nationale Superieure des Beaux-Arts, but was later asked to leave. He wanted to be a painter but indiscipline prevented him from fulfilling that aim. During the Second World War he and his family wore yellow stars, kept a low profile and survived. Serge spent some time after the war working as a student teacher in a Jewish school. He then became a pianist in the bar of a Paris saloon. It kept body and soul together and provided plenty of time for composition. In 1959 came his hit, *Du Chart a la Lune*. By now he was Serge Gainsbourg. He wrote songs for the singers of his day: Juliette Greco, Petula Clark and the like. In 1965 his song 'Poupee de cire, poupee de son' won the European Song Contest and Serge was on his way. He diversified, making promotional films for Brigette Bardot, including the hit *Harley Davidson*. When BB rejected his composition 'Je t'aime . . . moi non plus' he turned to Jane Birkin. He and she, over a musical background, gasped and grunted their way through a sexually explicit song that swept them to worldwide fame, albeit based on notoriety. Thanks to the Vatican, the song was banned in Italy; success was ensured. The sixties was the perfect time for 'Je t'aime', and although it was banned on many of the world's radio stations the record sold in millions and the radio stations caved in.

Gainsbourg acted in and produced films, including *Charlotte Forever*, which had incest as its theme; he brought out a reggae version of *Le Marseillaise* and sneered at the right-wing protests that followed. However, it wasn't just society he attacked; he attacked himself. He literally smoked and drank himself to death. It affected the way he looked, yet he would laugh about it and once declared: 'Ugliness is superior to beauty because it lasts longer.' The majority adored him. Alan Coren, who wrote his obituary for *The Times*, began it by describing Gainsbourg 'spreadeagled between his last drink and his last dog end', and ended it by giving thanks for him, declaring that on behalf of the pot-bellied unshaven male, 'he gave our fantasies credibility. That's more than Robert Redford ever did.' He married once and also had two long-term relationships, with Jane Birkin, which resulted in a daughter, Charlotte, and with Caroline von Paulus, resulting in a son, Lucien. Gainsbourg died of a heart attack in Paris on March 2nd, 1991. President Mitterrand was 'desolated'. Chirac, the mayor of Paris, spoke of 'his personal loss' and Brigitte Bardot spoke on something other than animal welfare for the first time in twenty years and said 'she wasn't surprised' - referring to his lifestyle. In 1996 the actress Charlotte Gainsbourg, star of the film *Jane Eyre*, announced she was planning to open a museum dedicated to her father in Paris. She has already bought his old house on the Left Bank, where he died.

Abram Games was born in Whitechapel in the East End of London on July 29th 1914. His father, a photographer, had migrated to England from Latvia a decade earlier. While at primary school Abram excelled at art; consequently, following a secondary education at the Grocers' Company School in nearby Hackney Downs, in 1930 he enrolled at St Martin's School of Art in Central London. However, after two terms there Games believed he could learn more elsewhere. He worked for his father and attended evening classes. In 1936 he won first prize in a poster competition. He became a freelance poster designer and was chosen to design posters for the London Underground. Shell Oil and the Post Office followed in the demand for his skills. Upon the outbreak of the Second World War Games joined an infantry regiment of the army. However, he was soon transferred to the public relations section of the War Office where, for the remainder of the war, he worked in an attic studio in Whitehall, designing posters. His style was distinctive and powerful and often reflected the surrealist principles of Dali and Max Ernst. Although he produced some 100 wartime posters covering all aspects of wartime society, he was not always free from government interference. One such instance was when Games designed a recruiting poster for the Auxiliary Territorial Service and showed the girl, a member of the Women's Royal Naval Service, in a too glamorous pose. However, a study of his wartime work is still most emotive, as memories of those days are evoked. The war over, Games appeared to specialize in areas of moral and public concern such as Jewish relief and the work being done for displaced persons and in public health, warning about the spread of VD. His commercial poster designs over the next four decades have become a constant art exhibition. Probably his best-known work was the symbol for the 1951 Festival of Britain. His work entitled 'Top People Read *The Times*' was only one part of his portfolio. In 1957 he was awarded the OBE for his graphic design work and two years later was appointed a Royal Designer to Industry. He died in London on August 27th 1996.

GAMES,
Abram
(1914-96)
British designer

Born Julius Garfinkle on March 4th 1913 on New York's Lower East Side, he was a difficult child, often in trouble with the law, following the early death of his mother. Persuaded by a progressive child psychologist to study acting, he changed his name and went to a drama school. John liked them and they liked John. He was later invited to join the Group Theatre Company. He played on Broadway in *Counsellor at Law* (1931) by Elmer Rice and worked his way up the billing ladder until in 1937 he played the lead in Clifford Odet's (*qv*) *Golden Boy*. This role led to a film career, generally as the 'tough guy', although sometimes he was the hero. His acting was fiery and memorable. His first film, *Four Daughters* (1938) brought him an Oscar nomination for Best Supporting Actor. He never made the top rank of stars but he was well on his way when he died suddenly on May 21st 1952. He was only 39.

GARFIELD,
John
(1913-52)
US actor

GARY,
Romain
(1914-80)
Russian/French
writer

He was born Romain Kacew in Vilnus, Russia, on May 8th 1914, to parents who were part Jewish, part Cossack and part Tartar. In 1921 the family moved to Poland and seven years later to Nice, France. Already a holder of a pilot's licence, on the outbreak of the Second World War Gary joined the French air force and became a fighter pilot. When France fell to the Germans in 1940, he escaped to England, joined the Free French forces under de Gaulle, and saw service in North Africa, where he won the Croix de Guerre. Following the war he returned to Nice, to find his father had been shipped off to Germany and the gas chamber. His mother became a force in his life and it was she who persuaded him to make his living as a writer. However, fearful of failure (although his first novel, *Forest in Anger*, had been published and well received), he joined the French Foreign Service and became the French Consul in Los Angeles from 1956 to 1960. Whenever he had time he would write. *The Colours of the Day* (1953) drew on his childhood in Nice. *The Dance of Genghis Cohn* (1968), about the ghost of a Jewish stand-up comedian that takes possession of a German executioner, became an international best-seller. *The Roots of Heaven* won him the Prix Concourt. It is a tale of freedom and justice against man's cruelty and greed. He was married to the actress Jean Seberg. After she died in Paris, in mysterious circumstances, on December 2nd 1980 Romain Gary committed suicide.

GANCE,
Abel
(1889-1981)
French
film-maker

Gance, born in Paris on October 25th 1889, became one of the most important figures in the world of film and is now universally recognized as one of the 20th century's greatest directors. The imagination, and sometimes extravagance, he has shown in his productions left his audiences gasping. At first Gance was not interested in the new wonder of movies; his first love was the theatre. However, in 1911 he agreed to direct his first film, *La Dique*, and enjoyed the experience and the result. He made a couple more films but the First World War interfered with his plans. After the war, Gance decided to concentrate solely on making films. In 1918 came *J' accuse!* He had begun work on it while the war was still on; in the event, Gance made it into a anti-war film that received worldwide critical acclaim. Anyone who has seen it can never forget the spectacle of thousands of dead soldiers rising from the battlefields and wandering through the country, to see if their ultimate sacrifice had been worthwhile. Now Gance was the greatest director in France; following his next two films, *La Roue's* (1922) and *Napoleon as Seen By Abel Gance* (1927), he was the greatest in Europe. These masterpieces are considered to be the among the greatest films of the century. The advent of the 'talkies' did not include Gance. He made a few unremarkable films in the 1930s, and in 1942 was forced to flee to Spain when the Germans started rounding up Jews. Following the Second World War he made a few good historical films, including *La Tour de Nesle* (1954), *Austerlitz* (1960) and *Cyrano et d'Artagnan* (1963). However, *Napoleon* is his greatest work. Filmed in a three-dimensional technique, it took him four years to produce and was some six hours long. In 1979 this epic was reshown, complete with orchestra and film music especially composed by Carl Davis, at the Edinburgh Festival. It has since thrilled modern audiences all over the world. Gance died in Paris on November 10th 1981.

Gasser was born on July 5th 1888 in Platteville, Wisconsin. In 1916 he was appointed professor of pharmacology at Washington University in St Louis. Here he met Joseph Erlanger (*qv*). The two men decided to collaborate in the study of very slight electrical impulses, carried by rare mammalian nerve fibres. In 1924 they adapted the oscillograph, which allowed them to see amplified nerve impulses on a fluorescent screen. They were thus able to demonstrate that different nerve fibres exist for the specific transmission of impulses such as cold, heat and pain. In addition, their work paved the way for medical machinery of all kinds that was needed for diagnostic purposes. In 1935 Gasser was appointed director of the Rockefeller Institute in New York, where he remained until 1953. In 1944 Gasser and Erlanger were jointly awarded the Nobel Prize for Physiology. Herbert Gasser died in New York on May 11th 1963.

GASSER, Herbert (1888-1963) US neuro-physiologist

Gaster was born in London on 21st July 1906. His father was a rabbi who lost his sight and relied on his son to read to him. As a result Theodor received a wide knowledge of Jewish life and literature, customs and myth. Educated at London University, where he obtained a BA and then an MA, he received his PhD from Columbia University in 1943, having emigrated to the US in 1939. Gaster rejected all religion. Paradoxically, however, he probably made more of a contribution to the understanding of Jewish history and culture than anyone else. He became known internationally as a result of his work on the Dead Sea Scrolls, discovered in the late 1940s and early 1950s in caves near Qumran, Jordan. Gaster worked on these scrolls and published a book on the subject: *The Dead Sea Scrolls in English Translation* (1956). It was literate, had popular appeal and sold a quarter of a million copies. Criticized for not being entirely accurate, Gaster was, however, able to justify his facts. His command of 29 languages and his unique and vast card index system, as well as his insistence on checking details, stood him in good stead. Gaster's approach was based not on religion but rather on anthropology. He wrote many other books, including *Thespis: Ritual, Myth and Drama in the Ancient Near East* (1950) and *Myth, Legend and Custom in the Old Testament* (1969). Gaster was a loner who preferred not be involved with others in any of his writings. This attitude was reflected in his approach to teaching and his tendency to regard students as a nuisance to be avoided if possible. He died on February 3rd 1992 in Philadelphia.

GASTER, Theodor (1906-92) British/ American historian

Arthur Gavshon was born on August 28th 1916 in Johannesburg. His parents were Jewish immigrants from Lithuania, his father a professional soldier in the army of the Tsar, his mother a teacher. Both were poor. Arthur was educated at Pretoria High School for Boys until shortage of money forced him to leave. He found a job as a labourer in a flour mill. A while later, because of his fluency in Russian, he was offered a job on the South African *Daily Express* in Cape Town. He later became that paper's parliamentary correspondent. He was also busy editing the magazine *Libertas*, a rare journal that fought racial discrimination. In 1943 Gavshon joined the army and was posted to the 23rd Field Artillery of the Sixth South African Division, which took part in the Italian campaign. Demobbed in London, he decided to stay,

GAVSHON, Arthur (1916-95) South African journalist

only to have all his worldly possessions stolen. He took the only job offered, a temporary sub-editing job for Associated Press of America. At that time, the leading members of both main British political parties were mostly ex-service and Gavshon found he had a natural rapport with them. This sphere of influence was sufficient to provide him with many inside stories. He would often spend whole nights researching the oddest of facts. One of his scoops was deducing that an old hulk once named, *President Warfield* and now known as the *Exodus* was, according to *The Shipping News,* on its way from south-west France to Tel Aviv. Further investigation by Gavshon revealed that this was in fact a Jewish ship bringing Holocaust survivors to Palestine, in breach of British immigration laws.

Over the next four decades Gavshon was credited with more original news than any other Fleet Street journalist. In 1963 he published his book *The Last Days of Dag Hammarskjold,* in which he claimed that the Swedish-born United Nations Secretary-General had not died in an accident but had been murdered. In 1984 he wrote about the sinking by the British Navy of the Argentine battle cruiser *Belgrano,* when that ship posed no danger to the British forces in the Falklands War. Gavshon never lost sight of what was happening in South Africa. He remained an opponent of apartheid all his life and relished the moment Nelson Mandela won a democratic victory to become President. Married with three daughters, Arthur Gavshon died in London on July 24th 1995.

GELFOND, Alexander (1906-68) Russian mathematician

Alexander Gelford was born in St Petersburg, Russia, on October 24th 1906. He taught mathematics at the Moscow Technological College (1929-30) and thereafter held various chairs connected with mathematics at Moscow State University. In 1934 Gelford originated basic techniques in the study of transcendental numbers, i.e. the numbers that cannot be expressed as the root or solution of an algebraic equation with rational coefficient. He proved that ab is transcendental if a is an algebraic number not equal to 0 or 1 and b is an irrational algebraic number. This statement, that has become known world-wide as Gelford's Theorem, was used positively to solve the seventh of the famous 23 problems posed by David Hilbert in 1900 while at the International Mathematical Congress in Paris. Some have remained unsolved, including the solution to the Riemann hypothesis. Therefore the world of mathematics went quite wild when Gelford came up with his theorem. In 1952 he published *Transcendental and Algebraic Numbers*. He died suddenly in Moscow on November 7th 1968.

GELLER, Uri (1946-) Israeli entertainer

Uri Geller was born in Tel Aviv on December 20th 1946. He became a celebrity in the early 1970s with what he claimed was the power of mind over matter or psychokinesis. The main manifestation of this power was the ability to cause forks and spoons to bend, and he has performed all over the world. The result appears to be that many canteens of cutlery have been deformed and clocks permanently stopped, but his audiences are most impressed. Geller is voluble concerning the origin of his powers and espouses theories on extra-terrestrial activities. He is still news, still bends cutlery and no one appears to care that there is probably a rational explanation of all that he does.

Born in New York City on September 15th 1929, **Murray** was the son of an Austrian-Jewish immigrant. At the age of fifteen he was at Yale University, receiving his BS in physics at nineteen and a PhD from Massachusetts Institute in 1951. The work he did for his doctorate was later influential in Eugene Wigner's work on subatomic particles, for which he was awarded the Nobel Prize in 1963. In 1952, Gell-Mann was at the Institute for Nuclear Studies at the University of Chicago, and in 1953 introduced the idea of 'strangeness', which he adopted, as a quantum property that accounted for previously puzzling decay patterns of certain mesons or unstable subatomic particles. Gell-Mann explained that the 'strangeness' binds the components of the atomic nucleus. In 1961, together with Yuval Ne'eman, an Israeli physicist, he suggested a scheme for classifying previously discovered interacting particles into an orderly and simple arrangement, which they published under the title *Eightfold Way* (1965). The title recalled Buddha's eightfold route to nirvana or heavenly bliss. Gell-Mann later suggested it should be practical to explain certain known particles in terms of building blocks. These they later called 'quarks', from James Joyce's novel *Finnegan's Wake*. Of the six quarks so far predicted, five have indirectly been detected. For this work Murray Gell-Man was awarded the Nobel Prize for Physics in 1969.

GELL-MANN, Murray (1929-) US physicist

Gellner was born on December 9th 1925 in Paris. His parents were Czech Jews. His education was begun at Prague's English Grammar School and completed at St Albans County Grammar School in England. A soldier in the Czech Armoured Brigade during the Second World War, he went after the war to Balliol College, Oxford and took a first in PPE in 1949. He joined the London School of Economics as a junior lecturer and stayed for 35 years. In 1962 he was appointed professor of philosophy. He completed his PhD on the Berbers, the aboriginal people of North Africa.

Gellner was a highly controversial person, from his book, *Words and Things*, written in 1959, to his appearance on a BBC show in 1994 in a debate concerning Salman Rushdie's *Satanic Verses*. His early writings declared that philosophy should have something to say about the existing world. In *Saints of the Atlas* (1969) he attempted to extrapolate a theory about Islam. In 1974 he published *Contemporary Thoughts in Politics,* investigating the inter-relationship between democracy and industrialization. He wrote on subjects which interested him, and his range of interests was large. He would often smile apologetically and admit he was, 'writing yet another book'. In his early work he mounted a closely argued attack on Oxford linguistic philosophy, contending that this format was responsible for closing the mind to more abstract modes of knowledge. It resulted in considerable acrimony that spread into the correspondence columns of *The Times.* Regarding Rushdie, some 35 years later, Gellner argued that one society could not be judged by the yardstick of another. Married with three children, Gellner died in London on November 5th 1995.

GELLNER, Ernest (1925-95) British anthropologist

GERCHUNOFF,
Alberto
(1884-1950)
Argentinean
writer

Alberto Gerchunoff, born in Buenos Aires, grew up in Moises Ville, a Jewish agricultural village founded by Baron de Hirsch. He became a journalist in Buenos Aires and worked on the daily paper *La Nacion* for some 40 years, eventually becoming its editor. His writings resulted in his becoming the best-known Spanish writer in South America. Among his books is *The Jewish Gauchos of the Pampas* (1945). Gerchunoff was the founder and first president of the Argentine Writers' Association.

GERNSBACK,
Hugo
(1884-1967)
Luxembourgeois/
American
inventor/
publisher

Hugo Gernsback, born in Luxembourg on August 16th 1884, is now credited as being the person more responsible than any other for the establishment of science fiction. He was educated in Luxembourg and Germany and, by 1904, had invented a superior type of dry battery. He travelled to the US in an attempt to sell his invention and four years later founded *Modern Electrics*, later to be known as *Popular Science*, an early magazine for radio fans. In 1926 Gernsback founded and edited another magazine: *Amazing Stories* was the first magazine devoted entirely to stories relating to science fiction, or scientifiction, as it was often called. It was later renamed *Wonder Stories.* From these most humble beginnings the genre has grown. Today it is an industry that his spawned thousands of novels as well as feature films that are both box office successes and critically acclaimed. In recognition of the part Gernsback played in all this, the annual award for the best science fiction novel is known as the Hugo Award. Hugo Gernsback died in New York on August 19th 1967.

GERO,
Erno
(1898-1980)
Hungarian
politician

Born Erno Singer in Budapest, he joined the Communist Party on his 20th birthday. Active in the revolution headed by Bela Kun (*qv*), he was lucky, a year later, to escape to Germany. He secretly returned to Hungary to edit an underground newspaper. During the Spanish civil war (1936-39), he fought on the Loyalist side in Catalan. The next time he saw his native country was in 1944, when he was part of the liberating Red Army. He became heavily involved with the new regime and, as Minister of Transport, was responsible for rebuilding an infrastructure that included bridges over the Danube. He subsequently held the portfolios of Finance, State, and Foreign Trade. He was appointed Deputy Prime Minister and became a member of the Politburo. He was also appointed First Secretary of the Communist Party when Matyas Rakosc (*qv*) was ousted. He tried unsuccessfully to stop the uprising of 1956, warning that it would set off a wave of anti-Semitism as remnants of the old fascist regime and the right-wing church joined forces. Events unfolded as he predicted and Erno Gero called on the USSR to help save his country and government from an anti-Communist coup. The tanks arrived and restored the status quo. But Gero was no longer welcome. Unwanted on all sides, he left on the last tank out of Budapest. For a number of years he lived quietly in Moscow. In 1962 the bar against him was removed and he returned to Hungary to spend his last years in retirement, bitter that he had been expelled by the Party for which he had given his life.

Gershwin was born in Brooklyn, New York, on September 26th 1898 and named Jacob. He was the son of Russian-Jewish immigrants who had arrived on Ellis Island with the surname Gershovitz. By the age of six, George was having piano lessons. Later he studied with Wallingford Riegger. His compositions were to become synonymous with the 20th century. Fame arrived overnight in 1919 with the composition he called 'Swanee', sung by Al Jolson. Commissioned by Paul Whiteman (*qv*) to write a classical work, Gershwin came up with *Rhapsody in Blue* (1924). When he played it for the first time, the audience included Rachmaninov, Stokowski and Heifetz. He went on to write extensively, including *An American in Paris* (1928) and *Cuba Overture* (1932). His last great work was *Porgy and Bess*, with lyrics by his brother Ira Gershwin (1896-1983), an opera among the greatest written this century. Besides his classical work, some of the songs he composed, with lyrics by Ira, have become standards, among them 'Lady Be Good', 'The Man I Love', 'S'Wonderful', 'I Got Rhythm', 'Embraceable You', 'A Foggy Day', 'Fascinating Rhythm', 'Let's Call the Whole Thing Off', 'Our Love is Here to Stay', 'Love Walked In', 'Nice Work If You Can Get It', 'Somebody Loves Me', 'Someone to Watch Over Me', 'Strike Up The Band', 'They Can't Take That Away From Me'. His songs appear to sing themselves. In 1931 he and Ira wrote the musical satire, *Of Thee I Sing*. It won the first Pulitzer Prize ever awarded to a musical. The sheer enjoyment the Gershwins have given to the 20th century is immeasurable. It is hard to imagine the century without their contribution. George died from a brain tumour in Hollywood on July 11th, 1937. He never married.

GERSHWIN, George (1898-1937) US composer

Although **Gertler** was born in London on December 9th 1891, he spent much of his childhood living in poverty in Poland. Deserted by his father, he and his four siblings were cared for by their mother, who supported them by working in a café and giving her offspring the leftovers from customers' plates. Back in London, the family lived in one room in Whitechapel, supported by the Jewish Board of Guardians. Tuberculosis was a scourge and Mark's health suffered, leading to depressions which would affect him all his life. Mark Gertler went to school at eight speaking only Yiddish. At fourteen he left and went to work for a firm of glass painters. In the evenings he attended art classes. In 1908 Sir William Rothenstein (*qv*) sent him to the Slade School of Art. In 1916 he painted *Merry-Go-Round*, described by D. H. Lawrence as 'the best modern picture I have seen; I think it great and true. But it is horrible and terrifying.' The painting shows men and women riding a carousel, the men as soldiers in the war around them. Another of Gertler's paintings, *The Artist's Mother*, hangs in the Tate Gallery, London. Handsome, volatile and an excellent conversationalist, by the 1920s Gertler was a leading British painter and part of the Bloomsbury set, A confidant of Lytton Strachey and in love with Dora Carrington, a fellow artist, with whom he lived for five years. Gertler's style was influenced by the French post-impressionists, in particular by Derain. He seemed destined for greatness, but worsening ill-health led to professional decline and consequent financial problems. On June 23rd 1939, his depressions increasing with reports of Hitler's purge of Jewish artistic life, Gertler committed suicide.

GERTLER, Mark (1891-1939) British painter

**GERTZ,
Elmer
(1906-)
US lawyer**

Gertz was born in Chicago and practised law in that city from 1930. He became internationally known for the forceful way he fought for those of his clients who faced the death penalty. Gertz was opposed to capital punishment and the constant breaches of civil liberties he encountered. He was instrumental in obtaining a parole for Nathan Leopold who, together with Richard Loeb, had murdered a young man for the fun of it while in their teens. Leopold had by then spent thirty-four years in prison. In 1962 Gertz had the death sentence on William Crump cancelled on the basis that during the period between sentence and execution day (a period of many years) Crump had become a rehabilitated person. William Witherspoon was another Gertz saved from the gallows, the Supreme Court upholding his contention that jurors should not have been challenged over their views regarding the death penalty. In 1966 Gertz had the death penalty imposed on Jack Ruby (*qv*) set aside. It was not, however, only capital crimes that interested him. He was also vehemently opposed to many censorship rulings. He was responsible for Frank Harris's *My Life and Loves* becoming available for everyone to read, as well as Henry Miller's *Tropic of Cancer*. Gertz even persuaded the courts that the work of the Marquis de Sade would not lead to wholesale degradation in society, if only because the works were so boring. Gertz wrote many books concerning his cases, including *The People v Jack Ruby* (1968).

**GETZ,
Stan
(1927-91)
US musician**

Stan Getz was born in Philadelphia on February 2nd 1927. His grandfather was a tailor who walked from Russia across Europe to the English Channel, where he took a boat to England and settled to live and work in Whitechapel. Stan would later look for where his grandfather lived, and where his father was born, but the house had been destroyed in the Blitz during the Second World War. In 1912 the family decided to leave England for the US. They tried to book on the *Titanic*, but even the steerage fare was too expensive. They settled for the *Lusitania*, which took them safely to New York.

Stan began playing the saxophone when he was twelve, and a little later switched from alto to tenor. Shorty Rogers was running a youth band in New York and Stan joined them. Coleman Hawkins was his hero until he came under the influence of Lester Young. During the Second World War, because of the call-up, the big bands were short of players. Getz, not yet old enough for the armed forces, joined Jack Teagarden and learnt his craft. In 1944 he played briefly with Stan Kenton, before leaving for Benny Goodman's band, with which he stayed until 1947, often being featured on recordings. Then he moved to Los Angeles and met up with Woody Herman and his 'Second Herd', becoming part of the famous Four Brothers saxophone section on tenor sax. Their style was derived from Lester Young, light and cool. In 1949 Getz formed his own group, a quartet of sax, piano, bass and drums. This small group was to become a major influence on jazz playing all over the western world. Many a musician who is now famous started off with Getz, among them Al Haig, Duke Jordan, Lou Levy, Horace Silver, Kenny Barron and many more. In 1951 he toured Scandinavia. There he met his future wife Monica, and Getz lived and played in that part of Europe for the next decade. He received a

Grammy award for *Desafinado* in 1962. His best-known recording is probably *The Girl from Ipanema* (1964) while his best-known jazz album was *Gertz/Gilberto* (1964). Although he knew he had cancer, he played and recorded for as long as he was able. When he died in Malibu, California, on June 6th 1991 he was cremated and his ashes were scattered into the sea, off Catalina Island, from Shorty Rogers' boat.

Arthur Gilbert was born in Golders Green, a north-west London suburb, in 1913. His father, a fur merchant, was an immigrant from Poland who had arrived in 1893. Arthur, who had a business in London manufacturing evening wear, moved to Los Angeles in 1950. Preferring to live in the sun, he established a financial and property business in Beverly Hills. The project was most successful and allowed Gilbert to indulge his hobby of collecting antiques. The result has been the largest and most comprehensive collection of antique gold and silver objects, now reckoned to be worth some £80 million. Gilbert is a world authority on Florentine mosaics, made in the 18th and 19th centuries from natural and semi-precious stones. In 1996 Arthur Gilbert stunned the museum world, especially in America, with the announcement that his whole collection would reside for ever in Great Britain. Because so much of his treasure originated in Britain, Gilbert decided that was where his collection belonged. It is to be housed in a special museum, created from the vaults of Somerset House in London. It is the largest collection of decorative art ever given to a country. Gilbert's wife, Rosalinde, who helped build the collection, died in August 1995 after a marriage of 61 years.

Martin Gilbert was born on October 25th 1936, in London, to middle-class Jewish parents. Educated at Highgate School and Magdalen College, Oxford, he decided upon a career as a biographical and historical writer. Probably his most important work has been as the official biographer of Sir Winston Churchill. The six volumes he has written on Churchill have brought him world-wide recognition. In addition, the publication of his book *The Second World War* (1989) is thought to be the best written and most readable on the subject. It is presented in a style that enables the reader to understand a complex period in history. Gilbert has also written, most authoritatively, on the Holocaust and the First World War. A much-admired historian, he was awarded a knighthood in 1995. In 1996, he published *The Boys*, a brilliant narrative of the true story of some 700 Jewish boys, survivors of the concentration camps, who were flown to Britain to start new lives within months of the Second World War ending.

Walter Gilbert was born on March 21st 1932 in Boston, Massachusetts. He obtained a BA in 1953 and an MA the following year, both from Harvard University. Thus armed, he went to England to work for a PhD from Cambridge University, which he obtained in 1957. Returning to the US, he joined the staff at Harvard and gradually climbed the teaching ladder from assistant professor in 1959 to associate professor in 1964 and professor of microbiology in 1969; he remained there until

1972. Gilbert's field of research is in biophysics and is connected with DNA. His work resulted in his being awarded the Nobel Prize for Chemistry in 1980, together with Paul Berg (*qv*), for determining the sequence of nucleotide links in the chainlike molecules of nuclear acids. In 1979 he joined the commercial research corporation Biogen. In 1966 he first achieved fame by isolating a sample of the elusive repressor substance that is centrally involved in controlling gene action.

**GILELS,
Emil
(1916-85)
Russian pianist**

Emil Gilels was born on October 19th 1916 in Odessa, Russia. At the age of six he was having piano lessons and in 1929, at the age of thirteen, he gave his first public concert. He graduated from the Odessa Conservatory in 1935 and moved to Moscow to continue his studies. In 1938 he won first prize at the Ysaye International Festival, Brussels, and returned to be appointed assistant professor of Moscow Conservatory. Following the Second World War he was the first Russian pianist to tour the West. He gave concerts in New York (1955) and London (1959) to critical acclaim. He proved to be the greatest in Soviet Russia and covered a wide repertory. He was responsible for introducing the works of Russian composers to American and European audiences and awarded with the Lenin and Stalin Medals of Honour. A charismatic, chunky figure, his musical interpretations were hailed by the critics and public alike. Although he died in Moscow on October 14th 1985, he has once again become a world favourite, following the release of his recordings on CD in 1996.

**GINSBERG,
Allen
(1926-97)
US poet**

Ginsberg was born on June 3rd 1926 in Paterson, New Jersey, the son of Louis Ginsberg, an English teacher who published two books of poetry. Allen graduated from Columbia University, where his radical activities often upset the faculty. Later he would have the FBI to contend with when they registered him as 'potentially dangerous'. He worked in a wide variety of jobs while writing his early poetry, and when touring the coffee shops, reading his poems, would gratefully accept any contributions offered. In 1955 he published his first book of verse, *Howl and Other Poems*. This book involved the publisher in a highly publicized obscenity trial and brought Ginsberg much fame. It meant having his poetry read by tens of thousands of people instead of a few hundred. Other works followed. *Kaddish and Other Poems* (1958-60) was dedicated to his mother, who had spent many years in a mental home. In this work Ginsberg tries to come to terms with life, death and the mother, a left-wing immigrant, he mourns. It is probably the best work Ginsberg wrote and, along with other poems, established him as one of the finest poets of his generation.

Ginsberg's poetry draws heavily on oriental mysticism and often uses mantric breath meditations. Ginsberg was the leader of the 1960s 'Beat Movement'. A homosexual who experimented with drugs, he was among the few who led the social movement away from the strictures and censorship of middle-class morality. Paradoxically Ginsberg, an anti-establishment figure, has accepted many - and well-deserved - honours and awards. An opponent of the Vietnam War, he wrote in *From The Fall Of America* in 1973 'What if someone gave a war and nobody came?' In 1986 he published *White Shrouds: Poems 1980-1985*. In 1996, Ginsberg, together with The Fugs, was a star of Woodstock 2, receiving a rapturous reception from the sell-out audience. Also in 1996 he published *The Ballad of the Skeletons*, a collection of poems concerning homelessness. His last poem, entitled *On Fame and Death* was written three days before his death. He died at home in New York on April 5th 1997 surrounded by family and friends.

Morris Ginsberg was born in Lithuania on May 14th 1889. He was twenty-one when he emigrated to the UK and became an undergraduate, reading philosophy, at University College, London. Many Jews were arriving in Britain from Eastern Europe at this time, but Yiddish-speaking Talmudic scholars at English universities, having little or no English, were rare. Three years later Ginsberg had a obtained a BA in philosophy with first class honours. Two years on and he had his MA. In 1914 he was invited to be an assistant to L. T. Hobhouse, professor of sociology at the London School of Economics. For Morris Ginsberg it was the beginning of a 40-year association with the School. Ginsberg reached a remarkable level of knowledge to arrive at the degree of sophistication he attained as a leading sociologist, and in so doing exceeded the brilliance of the brightest among his contemporaries. He wrote much. In his last work, *On Justice in Society* (1965), he makes an analysis of the concepts of justice, equality and general rights and their applications to criminal law and international relations. Goldberg's contribution to the ethical problems in society earns him an exceptional place in 20th century learning. An academic giant, he received many awards and honorary degrees and, in 1953, was admitted as a Fellow of the British Academy. He was described as 'a small, quiet, serious, yet friendly man, curled up in an old armchair, surrounded by walls of books, looking as if he had grown out of them'. He died in Highgate, London, on August 31st 1970.

Natalie was born on July 14th 1916 in Palermo, Sicily. Her father was Guiseppe Levi, a Jewish professor of anatomy, her mother a Gentile. Natalie was absorbed by her family and this showed in her writings. She was the youngest of a large family and received her early education at home with a governess. She then studied in Turin, where her friends were fellow Jewish anti-fascist intellectuals. Following university, she went to work in the publishing house of Giulo Einaudi. Here she met her husband, Leone Ginzburg. During the Second World War the Ginzburgs were exiled within Italy to Abruzzo, where Natalie completed her first novel, *The Road to the City*, although it was not published until 1948.

Leone Ginzburg was arrested during the German occupation of Italy and murdered in 1944. Natalie's published novel was a success and she returned to Einaudi. Her books continued to be about family life and personal scenes and were constantly acclaimed, although a small faction were critical of her not writing on a larger canvas. Her first novel, and one or two later books, appeared under the pseudonym of Alessandra Torrimparte. *Voices in the Evening* (1963) was a study of death and sadness, but relieved by family love and a delicate humour. Probably her best novel is *Family Sayings* (1967), a psychological story that covers several

GINSBERG, *Morris* *(1889-1970)* *British* *philosopher*

GINZBURG, *Natalie* *(1916-91)* *Italian writer*

generations and is based upon her own family experiences. It is often used in senior school work as a text for examinations. In 1950 she remarried, but kept the name Ginzburg. In 1955 she came to live in London. There, in 1968, she wrote the play, *The Advertisment*. It was produced at the National Theatre in London by Laurence Olivier and starred his wife, Joan Plowright. In 1983, back in Italy, she became active in politics. She was elected to the Senate on a left-wing Independence Party ticket. She told an American interviewer: 'I did it because I like to learn about things. I like to learn about them so I can write about them.' She died in Rome on October 7th 1991.

GLASER,
Donald
(1926-)
US physicist

Born on September 21st 1926, in Cleveland, Ohio, at school **Donald** needed the services of a child analyst to create an atmosphere of study. Whatever method the analyst used, it must have worked, because Glaser went on to take a degree in physics at the California Institute of Technology. He then moved to the University of Michigan and taught physics. During his research work with nuclear physics, Glaser discovered limitations surrounding the cloud chamber apparatus that was used to record very high speed nuclear particles. He therefore designed what he came to call a 'bubble chamber' and in effect reversed the process previously used. He implemented the idea in 1952, and it became the foundation for an essential aid in nuclear research. It also won him the Nobel Prize for Physics in 1960 at the young age of 34. He later became professor of molecular biology at the University of California.

GLASHOW,
Sheldon
(1932-)
US physicist

Sheldon was born in New York City on December 5th 1932 and graduated from Cornell University in 1954. In 1955 he received his MA and in 1959 a PhD, both from Harvard University. Following periods of teaching at Stanford (1961) and the University of California at Berkeley (1961-66), he returned to Harvard as a professor. A member of the National Academy of Science, he is a successful researcher in the field of nuclear physics. Together with Steven Weinberg whom he first met when they were schoolmates at Bronx School of Science in 1950, and Abdus Salam, he was awarded the Nobel Prize for Physics in 1979. Their work was in the development of the 'electroweak theory'. This theory marries two of the basic interactions of nature, electromagnetism and the weak nuclear force, into a single gauge theory. At Harvard, Glashow was Higgins professor of physics in 1979 and Mellon professor of sciences in 1988.

GLASS,
Philip
(1937-)
US composer

Philip Glass was born in Baltimore, Maryland, on January 31st 1937. As a boy he studied music; then, aged fifteen, he entered the University of Chicago and there studied mathematics and philosophy. He graduated in 1956 and found the interest he had had for music while a child was still the dominant feature of his life. It led him to join the Juilliard School of Music in New York and study composition. Armed with a degree in music, Glass went off to Paris to study with Nadia Boulanger. In Paris he met up with the now famed Indian sitar player, Ravi Shankar. Shankar had a decisive effect on Glass's style of composition, resulting in small ensembles playing his radical minimalist music to small but enthusiastic audiences in the 1960s. It was not until Glass composed the opera *Einstein on the Beach* (1976) that he reached a much wider audience and received a certain amount of critical acclaim. Although this opera still reflected his original radical style, it was tempered by the inclusion of more Western-style rhythms. His opera *Satyagraha* (1980) is far more in the accepted operatic mould, albeit with a strong Indian message. In 1992 his opera *The Voyage*, commissioned by the New York Metropolitan Opera, received mixed reviews. However, the opera was to commemorate the 500th anniversary of Columbus discovering America, and by choosing Glass, the music establishment confirmed his acceptance as a major composer.

Reinhold Gliere was born to middle-class Jewish parents in Kiev, Russia, on January 11th 1875, the son of a musician and instrument-maker. In 1900 he graduated from the Moscow Conservatory. He spent a while teaching in Moscow, then studied conducting in Berlin (1905-07). He was conducting in Moscow in 1908 when he introduced his tone poem, *The Sirens*. It received enthusiastic applause and critical acclamation. In 1920 he was appointed professor of music at Moscow Conservatory and took up collecting and researching Russian folk music. This resulted in his opera *Shah Senam* (1934), featuring music from the Azerbaijan region, which had a large Jewish population. Music from the Uzbek region was featured in his music drama *Hulsara* (1936). He was involved with the Moscow Union of Composers and taught at state music schools. Among his pupils were Sergey Prokofiev, Nikolay Myaskovsky and Aram Khachaturian. His music is still popular in Russia, and his ballet *The Red Poppy* (1927) was internationally performed. He died in Moscow on June 23rd 1956.

Gluckman was born in Johannesburg on December 14th 1914. He was educated at the University of the Witwatersrand and qualified as a doctor, after which he worked at St Bartholomew's Hospital in London. He remained there throughout the Second World War, doing pathology work at which, by the time the war was over, he was an expert at. Back in South Africa, he established a general practice and ran it for 25 years. His reputation as an eminent pathologist lent force to his attacks on the medical establishment and its relation with the state. He was particularly concerned with the number of suspects dying while in police custody. In 1977 the family of Steven Biko asked Gluckman to perform a post-mortem on Biko, a healthy man who had mysteriously died while detained by the South African police. His findings were contrary to those of other doctors. He found that Biko had died after being brutally tortured and suffering brain damage from the resulting trauma. At considerable risk to his life, Gluckman made his findings public. The resulting publicity caused an international political furore. The government tried to distance itself publicly from what it described as 'renegade police'. Gluckman received numerous death threats. As a Jew, he was a figure the Boers could really hate, a convenient scapegoat now that their cause of apartheid was beginning to crack. Gluckman ignored the threats and continued conducting autopsies and investigating deaths at the request of the families of victims of state violence. He set his fees according to what families could afford to pay, doing much work for no payment. He refused to be intimidated by the police bugging his phone and following him everywhere he went. He was asked to join Medical Rescue International, a group of doctors dedicated to battling against government-sanctioned persecution. In 1979, although 65 and ready to retire, he continued working harder than ever, investigating the cause of death among an increasing number of police victims.

Gluckman was able to draw upon his the Second World War experiences when examining bodies for which the official report stated one reason for death while Gluckman's vast knowledge indicated quite another, often sinister, cause. Gluckman was well aware that if he were to publish his findings he could well meet with a fatal accident. Instead he went directly to the President, F.W.de Klerk. However, in 1992 de Klerk refused to acknowledge Gluckman's information and the police killings continued. Gluckman then went public and announced that of the 200 bodies he had examined, 180 showed evidence of torture and fatal wounds that could only have been caused by the police. Eventually the Law and Order Minister admitted that 30 per cent of the people listed by Gluckman had been secretly murdered by the police. A year later, Gluckman had an operation for a back problem. The operation was successful but he suffered a post-operative heart attack and died in a Johannesburg hospital on May 25th 1993. There is little doubt that the work undertaken by Dr Gluckman hastened political change in South Africa.

GLUCKMAN,
Max
(1911-75)
South African/
British
anthropologist

Gluckman was born on January 26th 1911 in Johannesburg, South Africa and was a Rhodes Scholar at Oxford University in 1934. Gluckman has distinguished himself by his extensive work on political anthropology, especially his analysis of the political systems appertaining to African tribes. His book *Custom and Conflict in Africa* (1955) explains the relations of tribes to each other in respect of feuds and change, both political and cultural. Following a spell in Zululand (1936-38), he joined the Institute of Northern Rhodesia and made several studies on different tribal areas. Between 1947 and 1949 he was a lecturer in social anthropology at Oxford; he then went on to Manchester University. The anthropological work done by Gluckman in the late 1930s and early 1940s laid the foundations for the understanding required to facilitate the independence of Africans from the colonial ties of Britain, Belgium and France. He wrote many books on his subject, including *Rituals of Rebellion in South East Africa* (1954), *Politics, Law and Ritual in Tribal Society* (1965) and *The Allocation of Responsibility* (1972). Gluckman was chairman of the Association of Social Anthropologists of the British Commonwealth. He died in Jerusalem on April 13th 1975.

GODDARD,
Paulette
(1911-90)
US actor

Born Pauline Marion Goddard Levy on June 3rd 1911 in Long Island, New York, she experienced considerable anti-Semitism and attempted to allay this by changing her name. Professionally, she had little success until picked by Charlie Chaplin for his feature film *Modern Times* (1936). The two fell in love during the making of the film and married. The next film she made with Chaplin was *The*

Great Dictator (1940). In 1944, having divorced Chaplin, she married Burgess Meredith and they co-produced and co-starred in *Diary of a Chambermaid* (1946). In 1958 she married her final husband, the writer Erich Maria Remarque, author of *All Quiet on the Western Front*. Goddard was very popular during the 1940s and early 1950s. A happy-go-lucky type, she had the bubbly personality ideal for the romantic comedy so popular in the films of the 1930s. She made many run-of-the-mill films but was once nominated for an Oscar as Best Supporting Actress for *So Proudly We Hail* (1943). She made her final film in Italy in 1964. She died on April 23rd 1990 in Switzerland.

Arthur Goldberg was born on August 8th 1908 in Chicago, Illinois, the youngest of eleven children. He graduated from Northwestern University Law School and practised in Chicago from 1929 to 1948, establishing himself as a labour lawyer. He came to public notice when he acted as counsel for the Chicago Newspaper Guild during the 1938 strike. He was appointed Secretary of Labour and served in this position from 1961 to 1962, raising the minimum wage and improving unemployment benefits. In August 1962 President Kennedy appointed him to the Supreme Court; he stayed there until 1965, at which time President Johnson asked him to be the US ambassador to the United Nations. During his term on the Supreme Court he wrote the historical decision that 'every accused prisoner has the right that a lawyer be present during police interrogation'. Goldberg resigned his ambassadorship because of the escalation of US involvement in the Vietnam conflict. In 1970 he stood as Democratic candidate in the election for Governor of New York State and lost. A year later he returned to basics and Washington DC, where he continued as a lawyer in general practice. In 1977 and 1978, during the presidency of Jimmy Carter, Goldberg acted as a roving ambassador. His final years, while in retirement, were spent on human rights cases. He was a calm, courteous man who invariably put people at their ease. He died on January 19th 1990 in Washington DC.

GOLDBERG, Arthur (1908-90) US lawyer

Reuben Goldberg was born in San Francisco, California, on July 4th 1883. His father, the San Francisco Fire and Police Commissioner, guided his son towards a career in engineering. Rube studied at the University of California, gained a BS and got a job designing sewer pipes. He soon left and joined the *San Francisco Chronicle* (1904-5). Then he went east to the *New York Evening Mail*. Here he created three long-running cartoon strips and the character Professor Lucifer Gorgonzola Butts, was an inventor of contraptions that accomplished simple ends in a long, roundabout manner. In 1938 he left the *Mail* and spent the next ten years freelancing. He won the 1945 Pulitzer Prize for the best editorial cartoon. *Peace To-day* was a warning against atomic weapons that won the 1948 Pulitzer Prize. In 1959 he wrote *How to Remove the Cotton From a Bottle of Aspirin*. He retired in 1964 and took up sculpting, winning critical acclaim for his bronze work. The annual award of the National Cartoonists' Society is known as 'The Reuben'. Rube Goldberg died in New York on December 7th 1970.

GOLDBERG, Rube (1883-1970) US cartoonist

GOLDING,
Louis
(1895-1958)
British writer

Golding was born in Manchester on November 19th 1895, the son of impoverished parents recently arrived from Russia. Educated at the prestigious Manchester Grammar School and Queens' College, Cambridge, he started writing while at university. His career was interrupted by the First World War, during which he fought in the Salonika campaign. However, the war years gave him his creative ammunition and in 1920 he published his first novel, *Forward from Babylon*. Like many ex-soldiers, he was restless and, as a result, spent much of the 1920s travelling and getting the dust of war off himself. His lasting reputation was made with a series concerning working-class Anglo-Jewish life. The stories centred on the Manchester area, thinly disguised as the town of 'Doomington'. *Magnolia Street* appeared in 1931 and was an instant success. 'Doomington' became so real that railway ticket clerks had to be instructed accordingly. Each novel, concerning the same family and their friends, was set against a different background. They included *Five Silver Daughters* (1935) *Mr. Emmanuel* (1939); later a film was made, *The Glory of Elsie Silver* (1945). Golding wrote other novels as well as short stories, film scripts and books on boxing. He died in London on August 9th 1958.

GOLDMAN,
Emma
(1869-1940)
Russian/
American writer

Emma was born on June 27th 1869 in Kaunas, Russia, and grew up there and in St Petersburg. In 1885 she and her family emigrated to the US. Her long association with Alexander Berkman was of great significance in her life. It led her to think for herself and to appreciate anarchist philosophy. During her active life she was constantly in the news, starting in 1901 when she was accused of inspiring a fellow anarchist, Leon Czolgosz, to assassinate President McKinley in Buffalo, New York. Her thoroughly researched book *Mother Earth* (1906-18) brilliantly exposes the injustice and immorality of American society. The fact that American society, at that particular time, was head and shoulders above most other societies only serves to emphasize the enormity of Emma Goldman's conclusions. She was a compelling advocate of birth control before the First World War and, as a result, acquired a certain infamy; as if this were not enough, she was violently opposed to conscription and US entry into the First World War. Her activities led to her imprisonment. Worse, the government banned her book from being sent through the postal system. Emma Goldman continued her radical ways and the government now played its trump card, declaring her an undesirable alien and deporting her back to Russia. The order included Alexander Berkman. However, it was now 1919 and Russia was the Soviet Union; Goldman and Berkman were quite looking forward to their return.

Two years later, disillusioned by Russian Communism, Goldman escaped and wandered Europe. For a while she settled in England, but later moved on to Canada. She was in Spain during the civil war and earnestly supported the efforts of the Catalonian anarchists. She wrote *My Disillusionment in Russia* (1923) and her biography, *My Life* (1931). Her constant fight was for individual freedom. She hated capitalism because it enslaved a working class and was therefore full of inequality. For her, Communism was the ideal, but she saw that in practice it was corrupt. As a result, she found that, for her, anarchism was the answer. This, she thought, could prove to be a workable system by the free co-operation of the masses. Emma died on May 14th 1940 in Toronto, Canada.

Goldschmidt was born in Hamburg on January 18th 1903. Growing up in a flat over his father's hardware shop, he fell in love with music and he remained faithful to that love all his long life. From the age of fifteen he had private music lessons from the conductor of the Hamburg Opera Company, and later Schoenberg (*qv*) had a place for him in his master class. Goldschmidt, however, preferred Berlin and the Hochschule für Musik, although it was a time of violent inflation and political upheaval in Germany. Some early success as a composer encouraged him. He played with the Berlin Philharmonic, wrote incidental music and conducted small musical groups. In 1932 he composed his first opera, *The Mighty Cuckold*. It was premiered in Mannheim and has the dubious distinction of being the last work of a Jewish composer to be performed in pre-war Germany.

Goldschmidt arrived in London in 1935 and bought a flat which would be his home for the remainder of his life. For Ballets Joos he wrote *Chronica*, an anti-fascist work. He joined the BBC German Section in 1944 and gave piano lessons in his spare time. Then began a period of misfortune. A commissioned opera for Glyndebourne in 1951 was not performed, and his concertos for violin and cello and clarinet could not find a home. For many years he did little more than survive. In 1960 he conducted the first British performance of Mahler's Third Symphony. In 1964 he conducted the Mahler Tenth Symphony at the Proms. Then followed another long period of rest. Then, in 1982, Berthold Goldschmidt was taken out, dusted down and commissioned to write for the clarinet. *Clarinet Quartet* was the result and was much admired. Now work started coming in again: a concert in the US; a concert performance of his forgotten opera of 1951; enthusiastic performances of his works in Germany. Commissions followed for the Berlin festivals of 1987 and 1994. He was asked to write the music on the occasion of the opening of the Holocaust Museum in Schleswig-Holstein. In 1994 he composed a cycle of French songs as well as a variety of classical pieces. His music now reflected his life, serene and peaceful. A childless widower, he died in London on October 17th 1996.

GOLDSCHMIDT, Berthold (1903-96) German/British composer

It was **Richard Goldschmidt**, born in Frankfurt on April 12th 1878, who first told an unbelieving scientific world of his theory that chromosome molecules are the more decisive factors in inheritance. In 1904 he was a lecturer at Munich University and in 1913 was appointed head of the genetics department of the Kaiser Wilhelm Institute in Berlin. In pursuance of research on the gypsy moth he went to Japan. On his way back, the First World War broke out. He stopped off in the US and spent the period 1914-17 teaching at Yale University. Then the US declared war on Germany and Richard finished the war in an alien detention camp. After the war he returned to Berlin and the Institute, where he remained until 1936. By this time Goldschmidt was the leading geneticist in Europe, possibly the world. It made no difference. He was a Jew; he must leave Germany or go to a concentration camp. He left and returned to the US where he was appointed professor of zoology at the University of California (1936-48). His experiments in genetics led to his discovery that genetics are the reasons for geographical variations among animals. His was the first genetic explanation of this phenomenon. This work led him to theorize

GOLDSCHMIDT, Richard (1878-1958) German/ American biologist

concerning patterns of intersexuality. He coined the phrase 'phenocopy' to explain changes in the outward appearance of an organism caused by shock. Some of his theories were rejected by his fellow scientists; however they were still instrumental in paving the way for the advancement of genetic science and, later, genetic engineering. He died in Berekely, California, on April 24th 1958.

GOLDSCHMIDT,
Victor
(1888-1947)
Norwegian
mineralogist

Born in Zurich, Switzerland, on October 27th 1888, **Victor** became a Norwegian citizen in 1905. He followed his father Heinrich into the world of science. Victor was educated at the University of Christiania, Oslo, and, like his father, became a professor at the university. In 1929 he was appointed director of the mineralogical department at Gottingham. However, increasing anti-Semitism forced him to leave Germany in 1935 and return to Norway. Following the invasion of Norway in 1940, he was pursued by the Gestapo and was forced into hiding, keeping constantly on the move, until the Norwegian resistance movement smuggled him to Sweden in 1942. From there the British RAF flew him to England in a Mosquito fighter bomber, lying in the empty bomb bay. He spent the rest of the Second World War working in the arena of atomic energy, returning to Norway in 1946.

Victor Goldschmidt has been described as one of the greatest mineralogists of his generation and a continuing inspiration to students everywhere. In the course of a brilliant career he developed various ideas and theories, including an explanation of the distribution of chemical elements on the earth's crust; defining the laws that result from the natural factors in elements; the production of aluminium from silicates; the use of biotite as a fertilizer; and the use of olivine, a rock-forming mineral, as a material in the manufacture of items that require to be resistant to chemical reactions. All these, and more, have benefited mankind. In addition, he is the acknowledged founder of the science of geochemistry. He died in Oslo on March 20th 1947.

GOLDSTEIN,
Joseph
(1940-)
US geneticist

Joseph Goldstein, born on April 18th 1940 in Sumner, South Carolina, received his BS degree from Washington University in Lexington, Virginia. Four years later he gained his medical degree from the Southwestern Medical School at Dallas, Texas. He went to work as an intern at Massachusetts General Hospital between 1966 and 1968 and there met Michael Brown. Goldstein then spent four years researching at the National Institute of Health, specializing in genetically related factors that caused the accumulation of blood cholesterol in those prone to heart attacks. He later taught at the Southwestern Medical School and was reunited with Brown. Together they began studying the processes concerning the accumulation of cholesterol in blood. During this research they discovered that low density lipoproteins, which are primary cholesterol particles, are withdrawn from the bloodstream into the body's cells by receptors on the cell's surface. This new understanding, when developed, meant that new drugs could be established that would successfully lower blood cholesterol levels. In 1976 Goldstein was professor of medicine and molecular genetics at the University of Texas Health Science Centre at Dallas. In 1985 he and his old friend Michael Brown were jointly awarded the Nobel Prize for Physiology, in respect of their elucidation of the process of cholesterol metabolism in the human body.

Barry Goldwater was born on January 1st 1909 in Phoenix, Arizona, into an old Jewish family on his father's side; his grandfather, Michael, was the one who founded the family fortune. Barry worked in the Phoenix department store between 1937 and 1953, eventually becoming chairman of the company. He was elected to the US Senate in 1952 and again in 1958. A right-winger, he might have been dangerous in his warlike attitude to the USSR had not quieter voices prevailed. A Republican with set ideas, 1964 was his greatest year. Nominated as his party's choice to be the presidential candidate he fought the incumbent Democrat, President Johnson. The public said 'No' to Goldwater; they were afraid he and some bomb-happy generals might carry them into a third world war. In the event, Goldwater only took Arizona and five other states, all in the South. In 1968 he was re-elected to the Senate and continued to sit there until he retired in 1987. To his credit, he led a delegation of Republican senators who called on President Nixon to resign. His biography, *With No Apologies*, appeared in 1979. During his presidential campaign in 1964 his slogan was, 'In your heart, you know I'm right.'

GOLDWATER, Barry (1909-) US politician

Born Shmuel Gelbfisz in Warsaw on August 27th 1882 into a large and very poor family, by the beginning of the 20th century he had left Poland. Passing through much of Europe, he eventually surfaced in the US. Here he changed his name, choosing Sam Goldfish. He became a glove salesman. However, the current buzzword was 'the movies', and in 1910 he and his brother-in-law, Jesse Lasky, set up a film company. In 1913 they produced their first feature film, *The Squaw Man*. Its director was Cecil B. DeMille. In 1916 Goldfish and his company joined forces with another film entrepreneur named Adolph Zukor (*qv*): the result was called Paramount. In 1917 the two had a row and Goldfish left. He and the brothers Selwyn started a production company. They called it Gold-Wyn Pictures and Sam Goldfish now became Sam Goldwyn. The relationship lasted until 1922 when Goldwyn was manoeuvred out. The company he left took on Louis B. Mayer (*qv*) and changed its name to Metro Goldwyn Mayer or MGM. Goldwyn now decided he had enough of partners and became an independent producer. He used United Artists and RKO to distribute for him, while he concentrated on making films. Samuel Goldwyn Inc. went on to make some very important films. Goldwyn had the gift for finding talent among actors, writers and directors and joining them together. Some of his more notable films were *Roman Scandals* (1933); *Beloved Enemy* (1936); *Stella Dallas* (1937); *The Adventures of Marco Polo* (1938); *Wuthering Heights* (1939); *The Little Foxes* (1941); *The Best Years of Our Lives* (1946); *Guys and Dolls* (1955); and *Porgy and Bess* (1959). His illogical aphorisms are still with us: 'Include me out'; 'Anyone who visits a psychiatrist should have his head examined'; and ' Monogamy is OK in the office but at home I prefer white pine'. Probably the best known is, 'An oral contract is not worth the paper it's written on.' Goldwyn died in Los Angeles on January 31st 1974.

GOLDWYN, Samuel (1882-1974) US film pioneer

GOLLANCZ,
Sir Victor
(1893-1967)
British
publisher

Gollancz was born into a rabbinical family on April 9th 1893 in London. Educated at St. Paul's School, London, he left New College, Oxford without a degree in order to take part in the First World War. As an officer in the field he saw much action, before being sent home to train others. From 1920 to 1928 he worked in the publishing firm of Benn Brothers. At the beginning of the 1930s he set up his own house as Victor Gollancz Ltd, with the intention of publishing works in which he was interested. Among his authors were Harold Laski (*qv*), John Strachey, A. J. Cronin, Dorothy Sayers and John Le Carré. He supported many organizations and causes, mainly of the left, including among others pacifism, the abolition of capital punishment and the provision of decent social benefits. He was also an early opponent of fascism and for this purpose he launched his most successful Left Book Club to harness the work of intellectuals in a common purpose. Following the Second World War, he organized the 'Save Europe Now' campaign. He wrote much himself, including *Shall Our Children Live or Die?* (1942), *In Darkest Germany* (1947), *Our Threatened Values* (1947) and his autobiography, in three volumes, *My Dear Timothy* (1952). He was knighted in 1965. Victor Gollancz was said to be a man of great conscience. He helped lay the groundwork for the post-war Labour government and with it the British welfare state. Between 1960 and 1964 he headed the national campaign to abolish capital punishment and lived to see it achieve its aim. He died in London on February 8th 1967.

GOMBRICH,
Sir Ernest
(1909-)
Austrian/British
Art historian

Ernest Gombrich was born on March 23rd 1909 in Vienna and studied at the University of Vienna. His subject was the history of art, and his studies in this field have resulted in his receiving many honours and the accolade of having enriched the lives of millions of people all over the world. When he left Vienna, shortly after Hitler's arrival, he went to Britain and a job with the Warburg Institute as a research assistant. During the Second World War he monitored German broadcasts and translated them into English. The war over he began writing. The first edition of *The Story of Art* was published in 1950; since then there have been sixteen further editions, the most recent in 1995. These are reckoned to be the most famous and popular books on art ever published. The work, which has been translated into nineteen languages, is a friendly introduction to the history of art that does not intimidate those coming upon the subject for the first time. Other writings of Gombrich are more scholarly works for the specialist and academic reader. *Art and Illusion* (1960) explains and examines style, how it changes and develops. He challenges many orthodox views and does not shirk from exposing art shibboleths. Gombrich, who has received honorary degrees from universities the world over and been knighted by the British, is a modest, humorous man who makes clear to German and Austrian audiences his feelings about the recent past. J. M. Massing has written of Gombrich: 'For his scholarly method, his theoretical approach and his defence of cultural values, Gombrich will be remembered as one of the leading art historians of this century.' Gombrich is deemed one of those increasingly rare individuals, a genuine intellectual.

Born in Riga, Latvia, he was fortunate to have been away from that place and in the Russian armed forces when the Germans invaded his home and his fellow Latvians aided the Germans in killings his fellow Jews. Known as 'Sasha', Gomelsky is credited as being the father of modern basketball in the Soviet Union. More particularly, he was the coach of the gold medal winning Soviet team in the 1972 Munich Olympics: it was the first time the US had ever lost the gold. Gomelsky now became well known all over the basketball world. In the 1964 event at Tokyo Olympics, Sasha's men won the silver. Gomelsky has enjoyed numerous successes with the national team and, although on occasions relieved as coach, when his lads have lost, he was always being recalled to recreate his successes. He is well known and very popular in and out of the old and new Russia. The success of Soviet basketball in the international arena is directly attributable to Alexander Gomelsky.

GOMELSKY, Alexander (1926-) Russian basketball coach

Gompers was born on January 27th 1850 in London, left school at twelve and became apprenticed to a cigar maker. By the beginning of the 20th century the family had emigrated to the US and Gompers was vice-president of the National Civic Federation, set up to achieve stable labour relations via collective bargaining and personal contacts. He was the first president of the American Federation of Labour and remained in that position until his death. Gompers was responsible for building up the largest labour organization in the US. He was instrumental in winning support for trade union recognition from President Wilson, when the President needed the labour movement to back America's entry into the First World War. As a result, labour's interests were protected. Gompers often had the unenviable task of acting as a spokesman for views that differed from his personal opinions. Thus he had to tone down his efforts to make the labour movement anti-discriminatory and sacrifice his convictions about organizing black workers for the sake of getting some sort of agreement. Gompers' argued consistently throughout his life that improved conditions, wages and hours could only be achieved through the establishment of strong unions. He was not interested in political reform. He would explain to the movement that only by their collective efforts could they improve their poor conditions of work, and that the employer class would always be anti-union. His two-volume biography, entitled *Seventy Years of Life and Labour*, was published a few months after his death on December 13th 1924 in San Antonio, Texas. He once stated, 'the labour of a human being is not a commodity of commerce'.

GOMPERS, Samuel (1850-1924) British/ American trade unionist

Goodman was born on May 30th 1909 in Chicago. His father, a tailor, was very poor and had to take care of a large family. Benny was ten when he started taking lessons, on a borrowed clarinet, at the local synagogue. At fourteen he was making more money than his father by playing with a local band a few nights a week, and thoroughly enjoying it. Following school, Benny studied music. However, by the time he was sixteen, he was playing in California with the Pollack band. In 1933 Goodman had his own twelve-piece band; but it was just another band, and he would lay awake at night wondering how he could meet that week's wage bill. On August 21st 1935, Benny Goodman decided to include some of Fletcher Henderson's

GOODMAN, Benny (1909-86) US band leader and musician

arrangements at the Palomar ballrooms in Los Angeles. The crowd on the dance floor went crazy. The Benny Goodman band was a hit: that night Swing was born and Goodman was crowned its king. Playing a mixture of jazz and popular music, his band became the tops. The band was also the first to have black and white musicians playing together. Goodman, at his independent best, ignored the taboos. If the promoter wanted the Benny Goodman Band he had no choice but to accept black and white performing together. They played everywhere: theatres, night clubs, hotels, radio stations, recording studios, private parties and films. The Goodman band was featured in *Hollywood Hotel* (1938), *Stage Door Canteen* (1943) and *Sweet and Lowdown* (1944). It launched the careers of Peggy Lee, Gene Krupa, Harry James (*qv*), Lionel Hampton and Teddy Wilson. Although he was the established King of Swing, there was another side to Benny Goodman's music. Classical music had attracted him in 1938 and slowly taken over. Now he was often the soloist at a Mozart concert. Bela Bartok and Aaron Copland (*qv*) wrote clarinet concertos for him. In 1986 he was awarded an honorary doctorate from Columbia University. Benny Goodman, recognized as a genius of the clarinet, was the most recorded solo instrumentalist in history. Some of the hits he made remain standards of our time, among them 'King Porter Stomp', 'Stompin at the Savoy' and 'Sweet Georgia Brown'. Sinatra said of him: 'Working with Benny Goodman wasn't a job, it was an experience.' Goodman died in New York City on June 13th 1986.

GOODSON,
Mark
(1915-92)
US television
producer

Mark Goodson was born in Sacramento, California, on January 24th 1915. The son of poor immigrant Jews from Russia, the memory of the poverty of those early days lived with him all his life, even though by 1992 he was worth around $500 million. Educated at the University of California, he obtained a BA in 1937. Within weeks he was working as a disc jockey with KJBS, San Francisco. In 1939, Goodson launched his first radio game show, *Pop the Question,* and by 1941 was working in New York as a freelance announcer. While working on a WABC quiz programme called *Battle of the Boroughs* he met the man who would become his future partner in television, Bill Todman. They invented television game shows that would be shown all over the world. *Winner Take All* was launched with CBS in 1946, followed by *Stop the Music* and *Hit the Jackpot.* February 1st 1950 saw the first transmission of *What's My Line?*; CBS ran it for seventeen years and it is still playing somewhere in the world. The partners turned to drama and produced *The Richard Boone Repertory Theatre* for television. The partnership ended with Todman's death in 1979. By now Goodson was rich and famous had won three Emmy awards in 1951, 1952 and 1977 as well as the National Television Award of Great Britain. He died in New York on December 18th 1992. In an interview with the *Los Angeles Times,* Goodson once said: 'The game show business is essentially without status. I regret it and I resent it. There aren't many people at Yale drama school studying game shows.'

Nadine Gordimer was born on November 20th 1923 in Springs, Transvaal. The daughter of a Jewish watchmaker who had emigrated from Lithuania, she was educated at the University of Witwatersrand but did not stay to graduate. She had a love of writing which emerged when she was only nine years old, and had a short story published in *Forum* by the time she was fifteen. Her first book, *The Soft Voice of the Serpent*, published in 1952, was a collection of short stories. A year later she published a novel, *The Lying Day*, which concerned the tension of apartheid. *A World of Strangers* was published in 1958 and banned by the South African government. Two further novels, *The Late Bourgeois World* (1966) and *Burgher's Daughter* (1979), suffered a similar fate. In 1974 she won the Booker McConnell prize with *The Conservationist* . Her books were an indictment of the frustrations and stupidity of the apartheid regime as well as the cruelty used by the police in enforcing it. Gordimer refused to leave South Africa permanently, despite her life at times being in danger. During short trips abroad she exposed the regime. In 1971 she taught at Columbia University in New York. In 1987 she wrote *A Sport of Nature* about her experience of being Jewish. In 1991 Nadine Gordimer won the Nobel Prize for Literature. Not only was she the first woman to win this coveted prize for twenty-five years, she had the bizarre experience of, on the one hand, having her books banned by the South African government and, on the other, being publicly praised by the country's president for 'this exceptional achievement, which is also an honour to South Africa'. That statement was the more hypocritical of de Klerk because Gordimer was a co-founder of the Congress of South African Writers, 98 per cent of whose members were black and supported the Arts and Culture section of the ANC. In 1996 she published *Writing and Being,* the 1994 series of lectures she gave in the Charles Eliot Gordon series.

GORDIMER, Nadine (1923-) South African writer

Charles Goren was born in Philadelphia on March 4th 1901. While at McGill University, Montreal, he started his lifelong love affair with the game of bridge (Goren would have said the science of bridge). He sat down one afternoon with some young ladies, thinking he could play, and made a complete fool of himself. His girlfriend laughing at him was 'like putting a knife through me' - something any ordinary bridge player would sympathize with. However, Goren was no ordinary person. He not only read Milton Work's book on auction bridge, he memorized it. Goren's background was poor. He was a small child and podgy, and so looked healthy when he was in fact ill: so much so that he walked around for two weeks with mumps. He was a top student at Central High School, Philadelphia, and earned money tutoring younger students in Latin and Greek. He qualified as a lawyer and practised for thirteen years. Then, in 1936, he published his first book on bridge, *Winning Bridge Made Easy*, It made him so much money he gave up the law.

In the 1930s and 1940s, bridge reached obsessional proportions in America. In 1939 a housewife in Kansas, named Myrtle Bennet, shot her husband for miss-playing a lay-down contract. She pleaded not guilty and was acquitted. Until the late 1940s, the guru of bridge was Ely Culbertson. Then Goren introduced an improved system based on counting points: Ace = 4, King = 3, Queen = 2, Jack = 1, with 13

GOREN, Charles (1901-91) US bridge player

required to open the bidding. There are pluses and minuses, depending on the shape of the hand, but it all added to the game of bridge taking off. Goren had a weekly bridge column in many journals for many years and wrote upwards of 40 books. He was a bridge legend in his own lifetime and the world's most influential player. He died on April 7th 1991 in Encino, California.

GOROKHOV-SKAYA, Maria (1934-) Russian Olympic gymnast

Discovering her Jewish roots, **Maria Gorokhovskaya** moved from Russia to Israel in 1990. She found fame when, in the 1952 Olympic Games held in Helsinki, she won two gold medals and five silver in various gymnastic events, including vault, parallel bars, balance beam, floor exercise and team hand apparatus. One of her golds was for the combined exercises, the other for the team event.

GOSCINNY, Rene (1926-77) French writer

René Goscinny was born in Paris on August 4th 1926. His father was a Polish-Jewish chemist, his mother from a Jewish village in Russia. Two years later the family left France and settled in Argentina, where René was educated. In 1943 his father died and René had to leave university and became a clerk. However, his heart was in drawing and he tried to get a job in an advertising agency but failed. He left for New York. There he found the going tougher than he ever imagined. He did however work with Harvey Kurtzman and what became known as the 'Mad' Magazine team. He returned to Paris in 1952 and became involved in the publishing of humour comics. As the writer of the 'Lucky Luke' comic strip he became well known throughout France. In 1959 he founded *Pilote*, a comic magazine for students and adults alike. The same year, together with the illustrator Albert Uderzo, he created the cartoon character Asterix, the smart little Gaul who was always struggling against Caesar's conquest of Gaul. Asterix and his friend Obelix belonged to the only tribe that remained unconquered. Their Roman enemies were depicted as stupid and tactless. Goscinny went on to write other comic strips including *Les Dingodossiers* (1965-67). Asterix was published in newspapers and magazines all over the world. In the US over 100 newspapers carried the strip. When in 1959 Asterix was published as a book it sold over 18 million copies in fifteen languages. In 1967 Goscinny was made a Chevalier of Arts and Letters. He died in Paris on November 5th 1977 during a routine cardiological check-up.

GOTTLIEB, Adolph (1903-74) US painter

Born in New York City on March 14th 1903, **Adolph Gottlieb** studied at the Students' Art League of New York, and in Paris. Upon his return to New York in 1923, he studied at the Educational Alliance Art School. In 1935 Gottlieb became one of the founders of 'The Ten', a group with which he exhibited until 1940. He spent the years 1937-40 living in Arizona. The experience of isolation generated by the all-powerful desert would often be reflected in his work, lending surrealist overtones. When he returned to live in New York in 1941 he found many artists who were refugees from European fascism. They found they had much in common and co-exhibited. Gottlieb is probably best known for his 'pictographs', compartmentalized works filled with schematic shapes, sometimes Freudian, sometimes abstract or symbolist. During the 1950s, he concentrated on abstract landscapes, sometimes known as 'Imaginary Landscapes'. This led to his next style phase, 'Bursts', floats of sun-like forms floating above jagged areas. His paintings then became simpler and more precise, with fewer colours. Typical of this method are *Triad* (1959, The Lerner Collection), *Expanding* (1962, Chicago Art Institute) and *Orb* (1964, Dallas Museum of Fine Arts). His work can be seen at leading galleries and museums all over the US. A member of the New York School, he remains one of America's leading abstract expressionists. Gottlieb died in New York City on March 4th 1974.

Born Elliot Goldstein on August 29th 1938 in Brooklyn, New York, he decided from a young age that he would become a film star and has realized his ambition. He was eight when he started dancing and drama classes at the Charles Lowe School in Manhattan and only eleven when he danced professionally at the Palace Theatre. In 1960 he played in the stage version of *Irma La Douce* and received favourable notices. As a result he appeared in the Broadway musical *I Can Get It For You Wholesale* (1962) opposite Barbra Streisand (*qv*), whom he later married. He then took time off and studied with Lee Strasberg (*qv*) at the Actors' Studio. His big moment came when he played Ted in the very successful film *Bob and Carol and Ted and Alice* (1969), for which he received an Oscar nomination. Tall, often lugubrious, Gould dominates the silver screen. Considered a pleasure to watch, Gould has made relatively few films. However, those he has made are generally good and, in the case of a few, excellent. *M.A.S.H.* (1970), in which he plays Trapper John, has become a cult film. In 1971 Gould suffered a nervous breakdown and was unable to work. In 1973 he played the part of Philip Marlowe in the detective film *The Long Goodbye*; this was followed by the comedy *S*P*Y*S* (1974) and *California Split* (1974). His later films had a mixed reception, with only *Over the Brooklyn Bridge* (1983) reflecting his acting skills.

Morton Gould was born at Long Island, New York, on December 10th, 1913. His Jewish parents were immigrants; his father from Austria, his mother from Russia. An infant prodigy, he was giving piano recitals from the age of four. He was six when he wrote his first composition and aptly called it, 'Just Six'. At eight, he received a full scholarship from the Juillard School of Music when it was being run by Walter Damroch (*qv*). He was only fifteen when he graduated from New York University School of Music. During the depression of the early 1930s, he took any piano playing jobs he could find, including in the theatre, cinema and jazz clubs. He went on to compose both serious music in the grand manner and jazz-inspired light classics. The pavan from his Second American Symphonette (1935) is particularly popular. He composed 'Interplay' for the pianist and film actor Jose Iturbi; later, Jerome Robbins (*qv*) used it as the score for his ballet of the same name. In 1943 his first full symphony had its premiere and was much admired; however, his second was panned for what the critics called eclecticism. Gould persevered and over the next six years turned out many concert works. He was now being compared to Gershwin (*qv*) and Copland (*qv*), and by the early 1950s was one of the three most popular American composers. He worked hard. He established his own orchestra and recording studio as well as creating a music publishing business. He composed *A Cowboy Rhapsody*, which proved to be a great hit. Turning his attention to Broadway, he wrote two shows, *Billion Dollar Baby* (1945) and *Arms and the Girl* (1950). His popularity spread to Europe and he conducted the BBC Symphony Orchestra in London in 1966. In 1995 he was awarded the Pulitzer Prize for Music. He continued to work right up to the time he died, in Orlando, Florida on February 21st 1996.

GRADE,
Lord Lew
(1906-)
British film
producer

Born Lewis Winogradsky, he is now Baron Grade of Elstree and is known to everyone as **Lew Grade**. One of three successful brothers, he came to Britain with his family from Tokmak, Russia, at the age of six. At fourteen he was working at anything he could get, and at 20 he was a champion Charleston dancer with the name of Grade. Together with his brother Leslie, he opened a theatrical agency that by the early 1950s was the biggest in Europe. Grade turned to producing action adventure series for British television and export, including *Robin Hood*, *The Saint*, *The Avengers* and *The Prisoner*. All were highly popular and some are enjoying a second lease of life. His best series, however, was *The Muppets*. Through his company ITC he made feature films and came up with some well received successes: *The Tamarand Seed* (1974), *The Return of the Pink Panther* (1975), *The Eagle Has Landed* (1976) and *The Boys From Brazil* (1978). *On Golden Pond* (1981) took three Oscars, and *Sophie's Choice* (1982) gave Meryl Streep an Oscar for Best Actress. In 1969 he was knighted and seven years later was created a life peer. Of all the awards he has received in his lifetime, the one he is most proud of is his trophy as a Charleston dance champion.

GRAHAM,
Bill
(1931-91)
US entrepreneur

He was born Wolfgang Wolodia Grajonca in Berlin on January 8th 1931. His parents were Russian Jews and Wolfgang was their only son; he had five sisters. Two days after he was born his father was killed in a works accident. In 1939 he and a sister were sent to a Jewish orphanage in Paris. When the Germans arrived, all the children were taken by the Red Cross out of France and eventually reached Lisbon. His sister had become ill in Lyons and had to be left behind. She died there. After a tortuous journey that took in Casablanca and Cuba, he eventually arrived in New York. There a Jewish foster home was found for him in the Bronx. He graduated from high school and was then drafted into the army ready for the Korean war. Bill Graham's personality can be gleaned from his army war record. He was court-martialled twice for insubordination and won the Bronze Star and Purple Heart for bravery in combat. After the army he studied for a business administration degree by day and drove a cab at night.

In 1965 he was working as an office administrator in San Francisco. On a whim he decided to stage a benefit to aid the San Francisco Mime Troupe. He obtained the use of a large loft, and among those members of the arts community he persuaded to appear were Jefferson Airplane and Allen Ginsberg (*qv*). Now thoroughly involved, he gave up his job to become the poorly paid administrator of the Mime Troupe. He organized benefits and one night stands that featured, among many others, The Grateful Dead, whom Graham later managed. In 1966 Graham opened the Fillmore Auditorium in a an old run-down theatre. He soon had several Fillmores on both the East and West coasts. They featured most of the great names from the Woodstock era. After three years, disillusioned by the commercialism of rock music, he closed the Fillmores down. He later established Bill Graham Presents, which ran from 1976. He organized tours, benefits, festival promotions and major tours for great performers and causes. These included Bob Dylan (*qv*), George Harrison, the Rolling Stones, 30 Oakland open-air concerts, Live Aid, Amnesty International and more. Jewish charities in particular benefited from his expertise. He never recovered from the knowledge that his mother and several sisters died in the Holocaust. On October 25th 1991 he was killed in a helicopter crash at Sonoma County, California.

GRAHAM, Katherine (1917-) US publisher

Born Katherine Meyer in New York on June 16th 1917 and educated at Vassar College, she obtained a BA from the University of Chicago in 1938. She worked for a time on the *San Francisco News* and then in 1939 moved to the *Washington Post*. A year later she married Philip Graham, a law clerk. After service during the Second World War, Graham became an associate publisher on the *Post* in 1946 and in 1948 Eugene Meyer sold the newspaper to his daughter and son-in-law for a nominal amount. The new owners bought out *Newsweek* in 1961 and, following the suicide of her husband in 1963, Katherine took over and became president of the Washington Post Company. She remained in this position for the next ten years. During her time the *Washington Post* not only increased its circulation, it became the most influential newspaper in the capital and beyond. Graham agreed to the investigation by two of her journalists, Carl Bernstein (*qv*) and Bob Woodward, that led to the unmasking of the Watergate cover-up and in due course to the resignation of President Nixon. It was a very brave act by Katherine Graham, whose only interest was to secure democracy in the US against the threat represented by Nixon and his close associates. She remains on the board of the company and has other media interests in radio and television. In 1997 she published her autobiography, *Personal History*. It is a most candid self-portrait that opens up the most secret events of her life, including the suicide of her husband.

GREEN, Peter (1940-) British guitarist

Peter Green was born in London's East End early in WW2. From an early age he was found to be musically gifted. His parents encouraged him and it resulted in his becoming the leading blues guitarist by his early twenties. He became a legend who BB King would declare to be, the only British blues guitarist who 'brought him out in a sweat'. Green founded the group, Fleetwood Mac in July 1967 and quickly had a Number 1, 'Albatross'. This he followed with 'Mr Wonderful'(1968) and 'Then Play On' (1969). Gradually Green became uneasy with the problems of fame and left the group in May 1970 at the time his 'The Green Manalishi' was at Number 1. Peter Green, the man who wrote, 'Man of the World' and 'Black Magic Woman' (which was covered by Santana), sank into obscurity, played the drug scene and many records, before spending a year in a mental hospital. He spent the next twenty odd years working on a kibbutz, getting married and divorced, having a daughter and generally coming to terms with himself. Now he has reverted to his original name of Greenbaum, created 'The Splinter Group' and plays on tour to new generations and their parents who applaud his playing and adore his songs. Once again the crowds are screaming, "We love you Peter". This time around Peter Green appears able to handle the fame.

GREENBERG,
Henry, 'Hank'
(1911-86)
US baseball
player

Greenberg was born in New York City and educated at Bronx High School. A sporting enthusiast, his passion was baseball. A big man at six feet four inches and 215 pounds, he joined Detroit Tigers in 1933 as first baseman. A year later his team won the American League for the first time in 25 years and Greenberg was the leading scorer. In 1935 the Tigers won the title and Greenberg 'The Most Valuable Player' award. In 1936 he scored 183 runs; one more and it would have been the American League record. During the Second World War Hank Greenberg put baseball to one side as he served as a captain in the Army Air Force in India and China. He returned to the Tigers ground and a hero's welcome in July 1945. In 1947 he was transferred to the Pittsburgh Pirates, where he remained until he retired from first-class baseball. He then went into management, staying with the Chicago White Sox until 1963, when he gave up the game to work on Wall Street in New York. His career encompassed baseball's best years and Hank Greenberg was considered one of the greats. As a result he was elected to the Baseball Hall of Fame in 1956. He died in New York on September 19th 1986.

GREENE,
Lorne
(1915-87)
Canadian actor

Greene was born in Ottawa, Canada, on February 12th 1915. His Jewish parents, recent immigrants from Eastern Europe, could never have imagined that in adulthood their son would be instantly recognized by over half a billion people spread over some 80 countries. His mother had long decided her son would be a concert violinist. Not so Lorne, who blessed the rock he fell over and the twenty stitches his hand needed. He studied drama at Queen's University, Ontario, and this led to a scholarship to the Neighbourhood Playhouse School Theatre in Manhattan. He returned to Canada in September 1939 to join the Canadian Armed Forces. The army wasn't ready for him, so he joined the Canadian Broadcasting Company as a radio announcer. In 1940 he was chief news broadcaster for CBC. He became known as the 'Voice of Doom' because he always appeared to announce bad news. In 1942 the African campaign produced a victory and thereafter, with more good news than bad to announce, Lorne Greene was the 'Voice of Canada'. In 1943 he was in the army and on his return founded the Academy of Radio Arts. He invented a stop-watch that counted backwards; it is still used by announcers and others needing to know the time remaining on a programme. Between 1954 and 1958 he was a support actor in many Hollywood films. A guest appearance in *Wagon Train* resulted in his being cast as Ben Cartwright in a television series called *Bonanza*: the first filmed in colour. It premiered on September 12th 1959 and was laughed at by the critics. It survived two years of poor ratings, gradually improved and became

America's favourite 'soap'. It reached its US peak in 1964 and then sold around the world. That year Greene was asked to record a poem/song about a sheriff and a gunman. 'Ringo' became a hit and number one for the week of December 5th 1964. Greene was scheduled to begin work on a television feature film called *Bonanza; The Next Generation* when, on September 11th 1987, he suddenly died. His surviving legacy is Toronto's Academy of Dramatic Arts, of which he was the founder.

Greenspan was born on March 6th 1926 in New York City. An advocate of free market policies, he was educated at New York University. In 1971 he became a consultant to the Congressional budget office. He was a member of President Ford's Council of Economic Advisers (1974-77) and since 1977 has been a consultant to the US Treasury. Between 1981 and 1989 he was a member of the President's economic policy board and in 1987 was appointed chairman of the board of the Federal Reserve Bank. In 1988 Greenspan warned the Congressional Commission of the dangers of failing to balance the budget. In 1991 President Bush backed Greenspan to serve a second four-year term as chairman of the Federal Reserve, and in 1995 President Clinton backed him for a third term. In 1993 Greenspan endorsed President Clinton's deficit-cutting plans. Although Alan Greenspan appears to be at home with Presidents of both major parties, he is essentially his own man. In September 1996 he was responsible for the final ditching of the Milton Friedman doctrine, that has resulted in mass unemployment in capitalist countries in many parts of the world. With unemployment falling in the US, Greenspan repeatedly refuses to increase interest rates. His example has been copied in France, Germany and Britain. It is as a direct result of Greenspan's policy that America has fought back from the world recession during the 1990s. As the Federal Bank's chairman Greenspan alone decides the interest rate to be charged by the US banks and this has an ongoing effect all over the world. His influence and low interest rate has kept inflation at a low level in much of the world for most of the last decade. For a man who studied music at the Julliard Music Academy and played clarinet in a jazz band the responsibility is considerable.

GREENSPAN, Alan (1926-) US economic administrator

Haika Grossman was born in Bialystok, Poland, on November 20th 1919. An active member of the Hashomer Hatzair movement during the Second World War, she was one of those who joined the partisan movement and operated from the forests. She was a soldier in the August 1943 Bialystok ghetto uprising which held out against the brunt of the German army for four days. She survived the battle and continued the fight until the end of the war, one of the very few to come through it. After the war she rejoined Hashomer in the work of resettling concentration camp survivors, many of whom wanted to go to Palestine. Haika arrived in Israel in 1948 and joined Hashomer's kibbutz Evron, in the Galilee. Politically aware, she joined the Mapam party as an active member. In 1968 she was elected to the Knesset and for some 20 years thereafter took up the unpopular issues of the times: women's rights, civil rights and the problems of the poor as well as of newly arrived immigrants.

GROSSMAN, Haika (1919-96) Polish/ Israeli politician

In 1975 she was urged by Mapam to withdraw her private member's bill that would make provision for civil marriage. She refused. Later she sponsored an abortion bill that led to violence between religious and secular factions. Haika Grossman never surrendered her support for the disadvantaged, and in pursuance of that ideal she was a leading supporter of Palestine independence.

In 1988 she wrote *The Underground Army*, describing the desperate struggle of the Jews of Bialystok. At the time of the German occupation the city had a Jewish population of 50,000; when the war was over, only 900 survivors came out of hiding, the rest having been murdered by the Germans. Haika Grossman added her husband's name to her own and became known as Haika Grossman-Orkin. She died at her kibbutz on May 26th 1996.

GRUEN, Victor (1903-80) Austrian/ American architect

Victor Gruen was born in Vienna on July 18th 1903. He received training as an architect at the Technological Institute of Vienna before joining Peter Behrens as an assistant. He started his own practice in Vienna in 1933 but, as a Jew, was forced to leave the country in 1938. He went to the US and during the Second World War worked on various suburban projects including the Lederer Store in New York City. In 1950 he established the firm Victor Gruen Associates, an all-encompassing company that dealt with all matters relating to property development. He designed Northland, in Detroit, in 1952 and thereby created the world's first out-of-town shopping mall. The second was at Fort Worth, Texas (1955). Thus began a social revolution that would have echoes all over the world. This form of urban renewal opened up enormous retail expansion and enabled people to bring their cars and shop for much longer periods, often including Sundays. Other centres followed, including a master plan for the comprehensive redevelopment of Tehran, Iran. Following the fall of the Shah the scheme was dropped. Victor Gruen was the design consultant for cities worldwide including his birthplace, Vienna. In 1972 he was awarded the City of Vienna award for architecture. He retired in 1968 and spent the rest of his life working for the Victor Gruen Foundation for Environmental Planning. Among his publications was *Heart of Our Cities* (1964). He died on February 14th 1980 in Vienna.

GRYN, Hugo (1930-96) Czech/ British rabbi

Hugo Gryn was born in Berehovo, Czechoslovakia, on June 25th 1930 and received his early schooling at the Jewish school of Debrecen. His religious teaching came from his father in Auschwitz, where the family were sent in May 1944. Mr Gryn stressed to his son that survival depended on having faith. It was, however, Hugo's knowledge of carpentry that kept him alive and allowed him to work in slave labour rather than being sent into the gas chamber. Only he and his mother survived; his father died from typhoid three days following liberation. Together with other young survivors, Hugo was sent to Scotland. There his education resumed, eventually taking him to King's College, Cambridge where he studied mathematics and biochemistry. In 1948 he was a volunteer soldier in Israel's war of independence. He then went to the US and the Hebrew Union College in Cincinnati to study Reform Judaism. In 1957 he was ordained. He began his lifelong interest in intercommunal affairs while a minister at Jasper, Alabama, following a night he spent in prison with Martin Luther King. They had marched together and been arrested together in Jasper. He later spent three years as the rabbi of the Jewish Religious Union in Bombay. He returned to America in 1960 to become executive director of the World Union for Progressive Judaism. Two years later he took over the running of the American Jewish Joint Distribution Committee. In 1964 he returned to Britain and the West London Synagogue, where he remained for the remainder of his life. He worked hard for the betterment of relations with both Christians and Muslims and became most active in working with matters and people relating to the Holocaust. His warm and relaxed manner made him a natural for radio and television. Through his participation in the BBC's *Moral Maze* programme he secured a wide following for his reasoned argument and depth of understanding. In 1993 he was awarded the CBE for his inter-faith work. He was, however, unsuccessful in his attempts to draw together the strands of Anglo-Jewry. The shrinking Orthodox community wanted little to do with Gryn's work and were not represented at his funeral, following his death on August 18th 1996 in London. His standing was such, however, that his passing seemed to touch wide sections of the larger population, Jew and Gentile alike.

Peggy Guggenheim was born in New York on August 26th 1898, the niece of Solomon Guggenheim, founder of the New York museum that bears his name. Peggy was educated in Paris, where she became part of the international art world. In London, in 1938, she opened a gallery which she called Guggenheim Jeune. There she exhibited such artists as Jean Arp (the mistress of her ex-husband, Max Ernst), Brancusi, Kandinsky, Duchamp and Henry Moore. In 1941 she returned to New York and opened her gallery, Art of the Century, into which she put her significant collection. Her gallery received much support from important American painters, including Hofman, Rothko (*qv*) and Pollock. Following the Second World War, during which time Samuel Beckett was her lover, she moved her entire collection to her palazzo in Venice. Peggy Guggenheim has been termed 'one of the world's greatest patrons of modern art'. She wrote her biography, *Out of This Century*, and died in Venice in the same year it was published, on December 23rd 1979.

GUGGENHEIM, Peggy (1898-1979) US art patron

Gurevich, born in Rubashchina, near Kursk, Russia, graduated from the Kharkov Technological Institute in 1925. By 1933 he was an established aircraft designer and in 1937 was appointed Deputy Director to Artem Mikoyan at the Experimental Design Bureau. They went on to become the joint designers of the MiG fighter plane series which contributed substantially to the Soviet victories during the Second World War. During the post-war era he continued designing jet versions of the MiG that kept pace with those being designed by the West. He received the Stalin prize five times and the Lenin prize once. During the Second World War, Gurevich was a member of the Jewish anti-fascist Committee. He died in Moscow in 1976.

GUREVICH, Mikhail (1893-1976) Russian aircraft designer

GUTENBERG,
Beno
(1889-1960)
German/
American
seismologist

Beno Gutenberg was born in Darmstadt, Germany, on June 4th 1889. Between 1912 and 1923 he was assistant at the International Seismological Bureau at Strasbourg. Later, while teaching at Frankfurt University, he received an offer to take up the appointment as professor of geophysics at the California Institute of Technology at Pasadena. It was 1930 and Gutenberg, seeing the Nazi writing on the wall, accepted. In the event he was to stay at the Institute until 1957 and his retirement. He is considered one of the greatest men in the field of geophysics this century. His research area has been wide and productive. He is particularly noted for his analysis of earthquake waves and the information to be gleaned concerning the physical properties of the earth's interior. He developed a method to determine the intensity of earthquakes. He also used present day shallow equals and calculated that three-quarters of the energy occurs in the Circum-Pacific belt. This accumulated information has allowed others to acquire essential knowledge needed to understand the violence of our world's interior. Beno Gutenberg died on January 25th 1960 in Los Angeles.

Arlo Guthrie was born on July 10th 1947 in Coney Island, New York. His father was Woody Guthrie, a major figure of America's folk heritage and a leading socialist. He lived as he preached and had a great influence on a generation of artists that included Bob Dylan (*qv*). Woody also had a great influence on his son Arlo, who had a folk song bar-mitzvah. Arlo was raised during the thriving years of folk and this is evident in his lengthy ballad, 'Alice's Restaurant Massacre' (1967), part narrative and part humorous song. This he popularized at the 1967 Newport Folk Festival and it was the main track on his first album. It went on to inspire a feature film by Arthur Penn, *Alice's Restaurant*, in 1969. Arlo released his album *Running Down the Road* in 1969. *Washington County* followed in 1970. *Hobo Lullaby* (1972) included his top twenty hit, 'City of New Orleans'. *Last of the Brooklyn Cowboys* (1973) included Irish jigs and reels. In 1974 his album *Arlo Guthrie* included 'Presidential Rag'. Together with Pete Seeger, an old friend of his father, Arlo recorded *Together in Concert* (1975) The following year saw *Amigo* released. *Power of Love* (1980) was a welcome return to the charts. Although he rarely performed 'Alice . . .' he played it for nostalgia at the 1985 Newport Folk Festival revival. He has his own record label, Rising Son, which he used to document his father's work, *Woody Gutherie/Hard Travelin'*. Arlo is known as one of the most likeable people in music and one of the most important keepers of the folk flame. His material reflects optimism and humour rather than gloomy protest.

Camille Gutt, who came from an old Jewish family, was born in Brussels. He qualified as a lawyer and decided to make his career in politics. Following the First World War, he was appointed Secretary-General and head of the Belgian delegation to the Reparations Commission that existed between 1920 and 1924. In 1934, and again in 1939 and 1940, he was Finance Minister in the Liberal administration. When the Germans overran his country, Gutt, together with the rest of the Belgian cabinet, succeeded in escaping to London. Here Gutt held various posts in the cabinet of the

Belgian government in exile. Between 1946 and 1951 Gutt was head of the International Monetary Fund, which did essential work for Europe's recovery following the end of the Second World War.

Born in Upper Silesia, Germany, on July 3rd 1899, by early 1939 he was a well-known neurosurgeon working at the Jewish Hospital in Bristly. At that time he received an invitation to go to Britain and continue his research into rehabilitating persons suffering from paraplegia. At that time his methods of treatment were considered highly controversial. However, it was an invitation that came just in time and allowed Guttmann, a Jew, to leave Germany with his life, though with little else. He acquired British nationality and continued his radical programme for the treatment of those suffering spinal injuries. During the Second World War, the large numbers of war wounded prompted the government to suggest that Guttmann put his ideas into general practice. A hospital at Stoke Mandeville, Buckinghamshire, was provided and within a short time he was achieving remarkable results. Referred to as 'Poppa Guttmann' by his patients, his methods and patience won through and many of the wounded recovered sufficiently to lead useful lives that before Guttmann would not have been possible. He drastically reduced the death rate from some 80 per cent to around 10 per cent. It was Ludwig Guttmann who established the Stoke Mandeville Games, as an example of how paraplegics could lead useful and fulfilling lives. His example was copied by other countries, particularly Israel, which had large numbers of paraplegic soldiers following their several wars. The World Veterans' Association awarded him their Rehabilitation Prize for 1953. A grateful Britain awarded him the OBE, then the CBE and, in 1966, a knighthood. In 1972 President Heinemann presented Guttman with Germany's highest peacetime award. In 1996 it was announced that the first Olympic village in the world is to be built in Stoke Mandeville as a memorial to Guttman. In 1945 the then Minister of Pensions, in an all-party government, said with reference to Guttmann: 'Thank you, Hitler, for sending us men like these.' Guttman died in Aylesbury, Buckinghamshire, on March 18th 1980.

GUTTMANN, Sir Ludwig (1899-1980) German/British medical pioneer

Gyarmati, born in Budapest to Jewish parents, is regarded by those who know about these things as the best ever water polo player. Between 1948 and 1964 he competed in five Olympiads. The result was five medals, one per Games: silver, gold, gold, bronze, gold. He was a member of the Hungarian team that won the European Championships in 1954, 1958 and 1962. Ambidextrous, he could play in any position, and has won more medals than any other water polo player. Following his retirement from active participation, he became the coach of the national team that won the gold medal in the 1976 Olympics. He later became a member of the Hungarian parliament and coach to his wife and daughter, both Olympic champion swimmers. His daughter, Andrea, broke the world record for the 100m butterfly in 1972.

GYARMATI, Dezso (1927-) Hungarian water polo champion

Commemorative
Stamps

Mikhail Gurevich
Issued by USSR

Denis Gabor
Issued by Hungary

Rene Goscinny
Issued by Guernsey, UK

Rube Goldberg
Issued by USA

Benny Goodman
Issued by USA

Victor Goldschmidt
Issued by Norway

Ludwig Guttman
Issued by UK

Nadine Gordimer
Issued by Antigua and Barbuda

Fritz Haber
Issued by Sweden

H

Haber was born in Breslau, Germany on December 9th 1868 the son of a Jewish chemical merchant. Following a university education in Berlin, Heidelberg and Zurich he joined the family firm. Fritz didn't stay long preferring an academic career. He took up chemical research at Jena University but found it too confining. During the early part of the 20th century the modern world had a continuing need for nitrogen fertilizer to offset a world shortage of food. Haber, between 1907 and 1909 invented the process of synthesis of ammonia that guaranteed an increased supply of nitrogen fertilizer for the world at large. He passed his invention on to a large development company and got on with other research. In 1911 he was head of the Kaiser Wilhelm Institute for Physical Chemistry in Berlin. During the First World War he played a leading part in Germany's chemical production and in the development of mustard gas as a weapon of war. His view, as a fervent German patriot, was that as the Allies also had the gas it was a legitimate weapon. He did not mention that it was the Germans who on April 22nd 1915 first made use of gas; perhaps he didn't know.

After the First World War Germany's requirement to make reparations to the Allies disturbed Haber and he conceived the notion of extracting gold from seawater. Surprisingly, he succeeded, but the amounts obtained did not repay the costs of extraction and so the project was halted; but positive gains in scientific knowledge were made. In 1918 Haber received the Nobel Prize for Chemistry for his earlier work on synthesized ammonia. Haber's institute became the world's leading centre for research into physical chemistry. Haber was a world-renowned figure who played an important role in co-relating chemical discoveries with the needs of industry. In 1930 he opened a branch of his institute in Tokyo and was responsible for promoting cultural and economic ties between Germany and Japan. For this work he was made a Privy Counsellor of Germany. Haber was at the top of the ladder. Then came 1933 and, with the arrival of Hitler, the official era of anti-Semitism. Haber, who had never bothered himself with things Jewish, was astonished to be called 'Jew Haber'. With his authority and influence at a low ebb and his previous work for the fatherland ignored, he resigned and went to England. Now working in Cambridge, he took some time off to go on holiday. On his way to Italy he suffered a heart attack in Basle and died there on January 29 1934. During the latter part of his life Haber became strongly convinced by the creed that science was for the betterment of mankind.

HABER,
Fritz
(1868-1934)
German chemist

HADAMARD,
Jacques
(1865-1963)
French
mathematician

Born in Versailles, France, on December 8th 1865, **Hadamard** proved the prime number theorems. He was a professor at the Collège de France from 1897 to 1935. His early work was an important contribution to the world of mathematics and he obtained results in connection with the partial differential equations concerning mathematical physics. His book, published in 1910, *Lessons on the Calculus of Variations*, set the basis for the modern theory of functional analysis; indeed, it was Hadamard who introduced the term 'functional'. His work was essential for the understanding of the theory of integral equations. He was professor of mathematics at the Ecole Polytechnique when he retired in 1937. He continued to publish well into his eighties. In 1912 he was elected a member of the Academy of Sciences and in 1955 he was the first person to be awarded the Italian Feltrinelli Prize. This prize, in some way, compensated Hadamard for not having been awarded the Nobel Prize. When the Germans took over France in 1940 Hadamard, as a Jew, was in danger. After a very difficult journey he surfaced in the US. However, he was soon back in Europe where in England he engaged in operational research for the RAF. He died in Paris on October 17th 1963.

HAFFKINE,
Waldemar
(1860-1930)
Russian/French
bacteriologist

Born and educated in Odessa, Russia, he studied under Elie Metchnikoff (*qv*), who later invited him to work at the Pasteur Institute in Paris. While there, Haffkine developed an anti-cholera vaccine, which was tested successfully, and went on to produce the vaccine that resulted in an attack of bubonic plague being successfully halted in Bombay, India. As he continued to work in India, the British administration there granted Haffkine British citizenship. However, in 1902 the plague struck the Punjab and some of the people there died of tetanus. Haffkine was blamed and severely criticized. In fact there were just nineteen deaths among the tens of thousands who received Haffkine's inoculation. Despite an official inquiry it wasn't until the London *Times*, on July 29th 1907, published a long, detailed scientific defence of Haffkine and his work that the government exonerated him. Haffkine returned to India and continued his research in Calcutta until forced to resign at the age of 55. He then settled in Paris and continued his work there. In 1925 the Plague Research Laboratory he had founded in Bombay was renamed the Haffkine Institute for Bacteriological Research. It is still the most important institute of its kind in India: an acknowledgement that it was as a result of Haffkine's early work in producing the first effective vaccine against cholera that India was able to flourish.

HAHN,
Reynaldo
(1874-1947)
Venezuelan/
French
composer

Reynaldo Hahn was born on August 8th 1874 in Caracas, Venezuela. His French-Jewish parents decided to return to France in 1884 and a year later Reynaldo was a pupil at the Paris Conservatory, where he studied under Massenet. He wrote several operettas, often in the style of Offenbach, including *Cibonlette* (1923). He specialized in writing incidental music for plays and worked with playwrights such as Edmond Rostand and Sacha Guitry. Hahn's ballets include *La Fête Chez Thérèse* (1910) and *Le Dien Bleu* (1912). The poetry of Marcel Proust (*qv*) inspired Hahn to write his piano suite *Portraits de Peintres*. From 1934 to the German occupation of 1940 Hahn was music critic of *Le Figaro*. Following the Second World War,

Hahn resurfaced to become director of the Paris Opera. Hahn's music, melodious and graceful, is still included in concert repertoires. He died in Paris on January 28th 1947.

Alphonse Halimi was born to Jewish parents in Constantine, Algeria, on January 18th 1932. After a career in the amateur ranks he became a professional boxer. Between 1957 and 1959 he was undisputed world bantamweight champion. He lost his title in July 1959 to Joe Becerra in a tough, bruising fight. Halimi regained his European title in 1960, lost it in 1961 and regained it in 1962 in Tel Aviv: the first time a professional boxing match was ever staged in Israel.

HALIMI, Alphonse (1932-) Algerian/French boxer

Halsman was born and grew up in Riga, Latvia. He later studied electrical engineering in Germany. Between 1930 and 1940 he ran a studio in Paris specializing in fashion photography. With Hitler's Gestapo on his heels he moved to the US and joined *Life* magazine. He produced 101 covers for the magazine, setting a record that still stands. Although he took some 100,000 photographs in his long career, it was the psychological portraits of world celebrities that attracted most attention. He liked producing stunt photos, such as the one of Salvador Dali as a fetus in an egg. His *Jump Book* (1959), a collection of photographs of famous people caught on camera as they jumped up, brought him world attention. Halsman reckoned that at the peak of a jump the subject's real character was revealed. One of the subjects was Richard Nixon. Halsman died in New York in 1979.

HALSMAN, Philippe (1906-79) Russian/ American photographer

Armand Hammer was born in New York on May 21st 1898. The son of a doctor, Armand also qualified but never practised. His father was also a businessman who had a controlling interest in a pharmaceutical company. By a series of deals young Hammer made a million dollars for his father's company and decided he was 'on his way'. He visited the USSR in 1921 and organized aid for the victims of the famine that followed the invasion of Russia by Western powers. Lenin persuaded Hammer to become involved in joint deals that would open Soviet markets to Europe and the US. In the 1920s Hammer launched a number of manufacturing industries that covered a wide spectrum of sectors; in 1930 he sold his share to the Soviet government and returned to America. He took part of the proceeds in the form of *objets d'art*, paintings and jewellery once owned by the Romanov family. Hammer sold much of this treasure trove to finance his US projects, which ranged from whisky making to cattle farming. In 1956 Hammer retired. However, after four months he allowed a friend to persuade him to get involved in raising finance for an oil project in California owned by the near-bankrupt Occidental Petroleum Corporation.. Hammer agreed. He financed new production and they struck oil. Hammer increased his already substantial holdings and became chief executive and chairman in 1957. By the mid-1960s Occidental was big, powerful and rich. Diversity into chemical manufacturing boosted profits so much that the company soon became one of the 20 richest companies in America. Hammer's lifetime contacts with the USSR ensured his place as linchpin during the US-Soviet trade talks in the detente of the 1970s.

HAMMER, Armand (1898-1990) US entrepreneur

Hammer was all things to all people. He was an avid art collector and founded the Armand Hammer Museum of Art and Cultural Centre in Los Angeles in 1990. He acted as counsellor to numerous presidents as well as to Charles, Prince of Wales. Most important of all, he was instrumental in bringing together the USSR and the US. He died on December 10th 1990 in Los Angeles. In 1996, with Hammer some years dead, there are those seeking the limelight who have come out of the woodwork with statements and publications that purport to show that Hammer was a traitor, a fraudster and much more. They include ex-employees of Hammer, too busy enjoying their large salaries to speak out while he was alive.

HARBURG, Edgar, 'Yip' (1896-1981) US lyricist

Harburg was born on April 8th 1896 in New York on the Lower East Side. He was given the Yiddish nickname of 'Yiprel' (squirrel) and was known to one and all as Yip. He graduated in 1918 from New York University and began to write light verse before becoming a journalist in South America. He returned to New York to run an electrical supply business but it failed in the 1929 stock market crash. He started writing song lyrics and collaborated with Jay Gorney to produce the socially significant song 'Brother, Can You Spare a Dime?' It became the hit of the Depression and, recorded by Bing Crosby and Rudy Vallee, it went around the world. With Harold Arlen (*qv*) he wrote 'It's Only a Paper Moon' (1933) and later 'April In Paris'. Together they worked on several Broadway shows, including *Walk a Little Faster* with Beatrice Lillie and *The Ziegfeld Follies of 1934*. They also worked on several film musicals for Warners including *The Singing Kid* with Al Jolson (*qv*). They wrote 'When The World Was Young', which Frank Sinatra featured in what was probably his best album, *In The Wee Small Hours* . Harburg and Arlen wrote the hit songs for Judy Garland's *Wizard of Oz*, including the haunting 'Over the Rainbow', for which they won the Academy Award. They also wrote 'Follow The Yellow Brick Road' and 'We're Off to See The Wizard' for the same film. They worked with the Marx Brothers (*qv*) and wrote 'Lydia, The Tattooed Lady'. During the 1940s Harburg, with various partners (and sometimes alone), continued to write songs for films, including 'Moonlight Bay', 'Happiness is Just a Thing Called Joe' and 'Let There Be Music'. In 1947 he teamed up with Burton Lane for *Finian's Rainbow*. Their songs included 'How Things in Glocca Morra?', and 'Old Devil Moon'. The show ran for over 700 performances and the film version in 1968 starred Fred Astaire. During the McCarthy witch-hunt Harburg wrote the song 'The Eagle and Me', a passionate plea for racial equality and freedom. He continued writing lyrics for musical shows and films until his death as a result of a car crash in Los Angeles on March 5th 1981.

HART, Moss (1904-61) US playwright

Moss Hart, born in New York on October 24th 1904, was the son of very poor Jewish immigrant parents who lived on the Lower East Side. At seventeen, following a limited education, Hart landed a job as office boy to a theatrical producer. At evening classes he learnt directing and acting and during the summer holidays worked at stock directing and play writing. In 1929 he wrote the outline of a play with the working title of *Once in a Lifetime*, a satire on early Hollywood. Picked up by George S. Kaufman (*qv*), who gave it a polish, it became a success. The two men collaborated further and produced *You Can't Take It With You* (1938) and *The Man Who Came to Dinner* (1939). Hart wrote and directed *Lady In the Dark* in 1941. He also collaborated with Irving Berlin (*qv*) in *Face the Music* (1932) and with Cole Porter in *Jubilee* (1935). Hart also found fame as a Broadway director, his work here including *My Fair Lady* (1956) and *Camelot* (1961). He also wrote the screenplay for Danuk's *Gentleman's Agreement* (1947), starring Gregory Peck, which concerned post-war anti-Semitism. Hart's autobiography, *Act One* (1959), has been hailed as a 'moving human document'. Hart died on December 20th 1961 in Palm Springs, California.

Heinz Hartmann was born in Vienna and came to be one of the most important researchers in the field of what became known as Hartmann's psychoanalytic ego psychology. In 1939 he published his *Ego Psychology and the Problem of Adaption*. He emphasized the ego as being as important as the id. He illustrated the importance of adapting to change and environment as a function of the ego. Originally a student of Freud (*qv*), he emphasized and elaborated on the master's teachings. He spent the Second World War in Switzerland and the US, where he eventually settled. He was president of the International Psychoanalytic Association (1951-57), by whose members he was held in such high esteem that in 1959 he was appointed honorary president for life.

HARTMANN, Heinz (1894-1970) Austrian/ American psychoanalyst

Hartog was born in London on March 2nd 1864, the son of a Dutch Jewish father and an English Jewess from Plymouth. Educated at University College School, London, and at universities in France and Germany, by the turn of the century Philip Hartog was the academic registrar of London University. During the seventeen years he was in charge, the university developed into a top teaching institution. He made time to write and in 1907 published *The Writing of English*, which was widely acclaimed for giving a new outlook on the teaching of English composition. However, what Philip Hartog is particularly remembered for is his role in the founding of the London School of Oriental Studies. Without his imagination and dedication over a period of many years the project would not have become a reality. The school received its charter in 1916 with Hartog representing the Crown on the governing body. Thirty years later the school saluted its founder by awarding Hartog an honorary fellowship. From 1917 onwards his experience was eagerly sought by educational establishments in many parts of the world. He was a member of the Calcutta University Commission, the first Vice-Chancellor of Dacca University and a member of the Indian Public Service Commission. In 1930 he resigned and returned to England where he received a knighthood. He served for seven years on the committee inquiring into the reliability of examinations, a subject that is still hotly debated. He wrote much on education, including *The Marks of Examiners* (1936). His books set out the difference between tests designed to illustrate skills and those designed just to test educational progress. In 1933, on behalf of the Liberal Jewish Synagogue

HARTOG, Sir Philip (1864-1947) British educator

in London, Hartog travelled to Palestine to report on the activities and organization of the Hebrew University. During the Second World War he was chairman of the government unit to select linguists for war work. He died in London on June 27th 1947 while working on an updated sequel to *The Writing of English*.

**HASSAN,
Sir Joshua
(1915-)
Gibraltarian
statesman**

Hassan was born in Gibraltar on August 21st 1915 to a Jewish family that originated in North Africa. He became a barrister and practised locally until he decided to become a politician. He was Mayor of Gibraltar from 1945 to 1950 and Chief Member of the Legislative Council between 1950 and 1964. In 1964 he was appointed Chief Minister, a post he held until 1969, when he was defeated in the general election. During his mandate he was instrumental in ensuring that Gibraltar remained under British rule and was not transferred to Spain; 30 years on, that situation still remains. Hassan, a religious Jew, became a Queen's Counsel in 1954 and ten years later was knighted for his services to Gibraltar.

**HAUPTMAN,
Herbert
(1917-)
US
Crystallographer**

Born in New York on February 14th 1917, he was educated at the City College of New York. There he first met Jerome Karle. Hauptman graduated in 1937 and went on to Columbia University to study mathematics. Following receipt of his PhD he worked at the Naval Research Laboratory in Washington DC, and here he met up with Jerome Karle again. They decided to collaborate on the study of crystal structures. Although Hauptman became a professor of biophysics at the State University of New York at Buffalo in 1970, he and Karle continued their research and invented mathematical equations to describe the way numerous spots appear on photographic film as a result of a crystal diffraction of X-rays. Their work meant it was possible to understand the location of atoms within the crystal molecules, enabling them to be pinpointed following an analysis of the intensity of the spots. For some years their ideas were neglected but gradually crystallographers began using their theories to determine the three-dimensional structure of many thousands of small biological molecules, including those of antibiotics, hormones and vitamins. Their work resulted in Hauptman and Karle sharing the 1985 Nobel Prize for Chemistry.

**HAWN,
Goldie
(1945-)
US actor**

Goldie was born in Washington DC on November 21st 1945. Her mother is Jewish and her father a Protestant musician. Educated at the American University in Washington, she graduated in drama studies. She has a natural gift for comedy, as she so ably demonstrated in the television series *Rowan and Martin's Laugh-In*. She transferred to Hollywood and there made *Cactus Flower* (1969). The result was the Oscar for Best Supporting Actress. After several films that, though entertaining, were not memorable she turned to producing. Her first effort, in 1980, was *Private Benjamin*, a box office hit which brought a nomination for Best Actress. She continues to act and produce, and her happy go-lucky personality and lack of airs endears her to a wide and faithful audience. In 1991 she signed a seven-picture deal with Disney Pictures worth $30,000,000. In 1997 she was considered excellent in Woody Allen's (*qv*) *Everyone Says I Love You*.

Hays was born on December 12th 1881 in Rochester, New York, and educated at Columbia University, obtaining a BA in 1902 and a law degree three years later. Although his law practice flourished through the representation of large corporations, his heart was in helping the cause of those who suffered a loss of their civil liberties. He was the general counsel of the American Civil Liberties Union from 1912 onwards and was to be seen acting for the defendant in some of the great civil liberties trials, including the Scopes trial in Tennessee in 1925, the housing segregation case and the 1926 Street case, as well as the obscenity trial of the *American Mercury*, a magazine run by H. L. Mencken 1926 in Boston, and the world-famous 'anarchist case' of Sacco and Vanzetti in 1927, again in Boston. In 1931 he successfully appealed against the carrying out of the death sentence in the infamous Scottsboro case in Alabama. In 1933 he was in Berlin aiding the defence of those alleged to have set fire to the Reichstag. Following the Second World War, Hays worked with the Allied occupation forces to help establish democratic institutions in Germany. His autobiography *City Lawyer* was published in 1942. He died on December 14th 1954 in New York.

Hecht was born on February 28th 1894 in New York, the son of recently arrived Jewish immigrants from Minsk, Russia. The family moved to Racine, Wisconsin, where Ben received a high school education. He moved to Chicago and worked as a reporter on the *Chicago Journal* (1910-14) before moving to the *Chicago Daily News*, which made him foreign correspondent. Hecht was in Germany following the end of the First World War, reporting on the post-war upheavals. This experience gave him the workings for his first novel, *Erik Dorn* (1921). In 1922, back in Chicago, he wrote the novel *Fantazius Mallare*. It was seized by the police, who claimed it was obscene, and Hecht was fired by his newspaper. Undaunted, Hecht travelled to Hollywood and there secured a studio job as a screenwriter. In 1927 he wrote *Underworld*. It was the first real gangster film ever made, and won for Hecht the first Oscar ever awarded for an original screenplay. There followed some 100 films and Hecht became wealthy and famous. He was one of the very few writers who were given complete editorial control. He became a right-wing Zionist who wrote anti-British advertisements during the Palestine mandate years. Oswald Mosley, the British would-be Hitler, took advantage of the situation to organize violent demonstrations whenever a Hecht film was shown in Britain. As these included such hits as Hitchcock's *Notorious* (1946), Mosley was given short shrift by the British public. Hecht's autobiography *A Child of the Century* was published in 1954. He died in New York on April 18th 1964.

Jascha Heifetz was born on February 2nd 1901 in Vilna, Russia. He was three when he first started studying the violin and at six was performing the Mendelssohn Violin Concerto. At nine he was studying at the St Petersburg Conservatory under Leopold Auer. In 1912, at the advanced age of eleven, Heifetz was invited by Arthur Nikisch, conductor of the Berlin Philharmonic, to play the Tchaikovsky Violin Concerto. From then onwards he was constantly touring Europe.

In 1917 he made his first appearance in the US, on the stage at Carnegie Hall in New York. Although only sixteen, Heifetz knew what he wanted and he wanted to remain in America: in 1925 he became a US citizen. He toured the world many times, always enjoying great success with the greatest orchestras available. He recorded much and his records sold by the millions. He was known for his smooth, technical brilliance and inspired interpretation. In time his name became synonymous with musical perfection. Heifetz commissioned modern composers such as Sir William Walton and Louis Gruenberg to write violin concertos for him. He later taught music and held violin master classes at the University of Southern California in Los Angeles, and it was here that in 1975 the Heifetz Chair of Music was founded. He was often quite eccentric. He once gave a tea party; the guests were invited for 4 p.m., and at that hour he opened his front door, left it open for one minute and then closed it. He would sometimes disappear for long periods, many months at a time. This habit went back to 1947. By that time he had travelled over two million miles and had played some 100,000 concert hours. The only explanation he offered was: 'I started playing the violin at three and gave my first concert at six. I have been playing ever since.' When he finally stopped altogether he became a recluse and refused all interviews. He died in Los Angeles on December 10th 1987.

HEILBRON,
Dame Rose
(1914-)
British jurist

Rose Heilbron was born on August 19th 1914 to a prominent Jewish family living in Liverpool, England. Following university Rose decided on the law as a career. She was admitted to the bar in 1939 and only ten years later became a King's Counsel (KC). In 1956 she became the first woman in Britain to be appointed a Recorder. In July 1974 Rosie, as she was affectionately known, became only the second woman in Britain to be appointed a High Court judge, and that October she was created a Dame of the British Empire. After several years she was appointed to the family division, retiring in 1988. During her long and distinguished career she became the first woman barrister to argue a case before the British supreme court the House of Lords.

HELLER,
Joseph
(1923-)
US writer

Born on May 1st 1923 in Brooklyn, New York, he has become one of the best writers in the post- Second World War era. In 1961 he wrote *Catch-22* and the world became a different place as ordinary people everywhere identified with Captain John Yossarian. Heller was barely out of school when he joined the US Air Force. As a bombardier he flew some 60 missions over occupied Europe and Germany. Following the war he went to Columbia University and received an MA in 1949. He won a Fulbright scholarship that took him to Oxford University (1949-50). On his return to the US he became an English teacher at Pennsylvania State University (1950-52). From there he went to work as an advertising copy writer for *Time* magazine (1952-56) and *Look* (1956-58). He joined *McCalls* in 1958 and stayed for three years while writing *Catch-22* in his spare time. This story describes a real life phenomenon. A US Air Force regulation states that 'a man is considered insane if he willingly continues to fly dangerous combat missions but, if he makes the necessary formal request to be relieved of such missions the very act of making the request proves that he is sane and therefore ineligible to be relieved'. The term Catch-22 has thus entered the languages of the world to describe a situation in which, whichever way one turns, one is tripped up. Heller later wrote further novels, including *Something Happened* (1974), *Good As Gold* (1979) and *God Knows* (1984); for which he was awarded the French Prix Medici Etranger in 1985. They were all very good stories, but nothing he has done could be expected to be quite as brilliant as *Catch-22*. His 1968 play *We Bombed in New York* was well received.

HELLMAN, Lilian (1905-84) US writer

Born in New Orleans on June 20th 1905, she was educated at both New York University and Columbia University but failed to gain a degree. She later claimed it was because of her constant travelling between New Orleans and New York. It made little difference to her future career: a writer doesn't require a degree, as Lilian Hellman showed. During the 1930s she worked as a book reviewer and it was during this period that she divorced her husband, Arthur Kober, to begin her relationship with writer Dashiell Hammett. It was he who encouraged Lilian to write. She began by writing plays, and her topics appeared to cover the various forms in which evil appears, as in *The Children's Hour* (1934) and *Little Foxes* (1939), which she later adapted as a screenplay for which she received an Oscar nomination. *Another Forest* was produced in 1946. The play for which she received international recognition was *Watch on the Rhine* (1941), which told of the relentless pursuit of a Jewish family by German agents in the US. It won many awards. Her work was tightly constructed and gripping. Her later work included adaptions, translations and editing Anton Chekhov's *Selected Letters*. Unashamedly left-wing, in *Scoundrel Times* (1976) she details the problems she and her friends experienced during the McCarthy witch-hunt of the 1950s. When forced to testify in front of the House Committee on Un-American Activities in May 1952 she included in her statement the memorable phrase 'I cannot and will not cut my conscience to fit this year's fashion'. She died at Martha's Vineyard, Massachusetts, on June 30th 1984.

HENRIQUES, Sir Basil (1890-1961) British social worker

A descendant of the distinguished Quixano-Henriques family that originated in Jamaica, **Basil** was born in London on October 17th 1890 and educated at Oxford University. He served as an officer in the First World War until invalided out through war wounds. He then devoted the remainder of his life to helping underprivileged children in the East End of London. In 1915 he founded his first Boys' Club. As a magistrate and later as the head of the juvenile court, Henriques made every effort to understand the causes of delinquency in the young and developed progressive social programmes to combat what he saw as a disease. He lectured all over the world on his subject and was rewarded with a knighthood in 1955. He wrote several books that described his career, including *The Indiscretions of a Warden* (1937) and *The Indiscretions of a Magistrate* (1950). He died in London on December 2nd 1961.

HENRIQUES,
Robert
(1905-67)
British soldier
and writer

Robert Henriques, born in London on December 11th 1905, a relation of Basil Henriques (*qv*), distinguished himself in two careers. Following his entry into the Sandhurst Military Academy he successfully completed his officer's training course and was gazetted a regular army officer. He served for several years in various parts of the world until his retirement in 1933. He then started on his second career and in 1939 published his first novel, *No Arms, No Armour*. The book was a success and Henriques was awarded several prizes. When the Second World War began in September 1939 he returned to the army and the Royal Artillery before transferring to the Commandos. He then served as a colonel on General Montgomery's staff, specializing in Combined Operations. Following the war, during which he received the US Silver Star, he returned to his writing. In 1950 he wrote *Through The Valley*, another prize-winning novel based upon his war experiences. Though uninterested in things and events Jewish he was sufficiently impressed by Israel's planning and execution of the 1956 Sinai campaign that he wrote his famous book, *100 Hours to Suez*, about that episode. He also volunteered his services to the Israeli government in respect of his expertise in artillery warfare. He later became involved with 'The Bridge in Britain', a movement set up to promote friendship between ordinary citizens in Britain and Israel. He wrote an autobiographical novel in 1967 called *The Commander*, in which he gave an account of his experiences as a Commando. He died in London on January 24th 1967.

HERSKOVITS,
Melville
(1895-1963)
US
anthropologist

Herskovits was born on September 10th 1895 in Bellefontaine, Ohio, and educated at Chicago and Columbia Universities. From the latter he obtained his PhD in 1923. He was a lecturer at Columbia and Harvard before moving on to Northwestern in 1927; here he remained until he died and did all his great work, other than his fieldwork. He undertook a number of anthropometric studies of American Negroes in the US and Africa which led to his book *The Myth of the Negro Past* (1941). This exposed as myths a number of previously held views. He attacked the colonial view that Africa must follow Western ideas and be directed by Europeans. He argued that African tribes must be free and independent to follow their own culture, religions and intellectual paths, regardless of where these might take them and regardless of how it might compare to Western standards. Herskovits was a man of vision who wrote much, and prophetically, on his subject. His final book and probably his most important work was *The Human Factor in Changing Africa* (1962). He was the first anthropologist to grasp the nettle and open up the study of the New World Negro. It was a new field of research that led to the establishment at Northwestern University of the first chair of African studies in the US. He died in Evanton, Illinois, on February 25th 1963.

Gustav Hertz was born in Hamburg on July 22nd 1887. He was educated at the universities of Göttingen, Munich and Berlin before becoming an assistant lecturer in physics at Berlin University in 1913. Here, together with James Franck (*qv*), he began his research into the theory that energy can be absorbed by an atom only in defined amounts. In 1925 the pair were awarded the Nobel Prize for Physics. The same year Hertz was appointed professor of physics at the University of Halle. In 1928 he transferred to the Technische Hochschule in Berlin. In 1932 he attracted the attention of the world's scientific press with his discovery of a method of separating the isotopes of neon. He spent most of the Second World War in Russia, returning to East Germany in 1954 to be appointed professor of physics and director of the Physics Institute in Leipzig. He retired in 1961 and died in East Berlin on October 30th 1975.

Myra Hess was born in London on February 25th 1890 and educated at the Guildhall School of Music before winning a scholarship to the Royal Academy of Music. She made her performing debut in 1907 at Queen's Hall, London, where she played Beethoven's G Major concerto with Thomas Beecham conducting. Thereafter she began to experience depressions, apparently brought on by a marked lack of response from concert promoters requiring her services. She left home because of the constraints upon her from orthodox parents. For a time Myra flirted with Christianity and other philosophies, but nothing helped so she remained Jewish. She had a love affair with the violinist Aldo Antonietti, but it did not last very long. She rejected proposals from fellow musicians including Mischa Elman (*qv*) and Benno Moisewitsch (*qv*) because she wanted no distraction from her music. At last, in 1912, she was invited to play with the Amsterdam Concertgebouw, then as now one of the world's great orchestras. Her playing of the Schuman A minor under the baton of Mengelberg was sensational. The reviews were ecstatic and she was compared to the legendary Clara Schuman. She became famous all over Europe long before she found full recognition in Britain. American audiences loved her, and for some 40 years she regularly appeared there, from coast to coast. The greatest compliment she received in the US was that during the depression of the 1930s her audiences grew where others dwindled. However, it was during the Second World War that Myra Hess became a legend. Defying the Blitz on London, she played lunchtime concerts from the National Gallery. Often hers was the only performance available, and she gave some 1,700 recitals and concerts to help satisfy music lovers otherwise denied that pleasure. Hess was credited with keeping up the moral of bomb-torn Londoners. Her concerts were broadcast on the BBC World Service and were particularly valuable to those in occupied Europe. The Germans were greatly put out, and made it clear that when they overran Britain the 'Jew Hess' would be dealt with. In 1941 she was created a Dame of the British Empire. She was also given the Royal Philharmonic Society's Gold Medal. She lived in Golders Green in north-west London, close to Hampstead Heath, and when she wasn't involved with music she could be seen out walking in all weathers. She died in London on November 24th 1965.

HEVESY,
George
(1885-1966)
Hungarian/
Swedish chemist

Hevesy was born on August 1st 1885 in Budapest, Hungary, and educated at Budapest University and Freiburg University, from where he obtained his PhD in 1908. In 1911 he began working at Manchester University, under Rutherford, on the chemical separation of radium. This led him to research the use of radioactive isotopes as tracers. In 1920 he was in Copenhagen at the invitation of Niels Bohr (*qv*); here he discovered hafinum, a metallic element in the fourth group of the periodic system among ores of zirconium. Hevesy went on to become professor at Freiburg, where he continued his research. In 1934 his research revealed the dynamic state of the body constituents. As a Jew he was forced to flee Hitler and Germany and went to Denmark; when the Germans took over there, he fled further, to Sweden. In 1943 Hevesy became a professor at the Institute of Organic Chemistry in Stockholm. His work in explaining the chemical nature of life's processes earned him the Nobel Prize for Chemistry in 1943. Following the Second World War he returned to the University of Freiburg, where he died on July 5th 1966.

HEYSE,
Paul von
(1830-1914)
German writer

Paul von Heyse, the son of a Jewish mother, was born in Berlin on March 15th 1830. By the turn of the century he was an established writer, a traditionalist who refused to accept the growing Naturalist movement. His writings never portrayed the darker side of life and so his work never really reflected on what was going on around him. Notwithstanding, he was awarded the 1910 Nobel Prize for Literature. He died on April 2nd 1914.

HILDESHEIMER,
Wolfgang
(1916-91)
German writer

Hildesheimer was born on December 9th 1916 in Hamburg. In 1933 his Jewish parents, seeing what was happening to Jews in Germany, left for England, and Wolfgang completed his education at Frensham Heights in Surrey. Thereafter his parents moved on to Palestine, where, in the late 1930s, he started to study art, including stage design, furniture design and drawing. In 1939 he returned to Europe and toured France, Italy and Switzerland. Back in Palestine he worked as a teacher of English. By 1946 he had married and divorced. He needed new horizons and they came when he was appointed a simultaneous translator for the Nuremberg War Crimes Tribunal. The trials over, he edited the proceedings. The experience left him with a fatalist and sometimes pessimistic view of life and in 1949 he returned to Germany to live in Ambach am Starnbergessee in Bavaria. There he became a freelance artist. Then, on February 18th 1950, his life changed. It was a very cold day and Wolfgang picked up his drawing pad and moved closer to the fire. Instead of drawing something, he found he was writing: writing a story. Next day he wrote another story, and another and another until he found he couldn't stop even if he wanted to. Hildesheimer had found a new career. In German literary circles he came to be compared to Max Frisch as a writer of the absurd and to Gunter Grass as a pessimist. All this attention was national; his international reputation was made with his controversial biography of *Mozart* (1977), which exploded the conventional notion of the great composer. Previously, in 1957, he had married again and moved to Poschiavo in Switzerland. He wrote the play, *The Conquest of Princess Turandot*, for the theatre and television; an unusual fairy tale without a happy ending. All his writings are described as bizarre. Asked why, he said, in part, it was because life cannot be understood and the viewer who waits for meaning waits in vain; he should mock the object of the situation; in that is life itself. In the mould of master of the absurd he wrote a fictional biography: *Marbot* was published in 1981 and achieves the ultimate absurdity of turning fiction into reality. In his role of pessimist he gave up writing on the premise that as the world was destroying itself there was little reason to write as there wouldn't be anyone around to read. He returned to his paintings and died at his home in Poschiavo on August 21st 1991.

Hillman was born in Zagare, Lithuania, on March 23rd 1887 into a rabbinical family. He rejected his background and in 1906 emigrated to the US. He lived briefly in New York before moving to Chicago. He worked in a clothing factory and in 1910 became one of the leaders who closed down that city's clothing factories when 35,000 clothing workers went on strike. He went on to become one of the founders of the Amalgamated Clothing Workers of America and its president for 30 years. He was a founder of the Congress of Industrial Organizations and its first vice-president (1935-40). His original trade union became a model for other unions in the fields of housing, arbitration, social benefits, etc. His aim was to achieve reforms to benefit the worker by the means of negotiation rather than wild-cat strikes. He became involved with politics and in particular with the election of Roosevelt as President. The core of the New Deal was the minimum wage law and Roosevelt later acknowledged that it was the work of Sidney Hillman that realized this goal. Hillman died on July 10th 1946 at Point Lookout, New York.

HILLMAN, Sidney (1887-1946) US Labour leader

Hirszfeld was born in Poland and, having qualified as a doctor, spent the years 1907-11 in Heidelberg on research work. His particular field was blood groupings. He succeeded in demonstrating that the heredity of different blood groups was crucial. During the First World War, while serving as an army doctor in Serbia, he discovered the bacteria of paratyphoid C, now known as 'Salmonella Hirszfeldi'. This discovery was of the utmost importance and brought him international recognition. In 1924 he was professor of the Free University of Warsaw. During the Second World War Hirszfeld was fortunate to escape from the Warsaw ghetto, which he later described in his book *Historia Jednegzycia*. Following the war, in 1945 he reorganized the administration of the medical department at Wroclaw University, where he served as professor of microbiology. He established both the Institute of Immunology and the research centre at Wroclaw for pathology in pregnancy. Hirszfeld was a member of the Polish Academy of Sciences and promoted the study of seroanthropology. He wrote much on his subjects, his two best-known works being *Blood Groups in Relation to Biology* (1934) and *The Establishment of Paternity in the Light of the Science of Blood Groups* (1948).

HIRSZFELD, Ludwik (1884-1954) Polish microbiologist

**HODES,
Art
(1904-93)
US jazz pianist**

Born on November 14th 1904 in Niolayev, Russia, **Hodes** left for America when he was six months old, his parents being anxious to escape from the antisemitic gangs that followed the abortive 1905 revolution, inspired by he League of the Russian People and supported by the Russian royal family; the Romanovs, the church and the secret police. The Jews left Russia in their thousands, forced by the pogroms that abounded. As a consequence of these upheavals, Art Hodes grew up on Chicago's West Side. He studied music at Jane Addam's Hall House on the South Side. In 1926, when he was 22, he met Louis Armstrong. The two became firm friends and Hodes hung out with Armstrong, six years his senior, every night, working with the South Side band led by 'Kid' Org. Hodes drank in the music and learned all about blues music from the black piano players who specialized in the blues. He developed his own sound, a mix of 1920s blues and jazz improvisation. During the Great Depression of the 1930s Hodes worked with band leaders Floyd Town and Frank Snyder. In 1938 Hodes was living in New York and working in the jazz clubs of West 52nd Street, enjoying the experience of belonging to just one Musicians' Union that enabled black and white to play together; in Chicago there had been segregation. In 1940 Hodes formed his own band and they appeared regularly at Child's Restaurant. He co-founded and edited the *Jazz Record* (1943-47). He had his own record label called Jazzy Record. In the late 1940s Hodes was performing regularly at the top New York jazz clubs. In 1950 Hodes and his family moved back to Chicago. There he joined the Blue Nore Band, which featured Chippy Hill as singer. The band folded when Chippy was killed in Harlem by a taxi. During the 1960s Hodes hosted *Jazz Alley'* on television, his guests the cream of the jazz world. From 1977 Hodes toured internationally on a regular basis. His last concert was in 1992 in Park Forest, Illinois. He suffered a stroke a few months later and died on March 4th 1993. Jazz historian Rudi Blash said of him, 'among the most Negroid of all living white pianists is Art Hodes.'

**HOFFMAN,
Abbie
(1936-)
US radical**

Hoffman, born in Worcester, Massachusetts into a regular Jewish family and educated at Brandeis University, came to the attention of the world during the late 1960s. By his radical political activities he called attention to those who were the victims of capitalist greed. Never ashamed or embarrassed by his Jewishness, he would later turn on Judge Hoffman , a Jew but no relation, and cry out: 'You're a shanda to the goyim' - a shame in front of Gentiles. Throughout the 1960s he was a prankster with a serious purpose, and as his pranks were reported internationally so were the reasons for them. These included his backing for the civil rights movement in the Southern states of America and the plight of the poor, often dismissed as hippies, who lived in deprived circumstances, especially in the bigger cities. Hoffman was dubbed the 'Robin Hoodlike statesman'. In the 'Chicago conspiracy' trial Hoffman was one of seven defendants charged with conspiracy to incite a riot at the 1968 Democratic National Convention in Chicago. The case flushed into the open the tactics of Chicago's Democratic mayor, Richard Daley, accused by the seven of gerrymandering. Hoffman was convicted after a boisterous trial, but the conviction was overturned on appeal. In 1973 Hoffman was accused of possessing cocaine and went 'underground', surfacing at regular intervals to hold press conferences in order to protest at America's involvement in Vietnam. In 1980 he revealed the astonishing news that following plastic surgery he had become 'Barry Freed' and as such had lived openly in an upmarket area of New York State, had been a pillar of society, had been praised by the Governor, had testified before a Senate Committee and had led a crusade against nuclear weaponry. It was Hoffman's ultimate jape. In 1982 he resumed his real identity and continued his social work. He wrote much that reflected what he stood for, including *Revolution For the Hell of It* (1968), *Steal This Book* (1971), *Square Dancing in the Ice Age: Underground Writings* (1982) and his autobiography, *Soon To Be a Motion Picture* (1980). His work was always for others and often abused by those who should have known better. At Woodstock he was appealing for funds to aid imprisoned activists when he was chased off the platform by Pete Townshend of 'The Who' while he was under the influence of acid, complaining Hoffman was 'spoiling the fun'! Hoffman was the original 'yuppie' who made whoopee in his pursuit of a peaceful revolution that was bound to fail.

HOFFMAN, Dustin (1937-) US actor

Hoffman was born in Los Angeles on August 8th 1937. He was at Santa Monica City College when after a year he dropped out in favour of acting classes at the Pasadena Playhouse. In 1958 he was in New York looking for parts to play. He gradually climbed the theatrical ladder and in 1967 Hollywood called and his film career began in a film called *The Graduate*. Seldom has an actor made such an impact on his first outing. Over some 30 years he has shown an exceptional ability to play widely differing roles with believable scope and brilliance. He has starred in several of Hollywood's best films, including, as well as *The Graduate* (for which he received an Oscar nomination), *Midnight Cowboy* (1969 and another nomination), *Little Big Man* (1970), *Alfredo, Alfredo* (1973), *Papillon* (1973), *Lenny* (1974 and another nomination), *Marathon Man* (1976), *All the President's Men* (1976), *Kramer vs Kramer* (1979 and at last an Oscar), *Tootsie* (1982 and an Oscar nomination) and *Rain Man* (1988, with an Oscar for Best Actor). In 1984 he returned to Broadway and Arthur Miller's (*qv*) *Death of a Salesman*. His wasn't bad; but compared to the performance of Lee J. Cobb (*qv*) as Willy Loman there is rarely a contest. Dustin Hoffman remains a film star whose fans look forward to seeing him tackle extraordinary roles. His cameo performance in *Sleepers* (1996) was such a role. He followed with the filmed version of David Mamet's play *American Buffalo* in which he plays the part of Teach; pigtailed and greasy.

HOFFMANN, Roald (1937-) Polish/American chemist

Born in Zloczow, Poland on July 18th 1937, he spent the war years in a German labour camp. His father was executed for trying to escape. Then his mother smuggled him out to spend the rest of the war in hiding with a sympathetic Christian family before being liberated by the Red Army to emigrate to relatives in the United States in 1949. He studied at Columbia and Harvard universities and received a BA from the former and an MA from the latter. He obtained his doctorate in 1962 and since 1965 has been associated with Cornell University, where he was a professor of chemistry 1968-74. His work in the fields of research is considerable, a primary focus being on molecular orbital calculations and adjacent activities. His work earned him the award of the Nobel Prize for Chemistry in 1981. Hoffmann is a member of the US National Academy of Science who in 1997 stated that the cloning of a sheep by genetic engineering raises ethical questions. His latest book *The Same and Not the Same* enjoins science with the wider world.

HOFSTADTER, Richard (1916-70) US historian

Richard Hofstadter was born in Buffalo, New York, on August 6th 1916. Educated at the University of Buffalo, he obtained his BA in 1937. He then proceeded to Columbia University, from where he received his masters degree in 1938 and his PhD in 1942, and where he taught from 1946 until his death in 1970. His books on American history included several that became best-sellers, including *The American Political Tradition* (1948), *The Age of Reform* (1955, for which he received the 1956 Pulitzer Prize), *The Idea of a Party System* (1969) and *American Violence* (1970). In 1963 he published *Anti-Intellectualism in American Life*; it won the 1964 Pulitzer Prize and explained that the egalitarian expressions of democracy, themes that echoed and re-echoed throughout US history, have caused many to have a prejudice against intellectuals, often believing them to be an alien elite. He died in New York on October 24th 1970.

HOFSTADTER, Robert (1915-90) US physicist

Hofstadter was born in New York on February 5th 1915 and educated at Princeton University, from where he obtained his PhD in 1938. During the Second World War he worked on scientific research for the US Air Force. In 1946 he joined the staff of Princeton, where his research work was in the field of infra-red rays. He moved to Stanford University in 1950 and stayed there until 1985. At Stanford he was able to use a linear electron accelerator to measure the structure of atomic nuclei. He discovered that both proton and neutron have a central core, positively charged, that is encompassed by a double cloud of p1-mesons. In 1961 Hofstadter shared the Nobel Prize for Physics in recognition of the contribution he made in classifying sub-atomic particles. He died on November 17th 1990 at Stanford, California.

HOLLIDAY, Judy (1922-65) US actor

Judy Holliday, born Judith Tuvin on June 21st 1922 in New York, was one of the best performers Hollywood has produced: an intelligent actress who played the dumb blonde to her advantage. Educated at the Julia Richman High School in Manhattan, she then joined the staff of Orson Welles' Mercury Theatre. She did some revue work that was good experience but little more. In 1944 she signed a contract with 20th Century Fox. The studio agreed to allow her time off to appear in the lead of a new Broadway production called *Born Yesterday*. The play was a hit and Judy a star. When the film version was contemplated, Judy was not the first choice. The producers auditioned over 30 actresses before coming to the obvious conclusion. Judy Holliday was as brilliant in the film as she had been on the stage and deserved the Oscar she won for Best Actress. She continued to make films but was constantly dogged by ill-health, and finally fell victim to cancer on June 7th 1965 in New York.

Nat Holman was born on the Lower East Side of New York and learned to play basketball in the small concrete playgrounds of large blocks of tenement houses among which he lived. At high school he was an all-round athlete who in 1916 decided to become a professional basketball player. The following year he joined the US Navy to take part in the First World War. He later became coach to the City College of New York while continuing to play. At 6 feet and 165 pounds he came to be regarded as the best ball handler and set shot artist of his time. He played for the Whirlwinds of New York (1920-21) and then moved to the Original Celtics (1921-28). His City College was unique in having no scholarship players and in being the only team ever to win the National Collegiate title and the National Invitation Tournament in the same year. In 1949 Holman went to Israel to teach basketball. The foundations he laid helped the Israeli national team to become among the world's best. It was the beginning of a long association and in 1976 Holman received the Olympic Award. Holman, known as Mr Basketball, was the first player to average out in double figures. He died in New York in 1994. He was that rare double, a world leading player and world-class coach.

Hook was born in New York on December 20th 1902 and educated at Brooklyn College and Columbia University, from where he graduated with a doctorate in 1927. He taught at New York University (1927-69) and Stanford University (1973-89). He studied historical theory and compared it with American philosophy. He came to some definitive conclusions, namely that all forms of totalitarianism were unacceptable and that only a liberal democracy could benefit society. He wrote around 35 books, including some that analyse Marxism as a possible solution for the world's ills. He firmly believed that only by high standards of education could society advance. He objected to the teaching of religion in schools on the basis that there is no clear evidence that God exists. His autobiography, *Out of Step*, was published in 1987. Hook is judged to have been one of America's outstanding intellectuals and an international exponent of political thought. He died on July 12th 1989 in Stanford, California.

Leslie Hore-Belisha was born in London on September 7th 1893. His father, Jacob Belisha, died while Leslie was an infant. His mother remarried and Sir Adam Hore became Leslie's adoptive father. Later Leslie honoured him by adding his surname to his own. Educated at Clifton College (which has a Jewish house) and Oxford University, where he was president of the Union, during the First World War he served in the army in France with distinction and was mentioned in dispatches. Following the war he became a barrister and was called to the bar in 1923. He entered parliament as a Liberal and later joined the National Government of Ramsay MacDonald. When the Liberal Party left the coalition Hore-Belisha remained as a National Liberal. He was Minister of Transport (1934-37) and brought in several radical measures to reduce road accidents. Among these were pedestrian crossings distinguished by a yellow globe, illuminated at night, on top of a tall black and white pole. They are still in use all over Britain, known as 'Belisha Beacons'. In 1937 he was appointed Secretary of State for War (the post now known as Defence Secretary). At the War Office he introduced reforms to modernize the armed forces, especially among the upper ranks, and generally democratize the administration. His measures were bitterly resented and attacks on him contained elements of anti-Semitism. In the early part of 1939, seeing a war with Germany on the horizon, Hore-Belisha took the valuable precaution of introducing conscription. He resigned from the government in 1940 but continued as an Independent MP until 1945 when he lost his seat in the post-war general election. In 1954 he was created a peer. He achieved more in the ways of reform than at any time since World War One. He died in Rheims, France, on February 16th 1957.

HOROWITZ,
Vladimir
(1903-89)
Russian/
American
pianist

Horowitz was born on October 1st 1903 in Berdichiev, Russia. At the age of twelve he was at the Kiev Conservatory, and in 1920 he gave his first concert in Kharkov. His reputation grew and by 1923 he had given some 20 recitals in Leningrad, all different and covering some 200 works. He became an international star during the 1930s and married Arturo Toscanini's daughter, Wanda. He became a US citizen in 1944. For twelve years from 1953 he stayed away from the concert platform, though he continued to record and give master classes. The brief periods during which he returned to live performances therefore became great events. In 1982, after an absence of 30 years, he toured Europe. His concerts were full and television coverage was prominent. In 1986 he returned to the Soviet Union and gave two fantastic performances. Another European tour followed in 1987, during which he gave a series of piano recitals and television interviews. Horowitz was distinguished for his technique and flawless tone. His interpretations of modern masters, such as Rachmaninoff, Chopin, Prokofiev and others, were hailed as brilliant for their clarity and delicacy. He died in New York on November 5th 1989 and was buried in the Toscanini family vault in Milan.

HOUDINI,
Harry
(1874-1926)
US magician

Harry Houdini was born Erik Weiss on March 24th 1874 in Budapest, Hungary. He was the son of a rabbi who emigrated to the US when Harry was only a few months old and settled in Appleton, Wisconsin. At an early age Harry gave up school for the circus and later appeared, unsuccessfully, in vaudeville. From 1900 Houdini, aided by his wife Beatrice, began getting an international reputation as an escapologist. He would escape from chains, handcuffs, locked dungeons, coffins, prison cells and anything imaginative promoters could devise. Sometimes he would be placed manacled into a coffin and the coffin weighted down and thrown off a boat into the sea. Anxious minutes would pass; then up would pop Harry, none the worse for his perilous exhibition. He toured Europe and was a sensation in London, where he took on Scotland Yard and won. He was hailed as the world's greatest magician and the money flowed in. In Australia in 1910 he won a trophy for being the first man to fly an aeroplane on that continent. His acts became ever more dangerous and more and more sensational, as when he made an elephant disappear (1918). He had enormous physical strength and unusual skills in picking and manipulating locks and chains. He would boast that he could take any punch in the stomach. An unknown man took him at his word, but unfortunately Harry was unprepared, and suffered a stomach injury that led to peritonitis. Between 1916 and 1923 he made a number of short silent films. He devoted much time to debunking and exposing mind-readers and mediums, claiming they were simply charlatans preying on a gullible public. Houdini claimed they used all sorts of tricks and wrote books on the subject, including *Miracle Mongers and Their Methods* (1920) and *A Magician Among the Spirits* (1924). He died in Detroit on October 31st 1926. Harry and Beatrice Houdini made a pact to experiment with spiritualism. They agreed that whoever died first would attempt to get in touch with the survivor. Shortly before her death in 1943 Beatrice declared the experiment a failure.

Born Jacques Haussmann on September 22nd 1902 in Bucharest, following an English education he immigrated to the US in 1924. He studied all aspects of drama and in 1934 directed the modern opera, *Four Saints in Three Acts*. In 1935, he worked with Orson Welles and ran the Negro Theatre Project. In 1937 he and Welles founded the legendary Mercury Theatre that had so much success on Broadway and radio. Houseman wrote and produced for the company, including *Julius Caesar* for the stage (1937), the controversial radio play *War of the Worlds* (1938) and the outstanding film *Citizen Kane* (1941). He fell out with Welles over the authorship of *Citizen Kane* and in the event didn't receive a credit. He left the company and moved to Hollywood to work as a producer. He produced a total of nineteen feature films that included *Letter to an Unknown Woman* (1948), *They Live by Night* (1949), *The Bad and the Beautiful* (1952), *Julius Caesar* (1953, for which he was nominated for an Oscar), *Lust For Life* (1956) and *Two Weeks in Another Town* (1962). He also advised traditional acting companies, including the American Shakespeare Festival. In 1973 Houseman was in front of the camera acting the role of the cynical law professor in *Paper Chase* and winning the Oscar for Best Supporting Actor. He had starring roles in *Rollerball* (1975), *Three Days of the Condor* (1975) and Woody Allen's *Another Woman* (1988). His published memoirs are *Run Through* (1972), *Front and Centre* (1979) and *Final Dress* (1983). He died in Malibu, California, on October 31st 1988.

HOUSEMAN, John (1902-88) Romanian/ American actor/ producer

Leslie Howard was born Leslie Howard Stainer in London on April 3rd 1893, the grandson of a Hungarian rabbi. Educated at Dulwich College, he had a variety of jobs before obtaining a commission in the 20th Hussars in time for the First World War. He was badly wounded in France and invalided out of the army in 1917. Following a recovery he decided to try for the stage. His quiet, persuasive charm was perfect for the theatre and he gradually obtained better and more important roles. Howard accepted an offer to appear on New York's Broadway in the play *Just Suppose* in 1920. It was the first of many such invitations and Howard spent the 1920s shunting across the Atlantic to appear in both London and New York. If the 1920s were his theatrical years, the 1930s were his film years, although he still took time off filming to do theatre, starring in such plays as *The Petrified Forest* (1935) and *Hamlet* (1936). He made his Hollywood debut in 1930 in *Outward*

HOWARD, Leslie (1893-1943) British actor

Bound and in 1933 made *Berkeley Square*, for which he was nominated for an Oscar as Best Actor. In 1938 he was Professor Henry Higgins in Shaw's *Pygmalion* and was again nominated for an Oscar. In 1939 he starred in *Gone With The Wind*. Howard enjoyed directing and in *Pimpernel Smith* (1941) he both starred and directed to very good effect. During the Second World War he undertook a government mission to persuade cinema chains in Portugal and Spain to exhibit British war films. In this he was successful - perhaps too successful, because on June 1st 1943, while flying home from Lisbon in an unarmed passenger aircraft, the plane was shot down by German fighter pilots. Leslie Howard was long known as the archetypal English romantic gentleman. More importantly, his films in which actors played the parts of Nazis had them speaking normal English.

HUBERMAN,
Bronislaw
(1882-1947)
Polish musician

Huberman was born on December 19th 1882 in Czestochowa, Poland. Not only was he a child prodigy, at ten years of age he gave a command performance for the Austrian Emperor, Franz Joseph, in Vienna. Following this performance and others it was not long before Huberman was internationally known. He had learnt the violin because it was cheaper for his poor lawyer's clerk father than a piano. Huberman became a virtuoso who introduced Paganini's violin concerto at a concert in Genoa in 1908. He gave concerts all over Europe and was a particular favourite with German audiences. In 1933 Huberman, a socialist, cancelled his future concert programme in Germany. However, he continued playing in Austria, even after the Anschluss - but with a difference: at his concerts he would announce he was sending his fee to the families of the working-class victims killed by the Dolfuss government. He received an offer from the pro-Nazi conductor Furtwaengler to play with him. Huberman turned him down and later explained to the *Manchester Guardian* how people like Furtwaengler went along with the persecution of Jewish artistic life. He went to Palestine and soon realized that the large numbers of Jewish refugees included many first-class musicians.

So he started an orchestra, the Palestine Symphony Orchestra, which in 1948 changed its name to the Israel Philharmonic. His dream of a world-class orchestra had taken root in 1935, and he raised money from all over the world by fund-raising speeches at which he played his violin. He donated his fees and auditioned musicians from all over Europe. On December 26th 1936 in Tel Aviv his dream was realized when Arturo Toscanini conducted the first concert. Huberman was disappointed at being unable to play at the inaugural concert. He had suffered an air crash in which his hands were so badly injured that his doctors told him to retire from playing permanently. Huberman ignored their advice and spent many years having treatment and forcing himself to practise the violin. In 1945, at the age of 63, Huberman returned to the concert platform in Lucerne to play Brahms' violin concerto. The concert hall was packed and the performance was broadcast all over Europe. The street in Tel Aviv, where the Israel Philharmonic is based was renamed after him. In 1982, on the centenary of his birth, his Israel Philharmonic, with Zubin Mehta conducting, gave a celebrity concert. The concert included performances by the greatest violinists of the century, including Stern (*qv*), Handel, Gitlis, Perlman (*qv*) and Zuckerman (*qv*). The world standing of the Israel Philharmonic has exceeded even Huberman's dream. He died on June 15th 1947.

The son of a Jewish mother, **Fritz** was born in Vienna on December 15th 1928 as Friedrich Stowasser, but appears to have undergone a series of personality changes. The choice of the name Hundertwasser was made to illustrate some obscure point of view. Nevertheless, whatever he calls himself, he is one of Europe's best-known painters. His style is distinctive and very original. His images, by way of energetic linear forms, show ordinary figures, scenes and objects dissolving into complicated patterns. His paintings are often brightly coloured with a dream-like quality. He stands aside from contemporary art movements and generally works on a small scale and often in water colours. He has been compared to Klee and Klint, but the resemblance is only superficial. He is concerned about the dehumanizing of society and is outspoken in his criticism of modern architecture. In 1975 Austria reproduced his painting 'Modern Art Spiral Tree' on a postage stamp. In 1983 the United Nations issued a stamp honouring Hundertwasser on the occasion of the 35th anniversary of the Universal Declaration of Human Rights.

Born in Pogar, Russia, on April 9th 1888, **Sol Hurok** arrived in New York penniless in 1906. He took any job going but at the same time, almost as a hobby, he was organizing concerts for working-class socialists. His high point came when the famous violinist Efram Zimbalist played at a benefit Hurok arranged for the Socialist Party in 1911. By 1916 Hurok was staging concerts at the New York Hippodrome. He sponsored a number of differing artistic talents and introduced the Bolshoi Ballet to the US as well as Sadlers Well Ballet from London, the Ballet Russe de Monte Carlo, the Old Vic, the Comédie Française and others. Some of the greatest performers of the century brought their talents to the US via Hurok's company, S. Hurok Concerts Inc., with around 4,000 artists demonstrating their talents to US audiences, and by his efforts countless Americans have benefited from this cultural exposure. His autobiography, in two volumes, was published under the title *Impresario* (1948). In 1953 a film version of Hurok's life called *Tonight We Sing* gave even wider audiences the chance to see the value of Hurok's work. In the same year Hurok was created a Chevalier of the Legion of Honour for his work in promoting French culture overseas. He died in New York on March 5th 1974.

Hurst was born in Hamilton, Ohio, on October 18th 1889 into a middle-class, assimilated family. Following her education at Washington University and Columbia University, she took a variety of jobs for the experience of working. She was 25 when her short story 'Just Around the Corner' was published and widely acclaimed. During her lifetime she wrote some 40 novels including *A President Is Born* (1928), *Back Street* (1930) and *Any Woman* (1950). Her stories are often about the poor of New York, women's rights and the problems of immigrant families. Her family later lived in St Louis, well away from the areas Fannie wrote about, but she was well travelled and sensitive to what she saw on her travels. She was president of the

Authors' Guild of America (1936-7). Her autobiography, *Anatomy of Me*, was published in 1958. A number of her books became successful films, often with Fannie writing the screenplay. She died in New York on February 23rd 1968.

HURWITZ,
Stephen
(1901-1990)
Danish lawyer

Born and educated in Copenhagen, Denmark, **Hurwitz** went on to become a law lecturer at the University of Copenhagen. During the Second World War he managed to escape to Sweden, where he set up and ran an organization to aid the many refugees living in that country. Following the war Hurwitz was appointed the Danish representative to the War Crimes Commission. In 1950 he was appointed to head the Permanent Committee dealing with penal law and followed this with a spell as Parliamentary Commissioner for Civil and Military Administration. From 1953 to 1954 he was also vice-chancellor at the University of Copenhagen. Then, from 1955 to 1971, Hurwitz held one of the most important posts in Danish society, Ombudsman of the Danish Parliament. Among his writings was the textbook concerning the results of criminological studies carried out in Europe, Britain, the US and Scandinavia. *Kriminologi* (1948) was translated into several languages.

HYMANS,
Paul
(1865-1941)
Belgian
statesman

Paul Hymans was born in Brussels on March 23rd 1865. He was the son of Solomon Hymans, a poet and member of the Chamber of Deputies. Paul graduated as a lawyer and joined the civil service. In 1900 he was elected to the Chamber of Deputies, eventually becoming leader of the Liberal party. During the First World War he served in the coalition government. From 1915 to 1919 he was Belgium's ambassador to Great Britain. In 1920 he was appointed his country's Foreign Secretary and head of the Belgian delegation at the Versailles Peace Conference. He served three further terms as Foreign Minister and one as Minister of Justice. He was president of the League of Nations, having helped draft the original covenants that founded the body. He was intensely disliked by King Leopold II because Hymans, no respecter of persons, publicly criticized the manner in which the king used the Belgian Congo, creaming off millions of francs for his personal use. Paul Hymans died on March 8th 1941 in Nice, France. In 1965, to mark the anniversary of his birth, the Belgian Post Office issued a commemorative stamp.

I

She was born Janis Eddy Fink on April 7th 1951 in New York City. The daughter of a music teacher, she was taught the piano at three and the guitar at eleven, and by the time she was twelve she was writing and performing. She attracted much attention with *Society's Child*. This was a chronicle concerning an inter-racial romance that was most mature for a teenager. No one would touch it. She was featured on Leonard Bernstein's (*qv*) *TV Special* and at sixteen she was a hit. Her album, *All The Seasons of Your Mind* (1967) followed and a year later another album, *The Secret Life of J. Eddy Fink*, was released. She moved to California and wrote for other singers until 1971, when she released *Present Company*. *Stars* (1974) re-established her. She wrote, 'Jesse', and Roberta Flack took it to the top ten. Her album *Between The Lines* (1975) included the track 'At Seventeen', her sole chart-topper. She waned in the 1980s and some thought she had retired from music writing and performing. However, in 1991 she surfaced in England and gave her first concert for 10 years to rave reviews.

IAN, Janis (1951-) US singer/ songwriter

Ionesco was born in Bucharest, Romania, on November 26th 1912, the son of a French Jewess who brought him up in France. In his teens Ionesco returned to his father in Romania and there taught French. He married in 1936 and returned to Paris to obtain his doctorate in literature. The Second World War caught up with him in France. He kept a low profile and earned a living by proofreading for writers and publishers. He became a playwright almost by chance. While learning English he was astonished by the meaninglessness of cliches used in everyday conversation. From the nonsensical use of English sentences he created his play *The Bald Prima Donna* (1950), a showcase of the idiocy of daily life in bourgeois society. He was hailed as the founder of the 'Theatre of the Absurd'. More success followed with plays that have since become classics, for example *The Chairs* (1951), in which an elderly couple tell of their experiences to a crowd of guests who never appear, their presence shown by a stage of empty chairs. In *Rhinoceros* (1959) fascism is shown as a disease turning humans into rhinoceroses. In 1970 Ionesco was elected a member of the French Academy. He died in Paris on 13th March 1994.

IONESCO, Eugene (1912-94) Romanian/ French playwright

**ISAAC,
Jules
(1877-1964)
French
historian**

Born in Rennes, France, **Isaac** became an historian who wrote textbooks for the French educational system that were in common use until the German occupation of France in 1940, when they were banned because they were the work of a Jew. His work was distinguished and he became chief of history education at the Ministry of Education. During the Second World War his wife and daughter were taken away by the Germans and murdered in one of their numerous death camps. As a notable figure Jules Isaac was in hiding and so escaped their fate. Just before Madame Isaac was taken away she managed to get a note to her husband which included the sentence 'Save yourself for your work; the world is waiting for it.' Jules Isaac did just that. He studied the root cause of anti-Semitism and concluded it was rooted in Christian teaching that included contempt for the Jews and their culture. Following the end of the war he created an eighteen-point plan in order to purify Christian teaching as it related to Jews. He was influential, during the 1947 inter-faith talks at Seeligsberg, Switzerland, in getting approval of a ten-point plan that became the basis for further conferences. Pope Pius XII invited Isaac to an audience. Isaac told the Pope that the Holocaust had been brought about by anti-Jewish impulses of historic Christianity. This assertion caused the Pope to have an offensive anti-Jewish phrase removed from the Good Friday liturgy. Jules Isaac was the main influence in persuading Pope John XXIII to propose that the Vatican Council pass a declaration on Judaism that rewrote the traditional Christian declaration that the Jews of all time were guilty of deicide. This opened a new progressive age in Catholic-Jewish relations. Isaac wrote many books during his life, including one when aged 85, *The Teaching of Contempt* (1964).

**ISAACS,
Alick
(1921-67)
British scientist**

Alick Isaacs was born in Glasgow on July 17th 1921. His father, Louis, was a shopkeeper and his maternal grandfather was Jacob Lion of London. When his father's father arrived in Britain from Lithuania his surname was Galinsky, but a port official preferred Isaacs. At Pollokshields Secondary School Alick studied physics and chemistry and largely ignored biology. In 1939 he was at the Medical Department of Glasgow University and gained his MB in 1944. He moved away from general medicine and opted for research. Awarded a medical research scholarship to Sheffield University, he began his life's work: researching all aspects of influenza. In 1948, with the benefit of a Rockefeller scholarship, he was in Melbourne, Australia, working under Macfarlane Burnett. He stayed for two years during which time he pursued his own path, heavily influenced by the interference of cells principle. He went on to publish a series of papers that analysed the interference between active and inactive influenza viruses in the allantoic cavities of developing hen's eggs. He showed that the interference did not concern the uptake of the virus but was effective in the cell's interior. In 1951 Isaacs returned to Britain and an appointment to the National Institute for Medical Research at Mill Hill, London. Here he continued his work on interference and his experiments proved there was much interfering activity in the fluids surrounding the treated tissue. A complete and unusual defence mechanism had been discovered, which Alick Isaacs named Interferon. From these early beginnings great strides have been made in the use of interferon and some forms of the substance have been used as anti-cancer agents in clinical trials. Isaacs was elected a Fellow of the Royal Society in 1966. He died a year later in a London hospital on January 26th 1967. To Isaacs, the imaginative pioneer, must go the thanks of many generations.

Isaacs was born in Melbourne, Australia, and originally educated by his parents. Conventional schools followed, culminating in a law degree from Melbourne University. In 1901 he was elected to Australia's first federal parliament and in 1906 was appointed a justice of the Federal High Court, remaining there until 1930 when he was appointed Chief Justice of Australia. A year later the King appointed Isaac Isaacs Governor-General of the Dominion of Australia (1931-36). Isaacs was the first Australian to be so appointed. In 1937 he retired and wrote on many subjects, including matters of Jewish interest. He publicly declared his opposition to Zionism, claiming that Jews were a religious group and as such had no claim to their own country. When the German death camps were revealed Isaacs was a very old man of 90; even so, the news affected him deeply and he admitted he had been wrong to deny the Balfour Declaration.

ISAACS,
Isaac
(1855-1948)
Australian
statesman

Commemorative Stamps

Waldemar Haffkine
Issued by India

Gustav Hertz
Issued by East Germany

George Hevesy
Issued by Hungary

Bronislav Huberman
Issued by Israel

Paul Hymans
Issued by Belgium

Isaac Isaacs
Issued by Australia

Eugene Ionesco
Issued byRomania

Al Jolson
Issued by USA

Gary Kasparov
Issued by USSR

J

François Jacob was born on June 17th 1920 in Nancy, France. His education was interrupted by the advent of the Second World War. Following the German occupation of France, Jacob made his way to Britain, joined the Free French Forces and earned a distinguished war record. Returning to France, he obtained an MD from the Paris Faculty of Medicine in 1947 and a doctorate in 1954 from the Faculty of Science. He joined the Pasteur Institute and worked as a researcher, before eventually becoming head of the department concerned with cellular genetics. In 1965, he shared the Nobel Prize for Physiology in respect of his work on cellular genetic function and the influence of viruses concerning regulatory activities in bacteria. In 1977 he was a member of the Academy of Sciences. Jacob has continued to research many essential factors contained within the science of DNA.

JACOB,
François
(1920-)
French biologist

Jacobs was born on April 18th 1904 in New York City. From the age of eight he raised and raced pigeons. The hobby later became his work, until he took up training horses. He became famous as one of the great characters in American horse racing and a leading trainer. Known as the 'voodoo veterinarian', he was brilliant at turning losers into winners. He was an owner, who trained his own horses, as well as those owned by others. During his long career he saddled a total of 3,569 winners: more than anyone else in the history of Thoroughbred horse racing. His best year was in 1936, when he had 177 winners. During the years 1940 and 1960, Jacobs was the top money-earning trainer in the US. His most notable success was with Stymie, who won 35 races and nearly a million dollars between 1943 and 1947. Jacobs' earnings for himself and other owners amounted to over 15 million dollars. Perhaps it isn't surprising that Hirsch Jacobs, widely known in the racing circles of the world, is in the Turf Hall of Fame.

JACOBS,
Hirsch
(1904-70)
US horse trainer

Arne Jacobson was born in Copenhagen on February 11th 1902, into a middle-class Jewish family. Educated at the Copenhagen Academy of Arts, he began designing when the influence of modernism was sweeping America and Europe, a period when the work of Frank Lloyd Wright and Gropus was causing great excitement. However, in the 1930s Jacobson took a different path, mixing classical with modern and thus adding an elegance previously missing, to produce a distinct Danish style. His first major triumph, in 1933, was the Bellavista housing estate at Klampenborg, where every house has a view of the sea. Between 1938 and 1942 he specialized in simple, small and elegant suburban town halls. During the Second

JACOBSON,
Arne
(1902-71)
Danish architect

World War he found sanctuary in Sweden, returning to Copenhagen on the day the Danish king declared a national holiday to welcome back the country's Jews and continuing where he had left off. His design for the Munkegard school at Gentofte (1952-56) was considered 'brilliant'. In 1958, he achieved international recognition with his SAS hotel in Copenhagen. The Royal Hotel, a simple, elegant and very tall building, constructed using tinted glass, became the Mecca for architects from all over the world. In 1964 he designed a building for St Catherine's College, Oxford, which was not only individually distinctive but also blended in with the surrounding ancient buildings, exemplifying his dictum 'economy plus function equals style'. His furniture designs are legendary. His three-legged chair and egg chair, popular in the 1950s and 1960s, have been sold all over the world and are still selling 40 years on. His last design of note was that of the Kuwait Central Bank in Kuwait. At the time it was built it had the distinction of being the world's most expensive structure, with a gold leaf dome and vaults that would protect in the event of a nuclear explosion. Arne Jacobson died on March 24th 1971 in Copenhagen.

**JAFFA,
Max
(1911-91)
British musician**

Max Jaffa was born in London on December 28th 1911. The son of Russian Jews, Max won a scholarship to the Guildhall School of Music in London. At the age of thirteen he was playing in cinemas to the flickering of the silent films. While a student, he lived by playing in dance orchestras and at eighteen was leading dance bands at top venues such as the Trocadero and the Piccadilly. By 1931 he was a virtuoso of the violin and leader of the Scottish Symphony Orchestra. However, it was his blend of classics, ballads and music from popular musical comedies, all thrown together to become 'Palm Court' music, that brought Jaffa to universal notice. The Second World War interrupted his musical career: he joined the army as a gunner in the Royal Artillery, later transferring to the RAF where he qualified as a pilot before joining the Air Transport Auxiliary to pilot planes from factory to operational airfields. He was in the armed forces for six years, during which time he didn't touch the violin. To his horror, when he was demobilized, he found he couldn't put one finger in front of another and play. Jaffa turned to the Russian violin teacher Sasha Lasserson for help. Lasserson came to the conclusion that there was nothing physically wrong, but that Jaffa had lost his confidence. A year of rehabilitation followed during which Jaffa re-learnt his technique. He then began rebuilding his career. Together with Reginald Kilbey and Jack Byfield he formed the Max Jaffa Trio. They went from strength to strength, with frequent radio appearances and, in 1952, television. When, in 1956, they took over the very popular BBC show *Grand Hotel*, Jaffa knew exactly what was wanted. The music he chose ranged from musical comedy to Massenet's *Thais*. He never felt obliged to play the fashionable, and extremely popular, music of the 1960s and didn't worry about being considered old-fashioned: he was, and therein lay his strength. The Trio had another very popular programme with the television series *Music at Ten*. When Jack Byfield died in 1976, the trio disbanded. By this time Jaffa was one of the most famous personalities in Britain and well known overseas. For some 30 years he would spend seventeen summer weeks at Scarborough, playing his violin and directing the Spa Orchestra.

The Spa Grand Hall had a seating capacity of over 2,000 people, yet every performance was sold out and there were constant queues for 'returns'. There are few entertainers, anywhere in the world, who can claim that record. His last concert was at Cambridge in November 1990. He died in London on July 30th 1991, a few months after the publication of his autobiography, *Max Jaffa: A Life on the Fiddle*.

Irving Jaffee was born on September 15th 1906 in New York City. He first came to prominence during the 1928 Olympic Winter Games when, while Jaffee was in gold position, the 10,000 metres race was cancelled after only five heats. No matter: in the 1932 Winter Games at Lake Placid, New York, Jaffee took the gold medal in both the 5,000 metre and 10,000 metre speed skating events. In 1934 Irving Jaffee set a world record for the 25 mile skating marathon and won himself a place in the United States Skating Hall of Fame in 1940.

JAFFEE, Irving (1906-81) US Olympic speed skating champion

Roman Jakobson was born on October 11th 1896 in Moscow. He was educated at Moscow University, from where he received his PhD. In 1915 he co-founded the Moscow Linguistic Circle, which was set up to study folklore and language. This later became the Russian Formalism, concentrating on pure literature. He was a professor at Moscow's Higher Dramatic School when he was only 22. During the 1930s Jakobson was professor of philology and Czech literature at the Masaryk University in Brno, Czechoslovakia. With the arrival of the Germans in 1938, as a Jew he moved from one Scandinavian capital university to another, finally, in 1941, emigrating to the US. Between 1946 and 1949 he was a professor at Columbia University, and from 1949 to 1967 professor of Slavic languages and linguistics at Harvard University, where one of his students was Noam Chomsky (*qv*). Jakobson spent the rest of his teaching career at Massachusetts Institute of Technology. A prolific writer on his subject, his work includes *Studies in Child Language and Aphasia* (1941), *Preliminaries to Speech Analysis* (1952) and the six-volume *Selected Writings* (1971-82). In 1979 he published *The Sound Shape of Language*. He was fluent in six languages and could read twenty-five. He died in Boston, Massachusetts, on July 18th 1982.

JAKOBSON, Roman (1896-1982) Russian/ American linguist

Harry James was born Haag James on March 15th 1916 in Albany, Georgia. His parents were circus folk and his mother was still performing as an acrobat in the final months of her pregnancy. Harry was playing drums at the age of four and the trumpet at eight, and by the age of twelve was conducting one of the circus bands. He went on to play in a number of big bands, including Benny Goodman's (*qv*), where he was part of the power trio of James, Ziggy Elman (*qv*) and Chris Griffin, probably the most famous trumpet section in jazz history. He formed his own band in 1939 and became world famous with his Number One hit, 'You Made Me Love You'; this was followed by 'I Cried For You', 'I Don't Want to Walk Without You', 'I Had the Craziest Dream' and his signature tune, 'Ciribiribin'. In 1943 the headlines around the world were even bigger when James married actress Betty Grable. In 1950 he retired, after a fashion, constantly reappearing to play guest trumpet in

JAMES, Harry (1916-83) US bandleader

some band somewhere. Indeed, he played only weeks before his death. He made his home in Las Vegas, Nevada, and died there on July 5th 1983.

JHABVALA, Ruth (1927-) British writer

Ruth was born in Cologne, Germany, on May 7th 1927, into a middle-class Jewish family. To escape persecution the family moved to England in 1939. Ruth graduated from London University and married a visiting Indian architect. The couple lived in Delhi, India, from 1951 to 1975. The majority of her novels are set in India and she uses the approach of an outsider looking in. Her novels include *To Whom She Will Marry* (1955), *Esmond in India* (1958), *The Householder* (1960) and *Heat and Dust* (1975), which won the Booker Prize. She is also well known as a writer of screenplays for the Merchant-Ivory team. The list of their films is impressive and includes some based upon her own novels: *The Householder* (1963), *Shakespeare Wallah* (1965), *Roseland* (1975), *The Europeans* (1979), *Quartet* (1981), *Heat and Dust* (1983), *The Bostonians* (1984), *A Room With a View* (1986), for which she won the Oscar for Best Screenplay, *Mr and Mrs Bridge* (1990) and *Howard's End* (1992), which brought another Oscar. Ruth Jhabvala excels at introducing the reader to the caste and class system of India. In 1996 she published *Shards of Mystery*, a family saga that embraces East and West. Also in 1996 her screenplay for the film *Surviving Picasso* was a valiant effort to transform a poor book into a worthwhile film.

JOEL, Billy (1949-) US singer/ composer

Born **William Billy Joel** in Hicksville, Long Island, New York, on May 9th 1949, the son of a Jewish father, he was a dropout at school. In 1971 his album *Cold Spring Harbour* (1971) brought him widespread recognition. He followed this success with *Piano Man* (1973), *Turnstiles* (1976), *The Stranger* (1977) and *52nd Street* (1978). All feature autobiographical ballads. Joel has had several hit singles, including 'Just The Way You Are' and 'It's Still Rock'n'Roll to Me', which stayed at the number one spot for two weeks. In the late 1980s, he departed from the personal theme to move in the direction of protest; his 1982 album *Nylon Curtain* and the hit single 'Allentown' tell of the problems of the unemployed working class of America. In September 1983 'Tell Her About It' was at Number One for a week, and in 1986 'Uptown Girl' was a world hit. In 1987 he successfully toured the Soviet Union. In December 1989 his composition 'We Didn't Start the Fire' was at Number One for two weeks, and in 1993 *River of Dreams* was critically acclaimed. Seven of his albums are categorized as 'multiplatinum'. Elvis Presley has twelve and the Beatles eleven, so this is no mean total.

JOFFE, Abraham (1880-1960) Russian physicist

Joffe was born in Romny, Russia. From 1907 to 1913 he was occupied with research into the quantum theory of light. His work was greatly admired, with the result that he was appointed professor extraordinary of physics at the Polytechnique Institute in 1913. Here he specialized in researching semiconductors. In 1915, he received the top award from the Academy of Sciences. Following the Communist revolution in 1917, Joffe founded the Physical-Technical Institute of Leningrad, and remained its director for some 30 years, opening and developing branches in the

Urals, Dneproprtrovsk, Kharkov and Tomsk. A pioneer of physics in Soviet Russia, his work led directly to the successful launch of *Sputnik*, the world's first outer space chamber. He was held in high regard by colleagues and students alike as a man of wide learning and affable personality. A scientist of international repute, he was acknowledged by his country in his lifetime, winning the Stalin Prize in 1942, Hero of Socialist Labour in 1955, the Order of Lenin and the Hammer and Sickle Medal.

JOFFE, Adolph (1883-1927) Soviet diplomat

Joffe was born in Sinferopol, Russia, in 1883. A friend of Trotsky (*qv*) when both men were living in Vienna, he helped edit the Austrian *Pravda* and smuggle it out to Tsarist Russia. In 1912 Joffe returned to Moscow, where he joined the Mensheviks. He was sent to prison and only released following the 1917 revolution. Thereupon he joined the Bolsheviks and resumed his relationship with Leon Trotsky. Joffe led the Soviet delegation to the peace talks with Germany that would end their role as one of the Allies in the First World War conflict. However, he found the Germans truculent and non-cooperative, and withdrew from the conference. Trotsky replaced him, the talks continued and the war ended. In 1918 Joffe was appointed Soviet ambassador to Germany; six months later Germany asked that he be replaced. Two years later, Joffe was leading the Soviet delegation in their peace talks with Poland.

On January 26th 1923 the Sun-Joffe Manifesto was issued by Sun Yat-Sen, the revolutionary Chinese leader, and Adolph Joffe, representing the USSR. The manifesto provided a basis for future co-operation between the Soviet Union and Sun's Nationalist Party, the Kuomintang. This led to the founding of the Chinese Communist Party and military aid from the Soviets for Sun's continuing reforms. Joffe was convinced that a bourgeois revolution had to come about in China before China could turn to Communism. Other articles of mutual co-operation were included in the Manifesto, which was probably the most important work Joffe accomplished. In 1923-24 he was ambassador to Austria and in 1924-25 ambassador to Japan. In 1926 he became gravely ill and was told by his doctors that he needed treatment that was only available in the West; Stalin, however, refused permission for him to leave. A period of persecution followed and Trotsky and Zinoviev (*qv*) were expelled from the party. Joffe wrote a last letter to Trotsky, went to the Kremlin and there publicly shot himself. Among the thousands who attended his funeral was Trotsky: it was his last public appearance. During the Chinese talks of 1923, Sun agreed to send one of his assistants to Moscow to learn about Soviet military methods. His name was Chiang Kai-Shek.

JOLSON, Al (1886-1950) US entertainer

Born Asa Yoelson on May 26th 1886, in Svednike, Russia, he was seven years old when the family arrived in Washington DC. Following a minimal education, he was fourteen when he made his first stage appearance at a hall near his home. His father, a cantor, wanted his son to use his singing talents in the synagogue, but Al had other ideas. He and his brother, Harry, arrived unannounced in New York, determined to succeed. Al split from Harry and worked the vaudeville circuit. It was during a working stint in San Francisco that Jolson's career took off. His quip, 'All right, all right folks, you ain't heard nothing yet' was a passing reference to the recent earthquakes and the audiences loved it nearly as much as Jolson loved the applause. He had taken to blacking up his face, and Gershwin's (*qv*) 'Swanee' became his trademark. Jolson featured in many of Broadway's most successful hits of the first part of the 20th century. His hit songs included 'California Here I Come', 'April Showers', 'Mammy' and 'Toot Toot Tootsie'.

They became popular all over the world. Probably Jolson's main claim to enduring fame was his being featured in the world's first 'talkie' film, *The Jazz Singer*, in 1927: he sang and talked and the audiences were astounded. Other films followed, culminating in *The Jolson Story* (1946) and *Jolson Sings Again* (1949), film autobiographies with Jolson singing and the face of Larry Parks. Jolson, one of the world's leading recording stars, died in San Francisco on October 23rd 1950. In his will he left 90 per cent of his fortune to charity, with the instructions that it should be divided equally between Jewish, Protestant and Catholic institutions.

JONAS, Hans (1903-93, German/ American philosopher

Jonas was born on May 10th 1903 in Moenchengladbach, Germany. Educated at the Universities of Freiburg (1921 and 1923-24), Berlin (1921-23) and Heidelburg (1926), he obtained a PhD from Marburg in 1928. When Hitler came to power in 1933, Jonas decided to leave for Palestine, stating at the time: 'I will never return except as the soldier of a conquering army.' At this time Jonas was already well known as a teacher and scholar and a specialist in Gnosticism, which originated as a heretical Christian concept in the second century. Once in Jerusalem, he continued with his studies and followed up the philosophical work he had published in Germany with his second book on Gnosticism. His thinking on this subject was to change, as the 20th century changed. During the Second World War he went to Britain and joined the British army, serving in the Royal Artillery (1940-45). He kept his vow and his return to Germany was as a member of the British army of occupation. He returned to Palestine in time to serve with the Israeli army artillery (1948-49). He then became a philosophy professor at McGill University in Montreal before moving down to the US in 1951 and becoming a US citizen in 1961. He moved around the university circuit in the 1960s and 1970s, constantly adding to philosophical thought and practice. He waged an continuing battle against the ideas of the Aryan German philosopher Martin Heidegger, and accused him of supporting the Nazi creed. The work Jonas did in the 1960s on medical ethics was most important. His worry concerning technology, as posing the single greatest moral challenge in human history, is shared by many today. His book *The Imperative of Responsibility* was published in 1984. Jonas died in New Rochelle, New Jersey, on February 5th 1993.

JONG, Erica (1942-) US writer

Erica Mann Jong was born in New York City on March 26th 1942. Educated at Columbia University, she became an English lecturer at several universities. In 1973 her first novel, *Fear of Flying*, became an international best-seller. It offered a pragmatic attitude to female sexuality and introduced the reader to the character Isadora Wing. Jong used the same character in two subsequent books, *How to*

Save Your Own Life (1977) and *Parachutes and Kisses* (1984). Both deal with the heroine's attitude to her Jewish background. *Fanny* (1980) looks at the life of women in the eighteenth century. In 1990 she published *Any Woman's Blues*, while *The Devil at Large* (1993) deals with the life and work of Henry Miller. The suffering experience of being a woman and Jewish is a common theme in much of her writings. She has had an important influence on later generations of women trying to fulfil themselves in a man's world. *Fear of Flying* includes the thought-provoking statement: 'There is no such thing as an atheist on a turbulent aircraft.'

Brian Josephson was born in Cardiff, Wales, on January 4th 1940. He studied physics at Trinity College, Cambridge, and obtained his doctorate when he was 24. However, while on this road he discovered, at 22, a process that was reckoned to be so important to electronic development that it won him election as a Fellow of Trinity College. This discovery became known as the 'Josephson effect'. While still an undergraduate he published the results of his primary work, which dealt with certain aspects of the special theory of relativity and the Mossbauer effect. A brilliant student, no lecturer dare make a mistake in front of him; if he did, he would be gently taken to one side after the class while Josephson quietly and politely explained his error. Further research followed, concerning voltage applications, and in 1970 Josephson was elected a Fellow of the Royal Society. In 1973, for his work on the transistor, he became one of the youngest men ever to be awarded a Nobel Prize. In 1974 he was appointed professor of physics at Cambridge. In 1980, using Josephson's discoveries, scientists made an experimental computer with switch structures 100 times faster than previously possible with conventional silicon-based chips. Later, Josephson became interested in Eastern mysticism as it refers to scientific understanding. Following an international symposium he and his associate, V. S. Ramachandran, co-authored a book published in 1980 called *Consciousness and the Physical World*.

JOSEPHSON,
Brian
(1940-)
British physicist

Commemorative Stamps

Theodore von Karman
Issued by USA

Danny Kaye
Issued by The Gambia

Agnes Keleti
Issued by Hungary

Joseph Kessel
Issued by Republic of Niger

Janusz Korczak
Issued by Israel

Otto Klemperer
Issued by West Germany

Henry Kissinger
Issued by Guyana

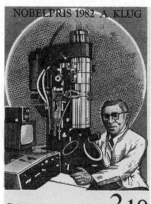

Aaron Klug
Issued by Sweden

Moshe Kisling
(Lady in Blue)
Issued by Israel

K

Endre Kabos was born on November 5th 1906 in Budapest. He went on to become the greatest fencer in Hungary's sporting history. In 1933 and 1934, Kabos was the world sabre champion. He also won a total of four Olympic medals for Hungary. In the 1932 Games, held in Los Angeles, he won a gold in the team sabre event and a bronze in the individual sabre, while in the 1936 Munich Olympics, held in the presence of Hitler, the Jewish member of the Hungarian fencing team won the gold for the individual sabre event and another gold in the team sabre event. Kabos is the only man ever to be the winner of a gold medal at the Olympics while reigning world champion two years running. A Hungarian sporting hero, Kabos was killed during the Second World War during an air raid on Budapest.

KABOS, Endre (1906-44) Hungarian world champion fencer

Lawrence Kadoorie was born in Hong Kong on June 29th 1899, the son of Sir Elly Kadoorie, an Iraq-born Jewish trader. Lawrence's life in Hong Kong mirrors the colony's existence. The colony came into British trusteeship in 1898 and reverted to China in 1997. Lawrence was educated in Shanghai and Britain. He grew up in an affluent atmosphere. By the age of nineteen he was working for the family-owned China Light and Power Company, as well as managing their Peninsular Hotel. In 1941 everything changed. The Japanese invaded and took over the island. The Kadoorie family were imprisoned, the Peninsular Hotel became the HQ of the Axis powers and Sir Elly Kadoorie died in a Japanese prison camp for lack of medical attention. With the war over, Kadoorie picked up the pieces. The family's Shanghai assets had been confiscated by the Chinese Communist Party. Although he was most busy, Lawrence Kadoorie found the time and energy to serve on the Legislature and advise the Cabinet. In the decades that followed Kadoorie was a benefactor of agricultural projects and built clinics and hospitals in the New Territories. Although the family fortune now stood at some three billion dollars, Kadoorie maintained a close relationship with Deng Xiaoping, the Chinese Communist leader, and used this influence to assist in ensuring a smooth reversion of Hong Kong to China. In 1987 Kadoorie became the first person born in Hong Kong to be elevated to the British peerage and he often visited the House of Lords when in London. At the age of 92 he retired and handed over to his son Michael. A year later, on August 25th 1993, he died on the island where he had been born. He used to describe himself as the last Victorian still around, while Sir David Ford, Hong Kong's acting governor, described him as 'a businessman of extraordinary vision and a driving force behind massive investment projects which will serve Hong Kong's interests well into the next century'.

KADOORIE, Lord Lawrence (1899-1993) Hong Kong industrialist

KAFKA,
Franz
(1883-1924)
Czech writer

Kafka was born in Prague on July 3rd 1883. His parents, middle-class Jews, had two previous children who died in infancy. Franz, therefore, was overprotected with the result that he grew to be mixed-up and influenced by his parents to an unacceptable degree. His enduring despair results from a persistent wish to withdraw from society, while at the same time desperately wanting to belong. Although he obtained a degree in law from Prague University, his hypersensitive personality prevented him from practising. Instead he became a writer of visionary novels, most of which were published after his death. His friends were mostly Jewish intellectuals and he spent much time in the company of women and falling in and out of love. His writings generally describes society as a pointless, dislocated organization into which the bewildered individual has mistakenly entered. In 1923, ill with tuberculosis, Kafka moved to Berlin in order to stay with Dora Dymant. Here he was happy, until his illness forced him to return home. He died on June 3rd 1924 in Kierling, a suburb of Vienna, and was buried in the family tomb at Prague's Jewish cemetery. In his will, Kafka instructed his friend Max Brod (*qv*), to burn all his manuscripts. Brod instead had them published, with the result that since his death Kafka has had an enormous influence on Western writers, as readers of Camus, Beckett and others can testify.

KAGANOVICH,
Lazar
(1893-1991)
Soviet leader

Born on November 22nd 1893 in Kiev, Russia, the son of a poor Jewish shoemaker, **Lazar** too was a shoemaker when he joined the Bolsheviks in 1911. At this period he was often in life-threatening situations and forced into hiding; but following the revolution of 1917, in which Kaganovich was a prominent figure, he quickly gained promotion in the ruling Communist Party. In 1920 he was the Soviet head in Tashkent, with orders to consolidate the new regime in the turbulent region of Turkestan. He was most successful, and Stalin spoke well of Kaganovitch and his achievements. He was then put in charge of overseeing party branches and the general party network, and in this role proved himself to be a most capable administrator. By 1930 he was a full member of the Politburo and belonged to Stalin's inner circle. He then became responsible for the construction of Moscow's underground train system, which later became a major tourist attraction. With Molotov, he was one of the main proponents in the Politburo of the policy of making no concessions to the peasants during collectivization. He was, at various times, responsible for Russia's heavy industry and transport and petroleum sectors. In 1938 he became deputy premier and leading member of the State Defence Committee that led the country's efforts in the Second World War. Neither Kaganovitch or Ehrenburg (*qv*) was ever involved in the post-war victimization of Jews by Stalin. Kaganovitch remained loyal to Stalin after the dictator's death in 1953, despite the prevailing fashion to abuse and discredit him. Under Khrushchev, he refused to accept the de-Stalinization programme as legitimate and, as a result, lost all his government posts other than a minor one in a far-away region which he was allowed to retain in order to have something to live on. In 1964 he was expelled from the Communist Party. His was a long, lonely and disillusioned retirement that lasted some 30 years, made bearable only by his memories of nearly 50 years at the centre of great events. He died on July 25th 1991 in Moscow.

Kahn was born on March 21st 1869 in Rhaunen, Germany, the son of a rabbi. In 1881 the family emigrated to the US. In 1902, following his experience of a year's trip to Europe, funded by his winning a competition in *American Architect*, Kahn decided to found his own firm. It was destined to become one of the biggest, and most important, in the history of architecture. In 1904 Kahn received a contract from the Packard Motor Car Company for an auto factory. The result enhanced Kahn's reputation as a radical designer, departing from traditional lines and building methods. He had developed a special structure that allowed clear floor space, large windows and skylights. The best feature was that everything happened on one floor, under a single roof. Over the next 30 years, Kahn was accepted as the leading architect for the expanding car makers. His firm developed over 1,000 projects for all the leading manufacturers, including the giant River Rouge assembly plant for Henry Ford. By the late 1930s his firm was responsible for 20 per cent of the industrial building development in the US. His designs were accepted all over the world and in 1925 Kahn built the giant tractor works at Stalingrad, Russia. This was the first of the 521 factories Kahn would build in the USSR. He became known as 'the father of modern factory design'. He died in Detroit on December 8th 1942.

KAHN, Albert (1869-1942) German/ American architect

Born in Versailles, France, into an old Jewish family, Kahn graduated with a degree in engineering. During the First World War Kahn commanded a battery of artillery during a battle in which he was wounded. He later became a marine engineer and as such was instrumental in equipping the French navy with the latest cruisers. Between 1928 and 1938 he was head of the air ministry's technical department. During this period he discovered a new method of map projection known to air navigators as 'transcontinental orthodrome itineraries'. He was also responsible for France having aircraft carriers ready when Germany invaded France in 1939-40; unfortunately these capital ships were not used prior to the fall of France. During the Second World War Kahn, now based in London, was in charge of naval construction for the Free French forces. He also devised new techniques for submarine warfare that were incorporated in the Allied plan. Following the war, Kahn was in charge of the operations required to reinstate over a million tons of scuttled ships and so restore navigation to many seaports. In 1950, he was promoted to general and head of the French armed forces. He took early retirement following a disagreement concerning the war in Indochina.

KAHN, Louis (1895-1967) French general

Kahn was born in Osel, Russia, on February 20th 1901. His parents emigrated to the US while Louis was an infant. He graduated from the University of Pennsylvania in 1924 and later toured Europe, sketching buildings and monuments. He was a pioneer of Functionalist architecture, sometimes known as the New Brutalist age, after completing the building of the Richards Medical Research HQ in Pennsylvania (1957-61). He was professor of architecture at Yale University from 1947 to 1957, and while there he designed the Yale University Art Gallery at New Haven, Connecticut. The completed building is considered a major contribution to American modern architecture. His design for the Salk Institute at La Jolla, California

KAHN, Louis (1901-74) US architect

has won international praise. Between 1969 and 1972 he built the Paul Mellon centre at Yale. His approach generally is known as the 'servant and served' method, by which the 'servant' elements such as stairwells, elevators and shafts are located separately from the 'served' areas where people work. His work, distinguished by his use of enormous, powerful forms, made Kahn one of the most discussed architects to emerge after the Second World War. He died in New York on March 17th 1974.

KAHN,
Otto
(1867-1934)
US benefactor

Otto Kahn was born on February 21st 1867 in Berlin and arrived via London in the US, where, by 1900, he was a partner in the banking firm of Kahn, Loeb and Co., with which he remained for 37 years. He amassed a great deal of money and with it made many worthy charitable donations. The recipients of his generosity included causes that were seen as unusual at that time. For example he was not only at one time the main support of the Metropolitan Opera Company in New York but also encouraged the emergence of black painters by creating generous prizes and insisting that the winning paintings be displayed at the Met. He also helped, through support of the arts, to bridge the wide gap between American capitalism and Russian communism. To this end he financed an American tour of the Moscow Arts Theatre. In addition to aiding the building of new theatres in New York; which enlarged the Broadway area to what it is today, he contributed to the restoration of the Parthenon in Athens. Kahn was a brilliant financial organizer, as he demonstrated when, almost single-handed, he radically reorganized six of America's railway systems. Kahn wrote on many topics, ranging from politics, finance and history to the arts. It was the arts, and his collection of paintings, sculptures and tapestries, that gave him the most pleasure and which he later donated freely to museums all over the US. What set Kahn apart from many other benefactors, Jewish and non-Jewish, was that he never insisted his name be attached to buildings or projects which he supported; unlike many other wealthy individuals of his time and ours, he had no wish to perpetuate his name. Self-publicity after death was of no interest to Otto Kahn, who died in New York on March 29th 1934.

KALDOR,
Lord Nicholas
(1908-86)
Hungarian/
British
economist

Nicholas Kaldor was born in Budapest to a middle-class Jewish family. He arrived in London in the early 1920s in order to study economics at the London School of Economics, from where graduated and where he returned in 1932 to teach until 1947. During the Second World War he served in both the British and US Stragetic Bombing Surveys. The results of his work had a profound effect on the nation's post-war defence policy. After the war he was appointed director of the Research and Planning Division of the Economic Commission for Europe. He became the tax adviser to the administrations of several countries, including Mexico, India, Turkey, Iran and Venezuela. In 1966 he became professor of economics at Cambridge University and in 1974 was created a life peer. The natural successor to J. M. Keynes, Lord Kaldor was an anti-monetarist, and his economic philosophy was in direct contrast to that behind Margaret Thatcher's policies, which led to the depression of the 1980s. He wrote much on his subject, including *The Scourge of Monetarism* (1982) and *The European Consequences of Mrs Thatcher* (1983). Lord Kaldor died in London in 1986.

He was born Lev Borisovitch Rosenfeld on July 18th 1883 in Moscow, the son of middle-class Jewish parents who had been active in the anti-Tsarist revolutionary movement of the 1870s. Educated in Moscow, he joined the illegal Social Democratic Party in 1901, before going over to the Bolshevik wing two years later. Kamenev collaborated closely with Lenin, and both men sought political asylum in Switzerland in 1908. Kamenev edited the Party's paper in exile until ordered to return to Moscow to edit the official Party newspaper, *Pravda,* as well as directing publicity activities in Tsarist Russia. A few months later the First World War began and Kamenev and other Bolshevik committee people were rounded up and sent to Siberia. Following the Revolution in 1917 Kamenev became chairman of the Moscow Soviet and a member of the Politburo - despite having formerly been at loggerheads with Lenin concerning the best methods to achieve the revolution. When Lenin died in 1924, Kamenev, together with Stalin and Zinoviev (*qv*), ruled Russia and the Party, fending off the important faction led by Leon Trotsky (*qv*). Then Stalin turned against his two comrades and Kamenev went through the see-saw process of being expelled, reinstated, expelled and reinstated, each time having to apologize for his 'anti-Party' views. The show trials of the 1930s, followed, and in August 1936 it was Kamenev's turn. Although the charges were obviously fabricated, Kamenev had had enough. He had become very depressed over the trials and disillusioned with the revolution. He pleaded guilty and was sentenced to death; he was executed by firing squad in Moscow on August 24th 1936. In 1988, he was posthumously cleared of all charges by the Soviet Supreme Court.

KAMENEV,
Lev
(1883-1936)
Soviet leader

Kantorovich was born in St Petersburg, Russia, on January 19th 1912. He was educated at Leningrad State University, where he received his doctorate at eighteen, and where he was a professor from 1934 until 1960. From 1961 to 1971 he was the head of the mathematics department of the USSR Academy of Sciences, before switching to head the government research department of the Institute of National Economic Planning (1971-76). In 1964 he was elected to the Academy of Sciences of the Soviet Union and a year later was awarded the Lenin Prize. He was an expert on the rational utilization of scarce resources and their optimal allocation. He pioneered the method of linear programming, as a part of economic planning. He went on to develop the concept known as resolving multipliers, in a country where critical analysis of Soviet economic policy differed from his ideas of practical economics. He maintained that the Soviet Union failed to achieve top economic growth because of failure to invest. His several publications include *The Best Use of Economic Resources* (1959). In 1975 he shared the Nobel Prize for Economics. He died on April 7th 1986 in Russia.

KANTOROVICH,
Leonid
(1912-86)
Soviet economist

Born in New York, **Kantrowitz** qualified as a doctor before deciding to specialize as a cardiovascular surgeon. During the time he was a director of surgery at Maimonides Medical Centre in New York, and later at the State University of New York, he began to pioneer products in the area of bioelectronics and bioengineering. He then developed a gadget that would help to alleviate heart problems:

KANTROWITZ,
Adrian
(1918-)
US surgeon

the auxiliary ventricle or artificial booster, to be inserted in a patient's body to help the work of the heart. He fashioned and built a machine that not only measured the volume of blood but, more importantly, recorded the patient's loss of blood during open heart surgery. His other inventions included equipment to aid paraplegics' bladder control and the balloon pump to treat cardiogenic shock following a heart attack. However, Kantrowitz's most important contribution to medical science was arguably the development of the heart pacemaker. Known as the Kantrowitz-General Electric pacemaker, it is a micro-transistorized instrument designed to stimulate and regulate the beat of a heart. It was the first pacemaker to be implanted directly into the heart.

KAPITZA,
Peter
(1894-1984)
Russian
physicist

Peter Kapitza was born in Kronstadt, Russia, on June 26th 1894 and studied at Petrograd and Cambridge universities. His mother was Jewish and his father a Russian army general. Between 1924 and 1932 he was assistant director of magnetic research at the Cavendish Laboratory at Cambridge. In 1934 he returned to Soviet Russia and was appointed director of the Institute of Physical Problems. His discovery, in 1938, that helium is a super fluid and has almost no viscosity set the world of science alight. In 1946 he was dismissed from his post for refusing to work on the atomic bomb project, but was reinstated in 1955, following the death of Stalin. For his work on high-intensity magnetism he shared the 1978 Nobel Prize for Physics. He later became a key figure in the Russian space programme. Kapitza died on April 8th 1984 in Moscow.

KAPLAN,
Chaim
(1880-1942)
Polish diarist

Chaim Kaplan was born in Gorodishche, Russia. After a secular and non-secular education, in 1902 he settled in Warsaw. He founded a Jewish primary school which he directed for 40 years. He wrote several books in Hebrew, as well as Hebrew books on grammar and children's textbooks on Jewish history. Kaplan was an introvert who claimed his best friends were the books on his shelves. From 1933, Kaplan began his personal diary, resolving from the beginning to make it a record of events for posterity. It was as though he had a premonition of the events that would follow. He carried out his task with a tenacity few would have thought possible and, as the years passed and the dreadful events of his time unfolded, they appeared to give him added purpose. Kaplan recorded everything that happened in the Warsaw ghetto in his diary, right up to the time it was finally liquidated. The diary is written from the heart of a tormented soul who saw the sufferings of children and suffered with them. He describes how the gypsies were brought to the ghetto, the Germans explaining it was a place for the inferior races. Kaplan's diary has a great feel for detail and it became his constant companion; in it he recorded not only the events around him but also snatches of conversation and gossip with friends. He also recorded the changing moods, as rumour fed upon rumour and the ghetto's inhabitants wondered about their fate.

When Chaim Kaplan realized that it would not be long before the ghetto was destroyed, he made arrangements for his diary to be smuggled out. His final entry was on August 4th 1942: 'if the hunters do not stop and if I am caught I am afraid my work will have been in vain. I am constantly bothered by the thought: If my life ends, what will become of my diary?' The fact that his last thoughts were for his diary, rather than for his two children safe in Palestine, is particularly poignant. One by one his precious notebooks were smuggled out by his friend Rubinszteyn, who worked every day as a forced labourer outside the ghetto. Rubinszteyn handed the notebooks over to an unknown Polish Gentile who kept them safe until the end of the war. Chaim Kaplan died in the horror of the destruction that followed. He would have died happily had he known his diaries would not only be preserved, but published in English, German, French, Danish and Japanese.

Louis Kaplan was born on October 15th 1901 in Kiev, Russia. He came to the US as a child and grew up on the Lower East Side of Manhattan. Unable to obtain work, he turned to boxing. After many fights he gradually climbed through the ranks to become undisputed world featherweight champion, a title he held from 1925 to 1927. At this time he was living in Meriden, Connecticut. Like many another boxer, he was forced to surrender his title when he was no longer able to make the maximum weight of 126 pounds. Kaplan then moved up a division to lightweight, only to find that the reigning champion, Sammy Mandell, refused to fight him. His record of 150 bouts yielded only seventeen defeats. He died in New York on October 29th 1970.

KAPLAN, Louis, 'Kid' (1901-70) US world champion boxer

Von Karman was born in Budapest on May 11th 1881 into a very old Jewish family, the third child of Maurice and Helen von Karman. His father was the first Jew to obtain a degree from the University of Budapest, where he later became a professor, before becoming a top civil servant at the Education Ministry. He suggested to his son that he become an engineer, and Theodore dutifully studied at the Royal Polytechnic University in Budapest before going on to the University of Göttingen for his doctorate. While in Paris preparing to submit his thesis, after a party that ended in the early hours a friend suggested to him that they watch Henri Farman, the French aviation pioneer, fly his plane. That was all it took to give von Karman his inspiration for his role in life. A little later Ludwig Prandtl, a pioneer of fluid mechanics, invited Theodore to be his assistant at Göttingen and work on dirigible research while completing his degree. Following a period of teaching, Karman became a consultant to Hungary's main engine manufacturer. He also conducted research and experiments on the strengths of various materials that would be vital if aircraft manufacturing ever became established. In 1911 von Karman made an analysis of various vortices in a fluid stream that became known as 'Karman's vortex street'. An example of the value of this analysis is its role in explaining the collapse, in very high winds, of the Tacoma Narrows Bridge in Washington State in 1940.

During the First World War, von Karman was in the Aviation Corps of the Austro-Hungarian forces and was seconded to the military aircraft factory at Fischamend in Austria, where he was responsible for developing the first helicopter capable of flight. Following the war, he became a visiting professor to aircraft establishments all over the world. His reputation grew and crowds flocked to his

KARMAN, Theodore von (1881-1963) Hungarian/ American aeronaut

lectures on aviation. In 1922, such was his reputation that when he called for a national conference on aerodynamics at Innsbruck, Austria, it was packed and eventually resulted in the formation of the International Union of Theoretical and Applied Mechanics, with von Karman as president. From 1923 until the Germans invaded the Netherlands, he lived with his sister near Aachen. Both of them subsequently managed to get to the US, where von Karman co-ordinated research on jet propulsion during the Second World War. In 1951 his sister died, which for some time left him in a deep depression. He gradually recovered and in 1956 helped to found the International Council of the Aeronautical Sciences and later, in 1960, the International Academy of Astronautics. In 1963 President Kennedy awarded him the first US national medal of science. At that time it was declared that it was von Karman's original work on rockets and rocket engines that had led to supersonic flights. During his lifetime, laboratories were named after him at the California Institute of Technology and the engineering development centre of the US Air Force at Tullahoma,Tennessee, as well as at the NATO Centre for Fluid Dynamics at Saint-Generius-Rode in Belgium. In 1970, a crater on the moon's surface was named after him. He was a man interested in literature and poetry and had a great sense of humour which he used to good effect when difficulties appeared insurmountable. He died on May 6th 1963 while on a visit to Aachen, Germany.

KASPAROV, Garry (1963-) Russian chess grandmaster

Garry Kasparov was born Harry Weinstein in Baku, Russia, on April 13th 1963. When he was six he began playing chess, when he was seven his Jewish father died and when he was twelve he changed his name to Kasparov, the Russian equivalent of his mother's Armenian surname. By the time he was thirteen he was the Soviet youth chess champion and at sixteen won his first international title. In 1980 he was an international grandmaster. He learned well under the tutelage of Mikhail Botvinnik (*qv*). In the years 1984-85 he took on Anatoly Karpov, the reigning world champion. Kasparov lost the first four games, but then defended so well that he exhausted Karpov. After 48 games the International Chess Federation, despite Kasparov's vehement protests, called a halt. Later, in 1985, they replayed and Kasparov won by a narrow margin, to become the youngest world champion ever. He continued as world champion into the 1990s, beating Karpov again in the 1991 final held in Lyon, France.

When he plays, Kasparov appears to crackle with energy and enthusiasm. His athletic build belies the sedentary game. He receives a million pounds every time he wins the championship, and he has won it five times. His lifestyle reflects his earnings, right down to his cashmere jackets and his hand-made shoes. His mother is his manager and inspiration. His intelligence is enormous. Not only does he speak fifteen languages, he is a political guru who can read and digest 100 pages on political theory in an hour. He married and had a daughter, but the marriage broke down in the mid-1990s. Ruthless at the chess table, he finds it hard to switch off. In 1996 he took on the greatest challenge yet: the IBM computer issued a challenge and Kasparov won 4-2. He also collected $400,000 and the knowledge that he had salvaged human dignity. In May 1997 there was a rematch which the computer,

Deeper Blue, won in the final of a controversial nine game series. Kasparov promises to return claiming the computer cheated

Katz was born in Leipzig, Germany, on March 26th 1911. In 1934, having received his medical degree from the University of Leipzig, Katz decided to leave Germany to the Hitler-lovers and emigrate to Britain. At London University he studied for his PhD and received it in 1938. He received a Carnegie Fellowship, and studied in Australia (1939-42). Katz then joined the Royal Australian Air Force, in which he served for the rest of the Second World War. He returned to University College London as a professor and head of the biophysics department (1952-78). While there, he discovered matters concerning the release of the neurotransmitter acetylcholine, which carries impulses from nerve fibre to muscle fibre, and was awarded a share of the Nobel Prize for Medicine in 1970. He was made a Fellow of the Royal Society in 1965 and knighted in 1969. In 1978 he became emeritus professor at University College. Among his writings are *Electric Excitation of Nerves* (1939), *Nerve, Muscle and Synapse* (1966) and *Transmitter Substances* (1969).

George Kaufman was born on November 16th 1889 in Pittsburgh, US, to Jewish immigrants newly arrived from Germany. Educated at schools in Pittsburgh and Paterson, New Jersey, he got himself a job as a salesman before turning to journalism, eventually becoming drama critic on the *New York Times* (1917-30). His first successful play, *Dulcey* (1921), was a satirical comedy co-written with Marc Connelly. Kaufman enjoyed writing in collaboration and wrote only one play solo: *The Butter and Egg Man* (1925). He worked with the Gershwin brothers on *Of Thee I Sing* (1931), with Edna Ferber (*qv*) on *Dinner at Eight* (1932) and with Howard Teicham on *The Solid Gold Cadillac* (1953). However, it was Moss Hart (*qv*), with whom he worked most happily. Their successes were many and varied, including *You Can't Take It With You* (1936) and *The Man Who Came to Dinner* (1939). Kaufman twice won the Pulitzer Prize. His strength was a feel for brilliant satire, combined with a caustic wit. He died on June 2nd 1961 in New York.

Born David Daniel Kominski on January 18th 1913 in New York, following a basic education he took the well-known route through the Jewish hotel circuit of the Catskill Mountains, known far and wide as the borscht belt. During the 1930s he was in cabaret of one sort or another all over the US. His quick-fire scat singing and wild physical movements marked him out. He then turned to Broadway, and success came immediately, with *The Straw Hat Revue* (1939) and *Lady In the Dark* (1940), where he introduced his amazing song 'Tschaikowsky' and mentions the tongue-twisting names of 50 Russian composers in less than a minute. He spent most of the Second World War entertaining Allied troops overseas. In 1944 he made the film *Up In Arms* and became a world star. More films followed, including *The Secret Life of Walter Mitty* (1947) and *The Inspector General* (1949); they were box-office successes, but he never won a major film award, save for the Special Award he received at the 1954 Academy Awards. In the late 1940s he became the greatest performer ever seen at the London Palladium. Tickets for his show were changing hands at 20 times their face value. Ten years later he was working full time for UNICEF. He was married to Sylvia Fine (1913-91), who wrote most of his original songs that made his so popular. Following his death on March 3rd 1987 in Los Angeles it emerged that he had had a love relationship with the English actor Laurence Olivier. Danny Kaye was a unique performer and an originator of ridiculous situations which appealed to all. No one has ever taken over his mantle.

KAYLAN,
Howard
(1947-)
and
VOLMAN,
Mark
(1947-)
'The Turtles'
US musicians

Howard Lawrence Kaplan was born on June 22nd 1947 in New York City; his friend Mark Volman was born in Los Angeles on April 19th 1947. Both grew up in Westchester, California and, although they went to different high schools, both had the same private music teacher. They became friends and together they created the group that came to be known as The Turtles. Other group members came and went but Kaylan, as he now called himself, and Volman remained constant during the six years the group lasted. The Turtles were born in 1965. In 1967 they had a number one hit with 'Happy Together', which remained at the top for three weeks and was a million-seller. In July 1967, while in the UK, they released 'She'd Rather Be With Me', which went to number 4. September 1967 produced 'You Know What I Mean', followed in December by 'She's My Girl'; both reached the top twenty. January 1968 started with their biggest-selling album, *The Turtles Golden Hits*, which became a gold disc. In November 1968, 'Elenore' reached number seven in the UK; it was their last British hit. On May 10th 1969 they were asked to play at the White House by Mrs Nixon. It was an invitation they couldn't refuse. They got their revenge by snorting cocaine on Nixon's desk. They were, after all, very young. In 1971, The Turtles disbanded. For some while Kaylan and Volman, still together, worked with Marc Bolan (*qv*) and his band T Rex. They also worked with Frank Zappa's imaginative band, becoming the characters Flo and Eddie. In 1982 Rhino Records began to re-issue all The Turtles' work, as well as material previously unpublished, all with Kaylan and Volman's assistance. In 1990, still together, Howard Kaylan and Mark Volman sued De La Soul for infringement of copyright and won. During the memorable 1960s, their harmony-faceted hits became some of the decade's best pop singles.

KEITEL,
Harvey
(1941-)
US actor

Keitel was born in Brooklyn, New York, on May 13th 1941. He was sixteen when he joined the US Marine Corps, later serving in the Lebanon. Army service over, he studied at the Actors' Studio under Lee Strasberg (*qv*) and with Stella Adler (*qv*). In 1965 Martin Scorsese was a student director at New York University's Film School. He ran a newspaper advert for actors in order to complete his graduation film. Keitel replied and a professional relationship followed that has included starring roles in *Mean Streets* (1973) and *Taxi Driver* (1976). His performances are impressive and he appears to have no problem with frontal nudity, as in the *Bad Lieutenant* (1992) and *Piano* (1993) - both films to whose success his brilliant acting made a notable contribution. His films with Quentin Taratino are memorable and include *Pulp Fiction* (1994). Keitel is considered an actor who is constantly developing his craft. If confirmation was ever required of his progress, his performances in *Smoke* (1996) and the sequel *Blue in the Face* (1996) provides it.

Agnes Keleti was born in Budapest on June 9th 1921. She became a fur worker before appearing in three consecutive Olympiads, 1948, 1952 and 1956. She won a total of eleven medals in gymnastics: five gold, three silver and three bronze. Four of her gold medals were for the floor exercises in 1952 and 1956, the asymmetrical bars in 1956 and the balance beam in 1956; the fifth was for a team event. In 1954 Keleti won the world championship for asymmetrical bars. Between 1947 and 1956 she was the all-round Hungarian champion every year. Agnes Keleti is Hungary's most successful Olympic competitor ever and she ranks as the fourth most successful female Olympian athlete of all time. In addition, she became the oldest female gold medallist in 1956, at the ripe old age of 37 and a half years. Following the end of her athletic and Olympic career, she became a professional cellist and went to live in Australia. She later emigrated to Israel, where she became coach to the national women's gymnastic team. It is salutary to note that during the Second World War her life was saved by the intervention of the Swedish diplomat, Raoul Wallenberg. However, her father and many of her family were murdered by a combination of effort between the Hungarian and German authorities as to which could get most Jews shipped to Auschwitz quickest.

To call **Hans Kelsen** a lawyer is far too bland; a more accurate description would be 'philosopher of law'. Born in Prague on October 11th 1881, Hans was fourteen when he moved with his family to Vienna. He was educated at the universities of Vienna, Heidelberg and Berlin, becoming professor of legal philosophy at Vienna University 1919-29 . In 1920 he drafted the constitution for the Austrian Republic and was a judge of the Supreme Court from 1920 to 1929). When Hitler arrived on the scene Hans Kelsen was a professor of law at Cologne University. He had previously been baptized and was internationally famous through his 'pure theory of law' philosophy, as detailed in his 1911 book, *Chief Problems of the Doctrine of International Law*. All this made no difference. He was considered to be a Jew, forced to resign his professorship and warned he faced a concentration camp if he spoke out. He went off to Switzerland and taught at the Institut des Hautes Etudes in Geneva until 1940, when he emigrated to the US, where he taught law at Harvard, Berkeley and the Naval War College at Newport, Rhode Island. His 'pure' theory has been criticized, and rejected in many legal quarters, but his view that law should be logically self-supporting, and not depend on extra-legal values, has greatly influenced legal jurisprudence this century. His later books include *General Theory of Law and State* (1945) and *The Law of the United Nations* (1950-51). He died on April 20th 1973 at Berkeley, California.

Robert Kempner was born in Freiburg, Germany, on October 17th 1899, into a professional middle-class assimilated Jewish family. He studied law at Berlin University and began practising while still in his twenties. During the Great Depression, Kempner found a position as a senior legal adviser to the police within the Prussian Interior Ministry. Following the Hitler riots in the late 1920s and early 1930s, Kempner demanded Hitler stand trial for treason. He called for the official disbanding of the Nazi party and the deportation of Hitler back to Austria, as an undesirable alien. Kempner was still in position at the Interior Ministry when he learned of the Nazi doctrine of 'getting rid of the useless eaters', viz. the mentally and physically handicapped, by killing them off. Kempner attacked his police chief, Wilhelm Frick, for supporting the move and Frick was replaced by Hermann Goring. Goring then had Kempner arrested. Upon his release Kempner went to Italy and at the start of the Second World War obtained a visa for the US.

A law lecturer at Pennsylvania University for twelve years, he was asked by the leader of the American team investigating Nazi leaders to join him. Robert Jackson was an associate justice on the Supreme Court but hadn't much idea of how to go about his new duties. Kempner provided the essential backgrounds to the people they were investigating. He was in charge of the team preparing the case against Goring at Nuremberg. Goring, convicted and sentenced to be hanged, became a bumbling wreck at the thought of the rope strangling him to death. SS comrades outside the prison managed to obtain a cyanide capsule and smuggle it in just before the deadline. Following the Nuremberg trials, Kempner continued his researches at the Bonn Foreign Ministry. In 1947 he found the file appertaining to a meeting held in January 1942. It was entitled the 'Wannsee Protocol' and contained details of the 'final solution' to the Jewish problem. This discovery changed the meaning of 'war crimes'. It was now proven that Hitler, with the willing compliance of many of the German people, had systematically murdered some six million Jews with the specific aim of genocide: the extermination of a race of people.

In 1951 Kempner opened a law practice in Frankfurt that concentrated on dealing with war crimes. In time, he proved that hundreds of war criminals had been helped to flee Germany, by sympathizers, the Catholic Church and senior officers of the occupation forces, in return for large sums of money supplied by the comrades of the SS. At the trial of Eichman in Israel in 1962, Kempner was an expert witness. He continued aiding the hunt for major German fugitives such as Mengele, Barbie and others. In 1986 he was instrumental in winning a settlement from the Flick industrial empire which had used young Czech and Hungarian women as slaves during the war. The payment, some $2 million, was split among 1,300 survivors. Frick's descendants refused to pay anything to the families of those who had died. In his autobiography, *Accuser of an Epoch*, published in 1983, Kempner responded to those who claim that the Nuremberg trials and other war crime prosecutions were illegal by stating: 'those who are against Nuremberg today are those who want war, are friends or successors of the war criminals or right wing extremists'. Kempner died on August 15th 1993 in Frankfurt.

Jerome Kern was born on January 27th 1885 in New York City. His musical education was international, covering New York, Heidelberg in Germany, and London. His father, a German-Jewish immigrant and New York businessman, wanted Jerome to enter the family business; however, he was also a pragmatist, and bowed to the musical ability of his son. In 1903, while living and working in London, Kern had considerable success with 'Mr Chamberlain'. The lyric was by P. G. Wodehouse, who later contributed to many of Kern's musicals. Kern's first great hit was in 1914: 'They Didn't Believe Me'. He wrote, co-wrote, produced and co-produced, many of the great musicals of the early 20th century, culminating with *Show Boat* in 1927. His hit songs include 'Smoke Gets in Your Eyes'; ''Ol Man River'; 'All The Things You Are'; 'Long Ago and Far Away'; 'Can't Help Loving Dat Man'; 'The Touch of Your Hand'; 'They Didn't Believe Me'; 'I Won't Dance'; 'Lovely To Look At'; 'A Fine Romance'; 'Look For The Silver Lining'; 'Dearly Beloved'; and many more. He won two Academy Awards, for 'The Way You Look Tonight' and 'The Last Time I Saw Paris'. His music has a natural rhythm and is often said to be folk music with a modern theme. However it is described, his music has become part of this century. He died in New York on November 11th 1945. The following year Hollywood made a film on his life entitled *Till the Clouds Roll By*.

KERN,
Jerome
(1885-1945)
US composer

Born to Russian parents on a Jewish run-farm in Clara, Argentina, **Joseph** was a small child when the family returned to Russia and only ten years old when his parents finally emigrated to France in 1908. After a conventional education, he trained as an actor at the Conservatoire Dramatique, before giving that up to become a journalist. During the First World War he lied about his age in order to join the French air force. He trained as a fighter pilot and won the Croix de Guerre. Following the war he became a reporter and at the same time started writing novels. His first novel, *The Crew*, was based upon his war experiences. Published in 1922, it became an immediate best-seller and Kessel went on to become one of the most popular authors in France prior to the Second World War. He escaped the German occupation by getting to London. There he joined de Gaulle's Free French air force and served as a captain in a bomber squadron. For his war work, he was awarded the Legion of Honour as well as receiving awards from Britain and the US. Kessel is particularly known for his best-selling novel *Belle du Jour*, later successfully adapted as a film. Many of his books, such as *Le Battallou du Ciel* (1947), feature stories about aviation. A holiday in Kenya resulted in a children's book, *Le Lion*, which has become a classic. In 1962 he was elected to the Académie Française, succeeding the Duc de la Force. The event was considered sensational. Kessel, a big, powerfully built man, wore a flowing green cape and carried a large sword emblazoned with a Star of David. He then set about telling his audience what his title would mean to certain people in certain places: 'You have chosen a man born and bred in Russia who in addition is a Jew.' He continued writing until his death in 1979 at his home in Avernes near Vexin.

KESSEL,
Joseph
(1898-1979)
French writer

KHARITON,
Yuli
(1904-96)
Russian
physicist

Yuli Khariton was born on February 27th 1904 in St Petersburg, the youngest son of a Jewish family; his father was a journalist, his mother an actress of the Moscow Arts Theatre. Yuli graduated from the Polytechnic Institute of Leningrad before going to Cambridge University to study under Ernest Rutherford and obtain a PhD. In 1939 he began working on nuclear fission and became part of the Russian team working on making an atom bomb. The team closely followed what was happening in the US and Khariton became responsible for building a nuclear laboratory 200 miles east of Moscow at Sarov.

When Stalin learned what happened at Hiroshima he understood that the USSR had to be a member of the world's most powerful club, which so far had only one member. In April 1946 Khariton was appointed scientific director, with the result that when the Soviets tested their atom bomb the US was most concerned that the Russian bomb was half the size of theirs and twice as powerful. It wasn't long before East and West were on level terms, and that the Soviet Union drew level was mainly due to Khariton's efforts. He was now the foremost physicist in Russia and remained so until he retired. He died on December 19th 1996 at Arzamas-16, the secret city he founded in the late 1940s. He was buried in Moscow at the cemetery reserved for the elite.

KING,
Carole
(1938-)
US singer/
songwriter

Neil Sedaka (*qv*) wrote a song for her, 'Oh Carol': it was a tribute to her for having written some of the best songs of the 1960s. Her well crafted songs, some written with Jerry Goffin, whom she married while both were at New York University, included, 'Will You Love Me Tomorrow?', 'Take Good Care of My Baby', 'I'm Into Something Good' and many more. King is particularly pleased with 'It Might As Well Rain Until September', a hit on both sides of the Atlantic. Singer James Taylor took Carole King's 'You've Got a Friend' to number one in July 1971. At the time Carole said: 'I didn't write it for James. It was one of those moments when I sat down at the piano and it wrote itself from some place other than me.' In 1972 her album *Tapestry* was a best-seller, as was *Jazzman* (1974). Carole King's soft rock was right for her time; the style was a showpiece for the songwriter/performer, who was such an important figure for the Vietnam War generation. In the image of a Jewish mother, she now wants her daughter, Louise Goffin, to have the limelight.

KING,
Larry
(1933-)
US broadcaster

Larry King, born in Brooklyn, New York on November 19th 1933 is now considered the world's most successful TV interviewer. His familiar style, no jacket and braces much in evidence, is seen by audiences all over the world. With Larry King the viewer feels , here is someone with a 'safe pair of hands' who will allow the person being interviewed all the latitude necessary to obtain the best possible result. He appears to enjoy himself and as a result encourages his subject to open out. Unlike most interviewers he rarely interrupts a flow and then only to encourage further answers to his original question. He doesn't bamboozle or lose his composure. His smiling admonishment of, 'don't go away' when the too frequent commercial breaks appear and his welcoming, 'we're back' when the programme re-appears are most convincing. King has won many awards for his work including the 1996

'Golden Plate Award'. He has probably interviewed more of the world's celebrities, and others, than any TV or radio interviewer, collecting some 30,000 on the way. His present programme, *Larry King Live* is seen around the world.

In 1987 he underwent heart surgery, as a result he now heads 'The Larry King Cardiac Foundation', created to help poor people obtain heart care. It is considered by some that the Larry King interviewing technique should be an required ingredient for both present and future interviewers.

**KIRSZENSTEIN-
SZEWINSKA,
Irene
(1946-)
Polish athlete**

She was born Irene Kirszenstein in Leningrad in 1946, to Jewish parents who left Russia for Warsaw shortly after Irene was born. At school, her sports ability soon became evident and her mother encouraged her to join an athletic club. By 1963 she was an established sprinter and long jumper. In Tokyo at the Olympic Games of 1964 the long-legged newcomer to international athletics picked up a silver medal in the women's 200 metres, silver in the long jump and a gold in the 400 metre relay. In the course of four Olympiads she collected seven Olympic medals: three gold, two silver and two bronze. Irene broke the world record for the 200 metres in 1968. In 1976 she did the same in the 400 metres. In 1977, during the International Amateur Athletics Federation World Cup, she clocked 22.72 seconds for the 200 and 49.52 for the 400 metres. She has been described as the greatest women's track and field athlete of all time. An Associated Press reporter who saw her run in Warsaw for Poland against the United States, a race in which she defeated two US Olympic champions, wrote: 'In her native Poland she's a national heroine and in their tens of thousands they stand and applaud her. They sing songs to her achievements. When Irene runs all Poland goes into a tizzy. When she walks on Warsaw streets, after the meeting, traffic stops, people look at her in awe and ask for her autograph. Anti-Semitic Poles even find it convenient to forget she is Jewish.'

In 1965 Tabs, the official Russian news agency, voted her the 'Outstanding Woman Athlete in the World', and in 1966 the British magazine *World Sport* voted her 'Sportswoman of the Year'. In 1967 she married Junusy Szewinska and tacked his name on to her own. She had a baby son in February 1970 and so missed the 1969/70 season. She came back in 1971, but her place at the top now belonged to Renate Stecher of East Germany. In 1974 Irene took on her rival and won. They met again in the European Championships and again Irene beat Renate in the 100 and 200 metre events. United Press International voted Irene Kirszenstein-Szewinska 'sportswoman of 1974'. She claims her most exciting medal was the gold she won in the 1976 Montreal Olympics for the 400 metres, during which she established a new world record of 49.29 seconds. It was her seventh and last medal. Her achievement of seven Olympic and ten European medals is a record unrivalled in the long history of women's field and track events. Yet once asked what her greatest joy had been, she replied, 'The birth of my son. No title could give me as much pleasure.' She is among those commemorated in the Jewish Sports Hall of Fame in Israel. She now works as a transport research executive in Warsaw.

KISCH,
Frederick
(1888-1943)
British soldier

Kisch was born in Darjeeling, India, on August 8th 1888. His father was a supervisor in the British-run Indian Civil Service. Frederick was educated at the Royal Military Academy, Woolwich, from where he graduated with top honours. He became a professional soldier and was commissioned into the Royal Engineers, with whom he served during the First World War. Wounded during one of the early battles in France, he recovered and was posted to Mesopotamia. Here he was again wounded and unable to continue active service. He was appointed to the War Office and Military Intelligence, becoming head of the section dealing with China, Japan, Russia and Persia. Following the First World War, Kisch, now with the rank of lieutenant-colonel, was the military adviser to the British delegation attending the Paris Peace Conference (1919-21). He was aggrieved not to have been appointed to the Staff College and suspected this was a reflection of an anti-Jewish bias left over from the days of General John Monash (*qv*).

Kisch resigned from the British army and spent some time as head of the political department of the Jewish Agency in Jerusalem. He left the Agency in 1931 to pursue business activities in Haifa. When the Second World War broke out, Kisch returned to the army and active service. In 1941 he was a brigadier and chief engineer of the Eighth Army in the Middle East. To Kisch fell the task of ensuring the essential and continuous supply of water for all of the Western Desert of North Africa: not only for troops and civilians but also for military construction work. He was also responsible for the layout of minefields as well as instructing how to clear them. Ironically, he was killed on April 7th 1943 while inspecting a captured German minefield. It is said of him that it was his exceptional efforts in ensuring water supplies that won the battle of El Alamein in November 1942, a victory which changed the course of the war. As a token of the esteem in which Kisch was held, a Moshav in Galilee named Kfar Kisch was founded by ex-Eighth Army soldiers.

KISLING,
Moise
(1891-1953)
Polish/French
painter

Moise Kisling was born in Cracow, Poland, in 1891 and studied art at the Cracow University of Fine Arts. In 1910 he emigrated to Paris, where he lived in abject poverty until his friend Sholem Asch (*qv*) contrived to get him an allowance from a wealthy patron of the arts. Now established in the Montparnasse, Kisling went to work. A friend of Modigliani (*qv*) and Chagall (*qv*), Kisling was influenced by Cezanne and Cubism. During the First World War, and not yet a French citizen, Kisling responded by joining the French Foreign Legion. He was wounded and invalided out of the Legion and resumed his artistic career. His style was elegant, polished and delicate; he used controlled colours when painting portraits, for which he had a particular talent. He used this talent to good effect when, during the period he spent in the US (1941-46), escaping from the Germans, he painted many portraits including Arthur Rubenstein, who was responsible for his rescue from France. His landscapes, still life and nudes demonstrated his great sensitivity. His work can be seen at galleries all over Europe.

Kissinger was born on May 27th 1923 in Fuerth, Germany. His father was a schoolteacher and the Kissingers, father and two sons, had the odd distinction of being thrown out of school on the same day. Their common offence was being Jewish. In 1938 the family saw the light, left Germany for the US and settled in New York. Henry combined learning and working and eventually graduated from high school at the top of his year. During the Second World War Henry served in the army, winding up with the occupation forces in Germany. Here he worked as an administrator and interpreter. In 1954 he obtained a PhD from Harvard University and stayed on there as a teacher. Subsequently he held a series of government posts and specialized in the role of peace negotiator.

In 1972 he was instrumental in organizing President Nixon's historic visits to Moscow and Peking. While these were probably designed to take the heat off Nixon, and distract attention from the Watergate affair, they did open the door that led to better relations between the Cold War superpowers. In 1973 Kissinger concluded the Vietnam War settlement, following his appointment as US Secretary of State, and for this achievement shared the Nobel Peace Prize for 1973 with Le Duc Tho, with whom he had negotiated the ending of the war. Le Duc Tho, however, refused the award. Kissinger continued his shuttle diplomacy concerned with the Middle East peace process. In the 1950s and 60s, Kissinger appears to have been the voice of reason among the hawks in American politics. He has been a consultant to several presidents and continues to be an influence.

The exact extent of his involvement in the Watergate scandal has never been fully explored. Perhaps he was 'Deep Throat'. His passion for football and attractive women is well known: he was recently photographed gazing wistfully into the cleavage of Britain's Princess Diana. He came into the open when, in an interview with the *New York Times* on January 1971, he said, 'Power is the ultimate aphrodisiac' In 1996 in Oliver Stone's film *Nixon*, Kissinger is shown as a hawk advocating an extension to the bombing campaign in Vietnam. His writings includes *American Foreign Policy* (1969), *The White House Years* (1979) and *For The Record* (1981). He now enjoys a lifestyle with an emphasis on parties, to which he escorts attractive ladies of the moment. It is said that his humour is at the root of his appeal. An ardent football fan, he is chairman of the North American Soccer League and a member of the Celtic Supporters Club.

Ronald Brooks Kitaj was born in Chagrin Falls, Ohio, on October 29th 1932. He studied art at the Cooper Union in New York and at the Academy of Fine Arts in Vienna. Following a period as a merchant seaman, and a spell in the US Army (1955-57), he settled in London, where he studied at the Ruskin School of Drawing and Fine Arts and the Royal College of Art. Although often mentioned as one of the prominent figures in the British Pop Art Movement of the early 1960s, he now claims he is not a Pop Artist. He met up with David Hockney and Allen Jones while at the Royal College and they all influenced each other. In 1975 he was living and working in Paris and there came to be inspired by the work of the Impressionist painter Degas. This influence led Kitaj to take up pastel, which he has used for

KISSINGER, Henry (1923-) German/ American statesman

KITAJ, R. B. (1932-) US painter

much of his subsequent work. Kitaj has been much preoccupied by his Jewishness and by the revelations of the Holocaust. He derives inspiration from literary sources such as Kafka (*qv*) and he creates large, often complicated paintings that reflect social themes. At his first solo exhibition at the Marlboro New Gallery, London, the critics praised Kitaj for bringing history painting back to the art scene and quoted the example of *The Murder of Rosa Luxemburg* . He claims that his objective is to bring art closer to the public and to this end he often includes explanatory footnotes to his hermetic inventions. Although Kitaj exhibited internationally during the 1970s, he also spent much time teaching. *Sandra 3* (1997) is a large canvas Kitaj painted in memory of his painter wife who died in 1994. It is a protest work against the critics whom the artist accuses of anti-Semitism.

KLARSFELD,
Serge
(1935-)
French lawyer

Serge Klarsfeld was born in Bucharest, Romania, on September 17th 1935. In 1943, while living in Nice, Serge, together with his mother and sister, were forced to hide from the Germans. His father, who had spent the two previous years fighting with the Resistance, was taken and entrained to Auschwitz, never to return. The war over, Serge studied history at the Sorbonne, before obtaining a law licence from the University of Paris. At the Institute of Political Studies in Paris he met Beate, a Gentile born in Berlin in 1939. They married in 1963. Serge, who had worked on a kibbutz in Israel, visited Auschwitz in 1966. A year later he was a volunteer in Israel, during the Six-Day War. At this time Beate made the headlines when she wrote a series of articles attacking the German Chancellor, Kurt Kiesinger, for his Nazi activities during the Hitler regime. In 1968 she became internationally known when she attended a meeting Kiesinger was addressing. Jumping on the platform, she succeeded in slapping his face. She was charged but released on probation. It was the beginning of a husband and wife team becoming the conscience of the world, systematically exposing the role of German war criminals and their French collaborators. They have succeeded in bringing to trial, or to the world's attention, many killers of Jews, culminating in Klaus Barbie, who was convicted of war crimes in 1987 and died in prison in 1991.

In 1987 Arno Klarsfeld, the couple's son, denounced Jean-Marie Le Pen, the French National Front leader, at a party meeting. In 1988 he went to Vienna and, dressed in Nazi uniform, protested at the meeting between a Polish Pope and an Austrian Nazi president. He was arrested and jailed. The Klarsfelds have repeatedly been threatened and their car has blown up, but they continue their campaign, often journeying to foreign capitals to urge governments to expel known German war criminals hiding in their countries. In 1994, Arno was part of the prosecution team during the trial of the war criminal Paul Touvier.

KLEIN,
Calvin
(1942-)
US designer

Klein was born on November 19th 1942 in the Bronx, New York. He studied at the Fashion Institute of Technology in New York and graduated in 1962. He then worked for various clothing companies and gained valuable experience before opening, together with his friend Barry Schwartz, his own firm in 1968. It was a time of economic depression, particularly in the world of fashion. Undeterred, Klein produced a range of simple, understated and elegant clothes that found favour with the fashion-buying public. Ten years on Klein had gained a reputation, not only for his formal coats and suits, but also for his casual and interchangeable separates fashioned from cashmere, linen and silk. By the end of the following decade his firm's turnover was in the region of 150 million dollars a year and growing. He has now added underwear to his range, as well as fashion for men and children and perfumes and toiletries for both men and women. The term 'designer jeans' was coined by Klein, and such garments, along with all his ranges, continue to appeal to those able to afford his high prices. He won three consecutive Coty Awards for women's wear (1973-5), the first designer ever to achieve this distinction, and in 1975 he became the youngest designer of ready-to-wear clothes to be elected to the Coty Hall of Fame. Probably Klein's real claim to fame is that his designs placed American fashion on a par with the collections of Paris, Milan and London. However, as the 20th century comes to an end Klein is having difficulty keeping up with the new designers from Europe and is having to come up with ever more radical designs and wider ranges.

Lawrence Klein was born on September 14th 1920 in Omaha, Nebraska, and graduated from the University of California at Berkeley in 1942. He then worked for a PhD from the Massachusetts Institute of Technology and received this in 1944. Between then and 1947 he did research in econometrics at the University of Chicago, after which he spent two years on the staff of the National Bureau of Economic Research. His researches have produced detailed accounts of economic changes. He invented macroeconometric models for economics of all kinds which won him the 1980 Nobel Prize for Economics. These models, known as Wharton models, have become very popular in forecasting gross national product, consumption, investment, etc. Klein also developed the Link Project, which incorporates data from a wide area and does multiple forecasts based upon political and economic policies. He has written much on his subject, including *An Economic Forecasting Model* (1967).

KLEIN, Lawrence (1920-) US economist

Melanie Klein was born in Vienna on March 30th 1882, the youngest child of a Viennese dental surgeon. She married at 21 and, although it was not a happy marriage, the couple had three children. While her children were still infants, Klein left for Budapest to train under Ferenczi, an associate of Sigmund Freud. In 1921 she worked with Karl Abraham at the Berlin Psychoanalytic Institute. Here she began working with children and adopted the method of free association, observing her young patients while they played with small toys and worked out their fantasies. The public of her time found it impossible to believe that small children could be capable of evil and great cruelty; but although she was often criticized, she proved the theory of Oedipus and the superego. In 1926 she moved to England where she founded the British Psychological Society. She later worked with adults, concentrating on the theory that paranoid behaviour had its roots in childhood. In 1945 she learned that most of her family had died in German death camps. Her book *Psychoanalysis of Children* was published in 1932; her other published works include *Envy and Gratitude* (1957) and *Narrative of Child Analysis*, published in 1961 and based

KLEIN, Melanie (1882-1960) Austrian/British psychoanalyst

upon detailed notes taken during the 1940s. She died on September 22nd 1960 in London.

KLEIN,
Yves
(1928-1962)
French painter

Yves Klein was born on April 28th 1928 in Nice, France. His first career was as a jazz musician. His second was to live in Japan for a year and become a world expert in judo, opening his own judo school in Paris in 1955. By this time he was already getting a name as an eccentric artist, and his third and final career was as a painter. He came to be judged the most unusual artist of the century. He had no formal training; he simply stated that his art was metaphysical and that was that. He held public demonstrations, where he would have naked models cover themselves in various coloured paints and then roll around on large, white, empty canvases. He would use a variety of materials on a canvas or sculpture and then use a flamethrower and stand back to admire the effect, seemingly oblivious of the sensation he was causing. In 1956 he exhibited at the Festival of Avant-Garde Art in Marseilles. His work is said to emulate that of Marcel Duchamp, displaying as it does a similar magical informality. Klein, who said he wanted to bring back some excitement into art, was one of the founders of the New Realism movement. Following his death from a heart attack while working at his Paris studio on June 6th 1962, his work has been rediscovered, and he is now proclaimed as one of the major artists of the 20th century.

KLEMPERER,
Otto
(1885-1973)
German
conductor

Klemperer, born in Breslau, Germany, on May 14th 1885, received his first music lessons from his mother. Later he studied in Frankfurt and Berlin. When he was 21 the person engaged to conduct Offenbach's *Orpheus in the Underworld* in Berlin fell sick, and Klemperer replaced him, to the pleasure of the critics. In 1917 he was appointed music director of the Cologne Opera. During the 1920s he was one of the leading conductors in Germany and was responsible for the introduction of new composers, including Stravinsky, Kurt Weill (*qv*) and Schoenberg (*qv*). He was also a great exponent of Mahler, whom he knew well as a young man. In 1933 he had an accident: on the podium during a rehearsal, he leaned back, the bar broke and he landed on his head. A year later the German authorities asked him to leave, explaining they would prefer an Aryan rather than a Jew to conduct Aryan musicians. He emigrated to the US to become music director of the Los Angeles Philharmonic.

By now Klemperer was suffering from constant headaches and in 1939 had an operation for a suspected brain tumour which left him partially paralysed and unable to conduct. Gradually he recovered sufficiently to become the director of the Budapest Opera House (1947-50); however, his health continued to worry him. He went to England, where by 1954 he was busy recording and guest conducting the London Philharmonic Orchestra. At the same time he was finding his health and vigour restored to such a degree that he was asked to become the orchestra's number one conductor. Now he sat when he conducted, and didn't bother with a baton; however, such was his power that he was constantly giving virtuoso performances. The critics raved and no one could explain the great change. He continued thus for the next ten years, always giving sparkling performances and receiving rapturous applause. In 1972 he called it quits and retired to Switzerland. A few months later, on July 6th 1973, he died in Zurich.

Franz Kline was born in 1910 in Wilkes-Barre, Pennsylvania, the son of Jewish parents. He studied at Boston University (1931-35) and at the Heatherly School of Art in London (1937-38). When he returned to the US, following a European tour of the art capitals, it was to New York. He began his artistic career as a painter of urban landscapes, but by the end of the 1940s he had turned to abstract art. Influenced by de Kooning, Kline developed an original style some thought extreme, using brush strokes that became bold black patterns on a white background, similar to oriental calligraphy. He held his first one-man show at the Charles Egan Gallery in New York, and his painting *Chief* was bought by the Museum of Modern Art. Later in his short life he would incorporate vivid colours into his work, although he preferred the black and white style he perfected. His 1958 painting *Mahoning* is in the Whitney Museum of American Art. Kline died in New York on May 13th 1962. He is now regarded as one of the top painters of the post-war abstract expressionist movement.

Kevin Kline was born on October 24th 1947 in St Louis, the son of a Jewish father and a Gentile mother. After graduating from Indiana University he entered the Juilliard Drama Centre in New York, acting with the school company in 1972. A gifted stage actor, he won two Tony Awards, for the Broadway musical *On the Twentieth Century* in 1978 and for *The Pirates of Penzance*. He starred in the New York Shakespeare Festival productions of *Richard III* (1983) *Henry V* (1984) and *Hamlet* (1986). He successfully transferred his talent to the screen, as his performances in *Sophie's Choice* (1982), *The Big Chill* (1983), *Silverado* (1985) and *Cry Freedom* (1987) illustrate. In 1988 he starred in the British film *A Fish Called Wanda* and deservedly won the Oscar for Best Supporting Actor. In the same year he headed a glittering galaxy of stars in the ill-conceived film *The January Man*, and in 1990 he starred in *I Love You to Death*, which didn't fare much better. However, in 1991 he starred in the critically acclaimed *Soapdish* and in 1992 made two films, *Grand Canyon* and *Chaplin*. In the political comedy *Dave* (1993) he played the role of impersonating the US President. In 1993 Kevin Kline, an actor's actor, was appointed artistic associate of the New York Shakespeare Festival, a position he takes very seriously but one that still allows him time to star in films.

Aaron Klug was born on August 11th 1926 in Lithuania. His parents emigrated as soon as they could to South Africa, the destination of so many Lithuanians prior to the Second World War. Aaron was educated at the University of Witwatersrand, Johannesburg, with the original intention of studying medicine; but he switched courses and took his degree in science. He then went to the University of Cape Town to do a doctorate in crystallography. However, he cut the course short, picked up an MA and took off for Trinity College, Cambridge, where he completed his PhD in 1953. He then won a research fellowship at Birkbeck College in the University of London, to study viruses connected with tobacco. In 1962 he returned to Cambridge and the

Medical Research Council, becoming head of the structural studies branch in 1978. His biological discoveries were in the field of crystallographic electron technique development. He proved that a series of electronmicographs, from various angles, can be combined to produce three-dimensional images of particles: a method used to study proteins and viruses. He was awarded the Nobel Prize for Chemistry in 1982 and knighted in 1988. He was also awarded the Order of Merit. In 1996, while President of the Royal Society, Klug made important contributions to the handling of problems connected with BSE in cattle.

KLUGMAN,
Norman
(1912-77)
British political
activist

Norman Klugman was born in Hampstead, London, to wealthy Jewish parents on February 27th 1912. In 1931 he was at Trinity College, Cambridge, reading modern languages. While researching his subject during the academic year of 1934-35, he became deeply involved with political communism and joined the Communist Party. His close contemporaries at Cambridge included some who would later become internationally known spies, including Anthony Blunt; Donald Maclean and Guy Burgess, as well as John Cornford, who was killed a year later while fighting for the Republican cause in the Spanish Civil War. It was Klugman, in his persistent fight against fascism, who expanded the Communist cell at Trinity and the Cambridge Socialist Society, and he ensured that similar groups in other universities were Marxist-led. Klugman became a full-time worker for the Party and often operated abroad. In 1935 he was secretary of the World Student Association, which waged a campaign against war and fascism from Paris. In this role he visited many parts of the world, including China, where he led a student delegation to Mao Tse-tung. During the Second World War, Klugman served in the Royal Army Service Corps before being commissioned into the Intelligence Corps. He later became a member of the Special Operations Executive (SOE). A captain in 1943, he was responsible for organizing resistance in Yugoslavia and liaising with Marshall Tito. Later he was promoted to major and parachuted into Yugoslavia for the final months of the war. He then spent a year working with the UNRRA mission trying to get Yugoslavia back on its feet. Back in England, he became head of the Party's education branch (1950-60). Despite his devotion to the party line, he was considered an easy-going, warm-natured and good-humoured person. It was therefore surprising that in his 1951 book, *From Trotsky to Tito*, he berated his one-time allies for what he describes as 'carefully concealed treachery'. When *Marxism Today* was launched in 1957, Klugman was assistant editor; in 1963 he became editor, and held the post until his death. He published his large work, *History of the Communist Party of Great Britain*, in two volumes in 1969. Although in an obituary in the *Labour Monthly* in April 1953 he called Stalin 'the world's greatest working class leader' and 'the man of peace and international fraternity', these views appear to be at variance with some of his later writings, especially in his *A Reader's Guide to the Study of Marxism*. Klugman died in London on September 14th 1977.

Koch, the son of Polish-Jewish parents, was born in New York on December 12th 1924. He qualified as a lawyer, graduating from New York University. Out of a sense of public duty, rather than self-aggrandizement, he entered local politics and was elected in the Greenwich district of New York. In 1966 he won election to the New York City Council, on which he served until 1968. He then won election to Congress, sitting from 1969 to 1977. During this period he was responsible for getting the mass transit operating subsidy bill passed in 1974. He has worked for equal opportunities, human rights and health care. In November 1977, he entered the election for Mayor of New York, and won. In 1981 he was victorious again with an overwhelming majority, and won again in 1985. He was defeated in the Democratic primary of 1989 by David Dunkins, who went on to succeed Koch as Mayor. During his mayoral terms Koch dealt with New York's problems in a masterly fashion, not shrinking from taking unpopular decisions when the situation demanded them. His autobiography, *Citizen Koch*, was published in 1992.

Arthur Koestler was born into a well-off Jewish family on September 5th 1905 in Budapest, Hungary. He was educated at Vienna University, where he joined the Communist Party. He chose journalism as his career and during the Spanish Civil War was war correspondent for the English *News Chronicle*. He was taken prisoner by Franco's fascists and sentenced to death as an alleged spy. The sentence caused an international outcry and was reduced to life imprisonment. In the event he was released some months later and lived for a while in Malaga. He later describes this ordeal in his book, *Spanish Treatment* (1937). Interned in a French detention camp in 1937, Koestler joined the French Foreign Legion, and when France fell in 1940 he escaped to England and the British army. His highly regarded *Darkness at Noon* (1941) tells of his despair at developments in the Russian Communist Party and the purges of the 1930s. In 1945 he was in Palestine as a correspondent for the London *Times*. This episode provided the background for his novel *Thieves in the Night*, probably his best known book. In later years Koestler was frequently at the centre of one controversy or another, generally through his journalistic writings. His later published work dealt with science and mysticism; *Act of Creation* (1964) is the best known example. In 1976 he wrote *The Thirteenth Tribe* about the origin of the Jewish people.. During the 1980s he became ill with cancer and Parkinson's disease; a long-time believer in euthanasia, he took his life on March 3rd 1983 in London. For reasons which remain unclear, his wife Cynthia committed suicide at the same time.

Mirra was born in Russia and arrived in the US with her family while still a young child. Having gained her doctorate, she began researching for the book that was eventually published in 1940 as *The Unemployed Man and His Family*. This book explored for the first time how the problem of what happens to the breadwinner affects the whole family, with repercussions often reaching into the next generation. Komarovsky was one of the principal pioneers of the modern women's movement. In 1946 her research produced *Cultural Contradictions and Sex Roles*, in which she explained the woman's life as one of great contradiction, torn between the demands of traditional and modern roles. She was professor of sociology at Columbia University, New York, and continued her writings into retirement. In 1953 *Women In The Modern World: Common Frontiers of the Social Sciences* was published, to become the bible of the women's equal opportunities movement of the early 1960s.

KOMPFNER, Rudolf (1909-77) Austrian/British engineer

Born in Vienna on May 16th 1909, he graduated from the Technische Hochschule zu Wien in 1931. It was already a difficult time for Jews and, through a British cousin-in-law, he was helped to London. There he joined his cousin's small building company, of which he later became the managing director (1936-41). He would spend his evenings reading in the Patent Office library, writing detailed notes. He began to acquire original ideas and in 1937 he patented his first: a television camera tube. During the Second World War, in June 1940, he was interned with other enemy aliens, Jew and non-Jew, on the Isle of Man. Just prior to his internment he had sent a paper concerning magnetrons to the editor of *Wireless Engineer*. It found its way to the Admiralty. Released six months later, Kompfner was asked to work at the physics department of Birmingham University. There he invented the travelling-wave tube, the first of a number of items he developed concerned with communications which are still used in radar and space programmes. In 1944, Kompfner was at the Clarendon Laboratory in Oxford; in 1947 he became a British subject. Having obtained a PhD in physics from Queen's College, Oxford, in 1951, he crossed the Atlantic and joined the communications division of Bell Laboratories. Here he became involved with super-magnetic conductors, lasers and optical communications, and was responsible for the design and launch of *Echo* (1960) and then of *Telstar*. He returned from Bell in 1973 and thereafter divided his time between Stanford, where he was research professor of applied physics, and Oxford, as a research professor of engineering science and a Fellow of All Souls College, where he worked on advanced microscopes. A gregarious man, he was considered an excellent companion. He died at Stanford, California, on December 3rd 1977.

KOOPER, Al (1944-) US rock musician

Kooper was born in 1944 in Brooklyn, New York. At sixteen, he was a professional guitarist in the group Royal Teens, who had a hit with 'Short Shots'. A musician's musician, he became a major part of the pop music scene in the 1960s and 1970s and has continued to be so through to the present day. An excellent keyboard player, he has worked with many of the stars of recent decades, including Gene Pitney, Bob Dylan (*qv*), Tom Rush, and Peter, Paul and Mary. As a soloist he released 'I Can't Keep From Crying Sometimes', and in 1966 his reading of 'Parchman Farm' was released as a single. In 1967 he founded Blood, Sweat and Tears, one of the original US jazz-rock groups. They made one album before breaking up in disharmony. His *Super Session* (1968), a recording of an informal jam session, was most successful. *I Stand Alone* (1969) was also well received. He established his own label, Sounds of the Earth, and became based in Atlanta, Georgia. In 1982 he completed his solo album, *Championship Wrestling*, since when he has been most active in recording computerized soundtrack music. In 1991 he produced *Scapegoats* for the Arizona-based group Green on Red. Kooper has been a major background personality in American rock for over three decades and his contribution has been, and continues to be, considerable. His autobiography, *Backstage Pass*, was recently published.

Janusz Korczak was born in Warsaw, into an assimilated household that had only tangential connections with things and people Jewish. After qualifying as a doctor, he began treating the poor, rather that the upper-middle-class group to which he belonged by birth and upbringing. His experience led to his book *Children of the Street* (1901), describing the horrific conditions in which the orphans of the Polish cities were living. Homeless and forced to steal to survive, they retained a dignity that was overwhelmingly moving. In *A Child of the Salon* (1906), he sharply contrasts the children of his previous book to the pampered and cosseted middle-class child. This work caused much controversy and resulted, in 1911, in his appointment as head of the newly established Jewish orphanage in Warsaw. Except for service in the First World War, when he was a medical officer with the Polish army, he remained head of the orphanage. He inculcated in his charges a radical and self-ruling regime that became a benchmark. He encouraged them to do most things for themselves, including the production of a newspaper called *Little Journal*. He also advised and aided non-Jewish orphanages, and by the outbreak of the Second World War, was considered an international expert in his field. An avid writer, he wrote and published many books. The last, published in 1938, was an autobiographical work called *Reflections*.

Following the German occupation of Poland in 1939, Korczak did whatever he could to protect his orphanage, but its days were inevitably numbered. The orphanage was transferred to the ghetto in 1940, and the numbers of children seeking asylum grew. In 1942 the Germans gave the order for the orphanage to close and its occupants to travel east. To calm the children, Korczak told them they were all going on a great picnic, deep into the countryside. When the train and its cattle trucks reached Treblinka the Germans, concerned that the death of Korczak could have international repercussions, told him he was free to leave and offered him a pass that would have allowed him to live in peace in the non-Jewish part of Poland. Korczak refused to abandon the children who were now terrified by what was happening all around them. He chose to stay and pacify them, going with them to their death. Today Korczak is regarded as the great exemplar of what sacrifice really means. His memory and deeds are commemorated in Israel and Poland where, in 1962, on the 20th anniversary of his death, postal stamps were issued. In Germany, in 1958, a book, *Dr Korczak and the Children* was published and a play produced.

KORDA,
Sir Alexander
(1893-1956)
Hungarian/
British film-
maker

Born Sandor Laszlo Kellner in Pusztaturpaszto, Hungary, on September 16th 1893, he completed his education at the Royal University in Budapest and became a journalist. In 1914 he published a film magazine called *Budapest Cinema*. He had spent a brief period in Paris during 1911-12, studying film-making, and thought he knew sufficient to produce his own. He made his first film in 1915 and eight more the following year. In 1918 he established Corvin Films, but a year later he left Hungary for political reasons. This was the time when Bela Kun (*qv*) was trying to free Hungary from its right-wing, antisemitic politics. Korda aided Kun and, as a result, served time in prison when the revolution failed. On his release in 1919, he headed for Berlin, where he made a few films for the UFA studios; then, it appears, someone in Hollywood heard about him and he was invited to cross the Atlantic. He spent three years in Hollywood (1927-30), and made *The Private Life of Helen of Troy* (1927). Then he went to England and formed his production company London Films. In 1933 he made *The Private Life of Henry VIII*; the film received a nomination as Best Picture and Charles Laughton won the Oscar for Best Actor. Korda continued to make excellent epic films, including *Catherine the Great* (1934), *The Scarlet Pimpernel* (1935) and *The Elephant Boy* (1937). During the Hitler era, appreciating, as a Jew, how lucky he was to be out of Germany, Korda did all he could to help others, especially when they came to him looking for work. Eventually he had to put up a notice to the effect that 'It's not enough to be Hungarian, or a Jew, you also need some talent.' At about this time Korda was in financial trouble, and as a result lost his studios at Denham. In 1942 he was awarded a knighthood, the first ever given to a member of the film industry. During the post-war period, he was involved in some of the best films of the 1950s, including *The Third Man, The Wooden Horse, Seven Days to Noon, The Sound Barrier* and *Richard III*. Alexander Korda helped launch the careers of many famous actors and was responsible for the continuing respect given to the British film industry. He died in London on January 23rd 1956.

KORNBERG,
Arthur
(1918-)
US biochemist

Kornberg was born in Brooklyn, New York, on March 3rd 1918. Having gained his PhD, he was appointed to the US National Institute of Health in Bethesda, where he was involved in, and later headed, the research into enzymes and intermediary metabolism. During this period, which spanned the years 1942-53, he was also responsible for the research concerning chemical reactions in cells that result in the making of flavine adenine: essential hydrogen, containing intermediaries in biological reductions. In 1953 he was appointed professor of microbiology at Washington University at St Louis, where he stayed until 1959. In that year he was a joint winner of the Nobel Prize for Physiology for his work on the synthesis of the nucleic acid DNA, which he found to be responsible for forming heredity-transmitting genes. Between 1959 and 1969 he was chairman of the department of biochemistry at Stanford University in Palo Alto, California. He has published several books, the best known being *Enzymatic Synthesis of DNA* (1961).

Korngold was born in Brno, Austria-Hungary (now in the Czech Republic) on May 29th 1897. He became a 'child prodigy', at the age of eleven writing the ballet *The Snowman*, which caused a sensation when it was premiered in Vienna in 1910. When his operas *Der Ring de Polykrates* and *Violanta* were produced in Munich he was still in his teens. At 23, he wrote one of the greatest operas of the century. *Die Tote Stadt* was produced in Hamburg in 1920 and brought Korngold world-wide acclaim. In 1934, he was persuaded to go to Hollywood. In view of what was happening to Jews in Europe, the timing of the invitation was perfect. He wrote the scores of many Hollywood films and won Academy Awards for Best Music for *Anthony Adverse* (1936) and *The Adventures of Robin Hood* (1938). He continued writing operas, but never repeated the success of his youth. In 1975 *Die Tote Stadt* was revived in New York and once again the plaudits were heaped on Korngold. Unfortunately he was no longer around, having died on November 29th 1957 in Hollywood.

KORNGOLD, Erich (1897-1957) Czech/American composer

He was born on June 14th 1933 in Lodz, Poland. His parents were Russian Jews, his father a university professor, his mother a concert pianist. Poland in 1939 was not the best place for a six-year-old boy to be alone in: however, that is what happened to Jerzy. In the upheaval of war he was sent to the Ukraine. He didn't arrive. He escaped the Germans by posing as a peasant boy and going from village to village begging. A small boy, he was only vaguely aware that it was open season on Jews. Often brutalized by Poles, by the time he was nine, he was so traumatized he became mute. The war over, he was reunited with his parents, regained the power of speech and got on with his education. At Lodz University he obtained an MA in political science and another in history. He became a high achiever and was soon assistant professor of sociology at the Polish Academy of Sciences. However, Jerzy hated the anti-Semitism he constantly came across. He and his parents tried leaving through legal channels; the state refused permission. It was now that Jerzy put to good use his wartime experiences. He invented four academics, in four different disciplines, and used these fictional people to sponsor him for a fictional research project in the US. It took him two years to obtain passport and travel documents.

KOSINSKI, Jerzy (1933-91) US sociologist and writer

In 1957 he arrived in America: alone, penniless and with little knowledge of English but with enough chutzpah to carry him through. He obtained a variety of jobs, scraping paint off ships, truck and cab driving, and as a cinema projectionist. He taught himself English with the object of obtaining a PhD. He read English books, did translations and went to the cinema; if he needed help with grammar during his night-time studies, he would dial O and ask the telephone operator for advice. In 1958 he achieved his aim with the receipt of a grant to study at Columbia University. He was thrilled by his newly acquired language. He used it to write his thesis under the pseudonym of Josef Novak. It was a case study concerned with collective behaviour. One of those who read it was Mary Weir, the rich young widow of steel magnate Ernest Weir. She wrote Jerzy a fan letter, telling him how strongly she agreed with his views. They agreed to meet, but shy Mary pretended to be her own secretary. Kosinski soon saw through her ploy and was quite charmed by it. They married in 1962; his gift to her was his novel *The Painted Bird*. The book caused a sensation. Kosinski denied it was autobiographical but confirmed every detail really happened. The book was acclaimed and Kosinski was awarded the French Prix du Meilleur Etranger. The story is of how a small boy is sent away to safety by middle-class parents and how, because he is dark, is taken to be Jewish or a gypsy and subjected by the peasants to much cruelty. He is suspended from the ceiling, while a vicious dog slavers beneath him. The story was too close to the truth. The book caused an outrage in Poland, where it was not published, because the peasants were shown in such a bad light. The critics found it haunting and were staggered by Kosinski's ability to express such shocking events in exquisite language. *Steps,* published in 1968, was described as an experimental, episodic novel. The critics couldn't make head or tail of it, describing it as cruel and pathological; nevertheless it won a National Book Award. In 1971 he wrote *Being There* and all was forgiven. The book became a film and Kosinski was now famous world-wide. The film won Peter Sellers (*qv*) an Oscar nomination Melvyn Douglas (*qv*) an Oscar for Best Supporting Actor. Jerzy wrote the screenplay and received a British Academy of Film award.

Kosinski was now the 'in man', mixing with the New York jet set and lecturing in English at both Princeton and Yale. At his first seminar at Yale in 1970 his talk was entitled '*Death and the American Imagination*': it was expected to attract twenty students and 2,000 turned up. He began his lecture by explaining that the seminar would confront the experience of death as realistically as possible through visits to morgues, hospitals and mortuaries. 'Regrettably,' he added, 'in order for the experience to be complete it will be necessary for one member of the seminar to die.' There was a mad rush for the exits and the class dwindled to twelve.

He wrote other books, but none to equal his earlier work. In the film *Reds*, which told the story of John Reed, Kosinski had a starring role as Grigory Zinoviev (*qv*) and received complimentary critical reviews. He was a guest at the party Sharon Tate attended immediately before she was murdered. His book *Blind Date* was the result.

On the evening of May 3rd 1991, Kosinsky held court at a crowded book party on Upper East Side. The next morning he was found dead in a bath half filled with water, a plastic shopping bag twisted around his head. The darkness of his life finally overwhelmed him.

KOSSOFF,
Leon
(1927-)
British painter

Leon Kossoff was born in Islington, London, in 1927 and grew up in Whitechapel. He left London's ghetto as an evacuee at the beginning of the Second World War and arrived in a different world, in the shape of King's Lynn, a small town in Norfolk. Before the end of the war he was back in London and attending St Martin's School of Art. Then came the army for the mandatory National Service. Then it was back to the London he knows and trusts. It has taken a long time, but Kossoff is now regarded as one of the finest British painters of the second half of the 20th century. David Bomberg (*qv*) encouraged the shy Kossoff in the days when his classes at the Borough Polytechnic in South London were the peak in art tutelage. Bomberg was a great artist well ahead of his time, producing work the critics could not understand, let alone appreciate. Bomberg was also an excellent and exciting teacher, and this excitement is expressed in the work of Kossoff. During the 1950s his style involved thick applications of paint. In the sixties his subjects appear to be suffering; a typical example is his *Woman Ill in Bed Surrounded by Family* (1965). In the 1970s his work reflected youth.

His paintings of situations generally manage to include poor weather and grim surroundings. His 1986 painting, *Outside Kilburn Underground 9 Nuclear Spring*, was a reflection of the Chernobyl disaster. Much of his work deals with ordinary life. When in the spring of 1995 he was chosen to exhibit his work at the British Pavilion of the Venice Biennale, it was thought to be no more than he deserved. The three-month retrospective exhibition of Kossoff's work at the Tate Gallery in London in 1996 proved to be a great success. The public's reaction to the 90 paintings on show proved Leon Kossoff to be one of Europe's leading artists.

Sandy Koufax was born on December 30th 1935 in Brooklyn, New York. In 1954 he became a professional baseball player and a year later joined the Brooklyn Dodgers, for whom he played as a left-handed pitcher in the National League from 1955 to 1957. However, it wasn't until 1959 that he found fame. The Dodgers played the San Francisco Giants and Koufax struck out 18 batters in a nine-innings game to equal a major league record. He went on to lead the Dodgers in three National League Championships as well as two World Series. In his career, which ended when he retired because of arthritis in 1966, he struck out 2,396 batters in 2,324 innings. In his final season, he recorded a 1.73 earned run average. In 1971, Koufax was the youngest player ever elected to the Baseball Hall of Fame and thought to be the game's greatest pitcher. When he retired, he became a sports presenter on national television. It was a fact that Koufax would never play baseball during the High Holy Days, regardless of the importance of the match.

KOUFAX, Sandy (1935-) US sportsman

Born in Kalinin, Russia, on July 26th 1874, he was baptized shortly after his bar-mitzvah because Jews were not allowed to live in the city of Moscow and Serge needed to study music there. It was a practical solution, which did not trouble him, and enabled him to become an established virtuoso of the double bass by the beginning of the 20th century. Ever the practical man, he married the daughter of a wealthy merchant. In 1905 he took the opportunity of fulfilling a long-cherished wish to become a conductor and in 1908 kicked off his new career by conducting the Berlin Philharmonic. He was soon established as a top conductor in both Russia and Europe. In 1921, in typically pragmatic fashion, he shrugged off the revolution and went to live and work in Paris. His big move and golden opportunity, which of course he seized with both hands, was the appointment to conduct the Boston Symphony Orchestra, a position he held on to for 25 years. Under his baton the Boston Symphony grew to become one of the top orchestras in the world, to the benefit of, among others, its conductor. Koussevitsky was among those who established the Berkshire Musical Centre in 1940 and the summer concerts at Tanglewood. He died on July 4th 1951 in Massachusetts.

KOUSSEVITSKY, Serge (1874-1951) Russian/ American conductor

KRAMER,
Stanley
(1913-)
US film-maker

Stanley Kramer, born on September 29th 1913 in New York, was educated at New York University. He is a producer, director and screenwriter of well-crafted films that have made a strong impact in the world of film-making. Having gained experience in all aspects of his craft, he began writing screenplays during the late 1930s. Following a spell as an associate producer, in 1948 he produced his first film: *So This Is New York*. Then came *Champion* (1949), *Home of the Brave* (1949) and *Cyrano de Bergerac* (1950). In 1952 he produced *High Noon,* and in 1954 *The Caine Mutiny*. His other films include *Not As a Stranger* (1954), *The Pride and the Passion* (1957), *The Defiant Ones* (1958), *Judgement Day at Nuremberg* (1961), *Guess Who's Coming to Dinner?* (1967) and more, many of them unforgettable. However, while several of his films have won Oscars for their actors, writers and other contributors, Stanley Kramer manages to avoid receiving one.

KRAVITZ,
Lenny
(1964-)
US rock
composer/singer

Lenny Kravitz was born in New York on May 26th 1964. His father was a top television producer. As a teenager he went to Beverly Hills High School. By 1987 his interest in music was uppermost in his thoughts of a future career. Kravitz favoured a return to basic instruments, without the benefit or need of digital computer influence. He produced '*Let Love Rule*', which was highly popular, and had a great success when Madonna recorded his song '*Justify My Love*', which topped the charts during the first two weeks of January 1991. Also in 1991, Lenny Kravitz wrote a new arrangement for John Lennon's '*Give Peace a Chance*': it was his comment on the impending Gulf War. He continues to impress with such compositions as '*Mama Said*' (1991).

KREBS,
Sir Hans
(1900-81)
German/British
biochemist

Hans Krebs was born on August 25th 1900 in Hildesheim, Germany, the son of a Jewish physician. He obtained an MD from the University of Hamburg in 1925 and joined the staff at the Kaiser Wilhelm Institute. There he worked under Otto Warburg, who at that time was researching metabolism. In 1932 Krebs was at the University of Freiburg when he discovered a series of chemical reactions known as the urea cycle, showing how ammonia is converted in mammalian tissue to urea and excreted by way of the urinary system. In 1933 Krebs was forced to leave Germany and found a ready place at Cambridge University (1933-35). He became a British citizen in 1939. From 1935 to 1943 he was at Sheffield University, where he did important research, especially in the field of carbohydrate metabolism; in 1937 he proved the existence of a chemical reaction cycle known as the tricarboxylic cycle, sometimes referred to as the 'Krebs cycle. In 1953 he was awarded the Nobel Prize for Medicine jointly with an old friend, Fritz Lipman (*qv*). From 1954 to 1967 Krebs held the Whitley chair of biochemistry at Oxford University. He was knighted in 1958 for services to science. He was a Fellow of the Royal Society and was awarded its Coply Medal in 1961. He retired in 1967 and died at Oxford on November 22nd 1981.

Kreiser, born in Russia, was the son of a Jewish cantonist or cadet soldier, forcibly taken at twelve or thirteen years of age for military training. By the time Jacob had graduated from university, the Russian Revolution was an established fact. He volunteered for the Red Army and, following preliminary training, was sent to an officer training school. By the time the Germans invaded Russia in 1941 Jacob was commanding the Moscow Proletarian Infantry Division. The bravery and skill he showed in defending the Moscow approaches earned him the award of Hero of the Soviet Union. Shortly thereafter, he was commanding the Third Army and fighting first on the Kalinin front and then on the Yelets front. The fighting was quite ferocious in the winter of December 1941, as the Russian troops took the full weight of the German advance. They held their ground, and then started counter-attacking on the 500 mile front, finally driving the enemy off and saving Moscow. Kreiser was then given command of the Second Army, which saw some of the fiercest fighting of the war on the Rostov and Donbass fronts. By now he was a colonel-general in command of the forces that liberated the Crimea and the Baltic states. He ended the war a full general. In 1962 he was a deputy to the Supreme Soviet, albeit still a serving general. He was also Commander of the Far East region, which he ran from his HQ at Vladivostok. He never retired and died suddenly from a heart attack at the age of 64.

KREISER, Jacob (1905-69) Russian soldier

Kreisky, born in Vienna on January 22nd 1911, is an enigma of our times. Who can understand, or ever imagine, how an antisemitic nation that welcomed Hitler with open arms and endorsed his treatment of the Jews would elect a Jew to be its Chancellor? The son of a wealthy textile maker, Bruno was continually in trouble with the authorities over his activities in the banned Socialist Party. In 1935 he was arrested, accused of treason and given a sixteen-month prison sentence; he was, however, freed a few weeks later. In 1937 he graduated with a PhD in law from the University of Vienna. At the time of the Anschluss he was arrested. Fortunate not to be sent to a concentration camp, he was instead ordered to leave the country as an unwanted Jew. Kreisky picked Sweden and there became a journalist. Following the end of the Second World War he joined the Austrian foreign service and promptly returned to Stockholm, where he served in the Austrian Legation (1946-50). In 1950 he returned to Vienna and the Foreign Office, only to resign in 1956 when he became a member of the Austrian parliament. Three years later he was in government as Austria's foreign minister.

In the 1966 general election, his Socialist Party was defeated and Kreisky undertook the implementation of long overdue party reforms. Not universally accepted by his comrades, he was lucky to be re-elected to the leadership in 1967. As chairman of the Social Democrats, he became Chancellor of Austria when his party won the general election of 1970. Kreisky's policy of keeping Austria free of alignment paid off handsomely. Austria grew economically wealthy by co-operating with the non-aligned countries of the world, particularly in Europe. His leadership was considered brilliant and he and his party were re-elected in 1975 and 1979. In 1983 he resigned rather than form a coalition, following his party's inability to win an overall majority.

KREISKY, Bruno (1911-90) Austrian statesman

During his chancellorship he allowed Vienna to be used as a half-way house for Jews leaving Russia on their way to Israel, but as if to balance his approach to the region also expressed support for the Palestinians. Kreisky regarded Begin and Sharon as 'semi-fascists' and argued that the Palestinians should have their own state in order to bring about a Middle East peace settlement. He was the first democratic leader to receive Yasser Arafat and give the PLO diplomatic recognition. This attitude caused Kreisky to be criticized by Jews, unable to appreciate his radical and far-sighted philosophy. The events of the middle and late 1990s, in the Middle East, have shown how correct his thinking was. He died in Vienna on July 29th 1990.

KRISS,
Grigori
(1940-)
Russian world
champion fencer

Grigori Kriss was born in Kiev, Russia, on December 24th 1940. He became internationally famous in the world of fencing, when he won the gold medal for the individual épée event at the 1964 Olympic Games held in Tokyo. In the 1968 Games in Mexico City Kriss won silver in two events, the individual épée and the team épée. In 1972, at the ill-fated Munich Games, he obtained a bronze medal in the team épée event. In 1971 Grigori Kriss became world épée fencing champion. His international competition days over, he now trains and encourages young people in the sport and art of fencing.

KROGER,
Peter
(1910-95)
American/
Russian spy

Peter Kroger was born Morris Cohen in the Bronx, New York. His parents were Jewish immigrants from Eastern Europe. He grew up in poor conditions to win a sports scholarship to the University of Mississippi in 1931. He became a star footballer and obtained a BSc. Four years later, during the Great Depression of the 1930s, he joined the American Communist Party and volunteered for the Lincoln Brigade that fought on the government side in the Spanish Civil War. Wounded in both legs during a fierce and sustained attack, he spent four months in hospital. During this period he was recruited by Soviet intelligence. He served in Europe with the US Army during the Second World War and after the war worked as a teacher. In the 1950s Kroger and his wife Helen left the US, created new identities for themselves and, after travelling the world, arrived in London.

The Krogers opened a bookshop in the Strand specializing in American literature. Their home was in Ruislip, a quiet dormitory suburb west of London. In 1961 the couple were arrested. The evidence found at their house was sufficient to send them to jail for 20 years each. In the event, they were freed after eight years and exchanged for the British spy Gerald Brooke, then in a Russian prison. The Krogers arrived in Warsaw and Peter spent some considerable time in a sanatorium, recovering from an illness he contracted while in Parkhurst. Following his recovery, the Krogers moved to Russia and for a while Peter was involved in training Soviet agents. In 1991 he took part in a British-Russian television documentary, in which he explained how keeping Russia on level terms with American nuclear innovations resulted in world peace. Kroger was at one time part of the Los Alamos spy group who made certain Soviet Russia was kept informed of the progress being made in the development of the atom bomb. This levelled the playing field and allowed the

Russians to test, four years later, an exact duplicate of the American bomb dropped on Hiroshima. Helen died in 1992 and Peter Kroger died alone in Moscow on June 23rd 1995.

Lily Kronberger was born in Budapest in 1887. Between 1908 and 1911 she was the world figure skating champion. She won the title four years running, a feat that has been beaten only once, by Norway's Sonja Henie (1927-36) - and she wound up a Hollywood star. When Lily won the world championship in 1911, she was the first skater whose free skating programme was accompanied by music. During the Second World War she disappeared into the abyss while attempting to escape from the German and Hungarian police, who wanted to send her to a concentration camp. Perhaps they succeeded.

Stanley Kubrick was born on July 26th 1928 in New York. At high school he became fascinated with photography and at seventeen was a staff photographer on *Look* magazine. After some well-made documentaries and a couple of low-budget also-ran feature films, he caused Hollywood to take notice of him in 1956 when he made *The Killing,* followed a year later by *Paths of Glory*. His brilliant style of direction won him great acclaim. He is also an excellent screenwriter and often acts as his own producer. His films are praised for showing great attention to detail and a formal visual style. His achievements and rewards have been considerable and many of his films have become cinematic classics. These include *Spartacus* (1960), *Lolita* (1962), *Dr Strangelove or How I Learned to Stop Worrying and Love the Bomb* (1963) and *2001: A Space Odyssey* (1968). *A Clockwork Orange* (1971) disturbed a lot of people and Kubrick has had it banned, although the violence in the film is mild compared to that routinely shown in the 1990s. *Barry Lyndon* (1975), *The Shining* (1980) and *Full Metal Jacket* (1987) have all been nominated for Oscars, as have many of his previous films, but Kubrick manages to avoid receiving the Academy Award himself, although many actors in his films have been so honoured. It is doubtful if a craftsman like Kubrick much cares about Oscars; he is too busy creating and giving other people, whose need is probably far greater, the chance to earn one. Known as a tyrant in a town where tyrants are commonplace, he bullies his actors, with the result that they achieve great results and rarely work with him again. In 1996, after an interval of ten years, he announced his intention to make a feature film starring the husband and wife team Nicole Kidman and Tom Cruise, both of whom are renowned for their large egos. *Eyes Wide Open* could well prove a prophetic title for all concerned.

Bela Kun was born on February 20th 1886 in Szilagyeseh, Hungary, the son of a Jewish clerk. He was educated at Kolozsvar University and joined the Hungarian Social Democratic Party when he was sixteen. He then worked as a journalist, before being conscripted into the Austro-Hungarian army during the First World War. In 1916 he was taken prisoner by the Russians and met up with Bolsheviks. At some time he must have come to the notice of Lenin, because he received special training and, on Lenin's direct order, returned to Budapest in November 1918 to take advantage of the political unrest that resulted from the collapse of the regime, following Hungary's defeat at the end of the First World War. Kun started a Communist newspaper and on December 20th 1918 announced the birth of the Hungarian Communist Party. In 1919 he was arrested and beaten up by the police when he spoke at an open-air meeting. Jailed, he continued directing his small party until his release a few months later. He gave workers and peasants some hope by promising to nationalize big business and banks and to split up the giant estates and redistribute the land. He created a Red Army, pledged to retrieve territory occupied by the Romanians and confirmed he had the promise of Soviet assistance.

Soon after his release from prison the Hungarian Soviet Republic was announced and took over the day-to-day running of the country. Kun was appointed commissar of military and foreign affairs. This effectively made him Hungary's leader. His army did recapture considerable amounts of territory but failed to retake all because the Soviets didn't appear. He failed to redistribute the land and instead, nationalized it into large collectives. The peasants thereupon revolted. The distribution of essential supplies broke down and there was no money to pay the soldiers. The short-lived revolution collapsed and Bela Kun escaped to Vienna and then on to Moscow. Between 1921 and 1936, Bela Kun was a member of the Third Congress of the Communist International and, during the 1920s, initiated revolutions in Germany and Austria, all to little avail, although they did delay the arrival of Hitler. During the Russian purges of the late 1930s Kun was accused of being a Trotsky supporter and subsequently executed in Butyrka prison on November 30th 1939.

Kun was a dedicated Communist who only wanted the proletariat to have their just rewards. His direct methods took little account of other people's views and he was unable to appreciate the problems of administration once in power. Following the end of the 1956 Hungarian uprising, Bela Kun's papers, articles and books were republished, appearing in 1958 and, to some extent, vindicating the work he did to rid Hungary of the corruption that surrounded big business and the military. In April 1964 he was rehabilitated and his Soviet medals and Order of the Red Banner were returned to his widow. At the same time a street and a school in Leningrad were renamed in his honour.

KUNSTLER, William (1919-95) US lawyer

William Kunstler was born in New York City on July 7th 1919, the son of a Jewish doctor. Following his graduation from Yale University, he joined the US Army and the Second World War. He served in the Pacific and by the end of the war was a major and holder of the Bronze Star. He enrolled at Columbia Law School and qualified as a lawyer in 1949. Strolling happily along in a private suburban law practice, in the mid-1950s he suddenly found himself with a client who had had his passport confiscated by the State Department because he was travelling to China. This led Kunstler to the American Civil Liberties Union and a professional life defending all sorts of people charged with a wide variety of offences. He got so deeply involved with his clients that at times his life was in danger. His exchanges with the trial judge in his 1968 defence of the 'Chicago Seven', all of whom were found not guilty of conspiracy, have since become famous, as has the sentence of four years and thirteen days imprisonment passed by that judge on Kunstler for contempt of court. The sentence was overturned on appeal.

Kunstler's list of clients was most eclectic. He defended Martin Luther King during his battle in Alabama against segregation; Stokely Carmichael and Bobby Seale of the Black Panthers; Jack Ruby, who killed the alleged assassin of President Kennedy; Lenny Bruce (qv) the comedian. He defended Sayyid Nosair, who was charged with the murder of Rabbi Kahane. Despite having to cope with witnesses who claimed they saw Nosair commit the murder, Kunstler was able to convince a jury otherwise and his client was acquitted of that charge. Kunstler lost, however, when defending the Mafia gangster John Gotti. He wrote several books, including *The Case for Courage* and *The Stories of Ten Famous Attorneys Who Risked Their Careers in the Cause of Justice* (1962). There was an eleventh: William Kunstler, who died in New York on September 4th 1995.

KUTNER,
Luis
(1908-93)
US lawyer

The son of immigrant parents, who had fled from Russia to escape the waves of anti-Semitism that followed the abortive 1905 revolution, **Luis** was born in Chicago on June 9th 1908. Educated at the University of Chicago from the age of thirteen, he began practising as an attorney in 1930, having graduated with a 'Juris Doctor' at 20. Early in his career he visited a former schoolfriend in jail: Nathan Leopold was serving life for murder as half of the pair Leopold and Loeb, who had killed for a thrill. Leopold told Kutner of two Chicago police detectives who had given false evidence to secure a conviction. Kutner interviewed the prisoners concerned, acted for them and, despite threats against him, secured their release. It was the beginning of his crusade to right wrongs. He obtained the release of the poet Ezra Pound from a mental institution after the government failed to proceed with charges connected with Pound's collaboration with Mussolini during the Second World War. His international casework included clients as dissimilar as Cardinal Mindszetny, jailed in Hungary for treason, and President Moise Tshomba of Congo, overthrown and illegally imprisoned. In addition to the famous, he aided poor and ignorant defendants whose trials had been mismanaged. However, Kutner is particularly famous for a legal document far removed from the publicity of the courtroom. Following the lingering death of a close friend, he spent several decades working on what has become known as a 'living will': a legal document instructing 'next of kin against using ongoing life support methods in the event the signer was unable to tend to his own affairs'. The Living Will got off the ground and found wide acceptance when Pope Pius XII endorsed the idea.

Kutner was although a painter of some distinction, who had work exhibited at the Metropolitan Museum of Art in New York, but his primary concern and interest was in the struggle for human rights. In 1961 he co-founded Amnesty International and worked closely with the organization thereafter. For his work he was nominated for the Nobel Peace Prize. Luis Kutner died in Chicago on March 1st 1993. Kenan Heise, in a *Chicago Tribune* article, wrote: 'In some parts of the world, especially where there are dictators, people are thrown in jail and can't get out. You are locked up and no writ can reach you. [Kuntner's] achievement was that he worked to change that throughout the world.'

KUZNETS,
Simon
(1901-85)
Russian/
American
economist

     Simon Kuznets was born on April 30th 1901 in Kharkov, Russia. He was 21 when he followed his family to the US, where his father had changed the family name to Smith. Simon preferred to keep his. He completed his education at Columbia University, from where he received his PhD in 1926. A year later he was working at the National Bureau of Economic Research, following publication of his thesis on the repeated cycle of retail business. While at the Bureau, he did exceptional work concerning US national income, especially during the years of depression when government required economic information on which to base forecasts and policy. He was able to define distinctly the relation of national product to national income and this formed the basis of future economic structure. His book *National Income and Its Composition 1919-1938* was published in 1941 and became the bible for economists world wide. He was a professor at Pennsylvania University (1930-54) and during the Second World War was also Director of the Bureau of Planning and Statistics on the War Production Board. He taught at John Hopkins University (1954-60) and Harvard (1961-71). He emphasized the complexity of gathering data and the relation of the data to historical situations. He explained the existence of cyclical variations in a growth rate and the factors that constitute that menu, known as the Kuznets cycle. In 1971 Simon Kuznets received the Nobel Prize for Economics for his work generating new and deep insights into the economic and social structure. He died on July 8th 1985 in Cambridge, Massachusetts.

L

Lafer was born in Sao Paulo, Brazil, the son of Lithuanian immigrants. He was educated at the Anglo-American School and the College of Law and Philosophy in San Paulo and graduated as a lawyer, before entering the paper-making industry. He later founded the Brazilian National Economic Development Bank and became Governor of the World Bank. In 1928, Lafer was Brazil's delegate to the League of Nations. He became a member of the Chamber of Deputies in 1934 and went on to represent his constituency for nearly 30 years. In 1933 he was influential in easing Brazil's immigration policy and so allowing Jews to find a haven from German persecution. He became Finance Minister in 1951, under President Vargas. He did much to open up north-east Brazil and created the Bank of the Northeast. Between 1959 and 1961 he served as Foreign Minister in the government of President Kubitschek. He died in Paris in 1965 and was later buried in San Paulo. He was posthumously honoured when a street and school in San Paulo were renamed after him following a special session of the Federal Parliament.

La Guardia was born in New York on December 11th 1882, the son of a Jewish mother. He grew up in Arizona, but at the age of sixteen his parents parted and mother and son left for Budapest, Hungary. Fiorello obtained employment with the US Consulate and went on to serve at the consulates of Trieste and Fiume. At Fiume, La Guardia started the first medical centre for would-be immigrants to the US. In 1908, he returned to the US and worked as an interpreter for the Immigration Service by day, and studied law at New York University by night. Admitted to the bar in 1910, he set up a law practice in 1912, specializing in the problems of the newly arrived immigrant. He was elected to the House of Representatives, on a progressive Republican platform, following his involvement in settling a garment workers' strike in New York. He was commissioned in the air force during the First World War, and with the rank of captain flew many missions in France before becoming a training officer at a base in Italy.

Back in the US after the war, La Guardia began to become well known. His name Fiorello translated into 'little flower', and it stuck. He served several terms in Congress, during which he opposed prohibition and supported child labour laws and the vote for women. In 1933 he became Mayor of New York on a Liberal Republican platform, so ending years of often corrupt Democratic rule. As Mayor, La Guardia earned a national reputation for honesty and laid the foundations for good urban government. He improved all the social services and did his best to weed out corrupt police force officials. He cleared many of the rat-infested slums and created low-cost housing. He held office for two terms and retired in 1945. New York's airport, built during his mayoralty, was named La Guardia. In 1946 he was appointed director-general of the United Nations Relief and Rehabilitation Administration. He died on September 20th 1947 in the New York he loved and for which he did so much.

**LAND,
David
(1918-95)
British
show-business
producer**

David Land was born in London on May 22nd, 1918, the son of Polish-Jewish immigrants, and educated at the local council school. On the outbreak of the Second World War, Land volunteered for the army and served throughout in the RASC. The war over, Land decided on a career in show business. He began by producing concerts that featured wartime favourites such as Vera Lynn and Anne Shelton. He then decided to become an agent/representative/administrator, furthering the interests of his clients. He looked after the Harlem Globetrotters in Europe and the Dagenham Girl Pipers everywhere. Together with Joe Collins, the father of Joan Collins (*qv*), he produced one of the first Beatles performances in London. It was Land who discovered the talents of Tim Rice and Andrew Lloyd Webber and became their personal manager. Recognizing a new talent, he signed a three-year contract with the pair, gave them each £30 a week and provided them with an office. He later co-produced many of their popular shows, including *Joseph and the Amazing Technicolour Dreamcoat* and *Jesus Christ Superstar*. Although there were many changes and large international agents brought in following the success of their shows, Tim Rice insisted David Land be involved on a continuing basis. More importantly, perhaps, Land was an important factor in revitalizing British theatre after the Second World War and establishing its enduring world reputation.. Between 1983 and 1991 Land was chairman of the Young Vic. In 1984 he bought the wreck that was the Theatre Royal in Brighton and turned it into the most successful regional theatre in the UK. He went on to found the David Land Arts and Studio Theatre, that would aid and promote both professional and amateur talent. He died in London on December 23rd 1995. The name of his firm was 'Hope and Glory', and he loved answering the telephone: 'Land of Hope and Glory'. At the 1997 Academy Awards in Hollywood Tim Rice in his acceptance speech, upon receiving the 'Best Song' Oscar, thanked David Land.

**LAND,
Edwin
(1909-91)
US inventor**

Edwin Land was born on May 7th 1909 in Bridgeport, Connecticut. He was a student at Harvard University, but left abruptly, having become interested in polarized light (i.e.light in which all rays become aligned in the same plane). In 1932 Land was able to report that he had made what he called Polaroid J sheet. It was deemed a tremendous advance on previous applications. Together with George Wheelwright, he founded the Land-Wheelwright Laboratories to develop different types of Polaroid. Land also developed the principle of instant X-ray photographs and special sunglasses to reduce glare. During the Second World War he invented special polarizing principles applicable to all sorts of military equipment, especially anti-aircraft gun sights. In 1947 Land started on his most ambitious project yet: the Polaroid Land Camera. It caught the public's imagination, producing a finished print in a minute. It meant that a tourist thousands of miles from home could have a photograph there and then. Commercial uses were developed, and even the camera in the American U2 spy plane used the Polaroid Land principle. Colour photographs followed and the price of the camera fell dramatically, as it was realized that increased profits from packs of film would more than compensate. During his long career, Land held more than 500 patents concerning light and plastics. He retired in 1980 from the post of president of the company but kept his seat on the board. After this point he spent most of his time at the Rowland Institute for Science, a non-profit organization founded by Land for research purposes. It was due to Land's perception theory that research led to the discovery that perception of light and colour is regulated essentially by the brain, rather than through a spectrum system in the retina of the eye, as hitherto believed. One of the richest men in America, Edwin Land died on March 1st 1991 in Cambridge, Massachusetts. He never did finish his degree course at Harvard.

Landau was born in Baku, Russia, on January 22nd 1908; his father was an engineer, his mother a doctor. At thirteen, Lev graduated from the Gymnasium and, too young for university, went to the Baku Technical School. In 1922 he did go to Baku University and two years later went on to the Leningrad State University and the centre of Russian physics. He graduated in 1927 and began a research programme at the Leningrad Physico-Technical Institute.

LANDAU, Lev (1908-68) Russian physicist

In 1929 Landau was offered the opportunity to study with Niels Bohr (*qv*) in Copenhagen. It is worth noting that nearly all the world's leading theoretical physicists of the 1920s and 1930s spent some time at Niels Bohr Institute for Theoretical Physics. Following Copenhagen, Landau looked in at Cambridge and Zurich before returning to the USSR. In 1932, he was head of the Theoretical Division of the Ukrainian Physico-Technical Institute. In 1937 he moved to Moscow to head the new theory division of the Institute of Physical Problems. There he researched the thermal conductivity of liquid helium, work which resulted in his receiving the Nobel Prize for Physics in 1962.

Landau was a tough, no-nonsense scientist who said what he thought. People either adored or hated him and Landau couldn't care less. On January 7th 1962 Landau was the victim of a car accident. He was unconscious for six weeks and several times declared clinically dead. Specialists world-wide helped to save his life and he gradually regained the use of his faculties; however, he never returned to his normal self. Landau received awards and honours from many countries. At home he received the Lenin Prize and was elected to the Academy of Sciences. He was a foreign member of the Royal Society in London and of the academies of The Netherlands, Denmark and the US. Landau died in Moscow on April 1st 1968.

Wanda was born on July 5th 1879 in Warsaw, into a highly cultured Jewish family to whom music was important. By the age of four she was learning to play the piano and making such progress that her teachers declared she was a budding genius. She studied composition in Berlin and by 1900 was living in Paris, married to Herbert Law, a folklore expert. In 1903 she discovered the harpsichord and devoted

LANDOWSKA, Wanda (1879-1959) Polish/American musician

the rest of her life to its revival for the 20th century. In 1909 she and her husband published their book *Musique Ancienne*, a study of 17th and 18th century music. In the years before the Second World War, Landowska was the pre-eminent authority and soloist on the harpsichord and the works of Bach. In 1925 she founded the school for the learning of old music at St-Len-La-Forêt near Paris. She escaped to the US in 1941, following the fall of France to the Germans. She continued her work in promoting the harpsichord and modern composers, including Manuel de Falla and Poulenc, wrote works for her. She died on August 16th 1959 at Lakeville, Connecticut.

LANDSTEINER, Karl (1868-1943) US pathologist

Karl Landsteiner was born in Vienna on June 14th 1868, the son of a newspaper publisher. He qualified as a doctor with a degree from the University of Vienna. While working at the university's hygiene department, he became interested in immunology. In 1901, he explained that there were at least three major types of human blood, distinguished by the antigens attached to the red blood cells. He labelled the types A. B and O, with an additional group AB in which the cells had both A & B antigens. In 1927 he followed with M & N. In 1923 Landsteiner joined the Rockerfeller Institute of Medical Research in New York, where he stayed until his death. In 1930 he was awarded the Nobel Prize for Physiology for his discovery of the major blood groups and the development of the ABO system of blood typing, which made blood transfusion a routine medical practice. In 1940 he discovered the Rhesus factor in monkeys. He died on June 26th 1943 in New York. His main writings based upon his work were published in 1936 under the title *The Specificity of Serological Reactions*. This work resulted in the establishment of immunochemistry.

LANG, Fritz (1890-1976) US film-maker

Fritz Lang was born in Vienna, Austria, on December 5th 1890. He had a Jewish mother and a Gentile father, who hoped his son would follow him into architecture. Lang studied the subject briefly, at the Technical University, but went off on his travels before finishing his course. For a time he was a painter in Paris, but on the outbreak of the First World War he returned home and joined the Austrian army. Invalided out after being wounded several times and losing the use of his right eye, he began writing screenplays. In Berlin after the war he met the film producer Erich Pommer, and drifted into directing silent films. He became increasingly interested in this new art form until he was judged to be an authority. Many of his films dealt with human destiny and were considered quite exceptional. His early work, *Dr Mabuse the Gambler* (1922), was a strong indicator of what was to come and *M* (1931) confirmed this. He went to France the same day he refused the offer of becoming boss of the Nazi film industry, fearing what would happen when it was revealed he was a Jew. He had left his wife, the writer Thea von Harbouv, because she was an early member of the Nazi party. In Hollywood before the Second World War, by 1950 he was bored by the place and the people and went back to Germany. He returned to the US in the 1970s to work on non-fiction films. He died in Los Angeles on August 2nd 1976. Among his better-known Hollywood films are *The Return of Frank James* (1940), *Man-Hunt* (1941), *Scarlet Street*

(1945), *Rancho Notorious* (1952), *The Big Heat* (1953) and *While the City Sleeps* (1956).

Meyer Lansky was born Maier Suchowlsansky on July 4th 1902 in Grodno, Russia. By 1911, he and his family had emigrated to the US and New York's Lower East Side. At sixteen he and Bugsy Siegel (*qv*), were running a floating crap game before graduating to stealing cars and selling them cheap, with no one asking any questions. These two were joined by 'Lucky' Luciano and together the three sought to control New York's underworld. Despite a police record, Lansky became a US citizen in 1928. During prohibition, he and Siegel had their own gang, known as the Bugs and Meyer Mob. They also formed a hit squad that later became known as 'Murder Incorporated', headed by Lepke Buchalter (*qv*).

In 1934 Lansky co-founded a national crime syndicate, in which his part was the legitimizing of illegal funds. It was the beginning of money laundering. In Cuba, Lansky had the criminal dictator Batista on his payroll when he directed Cuba's gambling empire. When Fidel Castro liberated Cuba and closed the casinos, Lansky moved on to the Bahamas. There, with local government assistance, he set up casinos in the 1960s on Grand Bahama and Paradise Island. Lansky was also involved in drugs, pornography, prostitution and general racketeering. He operated on an international level and was able to exist only because of the bribes he paid to politicians, judges, drug enforcement agencies and the police of many countries. Monies from illegal operations, once laundered, were used for legitimate purposes. Long-established merchant banks were provided with funds which they would advance for property development speculation. The source of the funds was often known to these pillars of financial society; it made little or no difference, except that they made very certain that interest was paid by the due date and principal funds repaid as agreed.

Lansky, when faced with the prospect of appearing before a Grand Jury, took off for Israel, demanding, as a Jew, to be allowed residence under the Law of Return. Israel, however, rejected his plea and returned him to the US, where in 1973 he was convicted of Grand Jury contempt. The verdict was overturned on appeal. He was also found not guilty of income tax evasion and released. In 1974 other charges were dropped when Lansky successfully played the 'chronic sickness' card. He lived for another decade, dying on January 15th 1983 in Miami Beach. Lansky was a killer, often admired for his financial manipulations. His life's motto was, 'is it good for Meyer?'. The only positive aspect of his career was that it prompted the law enforcement agencies in America, and in many other countries, to tighten up their operations and for Israel to re-examine 'The Law of Return'. It is interesting to note that Meyer Lansky had a special relationship with Jack Ruby (*qv*), who killed Lee Harvey Oswald, the alleged assassin of President Kennedy.

**LASKI,
Harold
(1893-1950)
British political
scientist**

Laski was born in Manchester, England, on June 30th 1893 into a middle-class Jewish family. He was educated at Manchester Grammar School and New College, Oxford; graduating in political science. He lectured at McGill University, Montreal, Canada from 1914 to 1916, then moved on to Harvard, where he met Oliver Wendell Holmes, the great American jurist. In 1920 Laski returned to England and the London School of Economics, first as a lecturer then, in 1926, as professor of political science, a post he held until he died. He was a leading light in the British Labour Party and sat on its National Executive from 1936. He became chairman of the party in 1945, when Labour won its great majority in the post-war general election. He continued to have a strong influence on the Fabian Society and wrote a number of political works. During the Palestine troubles leading to Israeli statehood he frequently clashed with Ernest Bevin, who lacked the intellectual ability to cope with his office of Foreign Secretary, let alone with the sort of intellect Laski possessed. He wrote *The American Democracy: A Commentary and Interpretation* (1948). In 1953, his 20 year correspondence with Oliver Wendell Holmes was published. He died in London on March 24th 1950.

**LASKIN,
Bora
(1912-84)
Canadian jurist**

Bora Laskin was born at Fort William, Canada, on October 5th 1912 and studied law at Toronto and Harvard universities. He later taught law at the University of Toronto for over 20 years, progressing from assistant lecturer to professor of law. He was appointed in 1965 to the Ontario Court of Appeals and in 1970 became a judge of the Supreme Court of Canada, the first Jew and the youngest person so appointed. Three years later he was the Chief Justice. Laskin, an expert on constitutional and labour law, published several books on his subject, including *British Tradition in Canadian Law* (1969). A federalist and a keen exponent of judicial reform, Laskin has had a continuing influence on law students all over Canada and beyond. He died on March 26th 1984.

**LAZAR,
Irving
(1907-93)
US artist's agent**

Irving Lazar was born in Stamford, Connecticut, on March 28th 1907. His parents were Russian-Jewish immigrants and Irving was brought up in the tough Brownsville area of Brooklyn, New York. He graduated from Brooklyn Law School in 1930 and obtained an LLB from St Lawrence University in 1931. For a while he hung around courthouses, picking up odd cases, until he decided to get involved in show business. This involvement initially took the form of booking acts for Catskill hotels and small vaudeville circuits. He then began representing big band jazz bands and personalities like Tommy Dorsey and Gene Krupa. He fell foul of the mobs running the clubs, and more than one knife fight ensued. Here his tough upbringing stood him in good stead. By 1936 Lazar was operating from Los Angeles and handling the interests of writers including Tennessee Williams, Noel Coward, Cole Porter, Clifford Odets (*qv*), Lillian Hellman (*qv*) and Ernest Hemingway. He sold manuscripts, ideas, plays and people by the simple method of going straight to the top. He was a tough, brash fast-talking New Yorker and had earned his nickname of Irving 'Swifty' Lazar, conferred by Humphrey Bogart when Lazar made five deals for the actor in one day. In all, Lazar would spend 60 years having lunches, courting clients and cutting deals. During the Second World War he served as a captain in the US Air Force (1942-45). After the war he returned to the West Coast and picked up the pieces. He was soon the number one agent (though he disliked the word, preferring 'artist's representative'). He was soon a power on both East and West coasts. His Academy Award parties became legendary. He and his wife would host a big party that started when the Oscar ceremonies ended. Only those who were personal friends or currently in the public eye would be invited. It was the party of the year and an invitation became the most sought-after ticket possible. Lazar was the most famous agent of the century. He would even make deals for writers and artists who never knew they were clients, until he told them what he had negotiated for them. He died in Beverly Hills, California, on December 30th 1993.

Pierre Lazareff was born in Paris and joined the staff of the *Paris-Midi* upon leaving school, eventually becoming its news editor. In 1931 he was head-hunted to become the editor of the new evening paper, *Paris-Soir*. The daily circulation at that time was 134,000. By using newspaper techniques he found in America, he increased the circulation to 2,500,000 a day, a record that has never been equalled. When France fell to the Germans in 1940, Lazareff went first to the US, where he headed the *Voice of America* programme, then to war-torn London to take charge of American broadcasts to German-occupied Europe. Following the Second World War he resumed control of *Paris-Soir* and repeated his successful formula.

LAZAREFF, Pierre (1907-72) French journalist

Paul Lazarsfeld was born in Vienna, Austria, on February 13th 1901. Following his PhD from the University of Vienna in applied mathematics, in 1925 he turned to social psychology and was appointed a lecturer at the university (1929-33). The offer of a research grant from the Rockerfeller Foundation in 1933 was opportune, considering Hitler had arrived on the scene and Paul was a Jew. He accepted the offer and eventually took US citizenship. Lazarsfeld was most interested by the influence of the mass media on society, and became an acknowledged expert on the subject. He carried out large-scale investigations that took in many aspects of the media, including, film, radio, newspapers and magazines. His work and results were of the utmost importance to sociologists everywhere. He wrote much upon his subject, including the textbook *An Introduction to Applied Sociology* (1975). He died on August 30th 1976 in New York.

LAZARSFELD, Paul (1901-76) Austrian/ American sociologist

Robert Lazurick was born in Paris in 1895, the son of recently arrived refugees from Russian anti-Semitism. He studied law and after graduating from the University of Paris worked as a civil servant. He was elected to the Chamber of Deputies in 1936 on behalf of the Socialist Party and served until the fall of France in 1940. At that time he succeeded in escaping to Morocco and safety. However, in 1942 he returned secretly to France and in Nice founded his newspaper *L'Aurore*, a name he borrowed from Clemenceau; it was the name of the paper in which he published Emile Zola's famous article, 'J'accuse'. *L'Aurore* continued after the war, becoming a leading French newspaper.

LAZURICK, Robert (1895-1968) French journalist

LEDERBERG,
Joshua
(1925-)
US geneticist

Lederberg was born on May 23rd 1925 in Montclair, New Jersey, into a rabbinical family. After obtaining his PhD from Yale University, he established a department of medical genetics at the University of Wisconsin and taught there from 1947 to 1959. He then transferred to Stanford Medical School and the Kennedy Laboratories of Molecular Medicine (1962-78). Subsequently he became president of Rockerfeller University, New York. As a result of his researches, in 1946 he was able to confirm that the association of two different strains of bacteria resulted in genetic recombination and therefore a new crossbreed strain of the bacteria. In 1952, while his earlier findings were still being considered by his colleagues, Lederberg came up with another 'first'. His paper *Genetic Exchange in Salmonella*, revealed that certain types of virus were able to carry a bacterial gene from one bacterium to another. This discovery was of the greatest importance in the field of genetic research. In 1958 he shared the Nobel Prize for Physiology.

LEDERMAN,
Max
(1922-)
US physicist

Max Lederman was born in New York on July 15th 1922. He was educated at the City College of New York, from where in 1943 he obtained a BS. He went on to Columbia University, where he gained his PhD in 1951 and stayed on to become a full professor in 1958. He later transferred to the Fermi National Accelerator Laboratory in Batavia, Illinois,. where he was director from 1979 to 1989. Lederman, together with Melvin Schwartz (*qv*) and Jack Steinberg (*qv*), researched the uses of neutrons and between 1960 and 1962 collaborated in an important experiment at the Brookhaven National Laboratory on Long Island, New York. They established that the neutrinos that produced muons were in fact a previously unknown and distinct type, and named them muon neutrinos. For their work all three shared the 1988 Nobel Prize for Physics. The high-energy neutrino beams that their researches produced have since become a basic tool in the study of subatomic particles and nuclear forces. The use of such beams has made possible the study of radioactive decay processes involving the weak nuclear force, one of the four fundamental forces in nature.

LEIBER,
Jerry
(1933-)
and
STOLLER,
Mike
(1933-)
US songwriters

Jerry Leiber, born in Baltimore, Maryland, on April 25th 1933, and **Mike Stoller**, born in New York on March 13th 1933, began their amazing songwriting partnership when they were seventeen. They based themselves in Los Angeles and complemented each other's talents: Stoller was a jazz pianist, Leiber a blues enthusiast. They gave the 1950s in general, and Elvis Presley in particular, some of the great rock'n'roll songs of the decade. 'Hard Times' was their first hit; 'Hound Dog' helped cement Presley's career, while 'Kansas City' was a hit for Wilbert Harrison. Leiber and Stoller founded their own record label, called Spark. They created a rhythm and blues group called Coasters (1955) that went on for decades and survived to play the 'oldies' circuit. During their heyday Leiber and Stoller wrote many hit songs; some went to Number One, all were in the Top Twenty on both sides of the Atlantic. These included, 'Down In Mexico'; 'Searchin'; 'Young Blood'; 'Yakety Yak'; 'Charlie Brown'; and 'Poison Ivy'. For Ruth Brown they wrote 'Lucky Lips', and for Lavern Baker, 'Saved'. Perhaps it was The Drifters who gained most from the duo of songwriters, with 'On Broadway', 'Spanish Harlem', 'There Goes My Baby' and 'Stand By Me'.

But the partners did not neglect Elvis Presley. They gave him songs that included 'Jailhouse Rock'; 'Baby I Don't Care'; 'Loving You'; 'Treat Me Nice' and 'His Latest Flame'. They also wrote 'I am a Woman' for Peggy Lee. They then became businessmen rather than songwriters, though remaining in the world of pop music. They semi-retired in the 1970s, during which time they staged a show called *Only In America*. During the 1980s the cartoon film *Hound Dog* featured Leiber and Stoller songs. They are members of the Rock 'n' Roll Hall of Fame (1987). In 1979 Robert Palmer wrote a biography of the songwriting duo: *The Legendary Leiber and Stoller*. In 1996, on Broadway and in London, the musical show *Smokey Joe's Cafe*, featuring the music of Leiber and Stoller, was a sell-out.

Benny was born Benjamin Leiner on April 7th 1896 in New York. Following a minimal education, he trained as a boxer. He came to be regarded as one of the finest defensive boxers in the history of pro-boxing. His parents disliked the idea of their son boxing for money, so when Benny had his first fight in 1911 he changed his name. In 1917 he fought Freddy Welsh of Wales for the world lightweight title and won. He held the title for eight years, retiring undefeated in 1925 at the insistence of his mother. Hit by the Wall Street Crash of 1929, Leonard, now 35, decided on a comeback. He retired finally in 1932, by now fighting as a welterweight, when he was knocked out by Jimmy McLaren. During his long career Leonard had 205 fights and won 200, 68 by a knock-out. During the Second World War, Benny Leonard was a lieutenant-commander in the US Navy. After the war he became a referee. During a fight at the St Nicholas Arena in New York, he had a heart attack and died. It was April 18th 1947. In 1980 Ray Arcel, the top boxing trainer, who had seen Leonard win his title in 1917, called him 'the greatest fighter who ever lived'.

LEONARD,
Benny
(1896-1947)
US world boxing
champion

Lerner was born in New York on August 31st 1918 to well-to-do middle-class Jewish parents, and educated at Beadales School in Hampshire, England. In 1940 he obtained a BS from Harvard University. He met his future partner and collaborator, Frederick Loewe, in 1942. Their first success was *Brigadoon* (1947), followed by *My Fair Lady*, probably the most successful musical ever. The 1964 film version received seven Academy Awards. *Camelot* (1967) and *Paint Your Wagon* (1969) were also great musicals of the sixties. In 1958 their film *Gigi* received a record nine Oscars, including one for Lerner for his adapted screenplay. On his own Lerner wrote the book and lyrics for *Love Life* in 1948, from the original story by Kurt Weill (*qv*). *An American in Paris* (1951) won him an Academy Award for Best Screenplay. Although Lerner collaborated with several distinguished musicians including Previn (*qv*) and Bernstein (*qv*), he never achieved the success he knew with Loewe. In 1978 Lerner published his autobiography, *The Street Where I Live*. He died in New York on June 14th 1986.

LERNER,
Alan
(1918-86)
US lyricist and
writer

LEVENE,
Phoebus
(1869-1940)
Russian/
American
chemist

Phoebus Levene was born Fishel Aaronovich Levin on February 25th 1869 in Sagor, Russia. By the 20th century Levene had left Russia because of persistent anti-Semitism, had changed his name and was living in New York City. He studied chemistry at Columbia University before becoming the head of the chemistry department of the Rockefeller Institute in 1907, where he taught and carried out research for the rest of his life. Levene's main claim to fame this century was the invaluable work he did on nucleic acids. In 1909 he succeeded in isolating the live-carbon sugar D-ribose from the ribonucleic acid molecule. In 1929 he discovered 2-deoxyribose, part of the deoxyribose DNA acid molecule. He also made other discoveries concerning nucleic acid components which were well ahead of his times. Later, scientists working on DNA and RNA realized the importance of the work of Phoebus Levene who died on September 6th 1940 in New York.

LEVI,
Carlo
(1902-75)
Italian writer

Carlo Levi was born on November 29th 1902 in Turin, Italy. Although he qualified as a doctor he never practised medicine. A founder of the underground anti-fascist party Justice and Liberty, he was arrested several times. In 1935, while speaking out against the Italian invasion of Abyssinia, he was ordered to live in exile in Lucansa in southern Italy. This experience became the backdrop for his famous first novel, *Christ Stopped at Eboli* (1945). It was acclaimed and translated into several languages. Levi left Italy during the Second World War for France and the French Resistance, but returned to Italy to fight there. He went on to write several books which were well received but were not as successful as his first novel. His left-wing views never deserted him and he served in the Italian Senate as a Communist between 1963 and 1972. Towards the end of his life, he devoted his time to painting; his works were well received and fetched good prices. He died in Rome on January 4th 1975.

LEVI,
Primo
(1919-87)
Italian writer

Levi was born in Turin, Italy, on July 31st 1919 and was brought up in the town's small Jewish community, attending the local school before going on to the University of Turin. Here he graduated top of his year in chemistry. In 1941, unable to get work because of the anti-Jewish laws, he worked secretly as a chemist through the help of Gentile friends. In 1943, when the Germans took over Italy, Levi tried to link up with an anti-fascist resistance group; unfortunately, he was captured and returned to Turin to become one of the 625 Jews who were sent to Auschwitz. There he was forced to become a slave labourer, working in the IG Farben factory. Because of his scientific qualifications, Farben used him for skilled work. Thus he was able to survive and return, in very poor health, to Turin, one of only 24 survivors from the original 625.

Although now working in his chosen field and the general manager of a large plastics company, Primo Levi felt the need to write of his experiences. He felt it was his duty to tell the world what he had witnessed. His first book was published in 1947 and entitled *If This Is a Man, or Survival in Auschwitz*. In this he shows amazing qualities of humanity and detached understanding, even when he is describing horrific events. In his next book, *The Truce* (1963), Primo Levi details his problems in getting home, following his release from Auschwitz. *The Periodic Table* (1975) is a series of 21 episodic experiences, each named after a chemical element. *If Not Now, When?* (1986) is a novel concerning a band of Jewish partisans. His final work was *The Drowned and the Saved*, a collection of essays detailing differing aspects of concentration camp life. He describes how he resisted praying in the camp, stating: 'a prayer under these conditions would have been blasphemous, laden with the greatest impiety of which a non-believer is capable'. On April 11th 1987 in Turin, Levi committed suicide, throwing himself down the stairs of the building in which he was born and had lived for most of his life. At the time of his death he was receiving medical treatment for severe depression.

Tullio Levi-Civita was born in Padua, Italy, on March 29th 1873. Much of his work was destined to become the foundation of Albert Einstein's (*qv*) theory of relativity. In 1917 Levi-Civita made his most important contribution to society, with the introduction of the concept of parallel displacement on general curved spaces. His concept became instrumental in the development of the modern differential theory of generalized spaces in topology. He made significant progress in his study of the three-body problem, which involves the motion of three bodies as they revolve around each other. In 1918 Levi-Civita became professor of mathematics at the University of Rome, from which position he was removed in 1938 with the introduction of the fascist anti-Jewish laws. His death was hastened by this act, because he couldn't get a new post in Italy and ill health prevented him travelling abroad. He died in Rome on December 29th 1941.

LEVI-CIVITA, Tullio (1873-1941) Italian mathematician

Rita Levi-Montalcini was born on April 22nd 1909 in Turin, Italy, one of a pair of twins, with an elder brother and sister, born to Jewish parents. She studied medicine at Turin University, where she remained after obtaining her MD to research the effect of peripheral tissues on nerve cell growth. Her work was interrupted when the Germans occupied Italy (1943-45), driving her into hiding. She later resumed her research work at Turin. However, in 1947 she accepted a position at Washington University, St Louis, to study with the eminent zoologist Dr Hamburger, then working on the growth of nerve tissues in chicken embryos. They worked together to discover that a nerve growth implanted into chicken embryos produced a nerve growth factor (NGF). Stanley Cohen (*qv*) now took the place of Hamburger. He and Levi-Montalcini went on to discover a bodily substance that stimulates and influences the growth of nerve cells. For this work they shared the 1986 Nobel Prize for Physiology. In 1961 Levi-Montalcini established a research medical laboratory in Rome and thereafter travelled constantly back and forth between Rome and the US. She holds joint citizenship and talks openly about her life in her autobiography, *In Praise of Imperfection*, published in 1988.

LEVI-MONTALCINI, Rita (1909-) Italian neurologist

LEVI-STRAUSS, Claude (1908-) French anthropologist

Born on November 28th 1908 in Brussels, Belgium, he was educated at the University of Paris, where he studied law and philosophy. While teaching at a secondary school in Paris, he became associated with Jean-Paul Sartre and an inner member of an intellectual circle. He left France to become a professor of sociology at the University of Sao Paulo, Brazil (1934-37). It was here that he first became interested in anthropology. His study of the Brazilian Indian was well received and led to an invitation to become a professor at the New School for Social Reform in New York (1941-45). Back in France, he became director of studies at the Ecole Pratique des Hautes Etudes in Paris (1950-74). In 1973 he was elected a member of the French Academy. He wrote much on his subject, including *Structural Anthropology* (1963), *The Savage Mind* (1966) and *The Elementary Structures of Kinship* (1969). *The Way of the Masks* (1975) analysed the art, religion and customs of the native Americans of the north-east coast.

Levi-Strauss's theories of structuralism profoundly influenced anthropology and cultural systems. These ideas are explained in his four-volume study, *Mythologiques* (1964-72). In this connection, the London *Times* commented, 'he established the great complexity and beauty of primitive cultures and questioned the assumed superiority of western logic and rationalism'. An intellectual, he was much amused by W. H. Auden's definition of the term: 'To the man in the street, who, I'm sorry to say, is a keen observer of life, the word "intellectual" suggests straight away a man who's untrue to his wife.' In 1991 Levi-Strauss was awarded the Legion d'Honneur.

LEVINAS, Emmanuel (1905-95) French philosopher

Emmanuel Levinas was born in Kaunas, Lithuania, on December 30th 1905, the son of a Jewish bookseller. In 1923 he went to Strasbourg to study philosophy and took as his topic the life of Husserl. A French subject by the beginning of the Second World War, he joined the French army. Captured by the Germans while in uniform, he was treated as a prisoner of war and so escaped the gas chambers. The war over, Levinas deliberately chose to become the director of a small Jewish school in Paris. Like many others who escaped the Holocaust, the revelation of what had happened affected him even more profoundly than those who actually suffered and survived. He brought all his philosophical and intellectual powers to bear on the aftermath of the Holocaust. He lectured frequently, and four of these addresses were published in 1968 under the title *Quatres lectures Talmudiques*. In 1972 his *Humanisme de l'autre Homme* attracted much attention. Although an important European thinker and held in high respect, he was not as well known as others in the circle of existentialists to which Levinas belonged, despite his having introduced into French intellectual circles the work of Husserl and Heidegger. He once wrote: 'If the State of Israel is to exist it needs the recognition of the Arab world.' Levinas died in Paris on December 25th 1995.

Jack Levine was born on January 3rd 1915 in Boston, Massachusetts. He trained first at the Jewish Welfare Centre in Roxbury, then at the Boston Museum of Fine Arts. Following the award of a scholarship, he studied art at Harvard University (1929-31). The Federal Art Project helped Levine set up a studio in the slums of Boston, and during the 1930s he became one of the leading Realist painters in the US. He used the backdrop of Boston, including the poor social outcasts, to satirize the greedy and corrupt politicians of the time. He came to the art world's attention with *Brains Trust* (1936) and *The Feast of Pure Reason* (1937). In 1939, he held his first one-man show in New York. His great works include *Gangster Funeral* (1952-3), *The Trial* (1954, now at the Art Institute of Chicago) and *The Patriarch of Moscow on a Visit to Jerusalem* (1975) His great triptych, *Panethuikon*, is his imaginary idea of the UN Security Council meeting in special session and was completed in 1978. All these paintings were in his satirical mode. Some of Levine's work was included in the State Department's 1959 exhibition to Moscow. President Eisenhower, who had shown himself to be a dithering Allied Commander and a second-rate president, now decided he was an art expert and objected to some of Levine's paintings being included. Levine's great surprise came in 1973 when the Vatican bought his painting *Cain and Abel* and he was told by Pope Paul VI that his work would always be welcome at the Vatican Museum. This was an unusual accolade for an American painter; it was almost unbelievable for a Jewish one. Jack Levine married a painter and their daughter has followed in her parents' footsteps.

LEVINE,
Jack
(1915-)
US painter

James was born on June 23rd 1943 in Cincinnati, Ohio. At the age of ten he was dubbed a 'child prodigy' when he made his piano-playing debut with the Cincinnati Symphony Orchestra. He went on to study piano and conducting at the Juillard School in New York. In 1965 he was invited to become assistant director of the Cleveland Orchestra, where he stayed until 1970. In 1971 came his big chance when he conducted the Metropolitan Opera Orchestra in *Tosca*. He has since become internationally famous for his work with the 'Met'. Appointed principal conductor in 1973, musical director in 1975 and artistic director in 1983, Levine has provided the 'Met' with the continuity it desperately needed. He has greatly improved the standard of Italian opera performance. Levine, who often makes guest appearances as conductor of the Chicago Symphony Orchestra, has made extensive recordings of the works of Brahms, Marler, Verdi and Mozart. His interpretations are said to be crisp and precise and he is known as a musician's musician. In July 1996 he conducted the concert in which the three great tenors, Domingo, Pavarotti and Carreras, appeared.

LEVINE,
James
(1943-)
US conductor

LEVINSKY,
Barney
'Battling'
(1891-1949)
US world boxing
champion

Born Barney Lebrowitz on June 10th 1891 in Philadelphia, he started his boxing career as Barney Williams, but in 1913 his manager, Dan Morgan, came up with the name 'Battling Levinsky' and a legend was born. In those days boxers fought often and Levinsky would fight several times a month. He was a light heavyweight who loved and lived to fight. The more the merrier appeared to be his motto. His record was 287 bouts of which he won 192, 34 of these by knock-outs. He sustained 52 losses, including fights with Gene Tunney and Jack Dempsey in the heavyweight division; 34 fights were drawn and the remaining nine were no-decisions. In April 1916 Levinsky took the undisputed world light heavyweight title from Jack Dillon of the US and defended it a record 59 times. He finally lost it to Georges Carpentier of France four years later. 'Battling' Levinsky died in February 1949.

LEWIN,
Kurt
(1890-1947)
US psychologist

Kurt Lewin was born on September 9th 1890 in Mogilno, Germany. He received his doctorate from the University of Berlin in 1914 and went directly into the German army. The First World War over, he taught at the Berlin Psychoanalytic Institute until 1933 when, like so many other Jewish teachers, he was ejected from his post. He emigrated to the US to teach at Stanford and Cornell universities, before becoming head of the Child Welfare Research Institute at Iowa State University. In 1945, he was responsible for the creation of the research centre for group dynamics at the Massachusetts Institute of Technology and was its director until his death two years later. Kurt Lewin became internationally known for his 'field theory of human behaviour'. This states that human behaviour is a function of the individual's psychological environment. To reinforce his theories, Lewin would use topologies or maps to illustrate various psychological patterns. The final years of his life were spent researching group dynamics to prove his theory that groups alter the individual's behaviour pattern. He died on February 12th 1947 at Newtonville, Massachusetts.

LEWIS,
Sir Aubrey
(1900-75)
Australian
psychiatrist

Aubrey Lewis was born in Adelaide, Australia on November 8th 1900, his father a watchmaker, his mother a teacher at the synagogue school. Educated at the Christian Brothers' College, he excelled at languages, physics and literature. He graduated from the Medical School at Adelaide University and received his MB when he was 23. Between 1923 and 1926 he conducted an anthropological study of Australia's Aborigines: a most detailed examination that included, for the first time, a social appraisal of the hopes and aspirations of the Aborigine in modern society. He then submitted a paper on his work to the Royal Society of South Australia. This work resulted in a Rockefeller research fellowship for Lewis and very little for the Aborigines. Lewis now trained in psychological medicine and nervous diseases. For two years he studied at divers places as varied as Boston, Berlin and London, and in 1938 became a Fellow of the Royal College of Physicians.

Remaining in London, Lewis became clinical director of Maudsley Hospital. During the Second World War he dealt in psychological medicine for the wounded, especially RAF air crew. The high reputation Maudsley earned before, during and after the war was due to Lewis's influence. The war over, Lewis achieved considerable recognition for his work on obsessions and depressions. Perhaps most importantly, he turned psychiatry from a purely clinical field into a recognized academic discipline. His international reputation was assured when hospitals all over the world came to be influenced by his methods of training and organizing research workers in psychiatry clinics. A keenly sought-after lecturer on both sides of the Atlantic, he was knighted in 1959 for his services to medicine. He retired in 1966 to indulge his interest in history and biography. He died in London on January 21st 1975.

LEWIS, Jerry (1926-) US actor

He was born Joseph Levitch on March 16th 1926 in Newark, New Jersey. Following a hotch-potch career as a stand-up comedian, he hit international stardom after teaming up with Dean Martin in 1946. They started off in night clubs and graduated to Hollywood in 1949. Their sequence of run-of-the-mill films ended when, in 1958, they broke up in disharmony. Lewis has since gone his own way, acting and often directing; he also lectures on the cinema. Some of his films have received critical acclaim, in particular *The King of Comedy* (1983) and *Funny Bones* (1993). In France he is regarded as a comic genius on a par with Chaplin, while in the US he is considered an acquired taste. In 1997 he starred in a theatrical revival of *Damn Yankees* both in the US and London.

LEWIS, Ted 'Kid' (1894-1970) British world boxing champion

Born Gershon Medeloff on October 24th 1894 in London's East End, he had his first professional fight the day after he left school at the age of fourteen. At seventeen, he was Britain's youngest ever boxing champion when he won the British featherweight title in 1913. A year later, he was European champion, and at 21 he was undisputed world welterweight champion. He held the world title for four years before losing it to the American Jack Britton. Between 1914 and 1924, 'Kid' Lewis was British Empire champion at featherweight, welterweight or middleweight. It is considered that, pound for pound, Ted 'Kid' Lewis was the greatest British fighter ever to hold a title. He died in London on October 20th 1970. He is the only British boxer enshrined in the Boxing Hall of Fame. He was the first boxer to use a mouthpiece to protect his teeth; it was designed by his ex-boxer dentist, Jack Marks, and continues to be standard boxing equipment.

LIBERMAN, Yevsey (1897-1983) Russian economist

Yevsey Liberman, born in Volga, Russia, in 1897, was educated at Kiev University and the Kharkov Engineering Economics Institute. At the outset of his career he worked in engineering factories all over the Soviet Union. It was this experience that resulted in his appointment as the head of the economic buildings industry at the Kharkov Institute (1947). In 1957 he received his doctorate and published his ideas for economic growth in a work entitled *The Planning of Profit in Industry*. His ideas of how to make the Soviet economy efficiently productive were noted by Soviet leaders but not acted upon until, in 1962, he wrote an article for *Pravda* entitled 'Plan, Profit and Bonus'. It received world-wide attention and the ideas in it were implemented in the Soviet Union, where Liberman was appointed professor of statistics at Kharkov University, forming the basis for wide-ranging economic reforms. The reforms won the approbation of the Russian people but were nevertheless difficult to put into practice, because they represented a radical departure from the old ways. Internationally regarded, he once graced the front cover of *Time* magazine (1965). Although he retired in 1963, he continued his outpourings of ideas in articles and lectures. When he died, his obituary stated that 'he was a great Soviet scientist whose ideas reflected the collective wisdom of the Party'.

LICHINE, David (1910-72) Russian/ American dancer/ choreographer

He was born David Lichtenstein in Rostov-on-Don, Russia. His family left Russia during the First World War and emigrated to France. At the Russian School in Paris he started dancing lessons under a prima ballerina from the Diaghilev company. He made his dancing debut with Ida Rubinstein's (*qv*) company. He joined the Ballet Russe de Monte Carlo in 1932, and there began his choreography career. He mixed dancing and choreography, creating Strauss's *Graduation Ball* to instant acclaim. In 1941 he and his wife were fortunate enough to escape from occupied France and get to America. There Lichine danced and choreographed for the American Ballet Theatre, first as a guest and later on a permanent basis. He invented dance routines for Broadway musicals including *Beat the Band* and *Rhapsody*, as well as doing film work. In 1947 husband and wife spent a year working in Argentina, before returning for the first time since the Second World War to Europe and France, where David created works for the Ballets des Champs Elysées. They returned to the US in 1952, to open and run a ballet school in Los Angeles. A man of great skill and enormous charm, Lichine was a great influence on mid 20th century ballet. He continued running his school until his death in 1972.

LIEBERMANN, Max (1847-1935) German painter

Max Liebermann, born in Berlin on July 20th 1847 to a wealthy family, spent his younger days in the Netherlands, painting that country's flat, austere landscapes. By 1900 he was back in Germany and an internationally acclaimed painter. He was a member of the Berlin Academy and a founder of Sezession and its president. Although still considered the most important of German painters, his radical style had been overtaken and he had come to be considered old-fashioned. When the Nazis came to power in 1933, Liebermann, as a Jew, was not permitted to continue as president of the Academy. His paintings were removed from all museums throughout Germany and his work declared 'degenerate'. His house was looted, while the police stood by laughing. His suffering, and the resulting stress, brought on an early death on February 8th 1935 and the later suicide of his wife.

LINDER, Max (1883-1925) French actor

Max Linder, born Gabriel Maximillian Leuvielle on December 16th 1883 in Caverne, France, completed his education at the acting academy of Bordeaux Conservatory. By 1910 he was the most successful screen comedian in France and indeed most of Europe. He influenced a generation of clowns, and in particular Charles Chaplin. His career was interrupted by the First World War, during which he joined the army and was twice wounded and suffered from mustard gas poisoning. Later, as an air force pilot, he crashed his plane and spent a long time recovering. He went to Hollywood at Chaplin's invitation and there directed and produced several films, of which only *Seven Years Bad Luck* was a box office success. He began to get depressions which became deeper and deeper. His last film, *Clown Aus Liebe* (1924), for which he wrote the screenplay as well as acting and directing, disappointed him; a few months later he, together with his wife, died in a suicide pact. That Max Linder was a genius was confirmed by the eloquence of those who spoke at his memorial service. It was summed up by Chaplin, who said: 'Linder was one of the truly great comedians of our time.'

LIPCHITZ,
Jacques
(1891-1973)
French sculptor

Jacques Lipchitz was born on August 22nd 1891 in Druskininkai, Russia, and studied engineering at Vilna University. In 1909 he was living in Paris and attracted by the avant-garde movement in sculpture. He studied the subject and, following service in the Russian imperial army (1912-13), returned to Paris to work on turning three-dimensional Cubism into sculptures. His first work of note was *Sailor with a Guitar* (1914), now at the Albright-Knox Gallery, Buffalo, New York. He worked on solid blocks of materials before, in 1926, producing a collection of sculptures that became known as 'transparents'. These included *Joy of Life*, a transparent dancing figure that Lipchitz mounted on a motorized pedestal so that it slowly turned about. *The Harpist* (1928) influenced a generation of sculptures. *The Couple* (1929) at the Rijksmuseum, Amsterdam, expresses as much emotion as a painting.

In 1941 he was in New York with an international reputation. He now turned to more substantial works, creating such masterpieces as *Prayer* (1943) and *Prometheus Strangling the Vulture* (1944-50). In 1952 tragedy struck when his New York studio was destroyed by fire. With help from the Museum of Modern Art, New York, his studio was rebuilt and Lipchitz later repaid MOMA with several works. In 1959 the Tate Gallery in London held an exhibition of his work. From 1962 he lived part of each year in Lucca, Italy, working and resting. On the occasion of his 80th birthday, the Metropolitan Museum in New York held an exhibition of his work. On the day of his birthday, Lipchitz was at the opening of the Tel Aviv Museum, to which he dedicated a set of 157 bronzes. He died on May 26th 1973 in Capri, Italy, and was buried in Jerusalem. His largest and final work, *Bellesophon Taming Pegasus* (1977), was dedicated to New York's Columbia University.

LIPMANN,
Fritz
(1899-1986)
German/
American
biochemist

Fritz Lipmann was born on June 12th 1899 in Königsberg, Germany. He received his MD in 1924 and his PhD in 1927 from the University of Berlin. Between 1932 and 1939, he did research at the Biological Institute of the Carlsberg Foundation in Copenhagen. With Hitler now on the scene in his native Germany, Lipmann accepted an offer from Cornell Medical School in New York to teach(1939-41). In 1941 he moved to the Massachusetts General Hospital in Boston, where he stayed until 1957. While there he discovered, together with Sir Hans Krebs (*qv*), coenzyme A, an essential catalytic substance present in the cellular conversion of food into energy. In 1953 the two men shared the Nobel Prize for Physiology for this work, which has proven to be of the utmost importance. In 1957, and until his death on July 24th 1986 in Poughkeepsie, Lipmann taught at the Rockerfeller University in New York.

LIPPMANN,
Gabriel
(1845-1921)
French physicist

Lippmann was born on August 16th 1845 in Luxembourg, of French-Jewish parents. By the beginning of the 20th century, Lippmann had researched the birth of colour photography, developing a technique known as the 'Lippmann process'. He had also invented the coleostat, an instrument that permitted long-exposure photographs of the sky by compensating for the earth's motion during the exposure. In 1908, Lippmann was awarded the Nobel Prize for Physics for producing the first colour photographic plate. He was later appointed president of the French Academy of Science. He died in Paris on July 13th 1921.

LIPPMANN,
Walter
(1889-1974)
US journalist

Lippmann was born in New York on September 23rd 1889. He studied for his BA at Harvard University and came under the influence of two philosophers, William James and George Santayana. He co-founded the *New Republic* in 1914 and worked on it as assistant editor. The magazine, published weekly, had a liberal slant and is said to have influenced President Wilson in formulating his fourteen-point plan after the First World War. Lippmann was an enthusiastic supporter of the principle of a League of Nations and was a US negotiator at the Treaty of Versailles (1919). Working on the *New York Herald Tribune* in the early 1930s he started his column, 'Today and Tomorrow'. It appeared in 250 papers in 25 countries, was syndicated coast to coast in the US and won him two Pulitzer Prizes, in 1958 and 1963. He travelled all over the world and formed various opinions, drifting from the socialism expressed in his book *A Preface to Politics* (1913) to the opposite view, expressed in *The Good Society* (1927). Although essentially a supporter of democratic ideals, he favoured a degree of government control. Over a 60 year career he became a most respected political columnist. He died on December 14th 1974 in New York.

LIPSON,
Ephraim
(1888-1960)
British
economic
historian

Lipson was born in Sheffield, Yorkshire, on September 1st 1888 to Jewish middle-class parents. In childhood he suffered a severe accident that left him disabled and fragile. Notwithstanding, he earned scholarships to the Sheffield Royal Grammar School and Trinity College, Cambridge. He achieved a first-class honours degree in history and departed to Oxford, where he became a tutor. In 1910 there was great and growing interest in the subject of economic history. It attracted many academics, was on the syllabus of all universities, and the most popular of the evening classes run by the Workers' Educational Association. Lipson saw that the textbook material for these courses was hopelessly out of date and set about redressing the balance. In 1915 he published *An Introduction to the Economic History of England: 1, The Middle Ages*. It was enthusiastically received; indeed, the reviews were overwhelming in their praise. Lipson, now very highly regarded, was appointed Reader in economic history at Oxford and a Fellow of New College. His lectures became so popular with students that larger halls were required to accommodate the numbers wishing to attend. By 1931 he had published parts 2 and 3 of his *Economic History*, describing the economic conditions that existed up to the beginning of the Industrial Revolution. Again, publication was greeted with enthusiasm and Lipson expected to be given the new chair in economic history at Oxford, the

Chichele professorship: however, the post went elsewhere and Lipson was shattered. While it was not likely that anti-Semitism played a part in the decision, it could not be ruled out. Lipson, hurt and angry, left Oxford. He declined to write volume 4 of his magnum opus and spent the next thirty years alternating between London in the summer and warmer climes in the winter. He kept busy by constantly adding to volumes 1, 2 and 3. Lipson never married but was very close to his elder brother, D. L. Lipson, who from 1937 until 1950 was the Independent MP for Cheltenham. Ephraim died in London on April 22nd 1960, his great books still the worldwide standard reference for students of British economic history.

He was born **Eliezer Markovich Lissitzky** on November 10th 1890 in Smolensk, Russia, where his parents made hats. As a Jew he was not allowed to study at the Academy of Arts in St Petersburg, so instead he went to Germany to study in Darmstadt. When the First World War broke out he returned to Russia. Following the Revolution in 1917, Lissitzky was allowed to continue his study of art when Chagall (*qv*) became head of the art school at Vitebsk. The following year Lissitzky succeeded Chagall as principal. At the same time, he began to paint what he called Prouns: geometrical abstractions that fused aspects of architecture with painting. His *Proun 2* (1920) is in the Philadelphia Museum of Art. In 1921 he was appointed professor at the Moscow Academy, but state interference angered him and he left the country. He returned to Germany where he contributed fundamental ideas to the Bauhaus and the Dada movement. It was largely through Lissitzky's efforts that abstract art in the form of suprematist and constructivist works was exhibited and appreciated in Western Europe. He designed and arranged the very important exhibition of abstract art at the Van Diemen Gallery. In 1923 he met Gropius, who pioneered the Bauhaus exhibition at Weimar. He was in Switzerland between 1923 and 1925, working and exhibiting, and at Hanover from 1925 to 1928. He then returned to Soviet Russia, where he devoted much time to typography and industrial design. He designed the Soviet Pavilion at the 1939 New York World Fair, causing a sensation. During his lifetime, he was rated the top abstract artist in the Soviet Union and one of the most important in the art world. He died in Moscow from tuberculosis on December 20th 1941.

Born Meir Wallach on July 17th 1876 in Bialystok, Poland, he received an elementary education which was followed by service in the imperial Russian army. In 1901 he was arrested as a revolutionary member of the Russian Social Democratic Workers' Party. He escaped to Britain, where he spent the next twelve years working closely with Lenin. Following the 1917 Russian Revolution, the new Bolshevik government appointed Litvinov their representative in Britain. A year later he was arrested for anti-British activities and later swapped for Robert Lockhart, who was doing the same thing in Moscow. Litvinov led the Soviet delegation to the League of Nations Disarmament Conference (1927-30) and proposed sweeping changes to end the arms race. At that time the Soviet Union needed to concentrate on peaceful growth. In 1930 he was appointed commissar for foreign affairs and led several

LISSITZKY,
El
(1890-1941)
Russian painter

LITVINOV,
Maxim
(1876-51)
Russian
diplomat

delegations to the League of Nations. He also attended the economic conferences held in London during the early 1930s, and was responsible for establishing diplomatic relations between the USSR and the US in 1934. Litvinov, a chubby fellow with a ready wide smile, never hid his Jewish roots and did not hesitate, at League meetings in Geneva, to criticize Germany for its treatment of the Jews. He resigned over the German-Soviet Treaty of Non-Aggression (1939) and only returned to the foreign ministry when Germany invaded his country in 1941. He served as the Soviet ambassador to the US from 1941 to 1943 and again in 1946. He spent the final years of his life actively supporting the work of the UN. He died in Moscow on December 31st 1951.

LOESSER,
Frank
(1910-69)
US composer

Frank Loesser, born on June 29th 1910 in New York, was to become one of the world's great songwriters. Educated at New York's City College, he left before graduating to become a self-taught pianist with a staff job at a music publisher. His first big hit came when he wrote the melody and lyrics of 'Praise the Lord and Pass the Ammunition'. Then came 'What Do You Do In The Infantry?', which became the number one army song. In 1948 the world was singing 'On a Slow Boat to China'. He wrote the hit show *Where's Charlie?* and followed it with *Guys and Dolls* in 1950, both shows winning him Tony Awards. For Danny Kaye (*qv*) he wrote 'Baby It's Cold Outside', which won the 1949 Academy Award for Best Song in a motion picture. He died on July 28th 1969 in New York, his ears still ringing from the plaudits he received for his last show, *How to Succeed in Business Without Really Trying*. It won him the Pulitzer Prize for the Best Musical.

LOEWI,
Otto
(1873-1961)
German/
American
physician

Otto Loewi was born on June 3rd 1873 in Frankfurt, Germany, to become yet another distinguished scientific benefactor who would later seek sanctuary from the Nazis in America. While in Austria, working and teaching in Vienna, Loewi shared the 1936 Nobel Prize for Medicine with Sir Henry Dale, for their discovery of related chemical transmission of nerve impulses. Prior to this award, Loewi's researches between 1921 and 1926 proved that chemicals were involved in the transmission of the body's impulses from one nerve cell to another. In 1938, when the Germans arrived in Austria, they arrested Professor Otto Loewi, now 65 and a Nobel Laureate, took away all his possessions and imprisoned him for two months. An international protest secured his release and he spent a year in Brussels and a year at Oxford before emigrating to the US in 1940. He became research professor at the School of Medicine at New York University, where he remained until his death 21 years later. He was a most humorous man who failed to be concerned that he had been stripped of all his worldly goods and not even allowed the use of his Nobel Prize money. In addition to his work on the nervous system, he researched diabetes and the action of the drug digitalis. He created a test for detecting pancreatic disease now known as the Loewi test. He died in New York City on December 25th 1961.

Peter Lorre was born Ladislav Loewenstein on June 26th 1904 in Rozahegy, Hungary. He acted on the stage and in small parts in several European films before gaining international stardom as the child murderer in Fritz Lang's (*qv*) 1931 film, *M*. It was perhaps inevitable that he became typecast as the villain. Concerned about the rise of Hitler, he was happy to accept an invitation in 1934 from Hitchcock to come to England and star as the kidnapper in his film *The Man Who Knew Too Much*. Lorre went on to make another film for Hitchcock, playing the same sort of role in *The Secret Agent* (1936). His first Hollywood role was in MGM's horror film *Mad Love* (1935). Between 1937 and 1939, Peter Lorre was the Japanese detective in the hugely successful *Mr Moto* films produced by 20th Century Fox. His superb character acting was never more evident than in the films he made in the early 1940s which, although originally 'B' movies, have become legendary: *The Face Behind The Mask* (1941), *The Maltese Falcon* (1941) and, of course, *Casablanca* (1942). In the 1950s Peter Lorre became ill and his weight increased considerably as a result. Nevertheless, he made several more films, including *Around the World in 80 Days* (1956). He also departed from his normal roles into comedy, for example in *The Raven* (1963). It is a pity that Hollywood did not recognize Lorre's diversity of talent earlier. His last film was *The Patsy* (1964), a Jerry Lewis comedy. It is said that Peter Lorre's performance in *M* remains the greatest in the history of the cinema. He remains one of the film world's most memorable personalities. He died in Los Angeles on March 23rd 1964.

LORRE,
Peter
(1904-64)
Hungarian/
American actor

Louis was born Vitali Yevgenyevich Lui in Moscow on January 5th 1928, and educated at the University of Moscow. A native Muscovite, and a Jew, he was still a student when he took a part-time job with the embassies of New Zealand and Sweden. The result was that he was arrested, charged with espionage and sentenced to 25 years in a Soviet labour camp. He was sent to Siberia and then Kazakhstan. After working in the 'Gulag' for seven years, he became the beneficiary in 1956 of a more liberal policy that followed the death of Stalin. His sentence was commuted, but not before the KGB had done a deal. Louis was fluent in English and the KGB assisted him in getting work with foreign news agencies in Moscow. For some time he was correspondent for *The Sunday Times*. Apparently the KGB had helped Louis in return for having the use of a conduit for information they wanted passed on to the West. Whatever the reality of any such arrangement, Louis proved himself a first-class journalist and he became a 'stringer' for several newspapers. He married an English woman working in Moscow, Jennifer Statham; this was unusual and gave further support to the theory that the KGB was backing him. The couple produced *Information Moscow*, a handbook for foreigners living in Moscow and for the increasing number of visitors. The handbook became most successful and, as it was constantly updated, was soon an essential item. This was further proof that Louis had friends in high places, as no private enterprise such as this handbook would have normally been permitted.

Louis became the source of 'scoops'. In October 1961, he revealed that the Politburo was demoting the mummified corpse of Stalin from alongside Lenin, and

LOUIS,
Viktor
(1928-92)
Russian
journalist

explained that Moscow students had led the demand for the removal. What was really happening was the world was being prepared for the process of de-Stalinization. It was Louis who in 1964 shook the world with the revelation that Nikita Khrushchev was on his way out. When Stalin's daughter, Svetlana, was preparing for publication of her book in London, Louis turned up with a Soviet-inspired version of Svetlana's memoirs and tried to find a publisher for 'the real thing'. He failed, but in the event it didn't really matter because the genuine version caused little if any stir. Louis continued to be a source of exclusive stories and hot tips well into the 1980s. Possibly the most important was his announcement of the imminent release of Anatoly Sharansky (*qv*). Now it was the era of Mikhail Gorbachev and the need for Louis's revelations diminished. Nevertheless, he was regarded with affection by those who maintained contact. He was charming and courteous and, although he lived in an ostentatious style, complete with a large house, private swimming pool and several cars, he never put on airs. He was always allowed to travel to the West and his two sons were educated at Oxford University. All in all, there can be little doubt that the wealth and lifestyle he acquired, and the privileges he enjoyed, could not have been obtained by a jobbing journalist. The possibility that Viktor Louis was indeed a KGB general cannot be ruled out. One day the files will be opened and the 'I told you so' pundits might have their field day. Louis died in London from a heart attack on July 18th 1992.

LUBETKIN,
Berthold
(1901-90)
Russian/British
architect

He was born in Tiflis, Russia, and studied architecture under Rodchenko and Tatlin in Moscow. At the Atelier Perret in Paris he came under the influence of Le Corbusier. There, in the late 1920s, he designed an apartment block at 25 avenue de Versailles which caused an architectural stir; his rhythmic horizontals were considered the poetry of architecture.. In 1931 he emigrated to England and set up his own firm, Tecton. His major works in Britain include the Penguin Pool at London Zoo (1933), Highpoint, blocks of luxury flats in Highgate (1933-38) and the Finsbury Health Centre (1935-38), all in London and all still in use. An important contributor to British architecture and beyond his buildings are examples of his genius. Highpoint was London's first all concrete apartment building and considered a breakthrough. Lubetkin in 1938 built a specialist bomb shelter that became the model for Government shelters in the Second World War. In 1951, and now a leading British architect, he left the capital for the heart of the Gloucester countryside and there buried himself for some 30 years. A committed Communist, he drove his children to become scholars; it was, ironically, the results of this pressure that later enabled his younger daughter, Louise Kehoe, to track down the mystery of her father. Lubetkin had a difficult temperament which, at times, kept his family at bay, and her father's indifference when Louise returned home from a traumatic holiday in Germany caused her to leave. However, after his death Louise investigated all aspects of her father's life and has published her findings in a recent book, *In This Dark House*. She discovered that her father was Jewish and that his parents died in Auschwitz. As a result of the war, and the revelation that so many of his family had died, Lubetkin had rearranged his past and refused to discuss any part of it with his wife and children. The loss of

Lubetkin's architectural artistry is overwhelming, when considering the examples we are left with. He died in the West Country on October 23rd 1990.

Zivia Lubetkin was born in Beten, Poland. An active Zionist, she was in eastern Poland when the Germans invaded her country. She immediately went to Warsaw, where she joined a small group of Jews who decided to form an armed resistance group, the Anti-fascist Bloc. Lubetkin fought the Germans in a small uprising in January 1943. She was in the forefront, and one of the leaders, of the fighting when the Warsaw ghetto rose up on April 19th 1943. On May 8th 1943, following the fall of the main bunker, she and others escaped the ghetto via the sewage system. Zivia Lubetkin and her husband Yizhak Cukierman were two of the four people who informed the Polish National Council in London of what had happened in the ghetto and warned of the fate that awaited the Jews in German-occupied Europe. Lubetkin and her husband fought with the partisans until the Red Army reached Warsaw. There they took part in the general uprising. Following the end of the war, she spent time helping survivors reach their homes or Palestine. She arrived in Palestine herself in 1946 and, together with her husband, founded Kibbutz Lohameiha-Getta'ot. She helped found the Ghetto Fighters' Kibbutz and was an executive of the Jewish Agency (1966-68). Her vivid testimony at the Eichman trial was most moving. Following her divorce, she married Yitzhak Zuckerman. They had met during the ghetto fighting and had remained close thereafter.

LUBETKIN, Zivia (1914-76) Polish fighter

Ernst Lubitsch was born in Berlin on January 28th 1892, the son of a bookkeeper. He studied acting and in 1911 met Max Reinhardt (*qv*), who gave him some minor theatrical roles. Lubitsch started directing one-reel film comedies and graduated to costume dramas. Spoken of as 'a man of pure cinema' by Alfred Hitchcock, a 'giant' by Orson Welles and 'a prince' by Truffaut, Ernst Lubitsch is obviously among the very best film-makers of the 20th century. His films have what has become known as the 'Lubitsch touch'. This is well illustrated by his version of *To Be or Not To Be* (1942). Lubitsch has that 'little something'. The film industry owes him a great deal. He was invited to Hollywood by Mary Pickford in 1923 to direct *Rosita* and stayed. In 1935 he was head of production at Paramount, but preferred directing his own productions. Three of his films were nominated for Academy Awards, all for Best Director: *Patriot* (1928), *The Love Parade* (1929) and *Heaven Can Wait* (1943). Several of his original films have been remade, but none has yet matched the master's work, let alone bettered it. He died in Los Angeles on November 20th 1947.

LUBITSCH, Ernst (1892-1947) US film-maker

Sid Luckman was born in Brooklyn, New York, on November 21st 1916 and graduated from Columbia University in 1939. Between 1939 and 1950 he played for the Chicago Bears. During this period he was one of the two top quarterbacks in the game. Sammy Baugh of the Washington Redskins was the other. During the years 1940-46 Luckman helped the Bears win four consecutive league championships, including the 74-0 rout of the aforementioned Redskins. Luckman directed the

LUCKMAN, Sid (1916-) US footballer

revolutionary T formation offensive and his forward passing feats became legendary. In 1943 he set a league record by passing for seven touchdowns in one game; the record still stands. He went on to become a successful coach and coached the Merchant Marine Academy for some 20 seasons. In 1965 he was elected to the Football Hall of Fame, judged one of the greatest players in American football history.

**LUKACS,
György
(1885-1971)
Hungarian
philosopher and
writer**

György Lukács was born on April 13th 1885 into a wealthy Jewish family of bankers living in Budapest, and was educated at the universities of Budapest, Berlin and Heidelberg. His early writings on literature and philosophy show the influence of Immanuel Kant and Max Weber, the German sociologist. Following the Soviet revolution of October 1917, Lukács joined the Hungarian Communist Party and was a member of the short-lived Hungarian government of Bela Kun (*qv*), serving as Minister of Education. Lukács fled to Vienna when Kun was overthrown in August 1919 and there wrote *History and Class Consciousness: Studies on the Marxist Dialect* (1923). This major work on Marxism was repudiated by the Russian Communist Party in the 1950s. From 1930 to 1945 he lived and worked in Moscow, editing the magazine *Literary Critcism*. He returned to Hungary to become professor of aesthetics and cultural philosophy at the University of Budapest (1945-58). He was often at odds with the Hungarian Communist Party in power and during the 1956 uprising became a minister in the temporary government. This presumed error of judgement was soon forgiven, following the restoration of the *status quo* after Russian forces restored the Communists to power. On the occasion of his 80th birthday in 1965 he was showered with honours and his numerous writings republished. Lukács' biography of Lenin (1924) is still the standard work on the subject. He died in Budapest on January 4th 1971.

**LUMET,
Sidney
(1924-)
US film-maker**

Lumet was born in Philadelphia on July 25th 1924, the son of a Jewish actor. He made his acting debut on the stage of the Yiddish Theatre in New York, thereafter graduating to Broadway. During the Second World War Lumet served in the US army, after which he joined CBS as a television director. He became one of television's best directors of drama until Hollywood beckoned. In 1957 Lumet directed one of the all-time great films, *Twelve Angry Men*. It was his first film and a taste of what was to come. Lumet became the master of psychodrama with *The Fugitive Kind* (1960), *The Longest Day* (1961), *Journey Into Night* (1962), *A View From The Bridge* (1962), *Fail Safe* (1964), *The Pawnbroker* (1965) and *The Hill* (1965). His tense modern dramas have included *The Anderson Tapes* (1971), *Serpico* (1973) and *A Dog Day Afternoon* (1975). In 1976 he made the brilliant satirical film, *Network*. Other important work includes *Equus* (1972) and *The Verdict* (1982). His works demonstrates how, time after time, he gets the most powerful performances from his experienced actors. It is said that when the history of American films made in the second half of the 20th century is written, Sidney Lumet will be among the top ten contributors.

Salvador Luria was born in Turin, Italy, on August 13th 1912. In 1935 he graduated in medicine from the University of Turin. Between 1935 and 1938 he was a medical officer in the army. He witnessed Mussolini's fascist dictatorship at first hand and did not like what he saw. By now a radiology specialist, he went to France in 1938. When the Germans arrived he left for the US. As a Jew he had little alternative. While in Paris he had worked at the Curie Laboratory. Now his considerable knowledge and experience were much in demand at American universities.

Although he became professor of bacteriology at the University of Illinois in 1950, it was not until he was professor of microbiology at the Massachusetts Institute of Technology (1959-64) that he really came into his own. He organized a new teaching and research programme and in 1972 founded the MIT Centre for Cancer Research, himself serving as its director until 1985. Luria's particular field was bacteriophages, sub-microscopic viruses that make bacteria. His work led him to DNA research and he contributed the discovery that viruses mutate, changing their form from one generation to another. Luria was also a political being, often a vocal one. He criticized the Vietnam War, biological weaponry and the Lunar Programme, in terms of the expense incurred for very little return. In 1969 he shared the Nobel Prize for Medicine, and donated $25,000 from his prize to anti-war groups. He was considered a remarkable man and an inspirational teacher. It was therefore all the more upsetting when, in 1969, his name appeared on a federal blacklist in the US because of his outspoken support for the peace movement. The government appeared unable to accept that Professor Salvador Luria was a scientific genius with a social conscience. He died of a heart attack in Lexington on February 6th 1991.

LURIA, Salvador (1912-91) Italian/ American biologist

Rosa Luxemburg was born on March 5th 1871 in Zamosc, Poland, the youngest of five children of a lower-middle-class Jewish timber merchant, and was brought up in Russian-ruled Poland. At high school she became involved in secret activities against the Tsar's police, and she spent the rest of her life fighting for the poor, the oppressed and the dispossessed. She became one of the original founders of the Polish Social Democratic Party, that would become the Communist Party. She was in favour of international socialism, while others could think no further than Polish independence. Their nationalism angered her. She argued the principle with Lenin, who came down in favour of national self-determination. The Russian revolution of 1905 was of overwhelming importance to her. She had been convinced that Germany was the country from which revolution would emanate first. Now she realized Russia was the prime candidate.

In her 1906 book, *The Mass Strike, The Political Party and the Trade Unions*, Rosa Luxemburg stressed the need for mass strikes all over the world as the best method of achieving the goal of revolution against capitalism. She argued against Lenin's belief that a tight party structure was essential, claiming that an acceptable organization would come about from the workers' struggle, once it was achieved. She opposed the Great War of 1914-18, and, together with her lover, Karl Liebknecht, formed the Spartacus League, dedicated to ending the war via revolution.

LUXEMBURG, Rosa (1871-1919) German radical

Her 1916 pamphlet *The Crisis in the German Social Democracy* was written while she was in prison in Germany. The influence of the Spartacus League was minimal as the war ground on. In December 1918, following the end of the war, Rosa and a few faithful comrades founded the German Communist Party. The following month, on January 15th 1919, she and Liebknecht were murdered by a group of right-wing army officers and their bodies thrown in the river. This group, the forerunners of the Nazi party, killed one of the greatest women of the century, a true believer in democracy and freedom of the individual in a socialist world.

LUZZATTI,
Luigi
(1841-1927)
Italian prime
minister

Born in Venice into an orthodox family, **Luzzatti** graduated with a law degree from the University of Padua. By 1900 he was a member of parliament; he served in this role until 1921, when he was promoted to the Senate. As treasury minister between 1904 and 1906, he was responsible for reducing the deficit, converting public debts and saving Italy from bankruptcy. In 1910 he became Prime Minister, Italy's first Jewish premier. He was a conservative and although he did put through some reforms they were insufficient. A year later he was defeated by the combined forces of the left in a general election. In later life he became outspoken on behalf of persecuted groups and wrote: 'I am a theist without a particular church and I will defend all who are persecuted for their faith.'

LWOFF,
André
(1902-)
French biologist

André Lwoff was born on May 8th 1902 in Ainay-le-Chateau, France, to Russian-Jewish immigrants. Educated at the University of Paris, he spent his entire working career at the research department of the Pasteur Institute in Paris. His work was interrupted by the Second World War, during which Lwoff actively fought in the French Resistance; for his efforts he was subsequently awarded the Medal of Resistance and created an Officer of the Legion of Honour. Following the liberation of France by the Allies in 1944, Lwoff resumed his work and contributed to the knowledge of lysogeny, a bacterial phenomena that generates subsequent bacteria by the original cell division. For his work Lwoff shared with Francois Jacob (*qv*) and Jaques Mond the 1965 Nobel Prize for Physiology.

M

He was born Al Rudolph in Rosenhayn, New Jersey. He reigned as middleweight champion of the world between 1914 and 1917. He constantly defended his title before losing it to Mike O'Dowd in October 1917. McCoy was the first 'southpaw' (a left handed boxer) ever to win a world title. He had a great and ongoing influence on sportspeople who were often instructed, in school and in the area of sport to stop being left handed and 'behave properly'. i.e. force themselves to become right handed. McCoy was the first example of a successful sportsman, anywhere in the world, to debunk this theory, encouraging left-handers to remain as they were and be natural; to-day, left-handers are among the champions throughout the sporting world.

Richard Maibaum, born on May 26th 1909 in New York, was a writer who specialized in screenplays. His parents were middle-class Jews and his father, an electrical engineer, viewed with some apprehension his son's decision to study drama at the University of Iowa. While studying for his degree Maibaum wrote plays. One, about a lynching, called *The Tree,* was staged on Broadway. *Birthright* followed in 1933; this came about following a trip to Europe on which he came into contact with some of Hitler's refugees. He left New York for Hollywood to become just another hack churning out mostly mindless film scripts. He was overqualified. The Second World War came and he joined the US army; as a captain he was transferred to the propaganda machine, where he remained until promoted to the rank of colonel and transferred to the Combat Film Division. The war over, Paramount invited Maibaum to join them. He went on to write some of the biggest box-office successes of the second half of the century, including *The Great Gatsby* (1949), *Cockleshell Heroes* (1955, considered one of the best the Second World War films made), *The Red Beret* (1953) and *Zarak* (1956). Many of these films concerned British forces during the Second World War, and many were produced by Warwick Films. One of the company heads was 'Cubby' Broccoli, who went on to co-produce the James Bond films. He asked Maibaum to write the screenplays. The first was *Dr No* (1962). After this he went on to write, sometimes on his own and sometimes with a co-writer, *From Russia With Love* (1963), *Goldfinger* (1964), *Thunderbolt* (1965), *On Her Majesty's Secret Service* (1969), *Diamonds Are Forever* (1971), *The Man With the Golden Gun* (1975), *the Spy Who Loved Me* (1977), *Octopussy* (1983), *For Your Eyes Only* (1985), *The Living Daylights* (1987) and *Licence to Kill* (1989). It is estimated that a quarter of the world's population have seen at least one Bond film that Maibaum wrote. He met Ian Fleming, the originator of James Bond, who couldn't understand why Maibaum injected a touch of levity into the stories. Fleming thought his stories were to be taken seriously. Richard Maibaum died in Santa Monica, California, on January 4th 1991. The best Bond film? Maibaum thought it was *From Russia, With Love*.

**MAILER,
Norman
(1923-)
US writer**

Norman Mailer was born in Long Branch, New Jersey, on January 31st 1923. Brought up in Brooklyn, he graduated from Harvard University in engineering in 1943. A year later he was serving with the US army in the Pacific. The war over, Mailer began studying at the Sorbonne in Paris. There he wrote of his war experiences, gave the book the title *The Naked and the Dead*, and thus was thrust into the public eye. He has been there ever since. He was 25 and great things were expected of him, but for some time it appeared that he was a one-novel writer. His frustrations led to anger which often hit the newspaper headlines; but he did not stop writing. He published three novels in the 1950s, to mixed reviews. In 1957, he published *The White Negro*, about social misfits known as hipsters. *An American Dream* (1965) and *Why Are We in Vietnam?* (1967) are important but not popular. Other novels include *Tough Guys Don't Dance* (1984) and *Harlot's Ghost*. Mailer has written much which lacks the entertainment appeal of the novel yet is essential reading for those who want to know what is happening. These works include *The Armies of the Night* (1968), about the 1967 peace demonstrations in Washington; Mailer was jailed for civil disobedience for his part in these events. *The Executioner's Song* (1979) is about the life of Gary Gilmore, a convicted killer, and *Oswald's Tale: A Reconstruction of His Life* is about Lee Harvey Oswald, and reflects once again Mailer's belief that there is evil in the system. He is the recipient of the Pulitzer Prize.

**MALAMUD,
Bernard
(1914-86)
US writer**

Malamud was born on April 26th 1914 in Brooklyn, New York, and educated at the City College of New York and then Columbia University. He taught literature at Harvard University until his novel *The Fixer* (1966) won him the Pulitzer Prize, when he gave up teaching to become a full-time writer. His novels, except for the *The Natural* (1952), which is about baseball, all have Jewish themes and deal with the trials and tribulations of everyday life. His short stories often have a dry humour that reduces the tensions he easily raises. Malamud gives the reader genuine insight into the life of the immigrant Jew, who comes from a European ghetto to one in New York. A brilliant writer whose characters come alive, he died in New York on March 18th 1986.

**MAMET,
David
(1947-)
US writer**

David Mamet was born in Chicago, Illinois, on November 30th 1947 and graduated from Goddard College in Vermont. He went on to study acting in New York. His subsequent writings are based on the experiences that arose from this training. His distinctive syntax, with half-spoken thoughts and quick-shifting moods, is a feature of his work and stems from his time at Sanford Meisner's New York Playhouse. His first plays, *Sexuality*, *Perversity in Chicago* and *Dutch Variations*, were produced off off Broadway in the early 1970s and confirmed Mamet as a 'new realistic' writer. In 1975 he wrote *American Buffalo*, a play set in a Chicago junk shop that was meant to represent capitalism in US society. The bleakness and anti-social explanations startled audiences and critics alike. *Glengary Glen Ross* (1983), a story of commission-hungry estate agents, was set in Chicago but it could have been anywhere in the world. In 1992 it became an award-winning film. Mamet's other successful plays include *A Life in the Theatre* (1977), *Speed the Plow* (1988) and *The Cryptogram* (1995). He works a lot in Hollywood, writing screenplays and sometimes directing. His work includes a reworking of *The Postman Always Rings Twice* (1981) that was not as good as the first version. He wrote the screenplay of *The Untouchables* in 1987 which resulted in Sean Connery receiving the Oscar for Best Actor. He wrote and directed *The House of Games* in 1988. It was his first effort at directing and won him critical acclaim.

MANDEL, Georges (1885-1944) French leader

Born Louis Georges Rothschild on June 5th 1885 into a well-known Jewish family living in Chatou, France, Mandel was a politician by conviction rather than as a career. He was on Clemenceau's staff between 1906 and 1909, and again during the difficult period 1917-20. As a deputy in the National Assembly, he was staunchly conservative and hated the left. He also hated the French right, who were pro-German and antisemitic. He was Minister of Posts (1934-36) and Minister of Colonies (1938-40); then Paul Reynaud, the Prime Minister, made him Minister of the Interior at the most dangerous time in French history. Mandel made it clear that he supported Reynaud's desire to continue the fight against Germany from the nation's African colonies. The resulting agreement between the Vichy fascists and Germany negated this possibility. Mandel refused to accept the dishonourable armistice and on June 21st 1940 he left France for Morocco. There he was arrested, returned to France and imprisoned. In November 1942 the Vichy regime handed him over to the Germans, who kept him in Buchenwald concentration camp. Following the D-Day landings on June 6th 1944, the Vichy French asked for his return. Mandel was duly delivered on July 4th 1944. Three days later, early on the morning of July 7th 1944, he was shot by Joseph Darnaud, the Vichy police chief. Six weeks later de Gaulle entered Paris.

MANDELSTAM, Osip (1891-1938) Russian writer

Osip Mandelstam was born on January 15th 1891 in Warsaw. He grew up in Leningrad and from the age of eighteen travelled through Eastern Europe to Paris, where he studied poetry. Back in Russia, he founded, together with Anna Akhmatova, the Acmeist Movement, the poetic principles of which were precision and concision, in marked contrast to Symbolism. Mandelstam was influenced by Greek culture and themes of classical Greece can be found in his poetry. His second book of poetry, *Tristia* (1922), confirmed him as a most important poet in a country which, following the Bolshevik Revolution of 1917, prized good poets. However, from around 1925 his popularity waned and he found it increasingly difficult to get his work published. It was fortunate that his wife Nadezhda, a translator, was kept busy, otherwise they might have starved. In 1934 he wrote an epic that was highly critical of Stalin. It was not one of Mandelstam's better ideas for a poetical theme: the result was arrest and exile to a provincial town. He was not allowed to return to Moscow until 1937; even then, he was not home for long before he was arrested again and in 1938 sent to a forced labour camp near Vladivostock. He died there during that winter, on December 27th 1938. Two volumes of his poetry, *Hope Against Hope* and *Hope Abandoned*, were published in 1970 and 1974 by his widow. They re-established Mandelstam's importance to post-Revolution Russia.

MANILOW, Barry (1946-) US singer

Barry Manilow, or Barry Alan Pinkus, was born in New York and lived in a six-floor walk-up in an East Side slum. He had his first break while working for CBS TV, writing music for the popular *Ed Sullivan Show*. In 1973 he was the arranger, producer and accompanist for Bette Midler (*qv*). The following year he became a solo artist. In 1976 he had a Number One single hit with 'Mandy' and a million-selling single, 'Looks Like we Made It', in 1977. 'Can't Smile Without You' and 'Copacabana' (both 1978) made Manilow a favourite with audiences everywhere. He became musically respectable when musicians like Sarah Vaughan and Gerry Mulligan sang and played with him in his jazzy album *2.00 a.m. Paradise Cafe* (1984). The middle-of-the-road pop he features in his television extravaganzas continues to bring him an enormous following in the US and Europe. In April 1996 Manilow became an ambassador to America on behalf of the Prince's Trust (organized by the Prince of Wales). In 1997 Manilow re-worked his previous hit 'I'd Really Like to see you To-night' into a modern technique version. A radical departure from his norm.

MANKIEWICZ, Joseph (1909-) US film-maker

Joseph Mankiewicz, the son of German-Jewish parents, was born on February 11th 1909 in Wilkes-Barre, Pennsylvania. He grew up in the shadow of his brother Herman, a brilliant writer, wit and founder member of the Algonquin Round Table. Herman also wrote *Citizen Kane* and won the Academy Award for it. Herman, twelve years older than Joseph, later became a drunk and a gambler. Joseph, for his part, became a screenwriter, producer and director. He has made some of the better Hollywood films and has earned a reputation for being an intellectual film-maker. Among his best have been *The Philadelphia Story*, which he produced in 1940; it won two Oscars. He produced *Woman of the Year* in 1942, and that too won an Oscar, for Best Screenplay. He wrote the screenplay for and directed *A Letter to Three Wives* (1948); it was a box office success and was nominated for the Oscars for Best Director and Best Screenplay. In 1950 he wrote and directed *All About Eve*, which won him two Oscars, for Best Screenplay and Best Director. Joseph Mankiewicz was at the top. However, unlike many successful Hollywood folk, he stayed at the top until he retired in 1972, just after he directed the award-winning *Sleuth*.

The 1950s was probably his best decade. It included *No Way Out* in 1950 and *Five Fingers* in 1952; in 1953 he wrote the screenplay for and directed *Julius Caesar*, and followed this up by writing, directing and producing *The Barefoot Contessa*. In 1955 he thought he would try writing and directing a musical and came up with *Guys and Dolls. The Quiet American* and *Suddenly Last Summer* completed the decade. Unfortunately, in 1963 he took over the direction of *Cleopatra* from Rouben Mamoulian, a volatile Russian director. Despite valiant attempts, Mankiewicz was unable to rescue the film which ended up becoming one of Hollywood's most expensive flops.

Daniel Mann was born in Brooklyn, New York, on August 8th 1912. Educated at the Professional Children's School in New York, he began his working career playing clarinet in a small band, before obtaining a scholarship to New York's Neighbourhood Playhouse, where he studied acting and directing. Following service in the US Army in the Second World War, during which he was a staff sergeant in Special Services, he enjoyed enormous success in bringing to the screen many of the stage hits of the 1950s, as well as other noteworthy and memorable films that cover three decades. He first directed *Come Back Little Sheba* on Broadway; in 1952 he turned it into a film, winning critical acclaim and the Best Actress Oscar for its star, Shirley Booth. In 1954 the same actress starred in his film *About Mrs Leslie*. He directed *The Rose Tattoo* on Broadway and was asked to film it. Anna Magnani had turned down the offer to play it on Broadway because of her poor English. Playing it before the cameras was far less of a problem, and indeed she won the 1955 Academy Award for Best Actress. That same year,1955, saw another Daniel Mann film, the weepie *I'll Cry Tomorrow*. In 1956 it was Marlon Brando's turn to star in a Mann film that had been a play: *The Teahouse of the August Moon*. Mann directed Paul Muni's (*qv*) last film, *The Last Angry Man* (1959); *Butterfield 8* (1960) was a hit and won Elizabeth Taylor the Oscar for Best Actress. The rest of the 1960s, however, did not bring any more films of note, and indeed it was not until he made *Lost in the Stars* (1974), a well-directed adaption of the Anderson-Weill musical, that Mann regained some of the prestige he had earlier enjoyed. He retired in the early 1980s, having made sufficient top films to justify his rightful place in film history. Known in the film world as an actor's director, He died in Los Angeles on November 22nd 1991.

Manfred Mann was born Michael Lubowitz in Johannesburg on October 21st 1941. He studied music at the Vienna State Academy and the Juilliard School of Music in New York. He then moved to England, where, together with drummer Mike Hugg and guitarist Mike Vickers, he formed the Mann-Hugg Blues Brothers. They signed with EMI in 1963 and called themselves Manfred Mann and the Manfreds, then diluted the name to Manfred Mann. They had their first hit with '5-4-3-2-1'; then they recorded 'Do Wah Diddy Diddy', which became Number One on both sides of the Atlantic. 'Sha La La' followed. In 1965 they made 'Come Tomorrow' and 'Oh No Not My Baby'. There was constant coming and going of musicians in the band, and for a time only Manfred Mann was constant. Rod Stewart sang with them for a brief time. In 1969 the group finally split up. However, Manfred Mann, on keyboards, formed Manfred Mann's Earth Band and on February 1977 they had a world hit with 'Blinded by the Light'.

MANN, Daniel (1912-91) US film-maker

MANN, Manfred (1941-) South African musician

MARCEAU,
Marcel
(1923-)
French
mime artist

      Marceau was born on March 22nd 1923 in Strasbourg, France, the son of immigrant Jewish parents. He has been termed the greatest mime artist of all time, his silent portrayals delivered with simplicity, perfection and grace. Following his education he served in the French army during the early part of the Second World War, joining the Resistance after the German takeover of France. After the war he studied at the School of Dramatic Art of the Sarah Bernhardt Theatre in Paris and later with Etienne Decroux. Marceau devoted himself to mime and developed the character of the white-faced Bip, adapted from the French 19th century Pierrot. With Bip, Marceau received world-wide recognition, and toured the world with his own show. He also created several mime-dramas, including *Mort avant l'aube* (1947) and *Le Manteau* (1951). *Don Juan* was produced in 1964 in Paris and his ballet *Candide* was first performed in 1971 at the Hamburg Opera House. In 1978 he founded the Ecole de Mimodrame de Paris at the Theatre de la Porte-Saint-Martin. However, his fame rests with the solo mime performances he gives hundreds of times each year. He has written a semi-autobiographical work entitled *L'Histoire de Bip*.

MARCUS,
David
(1902-48)
US soldier

      He was born **David Marcus**, though he was always known as Micky, in a New York slum where anti-Semitism was rife and Micky unequipped for the constant physical attacks he was forced to endure on the way to and from school. His answer was to build himself up to fighting fitness so that he could defend himself. He succeeded so well that he was later considered as a possible Olympic prospect. After an education that included New York City College, Marcus became a military cadet at West Point Military Academy. Here he won honours in the field of strategic planning and leadership. He graduated in 1924, was commissioned into the US Army and took leave to study law. As a lawyer he left the army for the Civil Service and joined the Attorney-General's office. The Mayor of New York, La Guardia (*qv*), appointed Marcus Commissioner of Corrections. In this role Marcus was confronted with the problem of the takeover of Welfare Island Prison by organized crime. Marcus masterminded the raid on the prison that broke up the underworld influence once and for all. In 1940, with American entry into the Second World War looming, Marcus rejoined the army with the rank of lieutenant-colonel. In 1942 he was head of training at the Havana Rangers Training School. He saw action at the Normandy landings in June 1944 and was at Dachau concentration camp when it was liberated.

      When asked by Ben-Gurion (*qv*) to plan the role of a future Israeli army, Marcus recalled Dachau and agreed. He left his law practice to arrive in Palestine in early 1948 and set to work designing a model army, preparing its training manuals and organizing training courses for its officers. He foresaw the military problems associated with a war on several fronts. To Marcus must go the tribute for Israel being ready to repel the invaders. He planned the building of the supply road to Jerusalem. On June 11th 1948, while wandering around outside the perimeter fence of his HQ at Abu Ghosh, he failed to heed the warning of a sentry who challenged him in Hebrew and fired a warning shot into the air. Marcus responded in English, kept on coming and climbed over the fence. The sentry shot Marcus, who was wearing a blanket to shield him from the cold Jerusalem wind, and Marcus fell dead. He had recently been appointed a brigadier-general or Aluf, the first Israeli soldier so appointed. The grief-stricken sentry tried to commit suicide but was prevented by his comrades; he was later held to be blameless. Marcus was buried at West Point with full military honours; his headstone bears the message: 'A Soldier For all Humanity'.

Rudolph Marcus was born on July 21st 1923 in Montreal, Canada. He obtained his doctorate from McGill University, Montreal, in 1946 and began work at the Polytechnic Institute of Brooklyn, New York (1951-64), followed by a period at Illinois University (1964-78). He then joined the California Institute of Technology in 1978. During the 1950s Marcus began investigating electron-transfer reactions. He published a number of scientific papers on the subject between 1956 and 1965 before concluding that subtle changes occur in the molecular structure of the reactants and the solvent molecules around them. He established that the relationship between the driving force of an electron-transfer and the reaction's rate is described by a parabola. Scientists were for a long time most sceptical of his conclusions, but in the 1980s they were confirmed, resulting in Marcus being awarded the 1992 Nobel Prize for Chemistry for his work on the theory of electron-transfer reactions in chemical systems.

MARCUS, Rudolph (1923-) Canadian chemist

Marcuse was born in Berlin on July 19th 1898. While a student at the University of Freiburg he took part in the abortive revolution of 1918-19. He stayed on to get his PhD in 1922 and continued conducting philosophical research until 1932. During this time he became a co-founder of the Frankfurt Institute für Sozialforschung. With the arrival of Hitler in 1933, Marcuse left for Geneva en route for the US. In 1934 he was teaching at Columbia University, and in 1940 became a US citizen. During the Second World War he was an intelligence analyst for the US Army and later headed the Central European Section of Intelligence Research. In 1951 he returned to Columbia University before moving to Harvard in 1954 and in 1955 to Brandeis, where he stayed for ten years. In 1966 he moved west to the University of California at San Diego for another decade of teaching. His Marxist critical philosophy and psychological analyses, strongly influenced by Freud, were popular among student left-wingers in Berlin, Paris and New York.

Marcuse believed that Western society was constrained and repressed; in his view, technology had brought complacency, as the masses took on big debts to acquire material goods that left them tied to the system, with the result that their intellectual powers were diminished. He wanted to promote resistance to this concept, even to the point of civil unrest. However, he appeared to draw the line at the violence that sometimes accompanied student demonstrations, stating: 'I still consider the American university an oasis of free speech and real critical thinking in the society. Any student movement should try to protect this citadel . . . try to radicalize the departments inside the university.' Among his writings are *Eros and Civilisation* (1955), *One Dimensional Man* (1964), *An Essay on Liberation* (1966) and

MARCUSE, Herbert (1898-1979) US political philosopher

Counterrevolution and Revolt (1972). In his time he was a hero of the New Left, especially during the student riots in Paris in the 1960s. Although he did not approve of that violence, he later decried the later lack of student involvement in society generally. He died on July 29th 1979 in Starnberg, Germany.

MARKOVA,
Dame Alicia
(1910-)
British ballerina

Born Lilian Alicia Marks on December 1st 1910 in London, she studied with Serafima Astafieva at her studio in King's Road, Chelsea, and made her debut at the age of fourteen, with the Diaghilev Ballet. Markova was soon dancing leading roles. In 1931 she joined Sadlers Wells Ballet and became its principal ballerina (1933-35). She was the first English dancer to dance the lead in *Giselle* and *Swan Lake*. Markova also appeared as a ballerina with Ballet Rambert and Ballet Russe de Monte Carlo as well as performing as a guest artist with the Metropolitan Opera. Together with Anton Dolin she headed the Markova-Dolin Ballet (1935-38) and London's Festival Ballet (1949-52). While her favourite role was *Giselle*, she was judged excellent in *Les Sylphides* and as the Sugar Plum Fairy in *The Nutcracker*. She also performed some of the early jazz ballets written by Massine, Antony Tudor and Ruth Page. In 1963 she retired from the stage, became director of New York's Metropolitan Ballet and was created a Dame of the British Empire. In 1970 she became professor of ballet at the University of Cincinnati.

MARKS,
Simon
(1888-1964)
British social
pioneer

Simon Marks was born on July 9th 1888 in Manchester, the son of Michael Marks who started the enterprise that became Marks and Spencer. When Michael died in 1907, M&S had 61 branches, albeit mostly market stalls or penny bazaars. Simon used these as foundations on which to create the M&S stores that now cover the UK as well as many countries overseas. Simon was appointed chairman in 1916 and stayed in that position until he died, his tenure interrupted only by the First World War when in 1917 he was called up to serve in the army. In 1924 he visited the US and studied modern methods of organization. Over the years, M&S has meant improved standards for working-class families in the areas of affordable clothing and household goods. In later years high-quality food products, usually associated with high-class stores, have been available at affordable prices. In 1926 M&S became a public company and the shareholders have profited from the success Simon Marks created. He provided employment by insisting that everything they sold be manufactured in the UK and he achieved a 99 per cent success rate in this aim. Knighted in 1944, he was created Lord Marks of Broughton in 1961. Simon was responsible for the company's trade mark of St Michael. The name Michael is in memory of his father; how a Jew can be a saint is not readily known. Simon Marks died in London on December 8th 1964.

MARSHALL,
David
(1908-95)
Singaporean
statesman

David Marshall was born in Singapore on March 12th 1908, the son of Baghdad Jewish immigrants. Qualifying as a barrister, he became highly successful as a criminal lawyer. He entered politics in the early 1950s, while Singapore was struggling to gain independence from Britain. A co-founder of the Labour Front, he was elected to the Legislative Assembly in 1955 and became the State's first Chief

Minister. Marshall led two delegations to London, in 1955 and 1956, and came away empty-handed on both occasions. He was informed that the independence he demanded was not as yet a realistic option. It was not until 1965 that Singapore became an independent republic, by which time Marshall's party, the Workers' Party, was no longer a political force. He stood as an Independent in 1963, but was beaten, and returned to his legal practice. He retired in 1978 but remained a public figure, being appointed in the same year as the Singaporian Ambassador to France. He continued his diplomatic work for the next fifteen years, becoming successively Ambassador to Spain, Portugal and Switzerland. In the latter part of his life he frequently criticized the government of Lee Kuan Yew, accusing it of abusing human rights. He died in Singapore on December 12th,1995.

The Marx Brothers, although individually famous, are most popular as a group. There were five to start off with, but Zeppo or Herbert (1901-79) later gave up and became a respectable agent, and Gummo or Milton (1893-1977) went in to business. The three remaining were to become the famous Marx Brothers. Chico was Leonard and born on March 26th 1886, Harpo was Adolph and born on November 21st 1888 and Groucho or Julius was born on October 2nd 1890. All the brothers were born in New York City. Their education was minimal and before long all five, plus their mother Minnie, were topping the vaudeville bill as 'The Six Musical Mascots'. Then Gummo left and Minnie retired and they became known as 'The Four Nightingales' before changing to the 'Four Marx Brothers'. Their first play on Broadway, *I'll Say She Is* (1924) was a huge success and was followed by *The Coconuts* (1925) and *Animal Crackers* (1928). These plays were later transferred to the silver screen with great success. Other films (but without Zeppo) included *Monkey Business* (1931), *Horsefeathers* (1932), *Duck Soup* (1933), *A Night at the Opera* (1935), *A Day at the Races* (1937) and *Room Service* (1938).

The Marx Brothers have a humour that has never quite been equalled. The perfect interplay between the brothers, Chico's piano playing, Harpo's playing of the harp, the continuous one-liners and asides to the audience from Groucho are as acceptable today as they were 60 years ago. Groucho sliding across the floor, a large cigar clamped between his teeth, and leering at Margaret Dumont is unforgettable. During the Second World War Chico was a band leader and entertained the forces. The brothers split up in 1949. Each appeared independently on radio and television. Groucho was probably the most successful, due to his long-running television quiz show, *You Bet Your Life* (1947-61). In 1954 Groucho married Eden Hartford, 40 years his junior. The marriage ended in divorce fifteen years later. Chico died in Hollywood on October 11th 1961. Harpo died on September 28th 1964, also in Hollywood, and Groucho died in Los Angeles on August 19th 1977. Three years before he died, Groucho accepted an honorary Oscar on behalf of the Marx Brothers.

MARX BROTHERS: Leonard 'Chico' (1886-1961) Adolph 'Harpo' (1888-1964) and Julius 'Groucho' (1890-1977) US actors

MATTHAU,
Walter
(1920-)
US actor

He was born Walter Matasschanskayasky in New York on October 1st 1920. His father, a Catholic priest from Russia, left the family soon after Walter was born, leaving him to be raised by his mother, Rose Berolskey, Jewish Lithuanian, in the Lower East Side. Walter was later educated at the Columbia School of Journalism and the Dramatic Workshop of New York. In 1942 he enlisted in the US Air Force, and it was not until the end of the Second World War that his acting career came into focus. Following a considerable stage career, he found his natural talent as the easy-going, wry, cynical and comical actor of many entertaining Hollywood films. Matthau has featured in some 100 films since his debut in 1955 in the best- forgotten *The Indian Fighter*. His better films include *Face in the Crowd* (1957), *Lonely Are the Brave* (1962), *Charade* (1963), *Fail Safe* (1964) and *Mirage* (1965). In 1966 he starred in *The Fortune Cookie* and won an Academy Award nomination for Best Actor. *A Guide For the Married Man* followed in 1967 and was judged to be one of the funniest films of the decade. *The Odd Couple* in 1968 saw the partnership of Matthau and Jack Lemon that continues on and off the screen. The 1960s ended with Matthau starring in *The Cactus Flower* and *Hello Dolly*. The 1970s kicked off with *Kotch* and another Oscar nomination. *Plaza Suite* (1971) was followed by *Charley Varrick* and *The Front Page* in 1973 and *The Taking of Pelham 123* in 1974. All starred Matthau, and were highly entertaining box office successes. In 1975 came the *Sunshine Boys* and yet another nomination for Best Actor. In 1981 he starred in *First Monday in October*, taking the part Henry Fonda played on Broadway.

In all these films Matthau has given brilliant performances. He is too good an actor for many of his other films, often badly written and with poor storylines. He and his son Charlie now have their own production company, the Matthau Company. In their recent production, an adaptation of Truman Capote's novel *The Grass Harp*, Walter plays the part of the judge and his son directs. Although a self-confessed cynic, he relishes the parts he plays and it shows. In 1990 he starred in the excellent film, *The Incident*, which tells the story of how a small-town lawyer takes on the defence of a German prisoner of war accused of killing a local doctor.

MAUROIS,
André
(1885-1967)
French writer

André Maurois was born Emile Herzog on July 26th 1885 in Elbeuf, France. His father was a well-off textile-maker and could afford to give his son a first-class education. Maurois' experiences in the First World War, in which he served as an officer and interpreter with a Scottish regiment and acted as liaison officer, led to his first novel, *The Silence of Colonel Bramble* (1918). His later novels centred on middle-class provincial life and the family and include *Bernard Quesnay* (1926) and *Climats* (1928). He is particularly known for his witty and popular biographies, written in a style more usually found in novels. These include *Shelley* (1923), *Lord Byron* (1930), *George Sands* (1952), *Victor Hugo* (1954) and more. He also wrote popular history, including a *History of England* (1937) and a *History of the United States* (1943). Maurois is generally considered the greatest French writer of modern times writing on British subjects. In 1949 he published *The Quest for Proust*, which is considered to be his most distinguished biography. Maurois died in Paris on October 9th 1967.

Robert Maxwell was born Jan Ludwick Hoch to Jewish parents in Slatinske Doly, Czechoslovakia, on June 10th 1923. His family were poor and religious and Jan was the third of seven children. It is doubtful if the world would ever have heard of him had not the Second World War blown down the walls that surrounded his small, narrow and poverty-stricken world. In the event he was propelled into a world he could never have remotely imagined during the sixteen years he lived with his family. Following Hitler's invasion of his country, the area in which he lived came under Hungarian control in 1939 and young Jews were being conscripted to work in labour battalions. Jan decided to leave home and get work in Budapest. It was the last time he ever saw his parents, who, along with most of his family, would later die in the Holocaust. A few months of living in Budapest convinced him that he had to escape to England. This achieved, he joined the Pioneer Corps. With a ready ear for languages he was soon ready to transfer to the North Staffordshire regiment. By the time of the D-Day landings in June 1944, Jan Hoch was Robert Maxwell and an officer in the Queen's Royal Regiment. He led his men into a German-occupied French village and, regardless of enemy fire, stormed, captured and liberated it. He was awarded the Military Cross.

At the end of the war Maxwell was part of the British Army of Occupation and came into contact with many engaged in scientific work. Captain Maxwell received his first taste of publishing when he supervised the founding of the Berlin paper *Der Telegraf*. It is now thought that at that time Maxwell was working for or closely associated with the British security service MI6, which provided the initial funds for Maxwell to set up Pergamon Press. This publishing company specialized in scientific publishing in the UK, with information from East European sources going straight to MI6. Maxwell and his company went from strength to strength; in 1959 he was selected as a Labour Party candidate, and in the 1964 general election he won a seat in Parliament. A man of great charm, Bob Maxwell was in his element; but it was not to last for long. Six years later the voters rejected him. Worse, the Department of Trade and Industry, while acknowledging Maxwell 'as a man of great energy, drive and imagination', declared him unfit to run a public company. In 1981 Maxwell took over the British Printing Corporation, which was on the point of collapse and whose shares Maxwell could not resist buying. He incorporated the company, together with others he owned, into Maxwell Communications Corporation. He replaced old-fashioned printing methods with computers and incurred and absorbed the wrath of the trade unions. He acquired the *Daily Mirror* group and founded *The European* in 1990. At this time Maxwell had one of the biggest media empires in the world, including American papers and publishing interests as well as television and film production companies. In 1991 he floated the *Mirror* group on the stock market.

What followed in the following summer and autumn is still shrouded in mystery. He died on November 5th 1991, drowning while his vessel cruised off the Canary Islands. Speculation concerning Maxwell's death continues. There has been an enormous outcry concerning the missing pension funds and while Robert Maxwell has posthumously borne the brunt of the attacks, his two sons Kevin and Ian having

MAXWELL, Robert (1923-91) British publisher

been found not guilty of involvement in any wrongdoing in connection with the missing monies, the British and Swiss banks have been shown to have acted badly by advancing monies on the basis of dubious security. Maxwell has been cast as the villain. The real truth is probably shrouded to protect greater interests. Although he later appeared to live in a fantasy world, his bravery never deserted him. He is buried on the Mount of Olives in Jerusalem. Following his death the laws concerning pension funds were tightened in Britain and elsewhere.

MAYER,
Daniel
(1909-97)
French
politician

Daniel Mayer was born in Paris on April 29th 1909 into a middle-class Jewish family, his father a commercial traveller, his mother a teacher. His education was minimal but sufficient to get him a job as a journalist on the left-wing daily newspaper *Le Populaire*. During the Second World War Mayer, a member of the National Council of the Resistance, was the leader in hiding of the Socialist Party. The war over, Guy Mollet became leader of the party and Mayer had to be content as the Minister of Labour; however, after a time he resigned in protest against Mollet's policies. In 1958 Mayer was elected President of the League of Human Rights and served in this position for seventeen years. He was never forgiven by the left of his party for insisting that the anti-Communist Mouvement Republicaon Populaire be part of the post-war coalition that came into being following the resignation of de Gaulle in January 1946. Mayer objected to plans for a European Defence Community on the grounds that it meant German re-armament. Following the row over Algerian independence, Mayer became one of the founders of the Parti Socialiste Unifié. In 1981 Mayer was a principal player in the election of Mitterrand to power as president. Later Mayer was President of the Constitutional Council. He died in Paris on January 10th 1997.

MAYER,
Helene
(1910-53)
German
Olympic fencer

Born in Offenberg, Germany, on December 20th 1910, the daughter of Dr Ludwig Mayer, she was only thirteen when she became German foils champion. In 1928, aged 18, she won a gold medal at the Amsterdam Olympic Games. Later the same year she was received by Mussolini in Italy, when she won the Italian championships. She was world champion in 1929 and 1931. In 1932, she was selected for the Los Angeles Olympics but because of illness failed to get a medal. She stayed on in the US to study law. In 1936, Helene Mayer accepted an invitation to represent Nazi Germany at the Berlin Olympic Games. Mayer appeared to be the epitome of Aryan womanhood, tall, slim and fair; a while later the Germans were considerably upset to discover that she was Jewish. However, they were prepared to overlook that fact in return for the probability of a gold medal. Mayer's decision to participate caused consternation among Jewish groups in America. In the event Mayer won the silver medal; the gold, to the dismay of the Germans, was won by the Hungarian Ilona Schacherer-Elek: another Jew. In 1937, at the world championships, the places were reversed.

As world champion, Mayer retired from international competitions and left Germany for the US, where she became an American citizen. Between 1934 and 1947 she competed annually for the US championships, winning first place eight times. Her long reach and classic style, together with a superb physique, put her on level terms with most male fencers of her time. She returned to Germany shortly before her death and died in Munich on October 15th 1953; she was only 43.

He was born Lazar Mayer on July 4th 1885 in Minsk, Russia; his family moved to Canada when Louis was a young lad. When he left school he worked at first in his father's scrap metal business, but in 1907 moved to Boston. He started a small nickelodeon theatre in Haverhill, Massachusetts, and by 1918 owned a chain of cinemas across New England. In order to provide products for his ever-expanding chain he went into film production in Hollywood. Louis B. Mayer became Metro Pictures Corporation, which in turn led to MGM. Mayer is credited with inventing the 'star system' and at one time had under contract most of Hollywood's top actors. Mayer relied on intuition rather than logical thought. He was a most unpleasant man, enormously disliked and, because of the power he wielded, feared. In 1950, when he was pushed out of MGM by Dore Schary, it was said that Hollywood had a smile on its face. He died on October 29th 1957 in Los Angeles, his funeral held in a large studio. The place was crowded, prompting a writer to turn to a colleague and say 'See: give the public what they want and they flock to it.'

MAYER, Louis B. (1885-1957) US film-maker

Born in Paris in 1895, he was educated at the Sorbonne and immediately after graduating joined the French army, fighting in the trenches during the First World War. He was later awarded the Croix de Guerre for bravery under fire. Between 1922 and 1932 he was a lecturer on political science at the Ecole Libre des Sciences Politiques. He was noted for his managerial abilities as well as for his keen political acumen, and it came as no surprise to those who knew him well when, in 1933, he was appointed administration director in charge of Air France. In 1937 he was the head of the SNCF, the French railway system.

Following the French collapse in 1940 and the anti-Jewish policies of Vichy France, Mayer joined the Resistance before escaping to Algeria. Here he continued his resistance work, this time on the committee of the Free French National Liberation Movement. Although a radical socialist, he accepted the post of Minister of Public Works and Transport in the de Gaulle provisional government of 1944. From 1945 to 1946 he was French High Commissioner for German Affairs. Between 1946 and 1952 he was a Deputy in the National Assembly and held various posts in the coalitions that ran French politics. For a brief period from January to May 1953, Renée Mayer was Prime Minister of France. He retired in 1957 following a two-year period as Chairman of the European Coal and Steel Authority, the beginning of what has now become the European Union.

MAYER, Renée (1895-1972) French statesman

Robert Mayer was born on June 5th 1879 in Frankfurt to wealthy Jewish parents. An excellent pianist, he began studying from the age of six at Mannheim Conservatory. When he was eleven, Brahms heard him play and advised a musical career. However, Mayer later doubted his ability and decided instead to go into business. He made a considerable fortune on the US and British stock exchanges

MAYER, Sir Robert (1879-1985) British music patron

and settled in London at the turn of the century. Following the First World War, Mayer decided he wanted to put something back into society. He began what became known as the Robert Mayer Children's Concerts. First held in 1923 under Adrian Boult, the concerts continued annually thereafter and introduced classical music to many children for the first time. In 1932 Mayer, together with Sir Thomas Beecham, founded the London Philharmonic Orchestra. On his 100th birthday a gala concert, attended by the Queen, was held at the Royal Festival Hall in London. He published his autobiography, *My First Hundred Years*, the same year. In 1980 he decided to re-marry at the age of 101. The marriage lasted until January 9th 1985 when he died aged 106 years old.

MEIR, Golda (1898-1978) Israeli stateswoman

She was born Goldie Mabovitch on May 3rd 1898 in Kiev, Russia. By the time she was eight she and her family were living in Milwaukee, Wisconsin. The family was poor. Her father was an odd job man and her mother ran a small grocery shop.. She managed to get to university and graduated as a teacher. In 1921 she married Morris Myerson and the couple left for Palestine and a kibbutz life. Constantly involved with Zionist affairs and trade union matters, Golda became more interested in politics than in being a wife and mother, and the Myersons separated. Gradually Golda progressed up the ranks of the Labour Party. Following Israel's achievement of statehood in 1948, she was appointed the country's ambassador to the USSR. Upon her return she was elected to parliament and became Minister of Labour and Housing. Within the government led by Ben-Gurion (*qv*), Golda Meir did her best work. She founded a secure social structure that helped absorb a million new citizens and provided national insurance and social services. For a decade from the mid-1950s to the mid-1960s she was Foreign Minister and in this role secured the co-operation of many African states. Meir became prime minister in 1969 and promptly gave Israel the dynamic leadership it had not seen since Ben-Gurion. However, time has shown that she made mistakes, particularly in domestic policy, by failing to identify the social problems of the ever-expanding Sephardic community. This would later have serious repercussions. She was nevertheless a superb leader during the Yom Kippur war of 1973 and, although by now in poor health, was a leading contributor to the peace process led by Henry Kissinger (*qv*). She died on December 8th 1978 in Jerusalem. Her autobiography, *My Life*, became a world best-seller.

MEISL, Hugo (1881-1937) Austrian football manager

Hugo Meisl was born in Vienna on November 16th 1881. His father, a wealthy Jewish banker, was so upset by Hugo's enthusiasm for sport in general and soccer in particular that he arranged for him to be exiled to Trieste. A player of average talent, he played for Austria FK but became more and more interested in the management of the game. In 1912 Hugo Meisl paid for Jimmy Hogan, the famous British coach, to come to Vienna. There they developed what was to become known as the Austrian 'Wunderteam'. During the early 1930s this was the top team of Europe. They beat Scotland 5-0, Germany 6-0 and only lost to England at Wembley (4-3). Meisl has long been recognized as one of the three great managers in the world of football, alongside Herbert Chapman of England and Vittorio Pozzo of

Italy. Meisl, known as the 'Father of Austrian Football' was also General Secretary of the Austrian Soccer Federation and in 1927 founded the 'Mitropa Cup', the first international competition at club level. His poor father must have really gone through the mill when his second son, Willy, also trod the football trail, in his case as an international goalkeeper before becoming an outstanding sports journalist. Hugo Meisl died in Vienna on February 17th 1937.

Lise Meitner was born in Vienna on November 7th 1878. Her father was a well-known lawyer with seven children, whose overriding principle was 'A Meitner must have a doctor's degree'. Having obtained her doctorate from the University of Vienna in 1906, Lise embarked on a career of research that would win her an international reputation, following her part in the discovery of uranium fusion. She studied under Max Planck and then joined Otto Hahn in researching radioactivity. This partnership led to their isolating the isotope protactinium-231. They followed this work by studying the effects of neutron bombardment of uranium, but then, as a Jew, Meitner was forbidden to continue working with Hahn. In 1938 she left for Sweden, where she stayed and worked for the next 20 years. There she and her nephew, Otto Frisch (*qv*), continued researching the physical characteristics of neutron-bombarded uranium. In January 1939 they called this process 'fission'. In 1949 she became a Swedish citizen, although her nickname of 'the German Madame Curie' remained.

Following the Second World War, Lise Meitner was credited with laying the foundation of the theoretical groundwork for the atom bomb through her work on discovering that the nucleus of an atom could be split and enormous amounts of energy thereby freed. But Otto Hahn received the Nobel Prize for the work; Meitner was ignored. She had to be content with the one-third share of the Enrico Fermi Award she received in 1966. She retired to England in 1960 to be with her nephews and nieces. Lise Meitner never married. She died in Cambridge on October 27th 1968.

MEITNER, Lise (1878-1968) Austrian/ Swedish physicist

Faina Melnik was born on June 9th 1945 in Bakota, Russia. She has set eleven world records for the women's discus - the total itself a record - ranging from 64.22m in 1971 to 70.50m in 1976. She was Olympic champion in 1972, but in the 1976 Games shocked a lot of people by coming only fourth, despite having won 52 successive discus competitions between 1973 and 1976. Her Olympic career was over when she failed to qualify for the 1980 Games. Paradoxically, however, she kept on winning domestic titles.

MELNIK, Faina (1945-) Soviet world discus champion

Born in Allenstein, Germany, on March 21st 1887, **Mendelssohn** became the leading exponent of German expressionist architecture. He was also known for his radical building ideas. Following training at Berlin and Munich universities, he was awarded a degree in architecture in 1912. In order to earn a living, while waiting for commissions, he worked in department stores, designing their windows. He also painted and was able to sell a few pictures by his association with the Blaue Reiter

MENDELSSOHN, Erich (1887-1953) German/ American architect

group of expressionist painters in Munich. During the First World War, while serving in the German army, he spent his leisure time creating a series of architectural drawings that, following the end of the war, led him to a commission to design what would become the Eisenstein Tower in Potsdam (1919-21). The result became a worldwide sensation, described as a living sculpture rather than a functional building. Many commissions followed and each was a radical departure from the past. He used a lot of glass for his horizontal applications: the Schocken Store in Stuttgart, built in 1927, was a typical example. In 1933 he was expelled from Germany by direct order of Hitler, who believed he had a flair for architecture and wasn't going to compete with Jews. Mendelssohn went to London via Brussels. In England he designed the De La Warr Pavilion in Bexhill, Sussex. The design included a glass-enclosed semi-circular stairway tower that a critic declared to be 'the last word in modern architecture'. Mendelssohn went to Palestine and built hospitals in Haifa and Jerusalem. In 1941 he settled in San Francisco and repaid the kindness he was shown by designing the Maimonides Hospital in 1946. He died in San Francisco on September 15th 1953.

MENDES-FRANCE,
Pierre
(1907-82)
French
statesman

Pierre Mendès-France was born into a well-known Jewish family in Paris on January 11th 1907. He graduated as the youngest ever French lawyer. He joined the Radical Socialist party at the age of sixteen and gravitated towards a life of politics. He was only 25 when he was elected the youngest deputy ever to serve in the National Assembly. In 1938 he was part of Leon Blum's (*qv*) government as Under-Secretary of State for Finance. At the outbreak of the Second World War he joined the French Air Force. Captured by Vichy troops and interned, he escaped in June 1941. Nine months later, after many adventures, he reached London, de Gaulle and the Free French Air Force.

Following the liberation of France in 1944, Mendès-France joined a coalition government headed by de Gaulle and served as Minister of National Economy, but resigned in April 1945 when his austere policies were rejected by his Cabinet colleagues. Re-elected to the National Assembly in 1946, he was a persistent critic of French policy, particularly over the wars in Indo-China and North Africa. He was elected Prime Minister on his pledge to end the Indo-China war within 30 days. As this followed the French defeat at Dien Bien Phu in May 1954, he was able to keep his promise and Indo-China became North and South Vietnam. A year later his ideas of giving independence to Morocco, Tunisia and Algiers, as well as bringing in radical economic measures, were unacceptable and he resigned. He continued in politics, playing an important part in Guy Mollet's successor government, but resigned over the policy of no independence for Algeria. Defeated in the 1958 general election, he was returned again in 1967. His best-known books are *The Pursuit of Freedom* (1956) and *Modern French Republic* (1963). He died at his desk in his Paris office on October 18th 1982. 'A man ahead of his time', 'a strong influence on French politics' and 'a man of peace' were some of the comments in the obituary columns.

Born in Melbourne in 1933, **June** was educated at Lauriston Girls' School. Her Jewish mother was a classical dancer who often took June with her went she went to work, where June would sit in a corner sketching those around her until it was time to go home. She knew from an early age that she wanted to be an artist. She left school and worked designing a wide variety of items, including book jackets and record sleeves. A while later, and by now living in Britain, June concentrated her talents on portrait painting. She prefers to use her mother's maiden name of Mendoza and is now considered one of the foremost portrait painters of the second half of the twentieth century.

Mendoza has probably painted more of the famous than any other living artist. Members of the British Royal Family abound, including the Queen, her mother, her daughter and Diana, Princess of Wales. Her formidable list of subjects also includes prime ministers, leading clergy, explorers, entertainers, writers, sportspeople, dancers and many musicians. She is a genius at painting very large groups in such a way that each individual is recognizable. One such work is her portrait of the House of Commons while in session, including 440 people: a most impressive portrait. She has made similar paintings, with lesser numbers, for the Australian parliament and the Council of the Royal College of Surgeons. In 1996 a portrait of the Queen by the artist Antony Williams caused much controversy. It showed the Queen with broken fingernails, looking somewhat grim and with veins standing out on her hands. June Mendoza, when asked to comment, said: 'People look at portraits only as portraits, they forget to look at them as paintings. This is a painting as well as a portrait'

MENDOZA, June (1933-) Australian/ British painter

Menuhin was born in New York on April 22nd 1916. He grew up in San Francisco, where he studied the violin from the age of four. At the age of seven he became world famous for his concert performance of Mendelssohn's Violin Concerto. He came under the influence and tutelage of Georges Enesco, who developed his talents considerably. Menuhin spent many years of his youth touring the world and playing with the top orchestras. When he was 20 he took eighteen months off to relax and study. In 1959 he moved to England where, in 1963, he opened the Menuhin School at Stoke d'Abernon for children who are musically inclined. Following the 1967 Six-Day War Menuhin was heavily criticized in the Jewish press for giving a concert in Jordan before going on to Tel Aviv. In the event, his Tel Aviv concert at the Mann Auditorium with the Israeli Philharmonic brought Menuhin sustained ovations. He performs all types of music with all sorts of musicians: jazz with Stefan Grappelli and duets with sitar-playing Ravi Shankar, among much else. He starred in the film *Raga* alongside George Harrison and Ravi Shankar. He also finds time to write and his autobiography, *Unfinished Journey*, was published in 1977. In 1985 he became a British citizen and eligible to use the title 'Sir' conferred upon him some time previously. In 1987 he was awarded the Order of Merit and in 1993 he became Lord Menuhin. In October 1996 Lord Menuhin was voted by *Gramophone* to have made the video of the year: *The Violin of the Century*.

MENUHIN, Lord Yehudi (1916-) British violinist and conductor

METCHNIKOFF,
Elie
(1845-1916)
Russian
biologist

Metchnikoff was born in Ivanovka, Russia, on May 15th 1845, the son of a Jewish mother and a Russian father who was an officer in the Imperial Guard. By the turn of the century Metchnikoff was researching the problem of biological ageing. He promulgated the idea that senile changes result from toxins produced by bacteria in the intestine. He advocated that to prevent or halt such unhealthy activity, a person's diet should include sour milk. He spent the rest of his life studying the effect of lactic acid producing bacteria as a means of increasing longevity. In 1908 he shared the Nobel Prize for Medicine for his work on immunity with Paul Ehrlich (*qv*). He died on July 16th 1916 in Paris.

MEYERHOF,
Otto
(1884-1951)
German
biochemist

Otto Meyerhof was born on April 12th 1884 in Hanover, Germany, and educated at Heidelburg University. In 1909 he received his MD. He was professor of physiology at Kiel University, where he researched the physical chemistry of the human muscle. In 1923 he and Archibald Hill shared the award of the Nobel Prize for Physiology. From 1929 to 1938 he was the head of physiology at the Kaiser-Wilhelm Institute; then, as a Jew, he was forced to flee and spent two years in France, until 1940 when the Germans arrived and he was off once again, this time to the US. He now became research professor of physiological chemistry at the University of Pennsylvania. His authoritative *The Chemical Dynamics of Life Phenomena* (1924) is still a standard work for students of his subject. Meyerhof died on October 6th 1951 in Philadelphia.

MICHELSON,
Albert
(1852-1931)
US physicist

Albert was born in Strelno, Germany, on December 19th 1852 and arrived with his family in San Francisco when he was two. By the turn of the century Michelson was known internationally for having fixed the speed of light at 186,329 miles per second. He was now appointed to be the first head of the department of physics at the University of Chicago, a position he held until he retired in 1929. He was awarded the Nobel Prize for Physics in 1907, the first American ever to receive the award for physics. In 1923 Michelson again attacked the problem of accurately measuring the speed of light. Following prolonged research, using the latest methods and instruments, he came up with a figure of 299,774 kilometres per second. Researchers in the 1970s, using far more advanced methods, came up with a result that varied by just two kilometres. On May 9th 1931 Michelson died in Pasadena, California. In 1973 his daughter Dorothy Livingstone published a biography of her father entitled *The Master of Light*.

MIDLER,
Bette
(1945-)
US entertainer

Bette Midler was born on December 1st 1945 in Honolulu, Hawaii. While still at high school she was a member of a professional singing trio. Further education followed at the University of Hawaii and the Herbert Berghof Studio, New York. Although she had a small part in the film *Hawaii* (1966), her big break came as a night-club entertainer and singer of outrageous, bawdy and funny songs. Her piano accompanist was Barry Manilow (*qv*). Her first album, *The Divine Miss M*, appeared in 1972 and won her a Grammy award as the year's best new artist. Her first Hollywood role was as a rock star in *The Rose* (1979); it won her an Oscar nomination for Best Supporting Actress. She continued her singing career alongside making films. In 1982 she starred in *Jinxed*; it was aptly named, for the film flopped and no one came out of it well. Bette Midler now had a spell at the Betty Ford Clinic for alcohol addiction. She returned fit and well to Hollywood and the management team at Disney. She starred in the successful *Down and Out in Beverly Hills* (1985), the hugely enjoyable *Ruthless People* in 1986, the comedy *Outrageous Fortune* in 1987, the weepie *Beaches* also in 1987, the raunchy *Big Business* in 1988 and the soap *Stella* in 1990, and in 1991 she co-starred with Woody Allen (*qv*) in *Scenes From a Mall*. In 1995 she hit the top with her performance in the film *Get Shorty*. In 1996 she was one of the three stars, alongside Diane Keaton and Goldie Hawn (*qv*) in *The First Wives Club*. All this has all added up to Bette Midler being one of the richest female stars in Hollywood. Not that it stops there. She has continued topping the pop music charts with *Wind Beneath My Wings* (1989), *From a Distance* (1990) and *Bette of Roses* (1995). Nor can anyone ignore her 1985 stand-up comedy album, *Mud Will Be Flung Tonight*. No one throws it quite as accurately as Bette Midler.

Lewis Milestone was born Lewis Milstein on September 30th 1895 in Chisinau, Russia. He was educated at the University of Ghent, Belgium, and graduated in engineering. He went to the US following the Russian Revolution of 1917. In Hollywood from 1920, Milestone directed his first film in 1925. In 1927 he directed *Two Arabian Knights* and won the Oscar for Best Director. In 1930 came the fame that would remain for ever with *All Quiet on the Western Front* - arguably the finest anti-war film ever made, and certainly the most influential. It resulted in another Oscar for Milestone. More important, it established his reputation as one of the best directors of all time. The following year he cemented that reputation with *Front Page*, still the yardstick for this genre. In 1933 he made a musical for the Depression, *Hallelujah, I'm a Bum*. Other Milestone films include *The General Died at Dawn* (1936) and *Of Mice and Men* (1939). In 1945 he produced and directed *A Walk in the Sun*, considered a return to his golden days of the early 1930s. His last film was the 1962 version of *Mutiny on the Bounty*, starring Marlon Brando. Milestone died in California on September 25th 1980.

MILESTONE, Lewis (1895-1980) Russian/ American film-maker

Darius Milhaud was born on September 4th 1892 in Aix-en-Provence, France. The son of a Provençal Jewish family, he studied at the Paris Conservatoire under Paul Dukas. In 1916 he went with Paul Claudel to Brazil and there discovered South American music with all its different forms. It made a deep impression on him, and his future was often influenced by what he had heard and seen here. Although he continued to act as guest conductor, he was principally a composer. During his life he composed over 400 pieces, ranging from chamber music to ballet and opera, as well as symphonies and Jewish religious music. His ballet *The Creation of the World* (1923) attracted the notice of the music world, as did the music he wrote for the *Greek Triple Tragedy* (1917-22). He developed the use of polytonality, or the simultaneous use of different keys, as well as incorporating jazz, soul and

MILHAUD, Darius (1892-1974) French composer

blues in his music. When the Germans invaded France, Milhaud left for the US where he became professor of music at Mills College, Oakland, California. From 1947 he taught at the Paris Conservatoire and divided his time between Paris and the US. Later in life he was crippled by rheumatoid arthritis and confined for long periods to a wheelchair. One of the most prominent composers of the 20th century, he died on June 22nd 1974 in Geneva.

MILKEN,
Michael
(1947-)
US criminal

Born in New York, **Milken** was to become known as 'the Junk Bond King'. Following the 1980s creed that 'greed is good for you', he invented a financial instrument that has caused innumerable downfalls in US financial circles. His creation of junk bonds allowed small companies with poor ratings to acquire bigger companies. This system allowed Rupert Murdoch to takeover the 2 billion dollar Metromedia television network, raised James Goldsmith to billionaire status and caused ructions in boardrooms across the corporate world. Milken was part of the Wall Street finance house of Drexel, Burnham, Lambert, where for a time at least everyone became seriously rich before the spree ended in bankruptcy. When Ivan Boesky became a government informer, the bottom fell out of the junk bond market. Milken was charged with fraud and insider dealing, found guilty and sentenced to ten years in prison plus a 200 hundred million dollar fine. Stock exchanges all around the world tightened their security, but it was a case of too little too late. Milken, now out of prison, is thought to have been the victim of powerful enemies. It is now argued that he never broke the law but was highly unorthodox in his constant pursuit of wealth. Professor Daniel Fischel makes this claim, and others, in his powerful book *Payback: the Conspiracy to Destroy Michael Milken and his Financial Revolution*. There is evidence that Rudi Guilliani, the New York prosecutor with political ambitions to be Mayor of New York (he succeeded), used this case to get a lot of publicity. Milken's enemies saw to it that Guilliani would do everything and anything to get a conviction; playing the antisemitic card was considered a fair tactic. The public were against Milken for his brash, arrogant ways and his crude displays of wealth. But were his actions illegal? The story will continue to run and Milken can be satisfied he turned financial institutions upside down. In 1995 Milken was featured in an education CD for children learning mathematics, called *Mike's Math Adventures* . His interest in the project, which he has part-financed, came about during the period he spent doing compulsory community service in a deprived inner-city area.

MILLER,
Arthur
(1915-)
US writer

Miller was born in New York on October 17th 1915 and grew up during the Great Depression. This experience was to provide him with the material to write *Death of a Salesman*, probably his greatest work and arguably the best play of the century. He worked in a warehouse to pay for his university fees and while at the University of Michigan began writing plays. *All My Sons* was produced in 1947 on Broadway and a year later was made into a powerful Hollywood film. In 1949 *Death of a Salesman* won every award in sight. The role of Willy Loman has made or broken more acting reputations than any other role of modern times. The film version of 1951, directed by Stanley Kramer (*qv*) was a masterpiece. In 1953 came

The Crucible, a play about the McCarthy witch-hunt of the 1950s thinly disguised as a story about the 1692 Salem witch trials. The film version was made in 1996-7. Miller became involved with the Un-American Activities circus when in 1956 he was ordered to appear before the House Committee. His refusal to name anyone led to his being cited for contempt, but Miller appealed and won. Miller's stand seriously damaged McCarthy's influence and a year later this sad period in American history was over. *A View From the Bridge* (1957) and *After the Fall* (1964) were plays focusing on personal relationships, while *The Price* (1968) concerned family. Miller's second wife was the actress Marilyn Monroe, who became Jewish for the role. Miller wrote the screenplay of *The Misfits* for her in 1961. The following year they divorced and a few months later she committed suicide. Around this time Broadway was looking for something radically different and Miller's new work was to be found off Broadway. It is now a fact that in some theatre, somewhere in the world, there is always an Arthur Miller play in production. In 1987 he published *Time Bands*, his memoirs, and in 1996 *Plain Girl*, his first novel for 20 years. He has been married three times and has four children.

MILLER, Jonathan (1934-) British stage and opera director

Jonathon Miller, born in London on July 21st 1934, is now a man of many parts. He first hit the headlines as actor in and co-writer of the popular satirical review, *Beyond The Fringe*. Educated at St John's College, Cambridge, and the University College School of Medicine, from where he received a degree in medicine, Miller went to the Edinburgh Festival in 1961 and there, together with Peter Cook, Dudley Moore and Alan Bennett, launched the hit show. It appeared in London (1961-62) and New York (1962-63). The show over, Miller now concentrated on writing television scripts and directing in the theatre. His interpretation of the classics gained him many friends and also some vocal foes. He directed at the National and Old Vic theatres and his production of *Alice in Wonderland* in particular brought him a deal of publicity. In 1976 he resigned from the National to enter the world of opera, and directed Tchaikovsky's *Eugene Onegin* to critical acclaim. In 1978 came the innovative thirteen-part television series called *The Body in Question*. It was a history of medicine and the human body, and one of the top features of BBC television. The series was accompanied by a popular book and followed up in 1982 by a series entitled *States of Mind*, reflecting Miller's chairmanship of the British Altzheimer's Society. In 1985 he became Research Fellow in Neuropsychology at Sussex University, and in 1988 he was appointed artistic director of the Old Vic. In 1996 Miller directed *A Midsummer Night's Dream* in London to excellent reviews.

Once, in a television interview, the subject of Miller's background came up. 'I'm not a Jew; I'm sort of Jewish,' he stated. His work in the theatre and opera house covers much of Europe and the US. Among his writings is *Subsequent Performances* (1986), an interesting dialogue about his work in the theatre. In 1995 came his production of *Carmen*, and in the same a year there was a production of *La Boheme* at the Opera Bastille in Paris that featured Roberto Alagna, commonly known as 'the difficult tenor'. An engaging personality, Miller continues both to be a radical director and to maintain his interest in neuropsychology.

**MILLER,
Mitch
(1911-)
US bandleader**

    Mitchell Miller was born in Rochester, New York, on July 4th 1911. He learned to play the piano at six and began studying the oboe when he was twelve. A student at the Eastman School of Music in Rochester, he graduated in 1932. For eleven years he was a soloist with the CBS Symphony Orchestra, thereafter playing with Andre Kostelanetz, Percy Faith and the Budapest String Quartet. He became musical director of Mercury Records in the 1940s and was responsible for producing most of Frankie Laine's hits (he had to work hard to convince Laine to record 'Mule Train'!). Mitch Miller recorded on his own in the 1950s, his solo work including the Israeli folk song 'Tzena, Tzena, Tzena' and 'The Yellow Rose of Texas', which in September 1955 climbed to the Number One spot, staying there for six weeks and becoming a hit in many countries. He also had a hit with his version of 'Colonel Bogey', following the popularity of the film *Bridge Over the River Kwai*. In the late 1950s he launched a series of albums entitled *Sing Along With Mitch* that featured an all-male choir singing old favourites. His work was often in the US top twenty and travelled well overseas.

    Throughout this period he was connected with Columbia records, who experienced ups and downs with Miller. He was not too keen on rock and he turned down Buddy Holly; however, he promoted Doris Day and Johnny Mathis as well as Tony Bennett and Vic Damone. The swinging sixties closed him down but during the previous decade he bestrode the stage of popular music like a colossus.

**MILLER,
Walter
(1890-?)
US champion
jockey**

    Walter Miller was born on the Lower East Side of New York City in 1890, his parents recent Jewish immigrants from Russia. Miller's way of getting out of his poverty-stricken environment was via horse riding. A small man, he was laughingly nicknamed 'the jockey', and so a jockey he became. In fact, he became the greatest jockey of the early twentieth century. He was just fourteen when, in 1904, he won his first race; by 1909 he had ridden 1,094 winners. During this period he had a total of 4,336 rides, over half of which were placed. He worked very hard, racing on average 722 times a year. He was national riding champion in 1906 and 1907. He rode for the James Keene stable and became the first jockey to ride more than 300 winners in a year. His record of 388 winners, during 1906, stood for over 40 years until it was broken by Bill Shoemaker in 1952. By 1910 it was all over. Miller was too big for American racing and he went off to Europe, where he kept going a little while longer. He disappeared during the late 1920s and the date and place of his death are unknown . However, for a while he was the king of the Turf, and this was recognized when he was elected to the Jockeys' Hall of Fame in 1957.

**MILSTEIN,
Cesar
(1926-)
Argentine
Immunologist**

    Cesar Milstein was born on October 8th 1926 in Bahia Blanca, Argentina, and gained a PhD from the University of Buenos Aires. He was on the staff of the National Institute of Microbiology in Buenos Aires from 1957 to 1963. Later he was at Cambridge University's research laboratory in Britain, where he met Georges Kohler and Niels Jerne. In 1975 they discovered a technique for producing monoclonal antibodies. This meant that large quantities of pure and uniform antibodies were able to recognize single antigence determinates. For this work the trio were awarded the Nobel Prize for Medicine in 1984.

Milstein was born on December 31st 1903 in Odessa, Russia. He trained initially under Leopold Auer in St Petersburg before continuing under Eugene Ysaye in Brussels. He went on to become one of the foremost violinists of the century, especially acclaimed for his interpretation of the Bach unaccompanied violin sonatas. Following the Russian Revolution he and Vladimir Horowitz (*qv*) toured the Soviet Union giving joint recitals to enthusiastic audiences. In 1928 he settled in the US, making his US debut the following year with the Philadelphia Symphony Orchestra, under the legendary conductor Stokowski. He made many recordings, wrote musical arrangements and violin cadenzas. In 1968 the French honoured Milstein by making him an Officer of the Legion of Honour.

Milstein was a happy-go-lucky individual, whose magical renderings reflected the Romantic music he enjoyed playing. It was Milstein who was responsible for the revival of Vivaldi, and it was Milstein who was reckoned to be the leading exponent of the Beethoven violin concerto. His style was such that after just a few notes the experienced listener knew who was playing. For many years he took master classes in Lausaune, Switzerland, where he told his students: 'A musician should not be an instrument operator. He or she should be a whole person.' He died in London on December 21st 1992.

MILSTEIN, Nathan (1903-92) Russian/ American violinist

'Honest' Ed Mirvish was born in Virginia, US on July 24th 1914. He was a small child when the family moved to Toronto, Canada where he received an elementary education. He grew up to become a businessman with a homespun philosophy that appears to have stood him in good stead. Ever since 1948 he has thrived on three points; 1, Fulfill a need. 2, Go against the trend and 3, Keep it simple. The result has been the 'Honest Ed' department store and numerous eating houses that feed large quantities of food to thousands of people, often at the same time. Mirvish, in 1962, saved the Royal Theatre in Toronto from demolition, restored it, and has continued operating it as an ongoing theatre staging plays, new and old. He became a property developer who included theatres in his developments, runs them as theatres and rewarded with the Canada Medal for so doing.

In 1982, following the public concern of stars such as Laurence Olivier and directors such as Tyrone Guthrie, Ed Mirvish bought London's famous Old Vic Theatre saving it from closure and possible demolition. Following a massive renovation programme, that restored the Old Vic to its' original glory in 1991, Ed Mirvish escorted the Queen Mother at the grand re-opening. The theatre, a legacy of Lilian Baylis (qv), continues to thrive and a grateful Britian awarded 'Honest Ed' with the CBE to become a Commander of the British Empire.

MIRVISH, Edwin (1914-) Canadian entrepreneur

Modigliani was born into a Jewish family in Leghorn, Italy, on July 12th 1884. His father was a merchant constantly concerned over his son's poor health. Forced to give up schooling because of reoccurring typhus, Amedeo turned to painting. He studied in Florence and Venice before going off to Paris. Here he was overwhelmed by the work of Cezanne. In 1908 Modigliani held a small exhibition at the Salon des Independants where he met Paul Alexander, who bought some of his work. He also

MODIGLIANI, Amedeo (1884-1920) Italian/French painter

met Constantia Braucuse, a Romanian sculptor. Modigliani now wanted to work and excel in this medium. He disliked the works of Rodin, preferring the style of African sculpture. He became known for simple, elongated pieces, with long necks and long noses that had a sexual rhythm. Amedeo's poor health was not improved by his having numerous mistresses and a penchant for drugs and an excess of alcohol. He had a turbulent affair with Beatrice Hastings, an English poet, with whom he lived for two years from 1914. Modigliani, a brilliant artist who followed none of the art movements of his time, is often portrayed as the epitome of the poor artist starving in a Paris garret surrounded by beautiful models. In Modigliani's case the image was reality. He was poor, and because of the First World War he was unable to sell his work. One of the models was Jeanne Hebuterne. She became his mistress and had a child in November 1918. She was pregnant with their second child when Amedeo died of tuberculosis. Jeanne, on learning of his death, jumped out of a window in Paris and died. Modigliani's work was well ahead of its time but he is now regarded as one of the most important artists of the 20th century.

MODIGLIANI, Franco (1918-) Italian/ American economist

Franco Modigliani was born in Rome on June 18th 1918. The son of a Jewish doctor, Franco studied law until 1939 when, to escape increasing anti-Semitism, he left Italy for the US. He studied economics at the New School for Social Research in New York, receiving his PhD in 1944. He later became a teacher at several US universities and in 1962 was appointed professor of economics at the Massachusetts Institute of Technology. He pioneered various aspects of economic theory and in 1985 received the Nobel Prize for Economics for the fundamental theories he produced that covered the fields of household savings and the dynamics of financial markets.

MOHOLY-NAGY, Laszio (1895-1946) Hungarian painter

Moholy-Nagy was born on July 20th 1895 in Bacsbarsod, Hungary. His Jewish parents encouraged him to take a law degree from Budapest University. While there he became entranced with poetry and joined the university artistic circle. This in turn led on to his interest in painting. In 1923 he was in Berlin and head of the metal department of the avant-garde Bauhaus School of Design. During the period 1923-29 he evolved the methods of training for which he became known, namely developing natural skills rather than pursuing specialist courses. He exhibited his work, which included sculptures, paintings and photography, at Berlin's Der Sturm Gallery. He was also responsible for stage settings for numerous Berlin productions. His photographic work mainly took the form of photograms created directly on to film. His 'light modulators' or oil paintings on transparencies had a mobile light effect. In 1933 he was forced to flee Germany following the election of Hitler. He arrived in Amsterdam in 1934 and in London a year later. In 1937 he was in Chicago and head of the New Bauhaus, which became the Institute of Design at the Illinois Institute of Technology. Moholy-Nagy, the originator of modern experimental art, died in Chicago on November 24th 1946.

Born on February 22nd 1890 in Odessa, Russia, **Moiseiwitsch** was training as a pianist before he could walk properly. At nine he won the Rubenstein Prize. He studied at the Imperial Academy of Music in Odessa and later continued his studies under Leschetitzy in Vienna. In 1908 he and his family moved to Britain, where he gave his first London concert in 1909. Afterwards he toured the world playing with the finest orchestras of the time. An exciting soloist with a caressing touch, he was a favourite with audiences everywhere, who loved the romantic Russian music he played. Benno Moiseiwitsch died in London on April 9th 1963.

MOISEIWITSCH, Benno (1890-1963) British pianist

Moissan was born in Paris on September 28th 1852. By the beginning of the 20th century he was an internationally known scientist who had devised and profited by the development of a system for commercially producing acetylene, previously thought impossible. Moissan developed the electric arc furnace and so was able to mix new compounds and vaporize substances that were had hitherto been infusible. He was professor of inorganic chemistry at the Sorbonne in Paris when, in 1906, he was awarded the Nobel Prize for Chemistry for the isolation of the element fluorine and the development of what was named the Moissan electric furnace. He died in Paris on February 20th 1907.

MOISSAN, Henri (1852-1907) French chemist

John Monash was born in Melbourne, Australia, on June 27th 1865, the son of Jewish immigrant parents from Vienna, where his father printed books in Hebrew. Monash was educated at Scotch College and Melbourne University, graduating in civil engineering and law. He was responsible for the building of Prince's Bridge across the Yarra river in Melbourne, and he pioneered the use of reinforced concrete for construction. A militia commander in 1900, he received a gold medal for his military articles published in the *Commonwealth Journal*. In the First World War he was the commander of the Australian Fourth Infantry Brigade at the time of the disastrous Gallipoli landings. The Australian and New Zealand forces were the principal casualties of the ill-conceived Gallipoli adventure (February 1915-January 1916), instigated by Winston Churchill. The infantry brigade, led by Monash, distinguished themselves and Monash Valley was so called to commemorate their bravery and the fact that, when ordered to evacuate their positions, they did so without a single casualty. Monash was a hero. In 1916 he was promoted to major-general and given command of the 3rd Division of the combined Australian and New Zealand Army Corps. For two years the division fought in France and, together with Canadian forces, eventually captured the strategic Vimy Ridge.

MONASH, General Sir John (1865-1931) Australian soldier

In May 1918 Monash was promoted to lieutenant-general and became Commander-in-Chief of all Australian and New Zealand Forces (ANZACS). Monash had from experience a poor opinion of the abilities of the British General Staff. The Commander-in-Chief, Field Marshall Haig, was a weak commander and his Chief of Staff, General Robertson, a failure. Monash saw how these generals played poker with their men's lives, while they lived in imperial splendour miles away from the mud-filled trenches, inadequate medical care and poor communications. Monash was a fighting general who knew what was required to launch a successful major offensive. In the spring of 1918, Monash was ordered to employ his army in the forthcoming summer offensive. Monash asked to see the overall plan. He then insisted upon alterations. The General Staff, in the shape of General Robertson refused, upon which Monash told him that under no circumstances would he allow his troops to become casualties because of inferior planning. Haig and Robertson raged against Monash, but Monash remained firm and had his way. The plans were altered and the offensive delayed until all the supplies Monash demanded were in place. In the event, after a long and hard campaign, Monash broke the German defences around Amiens which led directly to the Germans asking for an armistice. In this battle Monash used, for the first time ever, a combination of tanks and infantry as a single combat force. When the battle was over, King George V, much to Haig's and Robertson's disgust, visited Monash at his HQ at Bertangles Chateau and knighted him. It was the first time in over 200 years that a British monarch had knighted a commander in the field.

In the Victory Parade through London that followed the end of the war, the greatest cheers were for the ANZACS, led by Monash. After the war Monash was appointed chairman of the State Electricity Commission of Victoria and under his leadership the power resources of Victoria became entirely self-sufficient. In 1931 Monash was promoted to full general, the first Australian to achieve this rank. He wrote two books that describe his war experiences, *The Australian Victories in France in 1918* (1920) and *War Letters*, published posthumously in 1933. Monash, a practising Jew all his life, died on October 8th 1931 in Melbourne. He was given a state funeral, attended by 250,000 mourners, and buried with full military honours. In 1950 an equestrian statue was erected in Melbourne and in 1958 Monash University was established. In Israel, Kefar Monash was founded by Australian and New Zealand war veterans. In 1996 John Monash's picture appeared on the face of a $100 Australian banknote.

MONTAGU,
the Hon. Ewen
(1901-85)
British lawyer

Ewen Montagu, born March 29th 1901, was the second son of the second Baron Swaythling. Educated at Cambridge University, where he studied law, he was called to the Bar in 1924 and created a King's Counsel in 1939. Although he would later make his mark in law, it was his Second World War experiences that earned him international fame. When Britain declared war on Germany on September 3rd 1939, Montagu was an officer in the Royal Navy Volunteer Reserve. In 1941 he was head of Naval Intelligence at the Admiralty with special responsibility for counter-espionage. It was Montagu who dreamed up the operation that required the body of a Royal Marine officer to be found in Spanish waters complete with official Allied plans showing a landing in Sardinia instead of their real objective, Sicily. The ploy worked and many Allied lives were saved. In 1953 Montagu wrote *The Man Who Never Was*. It sold over 2 million copies and is considered to be one of the best spy books ever written. The film of the same name was equally successful. He continued practising as a lawyer after the war, becoming Judge Advocate of the Fleet. He also tried cases involving civilian crime and his comments from the bench, often cynical and caustic, were widely quoted. He died in London on July 19th 1985.

Ivor was born on April 24th 1904, the third son of the second Baron Swaythling and the brother of Ewen. No two brothers could have been more unalike. Ivor, after a public school and university education (he graduated in botany from the Royal College of Science, London, and in zoology from King's College, Cambridge), renounced his hereditary privileges and became a member of the British Communist Party; and there weren't many Honourables in the Communist Party. His journalistic career included periods as foreign correspondent on the *Daily Worker*, during which time he reported on the Spanish Civil War. Ivor Montagu was a leading light in the world of table tennis. It was his efforts and proletarian sympathies that, more than anything else, helped to turn the easy-to-learn and cheap-to-play game that was table tennis, also known as ping pong, into an important international sport. Indeed, one of the most important tournaments in the table tennis calendar is the Swaythling Cup, given by Ivor's mother, Lady Swaythling, in 1926. At the age of 22 Ivor was president of the International Table Tennis Federation and remained so for 40 years. An eccentric fellow, he would appear at press conferences in slippers and dressing gown. He had a commanding, almost hypnotic, personality, was a first-class linguist, a writer and a witty after-dinner speaker. He was also a film-maker who had accompanied Eisenstein on his 1930 trip to Hollywood. He went on to produce propaganda films on behalf of the Republican cause in the Spanish Civil War. Following the Second World War he worked with Ealing Studios and wrote the screenplay of *Scott of the Antarctic* (1948). Among his earlier productions were *The Man Who Knew Too Much* (1934), *The Thirty-Nine Steps* (1935), *Sabotage* (1936) and *Secret Agent* (also 1936). As a zoologist his research knew no bounds. He once travelled to the Gobi desert in order to research and write about the sex life of a rare camel. In 1960 he was awarded the Lenin Peace Prize. However, throughout his life and regardless of what he might be doing, his interest in table tennis was always in the forefront of his life. He died on November 5th 1984.

MONTAGU, the Hon. Ivor (1904-84), British journalist and administrator

Yves Montand was born Ivo Livi to Jewish peasants in a small Italian village near Florence on October 13th 1921. Avid Socialists, his parents moved to Marseilles when Mussolini came to power. Ivo was 2. He was 11 when he left school. Then came a wide variety of jobs until he became a music hall singer by night and a docker by day. At 18 he was in Paris working at the Moulin Rouge when he met the legendary Edith Piaf who became his lover and protector. Although a popular singer, with a wide following, it was as a screen actor that Montand received international acclaim. He made his debut in *Star Without Light* (1946). He made a considerable impact in *Les Portes de la Nuit* (1946) and *The Wages of Fear* (1953). During the latter half of the 1960s he starred in two films of Costa Gavras that reflected his left wing attitude: *Z* (1969) and *The Confession* (1970). He married Simone Signoret (qv) in 1951 and occasionally co-starred with her until her death in 1985. Neither relevations of his relationship with Marilyn Monroe or his Communist sympathies diminished his popularity. This reached a peak in 1986 when he starred in the internationally successful films: *Jean de Florette* and *Manon des Sources*. Yves Montand died in Senlis, France on November 9th 1991. In 1955 he published his biography, *Sunshine Fills My Mind* .

MONTAND, Yves (1921-1991) French actor

MORAVIA,
Alberto
(1907-90)
Italian writer

He was born Alberto Pincherle on November 28th 1907 in Rome to a Jewish father and Catholic mother. A sickly child, he spent many years living in sanatoriums. Confined to bed for long periods, he read books in French, German and English and in this way received a varied education. At the age of eighteen he was declared as fit as he was ever likely to be. He began writing and produced his first novel, *The Age of Indifference*, in 1929. It proved to be a sensation, attacking as it did nearly all that was holy to the middle classes. His anti-fascist views soon brought him into conflict with Mussolini and Moravia found it useful to be away for much of the 1930s, working for a newspaper as its foreign correspondent. During the Second World War, Moravia kept a low profile until in 1943 he learnt that the newly arrived Germans had him on their list of Jews they intended to round up in Rome. He and his wife, the famous writer Elsa Morante, spent the best part of a year hiding in a remote village and living in a goat-herder's cottage. This experience became a backdrop for his prize-winning novel *Two Women* (1957), later a film with Sophie Loren, who won the 1961 Academy Award for Best Actress for her performance as the daughter. His earlier novel, *The Women of Rome* (1947), is probably his best-known work. Although Moravia's constant theme is sexuality, he often uses it as a symbol to reflect the decadence of capitalistic life. A left-winger, he was elected to the European Parliament in 1983 and spoke out against injustice as he saw it. A most important figure in Italian literature, his stark style and narrative skill have won him admirers all over the world. He died on September 26th 1990 in Rome.

MORGENTHAU,
Henry Jr
(1891-1967)
US statesman

Morgenthau, born in New York City on May 11th 1891, had no need to worry about working for a living. However, he chose to become a farmer and went to New York State College of Agriculture at Cornell. There he developed typhoid and spent many months on a Texas farm recuperating. He and his father bought a large farm in Duchess County, New York, close to the Hyde Park estate of Franklin D. Roosevelt. Henry and Franklin became firm friends. During the First World War, although Henry was a serving lieutenant in the US Navy, he was also part of Roosevelt's presidential campaign. In 1922 Morgenthau founded the magazine *American Agriculturist* and was its editor until 1923. In 1934 Henry was appointed Secretary of the Treasury. His enthusiasm for the job was boundless. He reorganized the department and during his next twelve years in office, supervised the spending of $370,000 million that was raised in taxes from the time of the New Deal until the end of the Second World War - and without a single dollar going astray! He set up the Liaison Committee, the origin of the Lease-Lend arrangement essential for the British war effort at a time when that country stood alone in Europe against Hitler. Following the death of Roosevelt in April 1945, Morgenthau retired from public life to spend time on charitable causes and his farm. He died on February 6th 1967 in Poughkeepsie, New York.

He was born Samuel Joel Mostel in New York on February 28th 1915. Educated at New York University, he graduated in art and English. For some time he studied painting, following his decision to become a serious full-time painter. In order to buy art equipment and paints he took to becoming a party entertainer, and gradually this activity became more and more prominent. By 1942 he was working in night clubs and radio soon followed. Following the Second World War, he moved to Hollywood and the world of film. He had not been a film actor long when in 1955 he locked horns with the House Committee on Un-American Activities, with the result that his film career went into suspension. His Broadway stage career, by contrast, exploded, following his role as Leopold Bloom in Joyce's *Ulysses*. He won an award for his role in Ionesco's (*qv*) *Rhinoceros* in 1962. He had the lead in the musical *A Funny Thing Happened on the Way to the Forum*, followed by the lead in *Fiddler on the Roof* (1964). Hollywood once again embraced the big ,stooping man with the heavy-lidded eyes when Mel Brooks (*qv*) gave him the lead in *The Producers* (1967), arguably one of the ten best films of this century, in which Mostel was brilliant in his role as a crooked theatrical producer. He followed this with Woody Allen's (*qv*) *The Front* (1976), a film concerning the McCarthyite witch-hunt in which he had suffered. Throughout his life he continued his painting; he died in Philadelphia on September 9th 1977.

MOSTEL,
Zero
(1915-77)
US actor

Marie-Louise was born in Vienna on October 24th 1906 into high bourgeois Jewish society. While in her late teens, her passion for art was developed by Max Beckmann, with whom she studied in Frankfurt. Her *Self Portrait With Comb* (1924) was in the style of El Greco, and the earthy colours and paint application reflect this influence. When Hitler entered Vienna, Marie-Louise and her mother left for the Netherlands. At The Hague in 1939 she held her first exhibition, to critical acclaim. Soon after this mother and daughter left for England. Marie-Louise's brother Karl decided not to follow but to join the resistance. He later died at Auschwitz. In 1950 Marie-Louise painted a picture of her husband in the library of their home in Buckinghamshire talking to the emigré writer, Franz Steiner; it is entitled *Conversation in the Library* and hangs in the National Portrait Gallery, London. After the Second World War she moved to Hampstead, where she was surrounded by fellow Jewish refugees who treated her like an aristocrat.

Her style is unusual, influenced by Kokoschka who once painted her portrait. Marie-Louise painted a series of pictures of her mother, Henriette: smoking a pipe, gardening, cycling and holding her dog. Some of these are in the Tate Gallery, London. She also painted the portrait of the botanist, Miriam Rothschild (*qv* 1992), now in the National Portrait Gallery, London. She rarely exhibited and was quite indifferent as to whether or not she became famous. She was by no means prolific and often did not paint a stroke for many months on end. When she did exhibit, as she did in London in 1960 at Lessore's Beaux-Arts Gallery and in 1985 at the Goethe Institute, she was greeted by critics as a long-lost genius. Her last exhibition was in Vienna at the Belvedere in 1994. She died in London on June 10th 1996.

MOTESICZKY,
Marie-Louise
von
(1906-96)
Austrian/British
painter

MOTTELSON,
Ben
(1926-)
American/
Danish physicist

Ben Mottelson was born in Chicago on July 9th 1926. He obtained his doctorate from Harvard University in 1950 and then accepted a fellowship at the Niels Bohr Institute of Theoretical Physics in Copenhagen. He later became a Danish citizen. During the 1950s he worked with Aage Bohr, whose work led to the discovery that the motion of subatomic particles can change the shape of the nucleus. This was in the face of the previously held belief that all nuclei are constantly spherical. In 1975 Mottelson and Bohr were jointly awarded the Nobel Prize for Physics.

MULLER,
Hermann
(1890-1967)
US geneticist

Muller was born in New York on December 21st 1890. He was educated at Columbia University and while there became interested in the subject of genetics. In 1912 he began studying zoology. Following his classic paper in 1916 on the mechanics of crossing over genes, which established the principle of the linear linkage of genes in heredity, he obtained a PhD. In 1920 Muller became a professor at the University of Texas in Austin, where he stayed for twelve years. This was the most satisfying professional period of his life, as he studied and researched all possible biological mutations and established that these mutations were the result of chemical changes and that those changes could be artificially induced. Muller's work provided the foundation for future discoveries in molecular biology.

In 1931 he was elected to the US National Academy of Sciences. In 1932, however, as a result of personal problems, Muller had a nervous breakdown. As part of a rehabilitation programme he spent a year at the Kaiser Wilhelm Institute in Berlin. A year later he realized his mistake and left for Moscow, where he continued his genetic research with N. I. Vavilov. At this time the Russian biologist, T. Lysenko, who was to cause much scientific unrest, was also at work; Muller fought Lysenko's false doctrines but Lysenko was politically powerful, and in 1937 Muller left to return to the US. He then spent two years at Edinburgh University (1938-40), and following the Second World War became professor of zoology at Indiana University in Bloomington, where he stayed until his death. In 1946 he was awarded the Nobel Prize for Physiology and the resulting publicity allowed him to promote his warning concerning the dangers from radiation, for both present and future generations. He died in Indianapolis on April 5th 1967, content that Lysenko's theories had been demolished.

MUNI,
Paul
(1895-1967)
US actor

He was born Muni Weisenfreund on September 22nd 1895 in Lemberg, Austria. When he was seven, he and his family emigrated to the US and Chicago. At twelve he was an actor in the Yiddish theatre. As soon as it was legally possible he gave up school for the theatre and toured the Yiddish theatres of the US, eventually gravitating to the English-speaking theatre and Broadway. His role as an ex-convict in *Four Walls* brought him to the attention of Hollywood. Two unsuccessful films later, he was back in the theatre. Then in 1932 he received the script of *Scarface* and made the long haul back to Hollywood. The film was a great success and Paul Muni was an overnight star. He returned to Broadway and the play *Counsellor at Law* by Elmer Rice (*qv*) before signing a long-term contract with Warner Brothers. His first film for Warners was *I Am a Fugitive From a Chain Gang*: it won two

Academy Awards. He went on to star in many feature films, including *The Story Of Louis Pasteur* (1936) for which he received his only Oscar, and *The Life of Emile Zola* and *The Good Earth* (both 1937); Louise Rainer (*qv*) received the Oscar for Best Actress in the latter. He made several costume dramas, including *Song to Remember* in 1945, about Chopin and his love for George Sand. His final film, *The Last Angry Man* in 1959, earned him an Oscar nomination for Best Actor. Failing eyesight forced him to retire and he died in California on August 26th 1967.

He was born **Arthur Murray Teichman** on April 4th 1895 in New York City, where his parents owned a bakery. Educated at the Morris High School in the Bronx and the Georgia School of Technology, he would later explain how he became a dance teacher. 'I went to a dance at the Settlement House and asked a girl to dance. I didn't know how but figured it couldn't be that difficult. After a few steps she stopped, looked at me and said, "you dance like a truck driver driving".' That set Arthur learning how, and he later opened his dance studio to show others how. His business grew in line with the era's great bands and he soon had branches all over the world. Indeed, in 1952 he sold out for five million dollars and stayed on as president. He then went into the 'dance by mail order' business and franchised the Arthur Murray Dance Studio. He also had his own television show, the *Arthur Murray Dance Party*, which ran from 1950 to 1960. He wrote several books on dancing, including *How to Become a Good Dancer* and *Let's Dance*. Murray never forgot the poverty of his immigrant Jewish parents. He retired to Hawaii in 1964 and there ran an investment fund for the old friends and relations he had known in his impoverished days, making sure that they too were financially secure. He died from pneumonia at the age of 95 in Hawaii on March 3rd 1991. There is little doubt that dancing made Arthur Murray rich, famous and healthy. His advertising slogan was 'Arthur Murray taught me dancing in a hurry'. It became a popular song.

MURRAY, Arthur (1895-1991) US dance teacher

Michael Myers was born on September 7th 1873 in Motueka, New Zealand. He studied law at Wellington College and graduated from Canterbury University College. By 1900 he was a partner in a Wellington law firm and appeared for the Crown in a number of criminal and civil cases. In 1922 he was appointed a King's Counsel and knighted. He went into practice on his own and had a distinguished career at the Bar until 1929, when he was appointed Chief Justice of New Zealand. A man of vision and integrity, in 1936 he became the first New Zealander to sit on the judicial committee of the Privy Council. In 1946 he represented New Zealand on the United Nations Committee of Jurists and on several occasions acted as Deputy Governor-General. Myers had a strong sense of dignity and sense of occasion, never better illustrated than when he appeared on state occasions in court dress that included a velvet suit with white lace and ruffles together with knee breeches, buckled shoes and dress sword. He died on April 8th 1950.

MYERS, Sir Michael (1873-1950) New Zealand lawyer

Commemorative
Stamps

Jacob Kreiser
Issued by USSR

Otto Loewi
Issued by Austria

Bela Kun
Issued by Hungary

Karl Landsteiner
Issued by Austria

Lev Landau
Issued by St. Vincent and the
Grenadines

Rita Levi-Montalcini
Issued by Sierra Leone

Walter Lippmann
Issued by USA

Gyorgy Lukacs
Issued by Hungary

Rosa Luxemburg
Issued by USSR

N

Siegfried Nadel was born in Vienna on April 24th 1903. He went to Britain and decided upon a degree course at the London School of Economics. Here he met two fellow students taking courses in anthropology and decided to follow suit. His first expedition was to the Nupe area of northern Nigeria (1934-36). He wrote about his journey in *A Black Byzantine* (1942). He examined structures that he found to be constant among ten tribal groups, thereby making an important contribution to what was known of this area. He became a Reader in Anthropology at Durham University (1948-50) and then professor of anthropology at the University of Canberra (1950-56). Further writings were theoretical rather than ethnographical. In 1951 he published *The Foundations of Social Anthropology*, in which he claimed that the main purpose of anthropology is not only to describe but to explain behaviour, and that sociological facts emerge from psychological facts. In his *Theory of Social Structure*, published two years after his death, Nadel examines social roles and argues that they are crucial when analysing the general social structure. This book is regarded as one of the century's most important theoretical works in social science. Passionate about music, Nadel wrote the biography of the Italian composer Ferruccio Busoni and toured with his own opera company. He died on January 14th 1956 in Canberra, Australia.

NADEL, Siegfried (1903-56) Austrian/ Australian anthropologist

Elie Nadelman was born on February 20th 1882 in Warsaw. After studying at Warsaw Art Academy he left for Paris. His drawings and sculptures made while in France show an influence by Rodin as well as a simple form close to cubism. In 1905 he began working on geometric lines and published the results in *Toward a Sculptured Unity* (1914). He held his first one-man show in 1909 in Paris, to sensational reviews. Following his 1915 exhibition, he moved to the US and began making his now famous humorous manikins, such as *Man In the Open Air* (now in the Museum of Modern Art, New York) and *Tango* (1919, in the Whitney Museum of American Art, New York). Gradually he developed a more commercial style and towards the end of his life worked on small pieces of sculptures more suited to modern lifestyles. He died in New York on December 28th 1946.

NADELMAN, Elie (1882-1946) US sculptor

Ernest Nagel was born in Bohemia, part of the Austro-Hungarian empire, on November 16th 1882. Ten years later he was attending a local school in New York before going on to complete his education at Columbia University. Initially an exponent of logical realism, he reviewed his position and shifted to a philosophy of empirical

NAGEL, Ernest (1901-85) US philosopher

and theoretical philosophy of science, as expressed in *A Introduction to Logic and Scientific Method* (1934, with M.Cohen). In *The Structure of Science* (1961) he analyses the nature of the logic of scientific engineering. He taught philosophy at Columbia University from 1931 to 1970 - a record length of tenure. Nagel came to be recognized as one of the century's greatest philosophers of science. He died in New York on September 20th 1985.

NAMIER,
Sir Lewis
(1888-1960)
British historian

He was born Ludwick Bernstein Niemirowski on June 27th 1888 in Wolaokrzejska, Poland, and died Sir Lewis Namier in London. At the age of 18 he was at Balliol College, Oxford, becoming naturalized to serve in the British army during the First World War. A long and distinguished career in diplomacy followed, before a switch to a career in journalism. He spent much time on historical research and the result appeared in 1929. *The Structure of Politics at the Accession of George III* was a major work that caused a stir among historical academics. In 1931 he became professor of modern history at Manchester University, where he remained until 1952. His great reputation resulted in a Namier School of History being set up to examine and analyse the motivation of individuals in regard to their work in politics. He wrote much on historical themes, became a Fellow of Balliol College in 1948 and was knighted in 1952. His approach to history, while attracting many, also aroused opposition, particularly among historians who argued that he ignored certain historical elements while concentrating with the mechanics of politics. Whatever the merits of these positions, Namier is considered one of Britain's principal historians and a leading biographer. He died in London on August 19th 1960.

NATHANS,
Daniel
(1928-)
US
microbiologist

Daniel Nathans was born in Wilmington, Delaware, on October 30th 1928. He was educated at the University of Delaware and Washington University, St Louis, from where he gained a medical degree in 1954. His subsequent research work ran in tandem with his work as professor of microbiology at John Hopkins University, Baltimore (1962-72). Nathans used the restriction enzyme isolated from the bacterium *Haemophilias influenzae* by H. Smith and investigated the structure of the DNA of the Simian virus 40, the simplest virus known to produce cancerous tumours. Nathan's achievement, the creation of a genetic map of a virus, prepared the ground for the first application of the new enzymes that resulted in identifying the molecular basis of cancer. In 1978 Smith and Nathans, together with Werner Arber of Switzerland, shared the Nobel Prize for Physiology. Nathans is now one of the leading microbiologists in the world.

NEESKENS,
Johan
(1951-)
Dutch footballer

Johan Neeskens was born into a Jewish family living in Amsterdam on September 15th 1951. He would later make football history by being the first ever player to take a penalty in a World Cup final. Following school, Johan decided on a career as a professional footballer. He later became a key player for Ajax when that team won three successive European Cups in 1971-3. In 1974 came the moment when, playing in the World Cup in Munich, the Netherlands were awarded a penalty against their opponents, Germany. It was a heart-stopping moment for fans; but

Neeskens, radiating a calm he probably didn't feel, coolly scored from the spot. The game did not, though, have a fairy-tale ending as Germany went on to win 2-1. In 1975 Neeskens left Ajax for Barcelona, where he joined his long-time Ajax team-mate, Johan Cruyff. A Dutch international for many years, Neesken's fighting spirit, great strength and superb skills enabled him to score seventeen goals for his country. In 1979 he went to the US to play for the New York Cosmos. When time dictated his playing career was over he went into football management.

The English art critic, John Berger, said of him: 'Neizvestny is principally the first visual artist of genius to have emerged in the Soviet Union since the Twenties.' This was during the time of Khrushchev. His sculptures of the human body are his most outstanding works. He cast his bronzes himself on his own small furnace to get the best possible results - and also because state foundries became off limits to him, following a public row he had with Khrushchev concerning the validity of advanced art being held at a Moscow exhibition. Neizvestny's work, whether drawings or sculptures, is often described as 'wilfully abstract'. When Khrushchev was deposed, however, the two men became firm friends; so much so that Khrushchev requested his friend sculpt a headstone for his eventual grave. The sculptor agreed and the headstone over the former Russian leader's grave at the Novodevichi Cemetery in Moscow is Neizvestny's work. He has held very successful exhibitions in many countries including America; where he finally went to live and work.

NEIZVESTNY, Ernst (1926-) Russian sculptor

Born in New York on March 1st 1920 to middle-class Jewish parents, he was educated at Fieldston School, New York, and Harvard University, from where he obtained a BA in 1941. He joined the Canadian Royal Air Force and between 1942 and 1944 flew on North Atlantic missions. In 1944 he switched to the US Army Air Force to became operational in Europe. His post-war poetry reflects these years; some lines from his first book, *The Image and the Law*, read: 'They say the war is over. But water still Comes bloody from the taps.' He led a low-key life of teaching, some writing and much walking, and rejected the spotlight, yet was to become America's poet laureate in 1988. His life was only really disturbed when his sister, the famous photographer Diane Arbus (*qv*), committed suicide in 1971. No reader of his poetry would find any detail of his personal life in his writings. His poems are fictions; he takes the world as it is and tries to make some sense of it. He wrote much, and his *Collected Poems* won the Pulitzer Prize and the National Book Award of 1978. In 1987 he was awarded the National Medal of Arts. He died on July 5th 1991 in St Louis, Missouri. His non-fiction prose contained some of the most worthwhile comments on poetry ever written.

NEMEROV, Howard (1920-91) US poet

Von Neumann was born on December 28th 1903 in Budapest and while only a child showed extraordinary mathematical ability. He graduated from the Lutheran High School in Budapest and in 1927 received his PhD from Budapest University. In 1930, following a stint as associate professor at the universities of Berlin and Hamburg, he took up a visiting professorship at Princeton University in the US, becoming a full professor in 1933. Von Neumann's contribution to the advancement of mathematics is considerable. His greatest achievement in quantum theory was the foundation of the measurement theory of physical quantities. In this field Von Neumann was responsible for the development of operational research. Equally important was his contribution in the nascent field of computing; his explanation of the fundamentals concerning basic computer principles was instrumental in the development of MANIAC (Mathematical Analyser Numerical Integrator and Computer). He produced substantial writings on his subject and his *Collected Works* were published posthumously, in London and Paris, in six volumes between 1961 and 1963. He died on February 8th 1957.

Born in Vienna on April 8th 1891, **Richard Neutra** was to become one of the foremost architects in the United States. He was educated at the Technical Academy in Vienna and Zurich University. One of his earliest projects after qualifying as an architect was a city development in Haifa, Palestine, in 1923. The following year he joined the firm of Frank Lloyd Wright in Spring Green, Wisconsin, and remained in the US. An early design was the famous Lovell House in Los Angeles (1927-29). This was a unique project with expanses of glass and cable suspended balconies influenced by Corbusier. Neutra continued designing houses in the International style up to the Second World War, and was responsible for introducing this theme into the US. Following the war Neutra created his most notable works, including the Kaufmann Desert House in Palm Springs, California, in 1946-47. This was the forerunner of other fine establishments in the now famous International style. A feature of his work was the manner in which patios and terraces were integrated with the interior in a style designed to harmonize the living environment with nature. During the 1950s and 1960s Neutra's firm in New York and Los Angeles built offices, housing projects and colleges. His writings include *Survival Through Design* (1954), *Life and Human Habitat* (1956) and his autobiography, *Life and Shape* (1962). He died on April 16th 1970 in Wuppertal, Germany, while on holiday.

Louise Nevelson was born Louise Berliawsky in Kiev, Russia. She and her family moved to the US and Rockland when Louise was five years old. She pursued the usual life of a Jewish daughter and dutifully married Charles Nevelson, a businessman, when she was 21. She had a child and appeared to be settled; then, aged 29, she left her husband and child and took off for New York, where she studied sculpture at the Art Students' League under Kenneth Miller. In 1931 she moved to Munich, Germany, to study with Hans Hofmann. Louise Nevelson held her first exhibition in New York in 1941, showing models and sculptures in a variety of materials that included terracotta and plaster. She travelled much in Central

America and her work matured. She sold little, and consequently was often on the poverty line. Recognition and rewards came slowly from the 1950s onwards, and she began to receive critical acclaim. Her abstract forms won favour and she began to sell. Her small pieces of abstract work, sometimes single coloured or black, sometimes in white and gold, were acquired by galleries, museums and the public. She specialized in wall sculptures and from 1960 onwards became recognized as one of the foremost sculptors of the second half of the 20th century with such works as *Royal Tide V* (1960). During the 1970s and 1980s Nevelson worked in an ever-widening range of types of materials, including lucite, plexiglass and aluminium. She died in New York on April 17th 1988.

Barnett Newman, born in New York City on January 29th 1905, is probably the best-known artist of the New York School. However, although long associated with the abstract expressionists, his work was more austere than theirs and he gradually he found his own style.

NEWMAN, Barnett (1905-70) US painter

In the 1940s and 1950s he produced what he termed mystical abstraction, as notably exemplified by his *Onement 1* (1948), a solid colour canvas in dark red with a rough-edged strip in light red running down the middle. This was a recurring theme in his work. He was able to create a tension on the canvas that demanded attention. His series of fourteen black and white paintings entitled *Stations of the Cross* (1958-66) caused a stir as Newman eliminated form and an illusion of depth. His work has had a strong and continuing influence on abstract expressionist painters. He was also a pioneer of the very large format in which the picture dominates and occupies the whole visual field of the viewer; a magical experience. Newman created several pieces of sculpture, including the much admired *Broken Obelisk* (1963-67, Rothko Chapel, Houston, Texas). He died in New York on July 4th 1970.

Paul Newman was born into a non-religious family on January 26th 1925 in Cleveland, Ohio, where his Jewish father had a sports goods store. His education was interrupted by the Second World War, during which he served in the US Navy. In 1949 he graduated from Kenyon College, Ohio, and began acting in summer stock productions in Wisconsin and Illinois. In 1953 he went to New York and took classes at the Actors' Studio. During the run of *Picnic*, in which he made his Broadway debut, he came to the attention of Warner Brothers. In Hollywood he started at the top with the leading role in *The Silver Chalice* (1954) - a piece of miscasting so striking as to attract attention. His role as Rocky Graziano in *Somebody Up There Likes Me* (1957) shot him to stardom and he has remained there ever since. In 1958 he starred in *Cat on a Hot Tin Roof*, for which he received the first of many Academy Award nominations for Best Actor. He followed it with *Long Hot Summer* (1958), *Hustler* (1961), *Hud* (1963), *Hombre* (1967), *Cool Hand Luke* (also 1967), *Butch Cassidy and the Sundance Kid* (1969), *The Sting* (1973), *Absence of Malice* (1981) and *The Verdict* (1982). In 1986 he received his first Oscar as Best Actor in *Colour of Money*. In the 1960s he started directing: *Rachel, Rachel* (1968) received excellent reviews and four Oscar nominations. Away from

NEWMAN, Paul (1925-) US actor

acting, Newman excels in motor racing and produces a line in salad dressings that he sells world-wide, donating the profits to charity.

NEWTON-JOHN, Olivia (1948-) British actress/ singer

Olivia Newton-John was born on September 26th in Cambridge, England. Her grandfather had brought her mother to Cambridge to escape Jewish persecution in Germany following the election of Hitler in 1933; he was Max Born (*qv*), the German-Jewish physicist who was awarded the Nobel Prize for Physics in 1954. In 1960, when Olivia was twelve, her parents moved to Australia. There, in 1966, she won a television talent contest. The prize was a holiday to London. She stayed on, and became part of Tomorrow, a group set up to fill the vacuum left by the disbanded Monkees. When Tomorrow petered out she worked with Cliff Richards and the Shadows. She recorded a number of songs, including 'Take Me Home Country Roads', written by John Denver.

In 1973 her 'Let Me Be There' led to a television appearance in the US on the *Dean Martin Show* and a Grammy for Best Female Country Vocal. She went on to become one of the most popular artists singing country music. Greater fame came when she co-starred with John Travolta in the film version of the musical *Grease* (1978). In her career so far, she has achieved five Number One hits: 'I Honestly Love You' (October 1974 for two weeks), 'Have You Never Been Mellow?' (March 1975, one week), 'You're The One That I Want' (with John Travolta, June 1978, 1 week), 'Magic' (August 1980, four weeks) and 'Physical' (November 1981, 10 weeks). For her 1986 albums, *Soul Kiss*, Olivia changed her style from its original wholesome perkiness to a more sophisticated, even brash, image. In 1990 she released the album *Warm and Tender*, a collection of songs and rhymes for children. A star entertainer who is much sought after, she was awarded the OBE and continues to work despite her fight with cancer. Her fight has been a great example and comfort to others suffering from the same disease.

NICHOLS, Mike (1931-) US actor/ director

Mike Nichols was born Michael Igor Peschkowsky in Berlin on November 6th 1931. Educated at the University of Chicago, he rose to fame in the late 1950s as the partner of Elaine May. The pair were both Jewish, and their popular act, which ran from 1957 to 1961, was a satirical commentary on relationships between men and women. Mike Nichols then turned to directing on the Broadway stage and was an immediate success with the Neil Simon comedies *Barefoot in the Park* (1963) and *The Odd Couple* !965). He then turned to directing films. His first, *Who's Afraid of Virginia Woolf?* (1966), won him an Oscar for Best Director and Elizabeth Taylor, from whom he produced what is arguably the best performance she ever gave, an Oscar for Best Actress. The following year Nichols directed *The Graduate* and collected another Oscar. His style is often referred to as flashy and tends to concentrate on individual performances. Other films of note include *Catch-22* (1970), *Carnal Knowledge* (1971), *Silkwood* (1983, which he also produced) and *Heartburn* (1986). With *Biloxi Blues* (1988) Nichols again directed a Neil Simon comedy. It was the same year he directed the popular *Working Girl* and earned an Oscar nomination. Nichols started the 1990s with the excellent *Postcards*

From the Edge (1990). Although now famed as a film director, he has not neglected the theatre, and in 1984 he received a coveted Tony Award for his direction of Tom Stoppard's play *The Real Thing*. In 1997 he directed the controversial film, *Primary Colours*.

NIEDERLAND,
William
(1904-93)
German/
American
psychoanalyst

Born on August 29th 1904 in Schippenbeil, Germany, the son of a Polish rabbi, **William** was educated at the universities of Wurzburg and Genoa and obtained medical degrees from both. He was appointed the public health officer for Düsseldorf but later transferred to work in mental health. Driven out of Germany following the election of Hitler as German Chancellor, Niederland spent several years trying to find a new home. After being denied entry to the US and expelled from Switzerland, he set up a private medical clinic in Milan and there specialized in psychoanalysis. When Italy entered the Second World War on Hitler's side, Niederland was once again the wandering Jew. He tried to emigrate to Britain but the British imprisoned him as an enemy alien. After a short while they suggested a deal: he would be released if he agreed to become a ship's doctor on the British merchantman, SS *Dardanus*. Niederland agreed and spent the next two years travelling the world, including circumnavigating the globe twice. He would later use the experience and knowledge thus gained, together with his existing scholarship, to develop and pioneer the field of psychogeography; the study of how issues and experiences that result from growing up in a human body are later played out in the wider social and natural worlds that become the stages for these inner dramas. Victims of the Holocaust are particularly fertile subjects for such an approach.

While working as a ship's doctor he took unofficial leave of absence when the boat docked in the Philippines. He was teaching and missed the departure time of SS *Dardanus*. The boat left without him and was torpedoed by a Japanese submarine laying off the Philippine coast. There were no survivors. He described this incident, together with interviews with 2,000 survivors of concentration camps, accidents and natural disasters, when he produced his 'survivor syndrome' theory. Symptoms and problems associated with the syndrome included insomnia, inability to work, nightmares and psychosomatic illnesses. The syndrome was mentioned in professional journals and the further symptom of survivor's guilt feelings reported. Niederlander explained that severe depressions could result. He was accepted into the US in 1940 and qualified all over again, this time at the New York Psychoanalysis Institute. While teaching at the University of Tampa in the 1940s, Niederland set up an award-winning sample programme on instructing people in better group relations. He used this project to combat the Ku Klux Klan influence that was rife in the state. He was clinical professor of psychiatry at SUNY Medical Centre in Brooklyn, New York, from 1978 to 1993. He died in Englewood, New Jersey, on August 6th 1993.

NIMOY,
Leonard
(1931-)
US actor

Leonard Nimoy was born on Boston, Massachusetts, on March 26th 1931. He was educated at Boston College and then moved to California, where he learnt his craft at the Pasadena Playhouse. He appeared in several plays and had minor roles in television and low-budget films. Following army service (1954-56) he continued his studies. For a time, later on, he became a teacher and opened a studio based on the methods of Stanislavski. He continued acting for both stage and screen, and in 1966 his big break came when he was cast as 'Mr Spock' a humanoid alien and first officer of the Starship *Enterprise*, in a television science-fiction series called *Star Trek* (1966-69). Between 1969 and 1971 he starred in the television series *Mission Impossible* . He then spent time touring the US as Tevye in the musical *Fiddler on the Roof*, and in 1973 was on Broadway in *Full Circle*. Although Nimoy has starred in many theatrical plays, including works by Shakespeare, and although he writes and directs, it is his continuing role as Mr Spock in *Star Trek* that provides him with international fame. His first volume of biography was called *I am Not Spock*; the second volume, published in 1995, is called *I Am Spock* . His captain on the *Enterprise*, William Shatner (*qv*), is just four days older. It might interest the many millions of *Star Trek* fans to know that Mr Spock's characteristic hand gesture is in reality a Jewish sign of blessing.

NIREMBERG,
Marshall
(1927-)
US biochemist

Marshall Niremberg was born on April 10th 1927 in New York. He received his PhD from the University of Michigan in 1957 and joined the staff of the National Institute of Health in Bethesda. His research programme has been in the field of genetics and how genetic instructions in the cell nucleus control the composition of proteins. For his part in deciphering the genetic code, Niremberg shared the Nobel Prize for Physiology in 1968.

NOETHER,
Emmy
(1882-1935)
German
mathematician

Born to Jewish parents in Erlangen, Germany, on March 23rd 1882, **Emmy Noether** was to become one of the top mathematicians of modern times. She obtained her PhD from Erlangen University in 1907 with a thesis on algebraic invariants. In 1915 she was at the University of Göttigen and was asked by the eminent mathematicians Hilbert and Klein to stay there to work and teach. At that time, however, women were not allowed to hold academic posts, and as a result she did not take up the appointment until 1919. Even then she was not fully accepted and with the rise of Hitler and increasing anti-Semitism she emigrated to the US in 1933. An expert on non-communicative algebras, i.e. algebras in which the order by which numbers are multiplied affects the answer, she was readily accepted as professor of mathematics at Bryn Mawr College as well as lecturing on her subject at the Institute for Advanced Study at Princeton, New Jersey. Her later studies involved 'Noetherian Rings', an important facet of her work that continues to be invaluable to students of mathematics. She died at Bryn Mawr on April 14th 1935.

O

Ochs was born on March 12th 1858 in Cincinnati, the son of an immigrant rabbi. By the turn of the century he was the publisher and owner of the *New York Times*, which he had bought to save it from bankruptcy. Previously the owner of the *Chattanooga Times*, he built up *The New York Times* to become one of the world's leading newspapers, respected and authoritative. The newspaper's price was reduced to 1 cent and the circulation tripled, making it an essential outlet for the advertising companies. Ochs did not allow fraudulent advertising or let advertisers dictate editorial policy. He introduced radical printing and lay-out methods, including a review section to cover the theatre, opera and books. In 1913 Ochs was the first to introduce a financial section into his newspaper, calling it *The New York Times Index*. He also published *The Philadelphia Times*, with equal success. At the time of his death the daily circulation of *The New York Times* stood at 466,000. When he acquired the paper 35 years earlier it stood at 9,000. His banner headline became world-famous: 'All the News That's Fit to Print' . He died in Chattanooga, Tennessee on April 8th 1935.

OCHS, Adolph (1858-1935) US publisher

Phil Ochs was born in El Paso, Texas, in the same year as Bob Dylan (*qv*) and had the misfortune to live in Dylan's shadow. An international writer and performer, Ochs became one his generation's leading protest singers and wrote, among other pieces, 'I Ain't Marching Anymore', which became the anti-Vietnam War theme song. He also wrote 'There But For Fortune', which Joan Baez took to the charts. Ochs and Dylan never got on: Ochs thought of himself as a purist while Dylan went commercial. In one episode, when the two were travelling together in a taxi to a musical awards reception, they had such a row that Dylan ordered the taxi to stop and threw Ochs out. The best albums Ochs produced were probablys *Pleasures of the Harbour* and *Rehearsal for Retirement*. A mugging while on a visit to Africa resulted in injuries to his vocal cords; he became depressed and the depression grew as his writing block increased. His wrote his autobiography, *Chords of Fame*, in which he states: 'God help the troubadour who tries to be a star.' Phil Ochs hanged himself in 1976.

OCHS, Phil (1941-76) US composer/ singer

Odets was born on July 18th 1906 in Philadelphia into a poor, working-class Jewish family. Two years after he was born the family moved to the Bronx, New York, and his father found employment. Throughout his schooldays Odets was interested in acting, and in 1925 he formed a small group to air the radio plays he had

ODETS, Clifford (1906-63) US writer

written. For several years Odets studied to be an actor and joined the recently formed Group Theatre. He switched from acting to writing and in 1935 achieved his first great success with *Waiting For Lefty*, a play about a trade unionist denied his rights to strike by employers who used scab labour and bribed the police. This was followed by *Golden Boy*, a play about an Italian boy who rises from the slums by becoming a prize fighter. Odets, heavily influenced by the poverty he grew up with, had a natural leaning towards socialism that is often reflected in his writing. As a result, during the 1930s he was the leading dramatist of America's protest movement. From the later years of that decade through the 1940s and 1950s he was wrote and directed films in Hollywood. These included *The General Died at Dawn* (1936), which was directed by Lewis Milestone (*qv*) and nominated for three Oscars, and *None But The Lonely Heart* (1943), a box-office hit that gave Ethel Barrymore her only Academy Award. Odets wrote *The Sweet Smell of Success* in 1957; it was a major success and provided Burt Lancaster with one of his best parts.

Clifford Odets had a most stressful time during the McCarthy witch-hunt. Pressured and threatened, he finally agreed to testify but only mentioned names he knew the committee already had. His final play was *The Flowering Peach*, a pastiche of the Noah and the Ark fable portrayed in the manner of New York Jews, staged in 1954. Odets was both a great writer and a compassionate man who cared for those who were socially oppressed. He died in Hollywood on August 14th 1963.

OISTRAKH, David (1900-74) Russian violinist

He was born on September 30th 1900 in Odessa, Russia, into a musical family: his father was the choirmaster of the local operatic society, his mother was a singer. From the age of five David studied the violin. In 1926 he graduated from the Odessa Conservatory and in 1933 he gave his first Moscow concert. From 1934 he taught at the Moscow Conservatory, breaking off from time to time to tour the USSR, giving recitals and solo performances. During the Second World War Oistrakh would play to the troops while they rested between battles; and he played to audiences in battle-torn Leningrad during the time of the siege. In 1954 David Oistrakh was named People's Artist of the Soviet Union and in 1960 received the Lenin Prize. In 1953 he began playing overseas, first in Paris, then London and finally New York. He became recognized as one of the all-time great violin virtuosos and praised for his exceptional tone playing. David Oistrakh was one of the few Soviet greats who, having tested the fruits of Western rewards, never contemplated leaving his native country. He once told Yehudi Menhuin (*qv*), 'Russia is responsible for everything I have accomplished. It would be disloyal of me to live elsewhere.' He died on October 24th 1974 in Amsterdam, during an extensive tour.

OLIVETTI, Adriano (1901-60) Italian industrialist

Adriano Olivetti was born on April 17th 1901 in Ivrea, Italy. Following his education at Turin University, where he received a degree in industrial chemistry, his father, Camillo, who was Jewish and in 1980 had founded the typewriter company that bears his name, sent Adriano to America in order to study modern manufacturing methods and management techniques. When the son returned the company underwent radical changes, resulting in the marketing of a new typewriter, the M-

40, which became a world-wide best-seller. Adriano became president of the company in 1938 when his father retired, and so began the build-up to what would eventually become the largest manufacturer of typewriters and business machines in Europe.

The Olivettis made no secret of their anti-fascist views but were too important for Mussolini to arrest. Both were active in the Ponte Teresa affair, a short-lived attempt to topple Mussolini. During the Second World War Adriano was arrested for conspiring to end the war but released when Germany took over Italy. Wanted by the Gestapo, he went into hiding. When his father, hiding with peasants, died, he was heartbroken that he was unable to attend his funeral and grateful to the hundreds of non-Jewish Olivetti employees who risked their lives as they stood in the small rain-swept Jewish cemetery to pay their last respects to a man who had done much for them. Adriano escaped to Switzerland until the war was over. In his absence, his factory was the centre for the resistance movement, 24 members of which were killed by the Germans. After the war Adriano rebuilt his business, which soon became a world leader. He put his own money into the community, building centres that aided local populations. He was elected mayor of his home town, Ivrea, in 1956 and in 1958 formed his Community Movement Party, that put him into Parliament. He died on February 27th 1960, while travelling on the Milan to Lausanne express train. At that time his company was employing 25,000 people world wide.

OPHULS, Max (1902-57) German film-maker

Max Ophuls (or sometimes Opuls) was born Maximillian Oppenheimer in Saarbrücken, Germany, on May 6th 1902. For much of his life he was dealing with experiences resulting from being Jewish in a antisemitic world. His is a story of having to overcome poverty, eviction from two homelands, unemployment and under-appreciation of his work. However, he won through eventually to become known as a director whose masterly camera techniques gave his films a poetic flow. He started in the 1920s as an actor, but in 1932 directed his first film, *The Love Affair*, in Austria. It was well received across Europe, and Ophuls then went to live in Paris; here and in Italy and the Netherlands he made ten feature films, his best-known being *La Signora de Tutti* (1934). Following the German invasion of France in 1940, Ophuls and his family fled to Switzerland; however, the Swiss changed their minds and decided to return them all to France. They stamped each passport with a J and the Ophuls anxiously awaited the arrival of the Gestapo. Fortunately, before the Germans arrived, American interests changed the Swiss minds yet again, and the Ophuls family was dispatched to the US. Here Max was largely unemployed until 1946, when he made *Vendetta*, only for the film not to be released because of a studio row with the producer Preston Sturges.

Ophuls went on to direct four more films in Hollywood. *The Exile* (1947) is an historical film with an unusual directorial style. *Letter From an Unknown Woman* (1948) won critical acclaim. *Caught* (1949) caused a stir at the time because it was assumed the villain of the piece was a thinly disguised Howard Hughes. Ophul's direction of *The Reckless Moment* (1949) was described as 'electric'. Uneasy living in the US, he returned to France and in 1950 made *La Ronde*. A brilliant film, often described as one of the top ten of the century, it put Max Ophuls into the top rung of film-makers. *La Plaisir* (1952) won him yet more plaudits. His final film, considered by some to be his best, was *Lola Montes* in 1955. He died on March 26th 1957 in Hamburg, while negotiating a film production contract.

OPLER,
Marvin
(1914-)
US
anthropologist

Opler was born in Buffalo, New York, the younger brother of Morris Opler, who had a great influence in persuading Marvin to follow in his path as an anthropologist. Both brothers achieved excellent results in their research work concerning the American Indians in general and the Apache nation in particular. Marvin became the first anthropologist to link psychology and anthropology, so becoming the first cross-cultured social psychiatrist. As such he was appointed prefacer at the University of Buffalo School of Medicine in 1958. He pioneered research into psychotic disorders among ethnic minorities which resulted in psychiatrists being able to define and explain differences in mental disease. Opler explains his ideas and the result of his researches in his book *Culture and Social Psychiatry* (1967).

OPPENHEIMER,
Robert
(1904-67)
US physicist

Robert Oppenheimer was born on April 22nd 1904 in New York, where his German-Jewish father ran a textile importing business. A brilliant student, who at the age of eleven was exceptionally admitted to membership of the New York Mineralogical Society, in 1977 he wrote his doctoral thesis on the quantum theory and received a PhD from Gottingen University. Here he met, among others, Niels Bohr (*qv*). He also spent some time with Rutherford, of the Cavendish Laboratory, at Cambridge University before returning to the US. Oppenheim continued to work in the field of quantum theory and constantly developed and explored its significance. At the University of California at Berkeley he had the largest number of graduate and postgraduate students working on theoretical physics of any institution in the world.

In 1936, following the Spanish Civil War, Oppenheimer became most interested in left-wing politics. Although a rich man, following the death of his father in 1937, he supported anti-fascist causes everywhere. It was only Stalin's repression of scientists that prevented him from joining the Communist Party. Following the rise of Hitler and scientific talk about a possible race for a nuclear bomb, Oppenheim began to hunt for processes that would result in the separation of uranium 235 and thus pave the way for the ultimate weapon. In August 1942 the US government authorized the pursuance of such a weapon and Robert Oppenheimer was requested to head the operation, which was codenamed the Manhattan Project. For the development of the project he selected an area of New Mexico called Los Alamos. Oppenheimer now showed that besides being a brilliant scientist he was also an excellent organiser. The tall, thin chain-smoker gathered an international team around him and their results not only made history, when the A-Bomb was dropped on Japan in July 1945, but changed the course of the world for ever.

Like many of those who worked on the Manhattan Project, Oppenheimer felt that following the destruction of the heavy water plant in Norway in 1944 and the defeat of Germany in May 1945, it was not necessary for the project to continue. It was on the insistence of top US generals that the bomb was used. Their thinking was that Russia could well be their next problem and the A-Bomb would be their ace. Oppenheimer resigned in 1945, following the surrender of Japan in August. From 1947 to 1952 he was the Chairman of the Atomic Energy Commission. In October 1949 this committee rejected the development of a hydrogen bomb. It an attempt to vilify Oppenheimer, who by now had become a thorn in the side of the American right wing, he was falsely accused of association with foreign Communists. It was claimed that he had opposed the US developing a hydrogen bomb on the orders of Moscow. A special security hearing was held which ruled that Oppenheimer should no longer have access to military secrets. The Federation of American Scientists protested and Oppenheimer became the symbol of the moral scientist, concerned with mankind, being witch-hunted. By way of eventual apology President Johnston awarded Oppenheimer the Enrico Fermi Award worth $50,000, which he promptly gave away to charity. Oppenheimer's philosophies are best summed up in two of his books, *Science and the Common Understanding* (1954) and *The Open Mind* (1955). He was head of the Institution for Advanced Study at Princeton University until his retirement in 1966. He died in Princeton from throat cancer on February 18th 1967.

ORLOFF, Chana (1888-1968) French sculptor

Born in Staro-Konstant, Russia, **Chana** was destined to become the leading woman sculptor in France. As a sixteen-year-old she was living in Palestine where her father worked in the fields of Petah Tikva and Chana made clothes. At 22 she was busy in Paris, studying sculpture and living among the young artists of her time. One such was Modigliani (*qv*), who made a drawing of her entitled *Chana, Daughter of Raphael*. In 1913 three of her wooden sculptures were exhibited at the Salon d'Automme in Paris. In 1916 she married the poet Ary Justman, who died in 1920 during the flu epidemic that swept Europe after the First World War. Chana now had a baby son to care for. This she combined with executing commissions from all over the world, achieving the ultimate when asked to sculpt Picasso and Matisse. She went on to hold exhibitions in New York, Boston and Chicago, as well as in the capitals of most European countries. In 1935 she was awarded the French Legion of Honour. Back in France, her international reputation grew. Her work was realistic and stylized, surprising given that her contemporaries were influenced by cubism.

Following the German takeover of France in 1940, Chana Orloff was concerned that she was on the Vichy hit-list of persons to be handed over to the Germans. She and her son managed to escape to Switzerland, and her concern was vindicated: when the Vichy police and their German masters arrived to arrest her and found her gone they smashed her studio and all her work to pieces. Following the war, Orloff returned to rebuild her studio in Paris and during the following 20 years held many large-scale exhibitions in many places including Israel. It was during such an exhibition held at the Tel Aviv Museum that she collapsed and died.

**ORMANDY,
Eugene
(1899-1985)
US conductor**

Born Jeno Ormandy Blau on November 18th 1899 in Budapest, Hungary, he was introduced to music by his father and taught to play the violin. He went to the Budapest Royal Academy and by the age of seventeen was considered a professor of violin. There followed a tour around Europe giving concerts and recitals. Enticed to the US by the promise of a tour, he arrived to find the promoter had gone bankrupt. Ormandy, now aged 25 and in dire straits, got a job in a cinema with a small orchestra whose sole purpose was to accompany silent films. A week later he stood in when the conductor fell ill, and thereafter decided to exchange the bow for the baton.

Following a period during which he was an assistant to Toscanini, he was offered, and accepted, a contract to be the principal conductor of the Minneapolis Symphony Orchestra, a post he held from 1931 to 1935. A series of important recordings led to his sharing the conductor's baton with Stokowski at the Philadelphia Orchestra for two years. In 1938 he became principal conductor, and was still in place when he retired in 1980. Still a violinist at heart, Ormandy's trademark was to produce a full, fresh string section that became the Philadelphia's hallmark. In 1948 he was the first to conduct a full-length concert on TV. In 1973 the Philadelphia and Ormandy gave the first US concert in China. His fame as a conductor was known throughout the world and his students mourned his death in Philadelphia on March 12th 1985.

**OSIIER,
Ivan
(1888-1965)
Danish fencing
champion**

Ivan Osiier was born in Copenhagen on December 16th 1888. He holds the record of having represented his country at more Olympic Games events than any other athlete. His record covers the period from 1908 to 1948. He missed the 1936 Olympics because they were held in Berlin and in protest, as a Jew, he declined to participate. In all he participated in seven Olympiads, though he only won one medal; the silver for individual epee in the 1948 Games held in London. He was 60 years old. A doctor by profession, Osiier was Danish National Champion 23 times and in all three fencing events, epee, foil and sabre. This record was accomplished over a period of fifteen years. He also won a total of 38 Danish and Scandinavian fencing medals; a record that still stands. Dr Osiier was one of the few to be awarded the coveted Olympia Diploma of Merit. He died in Denmark on September 10th 1965.

**OZ,
Amos
(1939-)
Israeli writer**

Born Amos Klausner in Jerusalem on May 4th 1939 and educated at the Hebrew University in Jerusalem and at Oxford University, he fought in three of his country's wars, 1957, 1967 and 1973. This experience is often featured in his writings. His work reflects a cynical view of Israeli life and examines the Zionist dream. He is often at odds with those who are pragmatic about any failures in Israeli society and he brings an irony into the debate that some of his Israeli readers find disturbing. It is not, therefore, surprising that he is often praised abroad and criticized at home. His more important work includes *Else Where Perhaps* (1961), *The Hall of Evil Counsel* (1976), *In the Land of Israel* (1983), *Black Box* (1988) and *The Third State* (1991). Probably his best-known book is *My Michael* published in 1972. Oz is also widely known for his political essays.

P

Paley, was born in Chicago, Illinois, on September 28th 1901 to Ukrainian immigrant Jews. His father had a thriving cigar store and went on to become a multi-millionaire. Educated at the University of Pennsylvania, William discovered that he shared his name with a famous English cleric, and in order to avoid any possible confusion he added an S to become William S. Paley. He joined his father's business and within a short time was made a vice-president; he stayed in that role until 1928, when he bought into Columbia Broadcasting System (CBS), which was in financial trouble. Paley was set to turn an investment of $400,000 into a fortune of $350 million within a 60 year period. He knew the power of radio advertising from his experience as a cigar maker, and capitalized on this experience, building CBS into the world's second greatest radio and television network, surpassed only by the BBC. During the Second World War Paley, with the honorary rank of colonel, was deputy chief of the Psychological Warfare Division of the Allied Command in Europe. The war over, Paley took command of CBS, introduced long-playing records, made feature films and documentaries and went into publishing. CBS made many television shows that sold around the world, including *I Love Lucy* and *Gunsmoke*. An art enthusiast, Paley was president of the Museum of Modern Art in New York and owned a brilliant collection of French post-impressionist art. He retired in 1983 only to return four years later, at the age of 86, to sort out problems that had arisen while he was away. He died in harness on October 26th 1990 in New York.

PALEY, William (1901-90) US broadcaster

Panofsky was born on March 3rd 1892 in Hanover, Germany. Following his BA from the University of Freiburg, he joined the teaching staff of Hamburg University (1926-33), with a visiting professorship at New York University in 1931. Following Hitler's anti-Jewish crusade, Panofsky left Germany in 1935 to become professor of art history at the Institute for Advanced Study at Princeton, New Jersey. He went on to become an art historian whose writings on the subject were at once critical and erudite. His books are a must for all interested in the long history of art. Among his later works are *Pandora's Box: The Changing Aspects of a Mythical Symbol* (1956), *Renascence in Western Art* (1960) and *Tomb Sculpture* (1964). He died in Princeton on March 14th 1968.

PANOFSKY, Erwin (1892-1968) German/ American art historian

PAPP,
Joe
(1921-91)
US theatre
director

Joe Papp was born Joseph Pairofsky on June 22nd 1921 in Brooklyn, New York; his father was a luggage maker, his mother a seamstress. Papp was to become the greatest theatrical force in America during the second half of the 20th century. After high school he joined the US Navy and served throughout the Second World War; following his discharge in 1946, he used his demob money to buy a course on acting and directing from the Actor's Laboratory in Los Angeles. He had the lifelong notion, following an upbringing in poverty, that the people should have the pleasure of theatre and that theatre should be either free or very affordable. He practised what he said about free speech and in 1958 invoked the Fifth Amendment before the House Committee hearings during the McCarthy era. The result was that he was sacked by CBS TV. Papp fought this decision and a year later was reinstated following an arbitration ruling. Earlier, in 1954, he founded what he grandly called the New York Shakespeare Festival, which began life in the basement of a church. His productions were tagged 'American Shakespeare'. Papp's later open-air productions in New York's Central Park attracted actors of the calibre of Meryl Streep, Kevin Kline and Robert de Niro. They worked for nothing and that is how much the audience paid. It was the free theatre Papp had always imagined; but the standard of the productions was high. It wasn't easy going for Papp. He ran up against more bureaucracy than he ever thought possible; but in the end he got his way. He would never disappoint his public, which constantly grew.

Several of Papp's original productions transferred, when the old Astor library in Lower Manhattan was converted into a seven-theatre complex and renamed the Public Theatre. Here New Yorkers (and others) saw *Hair* and the longest-running show of all, *A Chorus Line*. When in the 1980s the Royal Court Theatre in London (with whose management Papp had a special relationship) was threatened with grant withdrawals by the Thatcher government, because their plays were too often anti-Tory, closure of the Royal Court was in the offing, Papp led the fight to save it. Papp's Public Theatre gave the chance of discovery to many a playwright, including David Mamet (*qv*), Caryl Churchill, David Hare and Steven Berkoff (*qv*). Papp introduced Black Theatre groups and became the first producer to use 'colour blind casting', with black actors playing roles previously reserved for white people.

Papp was a loner; he disliked committees and organizations, and the four years he spent running the Lincoln Center in New York was the most depressing period of his professional life. He received many awards, but the only one he ever valued was the acknowledgement that he never strayed from his original philosophy that the theatre is for the people. He was an eternal optimist whose cry was 'Don't tell me anything is impossible - let's try it first.' He died in his beloved New York on October 31st 1991.

PARISH,
Mitchell
(1900-93)
US lyricist

Mitchell Parish was born in Lithuania on July 10th 1900 and arrived in the US as an infant. He grew up in the Jewish ghetto that was the Lower East Side of Manhattan. He intended to be a doctor, but a friend was so impressed by Parish's ability to write lyrics to instrumental songs that were already successful that he introduced him to a musical publisher. The publisher was also impressed and gave him a job at $12 a week to write speciality lyrics to vaudeville songs. Although he wrote for performers like Al Jolson (*qv*), Eddie Cantor (*qv*) and Sophie Tucker (*qv*), it was 1922 before he knew the taste of success, when he wrote the words to 'Carolina Rolling Stone' for Columbia records. It was his first recording and an instant hit. He rapidly became a genius at setting words to well-known melodies and his work includes such standards as 'Sweet Lorraine', which launched Nat 'King' Cole. 'Star Dust' became a world hit two years after Hoagy Carmichael wrote and played it, and was recorded over 1,300 times after Parish added the words. Perhaps his greatest hit was with the Italian song 'Volare', a best-seller for Dean Martin. Other songs of note include 'One Morning in May' (1933), 'Sophisticated Lady' (1933), 'Stars Fell on Alabama' (1934), 'Stairway to the Stars' (1935), 'Deep Purple' (1939), 'Moonlight Serenade' (1939) and 'Tzena, Tzena, Tzena', the Israeli song that launched Mitch Miller's (*qv*) band career in 1952.

Parish never took lyric writing for granted as a career. From 1935 to 1945 he worked as a court clerk in a Manhattan criminal court. In 1947 he enrolled at New York University and graduated three years later at the age of 50. Nor did he ever subscribe to the notion that writing is a matter of sudden inspiration. In a 1991 interview for the *New York Times* he told Douglas Martin: 'The only time a songwriter gets up in the middle of the night is to go to the bathroom.' The inspiration came from the music. Mitch Parish died in New York on March 31st 1993. His life's work settled once and for all the answer to the question: which comes first, the music or the words?

Born Dorothy Rothschild in West End, New Jersey, on August 22nd 1893, she is probably quoted more often than any other writer, save for Shakespeare. The daughter of a wealthy Jewish father, who left her alone after her Scottish mother died, her education was poor though expensive: a case of the pupil outstretching the school. Her working career started when the magazine *Vanity Fair* took her on as their drama critic, something they came to regret when her piece on actress Billy Burke took her apart. Dorothy was fired. A book reviewer for *The New Yorker* for many years, she started writing on her own account in 1926 with a book of verse that became a best-seller. *Enough Pope* was followed by two more books and all three were later published in one volume as *Deep As a Well* in 1936. In 1929 she won the O. Henry Award for best short story of the year with *Big Blonde*.

By this time she was one of the writers who regularly met at what became known as 'The Round Table', at New York's fashionable Algonquin Hotel. Her witty comments are now part of the legend that grew up around her. She and her second husband Alan Campbell (she kept her first husband's name) became a Hollywood writing team that resulted in fifteen feature films. Active in left-wing politics following the Spanish Civil War, which she covered as a journalist, she was later to be a victim of the McCarthy witch-hunt by innuendo, the committee being too scared to call her to testify and put itself on the receiving end of her biting comments. Her attitude bothered the FBI, whose file on her ran to 1,000 pages. She continued to live off book reviews and royalties, but her heavy drinking caused the

PARKER,
Dorothy
(1893-1967)
US writer

work to begin to dry up. She became depressed as her friends died off one by one, and she died alone in New York on June 7th 1967.

Dorothy Parker's witticisms live on. 'Men seldom make passes at girls who wear glasses' brought her the enduring hatred of opticians. Of Katherine Hepburn, she wrote: 'She ran the whole gamut of emotions from A to B.' Hepburn, not known for her humour, bore a lasting grudge for this. Once, at a cocktail party, Parker confessed: 'One more drink and I'll be under the host.' When she heard that President Coolidge had died, she asked, 'How can they tell?' and when her friend had a baby Parker sent her a telegram reading 'Congratulations. We all knew you had it in you.' Parker was a tough journalist who considered herself the equal of any man and was not fazed by the famous. In her long-running hostile relationship with Hemingway, she gave far better than she got. This, together with an unfeminine appearance, led Noel Coward to say to her in public one evening: 'You almost look like a man.' Parker's riposte? 'So do you, Noel.' She was described by Alexander Woollcot as 'a blend of Little Nell and Lady Macbeth'.

PASCIN,
Jules
(1885-1930)
French painter

Although he was born Julius Pincas in Vidin, Bulgaria, on March 31st 1885 and later became a US citizen by naturalization, Pascin preferred to think of himself as French. His parents were Sephardic Jews from Italy and Serbia. By 1901 he was working for his father in his small trading business, but not for long; his father was spending too much money and time in the city's brothels. What his father didn't know, or if he knew didn't appreciate, was that his son was painting and sketching the girls his father was buying and that his dearest wish was to be an artist. On the small allowance Jules wheedled from the family he went off to study drawing in Vienna. Moving to Berlin, he drew satirical drawings for the magazine *Simplicissimus*, signing them Pascon so as not to upset his father. During the First World War he travelled the US and in 1915 exhibited at the Armory Show in New York. His travels also took him to South America and the Caribbean, and during the course of his voyaging he made hundreds of drawings which have a rare beauty, delicacy of line and gentle colours. Much of his work deals with erotic studies of the female form and has been favourably compared to Degas and Toulouse-Lautrec.

Pascin returned to Paris in 1920 and gradually the emotional side of his life became progressively unstable. By now he was financially secure but it made little difference to his increasing depressions; yet despite his erratic lifestyle he produced over 500 paintings. On June 2nd 1930, on the eve of an important one-man show, he slashed his wrists. To be certain of success, in this final sentence of his life, he also hanged himself - but not before he had given instructions for a Jewish funeral. Popularly known as the Prince of Montparnasse, Jules Pascin was attended at his funeral by over a thousand people. Shalom Asche gave a eulogy.

PASTERNAK,
Boris
(1890-1960)
Russian writer

He was born on February 10th 1890 in a small village near Moscow called Peredelkino. His father was the painter Leonid Pasternak and his mother the professional pianist Rosa Kaufman. Boris was brought up in a cultured Jewish atmosphere and his early ambition was to be a musician. However, a love of poetry took over and he chose to study philosophy at Moscow University. During the First World War he was a factory worker but following the Revolution of October 1917 he worked in a Moscow library. His book of poetry, *Over the Barriers* (1917), symbolized the new Russia. In a country of poetry lovers, the people loved Pasternak. His *My Sister, Life* (1922) and *Themes and Variations* (1923) were greeted with acclaim by critics and public alike. Then, gradually, his popularity waned as his poetry, now often politically incorrect, failed to get published. He relied on translation work as a means of earning his livelihood. In 1956 he presented his manuscript of *Dr Zhivago*, his first full-length novel, for publication in a leading magazine. It was rejected as being incompatible with the structure of the Soviet Union. In 1958, via an Italian publisher, *Dr Zhivago* was selling around the world in eighteen languages and being hailed as a masterpiece; but it was not available in Russia. The award of the 1958 Nobel Prize for Literature only added to Pasternak's problems. Now his membership of the Union of Soviet Writers was revoked and there were even orchestrated public meetings calling for his deportation and telling him to go back to Israel. Pasternak wrote to the Soviet leader Khrushchev, declaring: 'Leaving the Motherland will equal death for me.' Suffering from cancer and heart disease, he returned to the village where he was born and died there on May 30th 1960. His funeral was attended by thousands and his dacha and grave remain places of pilgrimage. In 1987 the Writers' Union rehabilitated Pasternak and the Russian people were at last permitted to read his book, albeit 30 years late, and see the film that had excited the world and won three Academy Awards. The absurd treatment of Pasternak was the direct result of the jealousy those in power had over those with talent.

In 1996 Olga Ivinskaya died. She was the role model for the character Lara in *Doctor Zhivago*; she was also Pasternak's mistress, and suffered for her love of the author. She was twice sent to labour camps, and as a result their baby was stillborn. The pair originally met in 1946 and although Pasternak refused to divorce his wife he spent every day with Olga, only going home to sleep. When Boris was dying, the Pasternak family refused to allow Olga to say goodbye. She spent the next 35 years living on memories and fighting through the courts for the return of her love letters. She lost after many years of bitter wrangling; now it no longer matters.

PAUKER, Ana (1890-1960) Romanian politician

Born Hannah Rabinsohn, the daughter of a kosher butcher in Bucharest, for a while she taught at a Jewish primary school until, following a love affair that went wrong, she went to Paris. There she met and married Marcel Pauker, a leading Communist. On her return to Bucharest to visit her family, she secretly organized a Communist cell. Although she was arrested in 1936 and imprisoned, and although her husband, while in Moscow, was arrested during a Stalinist purge and then executed as a 'Western spy', Ana Pauker never lost faith in the cause. She became prominent in the Comintern and during the Second World War was welcomed by Stalin to Moscow, where she remained until Russian forces liberated Romania from the German yoke. Following the Second World War, Pauker became a powerful

Communist leader and Secretary of the Central Committee; after the Communist takeover of Romania in 1947, she became Minister of Foreign Affairs as well as Deputy Prime Minister. Had she not been Jewish, albeit an atheist, she would have been Prime Minister; but anti-Semitism does not die, and however progressive a political party might be, the population is something else. However, Ana Pauker, who declared herself uninterested in matters Jewish, was instrumental in 100,000 Jews leaving Romania for Israel. The result was that in June 1952 she was accused of right-wing deviationism and of being pro-Zionist. She was stripped of all offices, expelled from the Communist Party and held under house arrest for some years. She was eventually allowed her freedom and she died shortly thereafter.

**PEERCE,
Jan
(1904-84)
US singer**

He was born Jacob Pincus Perelmuth in New York on June 3rd 1904 and only turned to singing after first studying medicine. He received some tuition, then decided to learn from experience. He joined a dance band, received a grounding and left for Radio City Music Hall in New York. It was here that Toscanini heard him and offered him the chance to sing with the NBC Symphony Orchestra in a performance of Beethoven's Ninth Symphony. In 1941 he had the leading tenor role in the Metropolitan Opera performance of *La Traviata*. He was to stay at the Met for over 20 seasons and sing in over 200 performances in some twelve roles. He toured extensively, both in the US and Europe, and in 1956 was the first American since the Second World War to sing at the Bolshoi Theatre in Moscow. He appeared on television and had minor roles in films. Peerce was a happy, jolly man who could hardly believe his luck at being discovered by Toscanini. When he landed the role of Tevye in the Broadway production of *Fiddler on the Roof* in 1971 it was the culmination of many years of hard but rewarding work. He died in New York on December 15th 1984.

**PEIERLS,
Sir Rudolph
(1907-95)
British physicist**

Born and educated in Berlin, he came to Britain in 1933 from Zurich, where he had held an appointment at the Institute of Technology. From 1933 to 1937, Peierls taught and researched at Manchester University before becoming professor of applied mathematics at Birmingham University. There he began work on the atomic energy project. It is fair to say that all Peierl's working life was spent on acquiring knowledge connected with aspects of atomic energy. At the outbreak of the Second World War, he and his close associate Otto Frisch (*qv*) concerned themselves with the theory of what chain reactions would occur, once the energy was released that had been contained in, say, a 5 kilogram bomb. They calculated that the resulting force would equate to several thousand tons of dynamite. They wrote a short paper, outlining these theories and including a possible method for the detonation of such a bomb. Peierls and Frisch were therefore the first people in the world to explain in scientific terms the practicalities of how to make an atomic bomb. The British government were sufficiently impressed to order a programme to commence, based on the guidelines set out in this paper. This was prior to the commencement of the Manhattan Project that would subsequently take over the UK programme and go on to produce the weapon. Peierls spent three years in the US as one of the leading scientists involved in the project. He later stated that his big fear was that the Germans would win the race to complete an atomic bomb; but by mid-1944 he realized there was no such danger. For him the dropping of the Nagasaki bomb was 'unnecessary and irresponsible'.

Following the war he returned to Birmingham, remaining there until 1963 when he became professor of physics at Oxford University. He was elected a Fellow of the Royal Society in 1945 and knighted in 1968. Between 1963 and 1974 he was Wykeham Professor of Physics at New College, Oxford. He retired in 1974 and died in London on September 19th 1995.

Penn was born in Philadelphia on September 27th 1922 and educated at Black Mountain College, North Carolina, and in Italy at the universities of Perugia and Florence. He also attended the Actors' Studio in Los Angeles, going on to become known as an actor's director, who achieved an astonishing range of performances from a variety of actors. Technically knowledgable, he understands and exploits the advantages of close-up filming. He is known as a director whose films examine the darker side of society. He started as a television director and made a name for himself in the series *Playhouse*. His stage direction on Broadway included *Two For the Seesaw* (1958) and *The Miracle Worker* (1959). In the 1960s he directed *All the Way Home, Toys In the Attic* and *An Evening with Mike Nichols and Elaine May*. His first film was *The Left-Handed Gun*, a different version of the Billy the Kid story. In 1962 he made the film version of *The Miracle Worker* and received an Academy Award nomination for Best Director. Other films of note include *Micky One* (1965), *Bonnie and Clyde* (1967, and another Oscar nomination) and *Alice's Restaurant* (a third nomination. *Little Big Man* in 1970 was a rare glimpse of what the real Wild West was about. *Mission Breaks* in 1976 with Marlon Brando and Jack Nicholson promised much but didn't deliver. In 1981 he made *Four Friends* and in 1986 his last film, *Dead of Winter*. His work following *Bonnie and Clyde* appeared to lack the vitality he had shown earlier, even though the later films were good in their own right. Penn promised so much, but the critics always expected more.

Irving is the older brother of the film-maker Arthur Penn (*qv*). Born in Plainfield, New Jersey, on June 16th 1917, he originally wanted to be a painter but instead got a job designing the cover of *Vogue* magazine. His style of bold graphic design and brilliant contrasts became his trademark. He has photographed many of the celebrities of our time, always drawing out of his subject some sparkle or sign of personality. He also took his camera out into the by-ways of America and photographed tramps, peasants and labourers in their dirty clothes, as well as the indigenous Indian. The results he published in several books: *Moments Preserved* (1960), *Worlds In a Small Room* (1970), *Inventive Paris Clothes 1909-1939* (1975) and *Flowers* (1980). Colour photography is a great feature of Irving's work and he uses radical techniques to capture unusual images of subjects as contrasting as wild flowers and industrial equipment. Penn is known as the commercial photographer who makes manufactured goods appear as an art form.

PENN,
Jack
(1909-)
South African
plastic surgeon

Jack Penn was born in Cape Town and educated at the University of Witwatersrand. Following medical school and qualification, Penn decided upon a career specializing in maxillo-facial surgery. During the Second World War his talent for rebuilding faces destroyed by war came to be internationally acknowledged. With the rank of brigadier he commanded the Brenthurst Military Hospital for Plastic Surgery in Johannesburg. Following the Second World War, and now recognized as one of the world's leading plastic surgeons, Penn opened his own clinic where he treated many Japanese victims of the atomic bombs dropped on Hiroshima and Nagasaki. During Israel's War of Independence in 1948, the Six-Day War of 1967 and the Yom Kippur War of 1973 Jack Penn brought his plastic surgery unit to Israel. He was later responsible for the founding of plastic surgery units all over Africa. His autobiography, *The Right to Look Human* (1976), covers it all.

PENZIAS,
Arno
(1933-)
US physicist

He was born on April 26th 1933 in Germany: no place for a new-born Jewish baby. Several years passed before his parents were able to settle, in 1939, in America. Arno received his doctorate in physics from Columbia University in 1962 and joined the Bell Telephone Laboratories in 1963. In collaboration with Robert Wilson, he started monitoring radio emissions from a ring of gas that surrounds the Milky Way galaxy. The two scientists were much surprised to discover a uniform static in the background that they identified as a residual thermal energy that spread throughout the universe. It is now universally agreed that this background static stems from the original explosion of billions of years ago from which our universe evolves. For their work Penzias and Wilson shared the 1978 Nobel Prize for Physics. Their work became known as the 'big bang' theory of creation. Penzias remains at Bell, where he is vice president in charge of research.

PERCHERSKY,
Alexander
(1919-)
Russian soldier

Perchersky was born in Rostov-on-Don, Russia, and called up to the Soviet Red Army when Germany invaded the USSR in the summer of 1941. In October of that year Perchersky, by now a lieutenant, was captured by the Germans but managed to escape. Some two years later he was again taken prisoner but this time the Germans, upon discovering he was a Jew, sent him to Sobibor concentration camp. It was a death camp staffed by Ukrainian guards and overseen by German SS officers. Perchersky was put to work labouring but knew what his ultimate fate would be. He gathered around him six other Jews, who had some military experience, and planned their revolt. A month after arriving at the camp, on the night of October 14th 1943, Perchersky made his move. The group attacked and killed 10 German officers, took their weapons, freed their comrades and went on to kill dozens of Ukrainian guards. Some 4,000 Jews escaped; half of them were blown up running across a minefield. A manhunt was launched by the Germans, ably assisted by Polish peasants, which resulted in most of the escapees being recaptured and immediately hanged. Perchersky and some of his companions were more successful and succeeded in reaching Russian Partisan forces. Perchersky rejoined the Red Army and took part in the fighting that later took place on German soil. In August 1944 he was seriously wounded and invalided out of the army. He was the leader of a heroic escape that caused the Germans to close down the Sobibor camp - but not before some quarter of a million Jews had died there.

The SJ stands for **Sidney Joseph**, who was born in Brooklyn, New York, on February 1st 1904. His father moved out of Brooklyn to Providence, Rhode Island where, as SJ said later, 'my father worked successively but not successfully at being a merchant, a machinist and a farmer'. Here SJ grew up. He studied at, but did not graduate from, Brown University, where he edited the school's humorous magazine. In 1925 he went to live in Greenwich Village in New York and got work as a cartoonist on the magazine *Judge*. He met the Marx Brothers and became caught up in their frenzy. He contributed to their scripts and in 1931 wrote *Monkey Business*, followed by *Horse Feathers* a year later. He was a regular contributor to *The New Yorker* and enjoyed this work so much he refused to call a halt even while working in Hollywood. A great humorist and wordsmith, he shared with James Poe and John Farrow the Academy Award for Best Screenwriter for *Around The World in 80 Days*. He wrote comedies for the Broadway Theatre, including *All Good Americans* (1934) and *One Touch of Venus* (1943). Perelman had a unique sense of cliché and literary parody. Nothing was sacred. He once said of dentists: 'For years I have let dentists ride roughshod over my teeth. I have been sawed, hacked, chopped, whittled, bewitched, bewildered, tattooed and signed on again; but this is cuspid's last stand.' He died in New York on October 17th 1979.

Shimon Peres was born Shimon Perski in Worozyn, Poland, on August 16th 1923. In 1934 he and his family left for Palestine, where he completed his education. During the Second World War he became active in politics, and when Israel became an independent state in May 1948 he was appointed head of the fledgling navy. He was just 25. In 1952 he began his climb up the ladder of the defence ministry, becoming deputy minister in 1959. Between then and 1965 he expanded the state's defence industry and began a nuclear research programme. A series of party changes and alliances resulted in Peres becoming Defence Minister under Rabin (*qv*) in 1974. In 1977 Peres was head of the Labour Party but remained in opposition while the Likud government ruled. In September 1984 an unsatisfactory power-sharing arrangement saw Peres as Prime Minister for two years after which Yitzhak Shamir took over the premiership and Peres served as his deputy and Foreign Minister. This arrangement continued until 1990, when Likud won a working majority. In February 1992 the leadership of the Labour Party reverted to Rabin, and when in July 1992 Labour won the general election Peres was Foreign Minister. In 1995, following the assassination of Rabin, Peres took over as premier until the 1996 general election, when he lost by the narrowest of margins to Likud in a result that jeopardized the peace process to which Peres contributed so much. In 1994 he shared the Nobel Peace Prize. In 1997 he resigned the leadership of the Labour Party.

PEREZ,
Victor 'Young'
(1911-43)
Tunisian world
champion boxer

Perez, born in Tunis on October 18th 1911, soon found that the best way of rising up from the poverty in which he grew up was to become a boxer. After years of fighting in the lower ranks, he won the French flyweight title in Paris in June 1931. In October of the same year he won the world flyweight title by defeating Frankie Genaro of the US. The following year he lost it to Jackie Brown of Britain. Perez now moved up a division to the bantamweight class and in February 1934 met Al Brown in a world title fight which Perez narrowly lost on points. He remained in Paris and continued fighting until December 1938. During the Second World War, he was included in a round-up of foreign-born Jews and sent to Auschwitz, where in February 1943 he was killed. Perez's professional boxing record was 133 fights, of which he won 92 including 28 knockouts, with 26 lost and 15 drawn.

PERLMAN,
Itzhak
(1945-)
Israeli violinist

Perlman was born in Tel Aviv, on August 31st 1945. He was struck down by polio in 1949 when he was four and Israel one. He was left with a total paralysis of the legs, but in 1958 was able to accompany his parents to New York and attend the Juillard School to continue his study of music. He had given his first public concert in Tel Aviv at the age of ten, and those who knew about such things had already singled out young Itzhak as destined to become a world-famous violinist. They were right, and today a concert with Perlman as the soloist is generally a sell-out. His obvious good humour and bouncy personality are infectious and his playing, and the audience's reaction to his playing, make for a happy occasion. Now one of the world's leading violinists, he holds master classes, has recorded most of the violin concertos worth recording and gives television interviews that leaves no one in any doubt that his handicap has in no way interfered with his life. By his example and his anecdotes, for example describing how, when he was a kid, he was always being asked by his friends to play football so that he could play in goal and use his sticks to help keep the ball out, he has given hope and comfort to others who spend their lives in wheelchairs.

PERUTZ,
Max
(1914-)
Austrian/British
biochemist

Perutz was born in Vienna on May 19th 1914 and educated at the University of Vienna until 1936, when he was advised that, as a Jew, it would be better for his health if he left. He continued his studies at Cambridge University and his research at the Cavendish Laboratory. Here he took his first X-ray diffraction pictures of haemoglobin crystals. In 1947 he and John Kendrew set up the Medical Research Unit for molecular biology at Cambridge. The two men's research into the structure of haemoglobin led to their being awarded the 1962 Nobel Prize for Chemistry for their work on the X-ray diffraction analysis of the structure of haemoglobin, the protein that transports oxygen from the lungs to the tissues via blood cells. From 1962 to 1979, when he retired, Perutz was chairman of the Medical Research Centre at Cambridge. A Fellow of the Royal Society, Perutz was also an authority in the field of crystallography and in 1938, while measuring the flow of glaciers, proved for the first time that the fastest flow occurs at the surface and the slowest near the bed of the glacier.

Pevsner was born in Orel, Russia, on January 18th 1886 and studied art in Kiev before going to Paris in 1911. In 1915 he joined his brother Naum Gabo (*qv*), also a sculptor and painter, in Oslo, Norway. Together the brothers experimented in art that was capable of utilizing emptiness and achieving liberation from the 'compact mass'. The brothers returned to Russia following the 1917 Revolution, and Pevsner became a professor at the School of Fine Arts in Moscow. While there he painted *Harmony In White* (1917), an extreme geometric piece of abstraction that led him on to develop his wire and glass sculptures. In 1920 the brothers issued the realist manifesto in which they introduced the term 'constructivism'. They established the idea of an art form that was a construction, that must have a social purpose and be purely abstract. Materials could be anything, including industrial types of plastic and glass. In 1922 those who ran the Soviet art world condemned this type of art and the brothers left the USSR; Gabo went to Berlin and Pevsner to Paris, where in 1930 he became naturalized. Pevsner co-founded the Realités Nouvelles group of artists who regularly exhibited, and devoted the rest of his life to producing sculptures in brass, zinc, copper, celluloid and much else. He produced plates of parallel pieces of bronze wire that he soldered together; the plates were then joined to form abstract shapes in lines that were both curved and straight. For Pevsner, constructivism was the only real form of art. Unassociated with Jewish life, Pevsner survived the German occupation. His *Torso* (1924-26) is at the Museum of Modern Art in New York, and there are examples of his work at the Tate Gallery, London, as well as in collections of modern art all over the world. He died in Paris on April 12th 1962.

PEVSNER, Antoine (1886-1962) Russian/French sculptor

Nikolaus Pevsner was born in Leipzig, Germany, on January 30th 1902 and educated at several German universities. When Hitler won the 1933 general election, Pevsner was a lecturer on art history and architecture at the University of Göttingen (1929-33). As a Jew, he knew his days in his job were numbered and, without waiting to be told to resign, he left. In England he made a new life, teaching both at Oxford and Cambridge universities (although not at the same time!). He is best known for his writings on architecture, especially his 46-volume county by county guide (1951-74) which he wrote and edited. It was a mammoth task and is now acknowledged as one of the greatest individual achievements of the century. He also conceived and edited the *Pelican History of Art*, the largest and most comprehensive, as well as the most scholarly, history of art ever published in English. Knighted in 1969, he died on August 18th 1983. In 1997 the BBC created a TV series under the title 'Travels With Pevsner' that examines his architectural guide.

PEVSNER, Sir Nikolaus (1902-83) German/British art historian

Picard was born in Wangen, Germany, and arrived in Palestine when he was 24. He was among the first students when the Hebrew University opened for business in 1925, and returned there as a lecturer in 1934. In between he was in Europe, completing postgraduate courses and progressing in his chosen field of geology. In 1936 he became a full professor at the Hebrew University and head of the geology department. His main contribution was his belief that underground water existed in hard limestone formations in sufficient quantities to make settlements possible. This

PICARD, Leo (1900-1991) German/Israeli geologist

would render habitable such arid places as Western Galilee, the Judaean Hills and the northern Negev. Theory became fact when deep drilling produced the vital water and the desert began to bloom. Picard became internationally known and his services required all over the world. It was due to Picard's work that development was discovered to be possible in large areas of Africa and Latin America.

PIJADE, Mosa (1890-1957) Yugoslav politician

Born in Belgrade, **Pijade** trained as an artist in Paris and returned to Belgrade to work as a teacher. In 1920 he joined the Yugoslav Communist Party, and a few years later was jailed when the party was banned. He was also imprisoned between 1925 and 1939, and during this long period he used his time to translate Karl Marx's *Das Kapital* into Serbian. The German invasion of his country in the Second World War was the beginning of a new life for Pijade. Although now over 50, he was to become a national hero while fighting with Tito and the Partisans. An outstanding organizer and tough resistance fighter, he became a legend. When Tito formed a government Pijade was on the Communist Central Committee. He attended post-war conferences and safeguarded Yugoslav interests. He was in the forefront of the drafting of the constitution. He was President of the Serbian Republic within Yugoslavia and was one of the country's four vice-presidents. It was due to the philosophy expounded by Pijade that Yugoslavia broke away from Moscow's influence and inclined more to the West. The year was 1948 and Tito was brave enough to take the brickbats that Stalin threw at him, safe in the knowledge that his economy was growing faster than before. Pijade, a key figure in the country's politics, now became Chairman of the National Assembly. Four-fifths of the Jewish population had died in the Holocaust and Pijade, always aware of his background, helped in reviving Jewish life and restoring some of the synagogues the Germans, and their Croatian allies, had destroyed. In Belgrade there is now a Jewish museum and Pijade is shown as a lifelong friend of Marshal Tito.

PINCUS, Gregory (1903-67) US endocrinologist

Gregory Pincus, born in Woodbine, New Jersey, on April 9th 1903, was to become known all over the world as 'the father of the pill', that is, of the first effective birth control pill. Educated at Cornell University and Harvard, gaining an MS from the former and a ScD from the latter, he also studied in England and Germany. In 1944, while serving on the teaching boards of several well-known US universities, Pincus, together with his friend and colleague Hudson Hoagland, founded the Worcester Foundation for Experimental Biology. The unit became an important location for the study of hormones and steroids. In 1951 Pincus and his team began working with synthesized hormones for pregnancy prevention. They were eventually able to discover that inhibition of ovulation was a practical way of preventing laboratory animals from becoming pregnant, and gradually progressed to perfect an oral contraceptive enabling women to prevent pregnancy. His discovery has led to a social revolution leading to the further emancipation of women. His books on his subject include *The Eggs of the Mammals* (1936) and *The Control of Fertility* (1965). He died in Boston, Massachusetts, on August 22nd 1967.

Harold Pinter was born in the East End of London on October 10th 1930. The son of a Jewish tailor, he grew up in an area that was often the scene of fascist intimidation led by Oswald Mosley. He spent two years at RADA, training to be an actor, but left to become a professional actor in a provincial repertory company that toured Britain, gaining valuable experience.

Albeit an acquired taste, Pinter is probably the most important British playwright of the latter half of the century. There is much depth and fine balances in Pinter's storylines and his dialogue is acutely timed. The first production of *The Birthday Party* (1958) received poor reviews and lasted a week. Later it was successfully revived. Perhaps Pinter was ahead of his time, or the audiences unsophisticated; in any event, *The Caretaker* (1960) gave Pinter an authority on which he could capitalize, and this he did in *Homecoming* (1965). He was now internationally known in the theatre and in films, following the successful transfer to the screen of his first two plays.

Besides writing for the theatre he also works as a director. His sensitively written screenplays sometimes differ from the original text but often give the story additional strength. They include *The Servant* (1963), *The Go-Between* (1971) and *The French Lieutenant's Woman* (1981), for which he was nominated for an Oscar. His play *Betrayal* became a successful film in 1982 and Pinter again received an Oscar nomination. In recent plays, which have been few and far between, he has been accused of creating caricatures of earlier works. In September 1996 his play *Ashes to Ashes* met with very mixed reviews. The *Times* reviewer claimed it showed Pinter as a continuing creative genius while the popular *Daily Mail*'s critic called it 'a dud . . . a biographical footnote '. His first wife was the actress Vivienne Merchant, who committed suicide after Pinter left her for the writer Antonia Fraser, whom he subsequently married.

Lucien Pissarro was born in Paris on February 20th 1863. the son of a famous Jewish father. Camille Pissarro, the impressionist pioneer, taught his son much of his craft. By the beginning of the century Lucien was living in London and married to Esther Bensusan, the daughter of an old English-Jewish family. Having been dissuaded by his father and Degas from attending the Slade School of Art, Lucien studied in the art museums when it was raining and painted outdoors when it wasn't. He learned about wood engraving and techniques concerning colour woodcuts. In 1902 he designed a type of his own that he called 'Brooks type' (he chose the name Brook because he was living at Stamford Brook Road, Hammersmith) and used for his beautifully illustrated books that his own Eragny Press produced.

Pissarro is acknowledged as the driving force in the introduction of impressionist art into Britain. His own impressionist paintings were well regarded and his work hangs in several galleries in Europe's capitals. He had his first one-man show at the Carfax Gallery in London in 1913. His style was a modified sort of pointillism not previously seen in Britain. In 1920 he founded the Monarro Group, an international society who stated objective was to concentrate on those artists who have derived inspiration from the leaders of the French impressionist movement, Claude Monet and Camille Pissarro. From 1922 Lucien would spend his winters in Provence, France, where he stayed with his ailing mother. There he would paint the landscape. These paintings were of a very high standard and a pure French product. Lucien died at Chard, Somerset, on July 10th 1944. His wife, Esther, herself an artist of some talent, divided her valuable art collection (it included a portrait of Lucien as a boy by his father) between the Tate Gallery, National Gallery, Ashmolean Museum and other institutions overseas.

PLISETSKAYA, Maya (1925-) Russian ballet dancer

Maya, born in Moscow on November 20th 1925, was destined to become prima ballerina of Moscow's Bolshoi Ballet. A niece of the renowned dancers Asaf and Sulamith Messerer, she graduated from the Bolshoi school in 1943. She went on to become one of the greatest ballerinas ever, renowned for technical brilliance, artistic expression and the unusual ability to integrate acting and dancing. She has been favourably compared to Anna Pavlova. She danced many famous roles but her greatest was probably that of Odette Odile in *Swan Lake*. She has performed all over the world and has made several films of the great ballets. In 1964 she received the Lenin Prize for the Arts. She has made many guest appearances, dancing for non-Russian companies. As a choreographer she has collaborated with Roland Petit and Albert Alonso and on her own created the ballet *Anna Karenina* in 1972. Very well received, it has given her a whole new career.

POLANSKI, Roman (1933-) French film-maker

Roman Polanski was born on August 18th 1933 in Paris. His parents were Polish Jews who decided to return to Poland in 1936. Following the German takeover of Poland, Polanski's parents were sent to a concentration camp and young Roman found refuge with a Gentile family. Polanski survived; his parents died. He appeared on the stage first in 1947 and later in films directed by Andrzej Wajda. In 1954 he began a five-year course at the Lodz Film School. A film he made there as a student, for an exam, called *Two Men and a Wardrobe* (1958), won five international awards and a bronze medal at the Brussels World Fair. His first full-length feature film was *Knife in the Water* (1962); it was not well received in Poland but proved a sensation elsewhere and won the Critics' Prize at the Venice Film Festival. It was also nominated for an Academy Award.

Polanski now realized that Poland was not the place to make the sort of films he wanted to make. He moved to England and made three first-class films in three years: *Repulsion* in 1965, *Cul-de-Sac* in 1966 and in 1967 the Dracula spoof, *The Fearless Vampire Killers or Pardon Me Your Teeth Are in my Neck*. Polanski now moved on to the US and his first Hollywood film, *Rosemary's Baby* (1968). It was a brilliant film, a box-office success, and it brought Ruth Gordon the Oscar for Best Supporting Actress and a nomination for Polanski. His happiness and success were short-lived. In 1969 his heavily pregnant wife, the actress Sharon Tate, was mindlessly murdered by Charles Manson. Roman needed time to get over this tragedy, and working was an aid. In 1971 he made *Macbeth*; it is interesting, given Polanski's recent trauma, to note how bloody a film it was. In 1974 came *Chinatown*, among the finest detective films ever made. Polanski, besides directing, also played the part of a gangster with considerable relish. The film won an Oscar for the writer Robert Towne plus six nominations. In 1976 came *The Tenant*, which Polanski wrote, directed and starred in. It had echoes of *Repulsion* and did not find much favour. In 1977 he was arrested and charged with unlawful sex with a minor, who looked much older than she was. Polanski pleaded guilty but before he could be sentenced left America for France. There, in 1979, he made the widely acclaimed *Tess*. In 1981 he returned to Poland to direct and star in a stage production of *Amadeus*. In 1988, in Paris, he made the hugely enjoyable film *Frantic*, with Harrison Ford (*qv*) searching for his kidnapped wife. Polanski allows his philosophies to be part of his work, adding an additional dimension to his films that varies from the deep dark abyss of despair and violence to a welcome sense of the absurd.

Bruno Pontecorvo was born in Pisa, Italy, on August 22nd 1913. His father was a well-to-do Jewish textile merchant and Bruno was one of eight children. He was only seventeen when he graduated, with honours, from Pisa University. A precocious youth, he was happiest when with his brothers and sisters during the short interval between the two world wars. Having become interested in the new and rapidly expanding field of nuclear science, he took his doctorate in nuclear physics at Rome University. While there he and five other like-minded enthusiasts wrote a paper called 'Artificial Radioactivity Produced by Neutron Bombardment'. This paper brought Pontecorvo to the attention of Enrico Fermi, the world's greatest authority on the subject. Together they conducted important experiments to produce radioactive isotopes. Pontecorvo received his PhD in 1933 and was establishing himself as a leader in his field when he ran up against Mussolini and his anti-Jewish legislation. It meant he was no longer able to work in Italy. It was now 1936 and he moved sideways to Paris to continue his work at the Curie Institute. Here he settled down and got married, never imagining that in 1940 France would collapse like a soufflé. The newlyweds took off for the US via Spain and Portugal. Overqualified for the work he was doing to keep two bodies and souls together, Pontecorvo was overjoyed when his old friend Enrico Fermi asked him to join the very secret British-Canadian atomic project in Montreal, a branch operation of the Manhattan Project going on in New Mexico.

In 1949, and now a British subject, Pontecorvo was working at the Harwell Institute in England and enjoying life to the full, playing sports, participating in the intellectual and social life of the Harwell set and happy to have received the offer of a professorship at Liverpool University. In 1950 the Pontecorvo family went on a trip to Italy and never returned. The family finally reappeared in the Soviet Union, much to the consternation of Britain and the US. Pontecorvo had a lot to tell his Russian friends but assured anyone who would listen that his information was limited to atomic energy for peaceful purposes. He reiterated his call for a ban on nuclear weapons, but it went unheeded by all concerned. He was never accused of espionage by any government and continued to enjoy life to the full. His time was now spent in teaching and researching nuclear physics. He was showered with honours, including the Order of Lenin, but more pleased that his work continued to be published abroad,

PONTECORVO, Bruno (1913-93) Italian physicist

especially *The Birth Processes of Heavy Mesons and Particles* (1955) and *Weak Reaction of Elementary Particles and Neutrinos* (1963). He died in Dubna, Russia, on September 25th 1993.

POPPER,
Sir Karl
(1902-94)
Austrian/British
philosopher

Karl Popper was born on July 28th 1902 in Vienna. He studied mathematics and psychology at the University of Vienna and obtained a PhD in 1928. Following the Anschluss, Popper left Austria for New Zealand and taught philosophy at Canterbury University College (1937-45). In 1945 he became a Reader in Logic at the London School of Economics, where he was later a professor until he retired in 1969. Popper's main contribution to the philosophy of science is his logical rejection of the inductive method in the empirical sciences. He successfully argued that hypotheses are deductively validated by what he termed the falsifiability criterion. Therefore, according to Popper, such so-called sciences as astrology and metaphysics are not empirical sciences because they fail to adhere to the principle of falsifiability. He maintained that no scientific theory can be conclusively established. His books *The Logic of Scientific Discovery* (1934) and *The Open Society and its Enemies* (1945) have become classics. His last work was *Postscript to the Logic of Scientific Discovery* in 3 volumes (1981-2). He was knighted in 1965 and died in London on September 17th 1994.

PRAAG,
Lionel, van
(1908-87)
Australian
speedway
champion

Lionel van Praag was born in Sydney and went to England in 1931 to join the Wembley Speedway Club, becoming club captain in 1935. In 1936 he took part in the first world speedway championships for individual riders. The event was held at Wembley before a capacity crowd. At the end of the programme van Praag was level on points with Eric Langton at 26 points all. There had to be a deciding lap and both men publicly vowed they would win. In the event it was van Praag who came through what was later described as the most exciting speedway race ever. Van Praag was in Australia when the Second World War was declared and immediately joined the RAAF as a transport pilot. In 1941 he was awarded the George Medal for bravery. The war over, van Praag returned to speedway racing at Wembley until 1954, when he returned to Australia. He retired from racing to become managing director of the Sydney International Speedway Club.

PREMINGER,
Otto
(1906-86)
Austrian/
American
film-maker

Preminger was born on December 5th 1906 in Austria, the son of the first Jew ever to be a senior law officer in the Austrian Empire. Otto dutifully studied law and received a doctorate from the University of Vienna, before becoming an assistant to Max Reinhardt (*qv*). In 1933 Preminger was in charge of a theatre in Vienna and was soon faced with the choice between converting to Christianity and becoming the director of Vienna's prestigious State Theatre, and remaining a Jew and leaving Austria. He chose the latter course and headed west for the US and Hollywood. Never an easy man to get on with, he soon fell foul of Darryl Zanuck, the studio head, and Preminger was out. He now returned to his first love, the theatre, directing himself and others in the successful play *Margin for Error*. Then he returned to 20th Century Fox and cemented his role as a major film director with

Laura (1944).

Preminger, always his own man, now embarked on three films that would emblazon his name all over the world and set the standard for future directors. In 1953 he filmed *The Moon is Blue*. With such words as 'virgin', 'pregnant' and 'mistress', it caused a scandal; it also received three Oscar nominations. In 1956 he made *Man With the Golden Arm*; its shocking portrayal of heroin addiction caused a sensation and won three Oscar nominations, including one for Frank Sinatra, who for the first time, revealed himself as a very good actor. The third in the triple scandal was *Anatomy of a Murder* (1959), which dealt with the subject of rape. It was also a very good film, as the seven Oscar nominations showed. Preminger was now king, and he asserted his royal credentials when, in defiance of the McCarthy witch-hunters, he insisted on crediting blacklisted Dalton Trumbo as the screenwriter of his epic, *Exodus* (1960). Preminger was not keen on musicals but he made two: *Carmen Jones* (1954) and *Porgy and Bess* (1959), which won two Oscars. He also had his flops, *Saint Joan* (1957) and *Rosebud* (1975). His last film was made in 1980, *The Human Factor*. It could have and should have been a winner, but the blame for its failure must lay with Otto Preminger, the enfant terrible of earlier days and one of the great directors of the century. He had an long-term affair with Gypsy Rose Lee that resulted in a child. He died on April 23rd 1986 in New York.

He was born Andreas Ludwig Previn on April 6th 1929 in Berlin. His father was a lawyer. One day a uniformed Gestapo man called at the office. He was an ex-client whom Previn had once defended on a criminal charge and got off. He was there returning the favour by warning him that the Gestapo would soon be calling for him, and that his family should leave that night. They did just that and Andre was only ten when the family arrived in Los Angeles, taking refuge from German hatred of the Jews. Previn is an all-round musician. He is equally at home conducting a symphony orchestra, playing piano jazz, writing film music or playing French impressionist music. He has been the principal conductor to some of the world's leading symphony orchestras, including the Houston Symphony (1967-70), the London Symphony (1968-79) and the Pittsburgh Symphony (1976-86). He was musical director of the Los Angeles Philharmonic between 1985 and 1989 and has been principal conductor to the Royal Philharmonic since 1987. A composer of a symphony, concertos and chamber music, he has also found time to be responsible for the musical direction of several major films, including *Three Little Words* (1950) and *Kiss Me Kate* (1953), both of which were nominated for Oscars. He provided the music for *Bad Day at Black Rock* (1954), *It's Always Fair Weather* (1955) and *Gigi* (1958), for which he won his first Academy Award for Musical Direction. In 1959 came another Academy Award for the musical direction of *Porgy and Bess*, and in 1964 he received his third Oscar for the musical direction of *My Fair Lady*. André Previn has done much for all branches of the music world as performer, conductor and composer, and has written books, including *Music Face to Face* (1971) and *Orchestra* (1979), explaining why. A football fanatic, he conducted a gala concert in London on the occasion of Euro '96. Perhaps he was also celebrating the award of a knighthood in January 1996.

PRINSTEIN,
Meyer
(1880-1925)
US Olympic
athlete

Meyer Prinstein was born on December 16th 1880 in Poland. He became the winner of five Olympic titles and one of the greatest performers in American track and field events. He took the gold medal for the triple jump in the 1900 Olympic Games in Paris with a jump of 14.47 metres, setting a new world record. In the 1904 Games at St Louis he won two more golds for the long jump event, with a new world record of 7.34 metres, and took two golds again in 1906 at Athens. Meyer was a graduate of Syracuse University and practised as a lawyer before his early death in New York on March 10th 1925.

PROUST,
Marcel
(1871-1922)
French writer

Marcel Proust was born on July 10th in Auteuil, France, his father a Gentile physician, his mother Jeanne Weill, the daughter of a wealthy Jewish family from Alsace. Marcel, by the beginning of the 20th century, was well established as one of the top novelists in French literature. Long influenced by his mother, his great work, the novel cycle *A La Recherche du Temps Perdu* (*Remembrance of Things Past*) was published between 1913 and 1927. It is often described as a letter to his mother; as it is in fifteen volumes this is probably something of an exaggeration. His father died in 1903 and his mother followed two years later. Marcel was heartbroken and rewrote the novel that would be hailed as a literary masterpiece. An asthmatic, he was constantly in need of medical attention. He often shut himself off from the world, then emerged to return to his friends who, like him, were snobs and homosexuals. Although in the world of letters he was often praised extravagantly, there were others who took a different view. Samuel Beckett described him briefly as 'the garrulous dowager of letters'. Proust wrote much and has remained popular, although during the Second World War the Vichy authorities, with German backing, banned his books because of his Jewish background. He had an enormous correspondence and over 3,000 letters have been published. To finish his great classic was a fight against time. He died in Paris on November 18th 1922.

PUGLIESE,
Umberto
(1880-1961)
Italian general

Umberto Pugliese, born in Italy, was the younger brother of Emanule, a hero of the First World War and also a general. Umberto trained as an engineer and naval architect and became known world wide for the battleships he built for the Italian navy. He went on to become General of the Naval Corps of Engineers and an expert on salvage operations. His 'Pugliese waterline' became the recognized method among salvage teams world-wide. In 1938, following the anti-Jewish laws, General Umberto Pugliese was forced to take early retirement. Living quietly in the country he was amazed to be summoned to Rome and there asked, by a desperate fascist government, to resume command of the Naval Corps of Engineers and raise the fleet sunk by the British Royal Navy at Taranto. The British action, codenamed Operation Judgement, had been launched on November 11th 1940 and consisted of 24 Fleet Air Arm torpedo-carrying bombers from the aircraft carrier *Illustrious*. Flying 170 miles to the Italian port, they sank the Italian battleship *Duilo* and left two more battleships and two heavy cruisers badly damaged and half sunk. Pugliese, ever the patriot, agreed, and when asked what payment he required answered, 'a return ticket home'. He also demanded the right to wear his uniform and medals throughout the operation. Pugliere completed his contract, after which he returned to a quiet retirement.

Q

'Ellery Queen' was the brainchild of two writers, Frederic Dannay, who was born Daniel Nathan in Brooklyn on October 20th 1905, and his cousin Manfred Lee, who was born Manfred Lepofsky, also in Brooklyn, on January 11th 1905. The boys, on an impulse, entered a detective writing competition in 1929; their central character was one Ellery Queen. They went on to write some 40 novels about the detective. A feature of their work was to leave sufficient clues for the reader to arrive at the solution before Queen. During the 1930s and 1940s, Ellery Queen was the most famous fictional detective apart from Sherlock Holmes. The stories became plays and films and delighted an international audience. Dannay and Lee published *Ellery Queen's Mystery Magazine,* and founded the Mystery Writers of America. Dannay died in White Plains, New York, on September 3rd 1982 and Lee on April 3rd 1971 at Waterbury, Connecticut.

'QUEEN, ELLERY': Frederic Dannay (1905-82) and Manfred Lee (1905-71) US writers

Commemorative Stamps

Georges Mandel
Issued by France

Lise Meitner
Issued by Austria

Darius Milhaud
Issued by France

The Marx Brothers
Issued by The Gambia

Bette Midler
Issued by Mali

Golda Meir
Issued by Santa Lucia

Osip Mandelstam
Issued by USSR

Laszio Moholy-Nagy
Issued by Hungary

Pierre Mendes-France
Issued by France

R

Isidor Rabi was born on July 29th 1898 in Rymanow, Poland. A year later he was breathing the air of New York's Lower East Side. Rabi received a BA from Cornell University in 1919 and his PhD from Columbia in 1927, where he became a professor of physics ten years later. In between he studied and worked in Europe and invented the magnetic resonance spectroscopy. During the Second World War he was leader of a group who were developing radar following its invention in Britain. A member of the committee advising the Atomic Energy Commission, he succeeded Robert Oppenheimer (*qv*) as its chairman in 1952. One of the founders of the Brookhaven National Laboratory in Upton, New Jersey, he went on to develop what is claimed to be the world's finest physics department at Columbia University. Rabi was only able to achieve what he did because of the reputation he earned during the 1930s. His researches became of the utmost importance as they provided the central method for all future molecular and atomic beam experimentation. His work resulted in his being awarded the Nobel Prize for Physics in 1944 for his 1937 invention of his method for observing atomic spectra. He died in New York on January 11th 1988.

RABI,
Isidor
(1898-1988)
US physicist

Rabin was born in Jerusalem on March 1st 1922. He was educated at a workers' school, an institution peculiar to Palestine where pupils and teachers were on first-name terms and agreed on the curriculum. Rabin wanted to become a farmer and only became a soldier by accident. While he was attending the Kadouri Agricultural College in the late 1930s the British began training and equipping the Jewish Settlement Police. Rabin became part of this force and later joined the Palmach branch of Haganah. In 1941 he was part of the unit, which included British and Australian troops, that invaded Lebanon, then under the control of Vichy France. Following the Second World War Rabin was active in securing, often by armed force, the release from detention camps of illegal Jewish immigrants, survivors of the Holocaust. Rabin showed his ability to lead and organize when he commanded the 1,500-strong Harel Brigade in the Israeli War of Independence in 1948. He was then transferred to become operations officer to Yigal Allon, the commander of the Palmach Brigade, who recognized his genius for planning. The result was a crippling defeat in Sinai for the Egyptian army, who were vastly superior in manpower and equipment. In June 1967 Rabin and Moshe Dayan were responsible for Israel's victory in what has become known as the Six-Day War. Rabin then became Israel's ambassador to Washington, the country's top diplomatic post. His success in this

RABIN,
Yitzhak
(1922-95)
Israeli
statesman

role often led to friction with Abba Eban (*qv*), Israel's Foreign Secretary, because Rabin would deal directly with his Prime Minister, Golda Meir (*qv*).

In 1974 Rabin, now head of the Labour Party, became Prime Minister. He resigned as a matter of principle following the disclosure that his wife had a $2,000 bank account in the US, contrary to Israeli law. In 1984 he was back in government as Defence Minister in a coalition government. In 1992, as leader of the Labour Party, he was premier once again, at the age of 70. His main political platform was the Israeli-Arab peace process and the world was amazed and delighted to see, on television, Rabin shake hands with Arafat on the lawn of the White House in Washington DC. In early 1995, Israel and Jordan took the first positive steps towards a peace treaty that was eventually sealed in September 1995. There was much opposition to the work Rabin was doing, from both Jews and Arabs. Rabin refused to be deterred by the bombs of Hamas, the Arab extremists or Israeli nationalists making death threats. In 1994 he, Shimon Peres (*qv*) and Arafat shared the Nobel Peace Prize. The end for Rabin came on November 4th 1995 when, having addressed a large peace rally, he was shot down by a young Jewish man, a student of religion.

RADEK,
Karl
(1885-1939?)
Russian
politician

Karl Radek was born Karl Sobelsohn to a Galician Jewish family in Lemberg, Russia. He went on to study at Krakow and Bern universities. By the age of 20 he had participated in the abortive Russian revolution of 1905 and was in a Russian prison. Released after a year, he worked on various Communist newspapers and acquired a reputation as a clever and witty political writer. In 1915, while attending a conference in Sweden, he met Lenin, who later invited him to return with him to Moscow. Instead, Radek stayed on in Sweden and then Germany, and only arrived in Russia in 1919. In 1923 he represented the Comintern and returned to Germany to pave the way for a Communist revolution there. Later, he was the secretary of the Comintern or Communist International. It was at this time that he fell foul of Joseph Stalin, who accused him of supporting Leon Trotsky (*qv*) and cited his failure in Germany as the reason for his dismissal from his post. In 1927 he was expelled from the party for supporting Trotsky and exiled to the Ural mountains. He subsequently made a full apology for all real and imaginary misdemeanours and was re-admitted to the Party, becoming strongly pro-Stalin. As a result he joined the Soviet newspaper *Izvestiya* and between 1931 and 1936 was a major commentator on foreign affairs. In 1935 he was part of the commission appointed to prepare the 1936 Soviet Constitution. However, in October 1936, he was arrested and accused with others of being concerned in a Trotsky-inspired conspiracy. Radek confessed to the fabricated charge and received ten years' imprisonment. Others denied the charges, were found guilty and executed. Radek died in prison, probably during 1939. In 1988 the Soviet Supreme Court found him not guilty and he was posthumously re-instated.

Arkady Raikin was born on October 24th 1911 in Riga to Jewish parents. He graduated from the Leningrad Theatrical Technical School in 1935 and worked in theatre and variety until 1939, when he opened his own theatre, the Leningrad Theatre of Variety. Here he offered his homespun philosophies and skits he called 'miniatures'. During the Second World War he took his show on the road and toured Soviet Army bases all over the country. The war over, he returned to his Leningrad theatre until 1984, when he moved to Moscow and opened the Satirikon Theatre. Raikin never suffered by ridiculing bureaucracy, Soviet inefficiency, shortages, politics and other aspects of life. A Jew who operated throughout the Stalinist era without any problems, he was probably the most popular comedian over a four decade period. In 1968 he received the title of Popular Artist and in 1981 the coveted award, Hero of Socialist Labour. He died in Moscow on December 17th 1987.

He was born in Ada, Serbia, on March 14th 1892, into a Jewish family. During the First World War he was a prisoner of war of the Russians, and by the end of it he was a Communist. A member of Bela Kun's (*qv*) short-lived Communist government in Hungary, he fled to Moscow when it was all over. He returned to Budapest in 1924 to rekindle the flickering flame of Communism, only to be arrested and spend many years in a Hungarian prison. Eight years later he was released, but was re-arrested on the same day. In 1934 he was sentenced to life imprisonment, his original death sentence for treason having been commuted. Released in 1940 and allowed to go to Russia, he returned in 1944. This time he had the Russian Red Army to assist him, and was soon the master of Hungary, with the title of Prime Minister. In 1953, following the death of his friend Stalin, he was forced to relinquish his powers in favour of the more liberal-minded Imre Nagy. However, Rakosi remained Party Secretary and in 1955 he managed to remove Nagy and return to power; but not for long. The following year, in an attempt to please the Yugoslav leader Marshal Tito, whom Rakosi had upset, the Russians dismissed Rakosi from all his posts. This led directly to the October 1956 uprising, when right-wingers came out of hiding to claim freedom and attack Jews and Communists. Rakosi, who was both, fled once again to Moscow. This time he did not return with the Russian Red Army who restored stability but kept to the small cottage in the Siberian fishing village of Ust Kamchtsk where he had been banished. He was expelled by both the Russian and Hungarian Communist parties. A witty and brilliant conversationalist who was fluent in six languages he kept busy by writing. Only towards the end of his life was he allowed to return to Hungary. On a trip back to Russia for medical reasons, he died in Gorky, on February 5th 1971.

She was born Cyvia Rambam on February 20th 1888 in Warsaw to a working-class Jewish family. Desperate to escape her roots and the endemic anti-Semitism of Poland, she found her answer in dance. In 1913, following a course with Jaques-Daleroze, the founder of eurhythmics, she was invited to teach the technique to the Diaghilev company, Ballets Russes. Rambert studied under the famous ballet teacher Enrico Ceccetti and later danced in London. Following her marriage to Ashley Dukes,

RAIKIN,
Arkady
(1911-87)
Russian
entertainer

RAKOSI,
Matyas
(1892-1971)
Hungarian
politician

RAMBERT,
Dame Marie
(1888-1982)
Polish/British
ballerina

a British playwright, in 1918 and using Ceccetti's teaching methods, Rambert opened her ballet school in London. In 1926 she staged a ballet choreographed by one of her students, Frederick Ashton. In 1930 she established the Ballet Club, which in 1935 became Ballet Rambert. With Rambert at its head, the company soon had a reputation for being willing to experiment. She presented many of the early works of such choreographers as Frank Staff, Andre Howard, Norman Morrice and others. She also launched the careers of dancers and designers and many others involved in dance. She relied on British talent, unlike other British companies who thought they needed foreign artists with which to pull in the crowds. Ballet Rambert is the longest-running British ballet company still performing. In 1962 the little Jewish girl from Warsaw was made a Dame of the British Empire. She died in London on June 12th 1982.

**RAMONE,
Joey
(1952-)
US musician**

Born Jeffrey Hyman on May 19th 1952 in Forest Hills, New York, in 1974 he founded The Ramones, a group that was partially responsible for the wave of punk music that swept through the Western world in the 1970s. At the Roundhouse in London in 1976 they created a sensation, and their albums *Beat On The Brat* and *Now I Wanna Sniff Some Glue* became winners. The Ramones continued playing through the 1970s and into the 1980s, enjoying success both in the UK and at home in America. August 1980 saw them begin a tour of Britain that lasted six weeks and culminated at the Edinburgh Playhouse during the Rock Festival Week. Between September 3rd and 5th 1981, they performed at the US Festival at San Bernando, California, in front of half a million people. In June 1985 they released 'Bonzo Goes to Bitberg': their protest at Reagan's visit to the grave of a Nazi in Germany. Six months later, Joey was part of the Artists United Against Apartheid movement. With *Brain Drain* in the 1989 charts, the Ramones began a comeback. In January 1990 Joey Ramones had an accident while at New York's Ritz Club that resulted in torn ligaments. Although the group had to cancel some engagements they were soon back on the road.

**RANK,
Otto
(1884-1939)
Austrian
psychologist**

Born Otto Rosenfeld into a poor Jewish family in Vienna on April 22nd 1884, he was educated at a training school with a view to becoming an engineer. At night he wrote. In 1907 he produced *The Artist*, in which he explains how art is linked to psychoanalytic analysis. The book brought him to the attention of Freud (*qv*), who helped to get him into the University of Vienna. There he received his doctorate in 1912. While at university he changed his name and published two more books, *The Myth of the Birth of the Hero* (1909) and *The Incest Motif in Poetry and Saga* (1912). In these works he attempts to show the numerous themes running through poetry and myth. In 1924 he published *The Trauma of Birth*, in which he argues that the transition from the womb to the outside world causes tremendous anxiety in the infant that can persist into adulthood. This work brought him into conflict with Freud and the Vienna Psychoanalytic Society, which expelled him. He went to Paris, where, during the 1930s, he developed the concept of the human will as the guiding force in personality development. This belief, and that in trauma at birth, are regarded as serious departures from the scientific base of psychoanalysis. However, his attitude concerning personal growth and self-actualization, as well as the application of psychoanalytic theory regarding the interpretation of art and myth, remains important. He died in New York on October 31st 1939.

RATHENAU,
Walther
(1867-1922)
German
statesman

Walther was born in Berlin on September 29th 1867, the son of Emil Rathenau, founder of the giant AEG combine. He studied at Berlin and Strasbourg, covering a large number of subjects ranging from philosophy to physics and engineering. By the outbreak of the First World War Walther was the boss of AEG. He convinced the German government of the need of a central resources unit that would monitor all German industrial strength. From August 1914 to May 1915 he headed such an organization, resulting in the conservation of essential raw materials. The importance of his work was evident when the British blockade bit. He then returned to his AEG empire and took no further direct action in the war until 1918, when, as it became clear Germany was in trouble, he urged a massive 'call to arms' directed at the civilian population in the attempt to turn defeat into victory.

Following the end of the war he co-founded the middle-class German Democratic Party and advocated an alliance with the Social Democratic Party. He became convinced that capitalism must change and his writings reflected his opinion that co-operation between government and companies that had a degree of worker participation was preferable to nationalization. He became Minister of Reconstruction in the government of Karl Wirth in 1921, and Foreign Minister in January 1922. In this role he negotiated the Treaty of Rapallo with the Soviet Union (April 1922). His diplomatic success was greeted with acclaim in most of Germany, because it once again established Germany as an independent state. Right-wingers, however, regarded Rathenau as a Jewish agent of Communism. He was murdered in Berlin on June 24th 1922, while journeying to his office at the foreign ministry, by fanatics who would later acclaim Hitler. Indeed, in July 1933, Hitler laid a memorial tablet to the assassins, calling them the 'champions of the new Germany'.

RAY,
Man
(1890-1976)
US
photographer

He was born Emanuel Rabinovitch on August 27th 1890 in Philadelphia. The son of a photographer and artist, he grew up in New York City, where he studied architecture and art and decided to become a painter. In 1915 Ray, as he now called himself, met Marcel Duchamp, the renowned French artist. They agreed to collaborate, and the Dada Group in New York was the result. They went on to found the Société Anonyme, set up to exhibit the work of contemporary artists from all over America. There were travelling exhibitions, too, and many ordinary working-class people, often living in remote parts of the country, had their first opportunity of seeing original art. It also established the first museum anywhere in the world devoted to modern art. In 1921 Ray went to live and work in Paris, where he became leader of the surrealist movement. He painted and made films in the surrealist manner until 1940, when the Germans entered his life and the US appeared to be a much better place for a Jew to be. He worked for a while in Hollywood, but in 1951 returned to Paris.

Man Ray is now regarded as one of the most important photographers of this century. During the 1930s he pioneered the 'raygraph' or 'photogram', a photograph produced without a camera by placing objects directly on to sensitized paper and exposing them to light. His solarization technique was the reversal of the tones of a photographic image. He was the first photographer to appreciate that with the equipment available, the photographer could be both a scientist and an artist. In 1975, on the occasion of his 85th birthday, a large retrospective exhibition was staged at both the New York Cultural Centre and the Institute of Contemporary Art in London. They showed the ingenuity and versatility of Man Ray. He died in Paris on November 18th 1976. Aged 86, he was still working up to the day he died.

REDDY, Helen (1941-) Australian singer

Helen Reddy was born on October 25th 1941 in Melbourne, Australia. Her father Max Reddy, a singer and comedian, and her mother, Stella Lamond, an actress. Helen was just four years old when she appeared with her parents at the Tivoli Theatre in Perth. In 1966 she entered a talent competition in which she defeated the other 1,358 contestants to win first prize: a trip to New York, $400 and an audition with Mercury Records. There was a row over the money and no audition. Helen, alone in New York, sang where she could and earned just enough to keep her head above water. Just before her 25th birthday she announced that she was going home to Australia. On her birthday, friends gave her a surprise party and each guest paid $5 to help raise funds so she might stay. There was a gatecrasher at the party: a William Morris Agency man called Jeff Wald. It was love at first sight and four days later Jeff and Helen were married. They moved to Chicago, where Helen became a 'filler-in': if a singer didn't show or cancelled, Helen stepped into the breach. Although husband Jeff knew the right people to call, it was six months before an executive of Capital Records found the time to hear Helen sing 'I Don't Know How To Love Him'. It became the B side of her first single. The A side was 'I Believe in Music'. However, DJs preferred the flip side and it became a hit. Capital then agreed terms for an album. It included the track 'I am a Woman', which not only reached Number One in December 1972 but became the anthem for the Women's Liberation movement of the 1970s.

In an acceptance speech upon winning the Best Pop, Rock and Folk Vocal Performance (Female) award for 'I am a Woman', Helen Reddy thanked her husband and others, 'and God, because She makes everything possible'. Her September 1973 release, 'Delta Dawn', was top of the Hot 100 and featured in her hit album, *Long Hard Climb*. The following year 'Angie Baby' was the Christmas present that took her to the top. She has since turned from writing songs to writing books, including a history of her native Australia.

Reich was born in Dobrzcynica, Russia, on March 24th 1897. He trained at the Berlin Psychoanalytic Institute before joining the teaching staff of the Vienna Psychoanalytic Institute in 1924. In 1927 he wrote *The Function of Orgasm*, arguing that the ability to reach orgasmic potency was essential for the healthy adult. Failure to dissipate pent-up sexual energy by orgasm could produce neurosis. Reich became a hero in the sexual-politics arena, populated by adherents of left-wing politics and sexual freedom. However, in 1933 he was forced out of Austria by increasing anti-Semitism and spent some years teaching in Scandinavia before emigrating to the US in 1939. Reich developed techniques for treating neurosis that had hitherto resisted the more usual methods. He believed that cosmic energy energized the nervous system and thought that mental illness could be treated by these means. His methods for treating serious illnesses, including cancer, brought him into open conflict with the American medical authorities. He was eventually convicted of contempt of court and sentenced to two years' imprisonment. He died a few months later on November 3rd 1957, still in prison. He left a sealed legacy, that was not to be opened before 2007. It is hoped the letter will unravel the mysteries of a brilliant mind.

In 1949, at the time he was battling against the US Food and Drug Administration, he wrote under the heading of 'Listen, Little Man': 'Whatever you have done to me or will do to me in the future, whether you glorify me as a genius or put me in a mental institution, whether you adore me as your saviour or hang me as a spy, sooner or later necessity will force you to understand that I have discovered the laws of the living.' It is to be hoped that someone has made a diary note for January 1st, 2007.

REICH, Wilhelm (1897-1957) Russian/ American psychologist

Born in Hamburg on September 26th 1891, between 1926 and 1933 he was professor of philosophy at Berlin University. Forced to resign by the advent of Hitler, he became a professor at Istanbul University from 1933 to 1938. In 1939 he was at the University of California, where he remained until he died. He is now regarded as one of the world's leading philosophers of science. The most important of his writings are *The Philosophy of Space and Time* (1927-28) and *The Rise of Scientific Philosophy* (1951). An early member of the Vienna School of logical postivists, he founded, together with Rudolph Carnap, the journal *Erkenntnis*, which ran from 1930 to 1938 and reappeared in the US in 1975. Reichenbach made an important contribution to probability theory, in which two truth tables are replaced by the multi-valued concept 'weight'. He died in Los Angeles on April 9th 1953.

REICHENBACH, Hans (1891-1953) German/ American philosopher

He was born on July 20th 1897 into a Jewish family in Wiociawek, Poland, and brought up in Switzerland. In 1933 he synthesized ascorbic acid (vitamin C) and in the same year began his work of isolating hormones manufactured by the cortex of the adrenal gland, the basis of cortisone. In 1938 he was appointed head of the Institute of Pharmacy at Basle University. In 1950 he received a share of the Nobel Prize for Medicine for his work on adrenal cortex hormones. From 1946 to 1957 he was professor of organic chemistry at Basle University and in 1968 was awarded the Copley Medal of the British Royal Society.

REICHSTEIN, Tadeus (1897-1980) Swiss chemist

REILLY,
Sidney
(1874-1925)
Russian/British
spy

He was born Sigmund Rosenblum, the son of a Jewish doctor, on March 24th 1874 in Odessa, Russia. Having studied chemistry in Vienna, he went to Brazil in 1900. There he changed his name to Sidney Reilly, following his meeting with British Army officers who recommended him to British Intelligence in London. Over the next decade he travelled to many parts of Europe, making deals and getting information and reporting back to his masters in Whitehall. His greatest coup appears to have been manipulating Persian oil concessions out of French hands and into British control. This ensured many years of continuing supply for UK oil companies. During the First World War he was in America, buying up huge amounts of munitions for Britain, as well as being involved in preventing German espionage of the factories concerned. He was most audacious and made several trips to Germany masquerading as an American businessman prior to America's entry into the war in 1917. It is said he even attended a German general staff meeting at which the Kaiser was present. In May 1918 he was sent to Moscow to persuade the new revolutionary government not to make a separate peace with Germany. He failed and ran for his life. In 1925, he was once again in Russia but now it was the USSR. When he was arrested on September 22nd of that year he disappeared for ever.

REINHARDT,
Max
(1873-1943)
Austrian/
American
director

Max Reinhardt, whose original surname was Goldman, was born in Baden, Austria, on September 9th 1873. He was the eldest child of orthodox Jewish parents who went on to give Max six brothers and sisters. His parents, who for their time were most understanding, allowed Max to play for long hours with his puppets, making up a variety of stories for them to play out. At working age, Max was an unhappy bank clerk who swapped the high desk for an acting school. By the 20th century Max was truly part of Vienna's theatrical scene and in 1902 he directed his first play, Oscar Wilde's *Salome*. The following year he produced *A Midsummer Night's Dream* and the plaudits came thick and fast. Still only 32, he was now famous. Buying the Deutsches Theater in Berlin for a million marks, he renovated it and installed the latest technical features. He brought his brother Edmond in to help him and by doing so erased the depressions from which Edmond was suffering. Probably Max's most spectacular work was *The Miracle*, which was premiered in London in 1911, then opened in New York, then Paris and then all of the major European cities. *The Miracle* involved as many as 2,000 people and is reckoned to be this century's greatest theatrical drama. Nothing remotely comparable has since been undertaken. The Salzburg Festival was his brainchild and entirely as a result of his early efforts remains an annual event. In the 1930s, Max was busy travelling between his castle in Austria and Berlin, Vienna and Salzburg, and was abroad when Hitler arrived. He wrote a letter to the new German government and, while acknowledging it had been democratically elected, berated them for their antisemitic creed. Bequeathing his theatrical empire to the German people, he left Germany for good.

After a while touring Europe he settled in America, where he opened a theatrical workshop in Hollywood in 1938. Reinhardt was a shy man and he found his new environment brash and frightening. He was a romantic who, all his working life, had combined German discipline with Viennese charm. Here in Hollywood, although much admired for the work he had done, there was little appetite for what he now had in mind to do. He became increasingly unwell and towards the end of his life lost his power of speech. He died in New York on October 31st 1943. His many obituaries included the judgement that he was one of the most outstanding and brilliant directors and producers of all time.

Judith Resnick was born on April 5th 1949 in Akron, Ohio. Her grandfather was a rabbi and she was educated at Carnegie-Mellon University, from where she obtained a degree in electrical engineering, subsequently gaining a PhD in the same subject from the University of Maryland. She had several jobs in industry, including a position as systems engineer with the Xerox Corporation. In 1978, still with Xerox, she was one of six people selected for training as an astronaut for the space shuttle programme. Resnick became only the second woman ever to travel in space when included as a specialist in the crew of the *Discovery* in 1984. As an acknowledged expert on solar power, she was one of the seven astronauts on the space shuttle *Challenger* when it lifted off from Cape Canaveral on January 28th 1986. Minutes later the spacecraft exploded and the entire crew was killed. Russian cartographers, in a tribute to Resnick, have named a crater on Venus in her honour.

He was born Elmer Reizenstein on September 28th 1892 in New York City and graduated from the New York Law School in 1912. Rice preferred writing to practising law, so it was most fortunate that his first play, *On Trial* (1914), was not only critically well received but earned him the then enormous sum of $100,000. The play, in which he used his legal training for the plot, was a radical departure from the norm in that it used the 'flashback' method so beloved of later film directors. In 1923 he produced *The Adding Machine*, using techniques from the German expressionist theatre to show the beginning of the dehumanization of man in favour of machinery. His play *Street Scene* (1929) was a realistic tragedy set in a New York slum and won him the Pulitzer Prize. *Counsellor at Law* (1931), *We The People* (1933), *Judgement Day* (1934), *An American Landscape* (1939) and *Dream Girl* (1946) were all first-class plays, even though not all found favour with the critics.

Rice was in the forefront of debates around the social issues of the century. He fought the internment of Japanese-Americans during the Second World War, as well as church-imposed morality. Censorship caused him to resign from the Federal Theatre Project during the depression of the 1930s. In the McCarthy era he opposed the blacklist and was himself accused of Communist connections. He resigned from the Playwright's TV Theatre over this, stating at the time: 'I have repeatedly denounced the men who sit in the Kremlin for judging artists by political standards; I do not intend to acquiesce when the same procedure is followed by political commissars who sit in the offices of advertising agencies of business corporations.' In 1963 he wrote his biography, *Minority Report*. In this he states his 'Decalogue of Principles': It is better to live than to die; to love than to hate; to create than to destroy; to do something than to do nothing; to be truthful than to lie; to question than to accept; to be strong than to be weak; to hope than to despair; to venture than to fear; to be free than to be bound. He died on May 8th 1967 in Southampton, England.

RICH,
Buddy
(1917-87)
US band leader

Born Bernard Rich on September 30th 1917 in New York City, from the age of two he was in show business, as part of his parents' act. At the age of six he was touring as a solo act, playing drums and tap dancing, and was not yet ten when he toured Australia. By the time he was an old boy of eleven he had formed his own band. From the age of 20 he began working with some of the top bands of the 1930s and 1940s. In this period he was the drummer with Joe Marsala, Bunny Berigan, Harry James (*qv*), Artie Shaw (*qv*) and Tommy Dorsey. Following service with the US armed forces during the Second World War, he formed his own band. Later he recorded extensively with Art Tatum, Lionel Hampton, Oscar Peterson, Dizzy Gillespie, Louis Armstrong and others. In the late 1950s he was appearing with his small band and singing. In the early 1960s, Buddy Rich was once again with Harry James, but by the middle of the decade had decided to try again and formed another big band.

For the next twelve years the Buddy Rich Band toured all over America and Europe. He was also a prolific record producer, producing 46 albums over a 40-year career, and rarely did a year go by without his releasing what generally proved to be a hit album. In his early career he was known for his short temper, and while playing with Dorsey he frequently clashed with the band's singer, who also had a short fuse: Frank Sinatra. Rich, known for his caustic wit, found it stood him in good stead when he appeared on television chat shows. His criticism of well-known pop singers worried the studios because they were often on the borderline of slander. He frequently came back from illness to hard work until in 1986 he was diagnosed as having a brain tumour. While being prepared for surgery, a nurse asked him if there was anything he was allergic to; 'Only country music,' he replied. Buddy Rich died on April 2nd 1987.

RICHLER,
Mordecai
(1931-)
Canadian writer

Richler was born in Montreal on January 27th 1931 and educated at Sir George Williams University. He then went to live in Paris where he met and was influenced by existentialist writers. Back in Montreal he published his novel, *The Acrobat* (1954), which he set in Spain. Richler then went to London and lived there for some 20 years before once again returning home. While growing up he experienced considerable poverty as well as anti-Semitism, aspects of his life which feature in many of his books, for example *Sons of a Smaller Hero* (1955) and *A Choice of Enemies* (1957). *The Apprenticeship of Duddy Kravitz*, a farcical tale of a young Jewish boy growing into manhood, was published in 1959 and filmed in 1974 with Richler writing the screenplay. Other works include *The Incomparable Atuk* (1963), *St Urbain's Horseman* (1971) and *Joshua Then and Now* (1980). *Solomon Gursky Was Here* (1990), a novel that spans five generations of the Gursky family, was short-listed for the Booker Prize. Richler, who also writes essays and books for children, is probably the greatest Canadian novelist of the second half of this century.

Burton Richter was born in Brooklyn, New York, on March 22nd 1931. Having received his PhD from the Massachusetts Institute of Technology in 1956, he was appointed a professor at Stanford University, California, and there started experiments to confirm the validity of quantum electrodynamics at short distances. In 1973, he completed construction of the Stanford Positron-Electron Asymmetric Ring, a colliding beam accelerator. This allowed Richter to discover a new subatomic particle that became known as the J-particle, the first of a newly discovered group of massive, long-lived mesons. In 1976, Richter was awarded the Nobel Prize for Physics.

Rickover was born in Makov, Russia, on January 27th 1900 and brought up in Chicago where his father worked as a tailor. In 1918, following high school, Rickover enrolled in the US Naval Academy at Annapolis, Maryland, graduating in 1922. He went on to study electrical engineering at Columbia University from where, in 1929, he obtained a MS. Submarine training followed and in 1937, after serving on several different types, he was given command of USS *Finch*, a minesweeper. During the Second World War, he headed the electrical section of the Bureau of Ships in Washington. In 1946, Rickover went on a course to Oak Ridge, Tennessee, to gain experience that would later enable him to advise and oversee the production of the US Navy's first nuclear submarine, USS *Nautilus*. He continued in the navy, but was involved in the development of the first full nuclear plant for civilian use at Shipping Point for civilian use.

Rickover was promoted to rear-admiral in 1953, vice-admiral in 1959 and full admiral in 1973. There was criticism over the time it took for him to reach admiral and anti-Semitism was not ruled out. Rickover was outspoken, tough and single-minded about the development of nuclear power for defence and domestic use. In 1982 he retired from the navy after serving as an officer for 63 years. This record followed an Act of Congress that exempted him from retiring at the time usually observed for senior admirals. Known as 'the father of the atomic submarine', he died in Arlington, Virginia, on July 8th 1986. Following his retirement, he openly regretted his part in nuclear proliferation and demanded the international abolition of nuclear weapons and reactors, saying: 'Humankind will probably destroy itself and be replaced by a wiser species.'

Lucie Rie, whose maiden name was Gomperz, was born in Vienna on March 16th 1902 and educated at the Vienna Gymnasium and the Arts and Crafts School. Her early work included such influences as neoclassicism, Jugendstil and modernism. In 1938, to escape from German persecution because of her Jewish background, she emigrated to England. In London, at her small workshop in Albion Mews, she specialized in creating ceramic buttons. She had her first exclusive show as a potter in 1949. In later shows in Rotterdam (1967) and Hamburg (1972) she collaborated with Hans Coper, who shared her studio in London. A major exhibition in Düsseldorf in 1978 was a great success, as was her show in London at the Victoria and Albert Museum (1981-82). In 1981 she was made a Commander of the British Empire. She died in London on April 1st 1995.

ROBBINS,
Jerome
(1918-)
US
choreographer

Born Jerome Rabinowitz on October 11th 1918 in New York City, he was drawn to the world of ballet while still in his teens. He danced with the Gluck Sandor-Felicia Sorel Dance Centre and toured with the Ballet Theatre before settling for a career as a choreographer. In 1944 he choreographed Leonard Bernstein's (*qv*) *Fancy Free*, which later inspired the Broadway musical and feature film *On The Town*. Major works as a choreographer included *Interplay*, *Les Noces* and *Dances at a Gathering*. In 1949 he joined New York City Ballet and combined dance and choreography. Over a period of ten years he choreographed nine ballets. He also worked on dance routines for the 1951 musical *The King and I*, *Peter Pan* (1954), *West Side Story* (1957), for the film version of which he received an Academy Award, *Gypsy* (1959) and *Fiddler on the Roof* (1964). Robbins is known as a versatile and imaginative creator and one of this century's truly great choreographers. Other important works include *Ballarde* (1952), *Goldberg Variations* (1971), *A Suite of Dreams* (1979), *Glass Pieces* (1983) and *Eight Lives* (1985). In 1983 Jerome Robbins succeeded Balachine as the New York City Ballet's master-in-chief. His blending of classical ballet with pragmatic, earthy styles has contributed to his success. In 1989 *Jerome Robbin's Broadway*, a staged compilation of his work, opened on Broadway. In 1990 Robbins resigned from the New City Ballet and retired.

ROBINSON,
Edward G.
(1893-1973)
US actor

He was born Emmanuel Goldenberg in Bucharest, Romania, on December 12th 1893. When he was ten years old his family emigrated to New York. While being educated at City College he decided upon an acting career, and first appeared on Broadway in 1915. Short and thickset, he looked ideal for the gangster roles he once appeared destined to take for ever. He made his film debut in 1923, having survived for nearly ten years in the theatre. In 1931 he was the trigger-happy gang boss Cesare Bandello in *Little Caesar*: thereafter he never looked back. During the 1930s and 1940s, he made numerous pictures including two directed by Fritz Lang (*qv*), *The Woman in the Window* (1944) and *Scarlet Street* (1945). Notable among the many films he starred in were *Dr Ehrlich's Magic Bullet* (1940), *Double Indemnity* (1944), *The Stranger* (1946), *Key Largo* (1948), *The Ten Commandments* (1956), *The Cincinnati Kid* (1965) and his last film, made in 1973, *Soylent Green*. The McCarthy hysteria, culminating in the evil Hollywood witch-hunt, damaged his career but he rode out the onslaught by returning to his first love, the theatre, appearing on Broadway in *Middle of the Night* to rave reviews (1956-58). During the Second World War he broadcast, in German, to the anti-Nazi underground and was the first Hollywood star to entertain the troops in France following the D-Day landings of June 1944. Robinson was a cultured man and an art connoisseur all his life, and his art collection was one of the finest private collections in America. His autobiography, *All My Yesterdays*, was published in 1973; on January 26th that year he died in Los Angeles. During his lifetime he received no Academy Awards or nominations; but he did receive one posthumously. Awards, however, never meant as much to him as his love of art. Films provided the finance for his paintings and the theatre the outlet for his love of acting.

Born on June 28th 1902 in New York, **Rodgers**, together with Oscar Hammerstein, was to compose some of the best musical shows of the century. At eighteen he entered Columbia University and there met Lorenz Hart. The two worked together on the university show, *Fly With Me* (1919). Then Rodgers went on to study music at the Juillard School of Music. The two men kept in touch and in 1925 produced their first professional show, *The Garrick Gaieties*, which included the hit song 'Manhattan'. In 1936 came *On Your Toes*, which included the jazz ballet sequence 'Slaughter on Tenth Avenue'. *Babe in Arms* (1937) included the hit songs 'My Funny Valentine' and 'The Lady is a Tramp'. From Shakespeare's *Comedy of Errors* they created *The Boys From Syracuse* (1938). The year 1940 saw *Pal Joey*, but in a form that didn't find favour, and it was only in 1952 that it was revamped to critical and public acclaim, including the song 'Bewitched, Bothered and Bewildered'. However, by that time Hart had died and Hammerstein was now Rodgers' partner. In 1943 they made *Oklahoma*, the first of the blockbusting musical comedies that went around the world following the end of the Second World War. It brought them the Pulitzer Prize and ran on Broadway for 2,248 performances. It included songs that have since become standards: 'Oh, What a Beautiful Morning', 'The Surrey with the Fringe on Top' and 'People Will say We're in Love'. The partnership would continue until Hammerstein died seventeen years later. During that time they wrote *Carousel* (1945), *South Pacific* (1949), *The King and I* (1951), *The Flower Drum Song* (1958) and *The Sound of Music* (1959). Many of these later became hit films. All three, Rodgers, Hart and Hammerstein, were Jewish, from European backgrounds, and together were responsible for America being seen as the home of the great musical shows. Rodgers also wrote many hit songs, in addition to those featured in his shows. These include 'Blue Room', 'Mountain Greenery', 'Thou Swell', 'With a Song in my Heart', 'Isn't It Romantic?', 'There's a Small Hotel', 'My Funny Valentine' and 'This Can't Be Love'. He also wrote the bewitching music for the documentary film *Victory at Sea* (1952). He died in New York on December 30th 1979. It has been calculated that if all of Rodgers' Broadway musicals were put on consecutively, in their original number of performances, they would run for 37 years.

Sigmund Romberg was born in Nagykanczsa, Hungary, on July 29th 1887. He was educated in Vienna as an engineer but his hobby was playing the violin and composing. In 1909 he went to New York and stayed. He ran a small orchestra in a high-class restaurant and introduced the dinner-dance concept to the US. In 1917 his operetta *Maytime* was produced and well received. In the 1920s there followed a series of operettas with romantic storylines and syrupy songs. They were most popular and included *The Student Prince* (1924). It became a silent film in 1926, and in 1954 was filmed again with Mario Lanza singing, but not playing: he was too fat. *The Desert Song* (1926) was produced in three film versions, and *The New Moon* was produced in 1930. Romberg's shows included the ever popular songs 'Deep in My Heart', 'One Alone' and 'Lover, Come Back to Me'. In the 1930s he switched to writing songs for films. In 1933 his operetta *Rose de France* was

RODGERS,
Richard
(1902-79)
US composer

ROMBERG,
Sigmund
(1887-1951)
Hungarian/
American
composer

produced in Paris. During the Second World War he had a radio series, *An Evening with Sigmund Romberg*. His last successful work was the musical comedy *In Central Park* (1945). He died in New York on November 9th 1951.

ROSENBERG, Harold (1906-78) US art critic

Harold Rosenberg was born in New York City on February 2nd 1906 and educated at New York's City College and Brooklyn Law School. He became responsible for the term, 'abstract expressionism' and championed the style of De Kooning, Pollack and Rothko (*qv*), to which he gave the name 'action painting'. He was art critic on the *New York Times* from 1967 and used his platform to clarify various concepts in the work of the new wave of painters. He was a controversial figure, and indeed many of the artists he befriended appeared to resent Rosenberg's incursion into their domain. He was accused of being obsessed with foreplay and apparently indifferent to the climax of the act itself, the canvas. He was however, a very powerful figure in the world of art and a positive and progressive presence, especially where abstract expressionist painters were concerned. He died in New York on July 11th 1978.

ROSENBERG, Isaac (1890-1918) British poet

Rosenberg was born in Bristol on November 25th 1890. His Jewish parents had come to England to escape religious persecution in Tsarist Russia. Shortly after Isaac's birth, the family moved to the East End of London. In 1911 Isaac went to the Slade School of Fine Arts and trained as an artist, winning several prizes. However, he later felt he could express himself better through words than through visual art. In 1915 he enlisted in the British Army and after minimal training was sent to France. He was to become famous for his 'Trench Poems', written between 1916 and 1918, which demonstrates his imaginative power and originality. In April 1918 he was killed in action. He also wrote a play, *Unicorn*. In 1922, the first volume of his poetry was published with an introduction by the eminent poet Laurence Binyon. His *Collected Works*, with a foreword by Siegfried Sassoon (*qv*), first appeared in 1937. A later, more extensive edition by Ian Parsons was published in 1979. It is generally accepted that much of Rosenberg's wartime poetry is not just realistic about trench warfare, incorporating a streak of romantic lyricism and a love of beauty, reminiscent of Blake, that makes Rosenberg's work stand out among early 20th century poetry.

ROSENBERG, Julius (1918-53) and Ethel (1915-53) US political victims

Julius Rosenberg was born on May 12th 1918 in New York and obtained a degree in electrical engineering in 1939. During the Second World War he served in the US Army Signal Corps. His wife, Ethel, was born on September 28th 1915, also in New York; her maiden name was Greenglass. In 1950 the couple were arrested and brought to trial on a charge under the Espionage Act of 1917. Despite world-wide pleas for clemency, they were executed at Sing Sing prison on June 19th 1953. Their trial, based mostly on circumstantial evidence, was considered at the time a sham more in keeping with the Russian show trials of the 1930s than with justice in a democratic state. The prosecution claimed the Rosenbergs were part of a complicated spy network and responsible for relaying secrets from the atomic bomb project in Los Alamos to the Russians. President Eisenhower actually foamed at the mouth as he bellowed, 'millions of dead would have their deaths attributable to what these spies have done', fuelling the hysteria of the time. It was noted in the more restrained elements of the press that this would be the first time in American history that civilians were executed for espionage in peacetime. Their trial was a travesty; Ethel was innocent and Julius framed, the whole calculated to flame Cold War propaganda. A lawyer at the time commented: 'the executions show the US is living under the heel of a military dictator garbed in civilian attire'.

The Rosenbergs were an ordinary American family, the father having connections with some of the other defendants in the trial and the mother manifestly innocent, plus two sons whom the state had no problem in making orphans. Following the execution the two boys, aged ten and six, were adopted by songwriter Abel Meeropol and his wife. Others involved in the case included Ethel's brother, who was coerced into giving evidence for the state and received fifteen years' imprisonment, and Harry Gold, a Swiss national and Russian courier, who got 30 years. Julius was a member of the legal American Communist Party and that appeared to be sufficient grounds for a conviction. Over the years, the general opinion has come to be that there was a gigantic miscarriage of justice that came from the very top. In the intervening years, nothing has emerged to support the verdict of guilty. The US government still refuses to release 100,000 pages of records that relate to the case. It is considered that one day the Rosenbergs will be posthumously reinstated, as have so many East Europeans since the fall of Communist regimes on that continent.

"......Always remember that we were innocent and could not wrong our conscience"

The Rosenberg's last letter to their children from Sing Sing's Death Row on June 18th 1953.

ROSENBLOOM, Maxie (1904-76) US world boxing champion and actor

'Slapsie Maxie' was born on September 6th 1904 in Leonard's Bridge, Connecticut, and given his nickname by Damon Runyon, who saw him as a colourful personality with a unique open glove style that was often a slap rather than a punch. Not that Maxie couldn't punch; he certainly could, and he punched himself to the very top, winning the world light heavyweight title in 1930, when he defeated Jim Slattery who had held it for only a few months. Not so Maxie; he was the reigning champion for four and a half years, defeating all-comers, until he met his fellow American Bob Olin and lost it. Maxie, who when young fought on average twice a month, now retired. He took a long holiday, then went to Hollywood on the off-chance. There he became a professional actor and appeared in some 100 films. A highly colourful character on and off the screen and in the ring, he had great talent for all he did. He died in Los Angeles in March 1976.

ROSS,
Barney
(1909-67)
US world
champion boxer

He was born Barnet David Rosofsky in New York City on December 23rd 1909. His father was a Talmudic scholar and did not approve of his son taking up boxing while in high school. He changed his mind when Barney won the Golden Gloves in 1929. In 1933 Ross became the first boxer to hold the lightweight and welterweight world titles simultaneously when he beat Tony Canzoneri and Jimmy McLarnin. The following year he gave up the lightweight title and lost the welterweight back to McLarnin. In 1935 he regained this title and kept it for three years until he lost to Henry Armstrong (US), but not before he was tagged 'the greatest welterweight of all time'. During the Second World War, he served in the Marines and was wounded at Guadalcanal during hand to hand fighting. Awarded the Silver Star, Ross was returned to the US for hospital treatment. During his recovery he became addicted to the drugs he was receiving. He overcame his problem and in 1957 published his autobiography, *No Man Stands Alone*. He died in January 1967.

ROTBLAT,
Joseph
(1908-)
Polish/British
physicist

Joseph Rotblat was born in Warsaw on November 4th 1908. In 1939, when the Germans invaded his homeland, Rotblat was working at Liverpool University. He stayed in Britain and later, from 1943, became part of the team that worked in Los Alamos, New Mexico, on the Manhattan Project that led to the manufacture of the atomic bomb dropped on Japan in 1945, to end the Second World War. Rotblat became most concerned to realize that atomic weaponry would become the basis of the Cold War and, together with Einstein (*qv*) and Bertrand Russell, signed the manifesto demanding that the scientists who invented the means of mass destruction be allowed a say in their future use. They were ignored.

In 1957 Rotblat organized a conference of like-minded scientists in a remote Canadian village on the coast of Nova Scotia, called Pugwash. Thus was one of the great movements of the second half of the 20th century. Pugwash members, with Rotblat at their head, warned the world of the dangers of unchecked nuclear manufacture and testing. He also warned of possible danger from some types of civil nuclear reactors. He scorned French nuclear testing in the Pacific and influenced the eventual ban on testing. In 1950, he was appointed professor of physics at St Bartholomew's Hospital Medical College in London and stayed here until 1976, specializing in the effects of radiation on living tissues. On October 13th 1995, Rotblat was awarded the Nobel Peace Prize. In October 1996 he hosted an international conference in Israel, for the purpose of securing the release from prison of Mordechai Vanunu, convicted in 1986 of revealing Israel's atomic secrets - which everyone knew about anyway. As Rotblat said at the conference, 'There is no reason to keep Vanunu in prison any longer because his revelations had no serious impact on Israel's security.'

ROTH,
Henry
(1906-95)
US writer

Henry Roth was born in Tysmenica, Russia, on February 8th, 1906 and was a small child when he and his parents arrived in New York. The family settled in Manhattan's Lower East Side, later dubbed by Roth a 'Jewish mini-state'. Roth was educated at De Witt Clinton High School and later at New York's City College. Here he was taught by Eda Walton, a critic, poet and academic. Twelve years his senior, she encouraged Roth to write and became his mistress. In 1934 he wrote his novel that was based upon his background and told the story of Jewish immigrant life. *Call It Sleep* was an instant best-seller and Henry Roth everyone's darling. His public eagerly awaited his next novel. Unfortunately most of that public died before their hope was realized. It took Henry Roth 60 years to produce his second novel. There were rumours that a previous effort was destroyed but these were never confirmed. *A Star Shines Over Mr Morris Park* was published in 1994. It was the first part of a six-volume work that was a mixture of autobiography and light fiction. The 60 intervening years had been spent learning Greek, Latin, Italian and German, falling in love with Marxism, falling out of love with Eda Walton, falling in love with Muriel Parker and marrying her. In 1952 he bought a small farm in Augusta, Maine, and here he reared and sold ducks and geese. He taught Latin and mathematics and lived very frugally.

In the 1960s, 30 years after it was originally published, *Call it Sleep* was republished, this time in paperback. It sold a million copies and once again Roth was in the money and in the limelight. The Arab-Israeli war of 1967 had an important impact on Roth. The support shown by the Communist Party for the Arabs annoyed him and he now felt 'a rational reunion with the Judaism of his earliest self'. He spent his last two years fighting arthritic pain and writing blocks. Shortly before his death, *Mercy of a Rude Stream* appeared. The title comes from Shakespeare's *Henry VIII* and refers to the fall of a once proud king from the heights of public attention into the depths of emotional turmoil. Henry Roth died in Albuquerque, New Mexico, on October 13th 1995. Published in 1997 the autobiography he completed shortly before his death was published: *From Bondage* in part attempts to explain his 60 year mental writer's block. It appears that he experienced ongoing sexual guilt following carnal knowledge of his sister, aged 11, and of his cousin when she was 14.

Philip Roth was born on March 19th 1933 in Newark, New Jersey. He obtained an MA from the University of Chicago and thereafter worked as a teacher. He first achieved fame with his novel *Goodbye Columbus* (1959), a story that depicts the materialism of a middle-class Jewish suburban family. It launched the career of the 'Jewish Princess'. In 1962 he wrote *Letting Go* and in 1969 he published *Portnoy's Complaint*, a brilliant story of an ordinary Jewish lad discovering sex and having to cope with a domineering mother. *The Ghost Writer* centres on an aspiring writer Roth calls Nathan Zuckerman; it hatched two further novels, *Zuckerman Unbound* (1981 and in 1983 *The Anatomy Lesson*. They all came together in *Zuckerman Bound* (1985). Roth is one of the best novelists of the second half of the century, and the Jewish character is integral to much of his work. He is, however, difficult to live with, according to ex-wife Claire Bloom (*qv*), and quite self-obsessed. In 1995 he published *Sabbath's Theatre*, the multi-faceted tale of Mickey Sabbath as he travels through life. In 1997 he published *American Pastoral* that brings 'Zuckerman' upto date.

ROTH, Philip (1933-) US writer

ROTHENSTEIN,
Sir William
(1872-1945)
British painter

Rothenstein was born in Bradford, Yorkshire, on January 29th 1872, the son of Jewish immigrants engaged in the woollen trade. William was educated at Bradford Grammar School and later studied at the Slade School of Fine Arts and the Academie Julian in Paris. By the turn of the century, Rothenstein was painting famous contemporary personalities. During the First World War, he was an official war artist and recorded the bloody battles in the trenches of northern France. In 1917 he was appointed a professor of art at Sheffield University, where he stayed until 1926. From 1927 to 1933 he was a trustee of the Tate Gallery, London, and until 1938 a member of the Royal Fine Arts Commission. He was probably better known as a teacher than a painter, but his earlier work such as *The Talmud School* (1904) and *Carrying the Law* (1909) is particularly well regarded. His *Dolls House* hangs in the Tate Gallery. Among his many writings is his three-volume, *Men and Memoirs*. During the Second World War, now aged 68, he worked as an unofficial war artist to the RAF. His paintings show the heroism of the youth of the time. Rothenstein died in Oxfordshire on February 14th 1945.

ROTHKO,
Mark
(1903-70)
US painter

He was born Marcus Rothkovitch on September 25th 1903 in Dvinsk, Russia. The family emigrated to Portland, Oregon, in the US and during his youth Mark dallied with politics. At Yale University he dropped out and wandered the country, finally in 1925 choosing to settle in New York. He took up painting and although he studied under Max Weber he was basically self-taught. His style became known as 'subway', the name he gave to a series of paintings showing the drab, seamy life of poor New Yorkers during the depression. His paintings show the social situation in the US from the New Deal era through the Second World War to the post-war years, though his *Baptismal Scene* (1945) at the Whitney Museum in New York is semi-abstract. By the early 1950s he had achieved a highly individualistic abstract form that did not rely on vivid brushstrokes but rather on melting colours that appeared to float around the canvas. An example is his *Red on Maroon* (1959, Tate Gallery, London). Rothko never really departed from this style; rather, he constantly refined it to become more simplistic. In the 1960s he worked on very large canvases, a series of fourteen that averaged around 5 x 3 metres each. These were serious pictures of a mystical quality. Rothko believed he had been forgotten by painters who had once learned from him, and these thoughts intensified his increasing bouts of depression. He committed suicide in New York on February 25th 1970. Following his death there ensued an ugly legal battle that lasted from 1972 to 1982. Rothko had saved over 700 of his paintings and his executors were accused by Rothko's daughter of having disposed of them for personal gain. The court found against the executors, who were fined or imprisoned. Thereupon the Mark Rothko Foundation came into being. Half of the works were distributed to museums in England, Denmark, America, Israel and Holland. The bulk can be seen at the National Gallery of Art in Washington DC.

Miriam Rothschild, the eldest child of Nathaniel and grand daughter of the first Lord Rothschild, was born on August 5th 1908 at the families estate in Ashton Wold near Peterborough. Her mother was Rozsika von Wertheinstein whose family later perished in the Holocaust. Miriam had little formal education until she was seventeen, having been educated by her father until his death when she was fifteen. Largely self-taught and without a university degree, she has gone on to become a world authority on fleas. She became fascinated by the flea at a young age and has catalogued some 30,000 types in a lifetime's work. She described, in some detail, how fleas, who exist entirely on blood, rely on breeding by attaching themselves to pregnant animals. The ability of a flea to continuously jump to heights as high as New York's Rockefeller Centre was her amazing discovery.

Dragonflies are another passion of Miriam Rothschild and one that has resulted in a museum at her birthplace. In 1992 she was presented with the Victorian Medal of Honour by the Royal Horticultural Society and elected president of the Royal Entomoligcal Society.

ROTHSCHILD, Miriam (1908-) British naturalist

Leon Rottman was born in Bucharest on July 22nd 1934. In the 1956 Olympic Games, held in Melbourne, Rottman won two gold medals, taking the 1,000 metres singles Canadian canoe race in a time of 5:05.3 and the 10,000 metres singles, also in the Canadian canoe. The Canadian canoe is the vessel propelled by a paddle with a single blade, from a half-kneeling position. It was the first time in the history of the Olympics that the 1,000 and 10,000 metre races were won by the same man; the achievement has never been repeated.

ROTTMAN, Leon (1934-) Romanian Olympic champion

Bernice Rubens was born in Cardiff and educated at the University College of South Wales. Following periods working as a teacher and writer of documentary films, she became a full-time novelist following the publication in 1960 of *Set on Edge*: *Madame Sousatzka* followed in 1962 and *Mate in Three* in 1965. These early novels show her Jewish background and portray family relationships. In 1969 she won the coveted Booker Prize with her novel *The Elected Member*, which tells the tale of the Zweck family. In 1979 she wrote *Spring Sonata*, this time about a Jewish family beset with the modern problems all families experience. Perhaps *Sheila Rosen* has slightly more. Later novels include *Birds of Passage* (1981) and *Kingdom Come* (1990). Like a good wine, Bernice Rubens improves with age. This is well demonstrated by her 1991 novel, *A Solitary Grief*, and her 1996 book, *Yesterday in the Back Lane*. She has a deftness in handling human behaviour, and her novels are full of surprises, often with a comic touch.

RUBENS, Bernice (1928-) British writer

Artur Rubinstein was born in Lodz, Poland, on January 28th 1887, and become world-famous as a repertoire pianist. He began studying the piano when was three, and at eight he was at the Warsaw Conservatory. In 1906 he made his US debut at the Carnegie Hall, where he was given a mixed reception. Fluent in eight languages, during the First World War he was a military interpreter, giving recitals in his spare time. Following the war he worked in Spain and South America,

RUBINSTEIN, Artur (1887-1982) Polish/American pianist

introducing works by de Falla and Albeniz. Here he was well received, unlike the US, where once again, although thirteen years had passed, his welcome was still tepid. It was only in the 1930s, following his marriage in 1932 to Amiela Mynarska, that he came to terms with his career and created the high calibre playing that would last for the next 50 years. His interpretation of Chopin has never been equalled. Rubinstein, a witty and engaging raconteur who could have made a fortune on the after-dinner speaker circuit, was also a serious performer whose concerts were always a sell-out. A US citizen from 1946, he was awarded the US Medal of Freedom in 1976. He wrote his autobiography in two parts: *My Young Years* in 1973 and *My Many Years* in 1980. He died in Geneva, Switzerland, on December 20th 1982.

RUBINSTEIN, Helena (1870-1965) Polish/American pioneer

She was born, one of eight daughters, to a middle-class Jewish family in Krakow, Poland, on December 25th 1870. In 1902 she went to Australia to visit relations in Melbourne, and while there she opened a beauty shop offering for sale a special cream, the ingredients of which she had brought with her from Poland. The business was a success and following specialist training in the field of dermatology, she opened a branch in London under the style of 'Maison de Beauté' in 1910. She followed this with her first venture in Paris, the capital of the beauty business. Leaving the First World War behind her, she arrived in the US and opened branches in all the principal cities. In 1917 she switched to manufacturing and distributing her products, via chemists, all over America and then all over the world. It meant that women everywhere could indulge their dreams at little cost and believe they could look like the stars they saw on the cinema screens. Her fortune, estimated at 100 million dollars, became the core of the Helena Rubinstein Foundation which she created in 1953 and directed until too ill to continue. The foundation's activities included caring for the needy as well as making endowments to art foundations. She had an enduring feud with Elizabeth Arden about whose products were the better. It afforded Rubinstein the greatest pleasure when hers were adjudged the winner. She died in New York on August 1st 1965.

RUBINSTEIN, Ida (1885-1960) French ballerina/ producer

Ida Rubinstein was born in St Petersburg, Russia and was soon the orphan of a wealthy Jewish family. Raised by her aunt, at 21 she inherited a fortune which she invested in the arts. She herself was an accomplished ballet dancer who had studied with Michael Fokine. He later choreographed *Salome* for her and in 1909 this caused such a sensation that the censor banned all future performances. She was renowned for her great beauty and Diaghilev chose her for the role of Cleopatra when the Ballet Russe began their first Paris season in 1910. Other members of this cast were Anna Pavlova and Nijinsky. In the later production of *Scheherazade*, she danced the role of Zobeide. The following year she formed her own dance company. She commissioned Ravel's *Bolero* in 1911 and later his *La Valse*. Debussy wrote the music for *The Martyrdom of St Sebastian*, in which Rubinstein danced the title role. She produced Stravinsky's *The Fairy Kiss* in 1928 and his *Persephone* in 1934. She also acted and appeared in several plays, including *Camille*, and commissioned works by Massine. At the beginning of the Second World War she retired to the South of France where she was left undisturbed. She died in Vence, France, on September 20th 1960. Jean Cocteau once said of her: 'she is too beautiful, like a perfume that is too strong'.

Yakov Rylsky was born on October 25th 1928 in East Kazakhstan, USSR. He is credited as being the father of modern fencing in the Soviet Union and of thrusting the USSR into Olympic fencing. A professional soldier, he is one of only three men in the world who have won the world individual sabre title three times (1958, 1961 and 1963). He represented his country at three Olympiads, in 1956, 1960 and 1964. He won a team bronze in 1956 and a gold in 1964. Rylsky has won the highest honour an athlete can achieve in the USSR as a Merited Master of Sports.

RYLSKY,
Yakov
(1928-)
Russian world
champion fencer

Commemorative Stamps

Paul Newman
Issued by Maldives

Boris Pasternak
Issued by USSR

David Oistrakh
Issued by USSR

Adriano Olivetti
Issued by Italy

Johann von Neuman
Issued by Hungary

Chana Orloff
(Mother and Child)
Issued by Israel

Dorothy Parker
Issued by USA

Shimon Peres
Issued by The Palestinian
Authority

Mosa Pijade
Issued by Yugoslavia

S

This was the pseudonym used by Umberto Poli, born in Trieste, whose Jewish mother was a member of the well-known Luzzatto family. Umberto experienced great poverty until, in 1908, he joined the Italian army. His verses *Versi militari* reflect those times and form part of his 1912 collection, *Coi miei occhi*, the book which brought him to prominence. He opened a secondhand bookshop in Trieste and this became a meeting-place for writers and poets. Although he wrote and published poetry for some 30 years, and although his work was well received, Saba was kept outside accepted literary circles. Often the victim of anti-Semitism, he emigrated to France and lived and worked in Paris for several years. In 1943 he smuggled himself back to Italy and stayed in hiding until the liberation. Back in Trieste, he wrote much that was a reflection of his life. He wrote about Trieste and compared pre- and post-war conditions. He wrote about the sailors, his wife, his daughter, his friends. He wrote about human suffering and animal suffering. His poetry is a mixture of pessimism and feeling; there is a warmth and an eagerness in his lines that enrich the reader, as well as a musical effect. *Canzoniere* (1964) is a mammoth collection of his poems from 1900 to 1954. Saba is considered one of the major Italian poets of the twentieth century. In 1983, the Italian postal authorities issued a stamp of Saba to mark the 100th anniversary of his birth.

SABA, Umberto (1883-1957) Italian poet

Albert Sabin was born on August 26th 1906 in Bialystok, Poland. In 1921 he and his parents emigrated to the US and in 1930 he became an American citizen. A year later, he received his MD from New York University, where he began his research into human poliomyelitis. The Second World War meant a temporary halt to his research into polio as the Rockefeller Institute, where he now worked, was asked to produce vaccines to aid servicemen serving in tropical areas, and in particular a vaccine against dengue fever. Sabin, now with the rank of lieutenant-colonel in the US Army, subsequently produced a vaccine to protect against debilitating diseases. He also developed a vaccine to combat encephalitis or inflammation of the brain, which was spread by insects. The Second World War over, Sabin returned to his first love, the protection of children from polio. At that time polio caused many deaths and paralyses every year all over the world, affecting rich and poor, young and old. In 1953, Jonas Salk (*qv*) developed a vaccine that was given by injection over a period of months, plus regular booster shots. It worked but it was not suitable for world-wide inoculation. Albert Sabin claimed that only by oral application, using weak live vaccine, could the real objective be reached. Highly motivated, Sabin had

SABIN, Albert (1906-93) Polish/American virologist

by 1957 produced such a vaccine. Field trials took place that confirmed its effectiveness and in 1960 the Sabin oral polio vaccine was approved for world-wide use, so becoming the main defence against the disease. The value of Sabin's work can be judged from the World Health Organization's report which states that, as at 1991, no deaths from polio had been reported. It is now possible that Sabin's prophecy that polio would be wiped out completely by the year 2000 will come true.

A pleasant, easy-going man away from the office, Sabin could be difficult and dogmatic at work, where he did not suffer fools gladly. His resignation from the presidency of the Weizman Institute of Science in Israel was said to be on the grounds of ill health, but this was essentially a smokescreen to cover up 'difficulties' with colleagues. He had little time for Jonas Salk, whom he tagged as a ' kitchen chemist', and in an interview once said 'I am too competitive to be gentle'. He spent the years 1972-84 as research professor at the University of South Carolina in Charleston. He died in Washington DC on March 3rd 1993. Sabin, hailed by the *Washington Post* as a 'hero of American medicine', would not have liked the tag. He would never allow nationalist claims on his work, which he always insisted must be used to benefit all the people of the world.

SACHS, Nelly (1891-1970) German/ Swedish writer

Her proper name was Leonie but she was always called Nelly. She was born on December 10th 1891 in Berlin, where her father was a wealthy merchant. She grew up in the very fashionable district of the Tiergarten and by the age of seventeen was an accomplished poet. During the 1920s her romantic and quite ordinary poems appeared in magazines and newspapers, happy to have something their minimally educated readers could easily understand. Following the arrival of Hitler her writings became outspokenly Jewish and it is surprising she waited as late as 1940 to leave Germany for Sweden. Her exit was assisted by the aid she received from the Swedish writer Selma Lagerlof, who in turn induced the King of Sweden to intercede with the German authorities. Now safe in Sweden, Nelly lived with her mother in a one-room flat, learnt Swedish and made a precarious living undertaking translations.

In 1946 she published her first book of poetry. It was called *In the Habitations of Death* and dedicated to 'my dead brothers and sisters'. Her now famous poem 'O The Chimneys' describes the body of Israel in smoke, as it drifts upwards in the German death camps. It was the title she used for the 1967 collection of her work translated into English. In 1965 she was awarded the German Publishers' Peace Prize. In 1967 Nelly Sachs, on her 75th birthday, was awarded the Nobel Prize for Literature jointly with the Israeli writer S. Y. Agnon (*qv*). Receiving her prize from King Gustav of Sweden, Nelly said: 'Agnon represents the State of Israel, I represent the tragedy of the Jewish people.' Much of her poetry reflects the horrors of the Holocaust and her style appears to be a mixture of Jewish and German passion. As a playwright, her best known work is *Eli: A Mystery Play of the Suffering of Israel*' (1943). Here she forges a link between the murder, by a German soldier, of a Polish child and the Jewish legend of the 36 saints who ensure the world's continuing existence. Nelly Sachs died in Stockholm on May 12th 1970.

Born in London on July 9th 1933, **Oliver Sacks** is a member of a well-known Jewish family of doctors. Although he completed his medical education in Britain, he moved to California to gain his working experience from 1960 to 1965. He then started to work at the Albert Einstein College of Medicine in New York and Beth Abraham, a small charity hospital. There Sacks discovered a group of patients who appeared to be in a constant trance-like condition. They were there following an epidemic of *encephalitis lethargica*, or sleeping sickness, which flew around the world following the First World War. In 1969 Sacks began treating these zombie-like humans with a new drug that was being successfully used on sufferers from Parkinson's Disease. His patients initially responded to the drug and awoke from years in a semi-frozen state to a wild and strange world that included everyday items like telephones, television, refrigerators and much more they knew nothing about. However, the drug had severe side-effects and most of the patients eventually reverted to their original condition. Sacks wrote about the experiment in *Awakenings* (1973). The book caused quite a furore and many in the medical community were concerned about aspects of his work. In 1990 the book became a film, giving a wider public an insight into what hospitals like Beth Abraham are about. In 1985 another book by Sacks appeared: *The Man Who Mistook His Wife for a Hat*. It is a collection of his more interesting case histories while a neurologist. Following a student uprising at Gallandet University, Sacks investigated the world of the deaf. His book *Seeing Voices* (1989) was the result. In addition to writing and working as a neurologist, in 1996 Sacks created a television series entitled *The Mind Traveller* that explains his work in layman's terms. In November 1996 Sachs published *The Island of the Colour-Blind*, in which he takes a romantic interest in the world of nature.

SACKS, Oliver (1933-) British neurologist

Moshe Safdie was born on July 14th 1938 in Haifa, Palestine. In 1955, now living in Israel, he emigrated to Canada to study architecture at McGill University in Montreal. He qualified in 1961 and went on to win international fame, following his revolutionary prefabricated housing design first exhibited at the Montreal Expo '67 show. He called the project 'Habitat'. His concept of low-cost building has won extensive favour all over the world. As a result, Safdie has designed many tailor-made projects, including among many others a unit of 300 houses in Puerto Rico (1968-72) and the Student's Union at San Francisco State College (1968). With architectural offices in Montreal, Jerusalem and Boston he has been responsible for many imaginative schemes, including, not least, the Wailing Wall Plaza in Jerusalem's old city in 1974. In 1978 he became professor of Urban Design at Harvard University. In 1988 he designed the National Gallery in Ottawa, where his tentlike pavilions of glass have been much admired. In the same year he built the Musée de la Civilisation in Quebec City. He has written much on his subject and his books include *Form and Purpose* (1982) and *Jerusalem: The Future of the Past* (1989).

SAFDIE, Moshe (1938-) Canadian architect

SALK,
Jonas
(1914-95)
US virologist

Jonas Salk was born on October 28th 1914 in New York City. In 1939 he received his MA from the New York University College of Medicine and soon thereafter was part of a team working on a programme of immunization against influenza. In 1947 Salk was associate professor of bacteriology at the University of Pittsburgh Medical School. Here he began his research into poliomyelitis. Following classification of various polio strains, Salk showed how a vaccine made from the killed virus could induce production of antibodies in monkeys. In 1952 he began limited field trials on humans, first on children who had recovered from polio and then on those who had not. Both trials were successful in that the children's antibody levels rose and no one contracted polio from the vaccine. Salk published his findings in 1953 in the *Journal of the American Medical Association* and in 1954 a mass field trial was conducted. The vaccine, injected by needle, was found to be entirely safe. The world breathed a little more easily when the vaccine was released for world-wide use in April 1955. This followed an edict by President Eisenhower that he wanted Salk to be the first recipient of the Congressional Medal for Distinguished Civilian Achievement. He also ordered that Salk should receive a pension of $10,000 for life and so be able to devote himself to research. In 1963 Salk became director of the Institute for Biological Studies in San Diego, California, later renamed the Salk Institute. In 1981, despite objections from his arch-rival Albert Sabin (*qv*), the Salk vaccine was once again being widely used in the US. In 1991 Salk claimed he was on the threshold of an AIDS vaccine using the same principles he used in his battle against polio. However, at the time of his death on June 23rd 1995 in La Jolla, California, the vaccine had not materialized.

SALMON,
Lord Cyril
(1903-91)
British judge

Cyril Salmon was born in London on December 18th 1903 into an affluent Jewish family. Educated at Mill Hill School, London, and Pembroke College, Cambridge, he was called to the Bar at the Middle Temple in 1925 and established a reputation in commercial law. His busy practice was interrupted by the Second World War, in which Salmon served in the Royal Artillery and was part of the Middle East Eighth Army campaign under General Montgomery. Following the end of the war Salmon took silk. His cases became more important and the public interest in them greater. Within twelve years he was appointed to the Queen's Bench Division of the High Court of Justice. Mr Justice Salmon came into the news when he presided over the trial of several white youths accused of beating up black immigrants in London's Notting Hill area. They were found guilty and given tough prison sentences which were meant to act as a deterrent. In 1964 Salmon was appointed to the Court of Appeal. There his judgments became famous, and his liberal approach sometimes controversial. He squashed the conviction of the publishers of *Last Exit to Brooklyn* and endeared himself to the women's movement by ruling that a woman could be a racehorse trainer and admitted to the Jockey Club. His was a lone voice that declared a journalist should be allowed to refuse to disclose his sources. He refused to accept that the law of any country required the execution of a prisoner for crimes committed when he was a minor. In 1972 he succeeded Lord Donovan as a Lord of Appeal in Ordinary; a lifelong ambition which gave him a seat in the

House of Lords. He was also made a Privy Counsellor. Although plagued for the last ten years of his life by illness that prevented him speaking in the upper chamber as often as he would have liked, he nevertheless argued strongly against the Police and Criminal Evidence Bill of 1984. He objected to an extension of the time a suspect could be detained and fiercely argued for all police interviews to be tape-recorded. Lord Salmon remained firm in defence of the rights of the individual. He died at Sandwich, Kent, on November 7th 1991.

Alice Salomon was born in Berlin on April 19th 1872. In 1906 she became the first woman to receive a PhD from the University of Berlin. Her thesis dealt with the inequality of pay between men and women doing the same work. In 1910 she created the first school to train social workers and set out its programme and training manuals. She remained president of the project until 1928, when it was renamed the Salomon Institute for Social Work. She was also one of the original founders of the International Congress of Women and its vice-president. In 1937, at the age of 65, she was thrown out of Germany for the crime of being Jewish. She spent the rest of her life in the US, lecturing on what she knew best: social work for the disadvantaged. She died in New York City on August 30th 1948.

SALOMON, Alice (1872-1948) German/ American social worker

Erich Salomon was born on April 28th 1886 in Berlin, the son of a Jewish banker. He obtained a law degree from the University of Munich but practised only briefly. In 1928 he began a career in photography as a freelance photographer. Equipped with one of the first miniature cameras, together with a high-speed lens, he was able to obtain good photos in poor light. He concealed the camera in a briefcase and took photos of a sensational murder trial in Berlin. These he sold so well that his next foray was to dress up in evening wear and gatecrash social gatherings, usually international conferences or diplomatic functions. His background and attitude easily persuaded those present of his right to be there and he concentrated on photographing pretentious people in unguarded moments. Eventually Salomon came to be invited to state dinners because it was judged that if he did not photograph the proceedings the function would be dismissed as unimportant. He visited England in 1929 and the US in 1930, photographing well-known people. In 1931 he published *Celebrated Contemporaries in Unguarded Moments,* a collection of 170 photographs. During the Second World War Salomon went into hiding in the Netherlands, but was eventually betrayed by a member of the Dutch SS when Salomon had no more money with which to buy his silence. In May 1944 he was sent to Auschwitz, and there, on July 7th 1944, one of the great European photographers was murdered for being a Jew.

SALOMON, Erich (1886-1944) German photographer

Felix Salten was born in Budapest on September 6th 1869. His original name was Siegmund Salzman. He started out as a journalist before becoming an influential theatre critic. However, following the First World War he turned to writing fiction, specializing in children's tales. In 1923 he won international fame with *Bambi,* a realistic story of a deer from his birth to his time as elder of the herd. The moral

SALTEN, Felix (1869-1945) Austrian writer

overtones were well established, and it was turned into a film by Walt Disney. Although *Bambi* is still a children's favourite, Salten's later work was probably better. *Florian, the Emperor's Stallion*, published in 1934, tells the tale of a proud horse who is later reduced to pulling a coach. In 1940 Salten published *Bambi's Children*. In 1939 he was living in Vienna; well known as a famous writer, he was also well known as a Jew, and had to flee for his life. His wealth gained him entry into Switzerland, where he died on October 8th 1945.

SALTZMAN,
Harry
(1915-)
Canadian film
producer

Born in St John, New Brunswick, Canada, on October 27th 1915 he made his name producing films that portrayed the post-war world. These included *Look Back in Anger* (1959), with a performance by Richard Burton, in the role of Jimmy Porter, that was among his best. *Saturday Night and Sunday Morning* (1960) was a critical success and heralded a new genre of films. Saltzman, having shown the way forward, now proceeded to make his fortune. He produced several of the James Bond films that have enthralled and delighted young and old all over the world. However, he still managed some productions in between, including *The Ipcress File* (1965), which launched Michael Caine, *Funeral in Berlin* (1966) - more Michael Caine - and *Billion Dollar Brain* (1967), with yet more Caine. All three films were box office successes. In 1969 he produced *Play Dirty* - starring Michael Caine. Described as a small-scale *Dirty Dozen*, it was a very good film. Also in 1969, Saltzman produced the all-star *Battle of Britain*, which could and should have been much better; in the event it lost ten million dollars worldwide. No matter; the eight James Bond films Saltzman produced easily covered it.

SAMUEL,
Lord Herbert
(1870-1963)
British
statesman

Born in Liverpool on November 6th 1870, with the proverbial silver spoon in his mouth, he was the fifth child of Edwin and Clara Samuel. When he was seven, his father died and Herbert was the product of his mother's upbringing. A legacy from his father made him financially independent. His mother was an orthodox Jewess who despaired when Herbert told her that, while he was proud to be a Jew, he could no longer believe in orthodox theology. Educated at University College School, Hampstead, and Balliol College, Oxford, he was 32 when, in 1902, he was elected to parliament as Liberal MP for Cleveland, Yorkshire. Six years later, in 1909, he became the first Jew to serve in the Cabinet, as Chancellor of the Duchy of Lancaster. In 1916 he was appointed Home Secretary, one of the three great offices of state. While he held this office the Easter Rising broke out in Dublin and Sir Roger Casement was arrested in Ireland and accused of treason (after this episode, Ireland would gain a large measure of independence and Casement would be hanged). Following the Balfour Declaration and the League of Nations granting Britain the Mandate over Palestine in 1920, Herbert Samuels was appointed the first High Commissioner. This followed assurances from the Colonial Office that as a Jew it would not be thought his impartiality would be impaired. He arrived to find the country 'almost derelict, politically and materially', as he noted in his 1945 memoirs. His term in Palestine was a success. He kept to a middle of the road policy and tried to fulfil the Balfour Declaration that would not deny Arab rights, while the establishment of a Jewish state was in progress. However, while Samuel was pleased Jewish immigration was progressing, he was disappointed that the Arabs refused to participate in political forums.

Samuel and his wife, his cousin Beatrice Franklin whom he married in 1897, wanted to retire to Palestine, but that idea was frowned upon by the British government and they opted for Italy instead. Fate, however intervened, and in 1929, past his retirement date, he was asked to stand for Parliament in that year's general election. Against the voting trend Samuel won Darwen, Lancashire, for the Liberal cause. Although Labour formed the government, they could govern only if the Liberals supported them. In 1931 rows within the Labour Party forced MacDonald to offer his resignation to King George V. By a strange quirk of fate, Lloyd George and Baldwin were both ill so Herbert Samuel, as deputy leader of the Liberals, went to Buckingham Palace to receive the King's request for the formation of a National Government or coalition to include all three parties. As a result, Samuel was once again in the Cabinet, and once again as Home Secretary. He was also leader of the Liberals; but that party was only a fraction of what it had once been. In the 1935 general election he stood and lost. He was now 65. Two years later he accepted a peerage and took his seat in the House of Lords as Viscount Samuel of Mount Carmel and Toxteth, Liverpool. He considered himself a meliorist, believing that the world would be a better place as a result of human effort. Unfortunately, dealing with people like Hitler was beyond the norm and Samuels lived to regret his support of the 1938 Munich Agreement. He was widely respected and admired and became even more generally known when he later took part in BBC Brains Trust programmes on radio. He died in London on February 5th 1963. In the House of Lords in December 1949 Samuel said 'Hansard is history's ear, already listening.'

SAMUELSON, Paul (1915-) US economist

Born on May 15th 1915 in Gary, Indiana, **Samuelson** was educated at the University of Chicago, from where he obtained a BA, and at Harvard, from where he received his PhD in 1941. Known as an outstanding economic theorist, he established a mathematical technique which became his problem solver. In 1947 he produced his *Foundations of Economic Analysis* which explained his thinking concerning the universal features of consumer habits as the mainspring of economic theory, in particular his mathematical formulation of the interaction of the multiplier and accelerator effects on economics. His best-selling textbook *Economics,* originally published in 1948, was updated in 1980. His contribution to world economics was recognized in 1970 when he was awarded the Nobel Prize for Economics.

SAPIR, Edward (1884-1939) US anthropologist

Edward Sapir was born on January 26th 1884 in Lauenburg, Germany, and was living in the US by the age of five. The son of a rabbi, Sapir was a graduate of Columbia University, where he came under the influence of Franz Boas (*qv*). As a result, Sapir developed a keen interest in linguistic anthropology. As an entomologist, Sapir devoted much time to studying the behaviour and language of the American Indians. In 1925 he joined Chicago University and in 1931 went to Yale, where he founded the department of anthropology. Sapir maintained that people saw the world mainly through language and wrote many articles on the correlation of language and culture. He did much research in comparative and historical linguistics. His books include *Language* (1921), and a collection of his essays entitled *Selected Writings of Edward Sapir in Language, Culture and Personality* was published posthumously in 1949. Sapir died on February 4th 1939 in New Haven, Connecticut. One of the greatest linguists and anthropologists of his time, he left behind a legacy of discovery.

SARNOFF,
David
(1891-1971)
US broadcasting
pioneer

Born in Minsk, Russia, on February 27th 1891 he intended becoming a rabbi but, fortunately for a lot of people around the world, changed his mind. In 1900 he and his family emigrated to the US and settled in New York City. While at school he contributed to the family funds by selling newspapers and running errands. In 1906 he became a messenger-boy with the Commercial Cable Company, and with his first wages he bought a telegraph instrument and taught himself Morse Code. Most unexpectedly, he found employment as a radio operator with the Marconi Telegraph Company. He spent some years at sea, working on ships, passenger and cargo, and in 1912 became the operator of the most powerful radio station in the world, sited on top of the department store owned by John Wanamaker in Manhattan, New York. There, while on duty on April 14th 1912, he found overnight fame when he picked up the distress signal from the *Titanic*. He immediately notified the shipping authorities, activated the rescue services and alerted the world to what was happening. He stayed at his post continuously for 72 hours, receiving and transmitting messages to and from the stricken liner, as well as other ships involved with the rescue. His reward was rapid promotion within the company. In 1916 he proposed the development of what he called the 'radio music box'; in 1921 his idea was accepted.

Sarnoff was now general manager of the Marconi Company. He demonstrated the potential of radio by broadcasting the Dempsey-Carpentier boxing match. It created a sensation, and within three years 80 million dollars' worth of radios had been sold. In 1926 Sarnoff formed the National Broadcasting Company (NBC) and later saw the potential of television. In 1928 he set up an experimental television station and in 1939 gave a demonstration at the New York World's Fair. By this time television was an established fact in Britain, with the BBC transmitting a regular schedule of programmes. As a result, Sarnoff engaged British technicians to help NBC launch their television network. From 1930 until his retirement in 1970, Sarnoff was chairman of RCA, one of America's top companies. He died in New York City on December 12th 1971.

SASSOON,
Siegfried
(1886-1967)
British soldier
and writer

Sassoon was born on September 8th 1886 in Brenchley, Kent, a member of a Jewish family that originated in India. He enlisted in the First World War and became a British army officer. Twice wounded, he was awarded the Military Cross for gallantry. His nickname of
'Mad Jack' came from his habit of making solitary reconnaissance into no man's land. In 1917 he published his book of anti-war poetry, *The Old Huntsman*,

which created quite a stir. He went further in his hatred of war, issuing a statement that he would no longer serve in the army and declaring himself a pacifist. The War Office could not tolerate such a radical situation. Their response was to declare Sassoon a victim of shell shock and confine him to a sanatorium where he was conveniently judged to be temporarily insane. In the hospital he met and influenced another war poet who would find fame: Wilfred Owen, whose works Sassoon published following Owen's death in the final stages of the war.

Sassoon returned to France and the fighting, only to be wounded once again. In 1918 he published *Counterattack*, another book of protest poetry, but by this time the First World War was over. He became literary editor of the *Daily Herald* and then spent the rest of his life writing. In the main his writings were autobiographical; they included *Memoirs of a Fox-Hunting Man*, which won the Hawthornden Prize; published in 1928, it is regarded as a classic. In 1930 came the brilliant *Memoirs of an Infantry Officer* and in 1936 *Sherston's Progress*. All three books were published under the collective title *The Memoirs of George Sherston*. *Siegfried's Journey* appeared in 1945 and *Collected Poems* in 1947. His last work was *The Path to Peace* (1960). He died on September 1st 1967 at Heytesbury, Wiltshire. During the Great War he wrote: 'Good morning, good morning, the General said when we met him last week on our way to the line. Now the soldiers he smiled at are most of them dead and we're cursing his staff for incompetent swine.' In December 1996 his only two grandchildren were killed in a car crash.

Vidal Sassoon (his surname was that of his stepfather) was born in London on January 7th 1928 and left school at fourteen to become apprenticed to a hairdresser. He was an early member of the 43 Group formed in 1946 to fight Fascism in London. In 1948 he was in Israel fighting in the war of Independence. In 1954 he opened his first salon in London's Bond Street and developed his unique technique of blow-drying hair. He introduced the 'blunt cut', but it was not until 1963, when his 'short at the back, long at the sides' style caused a sensation at a Mary Quant press show, that he took off. The following year his 'five-point ' haircut epitomized the Vidal Sassoon technique. During the 1960s he opened salons in the US and Canada, and by the end of the decade his school was running in the UK. Despite running around the world opening salons he found time to write a book: *Sorry I Kept You Waiting Madam* was published in 1969. His styles have been copied all over the world. His range of hair products is stocked everywhere and he is probably the foremost hair designer of the century. His second book, written with his now ex-wife Beverley, was called *Year of Beauty and Health* (1975). He is now a consultant to his company and content to be recognized as the man who has done so much for the well-being of both men and women. In 1958 the weekly *Hairdresser's Journal* stated: 'Vidal Sassoon is the big name in hairdressing this week. It is a name that might become bigger in years to come.' In 1982 the Vidal Sassoon International Centre for the study of Anti-Semitism and Related Bigotries was founded at the Hebrew University in Jerusalem.

SASSOON, Vidal (1928-) British hairstylist

SAVITT,
Dick
(1927-)
US champion
tennis player

Dick Savitt was born on March 4th 1927 in Bayonne, New Jersey. As a tennis player, he had his best year in 1951, when he won the Wimbledon singles title and the Australian singles and was picked for the American Davis Cup squad. In the event he was not allowed in the squad and the Americans lost to the Australians. Savitt had beaten the number one Australian, Ken McGregor at Wimbledon in three straight sets, as well as being the first non-Australian to win the Australian Open in thirteen years. In 1952 Savitt won the US national indoor singles championship, after which he retired. He has never explained his reasons, but it is assumed his treatment by the Davis Cup selectors influenced his decision. He returned to the tennis scene in 1956, and in 1958 and 1961 again won the national indoor singles title, thus becoming the first man ever to hold the title three times.

SCHECKTER,
Jody
(1950-)
South African
world motor
racing champion

Jody Scheckter, born on January 29th 1950 in East London, South Africa, was to become the first South African ever to win a world motor racing championship. His world was dominated by cars. His father was a Renault dealer and early on Jody was a stock car racer and motorbike racer before going on to become the number one driver in South Africa. By the age of 21 he was in Europe, and two years later began his Formula One career with Tyrrell. Laid back when off the track, tough and relentless when driving, in 1974 he won the British and Swedish Grands Prix and finished third in the overall championship. He was third in 1976 and in 1977 joined the Wolf racing team and came second. In 1979 he joined Ferrari and in that year won the Belgian, Monaco and Italian Grands Prix, becoming the Formula One world champion. The following year, 1980 was an unsuccessful one and at the end of it, aged 30, he retired. He has since become a most successful businessman. While driving, he was head of the racing drivers' association and worked hard for circuit safety. Michael Schumacher, when the reigning world champion, is on record as envying Scheckter more than any other racing driver past or present because Scheckter was the last man to win the world title while driving for Ferrari. It was said that Ferrari knew Scheckter was good because he wasn't interested in the glamour. When he won the championship in 1979 he did it in style, by beating the darling of the racing circuit, Giles Villeneuve, at Monza at his own reckless game. It was an exciting race the purists will never forget.

SCHICK,
Bela
(1877-1967)
Hungarian/
American
paediatrician

Born in Bolgar, Hungary, on July 16th 1877 and educated at Karl Franz University in Graz, Austria, **Schick** practised medicine in Vienna and went on to become professor of paediatrics at the University of Vienna. In 1923 he emigrated to the US, to become chief paediatrician at Mount Sinai hospital in New York (1923-42). He was also professor of diseases of children at Columbia University (1936-42). Although he made important contributions to the study of scarlet fever, tuberculosis and the nutritional needs of newborn babies, he is primarily and deservedly famous for what is internationally known as the Schick Test: a skin test that determines immunity or susceptibility to diphtheria. Countless children's lives have been saved as a direct result of Schick's unique work. He died in New York on December 6th 1967.

John Schlesinger was born on February 16th 1926 in London. He graduated from Balliol College, Oxford, and decided on an acting career. Before he could put that plan into operation, the Second World War arrived and he was in the Royal Engineers of the British Army. Renewing his pursuit of a stage career after the war meant spending long periods away from home, working in Australia and New Zealand, during the 1950s. After some 20 theatrical appearances and a few film parts, he switched to directing film. His documentary, *Terminus* (1960) won an award at the Venice Film Festival. His experiences as a repertory actor left him with an appreciation of an actor's worth and a skill at drawing out sensitive and sometimes great performances. His first three feature films as a director reflected the current English scene. *A Kind of Loving* (1962) was both a critical and a financial success and won the 'Golden Bear' at the Berlin Film Festival. It also pushed Schlesinger into the leading group of young British film-makers. He followed up with *Billy Liar* in 1963; this too was a critical as well as a financial success and led to a long-running television series. *Darling* (1965) was different, a satire on what was then known as 'swinging London'. The film was his entry into the world of international film-making; it also launched the career of Julie Christie, who won the Academy Award for Best Actress. Schlesinger had achieved that very rare double for a British film: success with both critics and box office.

Now in the US, Schlesinger made what is probably his best known film, *Midnight Cowboy*. It brought the sort of success that every film director must dream about: rich rewards, critical acclaim, an Oscar for Best Director and the film voted Best Picture. During the 1970s he made some excellent films, including *Sunday Bloody Sunday* (1971), an avant-garde film that told the story of a Jewish doctor and his homosexual relationship. *The Day of the Locust* (1975) was that rare find, a horror film to be believed. *Marathon Man* (1976) probably could not have been made by any other director, as it meant coping with the combined egos of Dustin Hoffman and Laurence Olivier. In 1983 he made *An Englishman Abroad* for television, one of his high-points of the 1980s, which also saw *The Believers* in 1987 and *Madame Sousatzka* in 1988. In 1990 he made *Pacific Heights*.

Schlesinger has maintained an interest in the stage, and in 1973 became a director of the National Theatre. In 1997 his film *Cold Comfort Farm* was premiered. Now over 70, he can look back with great satisfaction and see that he has both left his mark on the film world and provided a lot of people with an enormous amount of pleasure. He is recently quoted as saying, 'I'm only bald because I've used my head as a battering ram to get films made for the past 40 years.'

Artur Schnabel was born on April 7th 1882 in Lipnik, Austria. A child prodigy, he studied under the famous teacher Theodor Leschetizky. From 1900 he lived and worked in Berlin. A leading piano teacher at the State Academy of Music, he was dismissed by the Germans in 1933 because he was a Jew. He emigrated to Switzerland where he lived until 1939, after which he went to live and work in the US becoming naturalized in 1944. In pre-Hitler Berlin he gave concert performances of all Beethoven's sonatas; fortunately these concerts were recorded, and it is still

SCHLESINGER,
John
(1926-)
British
film-maker

SCHNABEL,
Artur
(1882-1951)
Austrian/
American
pianist

possible to appreciate his imaginative renderings that show such clarity and feeling. In 1939 he taught at the University of Michigan. He composed much and was influenced to some extent by Schoenberg (*qv*). His output includes three symphonies, a piano concerto, string quartets and various pieces of chamber music. He also found time to write about the world of music, in *Reflections on Music* (1933) and *Music and the Line of Most Resistance* (1942). Following the end of the Second World War Schnabel returned to Switzerland and there, in Axenstein, on August 15th 1951, he died.

SCHNEIDERMAN, Rose (1882-1972) US trade unionist

Born on April 6th 1882 in Sven, Russia, six years later she was living in New York's Lower East Side. A little later still, she and her two brothers were living in an orphanage, following the sudden death of her father and the poverty of her pregnant mother. She was thirteen before she returned home to become the family breadwinner. She was very small, 4ft 9in, and had to have cushions placed on her cashier's chair as she worked a 64-hour week in a downmarket store. A while later she was working in a cap-making factory; it was not as convivial but the money was better, although the hours were the same. That was her working background when in 1903 she organized Local 23 of the male-dominated United Cloth, Hat, Cap and Millinery Workers' Union. Henceforth Rose Schneiderman was a trade union organizer. A year later she was on the union's national executive. In 1913 she was in charge of the union's general strike following the 'Triangle Shirtwaist' fire of March 1911 in which 147 women died. She was a founder of the National Women's Trade Union League and held a series of posts culminating in the presidency, which she occupied until her retirement in 1949. A pioneer of women's rights, she was a delegate to the Paris Peace Conference following the First World War, presenting to those assembled a picture of American women striving for equal pay and opportunity. That remained her position, even when she was a member of President Roosevelt's political brains trust and had participated in the formation of the New Deal programme (1937-44). Rose died in New York City in August 1972. The *New York Times*, in an obituary, commented: 'a tiny, red-haired bundle of dynamite, Rose Schneiderman did more to upgrade the dignity and living standards of working women than any other American.'

SCHNITZLER, Arthur (1862-1931) Austrian writer

Arthur Schnitzler, son of a prominent Jewish physician, was born in Vienna on May 15th 1862. He qualified as a doctor but preferred writing. He went on to become known throughout the world for his descriptions of early 20th century Viennese society. *Anatol* (1911) depicts the many sides of love through the life and loves of Anatol, a wealthy playboy; *Playing With Love* (1914) tells the story of the poor working girl abandoned by her aristocratic lover. *Merry-Go-Round*, written in 1903, became in 1950 the very successful French film, *La Ronde*. Arguably his greatest work is *The Road to the Open*, in which he writes of the anti-Semitism prevalent at the time. He returns to the same theme in his play *Professor Bernhardi* (1927). Arthur Schnitzler was a most prolific author who had a major influence on young writers. He died in Vienna on October 21st 1931.

He was born Franz Walter Schoenberg on September 13th 1874 in Vienna, where his father Samuel had a small shoe shop. Although neither of his parents had any musical ability they, like most of their generation (long before the invention of radio) enjoyed music and visited concerts, operas and ballets. By the turn of the century, Schoenberg had composed his String Quartet in D Major, in the style of Brahms and the string sextet *Transfigured Night*, based on a poem by Richard Dehmel; hated by the public when it was first performed, it is now one of his most popular works. He moved to Berlin in 1911 and taught at the Stern Conservatory, before returning to Vienna to teach at Schwarzwald School, a post interrupted by brief periods in the army during the First World War.

By now Schoenberg had created a new method of composition based on a row of twelve tones: he called this method 'atonality', signifying its lack of a tonal centre. It was most radical and the most significant musical change this century. In the early 1920s he founded the Society for Private Musical Performances in order to play his own music and that of other avant-garde composers who found it difficult to get their work performed. Between 1925 and 1933 he taught at the Prussian Academy of the Arts in Berlin. By now his work was slowly being recognized, although musicians complained they had difficulty comprehending his unusual musical structures.

In 1933 Hitler gave orders for Schoenberg to leave the country or be sent to a concentration camp. He left for Paris and then the US, never to return to Europe. In the US he completed what is probably his greatest work, *Moses and Aaron*. Other works include a violin concerto (1935-36) and a Hebrew setting of *Kol Nidre* (1938). Schoenberg keenly felt the outrages being committed against his people and this is borne out in his later works, *Ode to Napoleon* (1942), and *A Survivor from Warsaw* (1947). His last years were dominated by the fight against sickness and financial worries. He was most depressed by the revelations of the Holocaust and the large family losses he suffered. He died alone in Los Angeles on July 13th 1951, mourned only by his students from the music department of the University of California, where he had taught for many years. Now his music is performed all over the world. Schoenberg always knew that his fundamental departure from the norm would take a long time to permeate the world of music. In addition to his other problems, he suffered from triskaidekaphobia, a fear of the number 13. In the event he died on Friday the 13th at 13 minutes before midnight.

Schwartz was born in Brooklyn, New York, on December 8th 1913. He was educated at New York University and Harvard, where he later taught. He was still a student when he made his debut as a poet. He caused quite a stir when in 1936 his poem 'Choosing Company' was published. His first book, *In Dreams Begin Responsibilities* (1939), brought him instant fame for a group of poems that were judged to be outstanding for the lyricism, beauty and imagination they showed. Thereafter he wrote *Shenandoah* (1941), a play in verse, *Genesis, Book 1* (1943) and *The World is a Wedding* (1948). In 1961 he wrote a book of short stories describing middle-class Jewish life, entitled *Successful Love and Other Stories*.

SCHOENBERG, Arnold (1874-1951) Austrian/ American composer

SCHWARTZ, Delmore (1913-66) US writer

Between 1955 and 1957 he edited *The New Republic*. Schwartz was depicted by Saul Bellow (*qv*) in the title role of his book, *Humboldt's Gift*. Schwartz, who suffered progressively from mental illness, died in New York on July 11th 1966.

SCHWARTZ,
Melvin
(1932-)
US physicist

Melvin Schwartz was born in New York on November 2nd 1932. He received his PhD from Columbia University, New York in 1958 and stayed on to teach until 1966. He became professor of physics at Stanford University (1966-83) but found time to serve as chairman of Digital Pathways, a company he founded to design computer security systems. Schwartz was part of the trio awarded the 1988 Nobel Prize for Physics, along with Max Lederman (*qv*) and Jack Steinberger (*qv*), for their work on muon neutrinos.

SCHWARZSCHILD,
Karl
(1873-1916)
German
astronomer

He was born on October 9th 1873 in Frankfurt-am-Main, Germany. In 1901 he was appointed professor and director of the observatory at the University of Göttingen, and in 1909 director of the Astrophysical Observatory at Potsdam. His achievements were well ahead of his time and his contemporaries found it difficult to understand much of his innovative work, including the precise method he used in photographic photometry. He investigated and questioned existing theories, while developing his own. His technique for determining stellar magnitude and colour, by means of a coarse grating, continued to be used long after his death. He defined, in precise terms, the principle of radioactive equilibrium and was the first person to appreciate in scientific terms the role of radiative processes in heat transport and stellar atmospheres. He developed basic methods for analysing the solar spectrum during eclipses. During the First World War he was in the German army and served on the Russian front. While off duty he wrote two papers on Einstein's (*qv*) general theory of relativity, thereby providing the first solution to the complex partial differential equation of the theory. He introduced what is now known as the Schwarzschild Radius, namely the principle that stars of a given mass must contract to reach the stage at the point when the gravitational field is intense. Stars that have contracted below the limit are now known as black holes. His contribution to 20th century science is of the highest value in both practical and theoretical terms, especially in astrophysics. He died, from an illness contracted while on active service, on May 11th 1916 in Potsdam. When Hitler, who fancied himself as an astrologer, came to power he ordered that all references to 'the Jew Schwarzschild' be deleted.

SCHWIMMER,
Rosika
(1877-1948)
Hungarian
activist

Born in Budapest, she was one of the early leaders of the feminist movement in Hungary. On the outbreak of the First World War she travelled to the US to plead with President Wilson to use his best endeavours and mediate an immediate end to hostilities. While in the US she co-founded the Women's Peace Party. Returning to Hungary in 1918, she accepted a post in the short-lived government of Count Michael Karolyi and served as Hungarian ambassador to Switzerland (1918-19), the first female diplomat to achieve the rank of ambassador this century. When Horthy, the right-wing antisemite, took over Hungary, Rosika Schwimmer had to be smuggled out to freedom. She returned to the US, where her pacifist views prevented her obtaining citizenship, despite an appeal to the Supreme Court. She continued her work for world peace, equal rights for women and world government, an idea that prefigured the United Nations. For nearly 30 years she lived in the US as an alien, continuing her struggle, until she died in New York City in 1948.

Julian Schwinger was born in New York on February 12th 1918. A child prodigy, he graduated from Columbia University with a PhD when he was just 21; he then spent two years (1939-41) working under Robert Oppernheimer (*qv*). In 1945, researching the theory of quantum physics, he went on to reconcile Einstein's special theory of relativity. He received the 1965 Nobel Prize for Physics for his pioneering work in quantum electrodynamics. In 1972 he was appointed professor of physics at the University of California.

SCHWINGER, Julian (1918-) US physicist

Ronnie Scott was born Ronnie Schatt on January 28th 1927 in the East End of London. His father, a saxophone player with a dance band, committed suicide aged 55 upon learning he had terminal cancer. Although Ronnie followed his father and became a sought-after saxophonist, albeit in the jazz idiom, it was as the founder, owner and operator of one of the world's greatest jazz clubs that he will best be remembered. Ronnie Scott's in London's Soho became the Mecca for the top jazz musicians and singers of the second half of the 20th century. Singers like Ella Fitzgerald and Sara Vaughan, and musicians of the calibre of Dizzy Gillespie, Coleman Hawkins and Buddy Rich (*qv*) crossed the Atlantic for a fraction of their usual fee and thought it a privilege to appear. Scott's jocularity when fronting his club was in marked contrast to the depressions he suffered. Dental and mouth problems began affecting his playing and he dreaded reaching his 70th birthday. Six weeks prior to that date, on December 23rd 1996, he committed suicide, so closing a chapter in modern jazz history. His two long-term relationships resulted in a son and a daughter with whom he had close ties.

SCOTT, Ronnie (1927-96) British jazz musician

Neil was born in New York City on March 13th 1939 and completed his education with a scholarship to study music at the Julliard School in New York. Howard Greenfield was a neighbour and a poet. He and Neil hit it off and wrote their first composition which they called 'My Life's Devotion'. It didn't break any records, but the boys decided to continue collaborating. In 1952 Sedaka talked Greenfield into writing a rock and roll song. He reluctantly agreed and they produced 'Mr Moon' - a hit by high school standards. They later wrote a song for Connie Francis called 'Stupid Cupid' which made it to number 14 on the Billboard's Hot 100. 'The Diary' followed with Sedaka singing; that too reached 14. Three hit singles then came in rapid succession: first 'Oh! Carol', written for Carol King (*qv*); then 'Happy Birthday Sweet Sixteen'; then, in August 1962, a Number One with 'Breaking Up is Hard To Do'. A few years later his singing career appeared to be over. He and Greenfield spent most of their time writing songs for others to sing: 'Puppet Man' for Tom Jones, 'Workin' on a Groovy Thing' for the Fifth Dimension, 'Is This the Way to Amarillo?' for Tony Christie. When that area dried up Neil Sedaka was

SEDAKA, Neil (1939-) US singer/ songwriter

seriously considering calling it a day. Then his agent suggested a trip to England might do something for his recording career. Sedaka agreed, the family arrived in London and Sedaka appeared at the Royal Albert Hall. His concert, a mixture of old and new, was a sell-out and led to an English album. *Solitaire* did much better in the UK than in the US. A new release in 1975 called 'Laughter in the Rain' got to number 15 on the UK chart. On February 1st 1975 it reached Number One in the US and Sedaka was back on track. By the end of the year he had an even bigger hit: 'Bad Blood' was a Number One hit and stayed at the top for three weeks, selling one and a half million records. In the 1990s Sedaka is still writing, singing and touring, one of the few artists to successfully span over four decades.

SEGAL,
George
(1934-)
US actor

George Segal was born on February 13th 1934 in Great Neck, Long Island. Educated at Columbia University he received a BA in 1955. His working interest in the theatre was interrupted by military service and resumed following his discharge. He received serious attention following his appearance in the Broadway production of *Rattle of a Simple Man* (1963). He switched to films and a sequence of major parts in several noteworthy films established Segal as a thoughtful star actor with a wry humour. This was in the 1960s and 70s. Unfortunately he later became a cocaine addict and it took several years out of his working life. In the early 80s, aided by his wife Linda Rogoff he finally kicked the habit and resumed his career. His best known films are; *The Young Doctors* (1961), *King Rat* (1965), *The Quiller Memorandum* (1966), *Who's Afraid of Virginia Woolf?* (1966 and an Oscar nomination), *No Way to Treat a Lady* (1968), *The Owl and the Pussycat* (1970), *A Touch of Class* (1973) and *The Duchess and the Dirtwater Fox* (1976).

SEGRE,
Emilio
(1905-89)
Italian physicist

Emilio Segre was born in Tivoli, Italy, on February 1st 1905. He originally set out to be an engineer and to that end he studied at Rome University in 1922. Later he switched and studied physics under Enrico Fermi, obtaining a doctorate in 1928. In 1932 he was assistant professor of physics at the University of Rome. In 1934 Segre and Fermi were experimenting on the effects of the neutron in relation to uranium bombardment, and the following year discovered that slow neutrons had important properties in relation to the operation of nuclear reactors. In 1937, while at the University of Palermo, Segre discovered technetium, a radioactive element found not in ores but among fission products of uranium. This most important find caused Segre to be invited to lecture in the US. While he was there, Mussolini announced his anti-Jewish laws and as a result Segre decided to remain in America. (In October 1943 Segre's father-in-law, Admiral Augusto Capon, and other relatives were rounded up by the Germans, taken away and murdered.) Further research by Segre contributed to the Manhattan Project that led to the A-bomb. In 1944 he became a US citizen and professor of physics at Berkeley (1946-72). For his part in the discovery of the antiproton Segre was awarded the 1959 Nobel Prize for Physics. He wrote much on his subject, including *Nuclei and Particles* (1964), *Enrico Fermi: Physicist* (1970) and *From Falling Bodies to Radio Waves* (1984). In 1974 he returned to Italy and, completing the cycle, became professor of physics at Rome University. Segre died in Lafayette, California, on April 22nd 1989.

Seligman was born in London on December 24th 1873. He originally trained as a doctor, but following an expedition to the Torrest Straight, as the doctor to the Cambridge University team, he fell in love with the science of anthropology. In 1904 he went to New Guinea; the resulting book, *The Melanesians of British New Guinea* (1910), remains a basic source. During the First World War Seligman served in the Royal Army Medical Corps and became convinced by the theories of Sigmund Freud (*qv*), which he later used while conducting experiments in the field trips he made to the Sudan (1919-22). This work provided the basis for *Pagan Tribes of the Nilotic Sudan* (1932). Seligman held the first chair of ethnology at London University, continuing as part-time professor until 1934. In 1938 he was visiting professor at Yale University in the US. Among his writings are *Races of Africa* (1930) and *Egypt and Negro Africa* (1934). His pioneering work in anthropology, with a psychological approach, had an enormous influence on later students of the science. He died in Oxford on September 19th 1940.

Peter Sellers was born in Southsea, Hampshire on September 8th 1925. The son of a Jewish mother, he was a direct descendant of the great British boxing champion, Daniel Mendoza (1764-1836). His uncle ran a small seaside theatre in Devon and at the age of fourteen Peter went to work there, all thought of further education forgotten. At eighteen, during the Second World War, he joined the RAF. The war over, Sellers decided he would become a comedian and in 1946 survived a six-week run at the famous Windmill Theatre in London. In the 1950s came *The Goon Show* a crazy comedy series that ran for many years and radically affected British humour. Sellers began his film career in 1951. In 1955 he starred in *The Ladykillers* and by the end of the decade he was one of Britain's favourite actors. In the early 1960s he was in Hollywood. Here he starred in *Dr Strangelove*, receiving an Oscar nomination for Best Actor. By the end of the 1960s he was an international star, if only for his portrayal of Inspector Clouseau in the *Pink Panther* films that continued into the 1970s. In 1979 Sellers made his final film, *Being There*; again he was again nominated for the Best Actor award, although in the event the film only took one Oscar, Melvyn Douglas (*qv*) taking the accolade for Best Supporting Actor. Although known world-wide for his films and broken marriages, Sellers will always be fondly remembered as one of the original Goons. He died in 1980 at the Middlesex Hospital, London, following a fifteen-year period of heart trouble.

Selznick was born in Pittsburgh on May 10th 1902. His father, a jeweller, ventured into film production; he became a major player, but was much disliked in the industry for his unscrupulous business methods. David, who learnt by his father's mistakes, was altogether a different person. Both he and his brother Myron suffered from their father's reputation: following his death in 1933, both boys were shunned by film people trying to punish a dead man. Arrogant enough to get himself noticed, David also knew how to be humble when the occasion demanded. After a series of inter-company battles, in 1933 David was at MGM, lured there by his father-in-law, Louis B. Mayer (*qv*). In the three years he stayed, Selznick produced, *Dinner at*

Eight, David Copperfield, A Star is Born and *A Tale of Two Cities*. He started his own production company in 1936, grandly calling it Selznick International Pictures. His publicity blurb claimed the company was 'dedicated to the ideal of artistic quality in picture making'. Perhaps it was. In a period of ten years he made *Gone With The Wind, Rebecca, Since You Went Away, Spellbound* and *Duel In The Sun,* each of which won at least one Oscar. He spent the rest of his career promoting the films of his second wife, Jennifer Jones. Selznick played an important part in creating the mystique and glamour of Hollywood and the films made there. He died on June 22nd 1965.

SERKIN,
Rudolph
(1903-91)
Czech/American
pianist

He was born on March 28th 1903 in Eger, Czechoslovakia, the son of working-class Jewish parents who had emigrated from Russia shortly before Rudolph was born. His father, who had to feed eight children, was a musician in his spare time, and it was he who taught Rudolph to read musical notation before he could read books. By the age of four he was a most able piano player: so much so that the Emperor's pianist urged Serkin senior to send his talented son to Vienna. At nine he became a pupil at the Music Academy, studying under Schoenberg (*qv*). At twelve he gave his first public concert when he played a Mendelssohn piano concerto with the Vienna Symphony Orchestra. The violinist Adolf Busch was a strong influence, as were Toscanini and Busoni. They told the now seventeen-year-old that he was ready to experience the concert platform. His partnership with Busch was a close and continuing one - so much so that when Busch moved to Switzerland in 1926 Serkin went also, and nine years later married his friend's daughter Irene, with whom he had six children.

Serkin made his debut with the New York Philharmonic under Toscanini in 1936, and he became a US citizen soon thereafter. In 1950 Busch founded the Marlboro Music School and Festival in Vermont. When he died in 1952, his son-in-law Rudolph Serkin became its president. His playing was most memorable and he was judged one of the greatest all-round pianists of the century. He toured the world and gave concerts with the finest orchestras. His incredibly extensive repertoire in no way diminished his performances of the music of the greats. The influence he had on his students at the Curtis Institute of Music, where he taught from 1939 to 1968, cannot be overestimated. A man of self-effacing personality and warm, gentle humour, he died in Guildford, Vermont, on May 8th 1991. Noel Goodwin, the eminent British music critic, wrote in the London *Independent*: 'a pianist friend said that if he were required to jettison, from a balloon, the six best pianists of the age one by one, he would save Rudolph Serkin to the last and after hearing him play the Andante from Mozart's C Major Concerto (K467) would jump out before him.'

Peter Shaffer was born on May 15th 1926 in Liverpool, England. Educated at St Paul's School and Trinity College, Cambridge, he worked for a music publisher before reviewing books and writing plays. His first performed play was the domestic drama *Five Finger Exercise* (1960). It made the critics sit up and the box office jingle. His *The Royal Hunt of the Sun* (1964), which told of the conflict between the native Inca and the Spanish invaders, is judged to be a masterpiece and confirmed Peter Shaffer's status internationally. *Equus* (1973), a disturbing play concerning a boy's obsession with horses, six of which he has blinded, became a successful film in 1977. *Amadeus* was the fascinating story of Mozart's relationship with his rival Salieri. Made into a film in 1984, it received four Oscars including one for Peter Shaffer. In 1987 his comedy play *Lettice and Lovage* was another winner on both sides of the Atlantic. His twin brother Anthony is also an important playwright, albeit not as prolific. He did, however, write the hit play and popular film *Sleuth*, which received four Academy Award nominations in 1970.

Ben Shahn was born on September 12th 1898 in Kaunas, Russia, and was eight years old when the family emigrated to America and settled in New York. Between 1913 and 1917, he worked as a lithographer's apprentice by day and studied at the High School by night. He would later study at New York University and the National Academy of Design. He worked at his trade until 1930, then took off for Europe and exposure to the current work of other artists. Shahn's first major work was in 1931-2, when he attracted much attention with his series of gouaches that illustrated issues of concern at the time: the aftermath of the Dreyfus Affair and the Sacco and Vanzetti trials. He expressed his sympathy in terms of emotion and satiric wit. In 1933 another series followed concerning the political scapegoat Tom Mooney. In the later 1930s, Shahn was involved in a number of New York projects, including a series of murals on public buildings showing the effects of Prohibition. Following the Second World War, he continued his paintings of social criticism but his influence had peaked. For much of his later life he therefore concentrated on lecturing and teaching. He died in New York on March 14th 1969. Once, when receiving one of his many awards, Shahn said: 'I hate injustice, I guess that's about the only thing that I really do hate, and I hope I shall go on hating it all my life.' His work is described as strong, his colours bright and the whole laid on with a sure hand.

Born in Boston on March 13th 1902, **Shapiro** was to become one of the first Americans to receive a doctorate in the field of physical anthropology. Early on in his career he specialized in problems attached to identifying humans badly damaged by fire, accident or hazard. He developed this field of study into what became known as forensic anthropology. His work was put to good use during the Second World War and Shapiro travelled to all the battle zones of Europe helping to identify dead soldiers for the American Graves Registration Unit. His methods were also used by police units to help identify murder victims. From 1943 Shapiro was professor of anthropology at Columbia University. He pioneered genetics relating to ethnic minorities and during the 1930s studied the descendants of the '*Bounty* mutineers' who survived and intermarried in Tahiti and Pitcairn. In 1960 he published *The Jewish People*, a work arising from the pioneering work he did on the biological history of the Jewish people, commissioned by UNESCO. It deals with the racial origins of the Jews and how they changed over thousands of years. His conclusions were that Jews have contributed part of their genes to a greater variety of people than any other group, and in return have taken in various strains that have enriched and diversified them. His lasting memorial will be the Hall of the Biology of Man. Shapiro died on January 7th 1990.

SHAPIRO, Henry (1906-91) Romanian/ American journalist

Henry Shapiro was born in Vaslui, Romania, on April 19th 1906. He grew up close to the border with Russia and by the time the Jewish family emigrated to the US in 1920 he was a fluent Russian-speaker. Living in New York City, he obtained a BA from City College in 1929 and a law degree from Harvard University in 1932. He practised for a year in New York; then, on a whim, he applied to Moscow University for permission to study there for a law degree. To his great surprise he was accepted. Upon reflection Shapiro decided to take up the offer. It was 1933 and the US had at last recognized the Soviet Union; Shapiro reckoned that if the result was mutual trade, a legal expert on Soviet law would be indispensable to American companies. Quite remarkably, Shapiro not only completed the course and obtained his degree, he also won the right to practise in the Soviet Union; the only Westerner who ever had this privilege.

While waiting for legal work, Shapiro took a job as Reuter's Moscow correspondent. His first scoop concerned the secret funeral of Sergei Kirov, the Communist leader of Leningrad who had been murdered in mysterious circumstances, thus providing Stalin with the opportunity to begin the purges of the 1930s. Shapiro was on the spot and his natural talent for rooting out the truth about what was going on became essential to the West. He was now the correspondent for the *New York Herald Tribune*, the London *Morning Post*, UPI and *Reuters*. With his reporting depending on the continuing information he received from his sources, Shapiro was becoming increasingly concerned not just for his own safety but for that of his partner, Ludmilla Nikitina, the daughter of his professor at Moscow University. There was no alternative but to stay and continue his reports, because the authorities would not allow Ludmilla to leave. His continuance showed bravery and intelligence in judging what to reject and what to believe and file. Accused by colleagues of having too close a relationship with the authorities, Shapiro would laugh and accuse them of jealousy.

When the Second World War arrived Shapiro came into his own. He was the first Western journalist allowed into Stalingrad in September 1942 to report on the siege and the fierce fighting. This battle was later confirmed as the one which turned eventual victory away from Germany. Following the war, Stalin became quite paranoid over the reporting of Soviet life. Journalists were constantly in fear of being arrested as Western spies. The American embassy advised Shapiro to leave; Shapiro told the embassy that if he did so Ludmilla would be sent to a labour camp.

He stayed, not daring to step outside of Moscow.

Five years later, in 1953, he had his reward. Shapiro had previously worked out his course of action ready for when Stalin died. He knew within minutes of it happening. Shapiro immediately telephoned London, knowing full well that the Moscow censor would be listening. 'Guess what happened here today,' Shapiro said. 'Stalin must have died,' came the excited response. 'Right!' shouted Shapiro, and the line went dead as the censor pulled the plug. The Soviet authorities refused to confirm the story for another twelve hours, by which time, as a result of Shapiro's call, the news was all over the world.

Shapiro's wide range of contacts proved invaluable when, at the Twentieth Party Congress in 1956, Khrushchev launched his critical analysis of the Stalin era. Western journalists were banned from the congress hall and it was Shapiro who got the details to the waiting world first. Throughout four decades Shapiro was UPI's man in Moscow. He left the Soviet Union on only three occasions: twice as a visiting professor to US universities and once to Israel to give a lecture. By 1973 he was ready to retire and return to the US. The rules had relaxed and Ludmilla was allowed to leave with him. Shapiro was immediately offered the chair of journalism at the University of Wisconsin, which he accepted. He remained associated with the university until his death in Madison, Wisconsin, on April 4th 1991.

SHARANSKY, Anatoly (1948-) Russian/Israeli activist

Sharansky was born in Russia in 1948. He was the most publicized of the many Russian-Jewish activists who led fierce campaigns on behalf of all Russians denied the right to leave the country. In 1978 he was accused of spying for the American CIA and sentenced to thirteen years' imprisonment. Released in 1986, he was finally allowed to leave Russia for Israel. In 1988 he published his autobiography, *Fear No Evil*, and during the 1990s he entered Israeli politics. He sees himself as the champion of the half million Russians living in Israel who left Russia for what they believed was the Promised Land, only to discover that the reality was rather different. His party, Israel Bealiya, won seven seats in the 1996 elections and became part of the right-wing Likud coalition; with Sharansky in the Cabinet as Minister of Trade and Industry. In 1997 he returned to Moscow as part of an Israeli trade delegation.

SHATNER, William (1931-) Canadian actor

William Shatner was born in Montreal, Canada, on March 22nd 1931 to Jewish parents. He is universally known for his role as Captain James Kirk in the television series *Star Trek*. There is, however, more to his credit. Educated at McGill University, from where he graduated in business studies, he decided upon a film career. His roles, other than that of Captain Kirk, have not been as many or as good as his talents deserve. He starred in the television series *T. J. Hooker*, several episodes of which he directed. To the *Star Trek* fan clubs around the world, William Shatner is a very important actor, particularly as a study of *Star Trek* fans resulted in the claim that one in ten fans are addicted to the programmes and suffer withdrawal symptoms if they miss a programme

SHAW,
Artie
(1910-)
US musician

Born Arthur Arshawsky on May 23rd 1910 in New York City, he began playing clarinet in the band at high school and became a professional when he left. Following a series of stops and starts, he formed his own band in 1937; a year later he became world famous with his rendering of Cole Porter's classic, 'Begin the Beguine', that has never been equalled. His recording in 1941 of 'Gloomy Sunday' was banned by the BBC, and in many other countries, because of the number of depressed people committing suicide after hearing it. His *Concerto for Clarinet* was a serious and successful attempt at a jazz concerto. He employed black musicians, including Billie Holiday, at a time when it would have been more convenient not to. During the Second World War, he led a US Navy orchestra and toured many parts of the world entertaining Allied forces. He wrote his biography, *The Trouble with Cinderella* in 1952 in which he revealed his disenchantment with popular music. In 1955 he retired from the music scene, but returned in 1983 to lead the Artie Shaw Orchestra. Married seven times, his wives included Lana Turner, Ava Gardner and Evelyn Keyes. He wrote a brilliant book that related to his marriages, entitled *I Love You, I Hate You, Drop Dead* (1965). Artie Shaw once said, 'I would have liked to have married the Fat Lady . She sings when it's over.'

SHAW,
Irwin
(1913-84)
US writer

Irwin Shaw was born on February 27th 1913 in New York City. Educated at Brooklyn College, where he was a football player, he began his writing career while working as a drama critic. Following the Second World War, during which he served in the army, he lived in Europe, writing and travelling. Pre-war success included writing short stories for the *New Yorker*. His play *Bury the Dead*, about a squad of dead soldiers who refuse to be buried, was produced in 1936 and well received. He wrote more plays after the war, but it was his war novel, *The Young Lions* (1948), which launched him as an important writer. The film version in 1958 gave him international status. His later novel, *The Troubled Air* (1951), exposed the McCarthy witch-hunt's work in the radio industry. He made a fortune from his best-seller *Rich Man, Poor Man* and the television series that followed, but his literary standing dropped. Nevertheless, other novels followed that proved popular, including *Beggarman Thief* (1977), *Bread Upon the Waters* (1981) and his last novel, *Acceptable Losses* (1987). In all, a staggering total of 14 million copies of his books, described as 'a jolly good read', were published in 25 languages. Shaw died in Davos, Switzerland, on May 16th 1984.

SHINWELL,
Lord Emanuel
(1884-1986)
British
politician

Shinwell was born in London to Jewish parents, his father from Russia, his mother from the Netherlands. The family moved to Glasgow, Scotland, and for the rest of his life Shinwell had a broad Scottish accent that became his trademark. His father had a small tailoring shop in a poor working-class area of the city, and it was here that Manny, as he was universally known, received his first political teachings. At seventeen he joined the Garment Workers' Union and in 1903 was a member of Keir Hardie's Independent Labour party. Manny threw himself into the fray and toured Scotland and northern England speaking at meetings. Self-taught and initially shy, he emerged over the following years as a fluent and influential speaker.

In 1916 he was elected to the Glasgow Town Council. In 1918 he stood for Parliament for the first time and lost. In 1919 he was sent to prison for five months, having been found guilty of incitement to riot when he was fighting police in a demonstration, demanding a shorter working week in the shipyards. In 1922 he reached Parliament as an Independent Labour MP and a year later was Minister of Mines in Ramsey MacDonald's Labour government of 1923. In 1924 he was out again, defeated in the general election. In 1928 he was back, and in 1931 he was again defeated. However, in 1935 he was returned to the House once more, and this time was to retain his seat for the next 35 years. In 1945 he was appointed Minister of Fuel and Power in the post-war Attlee Labour government - a very tough job. Shinwell had to pilot through Parliament one of the most important pieces of legislation: the nationalization of the coal mines. After decades of mismanagement and neglect of infrastructure, the mines needed large amounts of Britain's meagre post-war resources. Shinwell's efforts saw the mines saved to become among the best in the world.

Shinwell experienced anti-Semitism all his life and the House of Commons was no exception. In 1938, a right-wing Conservative MP and supporter of the fascist Oswald Mosley, named Bower, called across the chamber to Manny: 'Go back to Poland.' Shinwell left his seat, crossed the floor to the Tory benches and slapped him hard across the face. In 1952 he took on Winston Churchill, who accused him of 'owing a loyalty to an idea beyond his country's frontiers'. He meant Israel. Shinwell, whose temper could flare up in seconds, merely smiled broadly, and it was Churchill who looked away, most embarrassed. Shinwell wrote much, including his autobiography, *Lead with the Left: My First Ninety-Six Years* (1981). He died at the age of 102, his political life having spanned the turbulent twentieth century and reflected the changes he experienced.

Alexander Shulman was born on June 22nd 1915 in Toronto, where he was educated at Harbord Collegiate before obtaining his medical degree at the University of Toronto in 1939. After working for a while in Los Angeles, he joined the Army Medical Corps and saw action in France and Germany after D-Day. The war over, he returned to Los Angeles and private practice. In the early 1950s, Shulman burnt himself badly when he spilled burning grease on his hand. On instinct he plunged his hand into a bucket of very cold water. The pain relief was immediate and he left his hand in the water until he could withdraw it without suffering too much. Thereafter he felt no pain and the burn healed more quickly than he expected. At that time, the general treatment for burns was to apply butter or some similar substance. Shulman tried his new treatment on a girl who was brought to him having burned her hands. She was in great pain that was immediately relieved by the cold water. She refused to remove her hands for some time and she recovered without blisters. Shulman continued trying out his cold water treatments and, when thoroughly satisfied about their effectiveness, published his findings. Thereafter, what at first was regarded as a cranky idea became established practise for the treatment of emergency burns.

Later Shulman travelled to China, having become fascinated by Eastern

SHULMAN,
Alexander
(1915-96)
Canadian
physician

medicine. He wrote a book on the subject and promoted the use of heparin, a blood-thinning drug, to prevent heart attacks. He also preached the value of eating a high fibre diet and so preventing diverticulosis, and began practising a new type of treatment for hernia sufferers that proved to result in a high recovery rate. In 1991 he retired from general practice to become director of the Lichtenstein Hernia Institute. He wrote many medical articles for the *New York Times*, *The Lancet* and the *British Medical Journal*. Three days before he died in Los Angeles on July 7th 1996, he was made an honorary Fellow of the Royal College of Surgeons. He left a wife, a son, a daughter - and a brother, Milton Shulman, the theatre critic and journalist.

SHUSTER,
Joseph
(1914-92)
Canadian comic
strip artist
and
SIEGEL,
Jerry
(1914-96)
American comic
book writer

Joe Shuster was born in Toronto, Canada, on July 10th 1914 and was educated at John Huntingdon Polytechnical Institute and the Cleveland School of Art. When he was ten the family moved to Cleveland, Ohio, and there, at Glenville High School, he met **Jerry Siegel**, who was born in Cleveland on October 17th 1914. The two were to establish an enduring collaboration that would bring both world fame and poverty. When the two were at high school together they published amateur comic books, with Siegel writing the stories and Shuster doing the action drawings. In 1934 Siegel came up with an original idea, of a baby from another planet sent to earth and raised in Smallville, USA. Known as Clark Kent, he grows up, leaves home and gets a job as a reporter for the *Daily Planet*. Gentle Kent is a man with a secret. He has super powers, can fly, is bullet-proof and has superhuman strength. Superman was born. Shuster created the visuals. The All-American hero was tall, dark and handsome: a clean-cut, square-jawed paragon of everything good and wholesome. For four years the pair tried to find a newspaper who would run with it. There were no takers; 'too fantastic for our readers' was the common response. Eventually Detective Comics agreed a deal: Siegel and Shuster sold the rights to 'Superman' for $130. 'We were young. What did we know?' Shuster would later tell the *New York Times*.

From Superman's first appearance in June 1938 he was an instant success. Detective Comics made enormous profits on sales that exceeded millions of dollars a year. The originators took the company to court, suing for a fairer share. They lost the lawsuit and their jobs on the magazine. They tried creating new strips, and failed. They were unemployed and destitute. They had no funds to continue their fight. By now Warner Communications had acquired the rights, and in 1975 voluntarily gave Shuster and Siegel each a yearly pension of $20,000. In 1978 the first Superman film was made and Warners made a profit of $275 million. In a burst of great generosity Warners gave Shuster and Siegel each a bonus of $15,000. Shuster retired to California and isolation. He died in Los Angeles on July 30th 1992 of congestive heart failure - a euphemism for aggravation. Siegel, who lived a few blocks away, was quoted as saying that just the sight of a Superman comic book made him physically ill. Jerry Siegel died in Los Angeles on January 28th 1996.

Benjamin Siegel was born on February 28th 1906 in Brooklyn, New York. His respectable, middle-class, Jewish parents were never able to understand why their beautiful boy was so wild and unmanageable. Why he should rob people in the streets, steal cars and be part of a gang run by 'that nasty Meyer Lansky' (*qv*) - and all at the tender age of twelve? In time 'Benjamin' gave way to 'Bugsy' (but not to his face) and he participated in the fortunes made out of bootlegging during the Prohibition era. The gang was involved in all types of crimes, except drugs. They also ran 'Murder Incorporated' - in other words, murder for hire.

In 1937 Siegel was the syndicate's representative on the US West Coast. In Los Angeles he came into his own. As handsome as any of the actors he hobnobbed with, he enjoyed his new life. He successfully opened night clubs and gambling ships, anchored twelve miles off the coast, together with any illegal and legal enterprises the syndicate approved. All went well until Siegel got the vision of a gambling oasis in the Nevada desert. The tiny town was called Las Vegas. For some time Siegel tried to persuade Meyer Lansky to bring the syndicate round to his point of view and at last he was given the go-ahead. In 1945 work on the Flamingo Hotel and Casino in Las Vegas commenced. The original budget was $1,500,000 but it kept increasing as Siegel continuously demanded changes to the architect's original plans. He was also skimming off the top with his girlfriend, Virginia Hill, making frequent trips to Zurich. The syndicate's patience finally snapped: on June 20th 1947 Siegel was murdered and the syndicate took over the Flamingo operation. Siegel's dream blossomed and today Las Vegas is a thriving tourist attraction which is said to be gangster-free. Siegel must be laughing in his grave.

SIEGEL, 'Bugsy' (1906-47) US criminal

Don Siegel, born in Chicago on October 26th 1912, was educated in Britain at RADA and Jesus College, Cambridge. In 1934, following the consolidation of talkie films, Siegel arrived in Hollywood. He started at the very bottom and moved up through all the jobs connected with film-making until he was more than ready to direct his first feature film. *The Verdict*, made in 1946, featured Peter Lorre and was well received. It was a B film, and the studio system kept him in this category until in 1954 he made *Riot in Cell Block Eleven*. The critics hailed it and the studio took note. They soon came to realize that Don Siegel was a master of the violent action genre. *Baby Face Nelson* (1957) and *Madigan* (1968), which led to a television series, followed. Then Siegel and Clint Eastwood met. Their films included *Coogan's Bluff* (1968), *Two Mules For Sister Sara* (1970), *Dirty Harry* (1971) and *Escape from Alcatraz* (1979). Don Siegel died in Nipome, California, on April 20th 1991. Clint Eastwood once said: 'any ability I might have as a director I first learned from Don Siegel.'

SIEGEL, Don (1912-91) US film-maker

Born Simone Kaminker on March 25th 1921 in Wiesbaden, Germany, to French-Jewish parents, she was brought up in Paris and educated at the Sorbonne, where she espoused left-wing causes. Her parents were poor and the family lived in a tenement in a Paris slum. During the Second World War her father left the family, escaped to London and joined the Free French forces. Simone, following some

SIGNORET, Simone (1921-85) French actor

drama lessons at night school, took up acting and kept the family afloat. She married Yves Allegret, and this shielded her and her family from the attention of the German and French police when it came to rounding up French Jews for the journey to the gas chambers. After the Second World War she took feature roles, usually playing the 'fallen woman'. She was excellent when acting a woman in love. Particularly good performances among her many film roles were those in *La Ronde* (1950), *Diabolique* (1955) and the British film *A Room At The Top* (1958), which launched her as an international star when she won the Academy Award for Best Actress. She received an Oscar nomination for her performance in *Ship of Fools* (1965) and a French Cesar for *Madame Rosa* (1977). Her last film was *L'Etoile du Nord* (1982). In 1951 she married Yves Montand (*qv*), and they were still married when she died on September 30th 1985. Together they owned the hotel and restaurant at St Paul de Vence, France. The Colomb d'Or was her pride and joy, and when she was not working she would have her meals at her small table by the hotel entrance. Her autobiography, *Nostalgia Isn't What It Used To Be*, was published in 1976, and a novel, *Adieu Volodia*, in 1985.

SILLS,
Beverly
(1929-)
US singer

Her name was originally Belle Silverman and she was born on May 25th 1929 in New York. At the age of four she was already singing on the radio: a precocious child, she knew what she wanted from the time Estelle Liebling agreed to teach her to sing. In 1945 she toured with a Gilbert and Sullivan opera company and in 1947 made her operatic debut with the Philadelphia Civic Opera. Since then she has made great strides to reach the top. International recognition came in April 1969 when she sang the role of Pamira in Rossini's *The Siege of Corinth* at La Scala Opera House in Milan. The enthusiastic press called her, 'La Fenomena', and *La Stampa* went so far as to claim 'fine singing has finally returned to La Scala'. Between 1969 and 1975 she captivated audiences in London and Paris, and in April 1975 repeated her Milan triumph, in the same role, at the Metropolitan Opera House in New York, winning a fifteen-minute ovation and generous praise from the critics. She retired from singing in 1978 to become a director of the New York City Opera, where she stayed until 1989.

SILVERMAN,
Sydney
(1895-1968)
British
politician

Sydney Silverman was born in Liverpool on October 8th 1895 to poor Jewish parents recently arrived from Eastern Europe. By virtue of winning scholarships, he received a first-class education which resulted in his qualifying as a lawyer. During the First World War, Silverman, influenced in part by Bertrand Russell, registered as a conscientious objector. His stand resulted in his being sent to prison and this experience stood him in good stead in his later fight for prison reform. In his law practice he aided the poor of Liverpool in their constant fight with greedy landlords and corrupt police and their pursuit of compensation for working injuries. In 1932 he was a Liverpool councillor and soon won a reputation as a first-class orator. Invited to stand for Parliament, he accepted and in 1935 was elected Labour member for Nelson and Colne in Lancashire, a seat he retained until he died.

A small figure with a shock of grey hair and an overwhelming passion when he spoke, which he did with great frequency, he always stood out. To the left of prevailing Labour party policy, he was never offered any post, either in government or in opposition. He was a backbencher, there to fight for his constituents and those without a voice to speak for themselves. He campaigned vigorously for the abolition of capital punishment; it was his main platform and in 1957 he succeeded in having the death penalty restricted to particular types of murder. It was a step forward, but Silverman wanted what he called 'the loathsome practice' abolished entirely. He won through when, in 1960, he steered the Abolition of Death Penalty Bill through the House of Commons on a free vote.

The period immediately following the Second World War was particularly difficult for Silverman. The Holocaust convinced him that the survivors had won a right to live in Palestine and that a Jewish state was the only long-term answer. However, with Britain holding the Mandate over Palestine and a Labour government in power, Silverman was battling against his own party in general and an antisemitic foreign secretary, Ernest Bevin, in particular. Their clashes were frequent. As a leading member of the Campaign for Nuclear Disarmament he was a constant thorn in any government's side, but was always admired on all sides of the House for standing by his principles. He died on February 9th 1968 in Hampstead, London.

SILVERS, Phil (1911-85) US actor

Phil Silvers was born in Brownsville, New York, on 11th May 1911. Preferring stage and vaudeville to education, he was thirteen when he had his first professional part in the 1925 *Gus Edwards Revue*. He worked in the Minsky Burlesque Troupe between 1934 and 1939 and later in that year had his Broadway debut in *Yokel Boy*. As an MGM contract player he played a variety of balding, bespectacled, also-rans. After the war he played some notable Broadway shows, *High Button Shoes* (1947) and *Top Banana* (1951), for which he received a Tony Award. *The Phil Silvers Show* (1955-59) established him on television as Sergeant Bilko; the repeats are still popular all over the world. Further Broadway success came with *Do Re Me* (1960) and *A Funny Thing Happened on the Way to the Forum* (1972), which brought another Tony Award. Ill-health prevented him from continuing to act as much as he might have done; instead he wrote his autobiography, *The Laugh is on Me* (1973). He is however best known as Bilko a name that comes from the verb to bilk, to cheat; a loveable rogue so loveable he cannot be allowed to fade and actor Steve Martin has jumped onto the bandwagon only to fail; the fans only recognise Phil Silvers and he died on November 1st 1985 taking Bilko with him.

SIMON, Carly (1945-) US singer/ songwriter

Carly Simon was born on June 25th 1945, the third child of Richard Simon, co-founder of publishers Simon and Schuster. Her mother Andrea had studied music, and stressed to her children how important music was in life. Her childhood has had a strong effect upon her and this is reflected in her early Top Ten hit, 'That's the Way I've Always Heard It Should Be'. Her father was a Brooklyn Dodgers fanatic and he took Carly with him so often she became the team's mascot. At Lawrence College Carly and her elder sister, Lucy, formed a duet, calling themselves the Simon Sisters; they had a minor hit with 'Winkin', Blinkin' and Nod' in 1964. After college there was talk of promoting Carly as the female Bob Dylan, but the idea came to nothing and Carly pursued her own style.

Her career took off when in January 1973 she had a Number One hit that took the world's imagination by storm. 'You're So Vain' stayed at the top for three weeks. When asked who was the subject of the song, Carly Simon became most coy and refused to confirm or deny strings of names put forward that included Warren Beatty, Mick Jagger and Kris Kristofferson. Her second most successful single was 'Nobody Does It Better', which she wrote for the James Bond film, *The Spy Who Loved Me*. For her music videos, she persuades men to play impromptu cameos; these have included Jeremy Irons and Al Corley, as well as ordinary people she takes from everyday life. In 1989 she wrote her first children's book, *Amy and the Dancing Bear*. In 1990 her song 'Let The River Run' won the Oscar for Best Song in the film, *Working Girl*. Carly Simon, a multi-talented personality, published her second children's book, *The Boy of the Bells*, in 1991.

SIMON, Herbert (1916-) US economist

Herbert Simon was born in Milwaukee on June 15th 1916 and educated at the University of Chicago, from where he obtained his PhD in 1943. Various teaching posts in political science led him to a professorship at Carnegie-Mellon University in 1949. Simon is best known for his book *Administrative Behaviour* (1947). In this he coins the word 'behaviourism' to describe in practical terms the role of the entrepreneur who seeks the maximum profit, following the single decision via the multiple factors concerned. He later became deeply involved with the rise of computer technology and the possible creation of artificial intelligence. His work culminated in the award of the Nobel Prize for Economics in 1978. Among his writings are *Models of Man* (1973), *Models of Thought* (1979) and *Reason in Human Affairs* (1983). In 1986 he was awarded the US National Medal of Science.

SIMON, Neil (1927-) US playwright

Neil Simon was born on July 4th 1927 in New York. Educated at New York University, he worked as a comedy writer for several years. In the later 1940s and throughout the 1950s, he worked mostly on television shows. There is little doubt that Simon is an extremely popular playwright, never demanding much from his mainly middle-class audience; his characters, too, tend to be middle-class, with thinly veiled Jewish overtones. His work is commercial, amusing and pure escapism. The list of his Broadway successes is awe-inspiring and includes *Come Blow Your Horn* (1961), *Barefoot in the Park* (1963 and a film in 1967), *The Odd Couple* (1965 and a film in 1968 as well as a television series), *Plaza Suite* (1968 and a film in 1971), *Last of the Red Hot Lovers* (1969 and a film in 1972), *The Prisoner of Second Avenue* (1971, a film in 1975), *The Sunshine Boys* (1972, a film in 1975), *California Suite* (1976, a film in 1978) and *Chapter Two* (1977, a film in 1979). In the 1980s Neil Simon wrote an autobiographical trilogy: *Brighton Beach Memoirs* (1983), *Biloxi Blues* (1985) and *Broadway Bound* (1986). He also wrote the books of several well-known musicals, including *Sweet Charity* (1966), *Promises, Promises* (1968) and *They're Playing Our Song* (1979). A very talented fellow, he gives a lot of pleasure to a lot of people and is internationally respected.

Paul Simon was born in Newark, New Jersey, on October 13th 1941, **Art Garfunkel** in Queens, New York, on October 13th 1942. They met in a sixth-grade production of *Alice in Wonderland*: Simon was the White Rabbit and Garfunkel the Cheshire Cat. They would later join up to produce one of the greatest performing duos of the second half of the century. While still at high school together they made their plans. In 1957 they recorded a demo disc called 'Hey Schoolgirl' that scraped into the top fifty. Two more singles flopped, and they decided to go to college. Paul graduated in music from New York University and in English literature at Queen's College; in his spare time he recorded demos for publishers and earned $15 a day while learning about studio techniques. Garfunkel studied mathematics at New York University and architecture at Columbia University. In 1964, Simon and Garfunkel were on the Greenwich Village coffee-house circuit. Two years later, in January 1966, their album *The Sound of Silence* was a resounding hit and reached Number One in the charts. There can be few people who have not seen or heard about the film, *The Graduate* (1967); their song 'Mrs Robinson', written for the film, made them world-famous and was Number One for several weeks. It was not generally known that there was a tension in their relationship and they continued working only by compromise and genuine friendship. In February 1970 they produced their third Number One with 'Bridge Over Troubled Water'; it stayed at the top for six weeks, ran around the world, sold more than eight million copies and won a record six Grammy Awards. Then they decided to separate.

Even while they were working together, Art was becoming a film actor, and was busy in *Catch-22* while Paul was writing their songs. Their last album had eleven tracks, not the twelve originally planned. Art wanted a Bach chorale track to accompany 'Cuba Si, Nixon No'. Paul, who had written the song, said no; so they left it out. Paul Simon continued writing and performing solo. He experienced varying degrees of success with his 1976 and 1977 singles, 'Fifty Ways to Leave Your Lover' and his 1977 single 'Still Crazy After All These Years'. Art in his turn had two Number Ones in the UK charts with 'I Only Have Eyes For You' and 'Bright Eyes'. In 1982, the duo reformed for a concert in Central Park, New York. Once again on his own thereafter, Paul Simon had a worldwide hit with his album *Graceland*, which featured the rhythms of Black South Africa. In 1990 his *Rhythm of the Saints* was an exploration of Brazilian music. In December 1996 Art Garfunkel launched his solo album *Across America*. The title comes from Garfunkel's 12 year walk across the US. He walked a hundred miles in a week, returning home for a period before continuing his expedition.

He was born in Leoncin, Poland on July 14th 1904. His father was a rabbi and Singer was educated at the Tachkemoni Rabbinical Seminary in Warsaw. However, instead of following in his father's footsteps, he got himself a job as a proofreader and translator for *Literashe Bleter* a literary magazine. It was his older brother Israel, an aspiring writer, who lured Isaac away from a rabbinical calling and led the way. In 1935 Israel decided to seek his fortune in America and left. Disliking the way things were going for Jews next door in Germany, and missing his brother,

SIMON and GARFUNKEL: Paul Simon (1941-) and Art Garfunkel (1942-) US composer and singers

SINGER, Isaac Bashevis (1904-91) Polish/American writer

Isaac decided to leave his wife and son and follow Israel to the States. Later, his wife and child had a hellish time in Poland before eventually getting to Palestine via Russia. His marriage over, Isaac got a job on the Yiddish newspaper *Jewish Daily Forward* and in 1940 found a new wife. It wasn't until the sudden death of Israel, whom Isaac regarded as a surrogate father, in 1944 that he felt the urge to write fiction. With his wife working and his job undemanding, Singer worked in virtual isolation until the mid-1950s when Saul Bellow (*qv*) discovered him. Singer, who wrote in Yiddish and was translated by his nephew or his friend Elizabeth Shub, now began establishing himself as a major literary figure. His work appeared in magazines as varied as *Playboy* and the *New Yorker*. His books of short stories gave the reader insights into pre-war Jewish life in Poland. He pulled no punches and his description of Jewish life, showing its obsession with sex, dreams and ritual slaughter, did not go down well. A vegetarian, he was accused of equating the Holocaust with animal slaughter when he said 'all men are Nazis with respect to animals'. Singer refused to be blinded to people's shortcomings, and that included Jews as he shows in his writings. In 1978 he was awarded the Nobel Prize for Literature, which he accepted on behalf of all Yiddish writers. He died in Surfside, Florida, on July 24th 1991. Following his death his book *Meshugah* was published. It had been serialized in the *Jewish Daily Forward* during the 1980s under the title *Lost Souls*.

***SISKIND,
Aaron
(1903-91)
US
photographer***

Aaron Siskind was born in New York City on December 4th 1903. His parents were poor Russian Jews who lived in two rooms on the Lower East Side. Educated at DeWitt Clinton High School and New York City College, he graduated in 1926 and became a teacher of English. On his wedding day in 1929 one of the presents the couple received was to be highly significant: it was a camera. When a year later he joined the Communist Party, to become part of their Film and Photo League, the die was cast. Influenced by the likes of Paul Strand and Berenice Abbott (she also died in 1991 and was a lifelong friend), Siskind took as his life's work the defence of quality and sincerity in photography and the exposure of social injustice. A teacher by day, he was a photographer by night and week-ends. Within his home he built a small dark-room and developed his own work. He lived in this manner for 20 years, all the time learning his craft and fulfilling his work ethic. He created a book of photographs called *Harlem Document* which today is a part of photographic history. The images of black people living in slums, in crowded kitchens or lonely bedsits, and praying in leftover churches, demonstrates the social conditions existing during the Depression, as well as Siskind's extraordinary skill with a camera.

In 1941 he and the League fell out over the methods to be used when creating a living photo. The conflict had been simmering for many years; now Siskind was free to pursue his own course, the problem being that he was not certain which route to take. The answer came while on a visit to a small fishing village, Gloucester, Massachusetts. Idly walking along a deserted beach, camera over his shoulder, he chanced upon a collection of debris: an old rope, a couple of fish heads, an old glove and a couple of empty tin cans. Siskind, using a close-up lens, took photographs of what he would later call 'the drama of objects'. It was the beginning of his relationship with the surrounding physical world of the commonplace. Encouraged by abstract painter Franz Kline (*qv*), Siskind was persuaded to hold an exhibition of his work at the Egan Gallery of New York. It was so well received that he gave up teaching and surrendered himself full-time to photography. But the need to pass on his knowledge to the young remained strong and he began to teach creative photography at the Chicago Institute of Design, and later at the Rhode Island School of Design (1971). Exhibitions all over America and Europe brought Siskind much praise. Jonathan Williams of the London *Independent* posed the question: 'Has there ever been a greater photographer?' while a close friend described him as 'James Joyce with a tripod'. Siskind's photographic philosophy was quite simple: 'confrontation instead of documentation'. He died in Providence, Rhode Island, on February 8th 1991.

SLANSKY, Rudolf (1901-52) Czech politician

Born Rudolf Schlesinger, he rose in the ranks of the Czech Communist Party during the 1930s. Sometimes criticized for 'opportunism', and on occasion suspended from the party, he was given some very tough jobs to do during the Second World War, when his country was occupied by the Germans. In particular, he was in charge of training resistance groups that were parachuted in from Russia, where he worked for most of the war, when he wasn't inside Czechoslovakia, organizing and giving encouragement. He was responsible for the link-up of Russian and Czech partisan groups that spread fear and despondency behind the German lines. Slansky was involved with the uprising of August 1944 that resulted in Soviet forces fighting day and night to reach and liberate beleaguered Prague, despite the presence of American forces only 30 miles away.

In 1945 Slansky was appointed secretary-general of the Czechoslovak Communist Party, one post away from the chairman, Klement Gottwald. However, to all intents and purposes Slansky was in control. He was in charge of the army, the security services and the party machine. In 1951, on his fiftieth birthday, he was awarded the Socialism Decoration, the highest award possible. A few months later a plot was being hatched against him in Moscow. It resulted in his post being abolished. Slansky was appointed deputy prime minister in charge only of economic affairs, although still a member of the Politburo. On November 24th 1951 Slansky, on the evidence of Artur London, a former deputy foreign minister, was accused of leading a conspiracy. Two weeks he was out of office and expelled from the party. Slansky maintained his innocence even under torture. Eventually, having been chained to a wall for many months, he confessed. At his trial he and thirteen others, ten of whom were Jews, pleaded guilty to being 'Trotskyist, Zionist, bourgeois, nationalist traitors and enemies of the Czech people'. Slansky had suffered so much from continuous torture that he admitted everything, even matters he could not possibly have known about. He and ten others were sentenced to death and he was murdered in December 1952. In 1968 the Piller Commission found against the security services and called for the annulment of all charges and his posthumous rehabilitation. The report was filed away, but copies were smuggled out to the West and made public. The Slansky trial was called 'the most merciless and cruel and illogical trial ever'. There is no doubt that the whole affair was dictated by antisemitic feelings that originated in Russia. In 1990 Slansky's son was appointed Czech ambassador to Russia.

SLOVO,
Joe
(1926-95)
South African
politician

Slovo was nine years old when his parents made the long journey from Lithuania to South Africa. He studied law at Witwatrersrand University and during the Second World War volunteered for the South African armed forces. In the late 1940s Slovo joined the Communist Party and became increasingly active. In 1950 he and his wife, Ruth First, were cited in the Suppression of Communism Act. However, Slovo continued to act as a defence lawyer despite being banned from engaging in any political activity. He went underground and in 1955 drafted the Freedom Charter. In December 1956 he was one of 156 people arrested and charged with treason. Joe Slovo conducted his own defence and the trial was eventually abandoned two years later. In 1960, following the Sharpeville Massacre, he was detained without charge and upon release left the country. This meant he was not involved in the Rivonia trial, which led to leading members of the ANC receiving long terms of imprisonment.

In 1977 Slovo established the ANC headquarters in Maputo, Mozambique. There, in 1982, his wife was killed when she opened a parcel addressed to her. In 1985, in Lusaka, Zambia, he became the first white member of the ANC national executive. In 1990 he circulated a document entitled *Has Socialism Failed?* Now chairman of the newly legalized South African Communist Party, he argued that all should work for multi-party democracy in a post-apartheid South Africa. In July 1990 he was appointed ANC general secretary and was a major figure in the negotiations that abolished apartheid and led the way for free elections. In April 1994 Slovo was appointed Minister of Housing in the government of Nelson Mandela. He died from cancer on January 6th 1995, his death mourned by many, regardless of race. In 1997 his daughter Gillian in her book *Every Secret Thing: My Family, My Country* reveals the fact that Michael Sachs is her brother and son of Joe Slovo and Stephanie Kemp. When Gillian tried to question her father, shortly before his death, about the existence of Michael, Slovo told his daughter " I'm not going to tell you anything. You have no right. It's my life. My life. Not yours."

SOKOLOW,
Anna
(1915-)
US
choreographer

Anna Sokolow was born on February 9th 1915 in Hartford, Connecticut. She was brought up on New York's Lower East Side and trained as a dancer, despite her mother's resistance, in the basement of a settlement house. She joined Martha Graham's troupe in 1930 and stayed with them until 1938. She danced in some major works such as *Primitive Mysteries* as well as in her own pieces, which reflected a strong social conscience. In 1953 she created *Lyric Suite* with music by Alban Berg. Her choreography reflected the despair of the poor war victims and refugees. *Room* (1955) examined the isolation of people living alone in big cities. *Dreams*, in 1961, was a piece concerning the all-embracing Holocaust. In 1964 she presented *Steps of Silence,* a dance concerning political prisoners; it was revived in 1984. Her works live on in the repertories of many dance companies around the world. The students she taught from 1957 are everywhere, contributing to the world of dance what Anna Sokolow has inculcated.

Phil Solomon was born in Northern Ireland; his father Morris, was one half of the record distributors Solomon/Peres and an original investor in Decca Records. After a long period in Australia, Solomon returned to Northern Island and there became a pop concert promoter and artist manager. He was an important influence on the early careers of Nina and Frederick, and Ruby Murray. His first important discovery was The Bachelors; their later success was due to the early management of Phil Solomons and his wife Dorothy, one of the most respected agents in the music business. Phil was by inclination an entrepreneur, always working on his latest scheme: a new record label, something Irish, a new pirate radio station . . . It was Solomon who nurtured the early career of Van Morrison; the singer reciprocated by falling out with Solomon and ending up in court. However, of all Morrison's managers, Solomon was the most influential and beneficial and the only one who wouldn't stand for Morrison's temperamental and often inflated ego. In 1966, Solomon became a director of Radio Caroline, enabling him to publicize his string of artists further. He was responsible for importing Serge Gainsbourg's French hit, 'Je T'Aime . . . Moi Non Plus'. A gambler, he went bankrupt but came back to sign up The Dubliners for his new record label. He picked on David McWilliam to replace Van Morrison but to little effect, despite spending a fortune on publicity. By the end of the 1960s he was a spent force and he moved on. At his peak he was the equal of any manager, but he remains neglected in the history of pop music.

Robert Solow was born in Brooklyn, New York, on August 23rd 1924. He received his BA in 1947, his MA in 1949 and his PhD in 1951, all from Harvard University. He began a teaching career at the Massachusetts Institute of Technology in 1949, becoming a full professor in 1958. In the 1950s Solow developed a mathematical model that demonstrated the relative contributions of various factors to producing and sustaining economic growth. From the 1960s his work resulted in governments channelling funds into technological research to encourage economic growth. His researches resulted in his being awarded the 1987 Nobel Prize for Economics.

Solti was born on October 21st in Budapest, where, following a formal education, he studied music at the Liszt Academy. In 1930 he was at the Budapest Opera and eight years later he made his conducting debut. During the Second World War, as a Jew he was forced to leave his job and found sanctuary in Switzerland. Although only 27, he apparently had no urge to join any army to fight Nazism but instead won the 1942 Geneva International Piano Competition. Following the war, and the revelations of the Holocaust, Solti apparently had no difficulty in accepting the position of musical director of the Bavarian State Opera in Munich (1946-52) and for good measure he followed by running the Frankfurt Opera (1952-60). In 1961 he was appointed musical director of Covent Garden Opera; he stayed for ten years and collected a knighthood when he left. In 1972 he became a British citizen and musical director of the Chicago Symphony Orchestra. He took a second-rate orchestra to international fame: when he left in 1991, Chicago Symphony was in the top three of the world's orchestras. As a conductor with the London Philharmonic and the Paris Opera his great dramatic qualities give an added dimension to the music. His interpretations of Mahler are particularly brilliant; Bartok is another strength. Not only has George Solti won more Grammies than any other musical artist, as conductor of the Chicago Symphony he is the only person to have won awards for ten consecutive years (1974-83).

SONDHEIM, Stephen (1930-) US composer

Stephen Sondheim was born in New York City on March 22nd 1930. A precocious child, he showed an early aptitude for music, and received a musical education at Williams College in Massachusetts and at Milton Babbitt in New York. He was only 27 when he was introduced to Leonard Bernstein (*qv*) at a garden party and invited to write some lyrics for a modern opera he was writing. Sondheim agreed and the opera became *West Side Story*, premiered in New York on September 26th 1957 and still running at some theatre somewhere in the world. Sondheim then collaborated with Jule Styne (*qv*) on *Gypsy* (1959). He wrote the music and lyrics for *A Funny Thing Happened on the Way to the Forum* (1962): opening on May 8th 1962, it ran for 964 performances. Two years later his *Anyone Can Whistle* managed only nine. His list of hits is so impressive it beggars belief. His shows include *Follies* (1971), *A Little Night Music* (1973), *Pacific Overtures* (1976) and *Sweeny Todd* (1979). He has won many awards, including four Tonys as well as the Pulitzer Prize for *Sunday in the Park With George* (1984). In 1990 he won an Academy Award for his song 'Sooner or Later' featured in the film *Dick Tracy* and his shows are constantly being revived. In 1990 he spent six months as visiting Professor of Drama at Oxford University.

SONNINO, Baron Sidney (1847-1922) Italian statesman

Sonnino, the offspring of an Italian-Jewish father and an English Christian mother, was born in Pisa on March 11th 1847. He went on to qualify as a lawyer. By the turn of the century he was a well-known politician and diplomat. In 1906 and again in 1909-10 he was Prime Minister. However, it was while he was Foreign Secretary, from 1914 to 1920, that he became internationally known. When the First World War broke out in August 1914, Sonnino made certain demands on the Axis powers which were refused. As a consequence, Sonnino signed the Treaty of London and in May 1915 brought Italy into the world war on the Allied side. Following the end of the war he headed the Italian delegation to the Versailles Peace Conference in 1919. He was most disappointed when the conference refused to grant Italy portions of the now defunct Austro-Hungarian empire. In protest at the lack of support from the Italian government for his demands, he resigned. Made a Senator in 1920, he died in Rome on November 24th 1922.

SONTAG, Susan (1933-) US writer

Susan Sontag was born in New York on January 16th 1933. In 1935 her parents went to China, leaving Susan and her younger sister to live with their grandmother. In 1938 her father died in China and in 1939 her mother returned to take care of her children. Susan, an asthmatic, needed a healthier climate than New York so the family moved to Tuscon, Arizona. Later her mother remarried, and the family moved to a Los Angeles suburb. Susan studied at the University of California for a year before moving to the University of Chicago, from where she obtained a BA in Philosophy. She went on to Harvard to read English and gained an MA in 1954, as well as an MA in Philosophy in 1955. She then spent some time teaching before settling into a career of writing. Her first novel was *The Benefactor* (1963); her next, *Death Kit* (1967). *Against Interpretation and Other Essays* (1968) and *Radical Will* (1969) established Sontag's reputation as a provocative cultural critic, with a particular facility for the critical re-expression of European high culture. She had come to prominence with her 1964 *Notes on Camp*, in which she discusses questions of taste. In 1976 she spend a period in hospital being treated for breast cancer, an experience reflected in her 1978 book, *Illness As Metaphor* . She returned to the same theme for her 1988 book, *AIDS and Its Metaphors*. In 1993 she published her first novel for 25 years: *The Volcano Cover* is a short story about Horatio Nelson and his mistress, Emma Hamilton. It led Jonathan Miller (*qv*) to call her 'probably the most intelligent woman in America'.

SOUTINE, Chaim (1894-1943) French painter

Chaim Soutine was born in Minsk, Russia, the tenth child of a poor Jewish tailor. At the age of sixteen he went to Vilna and attended the School of Fine Arts for three years before going off to Paris. It was now 1913, and Soutine was fortunate immediately to meet with Chagall (*qv*), Modligiani (*qv*), and Lipchitz (*qv*). The art dealer Leopold Zborowski recognized Soutine's talent and financed his stay at Ceret in southern France. There Soutine painted the feverish landscapes that later marked him as one of the greatest exponents of expressionism during the first half of the 20th century. He returned to Paris, where his work was rarely shown because of his increasing belief that it was no good. Indeed, he often destroyed completed paintings. His attitude kept him in poverty until an American dealer, Dr Albert Barnes, bought several works in 1923. Soutine's style is of thick brushwork that shows a mixture of turbulence and tenderness. Many of his portraits depict twisted faces and distorted limbs, with an emphasis on one main colour, usually red. An exception was his famous *The Boy in Black* (1924), painted in oils on canvas. He painted everyday people: choirboys, cooks, hotel porters; anything or anyone that took his fancy. His painting *Side of Beef* (1925, Allbright-Knox Art Gallery, Buffalo) is a typical example and one of a series. To get the effect he needed Soutine would visit the nearby slaughterhouse and have fresh blood poured over the carcasses in order to create the right colour.

During the German occupation of France, Soutine refused to leave although he was offered a visa for the US. Often in hiding to avoid arrest, he had taken refuge in Chinon when in 1943 he was taken ill. The small local hospital diagnosed the urgent need for a special operation, available only in Paris. In order to avoid the French police, the ambulance was forced to take a route that added nineteen hours to what should have been a five-hour journey. The delay cost Soutine his life: at the hospital they operated at once, but he died the next day, August 9th 1943. His lover, Marie Aurenche, the ex-wife of the artist Max Ernst, was heartbroken. She had Soutine buried in her family plot in a Christian graveyard with a place reserved for herself. In 1960 she committed suicide and was buried alongside him. At Soutine's funeral, watched over by German and French police, there were few mourners. However, among those who did attend were Pablo Picasso and Jean Cocteau.

SOYER,
Raphael
(1898-1987)
US painter

Raphael Soyer was born in Russia on December 25th 1898. The family emigrated to the US in 1912 following the Tsarist pogrom of 1905. Raphael and his twin brother Moses (1898-1974) attended New York's art colleges. Raphael came to national prominence during the Depression of the early 1930s. For the subjects of his paintings he drew on the life surrounding him, the poor Italian and Jewish communities that in those days made up the Lower East Side of New York, very much a working-class area. His paintings exhibited the skill of the artist who produces work that reflects real life. His *Office Girls* (1936, Whitney Museum of American Art) is a famous example. The Soyers were also excellent teachers. Later, Raphael Soyer's work showed the lonely people of a big city and he became widely known as the 'dean of American realism'. He spent much of his last 20 years writing, and his work includes *A Painter's Pilgrimage* (1962) and *Homage to Thomas Eakins* (1966). In 1957 he was awarded the prestigious Merit Medal of the American Academy of Arts and Letters. He died on November 4th 1987.

SPARK,
Muriel
(1918-)
British writer

She was born Muriel Camberg in Edinburgh on February 1st 1918 into a middle-class Jewish family, and educated at James Gillespie's School for Girls and Heriot Watt College. She married in 1938 and went to live in Central Africa, returning from a broken marriage to London in 1944. She joined the British Foreign Office and worked in Intelligence. The war over, she became editor of *Poetry Review* (1947-49). She wrote *Memento Mori*, a black comedy, in 1959, followed in 1961 by her most famous novel. *The Prime of Miss Jean Brodie*, which brought fame and fortune after the book became a film in 1969 and won an Oscar for Maggie Smith as Best Actress. *The Ballard of Peckham Rye* in 1960 and *The Girls of Slender Means* in 1963 are humorous, while *The Mandelbaum Gate* (1965) tackles a weightier subject. In 1981 she wrote *Loitering With Intent*, which has been described as elegant and witty. *A Far Cry From Kensington*, published in 1988, describes London during the early 1950s. In 1996 she published *Reality of Dreams*. The opening lines convey succinctly the tone of the story: 'He often wondered if we were all characters in one of God's dreams . . .' When she was much younger and poor, Graham Greene paid her an allowance plus five bottles of wine. The only condition was that she didn't thank him or pray for him. She was created a Dame in 1996.

SPASSKY,
Boris
(1937-)
Russian chess
grandmaster

Spassky was born to Jewish parents on January 30th 1937 in Leningrad, Russia. As an infant he was fortunate to be evacuated out of the city and so escaped the bitter siege that marked one of the most heroic actions of the Second World War. He was sent to a children's home in Kirov and there he learned to play chess. He was still in his teens when he achieved the rank of 'international master'. Two years later he won the world junior championship and the title 'international grandmaster'. At this time he was studying journalism at Leningrad University. In 1966, still largely unknown outside the USSR, he challenged Tigran Petrosyan for the world title and lost. Three years later he won, subsequently holding the title until 1972 when, in a famously publicized and financially lucrative match in Iceland, he lost to Bobby Fischer (*qv*). Spassky's defence of his title encouraged a generation around the world to take up the game. In 1975 he married for the third time and went to live in Paris.

Phil Spector was born in the Bronx, New York, on December 26th 1940. When he was still a child the family moved to Los Angeles and there, while at high school, became immersed in pop music. He formed a vocal group and named it The Teddy Bears. In the late 1940s his father died and Spector was later inspired to write a song to him: 'To Know Him is to Love Him' took the Teddy Bears to Number One; the title came from the inscription on his father's headstone. In 1961 he started his own record label, Philles. He launched The Crystals and Gene Pitney and some of the other great names and sounds of the swinging sixties: The Ronettes, Bob B Soxx, The Blue Jeans, Darlen Love and the Righteous Brothers. In February 1965 Phil Spector wrote *You've Lost That Lovin' Feelin*, which reached Number One. He then retired for several years, although still dabbling in what interested him. He took a cameo part in the 1969 film *Easy Rider*. He worked with The Beatles, more particularly with John Lennon on his *Instant Karma* disc, and George Harrison on his Bangladesh album. He also worked with Cher, Dion and others. He financed the kung fu film of 1973, *Enter The Dragon*, which certainly made up for any loss of earnings from having taken early retirement. In 1997 Spector won a case in the English High Court over his claim for royalties for his debut hit *To Know Him is to Love Him*. Phil Spector now lives as a recluse; when the history of pop music is written, his will be a prominent place.

Born in Jaroslau, Austria, on November 11th 1903, he was educated at the University of Vienna. During the early 1920s he worked as a young pioneer in Palestine before going to Hollywood in 1927 to work as a translator. In 1930 he was in Berlin as the head of Universal Pictures' European operation. In 1933 he transferred to Vienna, but Hitler followed him there, so in 1939 he shut down the office and returned to the US. He now decided to become an independent producer. He kicked off with *Tales of Manhattan* (1942), written by Ben Hecht and including many of the great names of Hollywood. It wasn't bad but it certainly gave no inkling to the great things to come: Orson Welles' *The Stranger* (1946), Huston's *African Queen* (1951), *On The Waterfront* (1954), *The Bridge on the River Kwai* (1957), *Suddenly Last Summer* (1959), *Lawrence of Arabia* (1962), *The Night of the Generals* (1966), *Nicholas and Alexandra* (1971), *The Last Tycoon* (1976) and, in 1983, *Betrayed*. His films were generally large-scale productions filmed on locations that included jungles, deserts and rivers. Nothing was too much for Spiegel. He wanted realism and he achieved it. He must have done something right, for his films won more awards than those of any other producer in the history of film. He died on

SPECTOR, Phil (1940-) US music writer and producer

SPIEGEL, Sam (1903-85) Austrian/ American film producer

December 31st 1985 in St Martin in the Dutch Antilles. His fortune was around $16 million and he left it all to charity. His only child, Adam, was ten at the time; he was brought up by his mother, the English actress Ann Pennington, Spiegel's second wife and 43 years his junior.

SPIELBERG,
Steven
(1947-)
US film-maker

Steven Spielberg was born in Cincinnati, Ohio, on December 18th, 1947. He was educated at California State University and graduated in 1970. As a producer and director, he has become a household name all over the world and made some of the most popular films of the 20th century. He has also had his share of box-office flops. He is largely self-taught and was only sixteen when he made his first feature, a two hour sci-fi film called *Firelight*. He followed up with *Jaws* (1975), *Close Encounters of the Third Kind* (1977), *Raiders of the Lost Ark* (1981), *E.T.* (1982), *Indiana Jones and the Temple of Doom* (1984), *Empire of the Sun* (1987) and *Jurassic Park* (1993). It is, however, for *Schindler's List* (1995) that he will probably be best remembered. To produce a successful and acceptable film out of the horrors of the Holocaust is a staggering achievement. Spielberg has since embarked on producing the largest and most dynamic documentary in film history: he is recording the stories of some 200,000 Holocaust survivors. The results will probably be more memorable than any of the fine films Spielberg has so far made.

SPITZ,
Mark
(1950-)
US Olympic
swimmer

Mark Spitz was born on February 10th 1950 in Modesto, California. Following his education at Indiana University in Bloomington, from where he eventually graduated, Spitz dedicated his time and energy to becoming a champion swimmer. In the Olympic Games of 1968, held in Mexico City, he had rather pompously predicted that he would win six gold medals; in fact he won only two, both as a member of a relay team. He probably had not taken Mexico City's high altitude into consideration. In 1972 the Games were held at ill-fated Munich, where eleven Israeli sportsmen were murdered by terrorists. Undaunted, Spitz won a record seven gold medals. Undoubtedly the greatest swimmer in history, he held 27 world records for freestyle and butterfly between 1967 and 1972. Subsequently all his records have been broken and Spitz is now a businessman. However, it is doubtful if an athlete in any sport will ever equal his Olympic record of seven gold medals in one Olympiad. In 1996, at the Atlanta Olympic Games, Mark Spitz was honoured at the opening ceremony as the principal athlete of the 1972 Games.

STANLEY,
Paul
(1952-)
US singer/
musician

Born Paul Stanley Eisen on January 20th 1952 in New York City, in 1972 he introduced the world of rock music to a new sound. He and fellow musician Gene Simmons, who was born Gene Klein in Haifa, Israel, on August 25th 1949, founded a band that became known as 'Kiss'. The name came about when Stanley was driving on the Long Island Freeway. His worry was that Simmons, and the other two recently joined members, might object. However, their response was 'Yeah, that sounds pretty good' and Kiss were ready for launching. They had spent three months in a Manhattan loft experimenting with sounds, make-up and costumes. After a year's hard touring they were ready to record. The problem was that Kiss was a visual act. The guys would dress up on stage; Simmons was a blood-drooling Phantom of the Opera and Stanley a clown who wore glitter costume. A record couldn't convey the colour and flashing lights. They persevered and *Kiss Alive* sold a million records. Their single 'Destroyer' (1976) got to Number Seven and Marvel Comics published a *Kiss* comic book; and the PR hype did them no harm. Their fan club, Kiss Army Fan Club, now numbered several hundred thousand. *Love Gun* (1977) was at Number Four and *Kiss Unmasked* (1980) carried their imaginative work onwards. Several albums followed, all reaching the top twenty; *Asylum* (1985) and *Crazy Nights* (1987) were particularly well received. Paul Stanley is considered an excellent guitar player and an imaginative performer.

'**Steely Dan**' was the brainchild of Donald Fagen, who was born in Passaic, New Jersey, on January 10th 1948, and Walter Becker, born in New York State on February 20th 1950. The two boys met when they were both students at Bard's College. After college, from which only Fagen graduated, the two tried selling songs they had written while there, but without success. By June 1972 they had sufficient experience to start the group they called 'Steely Dan', a name they borrowed from a book by William Burroughs called *Naked Lunch*, which describes a steam-powered dildo. Over the next fifteen years they acquired an international reputation for jazz-influenced pop music and become renowned for perfection during production. Fagen played keyboards and sang, while Becker played bass. While the number of members of the group fluctuates, it is generally a duo. They disliked touring and largely ignored the singles market. However, all their albums were very popular and although they never reached the Number One spot it didn't appear to matter. By 1990 the duo had split, with Fagen living in New York and producing occasional live shows, Becker living and working in Hawaii as a producer. Their many fans all over the world believed nevertheless that they would get together again, and in 1996 it happened. 'Steely Dan' toured Europe to cheering, sell-out audiences.

'STEELY DAN'
US pop group

Rodney Stephen Steiger was born on April 14th 1925 in Westhampton, NY. His parents were in show business when they divorced. Steiger was a year old. At the time of WW2 he lied about his age and joined the US navy. As a torpedoman on a destroyer in the Pacific he saw much action. Following his four years in the navy Steiger joined the Civil Service and acted in their amateur theatre company. This experience decided his future. Taking advantage of the GI bill he studied drama at the New School for Social Research in New York and later at the Actors Studio. He made his Broadway debut in *Night Music* (1951) playing the part of a 55 year old detective. Steiger was 26 and highly praised.

He is however best known to the world for his film work. Among his better known films are, *On The Waterfront* (1954) for which he was nominated for an Oscar, *Al Capone* (1959) a role others have copied but never equalled. 1965 gave Steiger two of his greatest roles; *Dr Zhivago* and *The Pawnbroker* and another Oscar nomination. His performance in *In The Heat of the Night* (1967) earned a most deserved Oscar for Best Actor. Following the break up of his marriage

STEIGER,
Rod
(1925-)
US actor

to Claire Bloom (qv) Steiger, in the 1970s, experienced depressions and had a serious heart operation. He gradually returned to work and his portrayal of Mussolini in *Lion of the Desert* (1980) is considered masterly. In the 1990s he is as powerful an actor as ever.

**STIEGLITZ,
Alfred
(1864-1946)
US
photographer**

Steiglitz was born on January 1st 1864 in Hoboken, New Jersey. He was the elder son of a retired Jewish woollen merchant who subsequently took the family back to Europe in order to give them a better education than he thought they would get in America. In Berlin, Alfred discovered the camera and decided to spend his life fighting to have photography recognized as an art form, alongside painting and sculpture. Back in New York's art world he established the magazine *Camera Work* and often produced fine photographs of the newest work by famous painters. In 1916 he had a show of photographic art at the Albright Museum in Buffalo, New York. In 1924 the British Royal Photographic Society awarded him their highest award, the Progress Medal. Steiglitz, known as 'the father of modern photography', died at his studio in New York on July 13th 1946, knowing he had fulfilled his wish and that photography was indeed an acknowledged art form. He was also responsible, via his galleries and publications, of having introduced Americans to modern art. The most complete set of Steiglitz's work is held at the National Gallery of Art in Washington DC. Other collections are held at art museums all over the United States and Europe.

**STEIN,
Edith
(1891-1942)
Polish martyr**

Edith Stein was born on October 12th 1891 in Breslau, Germany. Her family were orthodox Jews. In 1904 she renounced her religion and became an atheist. While a student at the University of Göttingen she came under the influence of Edmund Husserl, founder of noumenology and an influential philosopher. She also came into contact with Catholicism. When Husserl moved to Freiburg University he asked Stein to be his assistant. There, in 1916, she received her PhD in philosophy and went on to achieve a reputation as a leading philosopher. Returning from a visit home in 1921, she read the works of the mystic St Teresa of Avila. This led to her conversion to Roman Catholicism. She was baptized on January 1st 1922 and went to teach at a Dominican girls' school in Speyer. There she translated St Thomas Aquinas' *On Truth* into German. In 1932 she was a lecturer at the Institute for Pedagogy at Munster, but was forced to resign because of the anti-Jewish laws passed by the new German government. In 1934 she entered the Carmelite convent at Cologne, taking as her new religious name Teresa Benedicta of the Cross. In 1938 she was transferred to the Carmelite convent at Echt in Holland. There she wrote her best-known work, *The Science of the Cross* . On July 26th 1942 the Dutch bishops publicly condemned German anti-Semitism. Hitler was furious. His response was to order the arrest of all non-Aryan Christians. Edith and her sister Roas, also a Catholic convert, were arrested by the Gestapo and entrained for Auschwitz. There, because they were considered Jews, they were murdered in the gas chambers on August 9th-10th 1942. On May 1st 1987 Edith Stein was beatified by Pope John Paul II.

Gertrude Stein was born in Allegheny, Pennsylvania, on February 3rd 1874. The daughter of a wealthy Jewish family, she grew up in California and graduated from Radcliffe College with a BA. She went to live in Paris on a handsome allowance from an indulgent father. For a while, from 1903 to 1912, she lived with her brother Leo, but when he left her lifelong companion, Alice B. Toklas, moved in. Under the guidance of Leo, Gertrude collected the works of the painters Picasso, who painted her portrait, Matisse, Braque and others. She created an atmosphere at her home where writers, especially American writers passing through, would congregate. Stein's first published book, *Three Lives* (1909), was hailed as a masterpiece. This book, and her bohemian way of life, were considered most avant-garde. During the 1920s, her home on the Rue de Fleurus was home to the literary giants of her time, including Hemingway, Fitzgerald and Anderson, among others. Her best-known book, however, is *The Autobiography of Alice B. Toklas* (1933), which is in fact her own autobiography. She wrote the book of the opera *Mother of us All*, based on the works of the feminist activist Susan Anthony. She was a legend in France, where in Paris she survived the German occupation by calling in the many favours she was owed; later she lived in obscurity in Belignin in the south of France. She wrote about these experiences, and about the liberating US soldiers, in *Wars I Have Seen* (1945) and *Brewsie and Willie* (1946). Gertrude Stein, an important influence on the literary and artistic life of the 1920s and 1930s, died on July 27th 1946 in Paris.

Born on November 26th 1862 in Budapest, by the beginning of the century he was established as an international archaeologist and teacher. *Chronicle of the Kings of Kasmur*, based on his travels in Central Asia, was published in 1900 and became a best-seller. Stein, who became a British subject in 1904, now began the expedition that took him through the west of China to Khotan. Three further expeditions were to follow, in 1906-8, 1913-16 (during which he covered 25,000 kilometres on horse and camel) and 1930. He was knighted in 1912. Stein was responsible for tracing the ancient caravan routes between China and the West. A quiet, friendly man, he spoke a number of languages and dialects. He made valuable contributions to the West's understanding of the little-known regions of this enormous area. He discovered many documents and artefacts, ranging from Neolithic stone tools to eighth-century textiles. Stein also found, near Tan Huang, the Cave of the Thousand Buddhas. Here, walled up since the beginning of the eleventh century, he found paintings and documents. Much of what he discovered is now in the Asian Antiquities Museum in New Delhi. In 1926, at Pir Sarai, near the Indes River, he identified the site of Alexander's storming of the near impregnable Rock of Aornos. He was 80 when he embarked on his last great adventure, the exploration of Afghanistan. However, shortly after arrival at Kabul he fell ill, and died on October 26th 1943. In his will he donated his personal library to the Hungarian Research Academy.

STEIN,
William
(1911-80)
US biochemist

Stein was born on June 25th 1911 in New York and received his PhD from Columbia College of Physicians and Surgeons in 1938. He joined the staff of the Rockefeller Institute for Medical Research and was made a professor in 1954. Stein spent the period between 1949 and 1963 working out how ribonuclease catalyses the digestion of food. He discovered new methods of analysing amino-acids obtained from proteins, and used the same method to determine the structure of ribonuclease. Stein and his colleague Stafford Moore shared the Nobel Prize for Chemistry in 1972. They celebrated by working out the complete sequence of deoxyribonuclease, a molecule twice as complex as ribonuclease. William Stein died in New York on February 2nd 1980.

STEINBERG,
Saul
(1914-)
Romanian/
American
painter

Saul Steinberg was born Saul Jacobson on June 15th 1914. Quite why he changed surnames isn't readily known, but it appears consistent with his general approach and the type of art for which he is famous. Born in Rimnicu-Sarat, Romania, he studied sociology at the University of Bucharest and architecture in Milan, and from 1933 made a living from selling his cartoons to an Italian magazine. In 1939 he decided to settle down at last and chose New York as his home. Here, as a freelance artist, he sold cartoons to *The New Yorker*. These works might fairly be described as abstract comedies. His laconic ink doodlings are considered quite brilliant and cause people to smile. They have smiled at his exhibitions in cities all over the US and in many parts of Europe. His subject is wide. It might be a wicker seat overtaken by its decorative twists or a hopeful, often tiny, figure on top of a question mark, sited on the edge of a ravine. A more imaginative artist would be hard to find.

STEINBERGER,
Jack
(1921-)
German/
American
physicist

Steinberger was born on May 25th 1921 in Bad Kissingen, Germany. In 1934 he left Hitler's Germany for the US, where he later studied physics at Chicago University, obtaining a PhD in 1948. At Columbia University, New York, where he was professor of physics from 1950 to 1971, he met Max Lederman (*qv*) and Melvin Schwartz (*qv*). The three researched the uses of neutrons, work culminating with their experiments establishing that the neutrinos that produced muons were in fact a previously unknown and distinct type, which they named 'muon neutrinos'. For this work all three shared the 1988 Nobel Prize for Physics.

STEINEM,
Gloria
(1934-)
US activist

Gloria Steinem was born on March 25th 1934 in Toledo, Ohio. Educated at Smith's College, she also studied at Delhi and Calcutta universities. In 1960 she had a job on the satirical magazine *Help!* and in 1963 worked undercover in Manhattan's Playboy Club, publishing her article under the title '*I Was a Playboy Bunny*'. In 1968 she began writing political articles for *New York Magazine*. This led her to the women's movement that was beginning to gather pace. Together with Betty Friedan (*qv*) and Bella Abzug (*qv*) she helped found the National Women's Political Caucus in 1971. The same year she produced the first issue of *Ms* with Pat Carbine as editor. Gloria Steinem has since become a role model for young women all over the world. She has promulgated the view that only when women are fully liberated will men become whole people. In 1986 she wrote *Marilyn*, a biography of Marilyn

Monroe. Her *Revolution from Within: A Book of Self Esteem* (1991), examines her innermost feelings in regard to the women's movement.

George Steiner was born in Paris on April 23rd 1929. He has become one of the most important man of letters in the second half of the 20th Century. He regrets what he sees as the passing of literature as a method of introducing civilisation. He has a passion for languauge and his book *After Babel* (1975) expresses his doubts as to the literary ability of contemporary writers. This book later became a TV series under the title *The Tongues of Men* (1977). In *Real Presences* (1989) he suggests that literature should be regarded with awe. His rhetoric is powerful and his university lectures are eagerly attended. He has been a Fellow of Churchill College, Cambridge since 1961 and associated with universities in France and America. In 1984 France honoured Steiner with the Chevalier de la Legion d' Honneur. A considerable writer his *The Death of Tragedy* (1960) is probably best known. He once stated, " We know now that man can read Goethe or Rilke in the evening, that he can play Bach or Schubert, and go to his day's work at Auschwitz in the morning ".

Isaac Stern was born on July 21st 1920 in Kremenets, Russia; a year later he was in San Francisco. Between 1928 and 1931 he studied at the San Francisco Conservatory and from 1932 to 1939 with violinist Naoum Blinder. He was 15 when he gave his first concert with the San Francisco Symphony and the critics claiming 'this is a real promise'. However, it was not until after the Second World War, following a hugely successful concert in New York, that he received international recognition, which has increased over the years. He is now recognized as one of the greatest violinists in the world. He has appeared with all the great orchestras at the world's great halls. He has played all the recognized concertos and has introduced many new composers. In 1960 he started a campaign to save Carnegie Hall from demolition with the result that the hall is now owned by New York City. Within the concert hall an auditorium named Isaac Stern was later created. His recordings are many and he is a favourite with concert-goers. His was the violin playing for *Fiddler on the Roof* . The documentary made for world television of his China concerts, entitled *From Mao to Mozart* (1979), won him an Oscar. In the 1990s Stern has been giving a series of worldwide concerts to celebrate his 70th birthday. Stern, during a Larry King interview in 1997 claimed, 'the violin is from the heart to the heart' . In 1975 France appointed him an Officier de la Legion d'Honneur.

Otto Stern was born on February 17th 1888 in Sohrau, Germany. Having obtained his PhD, he worked under Albert Einstein (*qv*) and taught at several universities. His research work was related to the development of the molecular beam as a tool to study molecular construction, and to measure the magnetic moment of the proton. He subsequently discovered it was two and a half times the theoretical notion. In 1933 the Germans, more concerned about racial matters than scientific ones, requested the Jewish Otto Stern to leave. He journeyed to the US, where he was welcomed by the Carnegie Institute of Technology at Pittsburgh (1933-45). In 1943 he was awarded the Nobel Prize for Physics in recognition of his work in the field of the molecular beam. He died in Berkeley, California, on August 17th 1969.

STONE,
Oliver
(1946-)
US film-maker

Oliver Stone was born in New York on September 15th 1946 and educated at Yale University and New York University, where he attended the film school. Stone first made his name as a writer. He wrote the screenplay for *Midnight Express* (1978) and received the Academy Award for Best Screenplay as well a Writer's Guild Award and a Golden Globe. Since then he has gone on to become one of today's most forceful directors, not afraid of tackling taboo subjects and making critically acclaimed films of them. His films include *Platoon* (1986), for which he wrote the screenplay and directed. It was a stark, tough criticism of the brutality and futility of the Vietnam War and was a box-office hit. Stone was nominated for an Oscar for his screenplay and won the Oscar for Best Director. *Salvador* (1986) exposed how right-wing regimes in Central America were supported by US government agencies. In *Wall Street* (1987) Stone shows the unacceptable face of capitalism. *Talk Radio* (1988) exposed the frailty of those often regarded as icons. *Born on the Fourth of July* (1989), an anti-Vietnam War film that well illustrates how dangerous jingoism can be, earned Oliver Stone the Oscar for Best Director. In 1995 he produced *Nixon*. Critics lined up to attack, not the film, but the portrayal of Nixon as a corrupt president. Worse criticism was to come when in 1996 he made *Natural Born Killers*, a brilliant film that clearly shows a residual sickness in a society that puts the creation of personal wealth before the education of children. Stone continues to produce films that entertain and inform.

STRANSKY,
Joel
(1967-)
South African
Rugby fly-half

Joel Theodore Stransky was born in Pietermaritzburg, South Africa on July 16th 1967. Following his education at Maritzburg College in Natal he became increasingly involved with rugby union. He has played for Northern Transvaal, Natal and Western Province as well as 23 times for South Africa scoring a record 240 points. He also spent some time playing for the L'Aquila and San Dona clubs in Italy. In the final of the 1995 World Cup Final, between South Africa and New Zealand, Stransky achieved world wide fame by kicking all of South Africa's points including the drop goal that clinched the cup and the world title for the Springboks. Named the 1995 Rugby Player of the Year he joined Leicester, one of England's top rugby clubs in December 1996. In only 8 games he scored over a 100 points and broke the club record. In March 1997 Stransky was responsible for Leicester getting into the final of the Pilkington Cup. In the event Leicester won the cup with Stransky kicking all their nine points.

STRASBERG,
Lee
(1901-82)
US
actor/teacher

He was born Israel Strasberg on November 17th 1901 in Budanov, Russia. When he was seven his family emigrated to the US and he grew up on New York's Lower East Side.. By the time he was fifteen he was acting in amateur plays and taking lessons at the American Laboratory Theatre. His teachers were exponents of the Stanislavsky method, in which Strasberg became an expert. A co-founder of the Group Theatre, he worked for ten years acting and directing. A period in Hollywood (1941-48) was followed by a return to Broadway and the Actor's Studio. He was a strong influence on a whole generation of actors who would climb to the top of their profession. These included Marlon Brando, Rod Steiger (*qv*), Marilyn Monroe, Paul Newman (*qv*) and Shelley Winters (*qv*). In 1969 he set up the Lee Strasburg Institute. More a teacher than an actor, he appeared in only a handful of films; however, he received an Oscar nomination for his part in *The Godfather Part 2* (1974). He died in New York on February 17th 1982. Elia Kazan described him as having 'the aura of a prophet, a magician, a witch doctor, a psychoanalyst and a feared father of a Jewish home'.

STREISAND, Barbra (1942-) US actor/singer

Barbra Streisand was born on April 24th 1942 in Brooklyn, New York. After graduating from high school she studied acting before becoming a night club singer. A highly talented entertainer, her energetic performance in the Broadway production of the musicals *I Can Get it For You Wholesale* (1962) and *Funny Girl* (1964) won her many fans. She has recorded many hit records and is one of the most popular singers in the world. As a film actress Streisand has her fans, and her performance in the screen version of *Funny Girl* (1968) won her the Academy Award for Best Actress. Other films have included *Hello Dolly* (1969) and *On a Clear Day You Can See For Ever* (1970). She turned producer for her film *Yentl*, adapted from Isaac Bashevis Singer's story, '*Yentl, the Yeshiva Boy*'. Singer tried to stop the 1983 production, in which Streisand plays Yentl; he failed, as did the film. Streisand is probably one of the top-selling record artists ever, having sold an awesome 60 million albums. In December 1992 she signed a long-term contract to film and record, said to be worth $2 million per annum for ten years, plus $5 million per record album, and the agreement is for six albums. In 1993, on New Year's Eve, she gave her first live concert for 27 years: she does not relish singing in front of a live audience. In 1997 her film, *The Mirror Has Two Faces*, was released. She produced, directed and starred. Inevitably, with Streisand the perfectionist, there were creative differences. Some fourteen people walked out or were fired during filming. According to the critics actress Lauren Bacall, who plays the part of Streisand's mother, takes the only acting honours.

STROHEIM, Eric von (1885-1957) Austrian/ American actor/ director

He was born Erich Oswald Hans Carl Maria **Stroheim** in Vienna on September 22nd 1885. His Jewish mother came from a well-to-do family and his Jewish father was a straw hat maker. Eric worked for his father until he went to the Military Academy in Wiener Neustadt. By the time he graduated he had acquired the ' von'. He emigrated to the US in 1909 and began his film career as a silent film actor. He invented a new family for himself to hide his true origins. He let it be known that he was a Catholic, that his father was a high military officer and that his mother held the Order of Elizabeth. During the First World War, with the US at war with Germany, the studio billed his film *Intolerance* (1916) as featuring 'the Hun you love to hate' and for Eric, with his large, bald, bullet head and overbearing military manner, the tag was just right. However, Eric wanted to be a director and in 1919 he made *Blind*

Husbands, which he also wrote and acted in. The film was very well received. He followed it with *Devil's Pass Key* (1920) and *Foolish Wives* (1922). Both were tales of adultery. He was criticized for the length of his films but objected to the studio editing his work. His great epic, *Greed* (1924), was originally ten hours long; it was later reduced by the studio to just two hours, although the premiere lasted seven. Robert Sherwood, the great American writer, declared: 'von Stroheim is a genius and *Greed* has established that beyond all doubt but he is badly in need of a stopwatch'. In 1928 von Stroheim directed *Queen Kelly,* with Gloria Swanson and financed by Joseph Kennedy, with such arrogance and high-handedness that Swanson had him fired and the film was never completed. Following the end of the silent era, von Stroheim began acting again and two of his films were great hits: these were *Five Graves to Cairo* (1943) and *Sunset Boulevard* (1950), in which he once again met up with Gloria Swanson and for which he was nominated for an Academy Award. He died on May 12th 1957 in Maurepas, France. In October 1985 the town honoured him by renaming a street after him.

STYNE,
Jule
(1905-)
US composer

He was born **Julius Kerwin Stein** on December 31st 1905 in London, England. The son of Ukrainian-Jewish parents, he was seven years old when the family emigrated to the US and settled in Chicago. Here, after school, he studied the piano. He was bent on becoming a classical pianist; however, needing to earn money he began playing in night clubs and writing music by day. In 1930 he changed his name so as not to be confused with Jules Stein, who was working in the same business. In 1934 he moved to New York, then west to Hollywood in 1937, to write film music. Styne, the music writer, met up with Sammy Cahn (*qv*), the lyric writer, in the early 1940s. They agreed to work together and produced many popular songs for Frank Sinatra in particular. The duo wrote the music for the film *Anchors Aweigh* (1945), which included the song '*I Fall in Love Too Easily*'. In 1949, with lyricist Leo Robin, Styne wrote the music for the Broadway show *Gentlemen Prefer Blondes*, which became a major Hollywood film in 1962. In 1956 he teamed up with Adolph Green to write the musical *The Bells Are Ringing*, filmed with Judy Garland in 1960. For *Gypsy* (1959), Stephen Sondheim was 'the words' and they both worked on the film version in 1962. Styne's last great Broadway success was *Funny Girl* in 1964, filmed in 1968 with lyrics by Bob Merrill. In a glittering career Jule Styne wrote or co-wrote over 1,500 songs that included '*Three Coins in the Fountain*' and '*I Don't Want to Walk Without You*'. All in all he has made a lot of people very happy.

SUZMAN,
Helen
(1917-)
South African
politician

Helen Suzman, the daughter of Lithuanian Jews, was born Gavronsky on November 7th 1915 in Germiston, South Africa and during the long years of apartheid was the only acceptable face of white South African politics to much of the world. Educated at the University of Witwatersrand, she obtained a Bachelor of Commerce degree, returning to her alma mater as a lecturer on economic history in 1945. She stayed there until elected to Parliament in 1953. In 1959, she and eleven other Liberal MPs broke away to form the Progressive Party. Two years later, following a general election, she was the only one to be returned. For thirteen years hers was a lone but loud voice as the only anti-apartheid MP, constantly fighting for the precious few rights the majority of South African citizens had. After serving 36 years as an MP, she retired in 1989. By then she was 71 and had fought the racial pass laws, unequal education, forced removal of blacks to ancient lands that were foreign to them, and many more discriminatory acts. Her first big moment came when, on June 19th 1986, Parliament voted 126 to 16 to scrap the pass laws. Her next was when free democratic elections were held in early 1994 to return Nelson Mandela as President of South Africa. In 1997 she was presented with South Africa's highest honour by Mandela.

SVERDLOV,
Yakov
(1885-1919)
Russian
politician

Sverdlov was born on May 22nd 1885 in Nizhny Novgorod, Russia, the son of a Jewish engraver. While still a teenager he was a full member of the Russian Social Democratic Party. When the party split in 1903, he joined the Bolshevik wing to follow the path of Lenin. Sverdlov worked for the cause in the Urals and as a consequence was often arrested, serving several terms of imprisonment. During his internal exile he was co-opted on to the Central Committee in 1912. Released from exile in March 1917, he was appointed head of the Party Secretariat, in effect the Party's chief organizer and in charge of personnel. Sverdlov's planning of the October 1917 revolution was all-important. Following the success of the revolution, he was elected chairman of the Central Executive Committee of the All-Russian Congress of Soviets, i.e. the recognized head of the USSR, on November 18th 1917. By his efforts all aspects of Russian life were brought under the control of the Bolshevik Party. Like Lenin, Sverdlov believed in a highly centralized polity and the two men dominated decisions made by the Central Committee. It was Sverdlov who gave the go-ahead for the execution of the Tsar and his Romanov family in Yekaterinburg in July 1918. The city was re-named Sverdlov in his honour when, on March 16th 1919, he died during the influenza epidemic that spread throughout Europe, killing more people than the First World War itself. Had Sverdlov lived, it is probable that the 20th century would have taken a radically different course, for he, and not Joseph Stalin, might well have succeeded Lenin when he died in 1924.

SVEVO,
Italo
(1861-1928)
Italian writer

Italo Svevo was the pseudonym used by Ettore Schmitz. Born on December 19th 1861 in Trieste, Italy, he was the son of Jewish parents, his father German, his mother Italian. Italo had to leave school early because his father, a glass merchant, had financial problems. He became a bank clerk and began writing in his spare time. His first two novels were published but ignored, and he gave up writing and went into his parents-in-law's business. In 1907 Svevo, having to make frequent business trips to England, decided to acquire an English teacher. He chose a young man of 25, named James Joyce, to come to Trieste and live and work at his home. The two men became friends and Joyce allowed Svevo to read some of his work in progress, later to be published under the title *Dubliners*. In return, Svevo shyly showed Joyce his two published novels. It was Joyce's unqualified admiration for his work that convinced Svevo that he should try again. In 1923 he published his most famous work, *Confessions of Zeno*, a brilliant tale of the relationship between a psychiatrist and his patient. Svevo published the book himself and, like his previous efforts, it proved a failure. A few years later James Joyce gave Svevo's book to two French critics who went on to praise it publicly, with the result that Svevo became internationally famous. He was working on a sequel when, on September 13th 1928, he was killed in a car accident. Much of his work, often written in secret, has been published posthumously in the 1950s and 1960s. His work graphically illustrates life in pre-Second World War Trieste. As time goes on, the work of Italo Svevo is increasingly appreciated. Joyce's character of Leopold Bloom in *Ulysses* is said to be based on Svevo.

SZABADOS,
Miklos
(1912-62)
Hungarian/
Australian
world table
tennis champion

Miklos Szabados was born in Budapest on March 18th 1912. He achieved a total of ten men's world titles: all doubles, often with Victor Barna (*qv*) as his partner, with the exception of 1931, when he was the world singles champion as well as the world men's doubles and mixed doubles champion. He was, however, the losing finalist on three other occasions; he once lost to Barna and once to Fred Perry, who went on to become the only Britain ever to win the Wimbledon lawn tennis singles championship. In 1937 Szabados toured Australia, fell in love with the country and never returned to Europe. He became an Australian citizen and that country's top player. He is recalled as a player whose superb footwork carried him through his matches; and his gentlemanly behaviour won him many friends. He died in Sydney on December 2nd 1962.

SZILARD,
Leo
(1898-1964)
Hungarian/
American
physicist

Born on February 11th 1898 in Budapest, **Szilard** received his PhD from the University of Berlin in 1922. He taught at the Institute of Theoretical Physics until the arrival of Hitler in power in 1933. Then he left for London, where he spent three years developing, together with T. A. Chalmers, the first method of separating isotopes of radioactive elements. In 1937 he was teaching at Columbia University in America. In 1939 Szilard was the prime mover in persuading his old friend Albert Einstein (*qv*) to write his famous letter to Roosevelt, urging the immediate development of an atomic bomb to counter Hitler's creation of such a weapon. The result of the letter was the establishment of the Manhattan Project and eventually the atomic bomb that was dropped on Japan in 1945, so ending the Second World War. In 1934 Leo Szilard had theorized the idea of a nuclear chain reactor. In 1939 he initiated research into the feasibility of a nuclear reactor using uranium. Now, following the end of the Second World War, he bitterly regretted the work he did on the making of the atom bomb and thereafter fought for nuclear disarmament and nuclear power for peaceful purposes. In 1959 he received the 'Atoms for Peace' award. In 1961 he published a collection of satirical pieces on the misuse of scientific information under the title *The Voice of the Dolphins and Other Stories* . He spent much time researching in the field of biophysics, and writing science fiction stories that were not nearly as exciting as his real-life scientific adventures. He died at La Jolla, California, on May 30th 1964.

Born Adina Blady, she qualified as a doctor and was working at Warsaw's Children's Hospital when the Germans arrived in September 1939. Recently married to Stefan Szwajger, she continued her work as a pediatrician. When the Germans created the Warsaw ghetto, the lack of supplies of food and medicine meant the hospital soon had many dying children. Adina worked around the clock but to little avail. When, in July 1942, the Germans began rounding up people in the ghetto to be shipped to the killing camps, Dr Szwajger had no doubt what lay in store for her little patients. The game the German soldiers played of catching babies on the end of their bayonets, as their depraved comrades threw them out of the upper windows, made it clear that no mercy would be shown. Over a short period the doctor fed the babies, lying in their cots, a lethal dose of morphine. By virtue of her Aryan looks and a false passport, she escaped the ghetto and fought with the Jewish resistance. Her husband was not so fortunate: the Germans eventually killed him in Auschwitz. During the 1944 Warsaw uprising, Dr Szwajger aided the wounded and, following the Russian liberation of Poland, returned to her work as a pediatrician specializing in treating children with tuberculosis. Forty years later she wrote her story. It first appeared as a series of articles in an underground magazine but in 1988 it was published in the West as a book, *I Remember Nothing More: The Warsaw Children's Hospital and the Jewish Resistance*. This gives a vivid and unsentimental account of her horrifying experiences, including incidents she had vainly tried to forget. She wrote it, she said, to explain why she wasn't able to live as others do, and to tell the world and her two daughters what it meant to be Jewish in the middle of the 20th century.

SZWAJGER, Adina (1918-93) Polish physician

Commemorative Stamps

Marcel Proust
Issued by France

Yitzhak Rabin
Issued by Uruguay

Matyas Rakosi
Issued by Hungary

Walther Rathenau
Issued by West Germany

Max Reinhardt
Issued by Austria

Judith Resnick
Issued by The Islamic Republic
of Mauritania

Ethel and Julius Rosenberg
Issued by Cuba

Arthur Rubinstein
Issued by Israel

Umberto Saba
Issued by Italy

T

She was born Helen Becker on April 24th 1905 in New York. Wanting to be a dancer she began by studying with Irene Lewisohn and developing a freestyle movement. Later she trained with Michel Fokine and at the Metropolitan Ballet school. She then danced with 'the Met' for some years, both at home and on tour. She gradually became disenchanted with traditional ballet and worked for a while with Isadora Duncan. However, this style was not what she wanted either, and she decided to found her own company. She and the new company successfully toured Europe between 1928 and 1930. Upon her return to the US she started her school, of which she was principal until 1945. She organized the Dance Repertory Theatre and produced jointly with choreographers such as Martha Graham and Charles Weidman. It was Tamiris who was responsible for the inclusion of dance in the New Deal Federal Theatre project. Her work was described as expressive and exuberant and she wrote much upon her subject. Between 1930 and 1945 she choreographed some 130 dances, many of them reflecting the social problems of the time. She created the dances for *Annie Get Yor Gun* (1946), *Touch and Go* (1949) and *Plain and Fancy* (1955). In 1960 she formed the Tamaris-Nagrin Dance Company with her husband and partner, the dancer Daniel Nagrin. Helen Tamiris died in New York on August 4th 1966.

TAMARIS, Helen (1905-1966) US dancer

Igor Tamm was born in Vladivostock, Siberia, on July 8th 1895. While a professor at Moscow University he studied the quantum theory of diffused light in solid bodies. His method of interpreting the interaction of elementary nuclear particles is now known as the Tamm method. He was passionate concerning nuclear energy for peaceful purposes and his later work centred on the control of thermonuclear reactions. He even went so far as to appeal for international disarmament on US television in 1963. Tamm was awarded the 1958 Nobel Prize for Physics for his work in interpreting the Cherenkov effect. He died in Moscow on April 12th 1971.

TAMM, Igor (1895-1971) Russian physicist

Born in Baltimore, Maryland, on October 13th 1925, he was the son of orthodox Jews who had left Russia following the Revolution. He studied at New York's Theological Seminary and gradually began to appreciate the need for tolerance and mutual understanding in the arena of Jewish-Christian values. He was ordained in 1950 and thereafter dedicated his life to improving inter-faith relations, much to the chagrin of orthodox Jewish leaders who thought his work too radical. In the early 1960s, Catholic-Jewish conversations were in the forefront of such efforts. In 1969,

TANENBAUM, Marc (1925-92) US rabbi

Tanenbaum realized that the virulent anti-Semitism that existed among many Catholics was caused in part by the standard teachings of the church. Tanenbaum was the only Jew who participated in the Second Vatican Council set up by Pope John XXIII. The resulting document was *Nostra Aetate*, which repudiated anti-Semitism and rejected the notion that all Jews were responsible for Christ's death. The decision was hailed as a victory for the forces of enlightenment and tolerance over ignorance and bigotry. Tanenbaum was credited by Cardinal Cassidy, quoted in the *New York Times*, 'as a great source of reconciliation and strength during moments of deep difficulty between our communities'.

It didn't stop there. Rabbi Tanenbaum went onto involve himself in other disputes, from the contentious idea of a Catholic convent at Auschwitz to questions of Palestinian rights. When Pope John Paul II offended Jews by meeting Austrian President Kurt Waldheim, the former Nazi army officer, Tanenbaum flew to Rome to mend fences. Orthodox Jews refused to call him 'rabbi' and accused him of aiding the conversion of Jews to Christ. Their bigotry was ignored by Tanenbaum, who had higher ideals. He died in New York on July 3rd 1992.

TARSKI, Alfred (1902-83) Polish/American mathematician

Alfred Tarski was born on January 14th 1902 in Warsaw. He obtained his PhD from the University of Warsaw in 1923 and taught there until 1939. He emigrated to the US just prior to the Second World War and continued his teaching there. He then moved to the University of California, where he was professor of mathematics until 1968. Here he moulded the careers of future mathematicians. He was a major figure in the world of modern mathematics and made significant advances to algebra measurement theory, as well as mathematical logic. Tarski is acknowledged with the advancement of the semantic method, a procedure for examining the relationship between an expression and the object to which it refers. He wrote much upon his subject, including *The Concept of Truth in the Languages of Deductive Sciences* (1933), *Introduction to Logic* (1936) and *Logic, Semantics, Mathematics* (1956). He died in Berkeley, California, on October 26th 1983.

TAUBER, Richard (1892-1948) Austrian/British singer

Born Richard Seiffert in Linz, Austria, on March 17th 1892, he first became noticed when he sang the role of Tamino in Mozart's *The Magic Flute* in 1913 at the Chemnitz Neues Stadt-Theater. The performance resulted in a five-year contract with the Dresden Opera. He went on to appear at the leading opera houses in Germany and Austria and his repertoire and reputation grew. In the 1920s he shifted from grand to light opera, with the result that he reached a far wider audience, particularly as the radio was now in fashion. His friend Franz Lehar wrote his most famous song for him: 'Yours is My Heart Alone'. It made Tauber the most famous singer in Europe. As a Jew, Tauber was disturbed by the anti-Semitism that was now rampant in Germany and Austria. In 1938 he moved to England where in 1940 he became a British subject. He appeared often at London's Covent Garden Opera House and on the BBC. At the end of the war he was devastated by news of the Holocaust in which he lost family and friends. He never really recovered and he died in London on January 8th 1948.

Edward Teller was born on January 15th 1908 in Budapest, Hungary. He was born into a family of prosperous Jews and received his PhD from Leipzig University in 1930. For his doctoral thesis he wrote on hydrogen molecular ions. His studies were interrupted by a street accident in which he lost a foot when he was run over by a tram. Equipped with an artificial foot, he studied under Niels Bohr (*qv*) in Copenhagen before teaching at the University of Göttingen (1931-35). In 1935 he and his wife moved to the US to teach at George Washington University in Washington DC. Here he established new rules for classifying the way in which subatomic particles can escape the nucleus during radioactive decay. When President Roosevelt called for scientists to defend the US against Nazism, Teller responded and accepted an invitation from the University of California at Berkeley to work on theoretical studies of the atomic bomb with Robert Oppenheimer (*qv*). Teller later joined Oppenheimer on the Manhattan Project in New Mexico.

Following the end of the Second World War, it was Teller who took the lead in pressuring the government to develop the hydrogen bomb. He met with a lot of opposition from Oppenheimer and other atomic scientists who had grave doubts about the morality of developing such a monstrous weapon. However, when President Truman was falsely told of Russian progress in this field, he believed what he heard and ordered the go-ahead. Teller made the hydrogen bomb a reality and received the dubious title of 'father of the H-bomb'. His testimony to the US government hearings, held in 1954, to decide if Oppenheimer was a security risk, included the comment: 'I would personally feel more secure if public matters rested in other hands.' Oppenheimer was dismissed, but his colleagues never forgave Teller for his betrayal. He became more right-wing and opposed the 1963 Nuclear Test Ban Treaty. In 1982-83 he was the main government adviser on nuclear weapons policy and a major influence on President Reagan's support for the Strategic Defense Initiative.

TELLER, Edward (1908-) Hungarian/ American physicist

Howard Temin was born in Philadelphia, Pennsylvania, on December 10th 1934. He obtained his doctorate from the California Institute of Technology and while working on his thesis began investigating how the Rous Sarcoma virus causes cancer in animals. One particular stumbling block was that the virus's main ingredient, ribonucleic acid (RNA) could not infect the cell if the synthesis of deoxyribonucleic acid (DNA) was halted. It was Temin who in 1965 suggested that somehow the virus turned its RNA into DNA, redirecting the reproductive activity of the cell and turning it into a cancer cell. That cell would then produce this DNA together with its own DNA, thus producing more cancer cells. Critics claimed that Temin's thesis contradicted the laws of molecular biology, i.e. that genetic information always passed from DNA to RNA and not the reverse. In 1970 Temin was proven correct and in 1975 was awarded the Nobel Prize for Physiology or Medicine, together with David Baltimore (*qv*). Howard Temin was later American Cancer Society Professor of Virol Oncology and Cell Biology.

TEMIN, Howard (1934-) US virologist

TENENBAUM,
Mordechai
(1916-43)
Polish war
leader

Born in Warsaw and educated at the university there, he was one of the heroes of the Second World War. In September 1939 he and his companions of the Zionist youth movement decided to make for Palestine. At the last moment, Tenenbaum waved goodbye to them, deciding to remain in Vilna and aid the Jewish community. On June 16th 1941 the Germans took over Vilna, and within hours masses of Jews were being rounded up and killed. Tenenbaum warned Warsaw Jews of what was happening and moved as many Zionist youth members out of Vilna as he could, taking them to Bialystok. On January 1st 1942 Tenenbaum began organizing armed resistance. Using forged documents, he moved around Poland organizing armed underground movements, especially in Grodno and Bialystok. In August 1943 he led the Bialystok ghetto revolt. Despite appeals to the official Polish underground for ammunition supplies, nothing was forthcoming. Their ammunition lasted three days; then the revolt was over and Tenenbaum committed suicide. His example of resistance spread and stiffened the Jewish fight against the Germans. His diary of events survived the war and was published in 1948.

THALBERG,
Irving
(1899-1936)
US film
producer

Irving Thalberg was known as the 'Boy Wonder of Hollywood'. His work rate was such that it was as if he knew he did not have long to live. Born in Brooklyn, New York, on May 30th 1899, by the age of 21 he was Universal Films' studio manager. Four years later he was head of production at MGM and responsible for such films as *The Barrets of Wimpole Street* (1934), *Mutiny on the Bounty* (1935) and *Romeo and Juliet* (1936). He was also the producer of the musical series starring Jeanette MacDonald and Nelson Eddy, beginning 1935 with *Naughty Marietta*. He pre-produced *The Good Earth* and *A Day at the Races*, but died before they were completed. He used the studio star system that discovered and developed much of MGM's talent. Married to the actress Norma Shearer, Thalberg was 37 when he died on September 14th 1936 in Santa Monica, California.

THOMAS,
Michael Tilson
(1944-)
US conductor

He was born Thomas Tomashevsky in Hollywood on December 21st 1944. His Jewish parents encouraged his musical aspirations; Thomas trained with Dahl and at Bayreuth won the Koussevitzky Prize. He was rewarded with a contract to conduct the Buffalo Philharmonic (1971-79). Known then as 'the young genius', he has since progressed to the point where he is now considered one of the most important conductors of the second half of the 20th century. He was director of the Young People's Concerts given by the New York Philharmonic, and has long been associated with the Los Angeles Philharmonic. He has also been guest conductor with most of the great orchestras in Europe and America. An acknowledged expert on the music of George Gershwin (*qv*), he is an ardent supporter of modern composers.

Timerman was born in the Ukraine on January 6th 1923. When Jacobo was five he and the family left the Ukraine because anti-Semitism, despite the Russian Revolution of October 1917, was still rife. They journeyed to Argentina, giving the family cause later to wonder whether their choice of country had been wise. Timerman was a teenager during the Second World War and was active in the Youth League of Freedom, which espoused the Allied cause. Unfortunately, the policy of the Argentinian government was pro-German. Following the war Timerman worked as a journalist, having given up his original idea of becoming an engineer. In 1971 he founded *La Opinion*, a liberal newspaper that denounced the right-wing government's terror campaign. The government was backed by German war criminals, who found refuge in Argentina by bribing antisemitic political leaders. In 1976 Timerman originally backed the military coup that removed the egotistical nationalist Isabel Peron from power. However, the military junta had a secret agenda and suspended civil liberties. A year later Timerman was arrested and the newspaper shut down. In prison he was beaten and tortured and incarcerated without trial for nearly three years. During this period he was the constant centre of an international human rights campaign. He was released in September 1979 and emigrated to Israel, where he received a hero's welcome. In 1981 he published a book based on his ordeals. *Prisoner Without a Name, Cell Without a Number* was an immediate best-seller and published in several languages. It was now the turn of the Israelis to be upset when in 1982 his book, *The Longest War: Israel in Lebanon*, appeared. With the resumption of free democratic elections in Argentina, which Raul Alfonsin won, Timerman returned to that country in 1984 to become chief editor of the daily newspaper, *La Razon*.

TIMERMAN, Jacobo (1923-) Argentinean publisher

Born on June 22nd 1909 in Minneapolis, his father a rabbi, he changed his name from Avrom Hirsch Goldbogen, and who could blame him? After all, he would later marry Elizabeth Taylor and it was so much in keeping for the producer showman he would become. He produced, in time for the Chicago Exhibition of 1933, a flame dance show. He went on to produce and sometimes co-write several Broadway shows, only some of which were financially successful. He was a flamboyant character who one day decided to invest in a new film technique. The result was a cinematic wide screen used to great effect in the film version of *Oklahoma* (1955). In 1956 he produced his one and only film using his new Todd-AO system: *Around the World in 80 Days* was a critical and financial success for the man who had made and lost several fortunes. In 1957 he married film star Elizabeth Taylor, who converted to Judaism for the part. A year later he died when a private plane in which he was travelling crashed on March 22nd 1958.

TODD, Mike (1909-58) US entrepreneur

Tolansky was born in Newcastle upon Tyne, England and educated at Imperial College, London, returning there in 1934 as an assistant lecturer in physics. He subsequently taught at Manchester University where during the Second World War he conducted important research work in atomic energy. He was professor of physics at London University in 1947 and in 1952 became a Fellow of the Royal Society. In

TOLANSKY, Samuel (1907-73) British physicist

the 1960s Tolansky was appointed a principal investigator for the US NASA Lunar Research Project. Following the successful Apollo moon landing, he was one of the first scientists chosen to evaluate and examine what the astronauts had brought back from the moon. He had predicted in 1969 that the moon was covered with glassy, marble-like forms. This was subsequently confirmed. He wrote much upon his subject; his writings, translated into several languages, include *Optical Illusions* (1964), *The Strategic Diamond* (1968) and *Revolution in Optics* (1968). He also published over 300 scientific papers. He died in London in 1973.

**TOLLER,
Ernst
(1893-1939)
German writer**

Ernst Toller was born on December 1st 1893 in Samotschin, Germany. He became involved with politics when, during the First World War, he saw at first hand the horror of modern warfare. Wounded and invalided out of the army in 1916, he launched a peace movement in Heidelberg. Viewed with alarm by the authorities, he was arrested, but escaped to Munich where he led a strike of munitions workers. They wanted more money, Toller wanted them to stop work permanently. Toller was again arrested and spent the rest of the war in prison. In 1919 he was elected president of the Central Committee of the revolutionary Bavarian Soviet Republic. The movement was suppressed and Toller received a five-year prison sentence. During his incarceration there was a plot to have him shot while attempting to escape. It was foiled by a sympathetic guard. In prison Toller wrote *Man and the Masses* (1920). Published while he was still imprisoned, it brought him widespread fame. Hard-hitting plays of social protest followed, including *The Machine Wreckers* (1922). His book of poetry, *The Swallow Book* (1924), added to his fame. In 1933 he felt his Jewish identity most keenly and left Germany. He toured Europe, lecturing against the evil of Hitler and Nazis, and in the late 1930s arrived in the US, where he continued his crusade against Hitler and where his autobiography, *I Was a German* (1935), was published. This was a vivid account of his life and caused a stir. Invited to Hollywood as a scriptwriter, Toller felt himself an alien and returned to New York. Here, depressed by his wife's desertion, his poverty, and the thought that his writings were passé, he hanged himself in his cheap Manhattan hotel on May 22nd 1939.

**TOPOLSKI,
Feliks
(1907-89)
Polish/British
painter**

Topolski was born in Warsaw on August 14th 1907, the son of a well-known Polish-Jewish actor, Edward Topolski. He studied art at the Warsaw Academy. After travelling through much of Italy and France, he settled in England in 1935. During the Second World War he was an official war artist and recorded in vivid fashion the work of Allied armies in the Middle East, Russia, the Far East and Europe. Several books published that show his wartime work. He was a brilliant mural painter and his commissions took him all over the world. Among this work is the 60ft x 20ft *Cavalcade of Commonwealth*, which he produced to mark the Festival of Britain. His *Coronation of Elizabeth II*, a 100ft x 4ft work, was done at the request of Prince Philip and is now at Buckingham Palace. The University of Texas commissioned 20 portraits of English writers and since 1953 he published *Topolski's Chronicle*, a hand-printed, pictorial broadsheet depicting current events.

In 1969 he made a television film: *Topolski's Moscow* was well received. In 1971 he started on his great painting, *Memoir of the Century*, for the South Bank Arts Centre in London. He died in London August 24th 1989.

Melvin Torme was born on September 13th 1925 in Chicago. Known as the 'Velvet Frog', he is one of the few singers who are sight-readers of music; a trained singer who is a musician, and appreciated as a 'singer's singer. Recognized as one of the greatest jazz singers of the second half of the 20th century, he was four when he first sang on radio. When he was nine he was touring with Chico Marx's band. In 1942 he formed a singing group called the Mel-Tones and recorded with Artie Shaw (*qv*). His hits are legendary. From 1949 onwards he has had more hits than any other singer save Frank Sinatra, who reckons Torme is the greatest. His films, a dozen or so, are pleasantly forgettable. His albums include many that have reached the top of the charts. *An Evening With George Shearing and Mel Torme* won a Grammy Award in 1982. He also published an autobiography, *It Wasn't All Velvet*. In the early 1990s, Torme was still getting rave reviews for record albums, new and re-released, and his personal appearances draw large crowds. His choice of material is perfection, and his repertoire shows great musical integrity that he refuses to compromise for any commercial reason. Torme once told Larry King (*qv*) " I wanted to be a drummer-then I heard Buddy Rich"

TREBITSCH-
LINCOLN,
Ignatius
(1879-1943)
Hungarian
adventurer

Few men have had such an unusual life as **Trebitsch-Lincoln**. Born into a Jewish family living in Paks, Hungary, in July 1879 he was, in succession, a Presbyterian missionary in Canada, where he married a German Gentile girl and brought up their son as a Jew, and an Anglian curate in England. As a Quaker, he was elected Liberal member of the British Parliament in 1910 and during the First World War he was a military censor. Suspected of spying for the Germans, he ran away to the US. He was deported back to England and found guilty of treason. Lucky not be hanged, he was given three years in jail. In 1920 he was in Germany, supporting the short-lived Kapp revolt against the new German republic. He narrowly escaped death by fleeing to the Balkans. In 1921 he turned up in China. In 1925 he was given permission to return to England in order to say farewell to his soldier son, who was sentenced to be hanged for murder. By the time he arrived the execution had taken place. He was most distraught and returned to China where he found comfort in Buddhism, shaving his head and being ordained as a monk in 1931. A year later, he was spying for the Japanese military intelligence and a member of the Japanese Black Dragon Society. It all came to an end in August 1943, when he was taken ill and died in a Shanghai hospital. He was an accomplished linguist and prolific writer. His books included *Revelations of an International Spy* (1916), *Can War Be Abolished?* (1932) and *The Autobiography of an Adventurer* (1931). During the Second World War he asked the German consul in Shanghai to arrange for him to meet Hitler, because of his supposed supernatural powers. The Consul was impressed and wired Berlin. Reinhard Heydrich replied, 'Beware, you should know he is a Jew.'

Trepper was born on February 23rd 1904 in Novy-Targ, Poland, the son of Jewish parents who ran a small general store and lived in three rooms above it. As a young lad, he joined the Hasomer Hatzair movement, before joining the Communist Party and becoming a local leader in 1920. In 1921 he was blacklisted by the right-wing police. Unable to get work he went to Palestine, only to discover that Jewish landowners were exploiting Arab labourers. By 1925 he was running the Palestine Communist Party. The Histadrut or trade union disliked the Communists and Trepper responded by founding the Ichud movement to unite Arab and Jewish workers. It was banned by the British at the request of the Histadrut. Trepper was jailed and eventually expelled in 1929. He went to Paris, where he started a Yiddish weekly, *Der Morgen*. An active Communist, he escaped arrest in Paris when, in 1932, the police alleged they had uncovered an espionage network. Now in Moscow, he and his wife were enrolled by the Comintern and trained at the Marchlevsky University for National Minorities.

Following Hitler's war on the Jews in Germany, Trepper volunteered to work for the Red Army Intelligence Services. In 1937 he was in Brussels as a French-Canadian businessman. Here he set up the 'Red Orchestra' that was to prove so valuable during the war that soon followed, its name conferred on Trepper and his colleagues by German counter-intelligence. The highest levels of the Luftwaffe and German High Command were infiltrated and a constant flow of vital information reached Moscow. Unfortunately, it was often neglected or rejected as unbelievable; an example was the exact time and place of the German invasion of Russia. Stalin claimed Trepper was a tool of the English and that Russia would not be invaded until 1944. In 1942 Trepper was jailed by the Gestapo, and released a year later after relentless questioning. Trepper returned to the Red Orchestra and worked with the French Resistance until the liberation in August 1944. Summoned to Moscow in 1945 to what he thought would be a hero's welcome, he was horrified to be put in prison and ordered to give a full account of everything he had done during the war. It would be ten years before he was released, and then only after Stalin had died and the Supreme Military Tribunal ruled that he was indeed a hero.

In 1957 Trepper was back in Warsaw with his family. He tried to revive the Jewish community, but following the Six-Day War of 1967 there was a wave of anti-Semitism in Poland and Trepper decided that the country would never be a place where Jews would be welcome. He applied to leave but was refused permission. It was only in 1973 that he was allowed to go to London, for essential medical treatment. A year later he was in Israel. While waiting to leave Poland he started his autobiography, *The Great Game* (1975), which tells the story of the Red Orchestra. The value and heroism of Leopold Trepper cannot be denied. Without the information he supplied, before and after 1939, the war in Europe might well have been lost. Trepper died in Jerusalem in 1982.

He was born Lev Davidovich Bronstein on November 7th 1879 in Yanovka, Russia, his father David a Jewish farmer who had long before settled in the steppe region. In 1902 he escaped from prison, where he was serving an indeterminate sentence for revolutionary activities, by using a false passport with the name of Trotsky. He went to London, where he joined Lenin and worked on the revolutionary newspaper *Iskra*. He returned to Russia in 1905 and was gaoled a year later. While in prison he wrote *Results and Prospects*. In 1907, in exile in Siberia, he escaped to Vienna and became a freelance journalist. He moved to the US in the early 1910s and in 1914 was in Hollywood, playing a small part in the spy drama *My Official Wife* (1914). In January 1917 he was in New York editing *The New World*. By mid-1917 he was back in Russia and in August he was once again in prison, this time put there by Kerensky. Elected to the Bolshevik Central Committee, he was released from gaol in September and ready for the revolution that began on October 24th. The workers' initial charges were repulsed by the Tsar's guards. Next day Trotsky took charge, the Bolshevik counter-attack succeeded and Petrograd was taken. In the weeks that followed, the revolution gained ground until the Red Army had knocked out all resistance. Trotsky was responsible for Russia withdrawing from the First World War, perceiving the need to buy time before the capitalist countries turned on the fledgling Soviet regime.

Following the Treaty of Brest-Litovsk in 1918, Trotsky resigned as Foreign Minister and devoted himself to reorganizing the army into a smaller, highly trained and professional force. In the early 1920s his work was vindicated when the revolutionary troops repulsed the White Russians and their allies in a campaign organized by Winston Churchill as British war minister. In 1919 Trotsky wrote the Comintern's Manifesto and by 1920 was the top man in the Soviet Union, alongside Lenin. In March 1921 internal bickering brought matters to a head. There was much agitation going on both in the country and within the party, and Trotsky found himself in a minority. However, when in May 1922 Lenin became very ill it was Trotsky who was the obvious candidate to take over. The majority on the Politburo conspired against him and a Troika consisting of Zinoviev (*qv*), Kamenev (*qv*) and Stalin became the Soviet leaders. Lenin's health recovered in the winter of 1922-23 and he turned to Trotsky for help in correcting the mistakes of the Troika. Just before his death in March 1923, Lenin urged Trotsky openly to attack Stalin, who had emerged as the most prominent of the Troika; but Trotsky preferred a waiting game - a choice that would prove fatal for a lot of people. Six months later Trotsky addressed the Central Committee and demanded changes. He lamented the lack of democracy in the party as well as the lack of economic planning. Although reforms were promised, Trotsky saw fit to publish an open letter listing his complaints. Stalin, by way of response, launched a fierce propaganda war against him and managed to have someone infiltrate Trotsky's household, so that he fell ill with an undiagnosed fever and was unable to reply to the attacks being made upon him. He was away recuperating when Lenin's funeral was taking place and too weak to prevent Stalin taking over. Attacks continued until, by a combination of political and antisemitic tactics, Trotsky was forced to leave, travelling to Turkey in 1929, France in 1933 and Norway in 1935. France expelled him for planning the 4th International while using the name Sodoroff. He finally settled in Mexico in 1936. Four years later Stalin's hand extended across the Atlantic and Trotsky, the real hero of the Russian Revolution, was murdered by Stalin's agent, a Spanish Communist named Ramon Mercader, who had previously won Trotsky's confidence and was a frequent visitor. The date was August 20th 1940, the place Coyoacan, Mexico. Trotsky's brilliance and intellectual ability worked against him. In an introduction to his book *Thought*, he states: 'The end may justify the means, as long as there is something that justifies the end.'

TUCHMAN,
Barbara
(1912-89)
US historian

She was born Barbara Wertheim in New York City on January 30th 1912, the daughter of a wealthy Jewish banker. Educated at Waldon School in New York and at Radcliffe College, she obtained a BA in 1933. She became foreign correspondent for *The Nation* magazine and covered the Spanish Civil War. In 1938 her first book on history was published: *The Lost British Policy: Britain and Spain Since 1700*. She married Lester Tuchman, had three children and settled down to being a mother and housewife. With the three children away at school, Barbara Tuchman went back to work and in 1956 published *Bible and Sword: England and Palestine from the Bronze Age to Balfour*. She followed up with *The Zimmerman Telegram* (1958), concerning Germany's romance with Mexico during the First World War. However, it was not until 1962 that she became internationally known with her book *The Guns of August*, that describes the first month of the First World War. It won her the Pulitzer Prize and worldwide acclaim. She won a second Pulitzer Prize for *Stilwell and the American Experience in China, 1911-1945* (1970). Her next book took her seven years to research and write. *A Distant Mirror: The Calamitous 14th Century* appeared in 1978. This brilliant journey into the past captivated all who read it, if only for the clarity with which she brought historical figures to life. Her final works were *From Troy to Vietnam* (1984) and *First Salute* (1988). She died in Greenwich, Connecticut, on February 6th 1989.

TUCKER,
Sophie
(1884-1966)
US entertainer

She was born Sophie Abuza on January 13th 1884, on board a passenger ship en route to America from Europe. Her father had a restaurant in Hartford, Connecticut, and here the precocious child would sing and eagerly scramble for the coins the diners threw to her. In 1906 she was in New York, and in 1909 making appearances in the Ziegfeld Follies. By the time she was 20, she was topping the bill at the Palace Theatre in New York; she remained at the top for the rest of her life. She toured the world and was billed as 'the last of the Red Hot Mammas'. She never failed to bring tears to the eyes of both men and women with her rendering of '*My Yiddisha Momma*' - and not all her audiences were Jewish! Her famous song 'Life Begins at Forty' brought hope to millions, and her tough, defiant, '*Some of These Days*' invariably brought the house down. During the Second World War, she not only toured army bases, but lent her name and support to a B52 bomber of the US Air Force which had an all-Jewish crew: it was emblazoned with a larger-than-life cartoon of her and called 'The Yiddisha Momma's Revenge'. She was still making stage appearances when she died at 78 in New York on February 9th 1966.

Julian Tuwim was born to orthodox Jews in Lodz, Poland, on September 13th 1894. Except for the years of the Second World War (he was fortunate to have been in Brazil on September 1st 1939), he lived all his life in Poland. In 1915 he published a futurist manifesto that set intellectual circles ablaze. He edited the monthly *Skamander* magazine, and books of his verse include *Lying in Wait For God* (1918), *Socrates the Dancer* (1920) and *The Seventh Autumn* (1922). These poems were full of youth and vigour and happiness at Poland's recently found independence from Russia. The realities of life soon made their mark, and he provoked the rich and greedy and the usurpers of power with *Words in Blood* (1926) and *The Czarnolesie Affair* (1929), in which his hero suffers from poverty and oppression. Tuwim became politically involved and attacked what was now a militarist and strongly capitalist regime in Poland. He earned friends and enemies when part one of *The Opera Party* was published in 1936. Paradoxically, Tuwim wasn't one of the poor himself, and when he was attacked, both as a socialist and as a Jew, he could afford to take himself off and preach anti-fascism from the safety of South America and the US. He was, however, most sincere and his epic poem, *Flowers of Poland* (1940-44), included a section known as 'A Prayer' that became the anthem of the Polish resistance movement. In 1944 he published a manifesto, *We Polish Jews*, of an inspiring fury, passion and irony. He returned to Poland in 1946 and devoted the rest of his life to literature and training young would-be poets. He died in Zakopane, Poland on December 27th 1953.

TUWIM, Julian (1894-1953) Polish poet

He was born Sami Rosenstein in Moinesti, Romania. In 1912 his first poems appeared in the literary review *Simboluc*, under the pen name of S. Samiro. In 1916 he left Romania for Zurich, arriving in 1919 in Paris, where he stayed to live and work. He was the founder of Dada, a nihilistic revolutionary movement of the arts that he originated while in Zurich during the First World War. Ably assisted by such artists as Jean Arp and Marcel Duchamp, the movement progressed. Tzara wrote poetry to match and *Seven Dada Manifestos* (1924) was the result. Dada was a sensation that dislocated rules of language and was considered anarchistic by the establishment. Around 1930 Tzara swapped Dada for surrealism. He also joined the French Communist Party. During the Second World War he was a leader in the French underground movement. His political liaisons brought him close to the working class and his experiences resulted in his becoming a lyrical poet. This is reflected in his poetry of the 1950s, including *Speaking Alone* and *The Inner Face*. These reveal Tzara's anguish as he is caught between revolt and wonderment at the human condition. He died on December 10th 1963 in Paris.

TZARA, Tristan (1896-1963) Romanian/ French poet

Commemorative Stamps

Albert Sabin
Issued by Brasil

Nelly Sachs
Issued by West Germany

Felix Salten
Issued by The Grenadines

Barbra Streisand
Issued by St. Vincent

Peter Sellers
Issued by UK

Phil Silvers
Issued by Grenada

Chaim Soutine
(Girl in Blue)
Issued by Israel

Eric von Stroheim
Issued by The Congo

Arnold Schoenberg
Issued by Austria

U

Born in Lemberg, Poland, on April 13th 1909, he received his PhD in 1933 from the Polytechnic Institute at Lvov. In 1936 he was working at the Institute for Advanced Study at Princeton, New Jersey. Between 1936 and 1940 he lectured at Harvard University and then taught at the University of Wisconsin from 1941 to 1943. Becoming an American citizen in 1943, he was recruited to work on the Manhattan Project at Los Alamos, New Mexico, where he stayed until 1965. Ulam was responsible for solving major problems while working on the fusion bomb. His theory, that compression was essential to explosion and that shock waves from a fission bomb could produce the required compression, was found to be correct. This, and other work, put him in the forefront of operational research. In particular, he was renowned for the advancement of the 'Monte Carlo method', a system for discovering likely solutions to problems by artificial sampling. Ulam remained at Los Alamos, unlike most of his colleagues, in order to work on the hydrogen bomb. He died at Santa Fe, New Mexico, on May 13th 1984.

ULAM,
Stanislaw
(1909-84)
Polish/American
mathematician

Leon Uris was born in Baltimore on August 3rd 1924. From high school, he joined the US Marines for the duration of the Second World War. Following the war, he had a job as a driver while working on his first novel, *Battle Cry* (1953). He followed up with *Exodus*, telling the story of the Jewish struggle against the British for the establishment of Israel. This novel became an immediate success and brought fame and fortune. In 1955 he wrote *The Angry Hills,* a story concerning the Jewish Brigade that fought, together with the British army, in Greece. The tragic story of the 1943 uprising of the Warsaw ghetto was harrowingly told in *Mila 18* (1961). *QBVII* (1970) was another story about Germany and the Jews and dealt with German war crimes. Uris left the Jewish scene in 1976 for Northern Ireland, and wrote *Trinity*, about an Irish family from 1840 to 1916. *The Haj* (1984) tells of the lives of Palestinian Arabs from the First World War to the Suez War of 1956. His prose style is an acquired taste, but he is a first-class story teller. *Exodus* became a hit film. Directed by Otto Preminger (*qv*), it ran for some four hours. At a preview performance, comedian Mort Sahl stood up after three hours and called across to Preminger, 'Otto, let my people go.'

URIS,
Leon
(1924-)
US writer

Commemorative Stamps

Mark Spitz
Issued by Liberia

Edith Stein
Issued by West Germany

Yakov Sverdlov
Issued by USSR

William Shatner
Issued by St. Vincent and the
Grenadines

Julian Tuwim
Issued by Poland

Tristan Tzara
Issued by Romania

Boris Volynov
Issued by USSR

Otto Warburg
Issued by West Germany

Selman Waksman
Issued by Gambia

V

Simone Veil, born on July 13th 1927 in Nice, France, was the youngest daughter of André Jacob, an architect. Simone graduated from the Lycée de Nice in March 1944. By this time the Germans were occupying the south of France, previously run by Vichy. Simone, her sister and mother were included in the German round-up of Jews and sent to Auschwitz. There her mother died of typhus. With the Russians rapidly advancing on the camp, the Germans shipped some of the survivors by cattle train to Bergen-Belsen in Germany. There, in May 1945, the sisters were liberated by British troops. Simone sought to escape her fourteen months of terror by completing her education. She studied law and political science at the Institute for Political Science in Paris. While there, she met her future husband, Antoine Veil. Marriage and three children followed. Her husband, a leading civil servant , encouraged Simone to continue working for her law degree and in 1956 she obtained it. Instead of practising, she joined the Ministry of Justice and stayed for seventeen years. Involved with drafting legislation concerning pension rights and prison administration, she also became an expert on the adoption of children. She suddenly sprang to prominence when, in 1974, Giscard d'Estaing appointed her Minister of Health, the first woman Cabinet minister in 30 years.

During an emotive debate concerning abortion, on a bill which Simone Veil was guiding through the National Assembly, an angry deputy demanded of her: 'Madame Minister, do you want to send children to the ovens?' The debate was being televised. Simone fought back her tears and retorted: 'You have no right to say that to me, of all people.' It transpired the deputy had no knowledge of what had happened to the minister and her family. In the event the bill was passed and France became the first Catholic country to legalize abortion. Veil has continued to be at the centre of controversial legislation. She is a strong advocate of European union and urges co-operation within the EU. In June 1979 she was elected to the European Parliament and resigned her seat as Minister of Health. Her greatest and proudest moment came when she was elected President of the European Parliament and dubbed 'President of Europe'. She 'reigned' until 1982, strongly aware of her minority status as a Jew, a woman and a victim. She is not part of the feminist movement; she once remarked, 'Sexual liberation doesn't help a woman if she hasn't got economic liberation and psychological liberation.' In 1995 Simone Veil was guest of honour at the 40th Women of the Year lunch in London. There she said: 'Women have not yet won equality at work despite legislation.'

VEIL, Simone (1927-) French politician

VEKSLER,
Vladimir
(1907-66)
Russian
physicist

Vladimir Veksler was born in Zhiomir, Ukraine. He moved to Moscow in 1931, where he obtained a diploma in electrical engineering. Following a period in X-ray research, he was appointed in 1936 to the Lebedev Institute of Physics in Moscow. There he studied cosmic rays. He then became part of the team that formed the expedition to the Pamur Mountains in Central Asia, discovering there a hitherto unknown type of reaction that was somewhere between high energy particles and atomic nuclei. It was in 1944 that Veksler came into his own, with his proposal of the principle of phase stability. It was the beginning of a new and powerful branch of particle accelerators. The sensational notion was the facility to simplify the existing cyclotrons. Although suffering to some extent from post-war anti-Jewish purges, Veksler nevertheless stayed with the project following his important discovery, designing large accelerators and supervising their construction. In 1956 he became director of the Joint Institute for Nuclear Research, a co-operative venture that embraced all the Warsaw Pact countries. He never shirked from praising scientists from Western countries, and he had an lasting friendship with Professor McMillan of the University of California whose work mirrored his own. The two shared the US 'Atoms for Peace' Prize in 1963. Veksler also received, in 1959, the Lenin Prize for his work on accelerator research. He died suddenly in Moscow in 1966.

VENGEROV,
Maxim
(1974-)
Russian/Israeli
violinist

Maxim Vengerov was born in Novosibirsk, Siberia, in 1974 into a Jewish musical family. His father played the oboe in the Philharmonic Orchestra, while his mother was the musical director of a national choir. Aged eleven, Maxim won a junior competition in Poland and made his recording debut. Now in his early twenties, he is regarded as the world's greatest young violinist. His violin is a Stradivarius and his bow once belonged to Jascha Heifetz (*qv*). Heifetz stipulated in his will that his bow should only be given to a violinist of truly outstanding ability. The winner of the 1995 *Gramophone* Record of the Year award, he was still a child when his mother was told by his teacher of the amazing talent her son had. 'It's a gift. Maybe once in a hundred years . . .' Maxim, like his father, is an Israeli citizen; however, he lives with his mother in Amsterdam. His recent recording of the Tchaikovsky and Glazunov violin concertos, with the Berlin Philharmonic under Claudi Abbado, has been hailed as a masterpiece.

VERCORS
(1902-91)
French writer

Vercors was the name under which Jean Bruller wrote. He was born in Paris on February 26th 1902, the son of Hungarian-Jewish parents. Educated at the University of Paris, he began a career as an engraving designer which continued until 1939 and the Second World War. He joined the French army and served as a lieutenant in an Alpine regiment. He suffered a broken leg during training and was sent to recuperate at a village near Grenoble, called Vercors. This was the name he adopted when he wrote *Le Silence de la Mer* in 1941. In this book he explained how the French should react to the German occupation. He advocated a policy of passive resistance. This advice became the norm and proved invaluable in keeping up the morale of the French people. His next novel, *Put Out The Light*, further explained the art of passive resistance as a way of retaining one's dignity, and the amount of humanity that could be shown the enemy. He also explained that the German plan was to leave the French to bicker among themselves until eventually they would be destroyed. Vercors reminded his French readers of the words of Racine: 'I embrace my enemy, but only to suffocate him.' It was Bruller who warned of the pleasant, courteous German soldier who, without warning or compassion and upon orders from a superior, would maim or kill mercilessly. When his book was finished, Bruller published it himself under the imprint of Dervignes, and printed and bound it under the name of Drieu. This was a jibe at Drieu La Rochelle, who was collaborating with the Germans in order to publish his *Nouvelle Revue Française*. Bruller was forced to exercise great caution. Each book was hand bound in secret. A copy was smuggled out to England and the Free French authorities there had thousands of paperback versions printed for the RAF to drop all over France.

Tragedy came in June and July 1944 when the village of Vercors and the surrounding forests were the scene of a German ambush resulting in the death of some 3,500 members of the French Resistance. They had been betrayed, following the infiltration of French Nazis. Following the war Bruller wrote to de Gaulle during the Algerian war, using his real name and complaining of the atrocities being committed by French forces. He was surprised by de Gaulle's reply: 'I remember you. You are Vercors . . .' His later books did not repeat the literary success of his wartime novels. The stress of the times was missing. His three-part autobiography was published in 1982 and this sheds light on the circumstances surrounding his wartime writings. At one time there was a suggestion of fulfilling Petain's dying wish to be buried alongside his soldiers who fell at Verdun during the First World War. Jean Bruller, however, observed that the hand of the Chief of State of Vichy France, which had signed the order for the arrest and deportation of French Jews, should be detached and be clearly exhibited elsewhere. He died in Paris on June 10th 1991.

Vishniac was born in Pavlovsk, Russia, on August 19th 1897 and studied biology at Russian universities, gaining a doctorate in zoology. In 1920 he left Soviet Russia for Berlin, where he worked as a biologist. He also studied optics and his photographic ventures included documenting the Jewish ghettos of Eastern Europe during the 1930s. Later, his books *Polish Jews* (1947) and *Life of the Six Millions* illustrated the pre-war Jewish life that is now extinct. He emigrated to the US in 1940, and there began experimenting in the field for which he would become world-famous. Photomicrography is the science of photographing live microscopic animals via a microscope. This led to his work in researching cytoplasmic circulation as it concerns photosynthesis, as well as photographing the formation of thrombosis in blood vessels. Placed against today's scientific instruments that do the same work, Vishniac's method must appear very basic, but he was the pioneer. In 1971 he published *Building Blocks of Life* and in 1983, *A Vanished World*. A recipient of many awards the one he prized the most was the coveted Eastman Kodak Gold Medal. He died in New York on January 22nd 1990.

VISHNIAC, Roman (1897-1990) Russian/ American photographer

VISSER,
Lodewijk
(1871-1942)
Dutch jurist

Visser was born in Amsersfoort, the Netherlands, into a well-known Jewish family who had lived in the country for several centuries. Even that distinction did not allow Visser, recently qualified as a lawyer, to enter the Dutch diplomatic service, however, because he was Jewish. In 1903 he was appointed a judge of the district court and in 1915 was elevated to the High Court. In 1939 he achieved his second ambition, when he was appointed President of the Dutch High Court. Besides his judicial work he was a member of the Netherlands Privy Council and Vice Chairman of the Royal Commission on Civil Legislation. When the Germans attacked the Netherlands, without warning, Visser appeared in the High Court and condemned what he called 'this treacherous attack'. By November 1940 he and all other Jewish state officials were dismissed. He was a regular contributor to the Dutch resistance newspaper, *Het Parool*, and he strongly disapproved of the Jewish Council which he claimed was collaborating with the enemy. The Council in their turn informed Visser that if he didn't cease his anti-German activities, he would be sent to a concentration camp. Visser wrote back: 'I have taken note of what you say and am quite overcome by the humiliation which you, who are well aware of the historical importance of these measures, have brought about.' Visser died suddenly three days later; the circumstances of his death are not readily known. Later, his wife and child were sent to concentration camps and killed by the Germans. In 1968, a square in Amsterdam was re-named Visser.

VOLTERRA,
Vito
(1860-1940)
Italian
mathematician

Volterra was born on May 3rd 1860 in Ancona, Italy. He would later be responsible for influencing the modern development of calculus. By the beginning of this century Volterra was professor of mathematical physics at the University of Rome. He 1905 he became a Senator. During the First World War, although aged 55 , he joined the fledgling Italian Air Force and, by experiencing at first hand the effects of flying, was able to help design and build airships as weapons of war for the Allied cause. He was the first to use helium in place of hydrogen as a far safer form of fuel. Following the war, he returned to the University of Rome and developed abstract mathematical models that had biological associations. In 1931 the fascist government of Mussolini required all university professors to take an oath of loyalty, promising to teach citizens to become industrious, honest, devoted to the nation and the fascist regime. In addition they had to swear they belonged to no organization incompatible with that duty. Twelve hundred professors signed; twelve refused, three of whom, including Vito Volterra, were Jews. It was not because he was Jewish that he refused to sign - many of the 1,200 were Jewish, nor was fascism in 1931 antisemitic; he refused because he was a democrat. He was dismissed and forced to resign from all Italian scientific organizations. He left Italy and lectured all over the world before returning home in early 1940. He died in Rome on October 11th 1940.

Boris Volynov was born in Siberia on December 18th 1934. His Jewish mother was Eugeniya Israelevna. Boris graduated from the Vorograd pilot school in 1956 and entered the Soviet Air Force Academy of Aviation. He was among the first group of cosmonauts selected in 1960. In January 1969 he was in command of the three-man Soyuz 5 that linked up with Soyuz 4 in space. Volynov's two companions walked in space to Soyuz 4, leaving him to land Soyuz 5 alone. This flight was the most historically significant space expedition in aeronautical history. In July-August 1976, Volynov was commander of the two-man Soyuz 21 spacecraft which linked up with Salyut 5 space station. On this flight he and his engineer spent 49 days in space.

VOLYNOV, Boris (1934-) Russian cosmonaut

Born on July 10th 1866 in Voronego, Russia, he was eighteen when he left home and settled in Paris. By the beginning of this century Voronoff was chief surgeon at a Paris hospital. In 1917 he was appointed director of the experimental laboratory in surgery at the Collège de France in Nice. There he began the experiments in tissue grafting that would later create such a furore. He gained an international reputation through his experiments in endocrine gland transplantation. He put into experimental practice the theory of transplanting glands from animals to humans. His initial purpose was to cure thyroid deficiencies; later it was to extend the human life span, and he was quoted as stating that people would live to be a 140 years old. Publication of his paper included the detail that the work included transplanting sex glands from primates to humans. His work excited the media, who called his work, 'monkey gland treatment'. As a Jew, he was forced to leave France when the Germans invaded. Following a difficult journey via Portugal, he eventually reached America. He returned to Europe after the war, and died in Lausanne, Switzerland, on September 2nd 1951. He was a prolific writer whose work was used as the basis for transplant work we now take for granted.

VORONOFF, Serge (1866-1951) Russian/French physiologist

Commemorative Stamps

Simone Weil
Issued by France

Chaim Weizman
Issued by Israel

Fernand Widal
Issued by France

Richard Willstatter
Issued by Sweden

Elie Wiesel
Issued by Sierra Leone

Rosalyn Yallow
Issued by Sierra Leone

Ossip Zadkine
Issued by France

Ludwik Zamenhof
Issued by Poland

Itzhak Zuckerman and Zivia
Lubetkin
Issued by Israel

W

Waksman was born in Priluka, Russia, on July 22nd 1888 to religious Jews. In 1910, to escape the anti-Semitism that followed the failed 1905 revolution, the family emigrated to the US, and in 1916 Selman became an American citizen. Two years later he obtained his PhD from the University of California. From then on most of his career was spent at Rutgers University, New Jersey. Here he was professor of soil microbiology (1930-40) and director of the department (1940-58). During the Second World War there was a continuous search for new anti-bacterial substances. Waksman was a leading scientist in this field and he concentrated on substances extracted from the soil. From these actionomycetes he took out what he called 'antibiotics'. These were valuable for their effects in killing off gram-negative bacteria. In 1943 he discovered, from a strain of fungus, streptomycin, which has since become a major factor in combatting disease. Waksman went on to isolate several other antibiotics, of which neomycin is the best-known. In 1952 he was awarded the Nobel Prize for Medicine or Physiology. His published writings include *Principles of Soil Microbiology* (1927) and his autobiography, *My Life With the Microbes* (1954). He died on August 16th 1973 in Hyannis, Massachusetts.

WAKSMAN, Selman (1888-1973) Russian/ American Biochemist

Anton Walbrook was born Adolph Wohlbruck in Vienna on November 19th 1900. His family were circus folk who constantly travelled Austria and Germany. Anton broke with tradition and, after some training, became a most successful stage actor. His striking good looks gave him the title of 'matinee idol'. In 1920 he turned to films. By the time Hitler took over Austria, Wohlbruck was sufficiently well known to take the main role in Hollywood's version of *The Soldier and the Lady*. It was 1937 and Austria wasn't the place for a Jew, even one as famous as Wohlbruck. In Hollywood he was Walbrook, and went to England to establish himself as an actor in the mould of an upper-crust European sophisticate. He starred in some memorable films, including *Victoria the Great* (1937), *Gaslight* (1940) and *49th Parallel* (1941). Walbrook was the star of the biggest box-office hit of the Second World War: *Dangerous Moonlight* (1941), which also gave the world the haunting music of Richard Addinsell's Warsaw Concerto. His last great film of the war era was *The Life and Death of Colonel Blimp* (1943). During the Second World War, British films were not considered for inclusion, when considering nominations for Academy Awards. After the war came *Red Shoes* (1948), *La Ronde* (1950) and *Lola Montes* (1955). Anton Walbrook died in London in on August 9th 1967.

WALBROOK, Anton (1900-67) Austrian actor

WALD,
George
(1906-)
US biochemist

George Wald was born in New York on November 18th 1906. While doing postgraduate work in Berlin on a National Research Council scholarship, Wald discovered that vitamin A is a vital ingredient of the pigment of the retina and therefore essential for vision. He researched further at Heidelberg, and the universities of Zurich and Chicago, before joining the staff at Harvard University in 1934. In the 1940s, Wald further discovered that people with cataracts, who have had the lenses of their eyes removed, can see ultraviolet light. He therefore concluded that the lens filters out the ultraviolet. He later succeeded in discovering the chemical reactions involved in the principle of sight, as applied to the way the retina is used for night vision. In the late 1950s he and Paul Brown identified the pigments of the eye that were sensitive to yellow-green light and red light, and then the pigment sensitive to blue light. They also discovered the role of vitamin A in forming the colour pigments and showed that colour blindness is caused by the absence of these pigments. All this work led to Wald sharing the Nobel Prize for Medicine or Physiology in 1967. In 1977 he was appointed professor emeritus at Harvard. During the Vietnam War Wald was an outspoken critic of American involvement.

WALLACH,
Otto
(1847-1931)
German chemist

Otto Wallach was born in Königsberg, Germany, on March 27th 1847. By the turn of the century he was the director of the Chemical Institute at Göttingen. Previously, while at Bonn University, he became interested in the composition of a group of volatile oils used in pharmaceutical preparations. Wallach was told it was impossible that these oils could be analysed. However, he was not to be so easily deflected. He spent many months repeatedly distilling in order to separate the components. He studied physical properties and was eventually able to distinguish one compound from another. He completed his work, having determined that most compounds belong to the class called isoprenoids. It resulted in Otto Wallach being awarded the 1910 Nobel Prize for Chemistry, in respect of his research into alicyclic compounds. Despite being Jewish in an increasingly antisemitic environment, he was elected to serve as president of the German Chemical Society. He died in Göttingen on February 26th 1931.

WALTER,
Bruno
(1876-1962)
German/
American
conductor

He was born Bruno Walter Schlesinger on September 15th 1876 in Berlin. By 1900 he was the conductor of the Berlin State Opera on a five year contract. On the advice of Gustav Mahler, a fellow Jew, Walter dropped his surname. He broke his contract with Berlin Opera when his friend Mahler invited him to Vienna to conduct the Vienna Opera. He stayed for several years and established himself as a leading conductor of opera. In 1923 he was back in Germany, this time as the conductor of the Munich Opera, giving performances of Mozart operas which are described as legendary and rarely equalled. Working with the Berlin Philharmonic, he established the Bruno Walter Concerts, which ran from 1921 to 1933 during the winter months, while his summers were spent conducting at the Salzburg Festival. In 1933 his career in Germany came to an abrupt end. He conducted orchestras in Amsterdam and Paris until, in 1936, he once again became the director of the Vienna Opera. This lasted until the Anschluss of 1938; thereafter he lived in Paris for a year and in

1939 emigrated to the US. He frequently conducted the Metropolitan Opera and was musical director of the New York Philharmonic from 1947 to 1949. He wrote two symphonies and wrote several books, including a biography of Gustav Mahler. Bruno Walter died in Beverley Hills, California, on February 17th 1962.

Wanamaker was born in Chicago on June 14th 1919, and educated at Drake University and later at the Goodman Theatre, where he learnt his trade. He acted in Chicago and on Broadway. In 1948 he made his film debut in England, and while there was subpoenaed by the House Committee on Un-American Activities. He decided to remain in the UK and continue making films, but McCarthy had a long arm and film-making became closed to him. It was not until the 1960s that Sam was off the blacklist. In the long interval he resumed his theatrical career, both acting and directing. He directed and starred with Michael Redgrave in *Winter Journey* by Clifford Odets (*qv*). He went on to direct plays and operas in both Europe and America. In 1973 he directed *War and Peace* at the Sydney Opera House. He will, however, be everlastingly remembered as the man who had the drive, dedication and ambition to rebuild Shakespeare's Globe Theatre in London, on the original site. No one believed it would happen; but Wanamaker overcame obstacles often thought to be insurmountable. He raised large amounts of money and anxiously watched as the Globe gradually took shape. His project was successful, and the theatre held its first production in August 1996, opening officially in spring 1997. Sadly, Sam Wanamaker, holder of the CBE, was not around to see the fruits of his labour; a kindly man with great personality, he died in 1993. On June 14th 1996 the Duke of Edinburgh, patron of the theatre, unveiled a bronze bust of Sam at the Globe Theatre. He stated that the date of June 14th, Sam Wanamaker's birth date, would henceforth be known as the theatre's Founder's Day.

WANAMAKER, Sam (1919-93) American/ British actor/ director

Otto Warburg was born in Freiburg im Breisgan, Germany, the son of Emil Warburg, a Jewish physicist who was baptized in order to be a professor. Otto received a doctorate in chemistry from the University of Berlin (1906) and another in medicine from Heidelberg (1911). He became internationally known following his work at the Marine Biological Station in Naples, Italy. Here he first conducted research into respiratory enzymes. The research culminated in the 1931 Nobel Prize for Medicine or Physiology. His appointment as head of the Max Planck Institute for Cell Physiology at Berlin followed. He continued with his research and investigated photosynthesis, becoming the first to discover that the growth of malignant cells requires markedly smaller amounts of oxygen than that of normal cells. All this took place both after Hitler came to power and after the Second World War had begun. Warburg, who never hid his Jewish heritage, though he had little connection with the Jewish religion, visited Palestine in 1938, travelling there with Leo Baeck, the Jewish religious leader, on the SS *Tel Aviv*. Now, in the middle of the Second World War, with all his Jewish friends and family either abroad, dead or in concentration camps, he was being allowed to continue his work and was still in place at the Institute. Indeed, in 1944 Warburg was awarded a second Nobel Prize.

WARBURG, Otto (1883-1970) German biochemist

Here Hitler drew the line. It was one thing allowing a Jew to work for the Nazi cause, quite another to allow him such a prestigious award. The Germans informed the Swedish Nobel authorities that, as Warburg was a Jew, he would not be allowed to accept such an honour; he already has a Nobel Prize; give it to someone else. Warburg remained head of the Berlin Institute and, ignored by the Gestapo, he survived the war. Indeed, he was still in place when, on August 1st 1970, he died. He once told a conference of Nobel prize-winners, 'cancer in most of its forms could be avoided if people would take the necessary preventive measures'.

WARNER BROTHERS (1923-69) US film-makers

The **Warner Brothers** constituted the four sons of Benjamin Eichelbaum, a Polish-Jewish immigrant and a cobbler. The brothers were Harry (1881-1958), Albert (1884-1967), Jack (1892-1978) and Samuel (1898-1927). Each brother had a defined area of responsibility. They started as travelling showmen, showing silent films in Ohio and Pennsylvania. In 1913 they started their own production company and in 1917 moved the operation to Hollywood. Then, in the mid-1920s, Warners were in financial trouble. They were saved by the genius of the youngest brother. Samuel saw the future and persuaded his brothers to invest and collaborate in a new process, called Vitaphone, that would make talking pictures possible.

The Jazz Singer was premiered in 1927 with both synchronized music and dialogue. It caused enormous excitement and Samuel, the hero of the hour, found it all too much: he collapsed and died the next day.

The enormous profits Warners earned from their early talkies made them a top studio. In the 1930s they producing some 100 films a year and owned around 300 cinemas in the US and over 400 overseas. It was Warners who identified the craze for gangster films that produced big profits, and Edward G. Robinson (*qv*) and James Cagney were their top stars. In the 1940s and 1950s they made some of the great films of the century, including *The Maltese Falcon* (1941), *Casablanca* (1942), *Watch on the Rhine* (1943) and *A Streetcar Named Desire* (1951). These were followed by such films as *My Fair Lady* (1964) and *Bonnie and Clyde* (1967). In 1972 the last Warner brother, Jack, retired and the company became known as Time Warner Inc.

WASSERMAN, August von (1866-1925) German bacteriologist

Born in Bamberg, Germany, on February 21st 1866 into a well-known Jewish family, he studied medicine and by the turn of the century was working at the Robert Koch Institute for Infectious Diseases in Berlin. In 1906 he was appointed its head. Wasserman was one of the founders of immunology. At that time syphilis was a killing disease. Wasserman, following his discovery of the reaction for the sero-diagnosis of syphilis, gave the world the first test ever known, enabling doctors to diagnose the disease and take appropriate action; death was no longer the inevitable result. This was in 1913; the test became known all over the world as the Wasserman test and is still used as the disease indicator. Wasserman was appointed director of the experimental department at the Kaiser Wilhelm Institute in Berlin, and he was still in situ when he died in Berlin on March 16th 1925. Although he went on to devise diagnostic tests for tuberculosis, and wrote much, he was really only famous for his syphilis test. When in 1933 Hitler came to power, he refused to allow the Wasserman test, the work of a Jew, be used in the German army and ordered his scientists to come up with an Aryan test. The scientists reported failure and, much to the chagrin of the Führer, he had the choice of allowing the test or forbidding his men to have sex; the Wasserman test won.

Max Weber was born on April 18th 1881 in Bialystok, Russia. In 1900 he was in New York studying at the Pratt Institute in Brooklyn. Five years later he was in Paris studying at the Academie Julian. Together with Henri Matisse, he exhibited at Alfred Stieglitz's '291' gallery. The hostile press he received, in contrast to the positive reception of the public, because of his style of radical abstraction did not bother him. Between 1909 and 1917 he painted much, including what would become his best-known works, *The Geranium* (1911, Museum of Modern Art, New York) and *Chinese Restaurant* (1915, Whitney Museum of American Art, New York). In America, Weber, more than any other painter, introduced the latest in European art, including the avant-garde movements of fauvism and cubism. Weber continued to create abstract paintings while teaching at the Art Students' League in New York City. In the 1920s and 1930s his work became more natural, with more emphasis on flowing lines and colour. In his latter years he returned to his roots, and much of his work centred on Jewish pre-war scenes of Eastern Europe. Weber died on October 4th 1961 in Great Neck, New York.

WEBER, Max (1881-1961) Russian/ American painter

Weidenreich was born in Edenkoben, Germany, on June 7th 1883. By the beginning of the 20th century he had received his MD from Strasbourg University (1899) and in 1904 was appointed a professor there. His abiding interest was anthropology, and to this end much of his writings and researches related to problems and explanations of the evolution of man from the primates. He was professor of anatomy at Heidelberg University from 1919 and later at Frankfurt University, until, in 1933, he was forced to leave because he was a Jew. The University of Chicago was pleased to receive him in 1934 and, with their agreement, he went to the Peking Union Medical College in China, where he conducted a detailed examination of what was then known as 'Peking Man'. Back in America, Weidenreich studied 'Java Man'. Both examples of primitive man yielded sufficient data for him to conclude that modern man had a more developed brain and decreased facial size. He brought all this work together in his book, *Apes, Giants and Man* (1946). Weidenreich played an important part in the study of human evolution and his descriptions of fossils are still without equal. He died in New York on July 11th 1948, overwhelmed by the revelation that so many of his friends and relations had died in the Holocaust.

WEIDENREICH, Franz (1883-1948) German/ American anthropologist

WEIL,
André
(1906-)
French
mathematician

André Weil was born in Paris on May 6th 1906, the older brother of Simone Weil (*qv*). He studied at the Ecole Normale Superieure in Paris and later at Rome and Göttingen universities. As a professor of mathematics, his influence was far-reaching throughout a teaching career that included periods at Aligarh Muslim University, India (1930-32), Strasbourg, France (1933-40), Sao Paulo, Brazil (1945-47) and Chicago University (1947-58). His research in the field of algebraic mathematics led to his establishing one of the most important central proofs in the theory of algebraic fields. He wrote much, including *Foundations of Algebraic Geometry* (1946) and *Elliptic Functions According to Einstein and Kronecker*. Weil was also part of a collective of intellectual mathematicians who published their works under the title 'Bourbaki'.

WEIL,
Simone
(1909-43)
French
philosopher

Simone was born in Paris on February 3rd 1909, the younger sister of André Weil (*qv*). Because of her brother's early influence, Simone was judged to be intellectually precocious. During the First World War, when she was only five years old, she refused sugar in support of French troops who had none. At six she was given to quoting Racine. Later, as a philosopher, she taught at several French schools and was repeatedly fired for her left-wing views and activities, that the school governors thought might have a prejudicial effect on her pupils. She practised first and preached later. For a year (1934-5), she worked and lived alongside working women in a car factory. Her experiences of the shattering noise of the machinery and poor working conditions led Simone to believe that such an environment produced mass slavery and drove out intellectual ability. For a complicated person, who allowed religious paradoxes to interfere with her logical thought processes, the Second World War brought the reality of the world to her doorstep. As a Jew she was in constant danger, so she left Paris for Marseille where she wrote for, *Cahiers d'Usa*. In 1942 she left, with her parents, for the US soon returned to Europe and England, where she joined the Free French army. Eager to be parachuted back into France, she was devastated when she was turned down. Exhibiting the same tendencies towards extremism she showed while a child, she starved herself in order to align herself with her French comrades living under German occupation. She died of self-neglect on August 24th 1943 in Ashford, Kent. Ironically the French, by and large, were not starving. However, it was long established that Simone Weil, an important figure in French intellectual circles, was always searching for something just outside her reach. In her book *On Science, Necessity, and the Love of God* she observes: 'The future is made of the same stuff as the present.'

WEILL,
Kurt
(1900-50)
German/
American
composer

Kurt Weill was born in Dessau, Germany, on March 2nd 1900. He studied at the Staatliche Hochschule für Musik in Berlin in 1921 and then under Ferruccio Busoni. Weill's first composition, although considered most avant-garde, established him as one of Germany's young promising composers, a status entrenched following his *Royal Palace* opera in 1924. In 1927, for the Baden-Baden festival, Weill teamed up with Bertolt Brecht, and *The Rise and Fall of the City of Mahagonny* was the result. A satire on modern America, it was a resounding success. A year later, *The*

Threepenny Opera explored the nature of Berlin's underworld. The resulting success established both Brecht and Weill. Weill's haunting music was the reason the libretto was published in eleven languages. *Mahagonny* now previewed in Dresden as a full-length opera, and is generally considered Weill's best work. It was the first time American ragtime/jazz had been blended with the conventional classical style. Weill, the Jew, was unwelcome in his homeland, now controlled by Hitler with the support of the majority of his fellow Germans, and his music was banned. With his wife, the singer Lotte Lenya, Weill left Germany in 1933 and the couple spent some time in France and England before arriving in America in 1935. There, Weill collaborated with several librettists on work including *Knickerbocker Holiday* (1938 with Maxwell Anderson) *Lady in the Dark* (1941 with Moss Hart (*qv*) and Ira Gershwin) *One Touch of Venus* (1943 with S. J. Perelman (*qv*) and Ogden Nash) and in 1947 a musical version of *Street Scene* with Elmer Rice (*qv*). Probably his best-known songs are 'Mack the Knife' from the *Threepenny Opera* and 'September Song'. Weill died in New York on April 3rd 1950. A year later, his violin concerto and two symphonies were revived to new critical acclaim. In 1997 *Lady in the Dark* was revived at London's National Theatre.

Steven Weinberg was born in New York City on May 3rd 1933. He was a pupil at the Bronx High School of Science and there, in 1950, met Sheldon Glashow (*qv*), with whom he would later share the Nobel Prize for Physics. Weinberg went on to Cornell University and later spent a year in Copenhagen at the Nordic Institute for Theoretical Atomic Physics. Then, in 1957, he obtained his PhD from Princeton University. He researched at Columbia University before joining the staff at the University of California in 1960, switching to Harvard University in 1973 and Austin's University of Texas in 1983. The award of the Nobel Prize in 1979 was for work in formulating a theory that explains the known facts of the electromagnetic and weak interactions in order to predict the outcome of new experiments in which elementary particles are made to impinge on one another.

WEINBERG, Steven (1933-) US physicist

Better known as Vicky, **Victor Weisz** was born in Berlin on April 25th 1913, the son of middle-class Jews who had come from Hungary. Vicky enrolled at the Berlin Art School but in 1928 his father died, forcing Vicky to become the family breadwinner. He managed to get a job on *12 Uhr Blatt* and, at fifteen years old, had an anti-Hitler cartoon published. He achieved popularity with his caricatures of theatrical, sporting and political personalities, but it was his political cartoons that caused him to lose his job when Hitler came to power in 1933. Overseas friends saw to it that Vicky and his family, who were in considerable danger from the Gestapo, escaped to England.

In 1938 he was working on the British trade union newspaper, *The Daily Herald*. He found this rather difficult, not only because he did not have a good command of English but because his style of humour was unsuitable for British tastes. He went freelance, but found this even more difficult. In 1939 Gerald Barry, editor of the now defunct *News Chronicle*, gave him a regular income, a crash

WEISZ, Victor 'Vicky' (1913-66) German/British cartoonist

course on the peculiarities of British humour and the reading matter Barry thought necessary to understand it: Dickens, Edward Lear, Lewis Carroll and A.A. Milne, plus back numbers of *Punch* and *Wisden* (Vicky could never understand what was funny about cricket). He listened to radio comedy and learned to appreciate throwaway lines, self-ridicule and British understatement. Comedians like Max Miller, Arthur Askey and Tommy Handley, plus Gilbert and Sullivan and football crowds, completed Vicky's education. In 1941 Vicky graduated and became the main cartoonist on the *News Chronicle*.

He resigned in 1953, following a new editor's refusal to publish a cartoon critical of British policy in Kenya. By now Vicky was Britain's number one cartoonist. He joined the *Daily Mirror,* whose stance was more in keeping with his own left-wing views. Five years later he was with the Conservative *Evening Standard*. To old Tory die-hards Vicky's cartoons often felt like having teeth drawn. He once explained: 'I don't make fun of a face. I make fun of what is behind that face.' In the last decade of his life, Vicky was the most important and eagerly read political cartoonist in the world. No pompous or egotistical politician was safe. A small bald man, with a large head and shaggy eyebrows, he wore thick glasses and often cartooned himself as the puzzled bystander at national and world events. He was constantly fighting for the underprivileged of the world. Outraged by the imperialist policy of a Labour government, which he felt disgraced the world socialist movement by supporting right-wing American involvement in Vietnam, he drew his last cartoon, took an overdose of sleeping tablets and died at his London home on February 23rd 1966. He was 52. His mother, aged 86, had a heart attack on hearing the news and died shortly thereafter. His wife, his fourth, whom he had married a few months previously, committed suicide on the ninth anniversary of his death. In December 1996 a blue plaque, dedicated to his memory, was erected on his house in London.

WEIZMANN, Chaim (1874-1952) Russian/Israeli statesman

Chaim Weizmann was born on November 27th 1874 in Motel, Poland (at that time part of the Russian empire), one of fifteen children. His father was a transporter of lumber: Motel was at the centre of great forests and the logs were sent downriver to the Baltic ports. By the turn of the century, Weizmann had obtained his PhD from Fribourg University in Switzerland and was teaching chemistry at Geneva University. He was also researching organic chemistry concerned with organic dyes. In 1904 Weizmann, his wife and two sons settled in England. Appointed science professor at Manchester University, his continued research resulted in a method of extracting acetone from maize. This was in 1916, in the middle of the First World War; acetone was an essential ingredient of cordite, which in turn was desperately needed by the munitions industry. He was highly respected internationally for his scientific work, and this was an important positive point in his later political life.

He took a leading part in the negotiations that led to the Balfour Declaration of November 1917. Lord Balfour was keen on the establishment of a Jewish national home in Palestine, if only to divert the ever-increasing immigration of Jews into Britain to somewhere else. Weizmann assumed the British promise to be positive and devoted the remainder of his life towards the goal of a Jewish state. He travelled the world talking, explaining and appealing for funds. He was a man who was constantly being let down. Some of his fellow Zionists accused him of being too friendly with Britain, now the Mandate power in Palestine. The Second World War was a hard time for him. He worked for a long time to bring about the formation of the Jewish Brigade. His son, Michael, was killed in action in 1942 while serving in the RAF, and he had the additional burden of knowing about the genocide of the Jews. He returned to his first love, research, and evolved methods of synthetic rubber production.

The war over, the extent of the Holocaust exposed the overwhelming need for an independent Jewish state. Weizmann's criticism of dissident groups fighting the British forces in Palestine cost him the presidency of the Zionist movement in 1946. Early in 1948, he went on a mission to Washington to see President Truman. As a result of Weizmann's efforts, Truman put pressure on the British to give up their Mandate and turn the issue of the partitioning of Palestine over to the United Nations. At their meeting, Truman promised Weizmann that, in the event the UN decided upon the creation of a Jewish state, the US would provide a $100 million loan to launch the new country. The man most Jews regarded as their leader was elected as Israel's first president in May 1948. Now suffering from poor health, he did his best to present a brave front to all those who came from all over the world to see him. He died in Rehovat on November 9th 1952. Prior to his state funeral, over 250,000 people filed past his coffin.

Roy Welensky was born on January 20th 1907 in Salisbury, Southern Rhodesia (now Harare, Zimbabwe). Welensky, the youngest of thirteen children, was the son of Michael, a Jewish trader from Lithuania. He received a minimal education and later became a professional heavyweight boxer. From 1925 to 1927 he reigned as heavyweight champion of Rhodesia, North and South. However, he once worked on the railways and always retained his union card. When he gave up boxing, deciding it offered too little money for too much pain, he became active in the union and was eventually elected to the national council. He gravitated to politics and in 1938 was elected to the Northern Rhodesia Legislative Council. In 1941 Welensky formed the Northern Rhodesia Labour Party. In 1953 he received a knighthood from Britain, which at that time controlled the Rhodesian colonies. He represented Northern Rhodesia at the talks that produced a federation of Northern and Southern Rhodesia and Nyasaland. In 1956 Sir Roy Welensky became Prime Minister as leader of the Federal Party and remained in office until 1963. The political scene changed radically when Ian Smith took over and declared his policy of independence from Britain and the creation of an apartheid state. UDI was a racial situation Welensky would not tolerate. Much to his delight, in 1979 Ian Smith capitulated and a multi-racial state came into being, with Northern and Southern Rhodesia coming together under the title of Zimbabwe. Welensky retired and subsequently moved to England where, in Blandford Forum, Dorset, he died on December 6th 1991. Welensky experienced considerable anti-Semitism, engendering in him a lasting sympathy with Africans among whom he had spent his slum childhood.

WELENSKY,
Sir Roy
(1907-91)
Rhodesian
statesman

**WERTHEIMER,
Max
(1880-1943)
Czech/American
Philosopher**

Max Wertheimer was born in Prague on April 15th 1880. By 1900 he had abandoned the notion of becoming a musician and entered Charles University in Prague to study law. It only took him a year to decide that he was more interested in the philosophy of law than the practise of it. The idea of the psychology of the court room prompted him to begin studying the larger subject at Friedrich Wilhelm University in Berlin. He received his PhD from the University of Wurzburg in 1904 and worked on the earliest known lie detector, as well as a method of word association to trip up anyone being interrogated. He carried out extensive field tests and discovered, inter alia, that simple-minded children can solve problems when they can comprehend the overall structure. This and other factors became the groundwork for Gestalt psychology, which Wertheimer co-founded in the late 1920s. In response to the early anti-Semitism he found on the streets of Berlin, Wertheimer left for the US. He became a professor at the New York New School for Social Research and stayed there until his death. During his lifetime, Wertheimer saw the Gestalt method of psychology, based on the principle of examining psychological phenomena as structural wholes, become accepted. He died at his home in New Rochelle on October 12th 1943.

**WESKER,
Arnold
(1932-)
British writer**

Arnold Wesker was born in London on May 24th 1932, and his plays reflect his working-class Jewish background. Probably his most interesting works are those that form the trilogy *Chicken Soup with Barley* (1958), *Roots* (1959) and *I'm Thinking About Jerusalem* (1960). However, his most famous plays are reckoned to be *The Kitchen* (1959) and *Chips With Everything* (1962). He is a co-founder of Centre 42, a group sponsored by trade unionists aimed at making culture attractive and available to working-class audiences. Wesker, unlike many of his contemporaries who mouth their message of protest but do nothing, went to prison for a month in support of his fight for nuclear disarmament. *The Wedding Feast* was produced in 1974, followed by *The Journalists* (1980), *Caritas* (1981) and, in 1986, *Whatever Happened to Betty Lemon? Love Letters on Blue Paper*, a book of short stories, was published in 1974 and staged at the National Theatre in London in 1978 with Wesker directing. Another book of short stories was published in 1978, entitled *Said the Old Man to the Young Man*. Wesker's plays have recently been in much demand overseas. In 1996 his play *Blood Libel* was produced. It deals with the false legend of Jews as killers of Christian children: the lie that led directly to the expulsion of the Jews from Britain in 1290 by Edward I.

**WEST,
Nathanael
(1903-40)
US writer**

He was born Nathan Weinstein in New York on October 17th 1903. Educated in New York, his first published work was *The Dream Life of Balso Snell*, published in Paris in 1931. Probably his most famous work was published the following year: *Miss Lonelyhearts* is a satirical novel concerning a lonely hearts columnist. There followed *A Cool Million* (1934), a satire on politics. *The Day of the Locust* (1939 and a film in 1975) takes the lid off Hollywood, where West once worked as a scriptwriter. He was 37 when he and his wife were killed in a car crash. His work, in which a streak of French surrealism is detectable, is more popular now than it was at the time of his death.

She was born Karola Ruth Siegal on June 4th 1928 in Frankfurt, Germany. In 1939 her orthodox parents sent her away for her safety and education to a Swiss school. It was meant to be a temporary arrangement whilst her parents arranged for the family to go to Palestine. In the event she never again saw her parents and believes they died in Auschwitz. Ruth completed her education and with the war over she fulfilled her father's plan and emigrated to Palestine. There she joined the Haganah and worked for an independent Jewish State. That accomplished she went to Paris in 1951 and the Sorbonne from where she obtained a degree in psychology. In 1956 she moved to New York and worked as a domestic whilst learning English. Attending evening classes she obtained a masters degree in 1959 from the New School for Social Research. In 1970 she received a Ph.D from Columbia University. In 1980 she began broadcasting on local radio and answered listeners sexual questions. The programme was called ' Sexually Speaking.' It later became a national TV show and exported internationally. She has an infectious and open personality and deals frankly with what is often a different subject.

Dr. Ruth practices as a family counsellor and has written several books on her subject including *First Love: A Young People's Guide to Sexual Information* (1985). *Dr Ruth's Guide to Married Lovers* (1986) and *The Art of Arousal* (1993). Her autobiography entitled *All In a Lifetime* was published 1993. She has had three husbands and two children.

WESTHEIMER, Ruth (1928-) US educator

Born on March 28th 1890 in Denver, Colorado, where his father was a well-known music teacher, **Whiteman** first learned classical violin and played in local symphony orchestras. During the First World War he organized the US Navy band. The war over, he formed his own band, which started life in Los Angeles and, via Atlantic City, arrived in New York. In 1920 he signed a record contract with RCA-Victor. By now a leader of modern jazz, he sailed the Atlantic in 1923 to appear in London to rave reviews. In 1924 he gave the first purely jazz concert in New York's Aeolian Hall. A contemporary of Whiteman gave the first performance of the work he had been especially commissioned to write for that concert: *Rhapsody in Blue*, with composer George Gershwin (*qv*) at the piano. Whiteman was the man of the moment, and gave concerts at Carnegie Hall and in most of the important capitals of Europe. He loved jazz and included in his orchestra the best white jazzmen of his time: Jack Teagarden, both the Dorseys, Bunny Berigan and Bix Beiderbecke. Now known as the King of Jazz, Whiteman discovered and featured Bing Crosby. Because of Paul Whiteman, jazz became acceptable; but it wasn't real jazz, it was sanitized jazz. Real jazz belonged to the small groups that played in New York's Harlem and Chicago's South Side and the blacks who played in New Orleans. Whiteman was never part of the Swing era; instead, he presented musicals for stage and film that featured jazz. By the 1940s, his large, full frame had turned to fat. He gave up his band and became musical director of ABC radio. Recently, much of Whiteman's music has been re-recorded, if only to capitalize on the work of Beiderbecke, the star sideman of the Whiteman era. Whiteman died on December 29th 1967 in Doylestown, Pennsylvania.

WHITEMAN, Paul (1890-1967) US bandleader

WIDAL,
Fernand
(1862-1929)
French
bacteriologist

Fernand Widal was born in Algeria on March 9th 1862, the son of middle-class Jewish parents who were doctors. By 1900 he was working as a professor of pathology at Paris University, where he remained until his death in 1929. He had already found international fame by developing the procedure known as 'the Widal reaction' for diagnosing typhoid fever. He had discovered that antibodies in the blood of an infected person caused the bacteria to bind together and form clumps. In 1906, he recognized the danger of kidney inflammation caused by sodium chloride, and cardiac edema resulting in an accumulation of excessive tissue fluid. In both cases he demonstrated that the effective treatment was to deprive the body of salt intake. During the First World War Widal discovered a vaccine against typhoid and paratyphoid that enabled the risk of soldiers contracting typhoid contagion to be reduced. In 1917, he was awarded the Grand Cross of the Legion of Honour and the Municipal Hospital in Paris was renamed Hospital Fernand Widal. He died in Paris on January 14th 1929.

WIESEL,
Elie
(1928-)
Romanian/
American writer

Elie Wiesel was born on September 30th 1928 in Sighet, Hungary, whose large Jewish population was not deported to the death camps until the latter part of 1944. Not that this made any difference; there were very few survivors. Elie was fifteen when he and his large family were divided up upon arrival. Elie, fit for work, went one way; his family, either too old or too young, another. He never saw them again. He has spent his life making sure the world never forgets the Holocaust. Following liberation and the end of the Second World War, he settled in France and studied at the Sorbonne. He became a journalist and worked on French and Israeli newspapers. In 1956 he went to the US and in 1963 became an American citizen. Elie Wiesel taught at City College, New York, and in 1976 became professor of humanities at Boston College. His first book was written in Yiddish in 1956. *And the World Has Remained Silent* is part autobiographical and deals with a young lad's spiritual reaction to Auschwitz. His books generally appear to ask 'why?': Why was the Holocaust allowed to happen?. In 1962 he wrote *The Town Beyond the Wall*, which examines apathy. *A Beggar in Jerusalem* (1968) deals with the philosophical questions attached to man killing man. *Souls on Fire* (1972) and *The Testament* (1980) are Hasidic tales. Wiesel has lectured all over the world and while the core of his message concerns the Holocaust, he uses this horror as a basis on which to condemn all violence, oppression and racial bigotry. In 1986 he was awarded the Nobel Prize for Peace. In 1996 he published part one of his memoirs, *All Rivers Run to the Sea*. This covers the period 1928-69. In May 1996, at the Cannes Film Festival, a 90 minute documentary film on the life of Elie Wiesel was shown in the 'Director's Fortnight' section. Directed by the Hungarian Judit Elek, it is an emotional tour-de-force.

Simon Wiesenthal was born on December 31st 1908 in Buczacz, Austria. Now the conscience of the world, following the Holocaust, he started his professional life as an architect. He received a degree in architectural engineering from the Technical University of Prague in 1932 and settled in Lvov, Poland. Lvov was an area of Poland that came under Russian rule following the non-aggression pact between Stalin and Hitler just prior to the Second World War. Until Germany invaded Russia in June 1941, the Jews of the city were either sent to Siberia, where by and large they survived, or allowed to remain. The arrival of the Germans meant the round-up of all Jews. Wiesenthal and his wife survived the concentration camps. In Simon's case it was little short of a miracle; on two occasions he was listed to be killed but escaped, and on recapture was put to work. Even two attempts at suicide failed. However, 89 members of their families died.

Having regained his health, Wiesenthal began helping the American army gather evidence with which to prosecute German war criminals. In Linz, Austria, in 1947, Simon Wiesenthal and 30 others opened the Documentation Centre on the Fate of the Jews and Their Persecutors. In 1954 the Centre was closed and the files transferred to Israel, and Wiesenthal went freelance in his hunt for those who had committed genocide. With the help of Israeli agents he was responsible, in 1959, for discovering that Adolf Eichman was alive and well and living in Argentina. In 1961 he opened the Jewish Documentation Centre in Vienna, in a building that was formerly the Gestapo HQ. For over four decades he has sought out German war criminals constantly on the run from him. In 1967 he discovered Fritz Stangl, the commandant of Treblinka and Sobibor concentration camps: a particular victory for Wiesenthal and a great loss to fugitive Nazis. He holds the rank of Chevalier de la Legion d'Honneur.

Wiesenthal has written a number of books, including *Concentration Camp Mauthausen* (1946), *I Hunted Eichman* (1961), *The Murderers Amongst Us: The Simon Wiesenthal Memoirs* (1967) in 1975, *The Case of Jaworska* was published and in 1986 *Every Day Remembrance Day*. He continues to take an active part in the continuing hunt for German war criminals and was most vocal when, in August 1996, an Italian court rejected the case against SS Captain Priebkes, claiming 'he was only obeying orders'. Wiesenthal then said, 'No Nazi murderer, however old, should be allowed to die in peace.' The hunt continues.

Eugene Wigner was born in Budapest on November 17th 1902 to middle-class Jewish parents. He was educated at the Berlin Technische Hochschule and obtained a PhD in engineering. Then followed a period at Göttingen University until 1930, when he received an invitation to teach at Princetown University in the US. With violent anti-Semitism rife in Germany, Wigner took up the appointment. In 1938 he was appointed Thomas D. Jones Professor of Mathematical Physics, a position he held until he retired. He was an early pioneer of nuclear power and from 1942 to 1948 worked on the Manhattan Project. His speciality was nuclear chain reactions connected with the atomic bomb. Wigner was one of the three Hungarian physicists, along with Szilard (*qv*) and Teller (*qv*), who persuaded Einstein (*qv*) to

WIESENTHAL, Simon (1908-) Austrian Nazi-hunter

WIGNER, Eugene (1902-96) Hungarian/ American physicist

write his now famous letter to President Roosevelt concerning Germany's potential to manufacture nuclear weapons. In 1956 Wigner received the Enrico Fermi Award and in 1960 the 'Atoms for Peace' award. In 1963 he was awarded the Nobel Prize for Physics for his introduction of the concept of parity into nuclear physics. His *Symmetries and Reflections: Scientific Essays* was published in 1967.

WILDER,
Billy
(1906-)
Austrian/
American
film-maker

Billy was born Samuel **Wilder** in Sucha, Austria, on June 22nd 1906. He was educated at various schools, ending up at the University of Vienna, which he left after a year to be a reporter, first in Vienna and then in Berlin. He spent the next few years writing film scripts for German and French films. After 1933 Wilder, as a Jew, was no longer welcome in Germany and he journeyed to Hollywood. In 1941 he wrote the screenplay for *Ball of Fire* and was nominated for an Oscar. The same year he wrote the screenplay for *Hold Back the Dawn* and won another Oscar nomination. In 1944 success came with *Double Indemnity*, which he wrote and directed. It brought him two Oscar nominations. In 1945 he wrote and directed *The Lost Weekend*, which took four Academy Awards, including Best Picture. He was now the toast of Hollywood and remained so for the next 40 years and more. Notable Wilder films include *A Foreign Affair* (1948), *A Song is Born* (1948), *Sunset Boulevard* (1950 and an Academy Award for Best Screenplay), *Ace in the Hole* (1951) and *Stalag 17*, which took the Oscar for Best Director. He wrote, produced and directed *Sabrina* in 1954; with 1955 came *The Seven Year Itch* and in 1957, *Witness For the Prosecution*. In 1960 he wrote, directed and produced *The Apartment* and collected three Oscars, for Best Picture, Best Director and Best Screenplay. In 1961 he made *One, Two, Three*, and in 1966 *The Fortune Cookie*; *The Private Life of Sherlock Holmes* followed in 1970 and *The Front Page* in 1974. *Buddy, Buddy* (1981) went to show that even the greatest of writer/directors could make a flop.

In 1986 the American Film Institute awarded Wilder the Lifetime Achievement Award, and at the 1988 Academy Awards ceremony he received the Irving Thalberg Award. In 1995 he was present in London when the musical version of *Sunset Boulevard* was premiered. It was generally agreed that Wilder's film was better. In May 1996, town officials of Sucha announced that one of the town's main streets had officially been renamed Billy Wilder Street. Wilder's comment? 'Well, I guess they wouldn't just grab anybody and name a street after him. They must feel that I deserve it. And God bless them.'

WILDER,
Gene
(1935-)
US actor

Gene Wilder was born Jerry Silberman in Milwaukee on June 11th 1935. Educated at the University of Iowa, he received his acting training at the Bristol Old Vic in England and the Actors' Studio in New York (one of only two actors selected from 1,200). He became internationally known following his role as the frenetic Leo Blum in the film *The Producers* (1967). This, however, was after many years as a most successful stage actor with performances that often resulted in awards, for example the Clarence Derwent award for Graham Greene's, *The Complaisant Lover* (1961). His selection for the role of Leo Bloom, came after he appeared with

Anne Bancroft in a performance of Brecht's *Mother Courage*. Miss Bancroft's boyfriend (and later husband) was Mel Brooks (*qv*), and it was Brooks who provided Wilder with the lead role in *Blazing Saddles* (1974); in the same year he appeared in *Young Frankenstein* and received his second Oscar nomination, this time for Best Screenwriter. In several of his subsequent films, Wilder wrote, directed and acted. Of these probably the best-known are *The Adventures of Sherlock Holmes' Younger Brother* (1974), *The World's Greatest Lover* (1977) and *The Woman in Red* (1984). His film partnership with the actor Richard Prior has been most successful from the first, *Silver Streak* being followed by *Stir Crazy* and then by *See No Evil, Hear No Evil*. In 1996, he toured England with Neil Simon's (*qv*), *Laughter on the 23rd Floor,* finishing the run in London to positive reviews.

Richard Willstatter was born in Karlsruhe, Germany, on August 13th 1872. By the turn of the 20th century he was researching the structure of cocaine as well as the structures of alkaloids. In 1905, he was a professor at Zurich University and working on the properties of chlorophyll. He discovered its structures and explained how the blood pigment theme bears a structural resemblance to the porphyrin compound found in chlorophyll. A professor of chemistry at Berlin University and director of the Kaiser Wilhelm Institute from 1912 to 1916, in 1915 he was awarded the Nobel Prize for Chemistry, for his study of chlorophyll and other plant pigments. The First World War brought a halt to his research into the pigment of fruit and nuts while he developed a gas mask. During the 1920s, his researches showed that enzymes are chemical substances and not biological organisms. In 1924, while working in Munich, he experienced such a marked increase in anti-Semitism that he left Germany for Switzerland. He never returned, dying in Locarno on August 3rd 1942.

WILLSTATTER, Richard (1872-1942) German chemist

Debra Winger was born in Cleveland, Ohio, on May 16th 1955, and was still a child when the family moved to Van Nuys, California. She graduated from high school in 1971 and went to Israel to live and work on a kibbutz. She served for some months in the Israeli army before returning home to the US. She became a student of sociology at California State University and worked at Magic Mountain amusement park in order to pay her way. There an accident partially paralysed her and it was while recuperating that she determined to make a radical career change. She left university and began studying drama. Following some work in repertory theatre she began appearing in television commercials. Small film parts followed until she received a feature role in *Urban Cowboy* (1980). The film was not well received but further parts came her way. She was most notable in the box-office success *An Officer and a Gentleman* (1982), for which she received an Oscar nomination. A series of starring roles followed in films including *Terms of Endearment* (1983 and another Oscar nomination), *Legal Eagles* (1986), *Black Widow* (1987) and *Everybody Wins* (1990). In 1993 she starred with Anthony Hopkins in *Shadowlands*. The film won critical praise and Debra Winger added another Academy Award nomination to her expanding CV. Her voice was one of two mixed to provide the voice for the character of ET in *ET: The Extra Terrestrial* (1982).

WINGER, Debra (1955-) US actor

**WINTERS,
Shelley
(1922-)
US actor**

Shelley Winters was born Shirley Schrift in St Louis, Illinois, on August 18th 1922. Educated at Wayne State University, she grew up in Brooklyn and received her acting tuition at the Dramatic Workshop in New York as well as the coveted Actors' Studio. In 1941 Shelley Winters made her Broadway debut and two years later starred as Ronald Coleman's mistress in *A Double Life*. A flashy and sensual actress, she matched Elizabeth Taylor frame for frame in *A Place in the Sun* (1951) and received an Oscar nomination for Best Actress. Several films followed, including *The Big Knife* (1955) and *I Am a Camera* (1955). Then she began studying with Lee Strasberg (*qv*). She shed her image and became one of Hollywood's leading character actors. Her performance in *The Diary of Anne Frank* (1959) won her the Academy Award for Best Supporting Actress. *A Patch of Blue* (1965) resulted in another Oscar. In *Lolita* (1962) she was memorable as the pathetic mother. She received an Oscar nomination for the box-office hit *The Poseidon Adventure* (1972). Her list of films is lengthy, but few are memorable. Those that are show Shelley Winters to be among the best film actresses of the post-war American cinema. Her biography, *Shelley; Also Known as Shirley* appeared in 1981 and was dedicated 'For Blanche, who has always made my reach exceed my grasp'.

**WINTON,
Nicholas
(1910-)
British
humanitarian**

Nicholas Winton, the son of Jewish parents who left the faith when they left Germany for Britain at the end of the 19th century, is today regarded as a hero and responsible for the saving of many Jewish lives immediately prior to the Second World War. Although he was born in Britain and baptized, at school Winton was on the receiving end of antisemitic barbs just like any other Jewish child of that time. In January 1939 he was a member of a fact-finding mission to Prague. Realizing the fate that imminently faced the Jews, he stayed and organized. By September 1939 when the Second World War began, Winston had arranged for the safe passage out of Czechoslovakia to England of 664 children in six trainloads. The preparation work involved was tremendous: passports, visas, money, carers, train times, guarantors and much more. Following service in the RAF during the Second World War, Winton became assistant director for reparations at the United Nations International Relief Organization. He has subsequently received many honours, including the Freedom of the City of Prague from President Havel in 1991 and a letter from President Ezer Weizmann of Israel expressing appreciation of a magnificent achievement. In 1983 he was awarded the British MBE, not for his *Kindertransporte* work but for his more recent charitable work in helping the weak and disabled.

**WITTGENSTEIN,
Ludwig
(1889-1951)
Austrian/British
philosopher**

Born in Vienna on April 26th 1889, the son of a Jewish steel magnate, **Ludwig** grew up in a sophisticated and intellectual atmosphere and was educated at the Technische Hochschule in Berlin, Manchester University and Trinity College, Cambridge. An interest in mechanics led him to the study aeronautics, but after reading Bertrand Russell's *Principles of Mathematics* he decided to study under Russell at Cambridge (1912-13). This led to the ideas he expressed in his now famous *Tractatus Logico-philosophicus* (1922). Wittgenstein wrote this work while serving in the Austrian army during the First World War, until taken prisoner by the Italians in November 1918. Also during the war he was influenced by Tolstoy, with the result that he gave away the large fortune he had inherited from his father. Until 1926 he worked as a teacher in a remote Austrian village, and from 1926 to 1928 as an architect in Vienna. By 1938 he had been living in London for a number of years and now became a British subject. The 80-page *Tractatus* concerns thought and language and demonstrated seven propositions, including 'a proposition is a model of reality as we think it to be'. His work influenced a whole generation of logical thinkers. A leading personality between the world wars in philosophy, Wittgenstein demonstrated two systems of philosophical thought: theories of logic and theories of language. Many of his writings were published posthumously, including *Philosophical Investigations* (1953). During the Second World War he worked as a hospital porter at Guy's Hospital, London, then as an assistant in a Newcastle medical laboratory. He was a gloomy, tortured individual, with a marked lack of faith in everything he did. He died in Cambridge on April 29th 1951.

Isaac Wolfson was born in Glasgow, Scotland, on September 17th 1897. His parents had emigrated to Britain from Russia in 1886 and settled in the Gorbals, the very poor part of the city. His father had a small cabinet-maker's workshop where Isaac worked after leaving Queen's Park School. He then spent some time working as a travelling salesman, before joining Great Universal Stores in 1930. He became a buyer and won a reputation for being very hard on small furniture manufacturers, squeezing their prices down as well as demanding long-term credit. He continued this policy after purchasing a controlling interest in the company. The years after the Second World War saw Wolfson tying up one deal after another until he had a virtual monopoly in certain fields. GUS grew until it was one of the top 100 companies on the British Stock Exchange and Wolfson a multimillionaire. He created the Wolfson Foundation and transferred a large amount of his shares to it. The result was that each year the Foundation received enormous sums of money which Wolfson directed towards charitable causes. In the 1970s and 1980s Wolfson spent most of his time directing the affairs of the Foundation and encouraging the belief that he ran the Jewish community in the UK. He didn't, but orthodox organizations fared well from his generosity by letting him believe he did. An egocentric, he was enthusiastic about creating new colleges at both Oxford and Cambridge universities provided they bore his name. At one time he was giving away £1 million a year to worthy causes, and this continued for some 20 years. He received many honorary degrees from universities all over the country. He was once asked by a friend what his abilities were, that had earned him so many honorary degrees. 'I'm a writer,' Wolfson explained. 'I didn't know you could write; what do you write?' continued his friend. 'Cheques,' responded Wolfson. He died in Rehovot, Israel, on June 20th 1991, following a long losing battle with Alzheimer's disease.

WOLFSON,
Sir Isaac
(1897-1991)
British
philanthropist

WOOLF,
Leonard
(1880-1969)
British writer

Leonard Woolf was born in Kensington, London, on November 25th 1880. His parents were early members of the Reform Movement in Judaism. Leonard was educated at St Paul's School, Hammersmith, and Trinity College, Cambridge, from where he graduated in 1904. Woolf entered the Colonial Service and was seconded to the Ceylon Civil Service. He was progressively promoted until, in 1911, he returned to England on leave. There he socialized with friends from his Cambridge days and met the members of the newly formed 'Bloomsbury Set'. Among those he met was Virginia, a daughter of Sir Leslie Stephen. A year later, Woolf left the Colonial Service, which by now he found to be politically unacceptable, to marry Virginia, a budding novelist. During the long nights when he was in Ceylon, Leonard had started writing. *The Village in the Jungle* was published in 1913 and was followed the next year by *The Wise Virgins*. In 1913 he joined the Fabian Society, becoming an avowed socialist and a lifelong supporter of the Co-operative Movement. However, his work began to be interrupted by Virginia's mental illness.

As a result of his own medical problems, Woolf was exempt from war service during the First World War. He turned to studying international relations and the evils of colonialism; his researches led him to write *International Government* (1916), which formed the basis for the British attitude to the later formation of the League of Nations. He followed with *Empire and Commerce in Africa* (1920), a devastating analysis of imperialist greed. From 1915 to 1924, the Woolfs lived at Hogarth House in Richmond, Surrey. There, in 1917, and more as a hobby to aid Virginia, who was recovering from a mental breakdown, they started their own publishing house. The Hogarth Press became quite remarkable. Among their authors were E. M. Forster, T. S. Eliot, Katherine Mansfield, Sigmund Freud, Maxim Gorki, J. M. Keynes and, of course, Virginia and Leonard Woolf. He continued to write extensively, including *Imperialism and Civilisation* (1928), *The Intelligent Man's Way to Prevent War* (1933), *Quack, Quack!* (1935), *Barbarians at the Gate* (1939) and, in 1940, *The War For Peace*.

The Second World War was a sad time for the Woolfs: for Leonard it meant the end of world sanity and for Virginia a more intense depression that ended in 1941 when she committed suicide, something she had threatened several times. They had had a particularly difficult marriage and during their many rows she would stoop to antisemitic remarks to wound him. Following her death, Leonard threw himself into work and activity. He had his writings, the Hogarth Press, the Labour Party and the Fabian Society; all this, plus his garden and a number of very good friends, gave him a happy old age. He wrote his biography, which was published in five volumes: *Sowing* (1960), *Growing* (1961), *Beginning Again* (1964), *Downhill All the Way* (1967) and *The Journey Not the Arrival Matters* (1969). He died at Monks House, Rodmall in Sussex, on August 14th 1969. A portrait of Leonard Woolf by Vanessa Bell hangs in the National Portrait Gallery in London.

Herman Wouk was born in New York City on May 27th 1915, the son of Jewish immigrants. Educated at Columbia University, he started his career writing radio scripts for, among others, Fred Allen. During the Second World War he served in the US Navy in the South Pacific. This gave him the experience to write *The Caine Mutiny* in 1951, which won him the 1952 Pulitzer Prize for fiction, as well as becoming a successful play and a hit film. Although *Marjorie Morningstar* (1955) and *Youngblood Hawke* (1962) were best-sellers, they were eclipsed by his first novel. However, *Winds of War* (1971) is considered important, as is *War and Remembrance* (1977). Both later became popular television serials. In 1985 he published the novel *Inside, Outside*. His non-fiction book, *This is My God*, written in 1959, is a study of orthodox Judaism. Wouk's novels are thoroughly researched and give the reader an accurate picture of the part of the world he is writing about.

William Wyler was born in Mulhouse, France, to Jewish parents, on July 1st 1902 and educated at the Ecole Supérieure de Commerce in Lausanne, Switzerland, and the Paris Conservatoire, where he studied the violin. He would probably have wound up as a haberdasher in Paris had he not, in 1920, met his mother's cousin over on a visit from New York. Carl Laemmie was the president of Universal Pictures. By the time he had finished telling the young Wyler about the world of film, Wyler was packing his case. He accompanied his cousin back to the US, where he was given a job in the New York office as foreign publicity assistant. Transferred to Universal Studios in Hollywood, he was, in rapid succession, office boy, script clerk, assistant casting director, assistant director and eventually, in 1925, director. In the next two years he dashed off some 50 Westerns. In 1936 he signed a deal with Samuel Goldwyn (*qv*), collaborated with Lillian Hellman (*qv*), and made *Wuthering Heights* (1939), *The Letter* (1940) and *Little Foxes* (1941). *Mrs Miniver* (1942) brought him his first Academy Award. During the Second World War he was a major in the US Army Air Force. Stationed in England, he undertook dangerous missions to collect war combat footage. Over Italy, his aircraft was hit and Wyler was left with a permanent partial deafness.

After the war, his last film for Goldwyn was probably his best: *The Best Years of Our Lives* (1946) won him the Oscar for Best Director. Wyler, together with Frank Capra, George Stevens and Samuel Briskin, then put together their own production company, Liberty Films. Wyler went on to make some of the best films of the next three decades, including *The Heiress* (1949), *The Detective Story* (1951), *Roman Holiday* (1953), *Friendly Persuasions* (1959) and *Ben Hur* (also 1959, winning an Oscar for Best Director). In 1965 came *The Collector* and in 1968 his first musical, *Funny Girl*: it was his touch that helped Barbra Streisand (*qv*) win her Oscar. In the post-war years Wyler stood up to the McCarthy witch-hunt and formed the Committee of the First Amendment. He retired in the early 1970s, and in 1976 was awarded the American Film Institute's Lifetime Achievement Award. He died in Beverley Hills, California, on July 27th 1981.

Some Quotes.

'*A kind word is no substitute for a piece of herring.*'
Shalom Aleichem

'*Vote for the man who promises least; he will be the least disappointing.*'
Bernard Baruch

'*Fascist dictatorship destroys the results of the political emancipation of the individual, in order to prevent the social emancipation of the individual, in order to prevent the social emancipation of the masses.*'
Otto Bauer

'*A cannibal is a man who goes into a restaurant and orders the waiter.*'
Jack Benny

'*There is no state of mind, however simple, which does not change every minute.*'
Henri Bergson

'*Around this studio the only Jews we put into pictures play Indians.*'
Harry Cohn

'*Irving Berlin has no place in American music. He is American music.*'
Jerome Kern

'*Never express yourself more clearly than you think.*'
Niels Bohr

'*Intellect distinguishes between possible and impossible; reason distinguishes between the possible and senseless: even the possible can be senseless.*'
Max Born

'*The greatest menace to freedom is an inert people.*'
Louis Brandeis

'*Nationalism is an infantile sickness. It is the measles of the human race.*'
Albert Einstein

Y

Rosalyn Yalow was born in New York on July 19th 1921. In 1941 she graduated from Hunter College and received her PhD in 1945 from the University of Illinois. She became a consultant in nuclear physics and in 1947 was at Bronx Veterans Administration Hospital. There, she and others investigated various medical applications of radioactive isotopes. She combined techniques from radioisotope tracing and immunology. This led to Rosalyn Yalow developing RIA or radioimmunoassay. This proved to be a simple and sensitive method for measuring minute amounts of biological and pharmacological substances in blood and other fluids. The RIA method was first applied in 1959, to study insulin concentration in the blood of diabetics. In 1976 Yalow became the first woman to be awarded the Albert Lasker Prize for basic medical research. In 1977 she was awarded the Nobel Prize for Physiology or Medicine for her part in developing RIA.

Lev Yashin was born in Moscow on October 22nd 1929, the son of Jewish parents. He started his sports career playing ice-hockey with Moscow Dynamos. However, he gradually developed as a soccer player. He joined the national team as the goalkeeper in 1954 and in 1956 was part of the team that won the Olympic gold medal. He won 78 caps, playing for the USSR between 1954 and 1967 and taking part in three World Cups. In 1960, he helped Russia win the European Championship. He was world renowned for his acrobatic skills as a goalkeeper and earned the nickname of 'Black Panther'. In 1963 he was voted European Footballer of the Year, the only goalkeeper ever to win the title. He helped Dynamo to win the Russian League title five times and the cup twice. Honoured by his country, he was Russia's most popular sportsman. When he retired in 1971, there was a testimonial match for him at the Lenin Stadium, with Yashin captaining the Dynamos against a Rest of the World eleven. The following day, he was appointed Dynamo's manager. When he died in Moscow in March 1990, from cancer, the soccer world mourned his passing.

Some more Quotes.

' *The Nazis stamped the yellow star on the Jewish dreamers to punish these usurers who have continuously endowed society with treasures of imagination, music, philosophy and religion and demand in return an exorbitant interest in currency of progress, revolutions and universal love.*'
Romain Gary

To the audience prior to a concert: ' *have a good cough and get it over.*'
Myra Hess

' *If you love the things you do you don't age, you always remain young. Age is for the calender. I hope to live to see the day when we have music on the moon.*'
Sol Hurok

' *My nation, which has given the world illustrious sages and brilliant thinkers, is also one that fights for its freedom.*' (*Jewish anti-Fascist Committee 1942*)
Jacob Kreiser

' *A true artist always compares what he does with what he intended to do*'
Wanda Landowska

' *An assimilated Jew and a hunchback were passing a synagogue. " I used to be a Jew once," said the Jew. " Yes- and I used to be a hunchback," came the reply.*'
Groucho Marx

' *Guns aren't lawful; Nooses give; Gas smells awful; You might as well as live.*'
Dorothy Parker

' *In the childhood of every German Jew there comes a moment, never to be forgotten, when he realises that he entered this world as a second-class citizen and that no personal merit of accomplishment can deliver him from that situation.*'
Walther Rathenau

' *The earth looks great.*' (*from the spaceship* **Discovery***)*
Judith Resnick

' *It takes two to make a marriage a success and only one a failure.*'
Herbert Samuel

Z

Zadkine was born in Smolensk, Russia, on July 14th 1890. His father, a professor of Greek and Latin, despaired of his son who was forever modelling pieces of clay. He sent him to be educated, after which Ossip worked for an ornament manufacturer. He moved to Paris at the time of the First World War and volunteered for the French army, serving as a stretcher bearer before being invalided out following a German gas attack. After the war, he stayed in France and studied at the Ecole des Beaux Arts. His style was cubist, unusually influenced by classical Greek art. Slowly his style developed and became most individual, as evidenced by his *Three Musicians* (1924). In 1939 he became internationally known with his *Christ*, a sculpture fashioned in elm wood and showing a writhing form with arms suggesting the limbs of a bare tree. During the Second World War, because of his Jewish parentage he left Paris for unoccupied France and subsequently the US. In America, he taught at the Art Students' League in New York. The war over, Zadkine returned to France. In 1947 he produced a complicated sculpture called *Birth of Forms*, a piece that combines convexities, lines and parallel planes to create a multidimensional unity. A visit to bombed-out Rotterdam produced his much-discussed *Destroyed City*. Unveiled in 1953, it takes the form of a larger-than-life figure of a man, his arms outstretched as in horror. At the 1950 Venice Biennale he received the Grand Prize for sculpture, and in 1960 he won the Grand Prix from the City of Paris. He produced statues for many city administrations, including Jerusalem. He died in Paris on November 25th 1967.

ZADKINE, Ossip (1890-1967) French sculptor

Zamenhof was born on December 15th 1859 in Bialystok, when Poland was part of the Russian empire. As a Russian-speaking Jew, he experienced a lot of racial antagonism from Polish antisemites. He qualified as a doctor and, for a hobby, began experimenting with the idea of a common language that would unite the world. He published his work under the pseudonym of Dr Esperanto. In 1905, the first international Esperanto congress was held at Boulogne, France. Following a series of congresses that firmly established Esperanto as a viable and continuing movement, Zamenhof retired. He was distraught by the enormous loss of human life occasioned by First World War, and died in Warsaw on April 14th 1917.

Esperanto draws on Latin, the Romance languages, English and German. It continues to be used in over 100 countries, and in Poland and China there are daily broadcasts. In 1996 the Congress was held in Prague. Over 3,000 people from 65 countries attended, all speaking Esperanto as their common language.

ZAMENHOF, Ludwik (1859-1917) Russian linguist

ZEVON,
Warren
(1947-)
US songwriter/
musician

Born in Chicago on January 24th 1947, **Warren Zevon** later moved to the West Coast.

In the mid 1960s he wrote songs for The Turtles (*qv*) and Nino Tempo. He is one of the few musician/songwriters to emerge from the swinging sixties and still be around in the late 1990s. In between, he has been at the core of the pop music business; writing, performing and recording. In 1965 he made an album, *Zevon: Wanted Dead or Alive*. One of the tracks, 'She Quit Me' was featured in the film *Midnight Cowboy*. He went on the road as the musical director to the Everly Brothers and by the early 1970s was working mainly as a songwriter. In 1976 he released his long-awaited second album, *Warren Zevon 1976*. It was critically acclaimed and showed his strong songwriting abilities. In 1978 came *Excitable Boy*, demonstrating further musical development. He became satirical in *Bad Luck Streak in Dancing School* (1980), particularly in the track 'Gorilla You're A Desperado', a dig at LA consumerism. 'Play it All Night Long' shows an anti-romantic side of so-called idyllic country life, as portrayed by Country and Western songwriters. Zevon's image is permeated by images of incest and disease: 'Daddy's doing sister Sally/Grandma's dying of cancer now/the cattle all have brucellosis/ we'll get through somehow.' With Bruce Springsteen, he co-wrote 'Jeannie Needs a Shooter'. Just as Zevon was set to establish himself as one of the best musical artists of the 1980s, he became beset with personal problems. An alcoholic, he needed a long period of therapy. In 1987 he returned to the music scene and *Sentimental Hygiene* was part of the result. He formed a band under the name Hindu Lovegods which released its first album in 1990. He is described as 'an inspiring force in pop music that caters for the more intellectual'.

ZIEGFELD,
Florenz
(1869-1932)
US theatre
producer

The son of poor Jewish immigrants, **Florenz Ziegfeld** was born in Chicago on March 21st 1869. He produced the first of his famous revues, *The Follies of 1907*, in New York and continued in the same vein for the next 23 years. Although modelled on the Folies-Bergère of Paris, Ziegfeld's versions were less provocative. The arrival of the Great Depression in the late 1920s ended the spectacle. Ziegfeld Follies was a showcase for talent and the likes of Marilyn Monroe, Leo Errol, Eddie Cantor (*qv*) and many others made their debut in this medium. Ziegfeld also produced *Show Boat* (1927) and *Bitter Sweet* (1929). In his lifetime he was the most famous of showmen. No one has taken up the mantle he shed when he died in Hollywood on July 22nd 1932.

ZINNEMANN,
Fred
(1907-1997)
Austrian/
American
film-maker

Fred Zinnemann was born in Vienna on April 29th 1907. Educated at Vienna University, he was destined to become a lawyer; instead, he went to the Ecole Technique de Photographie et de Cinematographie in Paris, and learnt to become a film director. He arrived in New York in 1929 aged 22 and as he later said " If I'd stayed I'd be dead by now- probably not even buried ". His parents died in the Holocaust. His outstanding career covers six decades, and includes some of the most important films of the second half of the century. He only made one Western; however, it was *High Noon* (1952), arguably the finest of the genre. His work is distinguished by craftsmanship and a meticulous attention to detail. His films include *The Men* (1950), in which Marlon Brando made his debut as a crippled Second World War ex-soldier, *From Here to Eternity* (1953), for which he won the Oscar for Best Director, *Oklahoma!* (1955), *The Nun's Story* (1959) and *The Sundowners* (1960). For *A Man For All Seasons* (1966), Zinnemann won two Oscars, Best Director and Best Picture. *The Day of the Jackal* was released in 1973 and *Julia* in 1977. In addition to the Oscars won, he was also nominated six times and is generally regarded as one of the 20th century's greatest film-makers. In 1963 he made his home in London where he remained for the remainder of his life. In 1992 he published his biography called simply, *Fred Zinnemann*. In 1996 he was invited to London, together with his fellow Viennese friend and director, Billy Wilder, to receive a lifetime achievement award from the Jewish Film Foundation and British Film Institute. He died in London on March 14th 1997.

Born Grigory Radomyslsky on September 11th 1883 in Yelisavetgrad, Russia, he first met Lenin when the two were political refugees in Switzerland. He returned to Moscow in 1905 and took part in the ill-fated revolution of that year. In the years that followed, Zinoviev became very close to Lenin and during the October 1917 revolution was in charge of the Petrograd Soviet. In 1919, he was chairman of the Communist International or Comintern and by 1921 a full member of the Politburo. Following the death of Lenin in 1924, he was part of the Troika set up to prevent Trotsky (*qv*) taking over the party leadership. With Trotsky safely out of the way, Stalin, one of the Troika, engineered Zinoviev's forced departure from the Politburo. In 1927, he was expelled from the Party. Then began a see-saw of expulsions and readmittances until 1935. At that time, he was arrested and convicted of treason and complicity in the assassination of Sergei Kirov (1888-1934). Zinoviev was executed on August 25th 1936.

While head of the Comintern in 1924, a letter allegedly written by him and inciting workers to rise up was sent to the British Communist Party. It was apparently intercepted, and published in the British press on the eve of the general election The result was thought to have caused the defeat of the Labour government. It is now believed the letter was a forgery by a person or persons who wanted to ensure the return of a Conservative administration. In 1988 the Soviet Politburo posthumously rehabilitated Grigory Zinoviev.

Sabine Zlatin was born Sabine Schwasts in Warsaw on January 13th 1907. Politically minded, she was sixteen years old when she was imprisoned for taking part in a workers' demonstration. Upon her release she went to live and work in France. She met and married Miron Zlatin and together they ran a poultry farm in northern France. In 1939 they became French citizens. Upon the outbreak of the Second World War, Sabine joined the French Red Cross and went to work in an army hospital in Montpelier. Dismissed by the government of Vichy France because she was Jewish, she began working with the organization set up to rescue Jewish children at risk, Oeuvre de Secours aux Enfants. In 1943 she set up a home for

Jewish children at Izieu, a small village some 70 kilometres from Lyons, overlooking the Rhone. Every so often Sabine organized trips that resulted in a few children being smuggled into Switzerland. In this manner she saved the lives of some 100 children. Then a neighbouring farmer, who wanted to extend his lands, did a deal with the French police. In return for the house and farm the French and Germans could have a group of Jewish children. The idea so excited Klaus Barbie, head of the German Gestapo in Lyons, that he took command of the operation and was present when the children were thrown into open lorries like sacks of potatoes. Staff members present, including Miron Zlatin, were also taken. Sabine, who was away at the time, immediately appealed to Vichy. They laughed her away. She turned for help to the Catholic church, but they refused to intervene. The children, aged between three and twelve, were sent to Auschwitz and murdered. Miron, and others, ended up in Estonia in front of a firing squad. Sabine joined the Resistance.

After the war she worked helping people rebuild their lives. Later, working as an artist and rare book dealer, she felt the need to trace those responsible for the tragedy at Izieu. In 1987 Klaus Barbie, whom Serge Klarsfeld (*qv*) had tracked down, was brought to trial. Sabine testified and helped secure a conviction. The house at Izieu has a small monument that records the names of all those who were taken away and killed. Barbie died in prison in 1991, unrepentant. In 1994 the farmhouse came up for sale. Sabine founded the association that raised the necessary funds to purchase the property, and subsequently turn it into a memorial museum. The museum was opened by President Mitterrand, whose role in working for the Vichy government and enduring friendship with René Bousquet, who was directly involved with the rounding up of Jews and their onward transportation to the gas chambers, has never been satisfactorily explained. In his speech at Izeau, Mitterrand did not say what Jews generally and French Jews in particular have waited 50 years to hear, namely an admission that the round-up of the Jews in July 1942, their deportation and subsequent murder was largely a French affair. That admission and apology came from President Chirac in July 1995.

**ZOREA,
Meir
(1923-95)
Israeli soldier**

Meir Zorea was born in Romania on June 24th 1923, while his parents were in transit from the Ukraine to Palestine. The family settled in Haifa, where Meir received his education. At sixteen he was a member of the Haganah, the illegal Jewish defence force that operated with the tacit approval of the British. During the Second World War he was a junior officer in the Jewish Brigade, part of the British army, which fought in Italy. During this campaign Zorea, while leading a small reconnaissance unit, ran into superior German forces. Although faced by heavy gunfire, Zorea and his men fought off the enemy and returned to their lines. For this action Zorea was awarded the Military Cross for bravery. Immediately after the war, Zorea became a founding member of a Jewish group known as The Avengers. This group, made up for the most part of former members of the Jewish Brigade, hunted down Germans against whom there was sufficient evidence to show they were guilty of murdering Jews. These Germans were killed out of hand. In later years he said: 'We never said anything before we killed them. Not why, nor who we were. We made no speeches claiming to come in the name of the Jewish people, or anything like that. We just killed them, like you would a bug.'

During the 1948 war in Israel, Zorea was a battalion commander in the hard battle for Jerusalem. Later he was sent to the British Staff College at Camberley, returning home to set up the Israeli Defence Forces Staff and Command College. Zorea was the establishment's first commandant. In 1962 he retired with the rank of major-general. In 1977 he turned to politics and entered Parliament as a member of the Democratic Movement for Change. A year later he quit politics, stating he saw all around him people willing 'to climb onto their mother's body if it lifted them 30 centimetres higher'. In 1984 Zorea was appointed to head an independent inquiry into the deaths of two Palestinians who died in suspicious circumstances after their capture, following a bus hijacking. Zorea reached the conclusion that the two men had been unlawfully killed. Later, Zorea was disgusted, and publicly voiced his protest, when a presidential pardon enabled several members of the security service to escape criminal prosecution. Zorea's stand won him international praise. Married with six sons, two of whom were killed in action in 1967 and 1973, he died on June 24th 1995 at Kibbutz Ma'agen Michael.

Victor Zorza was born in eastern Poland on October 19th 1925. When the Germans invaded Poland on September 1st 1939, Zorza took off for the Soviet Union. A short while later he tried to return in order to help his parents, only to be picked up and sent to Siberia. He escaped and eventually made his way to Britain. It was now 1942 and Zorza joined the Polish Air Force. The war over, he returned to Poland and searched for his large family; he failed to find any of them alive. He saw the heap of human misery around him and, concerned about the cooling off in relations between east and west, decided to concentrate on learning all there was to learn about the Soviet Union. He joined the BBC's Foreign Service and monitored Soviet broadcasts. At the same time he was providing the *Manchester Guardian* with articles on Russian subjects.

Nothing much happened then until Stalin suddenly died in 1953 and the *Guardian* discovered it had no obituary written up. It turned to Zorza, who provided them with the most comprehensive piece published in any newspaper. As a result he became the paper's Kremlinologist and in 1956 a member of its staff. Over the years, Zorza became an established spectator of the Soviet political scene, gleaning information and watching the signs. Thus equipped, he was able to forecast before anyone else the breakdown in relations between Russia and China. He was one of the few accurately to predict events in Czechoslovakia in 1968; when he wrote an article entitled 'The Czech regime is in danger', there was a retaliatory article in *Izvestia*. In 1971 he left Britain for the US to work on the *Washington Post*. His work was so valued that it was required reading by the President.

The death of his daughter in 1977 and the onset of heart problems brought him back to Britain. The doctors told him he had no more than a year to live. He had long meant to return to India and with time now short he did so. There he wrote about the problems of the poor, living in a basic hut somewhere in the Himalayas.

He wrote a regular column for *The Times* about what he saw and experienced. In 1989 he decided to return home to London. On the way he stopped off in Moscow, where his attention was directed to the Russian hospice movement. He was appalled by the condition of the terminally ill. Using his knowledge to circumvent Russian bureaucracy, he organized British nurses to train their Russian colleagues. His work resulted in two modern hospices opening in Russia, in Moscow and Leningrad. In 1994 Victor Zorza discovered that his sister had survived the Holocaust and had been searching for family remnants for 50 years. They were reunited, only to be parted again when Victor died on March 20th, 1996.

ZUCKERMAN, Itzhak (1915-81) Polish/Israeli resistance leader

Zuckerman was born in Warsaw. A member of Hehalutz, a collective of young Zionists, before the Second World War, he was present at a secret meeting, held in March 1942 at which, with the benefit of first-hand knowledge of the mass executions of Jews, Zuckerman urged the creation of an armed resistance force. Others present thought armed resistance would provoke the Germans further. However, by July of that year attitudes had changed. Jews were being shipped out to Treblinka for extermination. By setting up the Jewish Defence Organization under the leadership of Mordecai Anielewiez (*qv*), the Jewish Council went on the offensive. Zuckerman was the link man to the Poles outside the ghetto, and it was he who negotiated for the arms the ghetto so urgently needed. While a trickle of arms came from the official Polish resistance sources, the bulk were obtained from the Communist 'People's Guard'. The arms reached the ghetto defenders via the sewers that were common to all sections of Warsaw. When the actual fighting took place Zuckerman was outside the ghetto. He used the opportunity to spread the news of the uprising to the outside world; he also continued to smuggle in arms. Twenty days later the overall commander was killed when the Germans overran the command bunker. Zuckerman returned to the ghetto, took over command and led some 75 survivors of the fighting through the sewers to the Aryan side. He and the survivors continued their fight as part of the Polish Communist underground war against the Germans. Zuckerman survived the war and for some time was part of the organization set up to rescue survivors from the camps and settle them in Palestine. He and his wife, a survivor of the ghetto uprising, arrived in Palestine shortly before the State of Israel was created in 1948. They and others founded, in North Haifa, a kibbutz dedicated to the fighters of the ghetto uprising called Lohamei Hageta'ot. Zuckerman died in Tel Aviv on June 17th 1981.

ZUCKERMAN, Lord Solly (1904-93) South African/ British biologist

Solly Zuckerman was born on May 30th 1904 in Cape Town, South Africa. He obtained a degree in anatomy from Cape Town University in 1923 and moved to London three years later. There he studied medicine at University College Hospital and qualified in 1928. He became research anatomist to the Zoological Society in London (1928-32) and undertook the same work at Yale University in the US (1932-34). For ten years from 1935 to 1945 he lectured in anatomy at Oxford University. His work on investigating the social and sexual behaviour of primates resulted in his book *The Social Life of Monkeys and Apes* (1932). During the Second World

War he was a scientific adviser, heavily involved in evaluating the effects of bombing enemy cities and the resulting effects on their populations. In particular, it was necessary to decide the extent to which the human frame could withstand bomb blast damage. He went on to engage in active planning of bombing campaigns of German cities and later defended the absolute need to bomb Dresden, among other cities of concentrated populations, provided to do so would paralyse supply routes. After the war he served on several government committees; he was chief scientific adviser to the Ministry of Defence from 1960 to 1966, and from 1964 to 1971 to the government. A warm and cultured man, he was later created a life peer for his services. His writings include *A New System of Anatomy* (1961), *Scientists and War* (1966) and *Nuclear Reality and War* (1980). He died in London on April 1st 1993.

Bibliography:

Andre and Fleischer, *A Pictorial History of Boxing*, Hamlyn, 1982

The Annual Obituary, St James Press, 1980-1993

Boller and Davis, *Hollywood Anecdotes*, Ballantine Books, 1988

Briggs, Asa, *A Dictionary of 20th Century World Biography*, BCA, 1992

Chilvers/Osborne/Farr, *The Oxford Dictionary of Art*, Oxford University Press, 1994

Comay, Joan, *Who's Who in Jewish History*, Routledge, 1995

Dictionary of Biography, Wordsworth Reference, 1994

Dictionary of National Biography on CD-ROM, Oxford University Press, 1995

Dictionary of Political Biography, Chambers, 1991

Dictionary of World History, Chambers, 1994

Dormer, Peter, *Twentieth Century Designers*, Headline, 1991

Encarta, CD-Rom

Encyclopedia Judaica, Keter Publishing House, 1973

Encyclopedia Britannica, CD-ROM

Etkes and Stadtmauer, *Jewish Contributions to the American Way of Life*, Northside Inc

Greenberg, Martin, *The Jewish Lists*, Schocken Books, 1979

Greenberg, Stan, *Olympics Fact Book*, Guinness, 1992

Grollier, CD-Rom

Heatley, Michael, *The Ultimate Encyclopaedia of Rock*, CLB, 1994

1995 People Entertainment Almanac, Little Brown and Company, 1995

Magnusson, Magnus, *Chambers Biographical Dictionary*, Chambers, 1990

Matthews, Peter, *The Encyclopaedia of International Sports Records and Results*, Guinness, 1995

Matthews, Peter, *The International Who's Who of Sport*, Guinness, 1993

May, Robin, *History of the Theater*, Hamlyn, 1986

Monaco, James, *The International Encyclopaedia of Film*, Virgin Books, 1993

Morehead, Philip, *Dictionary of Music*, Bloomsbury, 1992

Morrison, Ian, *Boxing-The Records*, Guinness, 1987

Park, James, *Cultural Icons*, Bloomsbury, 1991

Parker, Peter, *The Reader's Companion to the Twentieth Century Novel*, Helicon, 1994

Read and Witlieb, *The Book of Women's Firsts*, Random House, 1992

Rees, Dafydd and Crampton, *Book of Rock Stars*, Guinness, 1991

Roth, Cecil, *The Jewish Contribution to Civilisation*, Macmillan, 1938

Scholes, Percy, *The Oxford Companion to Music*, Oxford University Press, 1991

Selby-Lowndes, Joan, *World Ballet*, Galahad Books, 1981

Siegel and Rheins, *The Jewish Almanac*, Banatam Books, 1980

Vernoff and Shore, *The International Directory of 20th Century Biography*, Sidgwick & Jackson, 1987

Walker, John, *Halliwell's Film Guide*, HarperCollins, 1995

Walker, Peter, *Science and Technology Dictionary*, Chambers, 1994

Wallechinsky and Wallace, *The Book of Lists*, Little, Brown, 1993
Wigoder, Geoffrey, *Dictionary of Jewish Biography,* Simon & Schuster, 1991
Zuccotti, Susan, *The Italians and the Holocaust*, Weidenfeld & Nicholson, 1989

Whilst effort has been made to trace and acknowledge all copyright holders Polo Publishing would like to apologise should there be any errors or omissions.

INDEXES

YEAR of BIRTH

1874
Baylis, Lilian
Cassirer, Ernst
Embden, Gustav
Erlanger, Joseph
Fleg, Edmond
Hahn, Reynaldo
Houdini, Harry
Koussevitsky, Serge
Reilly, Sidney
Schoenberg, Arnold
Stein, Gertrude
Weizmann, Chaim

1875
Elsa, Princess
Gliere, Reinhold

1876
Barany, Robert
David, Joseph
Litvinov, Maxim
Walter, Bruno

1877
Abraham, Karl
Elkan, Benno
Isaac, Jules
Schick, Bela
Schwimmer, Rosika

1878
Blum, Rene
Buber, Martin
Citroen, Andre
Goldschmidt, Richard
Meitner, Lise

1879
Adler, Friedrich
Einstein, Albert
Fox, William

Korczak, Janusz
Landowska, Wanda
Mayer, Robert
Trebitsch-Lincoln,
Ignatius
Trtsky, Leon

1880
Asch, Sholem
Bloch, Ernest
Bucky, Gustav
Joffe, Abraham
Kaplan, Chaim
Prinstein, Meyer
Pugliese, Umberto
Wertheimer, Max
Woolf, Leonard

1881
Adams, Franklin
Bauer, Otto
Deborin, Abram
Hays, Arthur
Karman, Theodore
Kelsen, Hans
Meisl, Hugo
Warner, Harry
(see Warner Brothers)
Weber, Max

1882
Born, Max
Courant, Richard
Franck, James
Frankfurter, Felix
Goldwyn, Samuel
Huberman, Bronislaw
Klein, Melanie
La Guardia, Fiorello
Nadelman, Elie
Noether, Emmy
Schnabel, Artur

Schneiderman, Rose

1883
Davidson, Jo
Fleischer, Max
Goldberg, Rube
Joffe, Adolph
Kafka, Franz
Kamenev, Lev
Linder, Max
Saba, Umberto
Warburg, Otto
Weidenreich, Franz
Zinoviev, Grigory

1884
Attell, Abe
Benatsky, Ralph
Bloch, Jean-Richard
Brod, Max
Brodsky, Isaac
Crohn, Burrill
Deutsch, Felix
Feuchtwanger, Lion
Funk, Casimir
Gerchunoff, Alberto
Gernsback, Hugo
Gutt, Camille
Hirszfeld, Ludwik
Meyerhof, Otto
Modigliani, Amedo
Rank, Otto
Sapir, Edward
Shinwell, Emanuel
Tucker, Sophie
Warner, Albert
(see Warner Brothers)

1885
Bohr, Niels
Burton, Montague
Delaunay-Terk, Sonia

Hevesy, George
Kern, Jerome
Klemperer, Otto
Lukacs, Gyorgy
Mandel, Georges
Maurois, Andre
Mayer, Louis
Pascin, Jules
Radek, Karl
Rubinstein, Ida
Stronheim, Eric von
Sverdlov, Yakov

1886
Ben-Gurion, David
Bloch, Marc
Broch, Herman
Jolson, Al
Kun, Bela
Marx, Chico
(see Marx Brothers)
Pevsner, Antoine
Salomon, Erich
Sassoon, Siegfried

1887
Andrade, Edward
Arnstein, Karl
Bllomfield, Leonard
Cassin, Rene
Chagall, Marc
Cohen, Morris
Fajans, Kasimir
Ferber, Edna
Fleischer, Nat
Hertz, Gustav
Hillman, Sidney
Kronberger, Lily
Romberg, Sigmund
Rubinstein, Artur

1888

Agnon, Shmuel
Baum, Vicki
Berlin, Irving
Cremieux, Benjamin
Gasser, Herbert
Goldschmidt, Victor
Hurok, Solomon
Kisch, Frederick
Lipson, Ephraim
Marks, Simon
Marx, Harpo
(see Marx Brothers)
Namier, Louis
Orloff, Chana
Osiier, Ivan
Rambert, Marie
Stern, Otto
Waksman, Selman

1889

Epstein, Jacob
Gance, Abel
Guttenberg, Beno
Hurst, Fannie
Kaufman, George
Lippmann, Walter
Wittgenstein, Ludwig

1890

Aaronson, Sarah
Baratz, Joseph
Bomberg, David
Dressler, William
Gabo, Naum
Henriques, Basil
Hess, Myra
Lang, Fritz
Lewin, Kurt
Lissitzky, El
Marx, Groucho
(see Marx Brothers)

Miller, Walter
Moiseiwitsch, Benno
Muller, Hermann
Pasternak, Boris
Pauker, Ana
Pijade, Mosa
Ray, Man
Rosenberg, Isaac
Whiteman, Paul
Zadkine, Ossip

1891

Alexander, Franz
Bacharach, Alfred
Bernays, Edward
Besicovitch, Abraham
Brice, Fanny
Cohn, Harry
Ehrenburg, Ilya
Elman, Mischa
Ernst, Max
Gertler, Mark
Kissling, Moise
Levinsky, Barney
Lipchitz, Jacques
Mandelstam, Osip
Morgenthau, Henry
Neutra, Richard
Reichenbach, Hans
Sachs, Nelly
Sarnoff, David
Stein, Edith

1892

Benjamin, Walter
Cantor, Eddie
Cohn, Edwin
Dassault, Marcel
Dubinsky, David
Lubitsch, Ernst
Milhaud, Darius
Panofsky, Erwin

Rakosi, Matyas
Rice, Elmer
Tauber, Richard
Warner, Jack
(see Warner Brothers)

1893

Behrman, Samuel
Bodenheim, Maxwell
Gollancz, Victor
Gurevich, Mikhail
Hore-Belisha, Leslie
Howard, Leslie
Kaganovich, Lazar
Korda, Alexander
Lafer, Horacio
Laski, Harold
Parker, Dorothy
Robinson, Edward, G
Toller, Ernst

1894

Fiedler, Arthur
Freed, Arthur
Hartman, Heinz
Hecht, Ben
Kapitza, Peter
Lewis, Ted
McCoy, Al
Soutine, Chaim
Tuwim, Julian

1895

Adler, Jankel
Bagritski, Eduard
Barnato, Woolf
Baron, Salo
Freud, Anna
Golding, Louis
Herskovits, Melville
Kahn, Louis
Lazurick, Robert

Mayer, Renee
Milestone, Lewis
Moholy-Nagy, Laszio
Muni, Paul
Murray, Arthur
Silverman, Sydney
Tamm, Igor

1896

Ardon, Mordecai
Balcon, Michael
Burns, George
Dietz, Howard
Fischer, Louis
Flanagan, Bud
Harburg, Edgar
Holman, Nat
Jakobson, Roman
Leonard, Benny
Tzara, Tristam

1897

Baruk, Henri
Buchalter, Louis
Fischer, Gottfried
Korngold, Erich
Liberman, Yevsey
Reich, Wilhelm
Reichstein, Tadeus
Vishniac, Roman
Wolfson, Isaac

1898

Eisentaedt, Alfred
Eisenstein, Sergi
Gero, Erno
Gershwin, George
Guggenheim, Peggy
Hammer, Armand
Kessel, Joseph
Marcuse, Herbert
Meir, Golda

1898 cont.
Rabi, Isidor
Shahn, Ben
Soyer, Raphael
Szilard, Leo
Warner, Samuel
(see Warner Brothers)

1899
Abrahams, Harold
Arlosoroff, Chaim
Avigur, Shaul
Benioff, Hugo
Bernstein, Sidney
Cukor, George
Ginsberg, Morris
Guttman, Ludwig
Kadoorie, Lawrence
Kempner, Robert
Lipmann, Fritz
Ormandy, Eugene
Thalberg, Irving

1900
Antheil, George
Aronson, Boris
Ashenheim, Neville
Benjamin, Ernest
Bergner, Elisabeth
Cohen, Henry
Copland, Aaron
Fromm, Erich
Gabor, Dennis
Krebs, Hans
Lewis, Aubrey
Nevelson, Louise
Oistrakh, David
Picard, Leo
Parish, Mitchell
Rickover, Hyman
Walbrook, Anton
Weill, Kurt

1901
Adler, Stella
Berman, Jacob
Clurman, Harold
Cohen, Harriet
Douglas, Melvin
Freedman, Barnett
Goren, Charles
Heifetz, Jascha
Hurwitz, Stephen
Kahn, Louis
Kaplan, Louis
Kuznets, Simon
Lazarsfeld, Paul
Lubetkin, Berthold
Montagu, Ewen
Nagel, Ernst
Olivetti, Adriano
Paley, William
Slansky, Rudolph
Strasberg, Lee

1902
Berg, Moe
Breuer, Marcel
Erikson, Erik
Hook, Sydney
Houseman, John
Jacobson, Arne
Lansky, Meyer
Levi, Primo
Lwoff, Andre
Marcus, David
Ophuls, Max
Pevsner, Nikolaus
Popper, Karl
Rie, Lucie
Rodgers, Richard
Selznick, David
Shapiro, Harry
Tarski, Alfred
Vercors

Wigner, Eugene
Wyler, William

1903
Abravanel, Maurice
Adorno, Theodore
Aub, Max
Bettelheim, Bruno
Goldschmidt, Berthold
Gottlieb, Adolph
Gruen, Victor
Horowitz, Vladimir
Jonas, Hans
Milstein, Nathan
Nadel, Siegfried
Neumann, Johann
Pincus, Gregory
Rothko, Mark
Salmon, Cyril
Serkin, Rudolph
Siskind, Aaron
Spiegel, Sam
West, Nathanael

1904
Bernstein, Edward
Burns, Arthur
Frisch, Otto
Hart, Moss
Hodes, Art
Jacobs, Hirsch
Khariton, Yuli
Lorre, Peter
Montagu, Ivor
Niederland, William
Oppenheimer, Robert
Peerce, Jan
Perelman, SJ
Rosenberg, Maxie
Singer, Isaac Bashevis
Trepper, Leopold
Zuckerman, Solly

1905
Arlen, Harold
Aron, Raymond
Balogh, Thomas
Berman, Pandro
Bloch, Felix
Bloch, Pierre
Canetti, Elias
Copeland, Lillian
Dannay, Frederic
(see Queen, Ellery)
Frankl, Viktor
Hellman, Lilian
Henriques, Robert
Koestler, Arthur
Kreiser, Jacob
Lee, Manfred
(see Queen, Ellery)
Levinas, Emmanuel
Newman, Barnett
Segre, Emilio
Styne, Jule
Tamaris, Helen

1906
Arendt, Hannah
Baker, Josephine
Bethe, Hans
Blume, Peter
Chain, Ernst
Chernyakhovski, Ivan
Dorati, Antal
Ferber, Herbert
Fortes, Meyer
Gaster, Theodor
Gelfond, Alexander
Gertz, Elmer
Grade, Lew
Halsman, Philippe
Jaffee, Irving
Kabos, Endre
Komarovsky, Mirra

Motesiczky, Marie-Louise
Odets, Clifford
Preminger, Otto
Rosenberg, Harold
Roth, Henry
Sabin, Albert
Shapiro, Henry
Siegel, 'Bugsy'
Wald, George
Weil, Andre
Wilder, Billy

1907
Deutscher, Isaac
Lazar, Irving
Lazareff, Pierre
Mendes-France, Pierre
Moravia, Alberto
Peierls, Rudolph
Tolansky, Samuel
Topolski, Feliks
Veksler, Vladimir
Welensky, Roy
Zinnemann, Fred
Zlatin, Victor

1908
Arega, Leon
Berle, Milton
Blanc, Mel
Blankstein, Cecil
Bronowski, Jacob
Fields, Jackie
Goldberg, Arthur
Landau, Lev
Levi-Strauss, Claude
Praag, Lionel van
Rotblat, Joseph
Rothschild, Miriam
Teller, Edward

1909
Baer, Max
Berg, Jack
Berlin, Isaiah
Borge, Victor
Buchthal, Hugo
Bunshaft, Gordon
Capp, Al
Cohen, Andrew
Dovator, Lev
Drucker, Peter
Goldwater, Barry
Gombrich, Ernest
Goodman, Benny
Kaldor, Nicholas
Kompfner, Rudolf
Kutner, Luis
Land, Edwin
Levi-Montalcini, Rita
Maibaum, Richard
Mankiewicz, Joseph
Marshall, David
Mayer, Daniel
Penn, Jack
Ross, Barney
Todd, Mike
Ulam, Stanislav
Weil, Simone
Wiesenthal, Simon

1910
Abramovitz, Max
Bazelon, David
Black, Misha
Burroughs, Abe
De Grunwald, Anatole
Dymshyts, Veniamin
Fortas, Abe
Kline, Franz
Kroger, Peter
Lichine, David
Loesser, Frank

Markova, Alicia
Mayer, Helene
Shaw, Artie
Winton, Nicholas

1911
Barna, Victor
Botvinnik, Mikhail
Calvin, Melvin
Cobb, Lee J
Dassin, Jules
Delvalle, Max
Gluckman, Max
Goddard, Paulette
Greenberg, Henry
Jaffa, Max
Katz, Bernard
Kreisky, Bruno
Miller, Mitch
Perez, Victor
Raikin, Arkady
Silvers, Phil
Stein, William

1912
Axelrod, Julius
Baum, Herbert
Bloch, Konrad
Brown, Herbert
Cohen, Israel
Cousins, Norman
Debre, Michel
Finniston, Monty
Friedman, Milton
Ionesco, Eugene
Kantorovich, Leonid
Klugman, Norman
Laskin, Bora
Luria, Salvador
Mann, Daniel
Siegel, Don
Solti, George

Szabados, Miklos
Tuchman, Barbara

1913
Atlan, Jean-Michel
Atlas, Jechezkiel
Begin, Menachem
Beloff, Max
Cahn, Sammy
Capa, Robert
Garfield, John
Gilbert, Arthur
Gould, Morton
Kaye, Danny
Kramer, Stanley
Pontecorvo, Bruno
Schwartz, Delmore
Shaw, Irwin
Weisz, Victor

1914
Adler, Larry
Boorstin, Daniel
Elman, Ziggy
Fast, Howard
Foreman, Carl
Games, Abram
Gary, Romain
Gluckman, Jonathan
Heilbron, Rose
Lubetkin, Zivia
Malamud, Bernard
Mirvish, Edwin
Opler, Marvin
Perutz, Max
Salk, Jonas
Shuster, Joseph
Siegel, Jerry
Steinberg, Saul

1915
Bellow, Saul
Bruner, Jerome
Dayan, Moshe
Eban, Abba
Goodson, Mark
Green, Adolph
(see Comden)
Greene, Lorne
Hassan, Joshua
Hofstadter, Robert
Levine, Jack
Miller, Arthur
Mostel, Zero
Rosenberg, Ethel
Saltzman, Harry
Samuelson, Paul
Shulman, Alexander
Sokolow, Anna
Wouk, Herman
Zuckerman, Itzhak

1916
Axen, Hermann
Bassani, Giorgi
Douglas, Kirk
Gavshon, Arthur
Gilels, Emil
Ginzburg, Natalie
Hildesheimer, Wolfgang
Hofstadter, Richard
James, Harry
Luckman, Sid
Menuhin, Yehudi
Simon, Herbert
Tenenbaum, Mordechai

1917
Auerbach, Arnold
Graham, Katherine
Hauptman, Herbert
Penn, Irving

Rich, Buddy
Suzman, Helen

1918
Bernstein, Leonard
Chaikin, Sol
Elion, Gertrude
Feynman, Richard
Kantrowitz, Adrian
Kornberg, Arthur
Land, David
Lerner, Alan
Modigliani, Franco
Robbins, Jerome
Rosenberg, Julius
Schwinger, Julian
Spark, Muriel
Szwajger, Adina

1919
Anielewicz, Mordecai
Balsam, Martin
Bergman, Richard
Bondi, Hermann
Comden, Betty
Cowen, Zelman
Feld, Bernard
Grossman, Haika
Kunstler, William
Perchersky, Alexander
Wanamaker, Sam

1920
Abzug, Bella
Asimov, Isaac
Benacerraf, Baruj
Celan, Paul
Franklin, Roaslind
Freedman, Maurice
Jacob, Francois
Klein, Lawrence
Matthau, Walter

Nemerov, Howard
Stern, Isaac

1921
Adelstern-Rozeanu,
Angelica
Arrow, Kenneth
Benzer, Seymour
Charisse, Cyd
Friedman, Betty
Isaacs, Alick
Keleti, Agnes
Montand, Yves
Papp, Joe
Signoret, Simone
Steinberger, Jack
Yalow, Rosalyn

1922
Baskin, Leonard
Bernstein, Elmer
Blake, George
Bohr, Aage
Caesar, Sid
Cohen, Stanley
Damm, Sheila van
Foss, Lukas
Freud, Lucien
Holliday, Judy
Lederman, Max
Penn, Arthur
Rabin, Yitzhak
Winters, Shelley

1923
Arbus, Diane
Avedon, Richard
Chayefsky, Paddy
Gordimer, Nadine
Heller, Joseph
Kissinger, Henry
Mailer, Norman

Marceau, Marcel
Marcus, Rudolph
Maxwell, Robert
Peres, Shimon
Timerman, Jacobo
Zorea, Meir

1924
Atlas, David
Bacall, Lauren
Bronstein, David
Caro, Anthony
Elek, Tamas
Koch, Edward
Lumet, Sidney
Solomon, Phil
Solow, Robert
Uris, Leon

1925
Blumberg, Baruch
Bruce, Lenny
Buchwald, Art
Charpak, Georges
Curtis, Tony
Daniel, Yuli
Gellner, Ernest
Lederberg, Joshua
Newman, Paul
Plisetskaya, Maya
Sellers, Peter
Steiger, Rod
Tanenbaum, Marc
Torme, Mel
Zorza, Victor

1926
Berg, Paul
Brooks, Mel
Ginsberg, Allen
Glaser, Donald
Gomelsky, Alexander

Goscinny, Rene
Greenspan, Alan
Klug, Aaron
Lewis, Jerry
Milstein, Cesar
Mottelson, Ben
Neizvestny, Ernst
Schlesinger, John
Shaffer, Peter,
Slovo, Joe

1927
Alechinsky, Pierre
Cranko, John
Falk, Peter
Getz, Stan
Gyarmati, Dezso
Jhabvala, Ruth
Kossoff, Leon
Niremberg, Marshall
Savitt, Dick
Scott, Ronnie
Simon, Neil
Veil, Simone

1928
Agam, Yaacov
Brookner, Anita
Chomsky, Noam
Fisher, Eddie
Gainsbourg, Serge
Hundertwasser, Fritz
Klein, Yves
Kubrick, Stanley
Louis, Viktor
Nathans, Daniel
Rubens, Bernice
Rylsky, Yakov
Sassoon, Vidal
Westheimer, Ruth
Wiesel, Elie

1929
Aloni, Shulamit
Bacharach, Burt
Edelman, Gerald
Feiffer, Jules
Frank, Anne
Gell-Mann, Murray
Previn, Andre
Sills, Beverly
Steiner, George

1930
Bart, Lionel
Becker, Gary
Friedman, Jerome
Gryn, Hugo
Pinter, Harold
Sondheim, Stephen

1931
Bloom, Claire
Doctorow, Edgar
Graham, Bill
Nichols, Mike
Nimoy, Leonard
Richler, Mordecai
Richter, Burton
Shatner, William

1932
Aimee, Anouk
Forman, Milos
Gilbert, Walter
Glashow, Sheldon
Halimi, Alphonse
Kitaj, RB
Schwartz, Melvin
Wesker, Arnold

1933
Brown, Georgia
Collins, Joan

King, Larry
Kosinski, Jerzy
Leiber, Jerry
Mendoza, June
Penzias, Arno
Polanski, Roman
Roth, Philip
Sacks, Oliver
Sontag, Susan
Stoller, Mike (see Leiber)
Weinberg, Steven

1934
Arkin, Alan
Cohen, Leonard
Epstein, Brian
Gorokhovskaya, Maria
Miller, Jonathan
Rottman, Leon
Segal, George
Steinem, Gloria
Temin, Howard
Volynov, Boris

1935
Abrahams, Ivor
Allen, Woody
Alpert, Herb
Klarsfeld, Serge
Koufax, Sandy
Wilder, Gene

1936
Gilbert, Martin
Hoffman, Abbie

1937
Ashkenazy, Vladimir
Berkoff, Steven
Bunke, Tamara
Cannon, Dyan
Cixous, Helene

Glass, Philip
Hoffman, Dustin
Hoffmann, Roald
Spassky, Boris

1938
Baltimore, David
Blume, Judy
Gould, Elliot
King, Carole
Safdie, Moshe

1939
Altman, Sidney
Brittan, Leon
Caan, James
Oz, Amos
Sedaka, Neil

1940
Brodsky, Joseph
Calmat, Alain
Goldstein, Joseph
Green, Peter
Josephson, Brian
Kriss, Grigori
Spector, Phil

1941
Brown, Michael
Diamond, Neil
Dylan, Bob
Ephron, Nora
Keitel, Harvey
Mann, Manfred
Ochs, Phil
Reddy, Helen
Simon, Paul

...ner, Aron
Barenboim, Daniel
Feld, Eliot
Ford, Harrison
Garfunkel, Art
(see Simon & Garfunkel)
Jong, Erica
Klein, Calvin
Streisand, Barbra

1943
Fischer, Bobby
Levine, James

1944
Bernstein, Carl
Bllomfield, Mike
Douglas, Michael
Kooper, Al
Thomas, Michael-Tilson

1945
Cohn-Bendit, Daniel
Hawn, Goldie
Melnik, Faina
Midler, Bette
Perlman, Itzhak
Simon, Carly

1946
Fabius, Laurent
Geller, Uri
Manilow, Barry
Stone, Oliver

1947
Bolan, Marc
Crystal, Billy
Guthrie, Arlo
Kaylan, Howard
Kline, Kevin
Mamet, David

Milken, Michael
Spielberg, Steven
Volman, Mark
(see Kaylan)
Zevon, Warren

1948
Dreyfuss, Richard
Fagen, Donald
(see 'SteelyDan')
Newton-John, Olivia
Sharansky, Anatoly

1949
Joel, Billy
Resnick, Judith

1950
Becker, Walter
(see 'SteelyDan')
Scheckter, Judy
Spitz, Mark

1951
Ian, Janis
Neeskins, Johan

1952
Ramone, Joey
Stanley, Paul

1955
Coen, Joel
Winger, Debra

1956
Alcott, Amy

1957
Edelstein, Jillian

1958
Coen, Etham
Day-Lewis, Daniel

1963
Kasparov, Gary

1964
Kravitz, Lenny

1965
Diamond, Michael
(see Beastie Boys)

1966
Horovitz, Adam
(see Beastie Boys)

1967
Stransky, Joel
Yauch, Adam
(see Beastie Boys)

1974
Vengerov, Maxim

OCCUPATION

Activists
Klugman, Norman
Schwimmer, Rosika
Sharansky, Anatoly
Steinem, Gloria

Actors
Aimee, Anouk
Arkin, Alan
Bacall, Lauren
Balsam, Martin
Bergner, Elisabeth
Bernhardt, Sarah
Bloom, Claire
Caan, James
Cannon, Dyan
Charisse, Cyd
Cobb, Lee J
Collins, Joan
Crystal, Billy
Curtis, Tony
Day-Lewis, Daniel
Douglas, Kirk
Douglas, Melvin
Douglas, Michael
Dreyfuss, Richard
Falk, Peter
Ford, Harrison
Garfield, John
Goddard, Paulette
Gould, Elliot
Greene, Lorne
Hawn, Goldie
Hoffman, Dustin
Holliday, Judy
Howard, Leslie
Keitel, Harvey
Kline, Kevin
Lewis, Jerry
Linder, Max

Lorre, Peter
Marx Brothers
Matthau, Walter
Montand, Yves
Mostel, Zero
Muni, Paul
Newman, Paul
Nimoy, Leonard
Robinson, Edward G
Segal, George
Sellers, Peter
Shatner, William
Signoret, Simone
Silvers, Phil
Steiger, Rod
Streisand, Barbra
Walbrook, Anton
Wilder, Gene
Winger, Debra
Winters, Shelley

Administrator
Cohen, Andrew
Cowen, Zelman

Adventurer
Trebitsch-Lincoln,
Ignatius

Agent
Lazar, Irving

Anthropologist
Boas, Franz
Fortes, Meyer
Freedman, Maurice
Gellner, Ernest
Gluckman, Max
Herskovits, Melville
Levi-Strauss, Claude
Nadel, Siegfried
Opler, Marvin

Sapir, Edward
Seligman, Charles
Shapiro, Harry
Weidenreich, Franz

Archaeologist
Stein, Mark

Architect
Abramovitz, Max
Blankstein, Cecil
Breuer, Marcel
Bunshaft, Gordon
Gruen, Victor
Jacobson, Arne
Kahn, Albert
Kahn, Louis
Lubetkin, Berthold
Mendelssohn, Erich
Neutra, Richard
Safdie, Moshe

Armed Forces
Ascoli, Ettore
Benjamin, Ernest
Chernyakhovski, Ivan
Cohen, Morris
Dovator, Lev
Dreyfus, Alfred
Kahn, Louis
Kisch, Frederick
Kreiser, Jacob
Marcus, David
Monash, John
Perchersky, Alexander
Pugliese, Umberto
Rickover, Hyman
Zorea, Meir

Art Dealer
Duveen, Joseph

Art Historian
Buchtal, Hugo
Gombrich, Ernst
Panofsky, Erwin
Pevsner, Nikolaus

Art Patron
Guggenheim, Peggy

Astronaut
Resnick, Judith
Volynov, Boris

Astronomer
Schwarzschild, Karl

Aviation
Arnstein, Karl
Berliner, Emile
Dassault, Marcel
Gurevich, Mikhail
Karman, Theodore

Bacteriologist
Ehrlich, Paul
Haffkine, Waldemar
Wasserman, August
Widal, Fernaud

Ballerina
Markova, Alicia
Plisetskaya, Maya
Rambert, Marie
Rubenstein, Ida
Tamiris, Helen

Benefactor
Kahn, Otto
Gilbert, Arthur

Biochemist
Bloch, Konrad
Chain, Ernst
Cohen, Stanley
Cohen, Edwin
Edelman, Gerald
Elion, Gertrude
Embden, Gustav
Funk, Casimir
Kornberg, Arthur
Krebs, Hans
Lipmann, Fritz
Meyerhof, Otto
Niremberg, Marshall
Perutz, Max
Stein, William
Waksman, Selman
Wald, George
Warburg, Otto

Biologist
Altman, Sidney
Berg, Paul
Gilber, Walter
Goldschmidt, Richard
Jacobs, Francois
Luria, Salvador
Lwoff, Andre
Metchnikoff, Elie
Zuckerman, Solly

Bridge
Goren, Charles

Cartoonist
Capp, Al
Feiffer, Jules
Fleischer, Max
Goldberg, Rube
Shuster, Joseph
Weisz, Victor

Chemist
Bacharach, Alfred
Baeyer, Adolph von
Brown, Herbert
Calvin, Melvin
Cohen, Ernst
Fajans, Kasimir
Haber, Fritz
Hevesy, George
Hoffmann, Roald
Klug, Aaron
Levene, Phoebus
Marcus, Rudolph
Moissan, Henri
Reichstein, Tadeus
Wallach, Otto
Willstatter, Richard

Chess
Botvinnik, Mikhail
Bronstein, David
Fischer, Bobby
Kasparov, Garry
Spassky, Boris

Choreographer
Cranko, John
Feld, Elliot
Lichine, David
Robbins, Jerome
Sokolow, Anna

Composer
Antheil, George
Arlen, Harold
Bacharach, Burt
Bart, Lionel
Benatsky, Ralph
Bernstein, Elmer
Bernstein, Leonard
Bloch, Ernest
Cohen, Leonard
Copland, aaron
Gershwin, George
Glass, Philip
Gliere, Reinhold
Goldschmidt, Berthold
Gould, Morton
Hahn, Reynaldo
Korngold, Erich
Loesser, Frank
Milhaud, Darius
Rodgers, Richard
Romberg, Sigmund
Schoenberg, Arnold
Sondheim, Stephen
Weill, Kurt

Conductor
Abravanel, Maurice
Damrosch, Walter
Dorati, Antal
Fielder, Arthur
Foss, Lukas
Klemperer, Otto
Koussevitsky, Serge
Levine, James
Ormandy, Eugene
Previn, Andre
Solti, George
Thomas, Michael Tilson
Walter, Bruno

Criminal
Buchalter, Louis
Lansky, Meyer
Siegel, 'Bugsy'

Critic
Berenson, Bernhard
Brustein, Robert
Clurman, Harold
Rosenberg, Harold

Crystallographer
Franklyn, Rosalind
Hauptman, Herbert

Designer
Aronson, Boris
Black, Misha
Games, Abram
Klein, Calvin
Sassoon, Vidal

Diarist
Frank, Anne
Kaplan, Chaim

Diplomat
Joffe, Adolph
Litvinov, Maxim

Director
Burrows, Abe
Cukor, George
Miller Jonathan
Nichols, Mike
Papp, Joe
Reinhardt, Max
Stronheim, Eric von

Drama Teacher
Adler, Stella
Strasberg, Lee

Economist
Arrrow, Kenneth
Balogh, Thomas
Becker, Gary
Bernstein, Edward
Burns, Arthur
Friedman, Milton
Greenspan, Alan
Kaldor, Nicholas
Kantorovich, Leonid

Klein, Lawrence
Kuznets, Simon
Liberman, Yevsey
Modigliani, Franco
Samuelson, Paul
Simon, Herbert
Solow, Robert

Editor
Cousins, Norman

Educator
Drucker, Peter
Flexner, Abraham
Hartog, Philip
Hook, Sydney

Endocrinologist
Pincus, Gregory

Engineer
Finniston, Monty
Kompfner, Rudolph

Entertainer
Baker, Josephine
Benny, Jack
Berle, Milton
Borge, Victor
Brice, Fanny
Bruce, Lenny
Burns, George
Caesar, Sid
Cantor, Eddie
Flanagan, Bud
Gainsbourg, Serge
Geller, Uri
Kaye, Danny
Midler, Bette
Raikin, Arkady
Tucker, Sophie

Entrepreneur
Bearsted, Viscount
Graham, Bill
Hammer, Armand
Mirvish, Edwin
Todd, Mike

Escapologist
Houdini, Harry

Financier
Milken, Michael

Film-Maker
Allen, Woody
Balcon, Michael
Berman, Pandro
Brooks, Mel
Coen Brothers
Cohn Harry
Dassin, Jules
De Grunwald, Anatole
Eisenstein, Sergi
Foreman, Carl
Forman, Milos
Gance, Abel
Korda, Alexander
Kramer, Stanley
Kubrick, Stanley
Lang, Fritz
Lubitsch, Ernst
Lumet, Sidney
Mankiewicz, Joseph
Mann, Daniel
Mayer, Louis B
Milestone, Lewis
Ophuls, Max
Penn, Arthur
Polanski, Roman
Preminger, Otto
Schlesinger, John
Siegel, Don

Spielberg, Steven
Stone, Oliver
Warner Brothers
Wilder, Billy
Wyler, William
Zinneman, Fred

Gastroenterologist
Crohn, Burrill

Geneticist
Benzer, Seymour
Brown, Michael
Goldstein, Joseph
Lederberg, Joshua
Muller, Hermann

Geologist
Picard, Leo

Historian
Baron, Salo
Beloff, Max
Bloch, Marc
Deutscher, Isaac
Gaster, Theodor
Gilbert, Martin
Hofstadter, Richard
Isaac, Jules
Lipson, Ephraim
Namier, Lewis
Tuchman, Barbara

Humanitarian
Winton, Nicholas

Immunologist
Milstein, Cesar

Impresario
Hurok, Solomon

Industrialist
Burton, Montague
Citroen, Andre
Kadoorie, Lawrence
Marks, Simon
Olivetti, Adriano
Wolfson, Isaac

Interviewer
King, Larry

Inventor
Land, Edwin

Journalist
Adams, 'FRA'
Bernstein, Carl
Buchwald, Art
Fischer, Louis
Gavshon, Arthur
Lazareff, Pierre
Lazurick, Robert
Lippmann, Walter
Louis, Viktor
Montagu, Ivor
Shapiro, Henry
Zorza, Victor

Jurist
Asser, Tobias
Bazelon, David
Heilbron, Rose
Laskin, Bora
Salmon, Cyril
Visser, Lodewijk

Trade Unionist
Chaikin, Sol
Dubinsky, David
Gompers, Samuel
Hillman, Sidney
Schneiderman, Rose

Lawyer
Ashenheim, Neville
Brandeis, Louis
Frankfurter, Felix
Fortas, Abe
Gertz, Elmer
Goldberg, Arthur
Hays, Arthur
Hurwitz, Stephen
Kelsen, Hans
Kempner, Robert
Klarsfeld, Serge
Kunstler, William
Kutner, Luis
Montagu, Ewen
Myers, Michael

Linguist
Bloomfield, Leonard
Jakobson, Roman
Zamenhof, Ludwik

Literary Critic
Steiner, George

Lyric Writer
Dietz, Howard
Harburg, Edgar
Lerner, Alan
Parish, Mitchell

Manager
Baylis, Lilian
Epstein, Brian
Meisl, Hugo
Solomon, Phil

Martyr
Stein, Edith

Mathematician
Besicovitch, Abraham
Bondi, Hermann
Bronowski, Jacob
Courant, Richard
Gelfond, Alexander
Hadamard, Jacques
Levi-Civita, Tullio
Neumann, Johann von
Noether, Emmy
Tarski, Alfred
Ulam, Stanislaw
Volterra, Vito,
Weil, Andre

Media
Bernstein, Sidney
Paley, William S

Meteorologist
Atlas, David

Microbiologist
Hirszfeld, Ludwik
Nathans, Daniel

Mime Artist
Marceau, Marcel

Mineralogist
Goldschmidt, Victor

Musician
Adler, Larry
Alpert, Herb
Bloomfield, Mike
Elman, Ziggy
Getz, Stan
Goodman, Benny
Green, Peter
Huberman, Bronislaw
Jaffa, Max

James, Harry
Kaylan, Howard
Kooper, Al
Landowska, Wanda
Mann, Manfred
Miller, Mitch
Ramone, Joey
Rich, Buddy
Scott, Ronnie
Shaw, Artie
Stanley, Paul
Whiteman, Paul
Zevon, Warren

Music Patron
Mayer, Robert

Naturalist
Rothschild, Marion

Nazi Hunter
Wiesenthal, Simon

Neurologist
Levi-Montalcivi, Rita
Sacks, Oliver

Neurophysiologist
Gasser, Herbert

Nurse
Zlatin, Sabine

Organiser
Avigur, Shaul

Orientalist
Barnett, Lionel

Otologist
Barany, Robert

Painter
Adler, Jankel
Agam, Yaacov
Alechinsky, Pierre
Ardon, Mordecai
Atlan, Jean-Michel
Bakst, Leon
Blume, Peter
Bomberg, David
Brodsky, Isaac
Chagall, Marc
Delaunay-Terk, Sonia
Ernst, Max
Freedman, Barnett
Freud, Lucien
Gertler, Mark
Gottlieb, Adolph
Hundertwasser, Fritz
Kisling, Moise
Kitaj, R.B.
Klein, Yves
Kline, Franz
Kossoff, Leon
Levine, Jack
Liebermann, Max
Lissitzky, El
Mendoza, June
Modigliani-Nagy, Laszio
Motesiczky,
Marie-Louise
Newman, Barnett
Pascin, Jules
Pissarro, Lucien
Rothenstein, William
Rothko, Mark
Shahn, Ben
Soutine, Chaim
Soyer, Raphael
Steinberg, Saul
Topolski, Feliks
Weber, Max

Paediatrician
Schick, Bela

Pathologist
Gluckman, Jonathan
Landsteiner, Karl

Patriot
Elek, Tamas

Pharmacologist
Axelrod, Julius

Philosopher
Adorno, Theodor,
Alexander, Samuel
Arendt, Hannah
Aron, Raymond
Basch, Victor
Benjamin, Walter
Bergson, Henri
Berlin, Isaiah
Buber, Martin
Cassirer, Ernst
Chomsky, Noam
Deborin, Abram
Ginsberg, Morris
Jonas, Hans
Levinas, Emmanuel
Lukacs, Gyorgy
Marcuse, Herbert
Nagel, Ernest
Popper, Karl
Reichenbach, Hans
Weil, Simone
Wertheimer, Max
Wittgenstein, Ludwig

Photographer
Arbus, Diane
Avedon, Richard
Capa, Robert

Edelstein, Jillian
Eisenthedt, Alfred
Halsman, Philippe
Penn, Irving
Ray, Man
Salomon, Erich
Siskind, Aaron
Steiglitz, Alfred
Vishniac, Roman

Physician
Benacerrak, Baruj
Blumberg, Baruch
Cohen, Henry
Dressler, William
Loewi, Otto
Shulman, Alexander
Szwajger, Adina

Physicist
Andrade, Edward
Bethe, Hans
Bloch, Felix
Bohr, Aage
Bohr, Niels
Born, Max
Charpak, Georges
Einstein, Albert
Feld, Bernard
Feynman, Richard
Franck, James
Friedman, Jerome
Frisch, Otto
Gabor, Dennis
Gell-Man, Murray
Glaser, Donald
Glashow, Sheldon
Hertz, Gustav
Hofstadter, Robert
Joffe, Abraham
Josephson, Brian
Kapitza, Peter

Khariton, Yuli
Landau, Lev
Lederman, Max
Lippmann, Gabriel
Meitner, Lise
Michelson, Albert
Mottelson, Ben
Oppenheimer, Robert
Peierls, Rudolph
Penzias, Arno
Pontecorvo, Bruno
Rabi, Isidor
Richter, Burton
Rotblat, Joseph
Schwartz, Melvin
Schwinger, Julian
Segre, Emilo
Steinberger, Jack
Stern, Otto
Szilard, Leo
Tamm, Igor
Teller, Edward
Tolansky, Samuel
Veksler, Vladimir
Weinberg, Steven
Wigner, Eugene
Yalow, Rosalyn

Pianist
Ashkenazy, Vladimir
Barenboim, Daniel
Cohen, Harriet
Gileis, Emil
Hess, Myra
Hodes, Art
Horowitz, Vladimir
Moiseiwitsch, Benno
Rubenstein, Artur
Schnabel, Artur
Serkin, Rudolph

Pioneer
Baratz, Joseph
Bernays, Edward
Castillo Y Albornoz,
Jose
Cohen, Israel
Fox, William
Goldwyn, Samuel
Guttmann, Ludwig
Rubinstein, Helena
Sarnoff, David
Wanamaker, Sam

Playwright
Belasco, David
Berkoff, Steven
Hart, Moss
Ionesco, Eugene
Kaufman, George
Miller, Arthur
Odets, Clifford
Pinter, Harold
Shaffer, Peter
Simon, Neil
Wesker, Arnold

Poet
Bagritski, Eduard
Bodenheim, Maxwell
Brodsky, Joseph
Celan, Paul
Ginsberg, Allen
Nemerov, Howard
Rosenberg, Isaac
Saba, Umberto
Sassoon, Siegfried
Tuwim, Julian
Tzara, Tristan

...cian
Adler, Friedrich
Aloni, Shulamit
Arlosoroff, Chaim
Axen, Hermann
Ballin, Albert
Bauer, Otto
Berman, Jacob
Bernstein, Eduard
Bischoffsheim, Ellen
Bloch, Pierre
Briscoe, Robert
Brittan, Leon
Dayan, Moshe
Debre, Michel
Delvalle, Max
Dymshyts, Veniamin
Eban, Abba
Gero, Erno
Goldwater, Barry
Grossman, Haika
Kaganovitch, Lazar
Kamenov, Lev
Koch, Edward
Lafer, Horacio
La Guardia, Fiorello
Laski, Harold
Mandel, Georges
Mayer, Daniel
Pauker, Ana
Pijade, Mosa
Radek, Karl
Rakosi, Matyas
Shinwell, Emmanuel
Silverman, Sydney
Slansky, Rudolph
Slvo, Joe,
Suzman, Helen
Sverdlov, Yakov
Trotsky, Leon
Veil, Simone
Zinoviev, Grigory

Political Victim
Rosenberg, Julius &
Ethel

Pop Group
' Beastie Boys '
' Steely Dan '

Princess
Princess Elsa of
Liechtenstein

Prime Minister
Ben-Gurion, David
Begin, Menachem
Blum, Leon
Fabius, Laurent
Hassan, Joshua
Kreisky, Bruno
Kun, Bela
Marshall, David
Meir, Golda
Mendes-France, Pierre
Peres, Shimon
Rabin, Yitzhak
Sonnino, Sidney
Welensky, Roy

Producers
Blum, Rene
Freed, Arthur
Goodson, Mark
Grade, Lew
Houseman, John
Land, David
Saltzman, Harry
Selznick, David
Spiegel, Sam
Thalberg, Irving
Ziegfeld, Florenz

Psychiatrist
Adler, Alfred
Baruk, Henri
Deutsch, Felix
Lewis, Aubrey

Psychoanalyst
Abraham, Karl
Alexander, Franz
Freud, Anna
Freud, Sigmund
Fromm, Erich
Hartmann, Heinz
Erikson, Erik
Ferenczi, Sandor
Klein, Melanie
Niederland, William

Psychologists
Bettelheim, Bruno
Bruner, Jerome
Erlanger, Joseph
Katz, Bernard
Lewin, Kurt
Rank, Otto
Reich, Wilhelm
Voronoff, Serge

Psychotherapist
Frankl, Viktor

Publishers
Fischer, Gottfried
Fried, Alfred
Gernsback, Hugo
Gollancz, Victor
Graham, Katherine
Maxwell, Robert
Ochs, Adolph
Timerman, Jacobo

Rabbi
Gryn, Hugo
Tanenbaum, Marc

Radical
Abzug, Bella
Bunke, Tamara
Cohn-Bendit, Daniel
Hoffman, Abbie
Luxemburg, Rosa

Radiologist
Bucky, Gustav

Reformer
Barnett, Louis

Resistance Leader
Anielewicz, Mordecai
Atlas, Jechezkiel
Baum, Herbert
Lubetkin, Zivia
Tenenbaum, Mordechai
Trepper, Leopold
Zuckerman, Itzhak

Scholar
Ehrlich, Eugen

Scientist
Isaacs, Alick

Sculptor
Abrahams, Ivor
Aronson, Naum
Baskin, Leonard
Bernstein-Sinaieoff,
Leopold
Caro, Anthony
Davidson, Jo
Elkan, Benno
Epstein, Jacob

Ferber, Herbert
Gabo, Naum
Lipchitz, Jacques
Nadelman, Elie
Neizvestny, Ernst
Nevelson, Louise
Orloff, Chana
Pevsner, Antoine
Rie, Lucie
Zadkine, Ossip

Seismologist
Benioff, Hugo

Singer
Bolan, Mark
Brown, Georgia
Dylan, Bob
Fisher, Eddie
Ian, Janis
Joel, Billy
Jolson, Al
Kravitz, Lenny
Manilow, Barry
Newton-John, Olivia
Peerce, Jan
Reddy, Helen
Sills, Beverly
Simon & Garfunkle
Tauber, Richard
Torme, Mel

Social Scientist
Durkheim, Emile
Henriques, Basil
Korczak, Janusz
Salomon, Alice

Sociologist
Komarovsky, Mirra
Lazarsfeld, Paul

Songwriter
Berlin, Irving
Cahn, Sammy
Diamond, Neil
Guthrie, Arlo
Kern, Jerome
King, Carole
Leiber & Stoller
Ochs, Phil
Sedaka, Neil
Simon, Carly
Simon & Garfunkle
Styne, Jule
Spector, Phil

Sportsperson
Abrahams, Harold
Adelstein-Rozeanu, Angelica
Alcott, Amy
Attell, Abe
Auerbach 'Red'
Bacher, 'Ali'
Baer, Max
Barna, Victor
Barnato, Woolf
Berg, Jack 'Kid'
Berg, Moe
Bergman, Richard
Calmat, Alain
Copeland, Lilian
Damm, Sheila van
Fields, Jackie
Flatow, Alfred
Gomelsky, Alexander
Gorokhovskaya, Maria
Greenberg, Hank
Gyarmati, Dezso
Halimi, Alphonse
Holman, Nat
Jacobs, Hirsch
Jaffee, Irving

Kabos, Endre
Kaplan, Louis 'Kid'
Keleti, Agnes
Kirszenstein-Szewinska, Irene
Koufax, Sandy
Kriss, Grigori
Kronberger, Lily
Leonard, Benny
Levinsky, Barney
Lewis, Ted 'Kid'
Luckman, Sid
Mayer, Helene
McCoy, Al
Melnik, Faina
Miller, Walter
Neeskens, Johan
Osiier, Ivan
Perez, Victor
Praag, Lionel van
Prinstein, Meyer
Rosenbloom, Maxie
Ross, Barney
Rottman, Leon
Rylsky, Yakov
Savitt, Richard
Scheckter, Jody
Spitz, Mark
Stransky, Joel
Szabados, Miklos
Yashin, Lev

Spy
Aaronson, Sarah
Blake, George
Kroger, Peter
Reilly, Sidney

Statesman
Baruch, Bernard
Cassin, Rene
Eisner, Kurt

Gutt, Camille
Hore-Belisha, Leslie
Hymans, Paul
Isaacs, Isaac
Kissinger, Henry
Luzzatti, Luigi
Mayer, Renee
Morgenthau, Henry
Rathenau, Walther
Samuels, Herbert
Weizmann, Chaim

Surgeon
Kantrowitz, Adrian
Penn, Jack

Voice-Over
Blanc, Mel

Violinist
Auer, Leopold
Elman, Mischa
Heifetz, Jascha
Menuhin, Yehudi
Milstein, Nathan
Oistrakh, David
Perlman, Itzhak
Stern Isaac
Vengerov, Maxim

Virologist
Baltimore, David
Sabin, Albert
Salk, Jonas
Temin, Howard

Agnon, Shmuel
Aleichem, Sholem
Arega, Leon
Asch, Sholem
Asimov, Isaac
Aub, Max
Babel, Isaac
Bassani, Giorgi
Baum, Vicki
Behrman, Samuel
Bellow, Saul
Benda, Julien
Bernard, Tristan
Bloch, Jean-Richard
Blume, Judy
Boorstin, Daniel
Brandes, Georg
Broch, Hermann
Brod, Max
Brookner, Anita
Canetti, Elias
Chayefsky, Paddy
Cixous, Helene
Comden & Green
Cremieux, Benjamin
Daniel, Yuli
David, Joseph
Doctorow, Edgar
Ehrenburg, Ilya
Ephron, Nora
Fast, Howard
Ferber, Edna
Feuchtwanger, Lion
Fleg, Edmond
Fleischer, Nat
Friedman, Betty
Gary, Romain
Gerchunoff, Alberto
Ginzburg, Natalie
Golding, Louis
Goldman, Emma

Gordimer, Nadine
Goscinny, Rene
Hecht, Ben
Heller, Joseph
Hellman, Lilian
Henriques, Robert
Heyse, Paul von
Hildesheimer, Wolfgang
Hurst, Fannie
Jhabvala, Ruth
Jong, Erica
Kafka, Franz
Kessel, Joseph
Koestler, Arthur
Kosinski, Jerzy
Levi, Carlo
Levi, Primo
Maibaum, Richard
Mailer, Norman
Malamud, Bernard
Mamet, David
Mandelstam, Osip
Maurois, Andre
Moravia, Alberto
Oz, Amos
Parker, Dorothy
Pasternak, Boris
Perelman, SJ
Proust, Marcel
'Queen, Ellery'
Richler, Mordecai
Rice, Elmer
Roth, Henry
Roth, Philip
Rubens, Bernice
Sachs, Nelly
Salten, Felix
Schnitzler, Arthur
Schwartz, Delmore
Shaw, Irwin
Siegel, Jerry
Singer, Isaac Bashevis

Sontag, Susan
Spark, Muriel
Stein, Gertrude
Svevo, Italo
Toller, Ernst
Uris, Leon
Vercors
West, Nathaniel
Wiesel, Elie
Woolf, Leonard
Wouk, Herman

COUNTRY OF BIRTH

ALGERIA
Halimi, Alphonse

ARGENTINE
Barenboim, Daniel
Bunke, Tamara
Gerchunoff, Alberto
Milstein, Cesar
Timerman, Jacobo

AUSTRALIA
Alexander, Samuel
Cowen, Zelman
Isaacs, Isaac
Lewis, Aubrey
Mendoza, June
Monash, John
Praag, Lionel van
Reddy, Helen

AUSTRIA
Adler, Alfred
Adler, Friedrich
Barany, Robert
Baron, Salo
Bauer, Otto
Baum, Vicki
Bergner, Elisabeth
Bergman, Richard
Bernays, Edward
Bettelheim, Bruno
Bondi, Hermann
Buber, Martin
Deutsch, Felix
Dressler, William
Drucker, Peter
Ehrlich, Eugen
Fleischer, Max
Frankfurter, Felix
Frankl, Viktor
Fried, Alfred
Freud, Anna
Freud, Sigmund
Frisch, Otto
Gombrich, Ernst
Gruen, Victor
Hartmann, Heinz
Hundertwasser, Fritz
Klein, Melanie
Kompfner, Rudolf
Kreisky, Bruno
Lang, Fritz
Landsteiner, Karl
Lazarsfeld, Paul
Meisl, Hugo
Meitner, Lisa
Motesiczky,
Marie-Louise
Muni, Paul
Nadel, Siegfried
Perutz, Max
Popper, Karl
Preminger, Otto
Rank, Otto
Reinhardt, Max
Rie, Lucie
Salten, Felix
Schnitzler, Arthur
Schoenberg, Arnold
Spiegel, Sam
Strasberg, Lee
Stronheim, Eric von
Tauber, Richard
Walbrook, Anton
Wiesenthal, Simon
Wilder, Billy
Wittgenstein, Ludwig
Zinnemann, Fred

BELGIUM
Alechinsky, Pierre
Gutt, Camille
Hymans, Paul

BRAZIL
Lafer, Horacio

BULGARIA
Canetti, Elias

CANADA
Altman, Sidney
Belasco, David
Bellow, Saul
Benjamin, Ernest
Blankstein, Cecil
Cohen, Leonard
Greene, Lorne
Laskin, Bora
Marcus, Rudolph
Richler, Mordecai
Saltzman, Harry
Safdie, Moshe
Shatner, William
Shulman, Alexander
Shuster, Joseph

CZECH
Benatsky, Ralph
Brod, Max
Forman, Milos
Gryn, Hugo
Kafka, Franz
Kelsen, Hans
Korngold, Erich
Maxwell, Robert
Nagel, Ernest
Schnabel, Artur
Serkin, Rudolph
Slansky, Rudolf
Wertheimer, Max

DENMARK
Bohr, Aage,
Bohr, Niels
Borge, Victor
Brandes, Georg
Hurwitz, Stephen
Jacobson, Arne
Osiier, Ivan

ECUADOR
Castillo Y Albornoz,
Jose

ESTONIA
Kahn, Louis

FRANCE
Aimee, Anouk
Arega, Leon
Aron, Raymond
Aronson, Naum
Atlan, Jean-Michel
Aub, Max
Baruk, Henri
Basch, Victor
Benda, Julien
Bergson, Henri
Bernard, Tristan
Bernhardt, Sarah
Bernstein-Sinaieff,
Leopold
Bloch, Jean-Richard
Bloch, Marc
Bloch, Pierre
Blum, Leon
Blum, Rene
Calmat, Alain
Cassin, Rene
Celan, Paul
Citroen, Andre
Cixous, Helene
Cohn-Bendit, Daniel
Cremieux, Benjamin
Dassault, Marcel

FRANCE cont.
Debre, Michel
Delaunay-Terk, Sonia
Dreyfus, Alfred
Durkheim, Emile
Fabius, Laurent
Gainsbourg, Serge
Gary, Romain
Gance, Abel
Goscinny, Rene
Hadamard, Jacques
Haffkine, Waldemar
Isaac, Jules
Jacob, Francois
Kahn, Louis
Kessel, Joseph
Klarsfeld, Serge
Klein, Yves
Lazareff, Pierre
Lazurick, Robert
Levi-Strauss, Claude
Levinas, Emmanuel
Linder, Max
Lipchitz, Jacques
Lippmann, Gabriel
Lwoff, Andre
Mandel, Georges
Marceau, Marcel
Maurois, Andre
Mayer, Daniel
Mayer, Renee
Mendes-France, Pierre
Milhaud, Darius
Moissan, Henri
Orloff, Chana
Pascin, Jules
Pissarro, Lucien
Polanski, Roman
Proust, Marcel
Signoret, Simone
Soutine, Chaim
Steiner, George

Veil, Simone
Vercors
Weil, Andre
Weil, Simone
Widal, Fernand
Wyler, William
Zadkine, Ossip

GERMANY
Abraham, Karl
Adorno, Theodor
Arendt, Hannah
Arnstein, Karl
Axen, Hermann
Baeyer, Adolph von
Ballin, Albert
Baum, Herbert
Benjamin, Walter
Berliner, Emile
Bernstein, Eduard
Bethe, Hans
Bloch, Konrad
Boas, Franz
Born, Max
Buchthal, Hugo
Bucky, Gustav
Cassirer, Ernst
Chain, Ernst
Courant, Richard
Damrosch, Walter
Einstein, Albert
Eisentaedt, Alfred
Eisner, Kurt
Embden, Gustav
Ehrlich, Paul
Elkan, Benno
Erikson, Erik
Ernst, Max
Feuchtwanger, Lion
Fischer, Gottfried
Flatow, Alfred
Foss, Lukas

Franck, James
Frank, Anne
Freud, Lucien
Fromm, Erich
Goldschmidt, Berthold
Goldschmidt, Richard
Graham, Bill
Gutenberg, Beno
Guttmann, Ludwig
Haber, Fritz
Hertz, Gustav
Heyse, Paul
Hildesheimer, Wolfgang
Jonas, Hans
Kahn, Albert
Kahn, Otto
Katz, Bernard
Kempner, Robert
Kissinger, Henry
Klemperer, Otto
Krebs, Hans
Lewin, Kurt
Liebermann, Max
Lipmann, Fritz
Loewi, Otto
Lubitsch, Ernst
Luxemburg, Rosa
Mayer, Helene
Meyerhof, Otto
Mendelssohn, Erich
Nichols, Mike
Niederland, William
Noether, Emmy
Ophuls, Max
Panofsky, Erwin
Peierls, Rudolph
Pevsner, Nikolaus
Picard, Leo
Previn, Andre
Rathenau, Walther
Reichenbach, Hans
Sachs, Nelly

Salomon, Alice
Salomon, Erich
Sapir, Edward
Schwarzschild, Karl
Steinberger, Jack
Stern, Otto
Toller, Ernst
Wallach, Otto
Walter, Bruno
Warburg, Otto
Wasserman, August
von
Weidenreich, Franz
Weill, Kurt
Weisz, Victor
Willstatter, Richard

GIBRALTER
Hassan, Joshua

GREECE
Abravanel, Maurice

HOLLAND
Asser, Tobias
Cohen, Ernst
Neeskens, Johan
Visser, Lodewijk

HONG KONG
Kadoorie, Lawrence

HUNGARY
Alexander, Franz
Auer, Leopold
Balogh, Thomas
Barna, Victor
Breuer, Marcel
Capa, Robert
Dorati, Antal
Elek, Tamas
Ferenczi, Sandor

Fox, William
Gero, Erno
Gyarmati, Dezso
Hevesy, George
Houdini, Harry
Kabos, Endre
Kaldor, Nicholas
Karman, Theodore von
Keleti, Agnes
Koestler, Arthur
Korda, Alexander
Kronberger, Lily
Kun, Bela
Lorre, Peter
Lukacs, Gyorgy
Moholy-Nagy, Laszio
Rakosi, Matyas
Romberg, Sigmund
Schick, Bela
Schwimmer, Rosika
Solti, George
Stein, Mark
Szabados, Miklos
Szilard, Leo
Trebitsch-Lincoln, Ignatius
Wigner, Eugene

INDIA
David, Joseph
Kisch, Frederick

ITALY
Ascoli Ettore
Bassani, Giorgi
Ginzburg, Natalie
Levi-Civita, Tullio
Levi, Carlo
Levi-Montalcini, Rita
Levi, Primo
Luria, Salvador
Luzzatti, Luigi

Modigliani, Amedo
Modigliani, Franco
Montand, Yves
Moravia, Alberto
Olivetti, Adriano
Pontecorvo, Bruno
Pugliese, Umberto
Segre, Emilio
Sonnino, Sidney
Svevo, Italo
Volterra, Vito

JAMAICA
Ashenheim, Neville

LITHUANIA
Hillman, Sidney
Shahn, Ben

LUXEMBOURG
Gernsback, Hugo

NEW ZEALAND
Barnett, Louis
Myers, Michael

NORWAY
Goldschmidt, Victor

PALESTINE
Aaronson, Sarah
Agam, Yaacov
Agnon, Shmuel
Aloni, Shulamit
Dyan, Moshe
Geller, Uri
Oz, Amos
Perlman, Itzhak
Rabin, Yitzhak
Zorea, Meir

PANAMA
Delvalle, Max

POLAND
Adler, Jankel
Ardon, Mordecai
Anielewicz, Mordecai
Asch, Sholem
Atlas, Jechezkiel
Begin, Menachem
Ben-Gurion, David
Berman, Jacob
Bronowski, Jacob
Charpak, Georges
Deutscher, Isaac
Fajans, Kasimir
Funk, Casimir
Goldwyn, Samuel
Grossman, Haika
Hirszfeld, Ludwik
Hoffmann, Roald
Huberman, Bronislaw
Kaplan, Chaim
Kisling, Moise
Korczak, Janusz
Kosinski, Jerzy
Landowska, Wanda
Lubetkin, Zivia
Nadelman, Elie
Peres, Shimon
Rambert, Marie
Rotblat, Joseph
Rubinstein, Artur
Rubinstein, Helena
Sabin, Albert
Schneiderman, Rose
Singer, Isaac Bashevis
Stein, Edith
Szwajger, Adina
Tarski, Alfred
Tenenbaum, Mordechai
Topolski, Feliks

Trepper, Leopold
Tuwim, Julian
Ulam, Stanislaw
Zlatin, Sabine
Zorza, Victor
Zuckerman, Itzhak

ROMANIA
Adelstein-Rozeanu, Angelica
Houseman, John
Ionesco, Eugene
Pauker, Ana
Robinson, Edward G
Rottman, Leon
Shapiro, Henry
Steinberg, Saul
Tzara, Tristan
Wiesel, Elie

RUSSIA/USSR
Aleichem, Sholem
Aronson, Boris
Asimov, Isaac
Ashkenazy, Vladimir
Avigur, Shaul
Babel, Isaac
Bagritski, Eduard
Bakst, Leon
Baratz, Joseph
Berenson, Bernhard
Berlin, Irving
Berlin, Isaiah
Besicovitch, Abraham
Black, Misha
Blume, Peter
Botvinnik, Mikhail
Brodsky, Isaac
Brodsky, Joseph
Bronstein, David
Burton, Montague
Chagall, Marc

RUSSIA/USSR cont.
Chernyakhovski, Ivan
Daniel, Yuli
Deborin, Abram
Dovator, Lev
Dubinsky, David
Dymshyts, Veniamin
Ehrenburg, Ilya
Elman, Mischa
Eisenstein, Sergi
Gabo, Naum
Gelfond, Alexander
Gilels, Emil
Gliere, Reinhold
Goldman, Emma
Gomelsky, Alexander
Gorokhovskaya, Maria
Grade, Lew
Gurevich, Mikhail
Halsman, Philippe
Heifetz, Jascha
Horowitz, Vladimir
Hurok, Soloman
Jakobson, Roman
Joffe, Abraham
Joffe, Adolph
Jolson, Al
Kaganovich, Lazar
Kamenev, Lev
Kantorovich, Leonid
Kapitza, Peter
Kasparov, Garry
Khariton, Yuli
Kirszenstein-Szewinska,
Irene
Komarovsky, Mirra
Koussevitsky, Serge
Kreiser, Jacob
Kriss, Grigori
Kuznets, Simon
Landau, Lev
Lansky, Meyer

Levene, Phoebus
Liberman, Yevsey
Lichine, David
Lissitzky, El
Litvinov, Maxim
Louis, Viktor
Lubetkin, Berthold
Mandelstam, Osip
Mayer, Louis B
Melnik, Faina
Metchnikoff, Elie
Milestone, Lewis
Milstein, Nathan
Moiseiwitsch, Benno
Neizvestny, Ernst
Nevelson, Louise
Oistrakh, David
Pasternak, Boris
Perchersky, Alexander
Pevsner, Antoine
Plisetskaya, Maya
Radek, Karl
Raikin, Arkady
Reich, Wilhelm
Reilly, Sidney
Rickover, Hyman
Rothko, Mark
Rubinstein, Ida
Rylsky, Yakov
Sarnoff, David
Sharansky, Anatoly
Soyer, Raphael
Spassky, Boris
Stern, Isaac
Sverdlov, Yakov
Tamm, Igor
Trotsky, Leon
Tucker, Sophie
Veksler, Vladimir
Vengerov, Maxim
Vishniac, Roman
Volynov, Boris

Voronoff, Serge
Waksman, Selman
Weber, Max
Weizmann, Chaim
Yashin, Lev
Zamenhof, Ludwik
Zinoviev, Grigory

SINGAPORE
Marshall, David

SOUTH AFRICA
Bacher, 'Ali'
Cranko, John
Eban, Abba
Edelstein, Jillian
Fortes, Meyer
Gavshon, Arthur
Gluckman, Jonathan
Gluckman, Max
Gordimer, Nadine
Mann, Manfred
Penn, Jack
Scheckter, Jody
Slovo, Joe
Stransky, Joel
Suzman, Helen
Zuckerman, Solly

SWITZERLAND
Bloch, Ernest
Bloch, Felix
Fleg, Edmond
Reichstein, Tadeus

TUNISIA
Perez, Victor

UK
Abrahams, Ivor
Abrahams, Harold
Andrade, Edward

Bacharach, Alfred
Balcon, Michael
Barnato, Woolf
Barnett, Lionel
Bart, Lionel
Baylis, Lilian
Bearsted, 1st Viscount
Beloff, Max
Berg, Jack 'Kid'
Berkoff, Steven
Bernstein, Sidney
Bischoffsheim, Ellen
Bloom, Claire
Bloomfield, Leonard
Bolan, Mark
Bomberg, David
Brittan, Leon
Brookner, Anita
Brown, Georgia
Caro, Anthony
Cohen, Andrew
Cohen, Harriet
Cohen, Henry
Cohen, Morris
Collins, Joan
Damm, Sheila van
Day-Lewis, Daniel
Duveen, Joseph
Epstein, Brian
Finniston, Monty
Flanagan, Bud
Franklin, Rosalind
Freedman, Barnett
Freedman, Maurice
Gabor, Dennis
Games, Abram
Gaster, Theodor
Gellner, Ernest
Gertler, Mark
Gilbert, Arthur
Gilbert, Martin
Ginsberg, Morris

Golding, Louis
Gollancz, Victor
Gompers, Samuel
Green, Peter
Hartog, Philip
Heilbron, Rose
Henriques, Basil
Henriques, Robert
Hess, Myra
Hore-Belisha, Leslie
Howard, Leslie
Isaacs, Alick
Jaffa, Max
Jhabvala, Ruth
Josephson, Brian
Klug, Aaron
Klugman, Norman
Kossoff, Leon
Land, David
Laski, Harold
Lewis, Ted 'Kid'
Lipson, Ephraim
Markova, Alicia
Marks, Simon
Miller, Jonathan
Montagu, Ewen
Montagu, Ivor
Namier, Lewis
Newton-John, Olivia
Pinter, Harold
Rosenberg, Isaac
Rothenstein, William
Rothschild, Miriam
Rubens, Bernice
Sacks, Oliver
Salmon, Cyril
Samuel, Herbert
Sassoon, Siegfried
Sassoon, Vidal
Schlesinger, John
Scott, Ronnie
Seligman, Charles

Sellers, Peter
Shaffer, Peter
Shinwell, Emmanuel
Silverman, Sydney
Solomon, Phil
Spark, Muriel
Tolansky, Samuel
Wesker, Arnold
Winton, Nicholas
Wolfson, Isaac
Woolf, Leonard

USA
Abramovitz, Max
Abzug, Bella
Adams, 'FPA'
Adler, Larry
Adler, Stella
Alcott, Amy
Allen, Woody
Alpert, Herb
Antheil, George
Arbus, Diane
Arkin, Alan
Arlen, Harold
Arrow, Kenneth
Atlas, David
Attell, Abe
Auerbach, 'Red'
Avedon, Richard
Axelrod, Julius
Bacall, Lauren
Bacharach, Burt
Baer, Max
Baker, Josephine
Balsam, Martin
Baltimore, David
Baruch, Bernard
Baskin, Leonard
Bazelon, David
Becker, Gary
Behrman, Samuel

Benioff, Hugo
Benny, Jack
Benzer, Seymour
Berg, Moe
Berg, Paul
Berle, Milton
Berman, Pandro
Bernstein, Carl
Bernstein, Edward
Bernstein, Elmer
Bernstein, Leonard
Blanc, Mel
Bloomfield, Mike
Blumberg, Baruch
Blume, Judy
Bodenheim, Maxwell
Boorstin, Daniel
Brandeis, Louis
Brice, Fanny
Brooks, Mel
Brown, Herbert
Bruce, Lenny
Brown, Michael
Bruner, Jerome
Buchalter, Louis
Buchwald, Art
Bunshaft, Gordon
Burns, Arthur
Burns, George
Burrows, Abe
Caan, James
Caesar, Sid
Cahn, Sammy
Calvin, Melvin
Cannon, Dyan
Cantor, Eddie
Capp, Al
Chaikin, Sol
Chomsky, Noam
Charisse, Cyd
Chayefsky, Paddy
Clurman, Harold

Cobb, Lee J
Coen Brothers
Cohen, Israel
Cohen, Stanley
Cohen, Edwin
Cohn, Harry
Comden & Green
Copeland, Lillian
Copland, Aaron
Cousins, Norman
Crohn, Burrill
Crystal, Billy
Cukor, George
Curtis, Tony
Dassin, Jules
Davidson, Jo
Diamond, Neil
Dietz, Howard
Doctorow, Edgar
Douglas, Kirk,
Douglas, Melvin
Douglas, Michael
Dreyfuss, Richard
Dylan, Bob
Edelman, Gerald
Elion, Gertrude
Elman, Ziggy
Ephron, Nora
Epstein, Jacob
Erlanger, Joseph
Falk, Peter
Fast, Howard
Feiffer, Jules
Feld, Bernard
Feld, Eliot
Ferber, Edna
Ferber, Herbert
Feynman, Richard
Fields, Jackie
Fischer, Bobby
Fischer, Louis
Fisher, Eddie

USA cont.

Fleischer, Max
Fleischer, Nat
Flexner, Abraham
Ford, Harrison
Foreman, Carl
Freed, Arthur
Friedman, Betty
Friedman, Jerome
Friedman, Milton
Fortas, Abe
Garfield, John
Gasser, Herbert
Gell-Mann, Murray
Gershwin, George
Getz, Stan
Gilbert, Walter
Ginsberg, Allen
Glaser, Donald
Glashow, Sheldon
Glass, Philip
Goddard, Paulette
Goldberg, Arthur
Goldberg, Rube
Goldstein, Joseph
Goldwater, Barry
Goodman, Benny
Goodson, Mark
Goren, Charles
Gottlieb, Adolph
Gould, Elliot
Gould, Morton
Graham, Katherine
Greenberg, Henry
Greenspan, Alan
Guggenheim, Peggy
Guthrie, Arlo
Hammer, Armand
Harburg, Edgar
Hart, Moss
Hauptman, Herbert
Hawn, Goldie

Hays, Arthur
Hecht, Ben
Heller, Joseph
Hellman, Lilian
Herskovits, Melville
Hoffman, Abbie
Hoffman, Dustin
Hofstadter, Richard
Hofstadter, Robert
Holman, Nat
Holliday, Judy
Hook, Sydney
Hurst, Fannie
Ian, Janis
Jacobs, Hirsch
Jaffee, Irving
James, Harry
Joel, Billy
Jong, Erica
Kantrowitz, Adrian
Kaufman, George
Kaye, Danny
Keitel, Harvey
Kern, Jerome
King, Carole
King, Larry
Kitaj, RB
Klein, Calvin
Klein, Lawrence
Kline, Franz
Kline, Kevin
Koch, Edward
Kooper, Al
Kornberg, Arthur
Koufax, Sandy
Kramer, Stanley
Kravitz, Lenny
Kroger, Peter
Kubrick, Stanley
Kunstler, William
Kutner, Luis
La Guardia, Fiorello

Land, Edwin
Lazar, Irving
Lederberg, Joshua
Leiber & Stoller
Leonard, Benny
Lerner, Alan
Levinsky, Barney
Levine, Jack
Levine, James
Lewis, Jerry
Lippmann, Walter
Loesser, Frank
Luckman, Sid
Lumet, Sidney
Maibaum, Richard
Mailer, Norman
Malamud, Bernard
Mamet, David
Manilow, Barry
Mankiewicz, Joseph
Mann, Daniel
Marcus, David
Marcuse, Herbert
Marx Brothers
Matthau, Walter
McCoy, Al
Michelson, Albert
Midler, Bette
Milken, Michael
Miller, Arthur
Miller, Mitch
Miller, Walter
Mirvish, Edwin
Morgenthau, Henry
Mostel, Zero
Muller, Hermann
Meir, Golda
Menuhin, Yehudi
Murray, Arthur
Nathans, Daniel
Nemerov, Howard
Newman, Barnett

Newman, Paul
Nimoy, Leonard
Niremberg, Marshall
Ochs, Adolph
Ochs, Phil
Odets, Clifford
Opler, Marvin
Oppenheimer, Robert
Paley, William
Papp, Joe
Parish, Mitchell
Parker, Dorothy
Peerce, Jan
Penn, Arthur,
Penn, Irving
Penzias, Arno
Perelman, S.J
Pincus, Gregory
Prinstein, Meyer
'Queen, Ellery'
Ramone, Joey
Ray, Man
Resnick, Judith
Rice, Elmer
Rich, Buddy
Richter, Burton
Robbins, Jerome
Rodgers, Richard
Rosenberg, Harold
Rosenberg, Julius and
Ethel
Rosenbloom, Maxie
Ross, Barney
Roth, Henry
Roth, Philip
Salk, Jonas
Samuelson, Paul
Schwartz, Delmore
Schwartz, Melvin
Schwinger, Julian
Sedaka, Neil
Segal, George

Selznick, David
Shapiro, Harry
Shaw, Artie
Shaw, Irwin
Siegel, Jerry
Siegel, 'Bugsy'
Siegel, Don
Sills, Beverly
Silvers, Phil
Simon, Carly
Simon, Herbert
Simon, Neil
Simon & Garfunkle
Siskind, Aaron
Sokolow, Anna
Solow, Robert
Sonheim, Stephen
Sontag, Susan
Spector, Phil
Spielberg, Steven
Spitz, Mark
Stanley, Paul
'Steely Dan'
Steiger, Rod
Stein, Gertrude
Stein, William
Steinem, Gloria
Stone, Oliver
Streisand, Barbra
Styne, Jule
Tamiris, Helen
Tanenbaum, Marc
Temin, Howard
Thalberg, Irving
Thomas, Michael Tilson
Todd, Mike
Torme, Mel
Tuchman, Barbara
Uris, Leon
Wald, George
Wanamaker, Sam
Warner Brothers

Weinberg, Steven
West, Nathanael
Whiteman, Paul
Wilder, Gene
Winger, Debra
Winters, Shelley
Wouk, Herman
Yalow, Rosalyn
Zevon, Warren
Ziefeld, Florenz

VENEZUELA
Benacerraf, Baruj
Hahn, Reynaldo

YUGOSLAVIA
Pijade, Mosa

ZIMBABWE
Welensky, Roy